D0848609

AMERICAN AND CANADIAN IMMIGRANT AND ETHNIC FOLKLORE

GARLAND FOLKLORE BIBLIOGRAPHIES
(General Editor: Alan Dundes)
Vol. 2

GARLAND REFERENCE LIBRARY
OF THE HUMANITIES
Vol. 275

Volume 2

Garland
Folklore Bibliographies

General Editor

Alan Dundes
University of California, Berkeley

AMERICAN AND CANADIAN IMMIGRANT AND ETHNIC FOLKLORE
An Annotated Bibliography

compiled by
Robert A. Georges
Stephen Stern

GARLAND PUBLISHING, INC. • NEW YORK & LONDON
1982

© 1982 Robert A. Georges and Stephen Stern

Library of Congress Cataloging in Publication Data

Georges, Robert A.
  American and Canadian immigrant and ethnic folklore.

  (Garland folklore bibliographies ; v. 2) (Garland
reference library of the humanities ; v. 275)
    Includes indexes.
    1. Ethnic folklore—United States—Abstracts.
2. Ethnic folklore—Canada—Abstracts. I. Stern,
Stephen. II. Title. III. Series. IV. Series: Garland
reference library of the humanities ; v. 275.
GR105.G43   1982   016.398′0971   80-9019
ISBN 0-8240-9307-0

KH
4-12-83

Printed on acid-free, 250-year-life paper
Manufactured in the United States of America

Dedicated to
RICHARD M. DORSON,
who led the way
and inspired others,
through his example and encouragement,
to follow

CONTENTS

	Introduction	xi
I.	General (GL) (1–82)	3
II.	Armenian (AR) (1–10)	24
III.	Austrian (AU) (1–6)	26
IV.	Basque (BA) (1–2)	28
V.	Belgian (BE) (1–3)	28
VI.	Bohemian (BO) (1)	29
VII.	Bulgarian (BU) (1–4)	29
VIII.	Celtic (unspecified) (CE) (1)	30
IX.	Chinese (CH) (1–28)	30
X.	Cornish (CO) (1–9)	36
XI.	Croatian (CR) (1–7)	38
XII.	Czech (CZ) (1–13)	40
XIII.	Danish (DA) (1–7)	42
XIV.	Dutch (DU) (1–28)	44
XV.	Egyptian (EG) (1)	49

XVI.	Filipino (FI) (1–6)	49
XVII.	Finnish (FN) (1–26)	51
XVIII.	French (FR) (1–119)	56
XIX.	German (GE) (1–775)	80
XX.	Greek (GR) (1–39)	230
XXI.	Gypsy (GY) (1–14)	240
XXII.	Hungarian (HU) (1–31)	242
XXIII.	Icelandic (IC) (1–4)	250
XXIV.	Indian (ID) (1–4)	251
XXV.	Iranian (IN) (1)	251
XXVI.	Irish (IR) (1–119)	252
XXVII.	Italian (IT) (1–86)	275
XXVIII.	Japanese (JA) (1–13)	293
XXIX.	Jewish (JE) (1–86)	296
XXX.	Korean (KO) (1)	317
XXXI.	Latvian (LA) (1–3)	317
XXXII.	Lebanese (LE) (1–4)	319
XXXIII.	Lithuanian (LI) (1–11)	320
XXXIV.	Macedonian (MA) (1–2)	322
XXXV.	Mongol (MO) (1)	322

XXXVI.	Norwegian (NO) (1–22)	323
XXXVII.	Pakistani (PA) (1)	327
XXXVIII.	Polish (PL) (1–87)	328
XXXIX.	Portuguese (PO) (1–22)	344
XL.	Romanian (RO) (1–7)	350
XLI.	Russian (RU) (1–24)	352
XLII.	Scandinavian (SA) (1–2)	357
XLIII.	Scottish (SC) (1–45)	357
XLIV.	Serbian (SE) (1–8)	364
XLV.	Slavic (SI) (1–2)	366
XLVI.	Slavonian (SJ) (1)	367
XLVII.	Slovak (SK) (1–10)	367
XLVIII.	Slovenian (SL) (1–3)	368
XLIX.	Spanish (SP) (1–16)	369
L.	Swedish (SS) (1–31)	372
LI.	Swiss (SW) (1–9)	379
LII.	Syriac (SY) (1)	380
LIII.	Syrian (SZ) (1–5)	381
LIV.	Turkish (TU) (1–5)	382
LV.	Ukrainian (UK) (1–35)	382

LVI. Welsh (WE) (1–8)   391

LVII. Yugoslav (YU) (1–10)   393

       Folklore Forms and Topics Index   397

       General Subject Index   421

       Geographical Index   427

       Author Index   449

INTRODUCTION

Nature and Scope

This is a bibliography of the folklore of European and Asian immigrants and their American- and Canadian-born descendants. It focuses upon examples and analyses of traditional expressive forms and behaviors observed among, recorded from, and concerned with members of the immigrant generations and their New World progeny. Included are books and essays which document Old World folklore remembered or perpetuated by the immigrants; transformations of immigrants' homeland traditions which have developed in American and Canadian locales; folklore generated as a result of the experiences of immigrating and adapting to New World environments; examples of traditional forms and behaviors created in the United States and Canada to express or maintain ethnicity; and folklore evolved by others to characterize their perceptions of, and reactions to, the immigrants and their offspring. Thus, one can find, side by side, works which document folktales that the immigrants learned in their homelands; New World versions of Old World ballads; personal experience narratives about the departure from the old, and the arrival and settlement in the new, country; festivals during which ethnicity is displayed through the costumes worn, the foods served, the music played, the dances performed, or the crafts sold; and jokes and slurs which stereotype the behaviors and values of those identified ethnically in particular ways.

The 1900 entries (many of which are multiple listings) cover a time period from 1888 through 1980. Books and essays cited are all published works written in English. Many contain data in other languages (some with, and some without, English translations); and a few are summaries or translations of works written in languages other than English. Most of the essays included appear in folklore periodicals; and most of the books listed either are authored by folklorists or contain information about, or examples of, the kinds of traditional expressive forms and behaviors upon which folklorists focus. (A listing of the periodical runs perused for the bibliography follows this introduction.)

General historical and ethnographic works on immigration and ethnicity are not included unless their authors either discuss or include specific examples of folklore; and unpublished theses, dissertations, conference papers, and research reports are excluded. (For relevant theses and dissertations, the reader should see *Folklore Theses and Dissertations in the United States*, compiled by Alan Dundes, Publications of the American Folklore Society, Bibliographical and Special Series, 27, Austin: University of Texas Press, 1976.) As noted above, this bibliography is concerned only with the folklore of European and Asian immigrants and their American- and Canadian-born descendants. Those interested in Mexican-American and Afro-American folklore should consult recent bibliographies which provide comprehensive coverage of the folklore of these peoples: Michael Heisley, *An Annotated Bibliography of Chicano Folklore from the Southwestern United States* (Los Angeles: UCLA Center for the Study of Comparative Folklore and Mythology, 1977), and John J. Szwed and Roger D. Abrahams, *Afro-American Folk Cultures: An Annotated Bibliography of Materials from North, Central and South America and the West Indies*, 2 volumes, Publications of the American Folklore Society, Bibliographical and Special Series, 31 (Philadelphia: Institute for the Study of Human Issues, 1978).

Organization

This bibliography is divided into fifty-seven (57) sections, with sections II through LVII arranged alphabetically according to ethnic designations. Section I (General) lists works which include data from multiple ethnic groups or which discuss theoretical or methodological issues relevant to immigrant or ethnic folklore studies in general. Entries in each section are identified by a combination of letters and numbers. For the most part, the letters in the entry designations are the first two letters of the ethnic grouping (e.g., CH = Chinese, IR = Irish, JE = Jewish). When duplication would have resulted from following this practice, alternative alphabetical codes were devised and employed to avoid confusion (e.g., FI = Filipino and FN = Finnish; SS = Swedish and SW = Swiss). The alphabetical codes for, and the number of entries in, each section are indicated in the section headings—e.g., I. General (GL) (1–82); XVIII. French (FR) (1–119). Because the compilers were influenced in designating ethnic groupings by titles of, and emphases in, essays and books, section headings sometimes overlap (e.g., Czech and Slovakian; Scandinavian and Danish, Norwegian, and Swedish; Yugoslavian and Serbian and Croatian). Hence, users are urged to explore the full listing of section headings in the Contents to determine which are relevant to their interests.

Entry designations preceded by asterisks are multiply listed, but full bibliographical citations and annotations are provided only once. Parenthetical remarks following the item indicate cross-listings and identify the entry which contains the full citation and annotation. Since many books and essays cited include data obtained from individuals of different ethnic backgrounds, the number of multiply-listed entries is sizable. While some might regard this procedure as unnecessarily duplicative, the compilers feel that it will facilitate users' finding data and studies which might otherwise go unnoticed or be difficult to locate.

Annotations

Annotations are provided for every entry in the bibliography. When possible, annotations for multiply-listed entries are included under the ethnic grouping to which the greatest amount of data or discussion is devoted. For example, Ruth Ann Musick's book *Green Hills of Magic: West Virginia Folktales from Europe* (Lexington, Ky., 1970) presents texts of folktales recorded in West Virginia from individuals of Armenian, Austrian, Czech, Hungarian, Irish, Italian, Polish, Romanian, Russian, Turkish, and Yugoslavian ancestry. Since the number of texts reported from individuals of Italian background is the largest (24), the annotation of Musick's book is provided in the Italian section (as part of entry *IT52); but the work is also listed (by author's name and title) in each of the other ten relevant sections of the bibliography, with instructions to users to see *IT52 for the full citation and annotation.

By contrast, when an equal or near-equal quantity of data or portion of a discussion comes from or concerns members of two or more ethnic groups, the compilers have decided arbitrarily under which section to provide the full citation and annotation. For instance, Pandora Hopkins' essay "Individual Choice and the Control of Musical Change" (*Journal of American Folklore* 89:354, 1976, 449–462) includes descriptions and discussions of an Irish-American traditional singer and an Icelandic-American musician, with approximately the same amount of space devoted to each. The annotation could have been included with either the Icelandic or the Irish entry for that work. The decision to annotate the essay in the Icelandic section (under *IC2) was thus arbitrary; but since the work is included under Irish (as *IR45) as well, users looking under either the Icelandic or the Irish heading will find the reference, though they will have to see the listing of the work in the Icelandic section to find the full bibliographical citation and annotation.

In the annotations, the compilers describe each essay and book specifically and succinctly, avoiding evaluative or judgmental statements. They also provide other kinds of information of interest to folklorists. Thus, when a cited work is based on its author's or someone else's fieldwork, the place at which, and dates on which, the field research was conducted are noted, if indicated in the publication. Moreover, when an entry includes examples of "folklore items," such as texts of proverbs or songs, the number of such items is usually indicated. Hence, users can generally discover from the annotations when and where data were obtained and how many examples of specific folklore forms or behaviors are included in a particular publication.

Indices

Following the main body of this work are four indices, designed to enable users to locate works on the basis of criteria other than ethnic designations. As its title implies, the Folklore Forms and Topics Index groups together publications containing examples, discussions, or analyses of various expressive forms and behaviors upon which folklorists focus (e.g., beliefs, customs, songs, tales); but it also indexes works according to topics commonly discussed in the folkloristic literature (e.g., baptism, courtship and marriage, death and the dead, occupational folklore, urban folklore, the weather, witches). By contrast, the General Subject Index includes headings which identify constructs usually employed in folkloristic research on immigrant or ethnic groups (e.g., culture change, ethnic identity); those which specify non-immigrant or ethnic group labels (e.g., Catholics, Hutterites); and those which designate a variety of other phenomena (e.g., cartoons, housekeeping, museums, phonograph records, snakes, modes of transportation, World War II). The Geographical Index brings together references to entries according to the provinces (Canada) and states (the United States) in which data were recorded or informants lived; and provincial and state designations are followed by subheadings identifying counties, regions, cities, and towns within these geopolitical units (arranged alphabetically rather than hierarchically). Finally, the Author Index presents an alphabetical listing (by last names) of the authors of all the entries included in the bibliography.

The organization of the citations under indexing headings follows the organization of the bibliography, with all references to the first section—General (GL)—coming first, followed by references according to ethnic group (in alphabetical order). Multiply-listed entries are indexed by the entry designations which contain the full bibliographical citations and annotations for the works, with cross-listings following them (enclosed in parentheses). When indexing headings are related in some way, cross-references are provided so users will know which additional indexing headings to consult.

Limitations, Resources, and Acknowledgments

Every bibliography is selective, and this one is no exception. The compilers have included only works which they were able to obtain and read. Items which could not be examined at first hand have not been included. This has obviously resulted in the exclusion of books and essays which might be relevant to users with interests in specific ethnic groups. Moreover, it has meant that coverage for the United States is more comprehensive than that for Canada, since a greater number of American and a lesser number of Canadian resources were available for the compilers' perusal. For these limitations, the compilers can only apologize and express their hope that any revision of this bibliography, or any successor to it, can include works with which the compilers are unfamiliar or of which they are aware but did not include because they could not obtain copies of them in time to consider them for inclusion.

Fortunately, the compilers had available to them the excellent resources of the many libraries on the campus of the University of California, Los Angeles (UCLA), as well as the services of the UCLA Interlibrary Loan Department. Particularly helpful were the extensive folklore holdings in the University Research Library and the Wayland D. Hand Library of Folklore and Mythology in the Center for the Study of Comparative Folklore and Mythology. The compilers also acknowledge, with deepest thanks, the assistance of colleagues and students who responded to requests for references and for bibliographies of their own publications on American and Canadian immigrant and ethnic folklore. Those who supplied such materials and who were often even kind enough to send reprints, course bibliographies, and syllabi are Samuel J. Armistead, Dan Ben-Amos, Carla Bianco, Jan Harold Brunvand, Larry Danielson, Linda Dégh, the late Richard M. Dorson, James R. Dow, Elsie Ivancich Dunin, Stephen Erdely, Gregory Gizelis, Wayland D. Hand, Philip Hiscock, Nathan Hurvitz, Alan Jabbour, Louis C. Jones, Barbara Kirshenblatt-Gimblett, Barbro Klein, Roberta Krell, Janet Langlois, Yvonne Lockwood, Jens Lund, Herminia Q. Meñez, George Monteiro, Willard B. Moore, Harry Oster, James Porter, Joanne B. Purcell, Charles Speroni, Robert Thomas Teske, and D.K. Wilgus. The compilers single out for special thanks Robert B. Klymasz, who not only provided immigrant and ethnic folklore bibliographies and copies of his own many publications on the subject but who also obtained for the compilers many out-of-print works on Canadian immigrant and ethnic folklore.

In any collaborative work such as this, there is always a necessary division of labor. Stephen Stern uncovered most of the entries for the German section, the largest single subdivision in the bibliography. Robert A. Georges compiled most of the entries for the other sections, ably assisted by Mary MacGregor-Villarreal, Clodagh Harvey, and Charmaine Grey. Clodagh Harvey's assistance was funded by a UCLA Academic Senate research grant awarded to Robert A. Georges; and Charmaine Grey worked on the bibliography for one quarter during which she held a research assistantship in the UCLA Center for the Study of Comparative Folklore and Mythology. The compilers acknowledge, with thanks, the support provided by the Academic Senate and Patrick K. Ford, Director of the Center.

The subject of this bibliography is one in which its compilers have a long-standing interest. Both wrote dissertations on immigrant folklore under the supervision of the late Richard M. Dorson at Indiana University—Robert A. Georges on Greek-American folk beliefs and narratives and Stephen Stern on Sephardic Jewish folklore in Los Angeles. They thank Alan Dundes, editor of this bibliography series, and Garland Publishing for providing them the opportunity to compile a work which both builds upon and extends their knowledge of this important field of American and Canadian folkloristics. The compilers hope that this bibliography will heighten researchers' awareness of the accomplishments and limitations of existing publications on American and Candian immigrant and ethnic folklore and that it will inspire others to expand the data base and to offer their insights into the ways in which the folklore of immigrants and their New World descendants facilitates cultural continuity, enhances the quality of social life, serves as an expressive outlet for collective accomplishments and frustrations, and reveals the distinctiveness of the human species.

We dedicate this work to the memory of Richard M. Dorson, who was a pioneer in American folklore studies. Professor Dorson was the first American folklorist to study systematically and rigorously the traditions of numerous ethnic groups in the United States, and he inspired many of his students—through his exemplary research and writings and his personal conviction of the importance of this field as a vital part of American folkloristics—to document and analyze ethnic traditions about which little was known or had been written. Because of Professor Dorson's industriousness and encouragement, the bibliography of American and Canadian immigrant and ethnic folklore is larger and richer at this point in time than it would have been had the field had a less insightful, resourceful, hard-working, or convincing leader or spokesperson.

Finally, the compilers express their deepest appreciation to their spouses, Mary Georges and Marilyn Stern, and their sons, Jonathan Georges and Alan Stern, for their patience, understanding, and support, without which this project would not have been possible. Mary Georges and Marilyn Stern aided their harried spouses inestimably as well by helping with indexing, proofreading, and typing at times when the pressures were greatest. For their encouragement, confidence, and assistance, the compilers are most grateful.

List of Periodical Runs Consulted for This Work

Following is a list of periodical runs consulted volume by volume and page by page for this bibliography (_not_ a complete listing of all periodicals from which bibliographical entries are taken). Those titles preceded by asterisks were checked through 1980 or through their terminal dates of publication, if the latter occurred prior to 1980. For those periodicals _not_ preceded by asterisks—that is, those for which all volumes and issues could not be checked through 1980 or for the full periods of their runs—information is provided following the citations to indicate which volumes and issues were or were not examined.

AFFword, Publication of Arizona Friends of Folklore, 3–4, 1973–75.
*_Alberta Folklore Quarterly_
Arv, 1–34, 1954–78
*_Canadian Folk Music Journal_
*_Canadian-German Folklore_
*_Colorado Folksong Bulletin_
Current Anthropology 1–15, 1960–74
*_Ethnomusicology_ and its forerunner _Ethno-Musicology Newsletter_
Folklore Forum, all issues _except_ 4:1–2 (1971) ; 5:1 (1972) ; 6:1–3 (1973) ; 7:1 (1974)

Folklore and Mythology Studies (UCLA)
French Folklore Bulletin, The
Hoosier Folklore
Indiana Folklore, all issues *except* 1980.
JEMF Quarterly (John Edwards Memorial Foundation, UCLA)
Journal of American Folklore
Journal of the Association of Graduate Dance Ethnologists, all *except*
    volume 1.
Journal of the Folklore Institute
Journal of the International Folk Music Council
Journal of the Ohio Folklore Society, all issues *except* for 1979–1980.
Journal of Popular Culture
Kentucky Folklore Record, all issues *except* 1980.
Keystone Folklore and its forerunner *Keystone Folklore Quarterly,* all
    issues *except* 23: 3-4 (1979) and issues for 1980.
Louisiana Folklore Miscellany, only checked 2:2 (1965).
Maledicta, The International Journal of Verbal Aggression
Mid-South Folklore, 1–6, 1973–78.
Midwest Folklore
Midwestern Journal of Language and Folklore, all issues *except* 1980.
Mississippi Folklore Register, 1–11, 1967–77.
New Mexico Folklore Record, 1–14, 1946–77.
New York Folklore and its forerunner *New York Folklore Quarterly,* all
    issues *except* 5: 3–4 (1979) and all 1980 issues.
North Carolina Folklore
Northeast Folklore, 1–19, 1958–78.
Northwest Folklore, 1–3, 1965–68.
Pennsylvania Dutchman
Pennsylvania Folklife
Polish Folklore
Publications of the Texas Folklore Society, all issues *except* 1980.
Southern Folklore Quarterly, all issues *except* 42:4 (1978) and
    1979–80.
Southwest Folklore
Temenos, 1–14, 1965–78.
Tennessee Folklore Society Bulletin
Western Folklore and its forerunner *California Folklore Quarterly*
Yearbook of the International Folk Music Council, all issues *except*
    1980.

BIBLIOGRAPHY

I. GENERAL (GL) (1-82)

GL1 Abrahams, Roger D. "Folklore." In *Harvard Encyclopedia of American Ethnic Groups*, edited by Stephan Thernstrom, Ann Orlov, and Oscar Handlin, pp. 370-379. Cambridge, Mass.: Harvard University Press, 1980.

Survey of folklore research among American ethnic groups, with characterization of the nature and functions of folklore; ways in which and reasons why folklore is maintained, generated, and evaluated; and insights that the study of ethnic folklore can provide into social and cultural processes. Includes discussion of the "creole continuum" and public presentations of ethnicity.

*GL2 Abrahams, Roger D. "Folklore in the Definition of Ethnicity: An American and Jewish Perspective." In *Studies in Jewish Folklore: Proceedings of a Regional Conference of the Association for Jewish Studies Held at the Spertus College of Judaica, Chicago, May 1-3, 1977*, edited by Frank Talmage, pp. 13-20. Cambridge, Mass.: Association for Jewish Studies, 1980.

Discussion of the contemporary concepts of ethnicity and ethnic identity in relation to the author's self-conception of his identities as American and Jewish. Notes that "ethnic identity turns on the very same kind of recognition of cultural difference as do stereotypes, but without the sense of either inferiority or superiority implied in stereotyping." Includes characterization and analysis of 1 Jewish joke. Warns that ethnicity today is becoming increasingly viewed as a consumable phenomenon rather than providing "individuals with any sense of their own traditions and history."
(Cross-listed as *JE1.)

GL3 Abrahams, Roger D., and Kalčik, Susan. "Folklore and Cultural Pluralism." In *Folklore in the Modern World*, edited by Richard M. Dorson, pp. 223-236. The Hague: Mouton Publishers, 1978.

3

Discussion of the growing awareness and public display
since the 1960s of ethnicity among non-Anglo whites in
the United States. Suggests that because folklore is
performance oriented, folklorists can contribute to an
understanding of the transition of traditional behaviors
to the realm of popular culture.

GL4 Algeo, John. "Xenophobit Ethnica." *Maledicta, The
International Journal of Verbal Aggression* 1:2 (1977):
133-140.

General discussion of derogatory English words and phrases,
with emphasis on those which reflect dislike of foreigners.
Includes examples of pejorative labels for members of some
immigrant and racial groups.

GL5 Barbeau, C.M. "Canadian-English Folk-Lore." *Journal of
American Folk-Lore* 31:119 (1918):1-3.

Brief commentary on folklore in Canada that remains to be
collected from non-French-speaking Canadians, namely the
English, Scottish, Irish, and Pennsylvania Germans. Notes
previous collecting and publishing efforts fostered by
the American Folklore Society in French Canada and the
establishment of branch societies in Quebec and Ontario.

GL6 Barbeau, C. Marius. "The Field of European Folk-Lore in
America." *Journal of American Folk-Lore* 32:124 (1919):
185-197.

Presidential address urging the study (with renewed interest and improved techniques) of the folklore of various
European immigrants and their descendants in America.
Notes briefly the presence of the "intrusive folk tradition"
of the Spanish, French, British, German, Dutch, and Swedish
in America and mentions some of the primary sources of
material already collected from these peoples. Stresses
the importance of obtaining more comparative data to be
able to answer questions of origins, particularly for
European material recorded among Afro-Americans and
Indians. Suggests that a plan and method for studying
European folklore in America must be established and
should include a faithful and complete record made in the
field, preferably by trained folklorists rather than by
amateurs.

*GL7 Barry, Phillips. "The Collection of Folk-Song." *Journal
of American Folk-Lore* 27:103 (1914):77-78.

Brief reminder that European material is abundant in
America and that much collecting has yet to be done.

References made to a few published folksongs collected
in America from native speakers of languages other than
English. Includes musical transcriptions of 3 French-
Canadian melodies, identified as "La Belle Canadienne,"
"Old Canadian French Song," and "La Fille blonde."
(Cross-listed as *FR23.)

GL8 Birnbaum, Mariana D. "On the Language of Prejudice."
     Western Folklore 30:4 (1971):247-268.

     General discussion of ethnic slurs or ethnophaulisms,
     with examples from Europe and the United States.
     Includes comments on possible reasons for the develop-
     ment, use, and perpetuation of such pejorative labels.

*GL9 Boswell, George W. "Ole Miss Jokes and Anecdotes."

     (Cross-listed as *IT12, *JE8, *PL7.)
     (See *PL7 for full citation and annotation.)

*GL10 Brunvand, Jan Harold. "Some Thoughts on the Ethnic-
     Regional Riddle Joke." Indiana Folklore 3:1 (1970):
     128-142.

     Discussion of possible models for, popularity of, and
     functions served by ethnic riddle jokes. Includes 1
     Jewish, 23 Polish, 13 Afro-American jokes. Based on
     archival data obtained at Indiana University in 1965.
     (Cross-listed as *JE10, *PL8.)

*GL11 Bryant, Margaret M. "Folklore in the Schools: Folklore
     in College English Classes." New York Folklore
     Quarterly 2:4 (1946):286-296.

     Discussion of the utility and value of using folklore
     in teaching college students, with commentary on
     proverbs and presentation of 14 proverb texts. Also
     includes 26 texts of children's rhymes, identified as
     counting-out (3), jump-rope (2), ball-bouncing (2),
     and miscellaneous (19), 5 of which constitute or
     include ethnic slurs against Jews, Afro-Americans, and
     Japanese.
     (Cross-listed as *JA1, *JE11.)

GL12 Christenson, Jackie. "Ethnic Folklore and the School
     Art Curriculum." New York Folklore 2:3&4 (1976):
     177-180.

     Drawing on experiences with Mexican-American students
     in San Antonio, Texas, argues that students' knowledge
     of folklore can be a valuable source for art work and
     can help bridge the gap between cultures.

GL13   Christiansen, Reidar Th. *European Folklore in America.*
        Studia Norvegica 12 (1962):1–124.

        States that most folklore in North America has British,
        Spanish, and French traditions as its sources and that
        imported narrative folklore has undergone changes that
        make it compatible with the New World environments and
        post-settlement eras. Asserts that this folklore is main-
        tained best in geographically-isolated areas and among
        those who continue to speak their homeland languages.
        Focuses principally on folktales, legends, and folk
        beliefs to exemplify these points.

GL14   Clements, William M. "Cueing the Stereotype: The
        Verbal Strategy of the Ethnic Joke." *New York*
        Folklore 5:1–2 (1979):53–61.

        Discussion of how and why ethnic stereotyping occurs in
        the United States, followed by a description of ways
        tellers of ethnic jokes "associate their jokes with
        the stereotypes with which they assume their audiences
        are familiar." Indicates that ethnic jokes are not
        always intended to denigrate particular ethnic groups,
        but may instead be directed at anyone considered to be
        an outsider.

GL15   Clifton, Merritt. "How To Hate Thy Neighbor: A Guide
        to Racist Maledicta." *Maledicta, The International*
        Journal of Verbal Aggression 2:1–2 (1978):149–174.

        Listing of 177 words and phrases common in American
        English that identify people according to racial,
        ethnic, geographical, or physical characteristics.
        Includes some examples referring to members of specific
        immigrant or ethnic groups.

GL16   Colombo, John Robert. "Canadian Slurs, Ethnic and
        Other." *Maledicta, The International Journal of Verbal*
        Aggression 3:2 (1979):182–184.

        Listing of 15 Canadian slurs, some pertaining to
        members of immigrant or ethnic groups.

GL17   Cray, Ed. "And Still More Derisive Ethnic Adjectives."
        Western Folklore 26:3 (1967):190–191.

        Presentation of 2 brief historical footnotes, offered
        as supplements to derisive ethnic adjectives noted in
        earlier essays by the author (see GL18, GL19).

GL18   Cray, Ed. "Ethnic and Place Names as Derisive Adjec-
          tives." *Western Folklore* 21:1 (1962):27-34.

       Listing of 77 expressions involving ethnic and place
       names, most used derisively. Based on fieldwork
       conducted in California. Includes some explanations
       and etymologies.

GL19   Cray, Ed. "More Ethnic and Place Names as Derisive
          Adjectives." *Western Folklore* 24:3 (1965):197-198.

       Listing of 23 words and expressions incorporating
       ethnic and place names and used derisively, for the
       most part. Recorded in Los Angeles and presented as
       a supplement to an earlier essay by the author (see
       GL18).

*GL20 Creighton, Helen. "Canada's Maritime Provinces: An
          Ethnomusicological Survey (Personal Observation and
          Recollection)." *Ethnomusicology* 16:3 (1972):404-414.

       Brief survey of folksong and folk music research among
       individuals of British, French, Micmac Indian, Afro-
       American, and other backgrounds in Canada's Maritime
       Provinces. Mentions names of selected fieldworkers
       and publications. Includes selected bibliography and
       discography.
          (Cross-listed as *FR46.)

*GL21 Curtin, Jeremiah. "European Folk-Lore in the United
          States." *Journal of American Folk-Lore* 2:4 (1889):
          56-59.

       General comments about the wealth of possibilities for
       collecting folklore in the United States from members
       of the Celtic, Teutonic, Slavic, and Latin divisions
       of the "Aryan race." Includes summaries of stories
       about the dead and dying told by Irish- and English-
       Americans.
          (Cross-listed as *IR16.)

GL22   Cutting, Edith E. "Community Folk Festival of the
          Triple Cities." *New York Folklore Quarterly* 6:2
          (1950):108-112.

       Brief discussion of events and activities of the
       Triple Cities Community Folk Festival, held annually
       in Binghamton, New York, and of the groups represented
       by crafts (Ukrainians, Afro-Americans, Germans, Welsh,
       Dutch, Lithuanians), by dances (Greeks, Palestinians),
       and by food (Armenians, Ukrainians, Dutch, Polish,
       British).

GL23 Danielson, Larry. "Introduction." *Western Folklore*
       36:1 (1977):1-5. Also published as *Studies in
       Folklore & Ethnicity*, edited by Larry Danielson,
       pp. 1-5. Los Angeles: California Folklore Society,
       1977, 1978.

       Distinction made between ethnic folklore ("the tradi-
       tional expressive behavior maintained consciously and
       unconsciously by a particular ethnic community") and
       the folklore of ethnicity ("the traditional expressive
       behavior used publicly and privately to demarcate one
       ethnic individual or community from another"), followed
       by remarks about 5 essays presented in the issue/work
       for which this essay serves as an introduction (see
       GL79, FI5, FN23, GY10).

GL24 Danielson, Larry, ed. *Studies in Folklore and Ethnicity.*
       Western Folklore 36:1 (1977):1-108. Also published
       as *Studies in Folklore & Ethnicity*, edited by Larry
       Danielson. Los Angeles: California Folklore Society,
       1977, 1978. Pp. 108, introduction, list of contri-
       butors.

       Presentation of 5 original essays concerning the
       articulation of ethnicity through folklore. Includes
       a general survey and analysis of American immigrant/
       ethnic folklore studies (see GL79), an essay on Rom
       Gypsy traditions (see GY10), a discussion of tales and
       taletelling in a Filipino-American community (see FI5),
       an examination of the Finnish-American sauna as a
       source and expression of ethnic identity (see FN23),
       and an essay on a Melungeon drama in Tennessee. Also
       includes an introduction by the editor (see GL23).

GL25 Dégh, Linda. "Approaches to Folklore Research among
       Immigrant Groups." *Journal of American Folklore*
       79:314 (1966):551-556.

       Notes that in many settlement areas, immigrants of
       varied national backgrounds interact and that newly-
       arrived immigrants settle among and associate with those
       who arrived much earlier. Suggests that researchers must
       consider these experiences and not approach immigrant
       folklore by collecting solely from arbitrarily selected
       single immigrant groups.

GL26 Dégh, Linda. "'Comment' to Marcus S. Goldstein,
       'Anthropological Research Action and Education in
       Modern Nations: With Special Reference to the U.S.A.'"
       Current Anthropology 9:4 (1968):256-257.

       Brief commentary on a *Current Anthropology* essay by
       Marcus S. Goldstein in which Dégh challenges the view
       that "very little anthropological attention has been
       given ... any ... contemporary industrial nations,"
       by noting the work of European ethnologists and folk-
       lorists in their own countries. Notes the potential
       for the study of ethnic groups in America and of the
       growing interest in interethnic research, as employed
       by the Indiana University Folklore Institute's
       "co-ordinated fieldwork in 15 ethnic groups in the
       Gary-East Chicago area."

*GL27 Dégh, Linda. "Prepared Comments by Linda Dégh."
       Journal of American Folklore 83:328 (1970):217-222.
       Also published in *The Urban Experience and Folk
       Tradition*, edited by Américo Paredes and Ellen J.
       Stekert, pp. 53-58. Publications of the American
       Folklore Society, Bibliographical and Special Series
       22 (1971).

       Commentary on Richard M. Dorson's presentation (see
       *GL34) concerning the study of folklore in urban areas.
       Compares and contrasts older and more recent conceptions
       of folk and folklore and characterizes her own fieldwork
       experiences among Hungarian-Americans in the Calumet
       area of Indiana, noting that their folklore reflects
       their perceptions and experiences in urban America.
       Views urban immigrant/ethnic folklore less as aesthetic
       creations and more as indicators of attitudes and
       ideologies.
       (Cross-listed as *HU6.)

GL28   Dégh, Linda. "The Study of Ethnicity in Modern
       European Ethnology." *Journal of the Folklore
       Institute* 12:2-3 (1975):113-130.

       Survey of studies of ethnic groups in Europe, with
       passing comparisons and contrasts between immigrant
       and ethnic groups and studies of them in North
       America and Europe.

*GL29   Dégh, Linda.   "Survival and Revival of European Folk
        Cultures in America."   *Ethnologia Europaea* 2-3
        (1968-1969):97-107.

        General discussion of settlement, acculturation, and
        assimilation processes among immigrants to America,
        with particular emphasis on findings from 1965-67
        fieldwork among Hungarian-Americans in the Calumet
        region of Indiana.   Includes brief mention of selected
        customs, religious practices, foodways, and traditional
        concepts and modes of interaction.
        (Cross-listed as *HU7.)

*GL30   Dorson, Richard M.   "The Ethnic Research Survey of
        Northwest Indiana."   In *Kontakte und Grenzen:
        Probleme der Volks-, Kultur- und Sozialforschung.
        Festschrift für Gerhard Heilfurth zum 60. Geburtstag*,
        pp. 65-69.   Göttingen: Otto Schwartz, 1969.

        Brief description of a field project undertaken by
        the Folklore Institute, Indiana University, in the
        Gary-East Chicago, Indiana, area, including comments
        by Linda Dégh and Andrew Vázsonyi on their life-history
        approach to Hungarian-American folklore.   Calls for a
        modification in folklore studies from an emphasis on
        traditional genres to a concern with life histories,
        personal experiences, and folk ideology.
        (Cross-listed as *HU12.)

GL31   Dorson, Richard M.   "Folklore and Cultural History."
        In *Research Opportunities in American Cultural
        History*, edited by John Francis McDermott, pp. 102-
        123.   Lexington, Ky.: University of Kentucky Press,
        1961.

        Survey of the accomplishments, limitations, and future
        prospects in American folklore studies, with brief mention
        of the few existing studies of and suggestions for future
        research among American immigrant and ethnic groups
        (pp. 117-118).

GL32   Dorson, Richard M.   "Hunting Folklore in the Armpit of
        America."   *Indiana Folklore* 10:2 (1977):97-106.

        Characterization of the work, experiences, and
        problems of a fieldwork team in the Calumet region of
        northwest Indiana, with passing reference to ethnic
        groups and their traditions.

GL33   Dorson, Richard M. "Immigrant Folklore." In *American
        Folklore*, pp. 135-165. Chicago: University of
        Chicago Press, 1959.

        Survey of selected folklore of post-Civil War immigrants
        to the United States, with examples from northern and
        western Europeans living in the Upper Peninsula of
        Michigan; Portuguese New Englanders; Japanese-American
        internees in Tule Lake, California, during World War II;
        Norwegians, South Italians, Greeks, Irish, and Poles.
        Includes texts of 8 dialect stories/jokes, verses from
        2 songs, summaries and characterizations of assorted
        folk beliefs and tales.

*GL34   Dorson, Richard M. "Is There a Folk in the City?"
        Journal of American Folklore 83:328 (1970):185-216.
        Also published in *The Urban Experience and Folk
        Tradition*, edited by Américo Paredes and Ellen J.
        Stekert, pp. 21-52. Publications of the American
        Folklore Society, Bibliographical and Special Series
        22 (1971).

        Report of a 23-day field trip to the Gary-East Chicago,
        Indiana, area in 1968, with brief description of the
        area; characterization of interactions with Afro-
        Americans, Serbians, Croatians, Greeks, Mexicans, and
        Puerto Ricans living there; and suggestions for con-
        ceptual schemes, research questions, and techniques
        to be used in studying folk cultures in urban and
        interethnic, as opposed to rural and monoethnic,
        communities. Notes that conventional folklore genres
        are absent or uncommon in interethnic urban America.
        (Cross-listed as *CR1, *GR5, *SE1.)

GL35   Dorson, Richard M. "Symposium on the Concept of
        Ethnohistory: Ethnohistory and Ethnic Folklore."
        Ethnohistory 8:1 (1961):12-30.

        Argues that the "function of ethnohistory ... is to
        provide a documentary history of the concealed and
        officially inarticulate ethnic groups in American
        history." General discussion of kinds of folklore
        examples (dialect stories, ethnic jokes, folksongs) to
        defend the thesis, with passing references to data
        recorded from and about American Indians, Afro-Americans,
        and members of several European immigrant groups.

GL36   Dorson, Richard M. "A Theory for American Folklore."
        Journal of American Folklore 72:285 (1959):197-215.

        Survey of folklore research, followed by presentation
        of a conceptual scheme recommended for studying American
        folklore in terms of "special historical conditions"
        unique to the settlement and development of America.
        Includes discussion of immigration as a source of and
        basis for the generation and perpetuation of folklore
        in the New World (pp. 206-208).

GL37   Dorson, Richard M. "A Theory for American Folklore
        Reviewed." *Journal of American Folklore* 82:325
        (1969):226-244.

        Review of reactions to the author's 1959 essay (see
        GL36). Asserts that criticisms of the theory do not
        invalidate it, and cites recent research and studies
        (including those on immigrant folklore, pp. 239-240)
        to illustrate further the defensibility of the con-
        ceptual scheme proposed.

GL38   Dundes, Alan. "Slurs International: Folk Comparisons
        of Ethnicity and National Character." *Southern
        Folklore Quarterly* 39:1 (1975):15-38.

        Characterization of 51 national and ethnic slurs
        (many from American informants and printed sources)
        in riddle, proverb, and joke forms, involving com-
        parisons of ethnic or nationality groups. Includes
        discussion of possible origins and significance of
        the act of stereotyping and of comparing or contrasting
        national character and ethnicity.

GL39   Eisiminger, Sterling. "A Glossary of Ethnic Slurs in
        American English." *Maledicta, The International
        Journal of Verbal Aggression* 3:2 (1979):153-174.

        Listing of 470 ethnic slurs found among American
        English speakers. Includes many examples pertaining
        to members of various immigrant and ethnic groups.

*GL40   Erdely, Stephen. "Ethnic Music in the United States:
        An Overview." *Yearbook of the International Folk
        Music Council* 11 (1978):114-137.

        Survey essay on ethnic music, based on the author's
        musicological research in Cleveland and northern Ohio,
        Boston, and Canada. Includes brief characterizations
        of "types" of ethnic music (singing societies, instru-

mental groups, liturgical music, folksinging), of
occasions for ethnic music (public events, community
affairs, family celebrations), and of "ethnicity in
ethnic music" (in the literature of choirs, in folksinging). Brief subsections devoted to Scottish bag-
pipers, Croatian and Serbian tamburitzan groups, Gypsy
ensembles, Greek and Armenian instrumental groups,
ancient instruments, fiddling, Jewish liturgical music,
Christian chants, folksinging.
   (Cross-listed as *AR5, *CR2, *GR7, *GY5, *JE22, *SC11,
*SE2.)

*GL41 Erdely, Stephen. "Research on Traditional Music of
       Nationality Groups in Cleveland and Vicinity."
       Ethnomusicology 12:2 (1968):245-250.

       Brief report on the author's research "on the musical
       folklore of nationality groups" in the Cleveland, Ohio,
       area, with mention made of music recorded from Hungarian
       and Slovakian choirs, the German Youth Choir, Croatian
       tamburitzan players, the Scottish Kilty Band, Finnish
       and Romanian singing groups, and Irish musicians. More
       specific characterizations of the Hungarian, Slovakian,
       and Irish collections (including descriptions of kinds
       of songs recorded from singing groups, instrumental
       groups, and individual musicians). Brief notes on
       Romanian, Finnish, and German songs and on American
       influences on ethnic music.
          (Cross-listed as *CR3, *FN11, *GE172, *HU14, *IR26,
       *RO3, *SC12, *SK4.)

*GL42 Evanson, Jacob A. "Folk Songs of an Industrial City."
       In *Pennsylvania Songs and Legends*, edited by George
       Korson, pp. 423-466. Philadelphia: University of
       Pennsylvania Press, 1949.

       General discussion of the Pittsburgh steel industry,
       including the interethnic mix of its workers. Emphasis
       on songs, with brief discussions of 3 Irish immigrant
       bards, presentation of 4 reprinted and 15 field-recorded
       song texts (the latter documented in 1942, 1945, and
       1947 and presented with musical transcriptions).
       Includes 2 songs in Slovak, 1 in Greek, 1 in Finnish
       (all with English translations) and 1 song recorded
       from an individual of German ancestry (in English).
          (Cross-listed as *FN12, *GE177, *GR8, *IR27, *SK5.)

*GL43   Foster, James R. "Brooklyn Folklore." *New York Folk-
        lore Quarterly* 13:2 (1957):83-91.

        Presentation of folklore items collected by the
        author's Long Island University students. Includes
        4 local legends (1 involving a New York Irish family),
        3 Afro-American magical tales, 2 Brazilian Portuguese
        tales from New York, 1 Brazilian changeling story, 2
        Greek tales, and 1 Jewish folktale from Poland. Also
        includes superstitions from individuals of the following
        backgrounds: West Indian (8), Brazilian (2), Italian (3),
        Cuban (1), Spanish (1), Jewish (8), and Afro-American (1).
           (Cross-listed as *GR9, *IR31, *JE24, *PL28, *PO6,
        *SP7.)

 GL44   Grame, Ted C. "Ethnic Music." *Carnegie Magazine*
        49:3 (1975):109-114.

        Brief sketch of various ethnic groups in Pittsburgh,
        Pennsylvania, with emphasis on their music, particularly
        that played in churches and religious community centers.
        Emphasizes the multicultural nature of Pittsburgh and
        suggests that it can serve as a model for the United
        States as a "multi-ethnic, pluralistic society that
        welcomes rather than ignores or discourages, cultural
        differences."

*GL45   Grame, Theodore C. *America's Ethnic Music.* Tarpon
        Springs, Fla.: Cultural Maintenance Association,
        1976. Pp. iv, 232, notes, introduction, bibliography.

        Survey of ethnic music in America and of immigrants'
        experiences as manifested in song and music. Includes
        texts of, and excerpts from, ballads and other tradi-
        tional songs recorded from individuals of varied ethnic
        backgrounds (most reprinted from other sources); one
        chapter (II) on ethnic music in Pittsburgh, Pennsyl-
        vania; a biographical sketch and description of the
        repertoire of a Scottish immigrant woman (chapter III);
        discussion of music and song that mark various rites
        of passage (e.g., marriage, death); discussion of
        ethnic musicians, ethnic phonograph recordings, ethnic
        radio, and ethnic popular music; and the role of music
        and song at ethnic festivals.
           (Cross-listed as *SC18).

GL46   Grame, Theodore C. *Ethnic Broadcasting in the United
        States.* Publication of the American Folklife Center
        No. 4. Washington, D.C.: The American Folklife
        Center, Library of Congress, 1980. Pp. ix, 171,
        preface, bibliography, 4 indices to ethnic radio and
        television stations and broadcasts (with geographical
        locations).

        Presentation of the results of the author's 1977-78
        traveling and research survey of ethnic radio and (to
        a lesser extent) television stations and programs in
        selected communities in Arizona, California, Colorado,
        Connecticut, Florida, Illinois, Louisiana, Maryland,
        Massachusetts, Michigan, Nevada, New Jersey, New Mexico,
        New York, Ohio, Pennsylvania, Texas, Ontario (Canada),
        and Baja California, Chihuahua, and Sonora (Mexico).
        Provides historical sketches of the development of
        ethnic radio and television broadcasts and stations
        and describes and assesses the economics, policy making,
        program content, audiences, and typical formats of
        ethnic broadcasting. Notes the emphasis on music,
        characterized as a mixture of old-fashioned, popular,
        and folk. Provides listings of stations and programs
        visited and studied, including their geographical
        locations and ethnic foci.

*GL47   Greenberg, Andrea. "Form and Function of the Ethnic
        Joke." *Keystone Folklore Quarterly* 17:4 (1972):
        144-161.

        Discussion of differences in function between ethnic
        jokes told by members of the group being depicted and
        those told by "outsiders" and of differences between
        ethnic jokes which are essentially narratives and those
        which occur in riddle form. Focuses primarily on jokes
        about Jews and Afro-Americans, comparing and contrasting
        their nature and functions. Includes characterizations
        or texts of 15 Jewish, 12 Afro-American, 30 riddle
        jokes (involving Morons, Italians, Texas Aggies, Poles,
        French-Canadians, plus a grape and a sick joke), most
        reprinted from other sources. Brief mention made of
        dialect jokes and their functions.
             (Cross-listed as *FR63, *IT27, *JE28, *PL33.)

*GL48   Halpert, Herbert. "Legends of the Cursed Child."
        New York Folklore Quarterly 14:3 (1958):233-241.

        Discussion of a group of legends about children who are
        cursed because their mothers are exposed to impression-

able experiences during pregnancy. Classifies, compares, and contrasts the tales and concludes that they constitute attempts to define a type of moral code through the use of negative models. Includes texts or characterizations of 14 such stories (from a variety of oral and printed sources), 2 identified as Irish, 1 as Scottish, 1 as English.
(Cross-listed as *IR37, *SC19.)

*GL49   Humphrey, Linda T. "'It Ain't Funny, Buster': The Ethnic Riddle-Joke at Citrus Community College." *Southwest Folklore* 4:2 (1980):20-25.

General discussion of ethnic riddle jokes contributed by introductory folklore students to the archive at Citrus Community College, Azusa, California, from 1976 to 1980. Includes examples of jokes about Mexican-Americans (5), Afro-Americans (5), Italians (5), American Indians (2), Chinese (1), Japanese (1), Irish (2), Swedes (1), Texans (1), Okies (1), Californians (1), and multiethnic jokes (5).
(Cross-listed as *CH13, *IR47, *IT32, *JA5, *SS17.)

*GL50   Jones, Louis C. "The Devil in York State." *New York Folklore Quarterly* 8:1 (1952):5-19.

Discussion of stories about the devil in American locales. Includes place names honoring the devil, descriptions of his appearance, relationship of American devil stories to the Faust legend, and beliefs about the nature of the devil and his relationship to human beings. Includes 13 tales involving the devil, 2 of which are identified as being German in origin, 1 identified as French-Canadian. Also includes a brief discussion of themes concerning the devil in French-Canadian tradition.
(Cross-listed as *FR69, *GE318.)

*GL51   Jones, Louis C. "The Evil-Eye among European-Americans." *Western Folklore* 10:1 (1951):11-25.

General discussion about causes, preventives, diagnoses, and cures for the evil eye, with characterizations of 5 personal experience narratives, recorded between 1940 and 1946, from American informants of Greek, Hungarian, Iranian, Irish, Italian, Jewish, Polish, Russian, and Syrian backgrounds.
(Cross-listed as *GR21, *HU17, *IN1, *IR50, *IT35, *JE35, *PL39, *RU10, *SZ2.)

GL52   Jordan, Rosan A. "Ethnic Identity and the Lore of
       the Supernatural." *Journal of American Folklore*
       88:350 (1975):370-382.

       Asserts that individuals relate to their ethnic groups
       in multiple ways (psychologically, socially, and
       culturally) and to varying degrees, often rejecting
       some and endorsing other views or behaviors. Indicates
       that the nature of one's ethnicity is often reflected
       in the folklore learned and attitudes toward folklore.
       Thesis developed with reference to a single female
       Mexican-American informant.

*GL53 Klymasz, Robert B. "The Ethnic Joke in Canada Today."
       Keystone Folklore Quarterly 15:4 (1970):167-173.

       Comparison and contrast of ethnic jokes in Canada and
       the United States, followed by an analysis of the kinds
       of functions ethnic jokes serve for members and non-
       members of ethnic groups. Includes texts of 7 ethnic
       jokes (1 each about the English, French-Canadians,
       Ukrainians, Jews, Newfoundlanders, Italians, Icelanders),
       and 13 riddle joke questions (without answers) about
       Ukrainians.
          (Cross-listed as *FR71, *IC3, *IT38, *JE40, *UK10.)

*GL54 Klymasz, Robert B. "From Immigrant to Ethnic Folklore:
       A Canadian View of Process and Transition." *Journal
       of the Folklore Institute* 10:3 (1973):131-139.

       Distinction made among immigrants' traditional (home-
       land) folklore, the lore which evolves as they resettle
       in new environments and must solve new problems (tran-
       sitional), and the folklore which emerges from com-
       bining elements of the old and new. Emphasis on
       language change as the most important factor in the
       transition from immigrant to ethnic folklore.
          (Cross-listed as *UK12.)

*GL55 Korson, George. "Coal Miners." In *Pennsylvania Songs
       and Legends*, pp. 354-400. Philadelphia: University
       of Pennsylvania Press, 1949.

       General discussion of the development of coal mining
       in Pennsylvania, including the interethnic mix resulting
       from European immigration. Emphasis on songs, with
       excerpts from 7 songs and presentation of 20 song texts
       (with musical transcriptions, recorded between 1940 and
       1947), 1 of which is Slovakian (with English transla-

tion). Includes 1 song identified as Irish, 1 as
Slovakian, 1 as Welsh.
(Cross-listed as *IR56, *SK7, *WE7.)

GL56   Kraut, Alan M. "Ethnic Foodways: The Significance of
       Food in the Designation of Cultural Boundaries
       Between Immigrant Groups in the U.S., 1840-1921."
       Journal of Popular Culture 2:3 (1979):409-420.

       Argues that foodways are an important indicator of
       immigrant values and patterns of social interaction.
       Analyzes the role of foodways among immigrants against
       the background of socioeconomic factors, influences of
       national origin, and functions of religious and
       ritualistic elements. Includes 1 cartoon depicting
       the pervasiveness of ethnic foods.

GL57   Landry, Renée. "The Need for a Survey of Canadian
       Archives with Holdings of Ethnomusicological Interest."
       Ethnomusicology 16:3 (1972):504-512.

       Presentation of results of a survey on musicological hold-
       ings in Canadian archives found in public institutions,
       educational institutions, associations and organizations,
       and private collections. Includes counts on holdings per-
       tinent to members of Canadian immigrant and ethnic groups.

GL58   McCadden, Helen M. "Folklore in the Schools: Folk
       Beliefs: Current Report." *New York Folklore
       Quarterly* 3:4 (1947):330-340.

       Presentation of miscellaneous superstitions gathered
       by a 9th grade class in New York City. Ethnic groups
       represented include Italian, Irish, English, German,
       and Jewish. Survey includes superstitions as follows:
       causes of bad luck, causes of untimely death, harbingers
       of death, omens of death, precautions against death,
       omens of good luck, remedies, methods to counteract
       bad luck, superstitions related to marriage, supersti-
       tions about babies, and occupational superstitions.
       No indication given of which items come from informants
       of which ethnic backgrounds.

GL59   MacMullen, Jerry. "Derisive Ethnic Names." *Western
       Folklore* 22:3 (1963):197.

       Supplement to an earlier essay by Ed Cray (see GL18),
       noting alternative meanings for 3 expressions involving
       ethnic names used derisively.

*GL60 Monahan, Kathleen. "The Role of Ethnic Record Companies
          in Cultural Maintenance: A Look at Greyko." *JEMF
          Quarterly* 14:51 (1978):145-147, 156.

          General discussion of companies that produced "foreign"
          music phonograph records between 1900 and the early
          1950s, with emphasis on the role they played in foster-
          ing multiculturalism in the United States. Detailed
          discussion of Greyko, an ethnic record company formed
          in 1952 by a man of Croatian (Yugoslavian) descent in
          Pittsburgh, Pennsylvania, and of the company's impact
          on emphasizing Croatian/Yugoslavian identity and stimu-
          lating others (such as various tamburitzan music and
          dance troupes) to form and perform.
          (Cross-listed as *CR7, *YU6.)

GL61   Monteiro, George. "And Still More Ethnic and Place
          Names as Derisive Adjectives." *Western Folklore*
          27:1 (1968):51.

          Listing of 11 expressions involving ethnic and place
          names, used derisively for the most part. Supplement
          to earlier essays by Ed Cray (see GL17, GL18, GL19).

GL62   Nettl, Bruno. *Folk and Traditional Music of the
          Western Continents*. Englewood Cliffs, N.J.:
          Prentice-Hall, Inc., 1965. Pp. 213, foreword,
          preface, bibliographies and discographies, index.

          Brief general survey, with commentary on the folk music
          and songs of European immigrants to the United States
          (pp. 194-200).

GL63   Nettl, Bruno. *An Introduction to Folk Music in the
          United States*. Rev. ed. Detroit: Wayne State
          University Press, 1962. Pp. v, 126, preface,
          bibliographical aids, notes, index.

          Brief introductory discussion of American folk music,
          including that of European immigrants (pp. 20-23,
          57-68). Includes 32 musical examples (8 of which are
          European folk music tunes, pp. 108-114).

GL64   Nettl, Bruno. "Preliminary Remarks on Urban Folk
          Music in Detroit." *Western Folklore* 16:1 (1957):
          37-42.

          General discussion of folk music in urban areas such
          as Detroit, noting that folk music "remains in the
          most real sense in the ethnic groups."

GL65   Paredes, Américo. "Tributaries to the Mainstream: The
        Ethnic Groups." In *Our Living Traditions: An Intro-*
        duction to American Folklore, edited by Tristram
        Potter Coffin, pp. 70-80. New York: Basic Books,
        Inc., 1968. Also published as *American Folklore:*
        Voice of America Forum Lectures, edited by Tristram
        Coffin, III, pp. 79-89. Washington, D.C.: U.S.
        Information Agency, 1968.

        Discussion of ethnic diversity in the United States,
        noting that the folklore of immigrants is best viewed
        not merely as a survival from homeland cultures, but
        rather as a source of identity and unity for members of
        ethnic groups and as a means of expressing and coping
        with aspirations and problems. Exemplifies these
        points principally with examples of Mexican-American
        folklore.

*GL66   Peacock, Kenneth. "Establishing Perimeters for
        Ethnomusicological Field Research in Canada: On-
        Going Projects and Future Possibilities at the
        Canadian Centre for Folk Culture Studies." *Ethno-*
        musicology 16:3 (1972):329-334.

        Survey of ethnomusicological research completed among
        immigrant and ethnic groups in Canada. Includes brief
        characterization of fieldwork among Chinese, French,
        Germans, Hungarians, Icelanders, Indian Sikhs, Italians,
        Japanese, Lithuanians, Norwegians, Russian Christian
        Doukhobors, and Ukrainians. Brief mention made of
        some musical instruments and songs, but no examples
        provided.
            (Cross-listed as *CH21, *FR91, *GE428, *HU25, *IC4,
        *ID2, *IT57, *JA9, *LI5, *NO19, *RU19, *UK32.)

GL67   Pelinski, Ramon. "The Music of Canada's Ethnic
        Minorities." *Canada Music Book* 10 (1975):59-86.

        General survey of contributions to Canadian music by
        "ethnic minorities" (excluding peoples of English,
        Scottish, Irish, and French ancestry), with emphasis
        on what has been recorded, in what quantity, and by
        whom.

GL68   Porter, James. "Introduction: The Traditional Music
        of Europeans in America." *Selected Reports in Ethno-*
        musicology 3:1 (1978):1-23.

        General survey of concepts, preoccupations, and
        problems in recording and studying immigrant or ethnic

folklore in general and traditional music in particular
in North America, with critical assessments of prevail-
ing assumptions and constructs found in a diverse body
of scholarly literature. Includes characterizations of
6 essays on traditional European music in America
presented in the volume to which this essay serves as
an introduction (see HU15, JE41, LA3, *SE3).

GL69   Porter, James, ed. *Selected Reports in Ethnomusicology*
       3:1 (1978). Pp. 259, introduction, bibliography,
       list of contributors.

Presentation of 6 original essays, on French music in
Louisiana (in French), fiddle tunes for the British-
American song "Bonaparte's Retreat," Hungarian-American
singers and their songs (see HU15), Nigun composition
in an American Hasidic community (see JE41), Bećar
music in the Los Angeles Serbian community (see *SE3),
and the Latvian kokle in America (see LA3). Includes
introduction by the editor (see GL68).

GL70   Porter, Kenneth. "More and Still More Ethnic and
       Place Names as Derisive and Jocular Adjectives."
       Western Folklore 26:3 (1967):189-190.

Listing of 20 expressions involving ethnic and place
names and used derisively. Supplement to earlier
essays by Ed Cray and Kenneth Porter (see GL18, GL19,
GL71).

GL71   Porter, Kenneth. "Still More Ethnic and Place Names
       as Derisive Adjectives." *Western Folklore* 25:1
       (1966):37-40.

Listing of 28 expressions incorporating ethnic and
place names and used derisively. Supplement to
earlier essays by Ed Cray (see GL18, GL19).

GL72   Rennick, Robert M. "The Inadvertent Changing of Non-
       English Names by Newcomers to America: A Brief
       Historical Survey and Popular Presentation of Cases."
       New York Folklore Quarterly 26:4 (1970):263-282.

General discussion (with assorted examples) of ways in
which and reasons why immigrants' surnames were changed
upon or shortly after their arrival in the United
States. Includes examples gathered by "personal
communication" between 1958 and 1968.

*GL73 Richman, Hyman. "The Saga of Joe Magarac."
           (Cross-listed as *HU27, *SI2.)
           (See *HU27 for full citation and annotation.)

 GL74 Sackett, Marjorie. "Folk Recipes as a Measure of
           Intercultural Penetration." *Journal of American
           Folklore* 85:335 (1972):77–81.

       Discussion of traditional recipes handed down in
       families, based on interviews with 20 women in Concordia,
       Kansas, in 1970. Concludes that despite interethnic
       interaction and the popularity of a local radio cooking
       program, there is little evidence of recipe exchange
       across ethnic lines, except among interviewees who are
       married to men of national backgrounds that differ from
       their own.

*GL75 Shoemaker, Henry W. "Neighbors: The Werewolf in
           Pennsylvania." *New York Folklore Quarterly* 7:2
           (1951):145–155.

       General survey of long-standing beliefs and stories
       about werewolves in Pennsylvania, including characteri-
       zations of 8 tales (1 French-Canadian and set in New
       York), 3 tales about heches (witches), a discussion of
       the French-Canadian tradition of the *loup-garou*, and
       3 stories about unusual wolves believed to be werewolves.
       (Cross-listed as *FR103.)

 GL76 Spicer, Dorothy Gladys. "Health Practices and Beliefs
           of the Immigrant Mother as Seen by a Social Worker."
           Hygeia, The Health Magazine 4:6 (1926):319–321.

       General description of miscellaneous traditional health
       beliefs and healing practices among immigrant women.
       Includes passing references to preventives, diagnoses,
       and cures for the evil eye, the use of midwives, and
       the strength of tradition in perpetuating these beliefs
       and practices. Includes 4 photographs of immigrant
       women.

 GL77 Spottswood, Richard K. "'Do You Sell Your Italians?'"
           JEMF Quarterly 15:56 (1979):225–229.

       General discussion of American phonograph recording
       companies and their early 20th-century developing
       interest in issuing "foreign" music for the consumption
       of immigrants. Includes photographs of 4 promotional

pieces, originally published in *The Voice of Victor*, suggesting why the market for foreign records was potentially great and how it could be developed.

GL78   Spottswood, Richard K. "Ethnic Music in America: First Progress Report on a Discography." *JEMF Quarterly* 15:54 (1979):84-90.

Progress report on a project funded by the National Endowment for the Arts to prepare a discography of ethnic music on records from 1895 to 1942. Characterizes the nature of coverage and kinds of source documents being examined. Includes photographs of phonograph company sheets, cards, and records that serve as sources of some of the information being compiled for the project.

GL79   Stern, Stephen. "Ethnic Folklore and the Folklore of Ethnicity." *Western Folklore* 36:1 (1977):7-32. Also published as *Studies in Folklore & Ethnicity*, edited by Larry Danielson, pp. 7-32. Los Angeles: California Folklore Society, 1977, 1978.

Survey of American immigrant and ethnic folklore scholarship (largely chronologically), with emphasis on the conceptual schemes, assumptions, and research orientations and techniques employed. Includes suggestions for future research.

*GL80   Thompson, Marion. "Folklore in the Schools: Collecting in Cortland." *New York Folklore Quarterly* 9:2 (1953):133-141.

Presentation of folklore items gathered by teachers at Cortland State College for Teachers in New York. Includes 1 tall tale, 8 weather sayings, 5 Irish boob tales, 1 Indian baptismal chant, 3 children's games, 2 children's song fragments, 7 Jewish proverbs, 3 Jewish retorts, 2 Italian stories, and 1 proverb with a fable explaining its meaning.
(Cross-listed as *IR105, *IT77, *JE77.)

*GL81   Walerstein, Marcia. "Ethnic Folklore in the Primary School Classroom." *Keystone Folklore Quarterly* 15:4 (1970):161-166.

Characterization and exemplification of the way folklore is used in a private primary school in San Francisco which is multiethnic in population and concerns.

Includes descriptions of typical activities during one
month in the Jewish class, selected examples of folklore utilized in Spanish and Afro-American classes, and
brief mention of ethnic slurs.
(Cross-listed as *JE79, *SP16.)

*GL82 Walker, Barbara K. "Folklore in the Schools: Collecting
       by Seventh Graders." *New York Folklore Quarterly*
       2:3 (1946):228-236.

Listing of miscellaneous folklore items recorded by a
7th grade class in Cornwall, New York. Groups represented in the survey, but not specifically cited as
sources of individual folklore items, include Austrian,
Czechoslovakian, Dutch, English, French, German, Italian,
Irish, Indian, Jewish, Afro-American, Polish, Scottish,
Spanish, Swedish, Swiss, and Welsh. Includes 1 tale
(in English) identified as German.
(Cross-listed as *GE700.)

II. ARMENIAN (AR) (1-10)

AR1   Bergen, Fanny D. "Borrowing Trouble." *Journal of
       American Folk-Lore* 11:40 (1898):55-59.

Presentation of summaries, from New York and Ohio, of
a tale about a young girl who laments the death of her
baby, imagined while she was daydreaming. Includes
1 text obtained from an Armenian immigrant woman.
Brief commentary about an ending formula and settings
in which stories are told in Armenia.

AR2   Borcherdt, Donn. "Armenian Folk Songs and Dances in
       the Fresno and Los Angeles Areas." *Western Folklore*
       18:1 (1959):1-12.

Description of folksongs and dances recorded from
informants of Armenian background in Fresno and Los
Angeles, California. Includes texts (in Armenian and
English translation), with musical transcriptions, of
5 songs, brief description of principal musical
instruments used and dances performed.

*AR3   Crosby, Rev. John R. "Modern Witches of Pennsylvania."
        Journal of American Folk-Lore 40:157 (1927):304-309.

   Brief characterization of Russian and Armenian immigrant
   members of the Thondrakian or Paulician sect living in
   Indiana County, Pennsylvania. Includes a short character
   sketch of one modern-day witch, 1 legend about a bewitched
   child, and 25 descriptions of beliefs, rituals, customs,
   and taboos, viewed by the author as survivals from pre-
   Christian and medieval times and as a means of avoiding
   the encroachment of Americanization.
   (Cross-listed as *RU6.)

 AR4   Edwards, G.D. "Items of Armenian Folk-Lore Collected
        in Boston." *Journal of American Folk-Lore* 12:45
        (1899):97-107.

   Collection (in English) of 11 dreams, 15 superstitions,
   13 cures for diseases, 12 riddles, 3 games (including
   1 counting-out rhyme in Armenian), various miscellaneous
   customs (including a description of holidays and the
   celebration of Easter). Comments on the need to record
   Armenian folklore in America before it is forgotten and
   on the various difficulties encountered in collecting
   such material, particularly language.

*AR5   Erdely, Stephen. "Ethnic Music in the United States:
        An Overview."

   (Cross-listed as *GL40, *CR2, *GR7, *JE22, *SC11,
   *SE2.)
   (See *GL40 for full citation and annotation.)

 AR6   Hoogasian, Susie, and Gardner, Emelyn E. "Armenian
        Folktales from Detroit." *Journal of American Folk-
        lore* 57:225 (1944):161-180.

   Presentation (in English) of texts of 9 folktales,
   recorded in Detroit from 1940 to 1942 from 8 informants
   of Armenian background. Includes tales identified as
   versions of "The Three Stolen Princesses," "The
   Cannibal," "The Ogre Beheaded (Polyphemus)," "Endless
   Tales," and a combination of "The Journey to God to
   Receive Reward," and "The Journey in Search of Fortune."
   Includes comparative notes, brief introductory sketch
   of storytelling among Detroit Armenians.

AR7   Hoogasian-Villa, Susie, collector and editor. *100*
       Armenian Tales and Their Folkloristic Relevance.
       Detroit: Wayne State University Press, 1966.
       Pp. 602, foreword, preface, 4 appendices (narrator
       sketches, motifs, bibliography of comparative sources,
       additional references), notes, 2 maps (of Armenia,
       one indicating birthplaces of the immigrant story-
       tellers).

       Presentation of texts of 40 *Märchen*, 14 moralistic
       tales, 7 anecdotes, 4 humorous tales, 11 tales of
       trickery and wit, 4 anti-feminine tales, 14 sagas and
       legends, 3 cumulative stories, 3 myths, all recorded,
       translated, and edited by the author, based on field-
       work in the Detroit area in 1940-42. Includes descrip-
       tion of fieldwork site, brief historical sketch of
       Armenia, characterization of Armenian folktales.

AR8   Kirwan, Lucile Vartanian. "Armenian Stories of Hodja."
       California Folklore Quarterly 2:1 (1943):27-29.

       Presentation of 8 Khodja (Nasreddin Hodja) tales told
       by an Armenian immigrant informant in California.

*AR9   Musick, Ruth Ann. *Green Hills of Magic: West Virginia*
       Folktales from Europe.

       (Cross-listed as *AU4, *CZ8, *HU24, *IR74, *IT52,
       *PL52, *RO4, *RU16, *TU3, *YU8.)
       (See *IT52 for full citation and annotation.)

*AR10 Thompson, Harold W. "Proverbs and Sayings."

       (Cross-listed as *IR104.)
       (See *IR104 for full citation and annotation.)

                    III.   AUSTRIAN (AU) (1-6)

AU1   Anderson, Jack. "Stories of Witches and Ghosts:
       The 'Evil Eye' and Hexing." West Virginia Folklore
       5:3 (1955):42-43.

       Characterization (in English) of 2 personal experience
       stories, recorded from an Austrian immigrant informant
       in West Virginia, concerning an afflicted man who is
       saved from death by the evil eye.

*AU2   Martens, Helen. "The Music of Some Religious Minorities in Canada."

> (Cross-listed as *DU13, *GE384, *RU14, *SW6.)
> (See *GE384 for full citation and annotation.)

*AU3   Musick, Ruth Ann. "European Folktales in West Virginia." *Midwest Folklore* 6:1 (1956):27-37.

> Presentation of 4 folktale texts, recorded in West Virginia from individuals of Czech, Italian (Sicilian), Hungarian, and Austrian backgrounds. Tales identified as variants of "The Dead Bridegroom Carries Off His Bride," "The Dragon Slayer," "The Magic Ring," and "The Smith Outwits the Devil."
> (Cross-listed as *CZ7, *HU23, *IT51.)

*AU4   Musick, Ruth Ann. *Green Hills of Magic: West Virginia Folktales from Europe.*

> (Cross-listed as *AR9, *CZ8, *HU24, *IR74, *IT52, *PL52, *RO4, *RU16, *TU3, *YU8.)
> (See *IT52 for full citation and annotation.)

*AU5   Musick, Ruth Ann. "West Virginia Stories: European Folktales in West Virginia." *West Virginia Folklore* 3:3 (1953):38-40.

> Characterization (in English) of 2 folktales, 1 from an informant of Polish background and 1 from an informant of Austrian background. Polish tale concerns a dead soldier whose corpse cannot rest in the grave or remain buried until a vow he made with a girl to be married is fulfilled. Austrian tale about some monks who steal a farmer's donkey, leaving one of their number in its place to tell the farmer he had been turned into a donkey as punishment for his sins.
> (Cross-listed as *PL53.)

*AU6   Webb, Wheaton Phillips. "The Wart."

> (Cross-listed as *GE703, *SS29.)
> (See *SS29 for full citation and annotation.)

IV.   BASQUE (BA) (1-2)

BA1   Bieter, Pat.   "Folklore of the Boise Basques."
          Western Folklore 24:4 (1965):263-270.

      Brief sketch of a Basque's immigration to Idaho and
      descriptions of dances, songs, card games, music, holiday
      celebrations that perpetuate Basque traditions in the
      New World.   Emphasis on the inevitability of change and
      assimilation.   Includes text of 1 song.

BA2   Robe, Stanley L.   "Basque Tales from Eastern Oregon."
          Western Folklore 12:3 (1953):153-157.

      Brief historical sketch of Basque immigration to Oregon,
      followed by texts of 4 tales (in English) recorded from
      a Basque immigrant narrator in 1948.

V.   BELGIAN (BE) (1-3)

BE1   Calkins, Charles F., and Laatsch, William G.   "The
          Belgian Outdoor Oven of Northeastern Wisconsin."
          Pioneer America Society Transactions 2 (1979):1-12.

      Description of outdoor ovens and adjoining summer
      kitchens in northeastern Wisconsin, built by Walloon-
      speaking Belgian immigrants who arrived in the area
      between 1855 and 1857.   Dimensions given and mode of
      construction described.   Includes 1 sketch of a summer
      kitchen with adjoining outdoor oven, 2 photographs (1
      of a Wisconsin summer kitchen with attached outdoor
      oven, 1 of a "typical" Belgian outdoor oven) and 1 map
      (showing geographical distribution of 18 known outdoor
      Belgian ovens in the state of Wisconsin).

BE2   Sackett, S.J.   "Flemish Folklore in Kansas."   *Western
          Folklore* 20:3 (1961):175-178.

      Brief description of difficulties involved in trying
      to elicit native folklore from a Belgian immigrant in
      St. Mary's, Kansas.   Emphasis on fact that immigrant
      folklore does not persist in the New World and must be
      collected quickly.   Includes 1 recipe, mention of
      lacemaking.   Based on 1959 fieldwork.

*BE3 Soland, Craig. "Ethno Cuisine: Serbo-Flemish Christmas
      Cookery."

      (Cross-listed as *SE7.)
      (See *SE7 for full citation and annotation.)

                    VI.   BOHEMIAN (BO) (1)

BO1 Lumpkin, Ben Gray. "The Storyteller at Podoli."
     Western Folklore 31:2 (1972):131-133.

     Characterization of a story learned by a Los Angeles
     informant of Bohemian ancestry in Chicago in the late
     1920s concerning a storyteller who obtains a free meal
     for telling his hosts a tale they have never heard
     before.

                    VII.   BULGARIAN (BU) (1-4)

*BU1 Dunin, Elsie Ivancich. *South Slavic Dance in California:
      A Compendium for the Years 1924-1977.*

      (Cross-listed as *YU2.)
      (See *YU2 for full citation and annotation.)

*BU2 Montgomery, Margaret. "A Macedonian Wedding in
      Indianapolis." *Hoosier Folklore* 7:4 (1948):101-104.

      Brief characterization of a Bulgarian (Macedonian)
      wedding in Indianapolis as observed by the author.
      Includes descriptions of the Eastern Orthodox wedding
      ceremony and the reception.
      (Cross-listed as *MA1.)

 BU3 Petroff, Louis. "Magical Beliefs and Practices in Old
      Bulgaria." *Midwest Folklore* 7:4 (1957):214-220.

      Description of beliefs and practices remembered by the
      author from his homeland Bulgarian village prior to his
      immigration to the United States in 1914. Includes
      descriptions of witchcraft, folk medicine, and rain-
      making practices.

BU4   Petroff, Louis. "Selected Bulgarian Proverbs and Pro-
           verbial Sayings." *Midwest Folklore* 9:3 (1959):163–167.

       Listing of 80 Bulgarian proverbs and proverbial sayings
       known to the author prior to his immigration to the
       United States in 1914, learned from other Bulgarian
       immigrants to America, and taken from published works
       by Bulgarian ethnologists and folklorists.

                    VIII. CELTIC (unspecified) (CE) (1)

CE1   Leach, MacEdward. "Celtic Tales from Cape Breton."
           In *Studies in Folklore in Honor of Distinguished
           Service Professor Stith Thompson*, edited by W. Edson
           Richmond, pp. 40–54. Indiana University Publications,
           Folklore Series No. 9. Bloomington: Indiana Univer-
           sity Press, 1957.

       Presentation of 12 tale texts (most recorded by the
       author in Celtic, but presented in English translation),
       documented in Cape Breton, Canada, in 1950. Includes
       stories involving giants, fairies, several tales
       hypothesized to be from the Finn cycle, and *Märchen*
       (one of which is identified as a male "Cinderella" tale).

                     IX. CHINESE (CH) (1–28)

CH1   Agonito, Rosemary. "Three Chinese Legends." *New York
           Folklore Quarterly* 28:3 (1972):234–240.

       Presentation (in English) of texts of 3 Chinese legends,
       recorded by the author in Syracuse, New York, from a
       native of mainland China and Hong Kong.

CH2   "Cantonese Riddles in San Francisco." *California Folk-
           lore Quarterly* 6:1 (1947):68–72.

       Presentation (in Chinese orthography and English trans-
       lation) of 12 Chinese riddles, recorded from unidentified
       source(s) in San Francisco.

CH3   Chapman, Mary. "Notes on the Chinese in Boston."
      Journal of American Folk-Lore 5:19 (1892):321-324.

      General ethnographic description of Chinese immigrants
      in Boston, including descriptions of living quarters,
      dietary habits, opium use, propensity for gambling,
      spending habits, modes of dress, and attitudes toward
      Christianity.

CH4   Culin, Stewart. "Chinese Secret Societies in the
      United States." *Journal of American Folk-Lore* 3:8
      (1890):39-43.

      Description of activities in meeting halls of Chinese
      secret societies in Philadelphia, with discussion of
      observations made at funerals of members.

CH5   Culin, Stewart. "Customs of the Chinese in America."
      Journal of American Folk-Lore 3:10 (1890):191-200.

      Plea for folklorists to study the lives and customs of
      Chinese immigrants to the United States, followed by a
      general survey of areas to be explored: language and
      dialect, home customs and traditions, funeral customs
      and beliefs about the dead, childhood customs and games,
      entertainment, holidays and festivals, diet, medical
      practices, and dress. Notes the tendency for Chinese
      immigrants to "borrow" Western customs and inventions
      that aid in material advancement.

CH6   Dow, James R. "Folklore from the *Frontier Index*,
      Wyoming Territory 1867-68." *Keystone Folklore* 18:1-2
      (1973):15-44.

      Characterization and exemplification of kinds of folk-
      lore found in the *Frontier Index*, a "press on wheels"
      which followed the construction of the Union Pacific
      Railroad, focusing on issues printed in 1867-68 in the
      then Wyoming territory. Includes characterization of
      pejorative references to Chinese immigrant railroad
      laborers, with 2 ethnic slurs.

CH7   "The Funeral Ceremonies of the Chinese in America."
      Journal of American Folk-Lore 1:3 (1888):239-240.

      Description of the burial preparation and funeral
      ceremony in New York for the wife of a Chinese merchant
      from New Orleans.

*CH8 Hand, Wayland D. "California Miners' Folklore: Above
      Ground."

      (Cross-listed as *CO5, *GE235, *IR39, *IT28, *SS15.)
      (See *CO5 for full citation and annotation.)

*CH9 Hoe, Ban Seng. "Asian-Canadian Folklore Studies: An
      Interdisciplinary and Cross-Cultural Approach." In
      Canadian Folklore Perspectives, edited by Kenneth S.
      Goldstein, pp. 39–52. Memorial University of New-
      foundland Folklore and Language Publications, Bibli-
      ographical and Special Series No. 5. St. John's,
      1978.

      General discussion of folklore and folklore studies of
      individuals of Chinese, Japanese, and East Indian
      descent in Canada, with emphasis on the necessity to
      study folklore in its sociocultural contexts.
      (Cross-listed as *ID1, *JA3.)

CH10 Hoe, Ban Seng. *Structural Changes of Two Chinese
      Communities in Alberta, Canada*. Canadian Centre for
      Folk Culture Studies, Paper No. 19. Ottawa: National
      Museums of Canada, 1976. Pp. xiv, 381.

      Discussion of general assimilationist tendencies of
      Chinese in Alberta, with brief descriptions of changes
      undergone by members of the immigrant and post-immigrant
      generations with regard to festivals, marriages, and
      funeral rites. Based on 1973 participant observation
      and life-history interviews with 20 Chinese informants.

CH11 Hoy, William. "Chinatown Devises Its Own Street Names."
      California Folklore Quarterly 2:2 (1943):71–75.

      Presentation of Chinese names for 10 streets (known
      officially by other names) in San Francisco's Chinatown.
      Includes explanations and etymologies for the names.

CH12 Hoy, William. "Native Festivals of the California
      Chinese." *Western Folklore* 7:3 (1948):240–250.

      Description of 7 Chinese festivals (New Year, Pure
      Brightness, Dragon Boat, Spirits, Moon, Chung Yang,
      winter solstice) as experienced and conceived by the
      author in San Francisco. Includes reasons for the
      perpetuation of the festivals in the United States and
      characterization of customs and foodways relevant to
      the festive occasions.

*CH13 Humphrey, Linda T. "'It Ain't Funny, Buster': The
       Ethnic Riddle-Joke at Citrus Community College."

       (Cross-listed as *GL49, *IR47, *IT32, *JA5, *SS17.)
       (See *GL49 for full citation and annotation.)

CH14   Langlois, Janet. "Moon Cake in Chinatown, New York City:
       Continuity and Change." *New York Folklore Quarterly*
       28:2 (1972):83-117.

       Brief sketch of Chinese immigration to the United
       States and New York City, with emphasis on the custom
       of preparing and consuming moon cakes and on stories
       behind the custom. Includes 10 tales (2 reprinted from
       other published sources) about the custom and its back-
       ground, descriptions of various ways moon cakes are
       prepared and distributed. Appendices provide list of
       informants (all interviewed in 1971), characterizations
       of interviews, transcription of 1 tape-recorded inter-
       view. Author states that the custom has been "de-
       ritualized" in New York City, losing much of its
       religious and social significance.

CH15   Lee, Jon. "Some Chinese Customs and Beliefs in
       California." *California Folklore Quarterly* 2:3
       (1943):191-204.

       Characterization of 1 festival at which individuals
       vie with each other for bamboo casings from exploded
       fireworks; of 6 stories dealing with individuals'
       descent to hell or the land of the dead, individuals'
       encounters with ghosts emanating from the burial sites
       of some dead persons, with the practice of burying
       a living child beside another child whom he or she has
       killed, with a mysterious lady who appears and offers
       drinks from inside a banana tree or banana. Auto-
       biographical presentation based on the author's recol-
       lections of his experiences in growing up in a Chinese
       family and community in California.

CH16   Lee, Jon. "The Tragedy of the Seventh Day." *Cali-
       fornia Folklore Quarterly* 1:4 (1942):337-357.

       Autobiographical account of Chinese New Year customs,
       foods, celebrations as remembered from the author's
       boyhood in San Francisco, with emphasis on the death of
       a cousin as foreshadowed by ominous events interpreted
       in terms of traditional Chinese beliefs. Includes
       description of foods prepared and consumed, gifts ex-
       changed, and fortune-telling.

CH17   Li, Lienfung. "Chinese Trickster Tales." *New York*
          Folklore Quarterly 6:2 (1950):69-81.

          Brief discussion of the contrast between formal
          literature of China and Chinese folksongs and folktales,
          followed by a characterization of 11 Chinese trickster
          tales, from the recollections of an informant of
          Chinese ancestry.

CH18   Li, Lillian. "Two Chinese Ghosts." *California*
          Folklore Quarterly 4:3 (1945):278-280.

          Characterization of 2 personal experience stories
          about sightings of returning ghosts of dead persons.

CH19   Loomis, C. Grant. "Chinese Lore from Nevada, 1867-
          1878." *California Folklore Quarterly* 5:2 (1946):
          185-196.

          Selection of reprinted articles from 19th-century
          newspapers concerning activities of Chinese immigrants
          in Nevada. Includes account of a temple dedication,
          description of a Chinese house of worship, reports on
          3 religious festivals, 2 articles on kite-flying, 1
          account of a superstition, 1 discussion of Chinese
          cursing, 1 description of opium-induced illusions,
          1 account of funerary rites, 1 report on a Chinese
          funeral, 1 account of an individual's encounters with
          a ghost, 1 description of a Chinese wedding.

CH20   Olsen, Louise P. "A Chinese Ghost Story." *Hoosier*
          Folklore 9:2 (1950):48-49.

          Transcription (from the author's shorthand notes) of
          a story about a young scholar visited nightly by a
          female apparition/ghost which disappears when a
          banana tree in the courtyard is destroyed by a priest
          and the landlord of the haunted house. Told by a
          Chinese student studying in the United States.

*CH21 Peacock, Kenneth. "Establishing Perimeters for Ethno-
          musicological Field Research in Canada: On-Going
          Projects and Future Possibilities at the Canadian
          Centre for Folk Culture Studies."

          (Cross-listed as *GL66, *FR91, *GE428, *HU25, *IC4,
          *ID2, *IT57, *JA9, *LI5, *NO19, *RU19, *UK32.)
          (See *GL66 for full citation and annotation.)

CH22   Riddle, Ronald. "Music Clubs and Ensembles in San
       Francisco's Chinese Community." In *Eight Urban
       Musical Cultures*, edited by Bruno Nettl, pp. 223-
       259. Urbana: University of Illinois Press, 1978.

       Survey of clubs and organizations of Chinese immigrants
       and their American-born descendants in San Francisco
       which teach, perform, and perpetuate Chinese traditional
       music. Includes discussion of social organization of
       clubs and organizations, teaching and learning of music,
       performance occasions, and instruments played. Based
       on 1973-74 research.

CH23   Sapir, Edward, and Hwa, Hsü Tsan. "Humor of the Chinese
       Folk." *Journal of American Folk-Lore* 36:139 (1923):
       31-33.

       Presentation of 7 "whimsies" written out by Hsü Tsan
       Hwa and edited for publication by Sapir.

CH24   Sapir, Edward, and Hwa, Hsü Tsan. "Two Chinese Folk-
       Tales." *Journal of American Folk-Lore* 36:139 (1923):
       23-30.

       Presentation of texts of 2 tales, written out by Hsü
       Tsan Hwa and edited for publication by Sapir. Source-
       author from Manchuria.

*CH25 Simmons, Donald C. "Protest Humor: Folkloristic
       Reaction to Prejudice."

       (Cross-listed as *JE73.)
       (See *JE73 for full citation and annotation.)

CH26   Spier, Robert F.G. "Tool Acculturation among 19th-
       Century California Chinese." *Ethnohistory* 5:2
       (1958):97-117.

       Discussion of 19th-century Chinese immigrants to
       California, with emphasis on occupations in which they
       engaged and kinds of tools and implements they used at
       work and in their homes. Demonstrates that in situ-
       ations over which they had little or no control or for
       which there was no homeland precedent or model, Chinese
       used American-made tools and implements, while they pre-
       ferred and employed "native" tools and implements for
       familiar work, such as fishing, and for daily living.

CH27   Wang, Joseph. "The Bill Collector: A Chinese Ghost
       Tale from New York City." *New York Folklore
       Quarterly* 1:4 (1945):231-232.

       Characterization of 1 ghost story set in China and
       recorded from a Chinese informant in New York City in
       1943.

CH28   Wong, Jason. "Ethno Cuisine: Gold Coin Soup."
       AFFword, Publication of Arizona Friends of Folklore
       3:2 (1973):44.

       Presentation of 1 recipe for "gold coin soup,"
       traditional in the author's family and from the
       Chinese heritage. Soup prescribed for nervousness.
       Contributor from Flagstaff, Arizona.

                    X.   CORNISH (CO) (1-9)

CO1   Bancroft, Caroline. "Cousin Jack Stories from Central
       City." *The Colorado Magazine* 21:2 (1944):51-56.

       Presentation of 15 anecdotes, numskull stories, and
       other humorous tales recorded in Central City,
       Colorado, from individuals of Cornish ancestry.

CO2   Dorson, Richard M. "Cousin Jacks." In *Bloodstoppers
       & Bearwalkers: Folk Traditions of the Upper
       Peninsula*, pp. 103-122. Cambridge, Mass.: Harvard
       University Press, 1952.

       Brief discussion of Cornish immigration to Michigan's
       Upper Peninsula, followed by texts of 3 songs, 2
       recipes, 9 tales, 5 beliefs, 12 proverbs and customs,
       all recorded by the author in 1946.

*CO3   Dorson, Richard M. "Dialect Stories of the Upper
       Peninsula: A New Form of American Folklore."

          (Cross-listed as *FN3, *FR53, *IR21, *IT17, *SS9.)
          (See *FR53 for full citation and annotation.)

*CO4   Dorson, Richard M. "Folk Traditions of the Upper
       Peninsula."

          (Cross-listed as *FN5, *FR54.)
          (See *FN5 for full citation and annotation.)

*CO5 Hand, Wayland D. "California Miners' Folklore: Above Ground." *California Folklore Quarterly* 1:1 (1942): 24-46; "California Miners' Folklore: Below Ground." *California Folklore Quarterly* 1:2 (1942):127-153.

Two-part survey of past and present beliefs, customs, sayings, anecdotes, and tales of California miners, based on the author's 1941 fieldwork. Includes passing references to beliefs, customs, and tales from or about individuals of the following backgrounds: Chinese (3), Cornish (19), German (3), Irish (4), Italian (2), Swedish (2).
(Cross-listed as *CH8, *GE235, *IR39, *IT28, *SS15.)

CO6 Hand, Wayland D. "Folklore from Utah's Silver Mining Camps." *Journal of American Folklore* 54:213-214 (1941):132-161.

Characterization of various customs, beliefs, stories, and other lore of Utah silver miners, with passing reference to folklore of probable Cornish origin.

*CO7 Hand, Wayland D. "The Folklore, Customs, and Traditions of the Butte Miner." *California Folklore Quarterly* 5:1 (1946):1-25; 5:2 (1946):153-178.

General survey of kinds and examples of folklore reported orally to the author and by others (in print) from Butte, Montana, miners. Includes 6 personal experience narratives/anecdotes, 2 superstitions, 1 expression, and descriptions of 3 foods of Cornish miners; 6 personal experience narratives/anecdotes and 1 superstition of Irish miners; 3 personal experience narratives/anecdotes and 1 superstition of Finnish miners; 1 superstition of Filipino miners; 1 personal experience narrative/anecdote of Serbian miners. For Butte miners in general and of mixed national backgrounds, includes a total of 52 personal experience narratives/anecdotes, 45 statements of belief/superstitions, 37 traditional expressions, 105 examples of cant and jargon terms, 16 examples of pranks played by miners on each other. Occasional comparisons made between Butte miners' lore and that of California and Utah miners. Includes reprintings of full or partial texts of 13 poems and ballads.
(Cross-listed as *FI2, *FN14, *IR40, *IT29, *SE4.)

CO8 Pinkowski, Edward. "Jack O'Lantern's Children."
     Keystone Folklore Quarterly 3:1 (1958):10-13.

     Brief discussion of the immigration of Cornish people
     to eastern Pennsylvania in the early 19th century and
     of their early work as canal builders and farmers,
     followed by a brief sketch of 1 Cornish woman who was
     known for her healing powers. Includes texts of 2
     charms for healing burns and sprains.

CO9 Rowe, John. "Cornish Emigration to America." *Folk-
     Life* 3 (1965):26-38.

     General discussion of Cornish immigration to America,
     with sketches of settlements, principally in California,
     Michigan, Montana, and Wisconsin. Includes characteriza-
     tion of 12 traditional beliefs, 1 tale, mention of the
     pasty and its importance as an ethnic food.

XI. CROATIAN (CR) (1-7)

*CR1 Dorson, Richard M. "Is There a Folk in the City?"

      (Cross-listed as *GL34, *GR5, *SE1.)
      (See *GL34 for full citation and annotation.)

*CR2 Erdely, Stephen. "Ethnic Music in the United States:
      An Overview."

      (Cross-listed as *GL40, *AR5, *GR7, *GY5, *JE22,
      *SC11, *SE2.)
      (See *GL40 for annotation.)

*CR3 Erdely, Stephen. "Research on Traditional Music of
      Nationality Groups in Cleveland and Vicinity."

      (Cross-listed as *GL41, *FN11, *GE172, *HU14, *IR26,
      *RO3, *SC12, *SK4.)
      (See *GL41 for full citation and annotation.)

CR4   Hoffman, David F., Jr. "The Meaning & Function of the
      Kolo Club 'Marian' in the Steelton, Pa., Croatian
      Community." *Keystone Folklore Quarterly* 16:3 (1971):
      115-131.

      Brief discussion of Croatian immigration to the United
      States and particularly to the Steelton, Pennsylvania,

area, followed by a brief biographical sketch of 1
Croatian immigrant woman and her family. Emphasis on
the founding in 1954 of a folk dance ensemble, the Kolo
Club "Marian," with description of its activities and
an analysis of the functions the performing group
serves for individuals of Croatian and other Central
and South European backgrounds. Includes 7 photographs
(1 each of a typical peasant setting in Croatia, of the
Steelton steel mill, of St. Mary's Croatian Catholic
Church, the Steelton Croatian lodge, of the woman whose
life is sketched and the kind of house she once lived
in and now occupies).

CR5 Jansen, William Hugh. "Tales from a Steel Town."
      Hoosier Folklore Bulletin 1:3 (1942):78-81.

Texts of 3 folktales recorded by the author, one of
which is from a Croatian informant living in East
Chicago, Indiana (titled "Be Kind to the Poor").

*CR6 March, Richard. "The Tamburitza Tradition in the
      Calumet Region." *Indiana Folklore* 10:2 (1977):127-138.

Description of the tamburitza musical tradition
prevalent in the Calumet, Indiana, area in 1975-76 and
as a source and symbol of ethnic identity for individuals
of Croatian (and, to a lesser extent, of Serbian) background. Includes distinctions between combos and performing musical groups, descriptions of principal musical
instruments used (illustrated with 4 photographs of
musicians and musical instruments).
      (Cross-listed as *SE5, *YU5.)

*CR7 Monahan, Kathleen. "The Role of Ethnic Record Companies
      in Cultural Maintenance: A Look at Greyko."

      (Cross-listed as *GL60, *YU6.)
      (See *GL60 for full citation and annotation.)

XII.   CZECH (CZ) (1–13)

CZ1   Atkinson, Robert. "The Kreutz Brothers: Craftsmen in
        Glass." *New York Folklore Quarterly* 25:2 (1969):
        100–118.

        Description and discussion of glassblowing, as carried
        out by four Czech immigrant men (brothers) in Southampton,
        Long Island, New York, based upon observations and inter-
        views carried out in 1969. Includes a brief family
        history of the craftsmen; description of the layout of
        their shop, their tools, and the glassblowing process;
        and discussion of their community and their role in it.
        Includes 16 photographs of the shop and of the craftsmen
        at work. Author notes the lack of "lore of the craft"
        among the Kreutz brothers and predicts the demise of the
        craft because younger generations are not learning it.

*CZ2   Babcock, C. Merton. "Czech Songs in Nebraska."
        Western Folklore 8:4 (1949):320–327.

        Presentation of texts of 10 Czech and Slovak traditional
        songs and ballads (some reprinted, some field-recorded)
        from Nebraska (in English only). Brief discussion of
        recurrent topics and themes in the songs.
        (Cross-listed as *SK1.)

CZ3   Buso, Mildred. "Czechoslovakian Holiday Lore in Onondaga
        County." *New York Folklore Quarterly* 8:4 (1952):
        311–313.

        Description of the meals held on Christmas Eve and New
        Year's Eve by the author's family in New York, followed
        by a brief discussion of Christmas and New Year's
        customs in Czechoslovakia. Includes 1 proverb text in
        English.

*CZ4   Cutting, Edith E. "Easter Eggs in the Triple Cities."
        New York Folklore Quarterly 12:1 (1956):21–25.

        Brief discussion of the pre-Christian roots of the egg
        as a symbol of life, followed by a discussion of the
        designs and techniques used in Easter egg decoration by
        the Moravians and Ukrainians. Also discusses some of
        the customs associated with Easter eggs in Moravia and
        in the Ukraine and indicates parallels in customs and
        decorating techniques to be found among those of Ukrainian
        and Moravian descent in the towns of Binghamton, Endicott,
        and Johnson City, New York.
        (Cross-listed as *UK2.)

CZ5   McLaughlin, Valerie. "Czech Tales." *New York Folklore Quarterly* 25:3 (1969):202-220.

Presentation (in English) of 18 memorates/personal experience stories, 2 wedding customs, 1 taboo against working on Sunday, recorded by the author from a Czech couple living in New York State. Tales concern death and the dead.

*CZ6   Musick, Ruth Ann. "Chapter 16, Immigrant Ghosts." In *The Telltale Lilac Bush and Other West Virginia Ghost Tales*, pp. 150-161. Lexington, Ky.: University of Kentucky Press, 1965.

Presentation of 5 ghost story texts (in English) recorded in West Virginia between 1948 and 1959 from individuals of Czech, Yugoslav, Italian, and Hungarian backgrounds. Includes stories about the return of a dead lover, a corpse that would not remain buried, corpses who return as flies and reveal their murderer. (Cross-listed as *HU22, *IT50, *YU7.)

*CZ7   Musick, Ruth Ann. "European Folktales in West Virginia."

(Cross-listed as *AU3, *HU23, *IT51.)
(See *AU3 for full citation and annotation.)

*CZ8   Musick, Ruth Ann. *Green Hills of Magic: West Virginia Folktales from Europe.*

(Cross-listed as *AR9, *AU4, *HU24, *IR74, *IT52, *PL52, *RO4, *RU16, *TU3, *YU8.)
(See *IT52 for full citation and annotation.)

*CZ9   Nettl, Bruno, and Moravcik, Ivo. "Czech and Slovak Songs Collected in Detroit." *Midwest Folklore* 5:1 (1955):37-49.

Presentation of texts of 13 Czech songs, 5 Slovak songs, 2 Czech children's rhymes recorded from a Czech immigrant in Detroit in 1954. Includes musical transcriptions, texts in both the original languages and in English translation, discussion of musicological features.
(Cross-listed as *SK8.)

*CZ10   Peacock, Kenneth. *Twenty Ethnic Songs from Western Canada.*

(Cross-listed as *GE429, *HU26, *RU21, *UK33.)
(See *RU21 for full citation and annotation.)

*CZ11   Pirkova-Jakobson, Svatava.   "Harvest Festivals among
         Czechs and Slovaks in America."   *Journal of American
         Folklore* 69:273 (1956):266-280.

         Comparative study of Czech and Slovak harvest festivals
         in Europe and America, with emphasis upon changes in
         meaning, function, symbolism, social interaction.
         Includes brief biographical sketches of selected
         immigrants and brief descriptions of harvest festivals
         held in such places as Hightstown, New Jersey, New
         York City, and Detroit, Michigan, in the early 1950s.
         Author concludes that harvest rituals of the Old World
         have been transformed into dramas or theatrical per-
         formances in the New World.
         (Cross-listed as *SK9.)

CZ12   Ryan, Lawrence V.   "Some Czech-American Forms of
         Divination and Supplication."   *Journal of American
         Folklore* 69:273 (1956):281-285.

         Description of 22 customs and beliefs recorded among
         Czech-Americans in Iowa and Minnesota, most centering
         around the Christmas and Easter holidays and relating
         to prophesying the future, insuring luck or bountiful
         harvest, protecting home and animals.

CZ13   Sackett, Marjorie.   "Folk Recipes in Kansas."
         Midwest Folklore 12:2 (1962):81-86.

         General discussion of some of the immigrant groups in
         Kansas and examples of traditional foods each prepares,
         followed by a comparison of 5 recipes recorded in
         1957-58 from Bohemian (Czech) informants for *kolaches*
         (a kind of sweet roll). Notes significant differences
         among the recipes and the discernible similarities that
         enable one to view them as alternative ways of making
         the same food.

                        XIII. DANISH (DA) (1-7)

*DA1   Barbour, Frances M.   "Some Foreign Proverbs in Southern
         Illinois."

         (Cross-listed as *DU2, *FR21, *GE33, *HU1, *IT3.)
         (See *GE33 for full citation and annotation.)

*DA2 Blegen, Theodore C. "Singing Immigrants and Pioneers."

(Cross-listed as *FN1, *IR10, *NO2, *SS3.)
(See *NO2 for full citation and annotation.)

*DA3 Cheney, Thomas W. "Scandinavian Immigrant Stories."
Western Folklore 18:2 (1959):99-105.

Presentation of texts of 8 personal experience stories
recorded in Utah from Mormon converts of Scandinavian
background. Includes brief discussion of kinds of
topics and themes presented in the tales.
(Cross-listed as *SA1, *SS4.)

DA4 Hubbard, Lester A. "Danish Numskull Stories."
Western Folklore 19:1 (1960):56-58.

Presentation of texts of 3 numskull tales recorded in
Utah in 1950 from a man of Danish background who learned
them from his immigrant father. Tales identified as
versions of "Marking the Place on the Boat," "Drowning
the Crayfish as Punishment," and a combination of
"Bringing Water from the Well" and "The Man Without a
Head in the Bear's Den."

DA5 Larson, Mildred R. "Danish Lore in Denmark and at
Troy, N.Y." *New York Folklore Quarterly* 10:4
(1954):266-273.

Discussion of the customs associated with the annual
festivals and holidays in Denmark, including Christmas,
New Year's, the Epiphany, Lent, Easter, *Store-Bededag*,
Ascension Day, Pinse (Pentecost), *Kyndelmisse* (February
2nd), *de 40 Ridder* (March 9), the Midsummer Festival
(June 24th--St. Hans Day), with a brief description of
the American counterparts of some of these customs as
observed in Troy, New York. Includes presentation of
2 children's song texts, 2 Christmas songs, and 1
weather rhyme (all in Danish with English translation).

*DA6 Lund, Jens. "The Legend of the King and the Star."

(Cross-listed as *GE380, *IT43, *JE44.)
(See *JE44 for full citation and annotation.)

*DA7 Wilden, Albin. "Scandinavian Folklore and Immigrant
Ballads."

(Cross-listed as *NO22, *SS30.)
(See *SS30 for full citation and annotation.)

XIV. DUTCH (DU) (1-28)

DU1   Anderson, Robert. "Tales of a Scholar." *New York*
      Folklore Quarterly 12:3 (1956):189-191.

      Characterization of 6 stories of the impractical-man
      type concerning the Dutch "minister-scholar-revolution-
      ist" Francis Adrian Van der Kemp, who settled in New
      York in the late 16th century.

*DU2 Barbour, Frances M. "Some Foreign Proverbs in Southern
      Illinois."

      (Cross-listed as *DA1, *FR21, *GE33, *HU1, *IT3.)
      (See *GE33 for full citation and annotation.)

*DU3 Barnes, Gertrude. "Superstitions and Maxims from
      Dutchess County, New York." *Journal of American*
      Folk-Lore 36:139 (1923):16-22.

      Collection of 21 weather signs, 13 planting and farmyard
      maxims, 48 good and bad luck signs, 5 rhymes of fortune,
      4 maxims, recorded by members of a folklore class at
      Vassar College. Informants of Dutch, German, English,
      and French ancestry.
      (Cross-listed as *FR22, *GE36.)

DU4   Bennit, Dorothy V. "Albany Preserves Its Dutch Lore."
      New York Folklore Quarterly 11:3 (1955):246-253.

      Brief discussion of St. Nicholas as the patron saint of
      various groups, how he is portrayed in tradition, the
      founding of the St. Nicholas Society (1835) and other
      societies concerned with preserving Dutch-related
      traditions, and of the customs which have evolved from
      Dutch traditions within these groups. Includes
      characterization of 2 legends about St. Nicholas, 1
      Dutch recipe from Albany, and presentation of 1
      children's song (in Dutch and English translation).

DU5   deKay, Eckford J. "Die Colonie Nieu Nederland."
      New York Folklore Quarterly 9:4 (1953):245-254.

      Description of family and community life in the Dutch
      settlement on Manhattan Island in the 17th century,
      covering such topics as structural floor plans, the
      training of children, typical daily meals, entertainment
      and recreation, civic responsibilities and projects,
      and major holidays and festivities, such as New Year's,

Epiphany, Pentecost, *Pass*, St. Nicholas' Day, and
Christmas. Also discusses briefly several societies
in New York involved in maintaining Dutch-related
traditions. Includes texts of 2 holiday songs (in
Dutch with English translation).

*DU6   Dorson, Richard M. "Personal Histories."

    (Cross-listed as *FR56, *IR22, *SS11.)
    (See *SS11 for full citation and annotation.)

DU7   Dorson, Richard M. "Yorker Yarns of Yore." *New York
    Folklore Quarterly* 3:1 (1947):5-27.

Presentation of 9 humorous tale texts originally
printed in the 19th century, dealing with picturesque
Yankee characters and/or Old World character types
(the Englishman, the Dutchman) or involving extravagant
exploits.

DU8   Freeman-Witthoft, Bonita. "Conflict and Awareness:
    Pool Search for Acceptance in Pennsylvania."
    Keystone Folklore 22:3 (1978):25-37.

Discussion of a group of people known as Pools residing
in Bradford County, Pennsylvania. Brief historical
sketch of their Dutch-native American (Indian) ancestry
and settlement in Pennsylvania, with emphasis on their
relative social isolation and on the abuse of and
condescension toward Pools by others in the area, with
consequent poverty status and negative self-image.
Includes characterizations of 5 pejorative tales about
the Pools' drinking, simple-mindedness, and mixed
racial background.

*DU9   Gardner, Emelyn E. "Folk-Lore from Schoharie County,
    New York."

    (Cross-listed as *GE197, *IR35.)
    (See *GE197 for full citation and annotation.)

DU10   Hand, Wayland D. "White Liver." *Journal of American
    Folklore* 59:233 (1946):323.

Brief note characterizing the attribution of the un-
expected death of a Salt Lake City Dutchman "to the
fact that his wife must have a white liver," with
comparative reference to a similar superstition reported
from Herefordshire, England, and with the question
raised as to how widely known this belief might be in
the United States.

DU11   Hondius, Katherine N. "The American Folk Idea of the
       Dutch." *Western Folklore* 11:1 (1952):29-31.

       Listing of 42 American English compounds and expressions,
       each containing the word *Dutch*, and a brief discussion
       of the mostly negative behaviors and values the expressions
       imply or attribute to the Dutch.

DU12   Huguenin, Charles A. "The Legend Martense's Land in
       Brooklyn." *New York Folklore Quarterly* 12:1 (1956):
       112-118.

       Characterization of a legend told by old Dutch residents
       of New York, which originally appeared in print in the
       Brooklyn Daily Eagle in the 1890s.

*DU13 Martens, Helen. "The Music of Some Religious Minorities
       in Canada."

       (Cross-listed as *AU2, *GE384, *RU14, *SW6.)
       (See *GE384 for full citation and annotation.)

*DU14 Norlin, Ethel Todd. "Present-Day Superstitions at La
       Harpe, Ill., Survivals in a Community of English
       Origin."

       (Cross-listed as *FR88, *GE424, *IR78, *SC30.)
       (See *IR78 for full citation and annotation.)

DU15   Prudon, Theodore H.M. "The Dutch Barn in America:
       Survival of a Medieval Structural Frame." *New York
       Folklore Quarterly* 2:3&4 (1976):123-142.

       Discussion of the history of the "Dutch" barn in Europe
       and America, with emphasis on continuities in America
       of structural features dating back to medieval times.
       Detailed descriptions of various structural features of
       barns. Includes photographs of 8 barns and their
       features, 10 sketches of same.

DU16   Reynolds, Neil B. "The Supernatural in Scotia." *New
       York Folklore Quarterly* 16:4 (1960):298-300.

       Presentation (with minor editing) of excerpts from a
       collection of historical material made by antiquarian
       Edwin Zachariah Carpenter of Glenville, New York, from
       1870 to 1890. Includes 3 stories about ghosts and 4 about
       supranormal events (1 associated with a Dutch family
       of Mohawk Valley, New York).

DU17   Scott, Kenneth. "Funeral Customs in Colonial New York."
         New York Folklore Quarterly 15:4 (1959):274-282.

         Discussion of funeral customs among the poor, the
         merchants, and the gentry of colonial New York and of
         reactions to certain excesses apparent in the customs.

*DU18   Shaw, Ann. "What's in a Name." *New York Folklore
         Quarterly* 14:4 (1958):305-308.

         Discussion of the origins of place names in Westchester
         County, New York, particularly names of Indian, Dutch,
         and French origin. Includes characterizations of 2
         local legends.
         (Cross-listed as *FR101.)

DU19   Smith, Agnes Scott. "The Dutch Had a Word for It."
         New York Folklore Quarterly 2:3 (1946):165-173.

         Discussion of the ways the Dutch heritage is still
         manifested by the people of Ulster County, New York,
         particularly in the village of Hurley. Provides
         examples of foodways, folk medicine, language. In-
         cludes presentations of 3 nursery rhymes, 2 five-finger
         rhymes, 1 nonsense rhyme, and 1 conversational poem
         (all in Dutch with English translations). Also in-
         cludes discussion of Dutch place names and 1 local
         legend (in English).

DU20   Smith, Agnes Scott. "Tales of the Shiftless Husband
         (Dutch)." *New York Folklore Quarterly* 8:2 (1952):
         132.

         Characterization of 1 folktale, recorded from an
         informant of Dutch ancestry in Woodstock, New York.

DU21   "Superstition Relating to Crossed Feathers." *Journal
         of American Folk-Lore* 10:36 (1897):76.

         Report of a previously published superstition from a
         Dutch town in Michigan about crossed feathers being
         a sign of the work of the devil.

DU22   Taylor, Archer. "Dutch in Proverbial and Conventional
         Use." *Western Folklore* 11:3 (1952):219.

         Listing of 4 English compounds and expressions contain-
         ing the word *Dutch*, used pejoratively. Supplements
         earlier essay by Katherine Hondius (see DU11).

DU23   Thompson, Harold W.   "President's Page."   *New York*
       Folklore Quarterly 2:4 (1946):245.

       Presentation of 1 proverb text (in Dutch with English
       translation) and a general discussion of the evolution
       of the figure of Sinte Klaas in the New World, including
       mention of his Afro-American servant, Black Pete.

DU24   Wacker, Peter O.   "Folk Architecture as an Indicator
       of Culture Areas and Culture Diffusion: Dutch Barns
       and Barracks in New Jersey."   *Pioneer America* 5:2
       (1973):37-47.

       Discussion of the introduction and diffusion of the
       Dutch barn and barrack in New Jersey during the 18th
       century.   Distribution of these two fading architec-
       tural forms traced from newspaper advertisements and
       Revolutionary War damage reports.   Indicates that the
       Dutch barn had a limited geographical distribution in
       New Jersey's Raritan Valley, while the Dutch barrack
       was widely imitated and adapted by non-Dutch, thus
       affording it a greater geographical diffusion in
       northern New Jersey.   Includes 3 distributional maps
       and 3 photographs (1 of a Dutch barn, 1 of a Dutch
       barrack, 1 a reproduction of an 1887 portrait showing
       a Dutch barrack on an Iowa farm).

*DU25 Webb, Wheaton P.   "Witches in the Cooper Country."
       New York Folklore Quarterly 1:1 (1945):5-20.

       General discussion of witch lore in Otsego County,
       New York, with examples of the beliefs of descendants
       of English, Irish, and "Schoharie Dutch" immigrants to
       the area.   Based on 1937-42 fieldwork.
          (Cross-listed as *IR113.)

DU26   Whiting, Clay.   "She Knew Her Onions."   *Keystone*
       Folklore Quarterly 2:3 (1957):79.

       Brief sketch of a Dutch woman from Gilmer County, West
       Virginia, with description of her use of onions as a
       means of forecasting the weather for a new year.

*DU27 Willis, Alice.   "Tales from a Mountain Homestead."
       New York Folklore Quarterly 3:4 (1947):302-312.

       Discussion and exemplification of types of tales found
       in South Gilboa, New York, a community whose inhabit-
       ants are largely of Scotch-Irish, Dutch, and Scottish
       descent.   Includes characterizations of 1 animal tale,

6 local legends, 1 humorous tale, 2 tales about witches,
1 tale about supranormal powers, and a miscellany of
anecdotes about the area.
(Cross-listed as *IR115, *SC41.)

DU28   Wright, Barbara. "Lore of Montgomery County." *New
       York Folklore Quarterly* 7:2 (1951):131-140.

Characterization of folklore recorded in Montgomery
County, New York. Includes 2 tales about actual events,
a description of funeral customs, 2 stories about
witches, 2 tales about wizards, 1 ghost story, a
discussion of weather lore, 1 love story, 1 Dutch
salutation, and 1 Dutch saying (both in English).

XV.   EGYPTIAN (EG) (1)

*EG1   Qureshi, Regula. "Ethnomusicological Research among
        Canadian Communities of Arab and East Indian Origin."

(Cross-listed as *ID3, *LE4, *PA1, *SZ4.)
(See *SZ4 for full citation and annotation.)

XVI.   FILIPINO (FI) (1-6)

FI1   "Filipino." *Journal of American Folk-Lore* 15:59
       (1902):293.

Suggestion that the word *Filipino* be added to the
dictionary of "political Americanisms" because of its
pejorative political meaning in Boston.

*FI2   Hand, Wayland D. "The Folklore, Customs, and Tradi-
        tions of the Butte Miner."

(Cross-listed as *CO7, *FN14, *IR40, *IT29, *SE4.)
(See *CO7 for full citation and annotation.)

FI3   Meñez, Herminia Q.   "Filipino-American Erotica and the
      Ethnography of a Folkloric Event."   In *Folklore: Per-
      formance and Communication*, edited by Dan Ben-Amos and
      Kenneth S. Goldstein, pp. 131-141.   The Hague: Mouton,
      1975.

      Description and analysis of a social event characterized
      by joking among participants (*risahan*) during which a
      4-line erotic verse was sung by 1 Filipino-American
      (in 1969 in California).   Includes a diagram of the
      setting and individuals involved and a transcription
      of the verbal (joking) exchange among participants,
      followed by a discussion of the rules for such communi-
      cation.

FI4   Meñez, Herminia Q.   "Juan Tamad, A Philippine Folktale
      Hero."   *Southern Folklore Quarterly* 35:1 (1971):83-92.

      Comparison and contrast between Spanish numskull tales
      of Juan Pusong and Philippine tales of Juan Tamad,
      followed by a discussion of the recurrent themes in
      the Philippine tales and correlations between the
      content of the tales and Philippine social relation-
      ships.   Includes commentary from Filipino-Americans
      from Philadelphia.

FI5   Meñez, Herminia Q.   "The Performance of Folk Narrative
      in Filipino Communities in California."   *Western
      Folklore* 36:1 (1977):57-69.

      Distinctions made between "tales of the old people,"
      about which Filipino-Americans can report but which
      they do not perform, and personal histories, ethnic
      jokes, and belief stories, which they do perform because
      these kinds of tales are closely bound up with their
      personal lives and experiences.   Includes transcriptions
      of 9 narrative texts, recorded in California in 1969-70.

FI6   Meñez, Herminia Quimpo.   *Folklore Communication among
      Filipinos in California*.   New York: Arno Press,
      1980.   Pp. xv, 257, bibliography.

      Analysis of the role of folkloric behavior among
      Filipino immigrants who resided in Delano city and
      Monterey County, California, in 1969-70.   Emphasis
      placed on ways in which folklore is communicated and
      performed, in terms of the "ethnography of communica-
      tion" approach.   Phenomena such as conversational genres
      (proverbs, beliefs, slurs), joking, storytelling, and
      singing viewed in native terms and in terms of events,

settings, and occasions for interaction. Introduction
surveys persistence and change in such cultural activities and phenomena as foodways, material objects, rites
of passage. Includes appendices of foods (16 dishes),
folk beliefs (6), supernatural beings, 4 narratives of
love magic and amulets, 16 additional narratives, 6
jokes, 1 transcript of an interview (in Tagalog).
Provides brief background on 24 informants and 2 maps.

XVII. FINNISH (FN) (1-26)

*FN1   Blegen, Theodore C. "Singing Immigrants and Pioneers."

(Cross-listed as *DA2, *IR10, *NO2, *SS3.)
(See *NO2 for full citation and annotation.)

*FN2   Dorson, Richard M. "Blood Stoppers."

(Cross-listed as *FR50, *GE160, *IR20, *SL1, *SS8.)
(See *FR50 for full citation and annotation.)

*FN3   Dorson, Richard M. "Dialect Stories of the Upper
       Peninsula: A New Form of American Folklore."

(Cross-listed as *CO3, *FR53, *IR21, *IT17, *SS9.)
(See *FR53 for full citation and annotation.)

 FN4   Dorson, Richard M. "Finns." In *Bloodstoppers &
       Bearwalkers: Folk Traditions of the Upper Peninsula*,
       pp. 123-149. Cambridge, Mass.: Harvard University
       Press, 1952.

Brief discussion of Finnish immigration to Michigan's
Upper Peninsula, followed by texts of 20 tales (identified as social tales, *noita* tales, fairy tales, seer
tales, tall tales, Savolainen jokes), all recorded by
the author in 1946.

*FN5   Dorson, Richard M. "Folk Traditions of the Upper
       Peninsula." *Michigan History* 31:1 (1947):48-65.

Survey of kinds of folklore obtainable in Michigan's
Upper Peninsula, with emphasis on anecdotes, jokes,
dialect stories. Includes characterizations (but no
actual texts) of 5 narratives from or involving individuals of French-Canadian backgrounds; 7 narratives,

4 superstitions, and 1 rhyme from informants of Cornish
background; and 11 narratives and 1 prayer for blood-
stopping from Finnish informants.
(Cross-listed as *CO4, *FR54.)

FN6   Edgar, Marjorie. "Ballads of the Knife-Men."
        Western Folklore 8:1 (1949):53-57.

        Characterization of 5 ballads about those who use
        woodsmen's knives as fighting weapons, popular among
        Finnish immigrants and their descendants in Minnesota.
        Includes 12 song couplets and stanzas (in English).

FN7   Edgar, Marjorie. "Finnish Charms and Folk Songs in
           Minnesota." *Minnesota History* 17:4 (1936):406-410.

        Brief discussion of homeland traditions remembered or
        perpetuated by Finnish immigrants in Minnesota.
        Includes texts of 1 chant, 2 charms to effect cures,
        and excerpts from 3 songs (including a variant of the
        ballad "Edward"), all in English.

FN8   Edgar, Marjorie. "Finnish Charms from Minnesota."
           Journal of American Folk-Lore 47:186 (1934):381-383.

        Presentation of texts of 7 charms and incantations
        (in Finnish, with English translations), recorded by
        the author in Crooked Lake, Winton, and other northern
        Minnesota communities.

FN9   Edgar, Marjorie. "Finnish Folk Songs in Minnesota."
           Minnesota History 16:3 (1935):319-321.

        Brief general description of the kinds of songs
        Finnish immigrants and their descendants in Minnesota
        remember and sing. Includes brief description of
        typical Finnish houses, saunas, and *Kalevala* songs and
        dramatizations.

FN10   Edgar, Marjorie. "Finnish Proverbs in Minnesota."
           Minnesota History 24:3 (1943):226-228.

        Listing of 42 proverbs (in English), recorded from
        individuals of Finnish descent in Minnesota.

*FN11   Erdely, Stephen. "Research on Traditional Music of
           Nationality Groups in Cleveland and Vicinity."

        (Cross-listed as *GL41, *CR3, *GE172, *HU14, *IR26,
        *RO3, *SC12, *SK4.)
        (See *GL41 for full citation and annotation.)

*FN12   Evanson, Jacob A. "Folk Songs of an Industrial City."

        (Cross-listed as *GL42, *GE177, *GR8, *IR27, *SK5.)
        (See *GL42 for full citation and annotation.)

FN13   Gronow, Pekka. "Finnish-American Records." *JEMF
        Quarterly* 7:23 (1971):176-185.

        Brief sketch of Finnish immigration to the United
        States, followed by a description of Finnish-American
        phonograph records issued from the early 20th century
        into the 1920s. Includes identification of some
        artists, excerpts from 5 recorded songs (2 in Finnish
        and English translations, 3 in English translations
        only), and a brief discography.

*FN14   Hand, Wayland D. "The Folklore, Customs, and Traditions
        of the Butte Miner."

        (Cross-listed as *CO7, *FI2, *IR40, *IT29, *SE4.)
        (See *CO7 for full citation and annotation.)

FN15   Jarvenpa, Robert. "Visual Expression in Finnish-
        American Ethnic Slurs." *Journal of American
        Folklore* 89:351 (1976):90-91.

        Brief discussion of anti-Finnish cartoons and jokes,
        focusing on one "visual cartoon" of a revolver, the
        nature and name of which suggest the stupidity and
        incompetence of Finns. Notes that anti-Finnish humor
        may be either amusing or denigrating.

FN16   Johnson, Aili Kolehmainen. "The Eyeturner (A Cycle of
        Finnish Wizard Tales from the Upper Peninsula of
        Michigan)." *Midwest Folklore* 5:1 (1955):5-10.

        Presentation and brief discussion of 7 tales involving
        illusory transformations, mostly by a wizard-trickster
        figure, Konsti Koponen. Based on fieldwork conducted
        in Michigan's Upper Peninsula in 1945-46.

FN17   Johnson, Aili Kolehmainen. "Finnish Labor Songs from
        Northern Michigan." *Michigan History* 31:3 (1947):
        331-343.

        Brief discussion of reasons for Finnish immigration to
        the United States and of Finns who settled in the
        vicinity of Ridge, Michigan, with emphasis on labor
        songs. Includes texts of 9 labor songs, 2 lullabies,
        and 1 anecdote (all in English).

FN18   Johnson, Aili K[olehmainen]. "Lore of the Finnish-
        American Sauna." *Midwest Folklore* 1:1 (1951):33-40.

        Brief sketch of the history and nature of the Finnish
        sauna in the United States, followed by a description
        of social customs and behavior associated with bathing.
        Includes texts of 1 nursery song, 2 anecdotes, 1 tale,
        1 proverb, brief discussion of a healing by massage
        and of blood-letting or "cupping." Based on fieldwork
        conducted in the Upper Peninsula of Michigan in the
        late 1940s.

FN19   Köngäs, Elli Kaija. "A Finnish Schwank Pattern: The
        Farmer-Servant Cycle of the Kuusisto Family."
        Midwest Folklore 11:4 (1961-62):197-211.

        Discussion of 3 generations of storytellers in a single
        Finnish-American family, based on 1960 fieldwork in
        Minnesota, Oregon, and Illinois. Notes that a cycle of
        farmer-servant tales known and frequently told by the
        immigrants in the family is unknown to their American-
        born children. Includes texts of 10 tales, 1 in both
        Finnish and English, the other 9 in English translations
        only. Includes 4 photographs of the storytellers.

FN20   Köngäs, Elli Kaija. "Immigrant Folklore: Survival or
        Living Tradition?" *Midwest Folklore* 10:3 (1960):
        117-124.

        Discussion of the tale repertoire of a Finnish immigrant
        woman interviewed in Vermont in 1959 who remembered
        stories from her homeland even though she had not told
        them to others for over 43 years. Notes that folklore
        which is not regularly communicated may still be
        remembered, but may not be subjected to usual changes
        expected with use and over time and may be merely a
        non-functioning survival. Includes texts of 3 legends
        (in English translations).

FN21   Köngäs, Elli Kaija. "Nicknames of Finnish Apartment
        Houses in Brooklyn, N.Y." *Journal of American
        Folklore* 77:303 (1964):80-81.

        Listing of 10 apartment house nicknames, with defin-
        itions and explanatory etymologies, recorded in 1961
        from Finnish-Americans in Brooklyn.

FN22 Köngäs-Maranda, Elli Kaija. *Finnish-American Folklore: Quantitative and Qualitative Analysis.* New York: Arno Press, 1980. Pp. v, 536, bibliography.

Analysis of folklore repertoires of Finnish-American informants, based on fieldwork conducted among 111 informants in 7 states (but principally in Virginia, Minnesota, and Astoria, Oregon) between 1959 and 1961. Presentation of data in quantitative and qualitative terms. Quantitative method isolates factors determining nature of folkloric repertoire, such as age, sex, place of birth, place of residence, and friendships and kinship contacts. Qualitative method draws on communication theory to explain how ethnic folklore is transmitted on the basis of content, function, style, and structure. Application of theory illustrated by the lives of 2 categories of immigrants--a family of 3 generations and an individual community leader--and considers such topics as joking, storytelling, values, language, beliefs, and religion. Appendices list informants, provide 80 Finnish texts (with English translations), a glossary of Finnish terms, 1 map of tradition areas in Finland, and a listing of tale types and motifs. Includes 9 maps and 5 photographs.

FN23 Lockwood, Yvonne R. "The Sauna: An Expression of Finnish-American Identity." *Western Folklore* 36:1 (1977):71–84. Also published as *Studies in Folklore & Ethnicity*, edited by Larry Danielson, pp. 71–84. Los Angeles: California Folklore Society, 1977, 1978.

Comparison and contrast of older and contemporary sauna structures and rituals, focusing on the social and enculturational aspects of sauna and on participation as a source and affirmation of ethnic identity. Based on fieldwork conducted in the Upper Peninsula of Michigan in 1976.

FN24 Sutyla, Charles M. *The Finnish Sauna in Manitoba.* Canadian Centre for Folk Culture Studies, Paper No. 24. Ottawa: National Museum of Man, 1977. Pp. iv, 115, bibliography.

Study of the sauna among Finnish settlements in Manitoba, conducted in 1976. Surveys the origin and transplantation of the sauna to Canada and analyzes similarities and differences in sauna practices in Manitoba. Presents case studies of several saunas in Rorketon Province, with detailed illustrations of the

physical structure and comments on the sauna's
significance by owners and users. Concludes with
observation that post-1950 immigrants have revived
a tradition dormant among immigrants who arrived in
Manitoba in the 1920s. Includes 85 photographs and
14 sketches.

FN25   Swanson, Kenneth Albin. "Music of Two Finnish-
         Apostolic Lutheran Groups in Minnesota: The Heide-
         manians and the Pollarites." *Student Musicologists
         at Minnesota* 4 (1970-71):1-36.

Musicological description of selected hymns and songs
of Heidemanian and Pollarite Finnish Lutherans in
Cokato and Crystal, Minnesota, based on research
conducted in 1964-65. Includes brief prefatory sketch
of the evolution of these religious groups.

*FN26 Wacker, Peter O., and Trindell, Roger T. "The Log
         House in New Jersey: Origins and Diffusion."
         Keystone Folklore Quarterly 13:4 (1968):248-268.

Discussion of log houses in New Jersey, particularly
in the northwestern and southwestern parts of the state,
with emphasis on their origins among 17th-century
Swede-Finns and German-Swiss. Includes data from early
records, descriptions of the physical characteristics
of selected houses, 2 maps indicating geographical
distribution, and 9 photographs of log houses.
    (Cross-listed as *GE699, *SS28, *SW9.)

XVIII.   FRENCH (FR) (1-119)

FR1   "Albino Robin." *Journal of American Folk-Lore* 17:66
         (1904):210.

Reprinting of a French-Canadian belief that one will
live to 100 years if one sees a white robin.

FR2   Ancelet, Barry Jean. "Talking Pascal in Mamou: A
         Study of Folkloric Competence." *Journal of the
         Folklore Institute* 17:1 (1980):1-24.

Characterization of a spontaneous storytelling tradition
in Mamou, Louisiana, which involves "a system of exagger-

ations, lies, and nonsense." Describes settings for
and participants in the taletelling and the characters
around whom the stories center. Includes transcriptions
(in French only) of 21 performances.

FR3   Anderson, Jay A. "The Early Development of French-
Canadian Foodways." In *Folklore of Canada*, edited by
Edith Fowke, pp. 91-99. Toronto: McClelland and
Stewart Limited, 1976.

Brief historical sketch of peasants of northwestern
France and their immigration to the Quebec province
of Canada, with emphasis on food preferences and diet
developed in the Old World and continued and supplemented
with newly-available foods in Canada. Includes brief
description of kinds of foods grown, prepared, and
consumed. Argues that the "core diet" of these French-
Canadians has differed only slightly for more than three
centuries.

FR4   Atwood, E. Bagby. "Shivarees and Charivaris: Variations
on a Theme." In *A Good Tale and a Bonnie Tune*,
edited by Mody C. Boatright, Wilson M. Hudson, and
Allen Maxwell, pp. 64-71. *Publications of the Texas
Folklore Society* 32 (1964).

Discussion of the word and the custom of shivaree, with
emphasis on its general characteristics and its practice
in Lafourche Parish, Louisiana. Includes excerpt from
1 interview with a Louisiana informant of French descent.

*FR5   Augar, Pearl Hamelin. "French Beliefs in Clinton
County." *New York Folklore Quarterly* 4:3 (1948):
161-171.

Discussion of beliefs held by the inhabitants of Clinton
County, New York, the majority of whom are of French
descent. Topics include omens, the meanings of certain
insects, causes of accidents, warnings of death, general
beliefs, supernatural beings (witches, wizards, devils,
ghosts, and fairies) and stories about them. Also
includes a brief discussion of ballads, wedding customs,
religious customs, naming practices, remedies, and the
presentation of 1 proverb text (in English). Contains
several references to parallel beliefs in Irish tradition.
   (Cross-listed as *IR1.)

*FR6   Barbeau, C.M. "Folk Songs."

        (Cross-listed as *IR3, *SC1.) ·
        (See *IR3 for full citation and annotation.)

FR7   Barbeau, C. Marius. "The Blind Singer." In *Folklore
        of Canada*, edited by Edith Fowke, pp. 45-50. Toronto:
        McClelland and Stewart Limited, 1976.

        Characterization of the author's encounter with, and
        documentation of the repertoire of, a blind singer and
        storyteller in Charlevoix County, Canada, with brief
        characterizations of the kinds of songs he sang and
        tales he told in the community. Reprinted from a
        1936 publication.

FR8   Barbeau, Marius. "Canadian Folklore." *The French
        Folklore Bulletin* 4:21 (1945):21-27.

        Brief survey of kinds of folklore to be found among
        French immigrants and their descendants in North
        America, in general, and Canada, in particular. In-
        cludes a survey (by titles and brief descriptions)
        of frequently recorded folksongs and excerpts from
        7 such songs (in French).

FR9   Barbeau, Marius. "Canadian Folklore II: Folk Tales."
        The French Folklore Bulletin 4:24 (1946):87-90.

        Brief discussion of kinds of folktales the author and
        others have recorded among French immigrants and their
        descendants in Canada, with emphasis on the antiquity
        of several selected tales (mentioned by title and with
        brief plot descriptions only).

FR10   Barbeau, Marius. "Canadian Folklore III: Legends."
        The French Folklore Bulletin 4:27 (1946):159-166.

        Presentation of excerpts from 5 narratives identified
        as legends, recorded in French Canada.

FR11   Barbeau, Marius. "Canadian Folk-Songs." *University
        of Toronto Quarterly* 16:2 (1947):183-187.

        Notes that "more than 9,000 folk-songs with over 5,000
        melodies have so far been recorded either for the
        phonograph or in musical script" in Canada. Focuses
        upon songs presumed to have come from France. Surveys
        such kinds of songs as love lyrics, drinking songs,
        and historical songs, giving titles and plot summaries.
        Includes excerpts from 6 songs (in French) to indicate
        stylistic features.

FR12   Barbeau, Marius. "Canadian Folk Songs." *Journal of the*
       International Folk Music Council 13 (1961):28-31.

       Brief survey of folksong collecting in Canada, particu-
       larly among individuals of French and American Indian
       descent. Includes brief mention of archives and of
       fieldworkers.

FR13   Barbeau, Marius. "The Ermatinger Collection of
       Voyageur Songs (Ca. 1830)." *Journal of American*
       Folklore 67:264 (1954):147-161.

       Presentation of the texts of 11 voyageur folksongs (in
       French, with musical transcriptions) found in an early
       19th-century manuscript of Edward Ermatinger, a Swiss-
       born fur trader who created "the first set of French
       folk songs of any type ever recorded in the New World."
       Also surveys other early recordings and collections of
       voyageur songs.

FR14   Barbeau, Marius. "Folk Songs of French Louisiana."
       The Canadian Music Journal 1:2 (1957):10-16.

       Characterization of a collection of French folksongs
       recorded in Louisiana by Elizabeth Brandon, with an
       inventory of the songs by titles and tune types. In-
       cludes sample tunes (with French texts) for 7 songs.

FR15   Barbeau, Marius. *Folk-Songs of Old Quebec.* National
       Museum of Canada, Bulletin 75, Anthropological Series,
       No. 16. Ottawa, n.d. Pp. 72.

       Presentation of 15 folksongs (in French, with English
       translations and musical transcriptions). Includes
       introductory essay (pp. 1-27), 5 pictorial sketches of
       folksingers and 2 of local scenes.

FR16   Barbeau, Marius. "How the Folk Songs of French Canada
       Were Discovered." *Canadian Geographical Journal*
       49:2 (1954):58-65.

       Sketch of how the author began to record French folk-
       songs and folktales near Quebec beginning in 1911.
       Includes brief descriptions of 2 traditional singers
       and listings (by descriptive titles) of the songs
       recorded from them. Also includes 11 photographs of
       selected informants.

FR17   Barbeau, Marius. "I Dressed Me All in Feathers."
       Journal of American Folklore 63:248 (1950):181-184.

       Discussion of the possible history of the song "I
       Dressed Me in Feathers," based upon 5 versions from
       central France and 6 versions from French Canada.
       Song attributed to a medieval *jongleur*. Includes a
       reprinting of 1 Canadian text (in French, with musical
       transcription), list of versions and variants.

FR18   Barbeau, Marius. *Jongleur Songs of Old Quebec*. New
       Brunswick, N.J.: Rutgers University Press, 1962.
       Pp. xxi, 202, preface, bibliography.

       Presentation of texts of 42 French-Canadian folksongs
       (in French, with English translations and tune tran-
       scriptions), recorded between 1915 and 1925, with
       comparative notes. Includes introductory essay titled
       "The Discovery of the Folksongs of French Canada."

FR19   Barbeau, Marius. *Roundelays: Folk Dances and Games
       Collected in Canada and New England*. National
       Museum of Canada, Bulletin No. 151, Anthropological
       Series, No. 41. Ottawa, 1958. Pp. 104.

       Presentation of texts (in French, with English
       translations) and 2 musical arrangements (transcribed
       tunes) for 21 dances and games, recorded from indi-
       viduals of French background in Canada and New England
       since 1912. Sources and instructions for playing and
       dancing provided in appended commentaries.

FR20   Barbeau, Marius, and Sapir, Edward. *Folk Songs of
       French Canada*. New Haven: Yale University Press,
       1925. Pp. xxii, 216.

       Presentation of 41 folksong texts (in French, with
       English translations and brief tune transcriptions),
       preceded by headnotes providing historical and
       comparative information and documentation. Some texts
       composites of multiple versions of songs. Brief
       documentation and informant data provided sporadically.
       Some texts recorded by authors, some by fieldworkers
       and previously published elsewhere.

*FR21 Barbour, Frances M. "Some Foreign Proverbs in
       Southern Illinois."

       (Cross-listed as *DA1, *DU2, *GE33, *HU1, *IT3.)
       (See *GE33 for full citation and annotation.)

*FR22   Barnes, Gertrude. "Superstitions and Maxims from Dutchess County."

        (Cross-listed as *DU3, *GE36.)
        (See *DU3 for full citation and annotation.)

*FR23   Barry, Phillips, A.M. "The Collection of Folk-Song."

        (Cross-listed as *GL7.)
        (See *GL7 for full citation and annotation.)

FR24   Beck, E.C. "'Ze Skunk.'" *Journal of American Folklore* 57:225 (1944):211-212.

        Publication (in English) of 1 text of "'Ze Skunk,' a bit of French-Canadian verse circulating in the lumberwoods." Recorded in Midland, Michigan.

*FR25   Bolton, Henry Carrington. "Fortune-Telling in America To-Day: A Study of Advertisements." *Journal of American Folk-Lore* 8:31 (1895):299-307.

        Examples and examination of various advertisements placed in the media by fortune-tellers, clairvoyants, and astrologers. Comments on the popularity of the services of such individuals. Notes that an interest in fortune-telling is related to the intelligence of the population. Provides examples of 1 German and 1 French advertisement, each from New York.
        (Cross-listed as *GE72.)

FR26   Brandon, Elizabeth. "A Study of a May-December Wedding Song in France and Louisiana." *Mid-South Folklore* 6:1 (1978):3-14.

        Comparison and contrast of versions of the song "Le vieux Mari" from France and Louisiana, noting the infrequency with which the song has been recorded in the United States and offering historical and cultural reasons. Includes texts of 3 Louisiana versions of the song and verses from 8 reprinted examples.

FR27   Brandon, Elizabeth. "Superstitions in Vermilion Parish." In *The Golden Log*, edited by Mody C. Boatright, Wilson M. Hudson, and Allen Maxwell, pp. 108-118. *Publications of the Texas Folklore Society* 31 (1962).

        General discussion of superstitions and related legends recorded from individuals of French descent in Vermilion

Parish, Louisiana, between 1950 and 1955. Includes
examples and discussion of conjuring, witchcraft,
fetishes, ghosts, will-o'-the-wisp (*feu-follet* or
fifollet and *loup-garou* or *roup-garou*). Includes
texts of 5 personal experience stories, 1 informant
description of the *roup-garou*. Emphasis placed on
blending of French and Black-African traditions and
its importance in perpetuating these beliefs.

FR28   Brassard, François. "French-Canadian Folk Music
        Studies: A Survey." *Ethnomusicology* 16:3 (1972):
        351-359.

A chronological sketch of French-Canadian folk music
studies since the 17th century.

FR29   Brown, Vonnie R. "Cajun Music--The Soul of Acadiana."
        Folk Dance Scene 12:12 (1977):9-13.

Brief general survey essay characterizing the kinds of
music, song, and musical instruments among Louisiana
Cajuns.

FR30   Carrière, Joseph M. "The Present State of French
        Folklore Studies in North America." *Southern Folk-
        lore Quarterly* 10:4 (1946):219-226.

Survey of research undertaken and remaining to be done
among individuals of French backgrounds in the United
States and Canada.

FR31   Carrière, Joseph Médard. *Tales from the French Folk-
        lore of Missouri*. Evanston and Chicago: Northwestern
        University, 1937. Pp. viii, 354, glossary, tale
        type and motif indexes.

Collection of 73 folktales recorded in longhand from
2 Creoles in 1934 to 1936 who resided in Old Mines,
Missouri. Stories of general French circulation
presented in French, with English summaries.

FR32   "Chansons d'Acadie." In *Folklore of Canada*, edited by
        Edith Fowke, pp. 70-75. Toronto: McClelland and
        Stewart Limited, 1976.

Presentation of texts (in French and English translations) of 3 French folksongs from the Maritime provinces
and Ontario (with tune transcriptions), reprinted from
works originally published in 1945 and 1946. One song
identified as version of "The False Knight upon the
Road" (Child 3).

FR33 "Chansons Franco-Ontarien." In *Folklore of Canada*,
      edited by Edith Fowke, pp. 75-81. Toronto: McClelland
      and Stewart Limited, 1976.

      Presentation of texts (in French and English transla-
      tions) of 3 folksongs (with tune transcriptions),
      recorded from individuals of French ancestry in Ontario,
      Canada, and reprinted from works originally published
      in 1950 and 1974. Songs identified as indigenous to
      the New World and not "imported" from France.

FR34 Claudel, Calvin. "A Comparison of the Folktales of
      Louisiana and Missouri." *Southern Folklore Quarterly*
      26:4 (1962):296-300.

      Brief comparison of kinds of French tales found in
      Louisiana and Missouri, noting similarities and differ-
      ences in animal tales, numskull stories, hero tales,
      romantic stories, rascal tales. Mention made of
      specific similarities and differences in particular
      tales, but no textual examples or plot summaries
      provided.

FR35 Claudel, Calvin. "The Folktales of Louisiana and Their
      Background." *Southern Folklore Quarterly* 19:3
      (1955):164-170.

      General survey of kinds of folktales found in Louisiana,
      with emphasis on their French background. Discussion
      by title of examples of 5 kinds of tales: numskull,
      clever and stupid animals, rascal or rogue, hero or
      heroine, and miscellaneous.

FR36 Claudel, Calvin. "Foolish John Tales from the French
      Folklore of Louisiana." *Southern Folklore Quarterly*
      12:2 (1948):151-165.

      Presentation of 4 translated Foolish John tales
      recorded in 1944 in Louisiana, with historical and
      comparative notes and discussion of major motifs.

FR37 Claudel, Calvin. *Fools and Rascals: Louisiana Folk-
      tales*. Baton Rouge: Legacy Publishing Company,
      1978. Pp. 78, introduction, bibliography.

      Presentation of texts of 47 narratives (in English),
      including tales involving Jean Sot or Foolish John,
      Lapin, and Bouqui, 27 of which are reprinted (some for
      the first time in English translation) from previously
      published sources or from unpublished theses. Tales

recorded in New Orleans and in the parishes of Avoyelles,
Iberia, Lafayette, Orleans, Pointe Coupee, and Saint
Bernard.

FR38   Claudel, Calvin.   "Four Tales from the French Folklore
       of Louisiana."   *Southern Folklore Quarterly* 9:4
       (1945):191–208.

       Presentation of 4 folktale texts from informants of
       French background in Louisiana.

FR39   Claudel, Calvin.   "Golden Hair."   *Southern Folklore
       Quarterly* 5:4 (1941):257–263.

       Presentation of text of 1 folktale, recorded from a
       Louisiana storyteller, presumed to be French.

FR40   Claudel, Calvin.   "Louisiana Tales of Jean Sot and
       Bouqui and Lapin."   *Southern Folklore Quarterly*
       8:4 (1944):287–299.

       Presentation of 7 folktale texts, recorded from
       informants of French background in Louisiana.

FR41   Claudel, Calvin.   "Mr. Doering's 'Songs the Cajuns
       Sing.'"   *Southern Folklore Quarterly* 8:2 (1944):
       123–131.

       Criticism of a published essay by J. Frederick Doering
       on Cajun songs (see item FR48 in this bibliography),
       emphasizing improper translations of poems and mis-
       leading statements about the Cajuns and their folklore.
       Includes 3 reprinted song texts to illustrate transla-
       tion problems.

FR42   Claudel, Calvin.   "A Study of Two French Tales from
       Louisiana."   *Southern Folklore Quarterly* 7:4 (1943):
       223–231.

       Presentation of 2 reprinted folktale texts, identified
       as variants of "Petit Poucet" or "Tiny Thumbkin"
       ("Tom Thumb") and of "Hansel and Gretel."

FR43   Claudel, Calvin, and Carrière, J.M.   "Three Tales from
       the French Folklore of Louisiana."   *Journal of
       American Folklore* 56:219 (1943):38–44.

       Presentation (in English) of texts of three folktales,
       recorded from author Claudel's French-speaking mother
       of Goudeau, Louisiana. Tales identified as versions

of "The Tarbaby and the Rabbit," "The Crop Division,"
and "The Wolf Overeats in the Cellar." Tales involve
the characters Bouqui and Lapin. Includes comparative
notes, some discussion of the meaning of *Bouqui*.

FR44 Claudel, Calvin A., and Carrière, Joseph M. "Snow
      Bella: A Tale from the French Folklore of Louisiana."
      Southern Folklore Quarterly 6:3 (1942):153-162.

      Presentation of 1 folktale text ("Snow Bella" or
      "Snow White"), recorded from a Louisiana informant of
      French background.

FR45 "Contes Populaires." In *Folklore of Canada*, edited by
      Edith Fowke, pp. 50-64. Toronto: McClelland and
      Stewart Limited, 1976.

      Presentation (in English) of texts of 6 folktales from
      French Canada, translated and reprinted from works
      previously published between 1916 and 1940. Comparative
      notes provided, including motifs and tale types.

*FR46 Creighton, Helen. "Canada's Maritime Provinces: An
      Ethnomusicological Survey (Personal Observation and
      Recollection)."

      (Cross-listed as *GL20.)
      (See *GL20 for full citation and annotation.)

*FR47 Cutting, Edith. "Peter Parrott and His Songs." *New
      York Folklore Quarterly* 3:2 (1947):124-133.

      Presentation of a miscellany of folklore materials
      recorded from an informant of French-Canadian descent
      living in Redford, New York. Includes 1 Irish *cante-
      fable* (text and tune, in English), 1 characterization
      of a tall tale, 2 texts of humorous songs (both un-
      titled), 2 summaries of short stories, 1 riddle text,
      1 rhyme text (presumably a children's rhyme), all in
      English, and 1 text of a children's rhyme (in French,
      with English translation).
      (Cross-listed as *IR19.)

FR48 Doering, J. Frederick. "Songs the Cajuns Sing."
      Southern Folklore Quarterly 7:4 (1943):193-201.

      Presentation of 8 song texts, all printed in dialect
      without English translations, recorded in Louisiana,
      some of which appear to be adaptations of well-known
      poems.

FR49   Dorson, Richard M.   "Aunt Jane Goudreau, *Roup-Garou*
       Storyteller."   *Western Folklore* 6:1 (1947):13–27.

       Biographical sketch of a female storyteller of
       Chippewa-French background living in Michigan's Upper
       Peninsula, followed by texts of 23 tales recorded from
       her in 1946. Includes personal experience stories of
       supernatural phenomena (the *loup-garou* or transformer,
       ghosts, specters) and religious jokes.

*FR50 Dorson, Richard M.   "Blood Stoppers."   *Southern Folk-
       lore Quarterly* 11:2 (1947):104–118.

       Characterization of faith healing, burn curing, and
       blood-stopping beliefs and experiences recorded by the
       author in 1946 in the Upper Peninsula of Michigan.
       Includes 16 statements of belief and 50 personal ex-
       perience narratives (the latter either told by patients
       or involving healers of the following national back-
       grounds: Finnish, 7; French, 15; German, 2; Irish, 1;
       Slovenian, 2; Swedish, 2).
           (Cross-listed as *FN2, *GE160, *IR20, *SL1, *SS8.)

FR51   Dorson, Richard M.   "Canadiens."   In *Bloodstoppers &
       Bearwalkers: Folk Traditions of the Upper Peninsula*,
       pp. 69–102.   Cambridge, Mass.: Harvard University
       Press, 1952.

       Brief discussion of French-Canadian immigration to
       Michigan's Upper Peninsula, followed by texts of 26
       narratives (identified as legends of the *loup-garou*,
       lutins, black magic, miracles, signs, beggars, strong
       men; as *contes*; and as dialect stories). Based on
       fieldwork conducted by the author in the Upper
       Peninsula of Michigan in 1946.

FR52   Dorson, Richard M.   "*Canadiens* in the Upper Peninsula
       of Michigan."   *Les Archives de Folklore* 4 (1949):
       17–27.

       Presentation of 6 personal experience stories/anecdotes
       and 18 tales about supernatural beings, phenomena, or
       happenings, recorded in 1946 in the Upper Peninsula
       of Michigan from individuals of French background.

*FR53 Dorson, Richard M.   "Dialect Stories of the Upper
       Peninsula: A New Form of American Folklore."
       Journal of American Folklore 61:240 (1948):113–150.

       Presentation of texts of 82 dialect stories, 1 song,
       1 poem parody, 1 dialect "no trespassing sign" in-

volving dialect speakers of Cornish, Finnish, French, Irish, Italian, and Swedish backgrounds, recorded by the author in 1946-47 in Michigan's Upper Peninsula. Includes characterization of the form, justification for studying dialect stories as a legitimate form of American folklore.
(Cross-listed as *CO3, *FN3, *IR21, *IT17, *SS9.)

*FR54   Dorson, Richard M.   "Folk Traditions of the Upper Peninsula."

(Cross-listed as *CO4, *FN5.)
(See *FN5 for full citation and annotation.)

FR55   Dorson, Richard M.   "Louisiana Cajuns."   In *Buying the Wind: Regional Folklore in the United States*, pp. 229-288.   Chicago: The University of Chicago Press, 1964.

Survey and exemplification of kinds of folklore found among Louisiana Cajuns.   Includes reprinted texts of 7 *contes populaires*, 12 riddles, and reprinted essays on Cajun folkways, folk healers, nicknames, country *mardi gras*, folk music, and descriptions of conjure, hoodoo, and *gris-gris*.

*FR56   Dorson, Richard M.   "Personal Histories."

(Cross-listed as *DU6, *IR22, *SS11.)
(See *SS11 for full citation and annotation.)

FR57   Doyon, Madeleine.   "Folk Dances in Beauce County."
Journal of American Folklore 63:248 (1950):171-174.

General sketch of various kinds of folk dances in Beauce County, Quebec, Canada, with mention by name of many dances, but somewhat detailed descriptions of 4.   Includes stanzas from texts of 2 sung dances (in French), brief description of musical instruments used for jigs.

*FR58   Eames, Frank.   "Landon's Ould Dog and Hogmanay Fair."
New York Folklore Quarterly 3:3 (1947):248-251.

Brief discussion of the Hogmanay Fair activities on the East Branch of the St. Regis River, and of the participants, who were largely descendants of Irish and Scottish immigrants, French-Canadians, or Indians. Presentation of 2 song texts (in English).
(Cross-listed as *IR25, *SC10.)

FR59   Fortier, Alcée. "Four Louisiana Folk-Tales." *Journal
        of American Folk-Lore* 19:73 (1906):123-126.

        Presentation of 4 tale texts in English. Footnotes
        indicate names of informants, original language of
        recordings (3 in Creole, 1 in English), and location
        of recording (St. Mary's Parish, Louisiana).

FR60   Fortier, Alcée. "Louisiana Nursery Tales. II."
        Journal of American Folk-Lore 2:4 (1889):36-40.

        Presentation of texts of 2 tales, "*Posson Dore*" ("The
        Golden Fish") and "Give Me," in Creole patois (with
        English translations). Provides brief notes on some
        aspects of content.

FR61   Fortier, Alcée. "Louisianan Nursery-Tales." *Journal of
        American Folk-Lore* 1:2 (1888):140-145.

        Presentation of 2 tale texts, "*La Graisse*" ("Grease")
        and "*Dezef ki Parle*" ("The Talking Eggs") in Louisiana
        Creole patois (with English translations). Footnotes
        provide explanations of language peculiarities and
        information on parallel tales.

FR62   Fowke, Edith Fulton, and Johnston, Richard. *Folk Songs
        of Quebec* (*Chansons de Quebec*). Waterloo, Ontario:
        Waterloo Music Company Limited, 1957. Pp. 96,
        introduction, bibliography, discography, index.

        Presentation of texts of 44 French-Canadian folksongs
        from Quebec (in French, with English translations and
        tune transcriptions), most reprinted from previously
        published sources.

*FR63   Greenberg, Andrea. "Form and Function of the Ethnic
        Joke."

        (Cross-listed as *GL47, *IT27, *JE28, *PL33.)
        (See *GL47 for full citation and annotation.)

FR64   Greenough, William Parker. *Canadian Folk-Life and
        Folk-Lore*. New York: George H. Richmond, 1897.
        Pp. xii, 199, illustrations by Walter C. Greenough.

        General description of life among French-Canadians in
        the area of Quebec, Canada. Includes "Part IV,
        Amusements--Contes and Raconteurs" (pp. 45-64) contain-
        ing texts or characterizations of 9 tales told by a
        single narrator (8 in English, 1 in French) with

accompanying sketch of the performer and his style,
and "Part IX, Chansons Canadiennes" (pp. 129-146),
including full or partial texts (with tune transcriptions) of 11 French-Canadian traditional songs (10 in
French, 1 in English).

FR65   Greenough, William Parker. "Tall Tales of Dalbec."
       In *Folklore of Canada*, edited by Edith Fowke, pp.
       82-83. Toronto: McClelland and Stewart Limited, 1976.

       Presentation (in English) of 4 tales, reprinted from
       Greenough's 1897 work, all told by a French-Canadian
       hunter named Dalbec. Tales identified as "fantastic
       yarns," all originally heard in Quebec.

FR66   Hatcher, Mattie Austin. "A Texas Border Ballad." In
       Rainbow in the Morning, edited by J. Frank Dobie,
       pp. 49-55. *Publications of the Texas Folk-Lore
       Society* 5 (1926).

       Presentation of text of 1 ballad (in French, Spanish,
       and English translation) about a fight between the
       French and Spanish that led to a 1795 lawsuit. Incident
       portrayed occurred along the Texas-Louisiana border in
       the vicinity of Natchitoches, Louisiana. Includes
       brief discussion of the incident and the ballad it
       spawned.

FR67   Huston, Nancy. *"Sacré Québec*! French-Canadian
       Profanities." *Maledicta, The International Journal
       of Verbal Aggression* 2:1-2 (1978):60-66.

       Discussion of profanity in French Canada (specifically,
       in Joual, the Quebec dialect), with emphasis on contrasts
       with, and transformations of, continental French pro-
       fanities.

*FR68 Jamison, C.V., Mrs. "Signs and Omens from Nova Scotia."
       Journal of American Folk-Lore 6:20 (1893):38.

       Listing of signs and omens learned in Nova Scotia from
       the Scotch and French nurses of the author's childhood.
       Does not note which items learned from which nurses.
       All items in English.
            (Cross-listed as *SC23.)

*FR69 Jones, Louis C. "The Devil in York State."

            (Cross-listed as *GL50, *GE318.)
            (See *GL50 for full citation and annotation.)

*FR70   Jones, Louis C.   "Italian Werewolves."

      (Cross-listed as *IT36.)
      (See *IT36 for full citation and annotation.)

*FR71   Klymasz, Robert B.   "The Ethnic Joke in Canada Today."

      (Cross-listed as *GL53, *IC3, *IT38, *JE40, *UK10.)
      (See *GL53 for full citation and annotation.)

FR72   Knipmeyer, William B.   "Folk Boats of Eastern French
      Louisiana," introduced and edited by Henry Glassie.
      In *American Folklife*, edited by Don Yoder, pp. 105-
      149.   Austin: University of Texas Press, 1976.

      Reprinting of an edited chapter from a doctoral
      dissertation (1956) in which six major types of boats
      common to Eastern French Louisiana are described.   In-
      cludes discussion of boat-building materials, tools
      and methods (illustrated with 31 photographs and 1 set
      of diagrams), and plots geographical distribution of
      boat types (illustrated with 7 maps).   Boats regarded
      generally as indicative of French influence, sometimes
      ultimately derived from Indian or French-Canadian
      models.

FR73   Kolinski, Mieczyslaw.   *"Malbrough s'en va-t-en guerre*:
      Seven Canadian Versions of a French Folksong."
      Yearbook of the International Folk Music Council
      10 (1978):1-32.

      Technical musicological analysis of 7 versions of the
      French folksong "Malbrough s'en va-t-en guerre" (about
      the military exploits of the English General John
      Churchill, Duke of Marlborough, 1650-1722), recorded
      in Quebec, Nova Scotia, and New Brunswick, Canada,
      between 1917 and 1965.   Includes texts (in French),
      musical transcriptions, graphs of melodic structures.

FR74   Lagarde, Marie-Louise; Chute, William S.; and Reinecke,
      George F.   "Six Avoyelles Songs from the Saucier
      Collection."   *Louisiana Folklore Miscellany* 2:2
      (1965):1-26.

      Presentation of 6 French folksong texts (in French and
      English translation, with musical transcriptions),
      recorded in Avoyelles Parish, Louisiana, from 4 in-
      formants in 1949 by Corinne L. Saucier, with compara-
      tive notes and discussion of literary relationships.

FR75   "Legendes." In *Folklore of Canada*, edited by Edith
       Fowke, pp. 58-64. Toronto: McClelland and Stewart
       Limited, 1976.

       Presentation (in English) of texts of 3 legends from
       French Canada, translated and reprinted from works
       previously published in 1920. Provides comparative
       notes, including motifs.

FR76   Le Moine, J.M. "On the Origin of Some Popular Oaths."
       Journal of American Folk-Lore 7:24 (1894):69-70.

       Brief note about the origins of euphemistic oaths used
       by French Canadians to avoid references to the divine.
       Puzzling meaning of a French-Canadian voyageur oath
       also noted (see item FR87 in this bibliography for
       additional comment).

FR77   "*Lutins* in the Province of Quebec." *Journal of
       American Folk-Lore* 5:19 (1892):327-328.

       Description of *lutins* or household spirits which take
       the form of animals and protect or annoy inhabitants
       with their activities, and examples of their powers,
       as told by the French-speaking of Quebec.

FR78   MacMillan, Ernest, ed. *Twenty-One Folk Songs of
       French Canada*. Ontario: The Frederick Harris Co.,
       1928. Pp. 53, preface, introduction.

       Presentation of 21 folksongs (in French, with English
       translations and tune transcriptions), recorded in
       Quebec province, Canada, from individuals of French
       ancestry. Most songs reprinted from previously
       published works.

FR79   Maranda, Elli Köngäs. "French-Canadian Folklore
       Scholarship: An Overview." In *Canadian Folklore
       Perspectives*, edited by Kenneth S. Goldstein, pp.
       21-37. Memorial University of Newfoundland Folklore
       and Language Publications, Bibliographical and
       Special Series, No. 5. St. John's, Newfoundland:
       Department of Folklore, 1978.

       General discussion of folklore societies, programs, and
       archives, and of the use of folklore in public educa-
       tion, cultural activities, and political movements in
       French Canada.

*FR80   "Maryland Superstitions." *Journal of American Folk-*
          Lore 20:77 (1907):159-160.

        Presentation of signs, cures, and superstitions, one
        of which was obtained from an Alsatian man in Washington
        County, Maryland. Reprinted from a previously published
        source.
          (Cross-listed as *GE385.)

*FR81   Mason, Wilton. "The Music of the Waldensians in
          Valdese, North Carolina."

        (Cross-listed as *IT47.)
        (See *IT47 for full citation and annotation.)

 FR82   Miller, William Marion. "A Boundary-moving Ghost."
          New York Folklore Quarterly 1:2 (1945):105-106.

        Characterization of 1 ghost story collected from an
        informant of French descent in Darke County, Ohio.

 FR83   Miller, William Marion. "'La Guignolee' in Southeast
          Missouri." *The French Folklore Bulletin* 4:23
          (1946):61-64.

        Description of a New Year's custom involving a group
        of "masked revelers" who parade through a southeast
        Missouri community singing and dancing at homes at
        which they stop and are given refreshments. Includes
        a text (with words in French and tune transcription)
        of 1 song sung (reprinted from a previously published
        source). Custom viewed as a continuity from medieval
        Europe.

 FR84   Miller, Wm. Marion. "How To Become a Witch." *Journal
          of American Folklore* 57:226 (1944):280.

        Description, based upon an account common among French
        settlers in Darke County, Ohio, "between 1830 and
        1850," of the way one can become a witch. Involves the
        killing of a black cat and planting of pea seeds in the
        cat's eyes in the separated head, with the eating of
        the harvested and cooked peas prescribed.

 FR85   Miller, Wm. Marion. "How To Catch a Witch." *Southern
          Folklore Quarterly* 10:3 (1946):199.

        Brief description of a way of finding a person who
        bewitches farm animals. Account provided by an inform-
        ant of French descent living in Ohio.

FR86   Monteiro, George. "*Histoire de Montferrand: L'Athlete
        Canadien* and Joe Mufraw." *Journal of American Folk-
        lore* 73:287 (1960):24-34.

        Discussion of the French-Canadian prototype Joe Mont-
        ferrand for the cook and sometimes opponent of Paul
        Bunyan, Joe Mufraw. Traces the evolution of this
        legendary character from an 1883 Canadian work through
        the character's transformation in the Bunyan cycle.
        Includes reprintings of 4 anecdotes about Montferrand/
        Mufraw (1 in French, 3 in English).

FR87   N[ewell], W[illiam] W[ells]. "A Remarkable Oath."
        Journal of American Folk-Lore 7:24 (1894):60.

        Traces the history of the custom on which an oath used
        by French-Canadian voyageurs is based. Oath first
        commented upon in a paper presented by J.M. Le Moine
        at the Annual Meeting of the American Folk-Lore
        Society, Montreal, September 14, 1893 (see item FR76
        in this bibliography).

*FR88   Norlin, Ethel Todd. "Present-Day Superstitions at
        La Harpe, Ill., Survivals in a Community of English
        Origin."

        (Cross-listed as *DU14, *GE424, *IR78, *SC30.)
        (See *IR78 for full citation and annotation.)

FR89   Oster, Harry. "The Evolution of Folk-Lyric Records."
        JEMF Quarterly 14:51 (1978):148-150.

        Autobiographical account of the author's fieldwork
        among Louisiana singers and musicians, some of French
        background and others Afro-Americans. Includes brief
        background on the preparing and issuing of early
        French Louisiana folksong and folkmusic phonograph
        records and albums, initially distributed through the
        Louisiana Folklore Society.

FR90   Oster, Harry. "Negro French Spirituals of Louisiana."
        Journal of the International Folk Music Council
        14 (1962):166-167.

        Brief characterization of *cantique* or hymn singing
        among French Catholic Afro-Americans in Louisiana,
        including mention of the nature of melodies (modal and
        regular in structure) and of language (approximates
        standard French), with brief comparison to the

Protestant Afro-American spiritual. Includes 1 reprinted 19th-century French text of "Madeleine au
Tombeau" (in French) and 1 1957 Louisiana text of
"Tombeau, Tombeau," recorded by the author and
presented in French.

*FR91   Peacock, Kenneth. "Establishing Perimeters for Ethno-
        musicological Field Research in Canada: On-Going
        Projects and Future Possibilities at the Canadian
        Centre for Folk Culture Studies."

        (Cross-listed as *GL66, *CH21, *GE428, *HU25, *IC4,
        *ID2, *IT57, *JA9, *LI5, *NO19, *RU19, *UK32.)
        (See *GL66 for full citation and annotation.)

FR92   Porter, Marjorie Lansing. "The Fifteenth of Redford."
        New York Folklore Quarterly 2:3 (1946):205-208.

        General description of a picnic held annually on
        August 15th in Redford, New York, by French residents,
        and those of French descent, in the area.

FR93   Prévos, André. "Some Louisiana Cajun Songs about
        Napoleon." JEMF Quarterly 15:53 (1979):44-51.

        Presentation of texts of 3 songs (in French and English
        translation), recorded in Cajun Louisiana, all re-
        lating to events surrounding the exploits of Napoleon
        Bonaparte. Comparison is made with similar songs from
        France and French-Canada (with excerpts from 2 and a
        full text of 1 additional song, all in French and
        English translation). Argues that Cajun songs probably
        were brought to Louisiana by post-Napoleon immigrants
        to the United States rather than via French-Canada.

FR94   Reich, Wendy. "The Uses of Folklore in Revitalization
        Movements." Folklore 82 (1971):233-244.

        Discussion of "the functions of folklore in periods of
        rapid social change" during which folklore serves as
        an "agent for change." Includes a brief characteriza-
        tion of 1 humorous tale involving interaction between
        an English-Canadian and a French-Canadian arising from
        language differences and preferences.

FR95   Reinecke, George F. "The New Orleans Twelfth Night
        Cake." Louisiana Folklore Miscellany 2:2 (1965):
        45-54.

        Description of the custom of serving a cake with a
        bean baked in it on the Twelfth Night (January 6,

Epiphany), as observed in New Orleans, Louisiana.
Includes discussion of the custom as depicted in art
and literature, with comparative notes to illustrate
its widespread distribution through time and space.
Implication that the practice in New Orleans is of
French derivation.

FR96   Rose, E.H. and H.J.   "Folklore Notes from the Province
       of Quebec."   *Folk-Lore* 23:3 (1912):345-347.

       Listing of 22 moon and calendar beliefs, interpretations
       of dreams, marriage omens, visitor signs, weather signs,
       miscellaneous beliefs, recorded by the author from a
       girl of French ancestry in Quebec, Canada.

FR97   Rose, E.H. and H.J.   "Quebec Folklore Notes, II."
       Folk-Lore 23:4 (1912):462-463.

       Listing of miscellaneous beliefs/superstitions,
       obtained by the authors from a girl of French ancestry
       in Quebec, Canada.

*FR98 Ross, Terri.   "Alsatian Architecture in Medina County."
       In *Built in Texas*, edited by Francis Edward Abernethy,
       pp. 121-129.   *Publications of the Texas Folklore
       Society* 42 (1979).

       Description of houses and buildings constructed by
       Alsatian immigrants who settled in Medina County,
       Texas, in the 1840s.   Emphasis on shape, physical
       features.   Illustrated with 13 photographs.
       (Cross-listed as *GE521.)

FR99   Saucier, Corinne L.   *Folk Tales from French Louisiana.*
       Foreword by Irene Wagner.   New York: Exposition
       Press, 1962.   Pp. 138, bibliography.

       Collection of narratives recorded in 1923 and again
       in 1949 from residents of Avoyelles Parish, Louisiana.
       Texts divided into 4 categories: 1) semi-legendary (1);
       2) fairy tales (19); 3) comical tales (12); and 4)
       animal tales (5).   Some variants of tales provided
       as well.   Appendices contain references to Aarne-
       Thompson motif index and Aarne tale type index, as
       well as parallels of tales to other collections.

FR100   Saucier, Corinne Lelia. "Little John and the Devil:
        A French Tale from Avoyelles Parish, Louisiana."
        Translated by Calvin Claudel. *The French Folklore
        Bulletin* 4:24 (1946):91-95.

        Presentation (in English translation) of 1 folktale,
        recorded in Avoyelles Parish, Louisiana, and included
        in an unpublished 1923 thesis.

*FR101 Shaw, Ann. "What's in a Name."

        (Cross-listed as *DU18.)
        (See *DU18 for full citation and annotation.)

FR102   Shoemaker, Henry W. "Neighbors: 'May Paulet et le
        Vieux Charlot,' A Pennsylvania-Huguenot Tale."
        New York Folklore Quarterly 9:4 (1953):307-313.

        Discussion of the origins of the French language as
        spoken by the Pennsylvania Huguenots and of its
        essential "privacy" as the main cause of its demise.
        Includes characterization of 1 tale collected in an
        area that retains some elements of the dialect.

*FR103 Shoemaker, Henry W. "Neighbors: The Werewolf in
        Pennsylvania."

        (Cross-listed as *GL75.)
        (See *GL75 for full citation and annotation.)

FR104   Shuttleworth, Barbara. "Supernatural Folk Stories in
        the French Canadian Tradition." *The French Folk-
        lore Bulletin* 7:40 (1949):1-4.

        Presentation of texts of 8 supernatural tales and 1
        supernatural belief, recorded from 2 informants of
        French-Canadian ancestry. Tales involve the devil,
        ghosts, and the "*loup-garou*."

FR105   Skinner, Charles M. "The Three Wishes: A Quaint
        Legend of the Canadian Habitants." *Journal of
        American Folk-Lore* 19:75 (1906):341-342.

        Retelling, in the author's words, of a story about
        Saint Peter and Christ, the latter of whom grants a
        shepherd 3 wishes by which he eventually captures the
        devil. Includes comments on the simplicity of French-
        Canadian folktales and the tendency for their tellers
        to refer to God.

FR106   Taché, Joseph-Charles. "La Complainte de Cadieux."
        In *Folklore of Canada*, edited by Edith Fowke,
        pp. 64-70. Toronto: McClelland and Stewart Limited,
        1976.

        Presentation (in English translation) of an 1863
        account of the death of Jean Cadieu (1671-1709), a
        French-Canadian voyageur-interpreter, who diverted
        the attention of a warring band of Iroquois Indians
        while a group of fur trappers escaped. Includes text
        of the "complainte" written by Cadieu shortly before
        he dug his grave and stretched out in it, the complainte
        being regarded as "the first song composed in Canada
        about a Canadian incident."

*FR107 Taylor, Archer. "An Old-World Tale from Minnesota."

        (Cross-listed as *GE682, *IR101.)
        (See *IR101 for full citation and annotation.)

FR108   Thériot, Marie, and Lahaye, Marie. "The Legend of
        Foolish John." *Southern Folklore Quarterly* 7:3
        (1943):153-156.

        Presentation of 3 texts of Foolish John (Jean Sot)
        tales from informants of French ancestry in Louisiana.

FR109   Thomas, Gerald. "A Tradition under Pressure: Folk
        Narratives of the French Minority of the Port-au-
        Port Peninsula, Newfoundland (Canada)." In *Folk
        Narrative Research: Some Papers Presented at the
        VI Congress of the International Society for Folk
        Narrative Research*, edited by Juha Pentikäinen and
        Tuula Juurikka, pp. 192-201. *Studia Fennica,
        Review of Finnish Linguistics and Ethnology* 20
        (1976).

        Brief historical sketch of the French minority of the
        Port-au-Port Peninsula, Newfoundland, Canada, followed
        by a listing of types of folktales recorded by the
        author during 1971-74. Emphasis on the demise of
        storytelling due to the influences of the English-
        speaking majority, American military personnel, the
        introduction of electricity and television. Views
        code-switching in storytelling and the rise of
        macaronic verse and prose traditions as results of
        these changes. Includes text of 1 song and maps of
        the study area (2).

FR110   Thomas, Rosemary Hyde. "La Guillonnée: A French
        Holiday Custom in the Mississippi Valley." *Mid-
        South Folklore* 6:3 (1978):77-84.

        Description and historical discussion of a French-
        derived custom of groups of singing and dancing
        disguised individuals going from house to house on
        New Year's Eve, singing the opening verses of an
        ancient French song, then singing the entire song
        and dancing as well if and when invited into the
        households for food and drink. Based on data obtained
        in several Illinois, Indiana, and Missouri communities.

FR111   Tremblay, Maurice. "Nous Irons Jouer Dans L'Isle."
        Journal of American Folklore 63:248 (1950):163-170.

        Brief discussion of a French-Canadian parish at
        Notre-Dame de l'Ile Verte south of Quebec and of
        kinds of parlor games played there (in English),
        followed by descriptions (including some rules, texts,
        and songs/verses) of 32 parlor games (in French only).
        (For English translations of the game descriptions,
        see FR112.)

FR112   Tremblay, Maurice. "Parlour Games in French Canada."
        In *Folklore of Canada*, edited by Edith Fowke,
        pp. 83-91. Toronto: McClelland and Stewart Limited,
        1976.

        Presentation of descriptions of 31 parlor games (in
        English translation), recorded in Quebec in 1948 from
        individuals of French ancestry. Reprinting of a 1950
        essay (see FR111).

FR113   Tucker, Philip C. "Le Loup Blanc of Bolivar's
        Peninsula." In *Follow de Drinkin' Gou'd*, edited
        by J. Frank Dobie, pp. 62-68. *Publications of the
        Texas Folklore Society* 7 (1928).

        Reconstruction from the author's memory of a story
        about *le loup blanc* or white wolf, told to him prior
        to 1900 by individuals of French descent living on
        Bolivar's Peninsula near Galveston, Texas, and pre-
        sented in a Cajun dialect of English.

FR114 Whitfield, Irène-Thérèse. *Louisiana French Folk Songs*.
       Reprint. New York: Dover Publications, Inc., 1969.
       Pp. xv, 171, appendix, bibliography, index of songs.

  Presentation of texts of 115 French folksongs from
  Louisiana (in French with tune transcriptions), some
  recorded by the author, some by other researchers and
  reprinted from previously published sources or transcribed from phonograph recordings. Songs classified
  into 3 categories: "Louisiana-French Folk Songs,"
  "Cajun Folk Songs," and "Creole Folk Songs." Reprint
  of a 1939 work, with a new preface and appendix of
  11 additional songs.

*FR115 Wintemberg, W.J. "Alsatian Witch Stories."

  (Cross-listed as *GE723.)
  (See *GE723 for full citation and annotation.)

FR116 Wintemberg, W.J. "French Canadian Folk-Tales."
       Journal of American Folk-Lore 17:67 (1904):265-267.

  Presentation of 5 tale texts (2 on transformation of
  humans into animals, 1 on the evil eye, and 2 about
  Jack with his lantern), related to the author by an
  informant from Toronto, who heard the tales from his
  French-Canadian mother.

FR117 Wintemberg, W.J. "Items of French-Canadian Folk-Lore,
       Essex County, Ontario." *Journal of American Folk-
       Lore* 21:82 (1908):362-363.

  Presentation of 8 folklore items (beliefs, cures, and
  superstitions) recorded from an informant of French
  ancestry in Toronto.

FR118 Wyman, Loraine. "Songs from Percé." *Journal of
       American Folk-Lore* 33:130 (1920):321-325.

  Brief description of the fishing village of Percé in
  Gaspé County, Quebec, its isolation from the "outside,"
  and the author's methods of conducting fieldwork.
  Includes 16 songs (in French, with musical transcriptions).

FR119 Zimm, Louise Hasbrouck. "Songs: Two Ballads of the
       French-Indian War, 1763." *New York Folklore
       Quarterly* 11:3 (1955):219-223.

  Presentation of 2 ballad texts (1 with tune transcription) from the French and Indian War which are anti-
  French in sentiment, taken from a 1763 manuscript.

XIX. GERMAN (GE) (1-775)

GE1   Albrecht, Henry F. "Troy Street Cries." *New York
        Folklore Quarterly* 1:4 (1945):238.

      Presentation of 3 texts of the street cries of a 19th-
      century German vegetable peddler from Troy, New York.

GE2   Alderfer, Harold F. "On the Trail of the Hex Signs."
        American-German Review 19:vi (August-September 1953):
        4-8.

      Discusses similarities between signs found in Greek
      churches and hex signs found on Pennsylvania German
      barns. Speculates on the universality of signs and
      paths of dissemination.

GE3   Allen, George. "A Note on Pennsylvania Dutch Art."
        'S Pennsylvaanisch Deitsch Eck, 19 March 1949.

      Criticism of the first known article on Pennsylvania
      Dutch folk art by Henry C. Mercer (titled "The Survival
      of the Medieval Art of Illuminative Writing among
      Pennsylvania Germans") and presentation of the main
      characteristics of the art in terms of scope, economic
      level of practitioners, and religious and non-religious
      uses.

GE4   "Amish Folk-Beliefs." *Pennsylvania Dutchman* 5:5
        (September 1953):3-4.

      Reprint from a chapter of George Smith's 1912 novel
      Amishman, which depicts folklife of the Pennsylvania
      Dutch in Ontario, Canada. Reprinted section character-
      izes conflicts between a father and son over planting
      by the sign of the moon.

GE5   Andrews, Jan. "Witchcraft in Enon Valley." *Keystone
        Folklore Quarterly* 7:1 (1962):40.

      Presentation of 2 stories from the Amish of Enon Valley,
      Pennsylvania, both concerning bewitchment and the
      counteractants prescribed to cast off the spells.
      Recollected by the author from childhood days.

GE6   "Auch, Die Lieber Augustine." *Colorado Folksong
        Bulletin* 2 (1963):44.

      Presentation of 1 song text (in German, with English
      translation), recorded in 1962 from a Boulder, Colorado,

woman who learned the song from family members of
German background among whom the song was traditional.

GE7   Aurand, A. Monroe. *Child Life of the Pennsylvania
       Germans*. Harrisburg, Pa.: The Aurand Press, 1947.
       Pp. 32.

       Description of folklife concerning childhood. Includes
       information on games and sports, foodways, industry,
       music, education, Halloween, the devil, and maturation.
       Includes 8 photographs.

GE8   Aurand, A. Monroe. *Cooking with the Pennsylvania
       "Dutch."* Harrisburg, Pa.: The Aurand Press, 1946.
       Pp. 32.

       Brief introduction to the nature of Pennsylvania Dutch
       cooking, followed by a book of recipes arranged
       according to type of meal. Includes 4 sketches
       illustrating food habits.

GE9   Aurand, A. Monroe. *Home Life of the Pennsylvania
       Germans*. Harrisburg, Pa.: The Aurand Press, 1947.
       Pp. 31.

       Description of traditions related to the home, with
       information on the role of parents and children; the
       art of curing, preserving, and cooking foods; house-
       hold furniture; lore concerning guests (such as the
       tailor, teacher, and cobbler); quilting parties; and
       music and dance. Includes 9 photographs.

GE10   Aurand, A. Monroe. *Little Known Facts about the Ritual
       of the Jews and the Esoteric Folklore of the
       Pennsylvania-Germans*. Harrisburg, Pa.: The Aurand
       Press, 1939. Pp. 108.

       Uses a rare 1753 London edition of Jewish rituals as
       a basis of comparison between Pennsylvania Dutch and
       Jewish folklore. Notes similarities and differences
       and explains similarities as due to a common Old
       Testament heritage (while also allowing for the possi-
       bility of contact in Pennsylvania). Includes a
       summary (in the appendix) of Pennsylvania Dutch lore
       related to the life cycle, circumcision, sex differ-
       entiation, moon lore, dreams, and witches.

GE11   Aurand, A. Monroe. *Popular Home Remedies and Supersti-*
       tions of the Pennsylvania Germans. Harrisburg, Pa.:
       The Aurand Press, 1941. Pp. 32.

       Listing of beliefs under such headings as childhood,
       luck, dressing and sewing, weather, seasons, witches,
       dreams, sex, marriage, and death.

GE12   Aurand, A. Monroe. *The "Pow-Wow" Book: A Treatise on*
       the Art of "Healing by Prayer" and "Laying of Hands,"
       Etc., Practiced by the Pennsylvania-Germans and
       Others; Testimonials; Remarkable Recoveries; Popular
       Superstitions; Etc. Harrisburg, Pa.: The Aurand
       Press, 1929. Pp. x, 85.

       A treatise on the art of powwowing, tracing the roots
       of the activity to America and relating powwowing to
       healing, psychology, and frugality. Includes reports
       of interviews with powwowers and skeptics. Discusses
       powwow manifestations in charms and amulets, and de-
       fends the rationality of "superstitious" beliefs.

GE13   Aurand, A. Monroe. *Quaint Idioms and Expressions of*
       the Pennsylvania Germans. 4th ed., rev. and enl.
       Harrisburg, Pa.: The Aurand Press, 1939. Pp. 32.

       Brief introduction to Pennsylvania Dutch dialect, with
       illustrations from 4 alphabetical lists: 1) 209 dialect
       words interspersed in English sentences; 2) 139 English
       words transformed by the dialect; 3) 64 expressions
       using a combination of English and dialect; and 4) 21
       additional expressions combining English and dialect.

GE14   Aurand, A. Monroe. *The Realness of Witchcraft in*
       America. Harrisburg, Pa.: The Aurand Press, 1942.
       Pp. 32.

       Traces introduction of belief in witchcraft to America
       and, in particular, to Pennsylvania Dutch. Cites
       famous witch cases and notes witchcraft beliefs on
       American and Pennsylvania Dutch holidays. Comments
       on the conflict between science and witchcraft.

GE15   Aurand, A. Monroe. *Social Life of the Pennsylvania*
       Germans. Harrisburg, Pa.: The Aurand Press, 1947.
       Pp. 31.

       Description of social customs, including marriage,
       funerals, games, taffy making (including 13 recipes),
       sleighing, medicine shows, and bundling. Includes
       8 photographs.

GE16 Aurand, A. Monroe. *Wit and Humor of the Pennsylvania Germans*. Harrisburg, Pa.: The Aurand Press, 1946. Pp. 32.

Presentation of 71 jokes and anecdotes (each with a distinctive title) and 8 humorous cartoons of the Pennsylvania Dutch.

GE17 Bachman, George. *The Older Order Amish of Lancaster County, Pennsylvania*. Norristown, Pa.: Pennsylvania German Society, 1942. Reprint. Lancaster, Pennsylvania German Society Publications 60 (1961):62–294.

Descriptions of Amish folklife, including mention of homes and furnishings, methods of transportation, weddings, funerals, cemeteries, holidays, music, and superstitions. Includes 11 photographs of Amish cultural life.

GE18 Bailer, Sophia. "How I Learned 'Powwowing.'" *Pennsylvania Dutchman* 4:2 (June 1952):8.

Description of how the author learned the art of powwowing, with comments on transmission and goals and presentation of 1 cure each for "liver grown" and bleeding, with 1 appropriate formula for each.

GE19 Bailer, Sophia. "How I Pow Vow for ... Rote Laufa." *Pennsylvania Dutchman* 4:3 (July 1952):5.

Letter to Don Yoder dated 15 April 1952 describing cure for inflammation, with 1 formula (in German, with English translation).

GE20 Bailer, Sophia. "How to Stop a Witch." *Pennsylvania Dutchman* 4:1 (May 1952):8–9.

Description of how author used powwow for a visitor who requested help for his ill wife and how she stopped the power of witchcraft.

GE21 Bailer, Sophia. "Witches ... I Have Known." *Pennsylvania Dutchman* 4:1 (May 1952):8.

Relates witchcraft experiences of the author's mother. Includes photograph of the author.

GE22 Baldwin, Sioux. "Amish Plain Costume: A Matter of Choice." *Pennsylvania Folklife* 19:4 (Summer 1970): 10–17.

Analysis of Amish plain costume through investigation and interviews with 3 members of an Old Order Amish

family of Lancaster County, in 1969. Focuses on aspects
of modernity in Amish dress. Contains transcription of
a conversation concerning costume. Includes in-depth
discussion of appropriateness of adult and children's
dress of both sexes in a variety of daily situations,
and comparison of differences between Amish and
Mennonite dress. Includes 5 photographs and 5 sketches
of dress.

GE23   Barakat, Robert A. "The Herr and Zeller Houses."
       Pennsylvania Folklife 21:4 (Summer 1972):2–22.

       Discussion of the use of two Pennsylvania Dutch homes,
       built during the colonial period (one in Lancaster,
       one in Womelsdorf), to demonstrate value of typologies
       in folklife studies. Argues that historical archaeology
       requires reconstruction of cultural and physical back-
       ground in order to place edifice in proper perspective.
       Elaborate detail of house structures, designs, and
       physical composition. Includes 26 photographs and 10
       diagrams of these homes and their parts.

GE24   Barba, Preston. "Christmas Lore." *'S Pennsylvaanisch
       Deitsch Eck*, 21 December 1968.

       Listing of 20 folk beliefs surrounding Christmas Eve.

GE25   Barba, Preston. "Greens." *'S Pennsylvaanisch Deitsch
       Eck*, 27 March 1954.

       Discussion of the history and use of greens, especially
       dandelion, for everyday cooking, as well as during Holy
       Week. Also notes placement of greens in salad mixture
       as cure or protection against pneumonia.

GE26   Barba, Preston. "Notes on Matteis Daag." *'S Pennsyl-
       vaanisch Deitsch Eck*, 5 April 1947.

       Discussion of the influence of St. Matthias on Pennsyl-
       vania Dutch, who associate the saint's day, February
       24, with weather, harvesting, marriage, and death, but
       most commonly in connection with termination of winter.
       Traces historical roots of the saint's day.

GE27   Barba, Preston. "Old Time Christmas Baking."
       'S Pennsylvaanisch Deitsch Eck, 8 December 1956.

       Discussion of the importance of food preparation for
       Christmas holiday celebration. Elements used in the
       making of Christmas baked goods provided, along with
       6 recipes.

GE28   Barba, Preston. "Pennsylvania German Tombstones."
       The Pennsylvania German Folklore Society, *Yearbook*
       18 (1953):1–228.

       Discussion of motifs found on Pennsylvania Dutch tomb-
       stones between the years 1750 and 1850, covering over 100
       graveyards. Recognizes universality of motifs, although
       notes strong concentration in Pennsylvania Dutch mother
       countries. Characterization of the general nature of
       folk art. Includes 196 pencil drawings of tombstones
       accompanied by notes.

GE29   Barba, Preston. "Pennsylvania German Tombstones."
       American-German Review 20:6 (August–September 1954):
       24–28.

       Study of Pennsylvania German tombstones found between
       the years 1750 and 1850. Categories of symbols discussed,
       as well as parallels drawn to European folk art.

GE30   Barba, Preston. "Pie and the Pennsylvania Germans."
       'S Pennsylvaanisch Deitsch Eck, 24 February 1951.

       Presentation of an excerpt from a book by Barba and
       Ann Hark entitled *Pennsylvania German Cookery* on the
       history, variety, and importance of pies and pie making
       to the Pennsylvania Dutch.

GE31   Barba, Preston. "Symbols and Stones." *Pennsylvania
       History* 23 (April 1956):241–247.

       Argues for universality of motifs commonly found on
       Pennsylvania Dutch tombstones by showing similarities
       to sun, spiral, and tree symbols found all over the
       world.

GE32   Barba, Preston. "Der Tambour Yockel: Pennsylvania
       German Folklore in the Making." *'S Pennsylvaanisch
       Deitsch Eck*, 16 July 1949.

       Presentation of the ballad "The Legend of Tambour
       Yokel" and a German variant. Speculation that events
       depicted in the ballad so horrified congregants of
       East Salisbury Church that they temporarily disbanded
       the church between 1791 and 1847.

*GE33 Barbour, Frances M. "Some Foreign Proverbs in Southern
       Illinois." *Midwest Folklore* 4:3 (1954):161–164.

       A collection of 47 German, 3 French, 1 Italian, 2
       Danish, 1 Hungarian, 1 Dutch proverbs from Southern

Illinois, with all but the Italian, Danish, Hungarian, and Dutch presented in both the original language and in English translation.
(Cross-listed as *DA1, *DU2, *FR21, *HU1, *IT3.)

GE34   Barbour, John. "Dick Harman Tales." *Pennsylvania Dutchman* 5:14 (15 March 1954):11.

Presentation of 7 stories of strongman Dick Harman, recorded from Earl Barger of Queenstown, Pennsylvania, on December 28, 1950. Tales recount Harman's feats as he personally remembered them.

GE35   Barker, Maxinne. "Schnitz Pie." *Pennsylvania Dutchman* 5:5 (September 1953):3, 14.

Reprint of article in which the popularity of schnitz pie, spareribs, sauerkraut, noodles, and coffee cake among Canadian Pennsylvania Dutch Mennonites is discussed. Includes 2 recipes.

*GE36   Barnes, Gertrude. "Superstitions and Maxims from Dutchess County, New York."

(Cross-listed as *DU3, *FR22.)
(See *DU3 for full citation and annotation.)

GE37   Barrick, Mac E. "'The Barber's Ghost': A Legend Becomes a Folktale." *Pennsylvania Folklife* 23:4 (Summer 1974):36-42.

Presentation of a well-known folktale among Pennsylvania Dutch, with discussion of distinctions between legend and folktale, and of influence of print on changing a story from legend to folktale. Includes 6 variants of tales.

GE38   Barrick, Mac E. "Cumberland County Death Lore." *Pennsylvania Folklife* 28:4 (Summer 1979):37-46.

Description of beliefs and practices surrounding death, from preparation through burial, to tombstones. Data based on interviews with informants in Cumberland County. Reports of interviews reflect informants' attitudes toward death customs which derive from dreams, herbs, and omens. Divides behavior concerning death into conceptual and organizational aspects. Includes 5 photographs.

GE39   Barrick, Mac E. "Finger Games and Rhymes." *Pennsyl-
        vania Folklife* 17:4 (Summer 1968):44-47.

        Study of finger rhymes and games practiced by young
        children on Pennsylvania Dutch farms as a means of
        entertainment. Over 15 examples of rhymes taken from
        9 informants. Scholarly footnotes provide parallel
        samples. Includes 7 sketches of finger positions.

GE40   Barrick, Mac E. "Folklore in the Library: Old Schuyl-
        kill Tales." *Pennsylvania Folklife* 23:3 (Spring
        1974):44-48.

        Plea for the folklorist to examine written descriptions
        of local history for their folkloristic content. Such
        is the case with Ella Zerby Elliott's *Old Schuylkill
        Tales*, which includes accounts of witchcraft, ghosts,
        Indian legends, memorates, folk beliefs, and folktales.

GE41   Barrick, Mac E. "Moon-Signs in Cumberland County."
        Pennsylvania Folklife 15:4 (Summer 1966):41-43.

        Discussion of almanacs as sources for folk beliefs
        concerning farming, especially relating to planting by
        signs of the Zodiac. Lists 47 beliefs derived from 3
        informants and compares beliefs to published sources.

GE42   Barrick, Mac E. "Pulpit Humor in Central Pennsylvania."
        Pennsylvania Folklife 19:1 (Autumn 1969):28-36.

        General discussion of pulpit humor of both preachers
        and laymen of Central Pennsylvania. Themes reflect
        image that preacher had of himself and that parishioners
        had of him. The latter revolves around preacher's
        exaggerated features, and the former concerns attempts
        to bring parishioners into the religious fold. Compari-
        son of Pennsylvania German preachers to Afro-American
        preachers, and contemporary humor to that of the immi-
        grant period and earlier medieval parallels. Includes
        4 photographs of preachers and 2 of title pages of
        books containing humor of preachers.

*GE43   Barrick, Mac E. "Racial Riddles & the Polack Joke."

        (Cross-listed as *IR4, *IT6, *JE4, *PL5.)
        (See *PL5 for full citation and annotation.)

GE44   Baver, Florence S. "Dutch Needlework." *Pennsylvania
        Dutchman* 5:11 (1 February 1954):15.

        Specially made footstools are discussed as evidence of
        Pennsylvania Dutch creativity and penchant for sewing.
        Includes 1 photograph of 2 footstools.

GE45   Baver, Russel S. "Corn Culture in Pennsylvania."
        Pennsylvania Folklife 12:1 (Spring 1961):32-37.

        Discussion of techniques of planting, chopping, and
        husking, as well as uses of corn. Illustrations drawn
        from 1 proverb, 2 rhymes, 1 humorous prayer, and
        mention of behavior of children around corn culture.
        Includes 2 photographs depicting families in corn
        fields and 2 sketches of tools.

GE46   Baver, Russel S. "Golden Fields in the Golden Years."
        Pennsylvania Folklife 9:4 (Fall 1958):12-17.

        Detailed description of the various processes involved
        in raising grains, including sowing, harvesting,
        reaping, threshing, winnowing, and marketing. Author
        adds experiences of friends and family and remarks on
        changes in various practices over the years. Includes
        5 photographs of grain raising and harvesting.

GE47   Baver, Russel S. "'H' is for Hinkle." *Pennsylvania
        Folklife* 13:1 (Fall 1962):13-18.

        Reminisces on the role of hens on the Pennsylvania Dutch
        farm, and describes processes involved in raising hens
        and taking care of egg laying, including starting a
        new flock, feeding baby chicks, and dressing chickens.
        Over 10 folk beliefs listed pertaining to egg lore.
        Includes 7 photographs illustrating care and feeding
        of chicks.

GE48   Baver, Mrs. Russel S. "Housebutzing." *Pennsylvania
        Dutchman* 5:7 (November 1953):7-8.

        Description of the role of house cleaning among Pennsyl-
        vania Dutch, including references to where and when
        house cleaned and to which tools were used. Discussion
        of the role of cleanliness for Pennsylvania Dutch
        housewife.

GE49 Baver, Mrs. Russel S. "Ironing Day." *Pennsylvania Dutchman* 5:2 (June 1953):6-7.

Process of ironing is described, from washing clothes to putting clothes away, from location of ironing board to placement of clothes during ironing. Mentions that there are few folk beliefs attached to ironing, and supplies 1 belief. Includes 5 photographs depicting historical changes in irons.

GE50 Baver, Mrs. Russel S. "Kitchen Glimpses." *Pennsylvania Dutchman* 5:4 (August 1953):10-11.

Continuation of previous article in which kitchen table was stressed (see GE51). Focus here on importance of stove. Functions of cooking, warming, and cleaning stove dramatized through reconstructed conversation between a mother and daughter. Includes 3 photographs of kitchen objects.

GE51 Baver, Mrs. Russel S. "Kitchen Lore." *Pennsylvania Dutchman* 5:3 (July 1953):8.

Role of kitchen among Pennsylvania Dutch discussed, especially the table on which foods were prepared and meals eaten. Reconstruction of typical conversation in German (with English translation) indicating styles of tables and their uses. Includes 3 photographs of various kitchen tables.

GE52 Baver, Mrs. Russel S. "Music in the Parlor." *Pennsylvania Dutchman* 5:9 (1 January 1954):5.

Discussion of the importance of parlor organ for fostering family togetherness and music appreciation. Includes 1 photograph of organ and 4 lines of a song typically sung and accompanied by organ.

GE53 Baver, Mrs. Russel S. "Of Brooms and Cleaning." *Pennsylvania Dutchman* 5:6 (October 1953):5, 12.

Discussion of the role of cleaning among Pennsylvania Dutch women. Mention of use of brooms and schedule for cleaning various rooms of the house, as well as windows and the outdoors. Importance of inculcating values of cleanliness to children is stressed. Includes 7 folk beliefs relating to broom, 1 photograph of 2 brooms.

GE54   Baver, Mrs. Russel S. "Washday Lore." *Pennsylvania*
           Dutchman 5:1 (May 1953):6-7, 15.

       Elaboration of custom of washing clothes on Monday,
       including description of washing locations (wash-houses,
       creek), washing process, soap making, and dress worn
       for the occasion. Reference to early washing machines
       and to 11 folk beliefs about the days and occasions on
       which washing certain types of clothing would or would
       not be appropriate. Includes 1 photograph of a washtub,
       and 1 of a stove for heating wash water.

GE55   Baver, Mrs. Russel S. "Wood and the Woodchest."
           Pennsylvania Dutchman 5:5 (September 1953):5, 14.

       Discussion of the importance of wood for completion of
       many farming chores, based on author's childhood
       reminiscences. Processes of cutting, drying, and
       storing wood (such as in wood chests) described, as
       well as the multiple uses of wood. Includes 3 photo-
       graphs depicting cutting and storing of wood.

GE56   Beck, Berton E. "Grain Harvesting in the Nineteenth
           Century." *Pennsylvania Folklife* 23:4 (Summer 1974):
           43-46.

       Description of harvesting process typical on a Pennsyl-
       vania Dutch farm, based on father's reminiscences.
       Processes described include: taking up and shocking
       grain, threshing, and flailing. Notes introduction of
       horse-powered threshing machines and the increasing
       trend toward mechanization.

GE57   Beckel, Clarence E. "Early Marriage Customs of the
           Moravian Congregation in Bethlehem, Pennsylvania."
           The Pennsylvania German Folklore Society, *Yearbook*
           (Section II) 33 (1938):3-32.

       Description of early weddings among Moravians based on
       manuscripts of the Moravian congregation in Bethlehem,
       Pennsylvania, dated in the 1740s. Main section in-
       cludes methods of choosing a wife and description of
       notable marriage ceremonies, especially that of the
       Great Wedding of 1749. All 56 attendees' names
       mentioned.

GE58 Bek, William G. "Survivals of Old Marriage-Customs among the Low Germans of West Missouri." *Journal of American Folk-Lore* 21:80 (1908):60-67.

Brief history of the settlement of the area around Johnson, Lafayette, Pettis, and Saline counties, Missouri, by Germans primarily from Hanover. Focus of article on a Low German marriage feast, with an explanation of some of its features as "survivals" of earlier customs and beliefs. Includes texts of 3 poems (in High German, with English translations) recited to invite guests to the wedding, and 1 poem recited to fetch the bride.

GE59 Bender, Rhoda. "Dutch Nicknames." *Pennsylvania Dutchman* 1:14 (4 August 1949):3.

Extracted from *The Mountaineer*, this article demonstrates the pervasive use of nicknames among the Pennsylvania Dutch. The 25 to 30 names presented fall into 3 categories: descriptive, distinguishing, and stigmatizing.

GE60 Berkey, Andrew S. "Christmas Customs of the Perkiomen Valley." *Pennsylvania Dutchman* 4:8 (December 1952): 2-3, 7.

Information on Christmas customs learned from interviews with Perkiomen Valley residents, focusing on such topics as Belsnickel, the Christ child, dew, cattle divination, Christmas tree, and Christmas cookies. Includes 1 photograph of old-time decorations on Christmas tree.

GE61 Berky, A.S. "Folktales." *Pennsylvania Dutchman* 3:6 (1 August 1951):2.

Presentation of 2 accounts reported to have taken place 120 years ago in Bechtelsville and in New Berlinville. One relates to use of magic, the other to fear of a corpse.

GE62 Berky, Andrew S. "Bread and Apple-Butter Day." *Pennsylvania Folklife* 12:3 (Fall 1961):42-43.

Explanation of use of bread and apple butter by Schwenkfelders for a thanksgiving service which is held on September 24, to commemorate their safe voyage to Pennsylvania. Description of change in customs sur-

rounding the thanksgiving service, especially with
regard to service of foods. Includes 1 map, and 1
photograph of a title page of a famous Pennsylvania
Dutch book.

GE63   Berky, Andrew S. "Buckskin or Sackcloth? A Glance at
       the Clothing Once Worn by the Schwenkfelders in
       Pennsylvania." *Pennsylvania Folklife* 9:2 (Spring
       1958):50-52.

       Traces the evolution in style of dress from "plain" to
       "fancy" among Schwenkfelders, including mention of
       debates over proper attire. Includes 1 photograph of
       3 women dressed in popular garb of 1830s.

GE64   Berky, Andrew S. "New Year's Eve." *Pennsylvania
       Dutchman* 4:9 (1 January 1953):3.

       Supplement to author's article on Christmas customs in
       Perkiomen Valley. Customs include "wishing," "shoot-
       ing," and visitation of friends. Information obtained
       firsthand from 4 informants. Mention made of 2 folk
       beliefs.

GE65   Berky, Andrew S. "Yesterday in Dutchland." *Pennsyl-
       vania Folklife* 8:1 (Summer 1956):10-15.

       Discussion of strengths and weaknesses of H. Winslow
       Fegley's photography of Pennsylvania Dutch rural life
       at turn of century. Comments on the role relationship
       of photographer and subject. Examples of his photo-
       graphy in 16 photographs of rural life.

GE66   Berwin, Solomon. "New Year's Celebration in Berks
       County in 1828." *Pennsylvania Dutchman* 3:15
       (1 January 1952):1, 4.

       Description of adventures of several boys who went to
       37 different farms to wish and shoot in the New Year,
       but whose activities ended in tragedy for one of the
       cows on a farm.

GE67   Best, Martha S. "Christmas Customs in the Lehigh
       Valley." *Pennsylvania Folklife* 22:2 (Winter 1972-73):
       15.

       Description of modern-day celebrations of Christmas in
       over 100 churches in Lehigh Valley, Pennsylvania.
       Forms of expression include church services, choral

programs, breakfasts, giving to the needy, musicals,
tree decoration, and contemporary *putzes*. Includes 8
photographs depicting various decorations and 1 recipe
for white cookies.

GE68 Best, Martha S. "Easter Customs in the Lehigh Valley."
Pennsylvania Folklife 17:3 (Spring 1968):2-13.

Report on Easter customs discovered while author took
2 children on a tour of the Pennsylvania Dutch area of
Lehigh Valley. First half of article describes Easter
days (including Palm Sunday, Passion Week, and Easter
Sunday). Second half focuses on various types, styles,
and uses of Easter eggs. Detailed description of
process of dyeing and carving eggs, with comparison
made between Pennsylvania Dutch and Ukrainian styles.
Discusses the artistry of several well-known egg
decorators. Includes 24 photographs of over 20 Easter
foods and varieties of Easter eggs.

GE69 Bittinger, Lucy Forney. "Pennsylvania German Folklore."
The Pennsylvania-German 9:iv (April 1908):171-173.

Listing of categories of folklore typically found in
York and Adam counties, with 1 or 2 examples under each
(holidays, powwowing, and signs of the zodiac).

GE70 Bixler, Leo H. "Pine Tar and Its Uses." *Pennsylvania
Folklife* 13:3 (July 1963):18-23.

Profile of a Pennsylvania farmer who resides with his
family in Hebe and who is well known for producing pine
tar. Presents a biographical sketch of Geirmon Straub
and tape-recorded reminiscences of his making pine tar.
Concludes with the author's summation of uses for pine
tar. Includes 5 photographs of Straub, his living
quarters, and 1 diagram of the tar-making process.

GE71 Bogusch, E.R. "Superstitions of Bexar County." In
Rainbow in the Morning, edited by J. Frank Dobie,
pp. 112-125. *Publications of the Texas Folk-Lore
Society* 5 (1926).

Listing of statements of belief/superstitions, most of
which were recorded from "German farmers of Bexar
County," Texas. Includes 45 weather signs, 13 superstitions about snakes, 20 statements of belief about
cats and other animals, 14 social superstitions, 31
superstitions concerning love and marriage, 19 signs

predicting death, 53 omens of misfortune other than
death, 33 good luck signs, and 12 wart cures.

*GE72   Bolton, Henry Carrington. "Fortune-Telling in America
        To-Day: A Study of Advertisements."

        (Cross-listed as *FR25.)
        (See *FR25 for full citation and annotation.)

GE73   Bomberger, Barbara B. "Simple Basics of Egg Decorating."
        Pennsylvania Folklife (Folk Festival Supplement 1974):
        12-13.

        Description of decorating process involved in scratch-
        carving Easter eggs. Highlights 3 methods: blocked,
        blown, and decoupage. Includes 1 photograph of a
        scratch carver.

GE74   Bomberger, C.M. "Bundling." *Pennsylvania Dutchman*
        3:6 (1 August 1951):7.

        Description of attitudes of Amish residents of Berks,
        Lebanon, Lancaster, Mifflin, and Snyder counties toward
        the custom of bundling. Also includes mention of other
        traditional Amish practices to which the author claims
        the Amish have held steadfast despite modern incursions.

GE75   Borneman, Henry S. *Pennsylvania German Illuminated
        Manuscripts: A Classification of Fraktur-Schriften
        and an Inquiry into Their History and Art.* Norris-
        town, Pa.: Pennsylvania German Society, 1937. Pp. 58.

        Discussion of the nature and variety of fraktur, in-
        cluding categories of manuscripts, methods of design,
        and types of implements and materials used. Illustrated
        by 38 plates.

GE76   Bowman, H.H.M. "The Use of Saffron in Pennsylvania
        Dutch Cooking." *Pennsylvania Dutchman* 1:6 (9 June
        1949):3.

        Explanation as to why saffron was used in some, but not
        all, Pennsylvania Dutch counties and why it is particu-
        lar to Swiss Mennonites who settled in Lancaster County.

GE77   Boyer, Walter E. "Adam und Eva im Paradies." *Pennsyl-
        vania Folklife* 8:2 (Fall-Winter 1956-57):14-18.

        Attempt to prove the popularity of the broadside "Adam
        and Eve" by historical references to early printings

and prototypes, artistry of illustrations, and appeal
to symbolic themes in the ballad. Includes 2 photographs of broadside sheets and 1 illustrating an Adam
and Eve scene.

GE78   Boyer, Walter E.   "The German Broadside Song of
          Pennsylvania." *Pennsylvania Folklife* 10:1 (Spring
          1959):14-19.

Decries the neglect of broadside research and argues
that the analysis of broadsides would demonstrate that
spirituals are of Germanic origin rather than stemming
from the Great Awakening, as Don Yoder claims. Discusses themes and the relationship of broadsides to
folk beliefs and art. Includes photographs of 4 broadsides.

GE79   Boyer, Walter E.   "The Meaning of Human Figures in
          Pennsylvania Dutch Folk Art." *Pennsylvania Folklife*
          11:2 (Fall 1960):5-23.

In-depth investigation of the human symbolism found in
baptismal certificates, based on a study of 6 certificates from well-known collections (photographs included).
Symbolism considered in terms of function of certificates, role of naming, general folk beliefs of the
Pennsylvania Dutch, and structural placement of symbols
on certificates.

GE80   Boyer, Walter E.   "The New Year Wish of the Pennsylvania
          Dutch Broadside." *Pennsylvania Folklife* 10:2
          (Fall 1959):45-48.

Discussion of 3 distinct types of New Year's wishes:
those identical with folk blessings, those distributed
by newspapers, and those personal ones sent from friend
to friend on greeting cards.

GE81   Boyer, Walter E.; Buffington, Albert F.; and Yoder,
          Don. *Songs Along the Mahantongo.* Lancaster, Pa.:
          The Pennsylvania Dutch Folklore Center, 1951. Pp. 23.

Examination of 62 songs recorded from informants in
the Mahantongo Valley, viewed in the broader context
of Pennsylvania Dutch culture and religion. Introduction relates folksong to the questions of origin,
instruments used, spirituals, dance, and lists prominent
informants, with brief identifying comments. Songs
arranged by subjects, such as childhood, marriage,

farm, tavern, American life, and campground. Includes
extensive notes and tune transcriptions for each song.

GE82 Brednich, Rolf Wilh. *Mennonite Folklife and Folklore:
      A Preliminary Report.* Canadian Centre for Folk
      Culture Studies, Paper No. 22. Ottawa: National
      Museum of Man, 1977. Pp. iv, 111, bibliography.

      Study of Mennonite folklife and folklore in the
      Saskatchewan Valley, undertaken in 1975. Emphasis on
      material culture, including barns, foodways, farm
      implements, and household objects. Based on interviews
      with 45 informants, author assesses continuities and
      discontinuities in traditional religion and cultural
      values through an examination of material culture,
      social customs, hymns and other folksongs, and narra-
      tives. Author discerns a lessening of traditions
      among second and third generations. Appendices present
      13 jokes, biographical sketches of informants, and a
      catalog to 18 tape recordings. Includes 34 photographs
      and 7 sketches.

GE83 Breininger, Lester. "Beekeeping and Bee Lore in
      Pennsylvania." *Pennsylvania Folklife* 16:1
      (Autumn 1966):34-39.

      Presentation of the history and lore of beekeeping in
      America, especially in Pennsylvania, together with
      descriptions of bee caring, honey extraction, and
      various types of beehives. Includes 1 custom, 1 poem,
      1 riddle, 2 recipes, and 10 beliefs.

GE84 Breininger, Lester. "Country Auctions: 'Going-Going-
      But Not Gone!!'" *Pennsylvania Folklife* 28 (Folk
      Festival Supplement 1979):25-27.

      Description of a typical auction prevalent in Pennsyl-
      vania Dutch counties. Provides reasons for attendance
      by different age groups, notes typical expressions
      used by auctioneer and audience, and comments on the
      relationship between "crier" and "buyer." Points out
      changes in auctioneering over the years.

GE85 Breininger, Lester. "The Lore of Tinsmithing."
      Pennsylvania Folklife 22 (Folk Festival Supplement
      1973):36-37.

      Short note on decorative art created from tin. Focuses
      on 2 craftsmen, noting how they became tinsmiths, what

their primary jobs are, and how they developed a hobby
of creating small objects from tin before beginning to
work fulltime in their occupation. Includes 3 photographs of the tinsmithing process.

GE86   Brendel, J.B. "Two Folktales." *Pennsylvania Dutchman*
        1:11 (14 July 1949):2.

        Presentation of 2 tales (1 in English, 1 in German)
        titled "A Promising Son?" and concerned with a test
        assigned by a boy's father and a Lancaster County
        minister to determine the boy's future.

GE87   Brendel, John B. "Johnnie Weitzel and His Two Old Maid
        Sisters." *Pennsylvania Dutchman* 4:1 (May 1952):11.

        Presentation of stories about Sammy Snook, who was
        known for his antics and freeloading and also because
        of his two miserly sisters.

GE88   Brendle, Thomas R. "Collecting Dialect Folk Songs."
        Pennsylvania Folklife 11:1 (Spring 1960):50-52.

        Argues that dialect folksong is not moribund, as some
        have claimed, and proceeds to enumerate 9 categories
        under which folksongs collected in 1935 by Brendle and
        Troxell can be classified. Includes a bibliography of
        German-language imprints of Pennsylvania containing
        folksongs for the period 1816-1903.

GE89   Brendle, Thomas R. "Customs of the Year in Dutch
        Country." *Pennsylvania Dutchman* 3:12 (15 November
        1951):1, 7.

        General listing of over 100 folk beliefs surrounding
        such religious holidays as Christmas, Good Friday,
        Easter, and Ascension Day.

GE90   Brendle, Thomas R., and Troxell, William S. *Pennsyl-
        vania German Folk Tales, Legends, Once-Upon-A-Time
        Stories, Maxims, and Sayings*. Norristown, Pa.:
        Pennsylvania German Society, 1944. Pp. 238.

        Collection of folk stories and other folklore
        originally recorded in German, but here translated
        into English and edited. Most narratives relate to the
        past, with some anecdotes, humorous tales, and tall
        tales referring to contemporary folk characters.
        Chapters divided into tales of long ago (15), plant
        legends (9), hidden treasure tales (8), selling oneself

to the devil (11), special days (5), proverbial stories
(5), place names (6), making a choice (5), items that
cannot move (5), the stupid Swabians (20), spirits of
the countryside (15), brauche and hexe (13), folk
characters (37), preachers (6), and 45 miscellaneous
stories, including tall tales. Total of 194 tales,
most in several versions each.

GE91 Brendle, Thomas R., and Troxell, William S. "Pennsyl-
      vania German Songs." In *Pennsylvania Songs and
      Legends*, edited by George Korson, pp. 62–128.
      Philadelphia: University of Pennsylvania Press, 1949.

      Brief historical sketch of the Pennsylvania Germans,
      followed by the presentation of 28 songs (in German,
      with musical transcriptions and English translations),
      recorded in Pennsylvania between 1936 and 1940.

GE92 Brendle, Thomas R., and Unger, Claude W. *Folk Medicine
      of the Pennsylvania Germans: The Non-Occult Cures*.
      Reprint. New York: Augustus M. Kelley, 1970. Pp. 303.

      Presentation of remedies common among rural Pennsyl-
      vania Dutch as cures for specific illnesses. Chapters
      arranged according to 37 types of illnesses, with over
      500 cures mentioned. Provides native terms for diseases.
      Within each section references made to 3 bibliographical
      sections which provide relevant sources for books (56
      entries), almanacs (37 entries), and manuscripts (50
      entries). Includes 18 photographs of title pages of
      household medical books.

GE93 Brendle, Thomas R., and Unger, Claude W. "Illness and
      Cure of Domestic Animals among the Pennsylvania
      Dutch." *Pennsylvania Folklife* 8:4 (Summer–Fall
      1957):36–47.

      Detailed description of animal diseases of the stomach,
      mouth, sores, lameness, eyes, plagues, fevers, head
      and nerves, hoofs and horns, lungs, skin, cuts, and
      madness, with accompanying cures (over 20 for each
      category), especially of bloodletting. Includes 2
      photographs of book covers.

GE94 Brendle, Thomas R., and Unger, Claude W. "Witchcraft
      in Cow and Horse." *Pennsylvania Folklife* 8:1
      (Summer 1956):28–31.

      Presentation of a chapter from an unpublished manu-
      script ("Illness and Cure of Domestic Animals among

the Pennsylvania Dutch") in which symptoms, causes, and
cures of animal bewitchment are discussed. Includes
5 photographs of manuscript pages concerning hexing
and 2 pertaining to magical objects.

GE95   Brenner, Scott Francis. *Pennsylvania Dutch: The Plain
        and the Fancy.* Harrisburg, Pa.: The Stackpole Co.,
        1957. Pp. vii, 244.

        Vignettes of Pennsylvania Dutch culture offered by a
        long-time participant in that culture. Recreates
        discussions with Pennsylvania Dutch concerning foodways,
        folk art, and beliefs concerned with hexing.

GE96   Bressler, Leo Albert. "Pennsylvania German Wit and
        Humor." *'S Pennsylvaanisch Deitsch Eck*, 23 March-
        25 May 1957.

        General introduction to the nature of Pennsylvania
        Dutch humor, to illustrate that the Pennsylvania Dutch
        do generate their own humor and are not simply the butt
        of others' jokes. Topics include themes, newspaper
        humorists, verse, linguistic devices (30 proverbs, 18
        hyperbolic formulae, 9 onomatopoetic words, 2 epithets
        and exclamations). Includes 3 sample German passages
        illustrating these phenomena and 10 jokes and anecdotes
        (in German, with English translations).

*GE97   Bronner, Simon J. "'We Live What I Paint and I Paint
        What I See': A Mennonite Artist in Northern Indiana."
        Indiana Folklore 12:1 (1979):5-17.

        Discussion of the work of a woman Mennonite folk artist
        of Swiss ancestry from Elkhart County, Indiana, who
        paints on ceramics, wood, and canvas. Indicates that
        the artist paints what will sell rather than what she
        prefers. Discussion of the scenes she paints ("familiar
        events marking Mennonite life as well as life in
        northern Indiana") and of the foci of the paintings
        ("selected activities ... and on cultural landmarks
        prevalent on the landscape"). Includes photographs of
        7 paintings.
        (Cross-listed as *SW1.)

GE98   Brown, Carleton F. "The Long Hidden Friend." *Journal
        of American Folk-Lore* 17:65 (1904):89-152.

        Introduction (pp. 89-100) discusses the popularity of
        hexing among the population of eastern Pennsylvania and

surveys some research on the subject. Provides historical information about John George Hohman, the author of *The Long Hidden Friend*, a handbook of charms and popular magic in use among eastern Pennsylvanians. Also discusses possible sources of information provided in the book in an attempt to show that the book is "a compilation of genuine traditional material." Introduction followed by a reprinting of *The Long Hidden Friend* in its entirety (pp. 101-152). Foreword and preface in both German and English, with the testimonials, the 187 "means and arts" (including cures, remedies, charms, safeguards, and prayers) and the table of contents in English only. Notes comment on the English translation, various editions, and some parallel material.

GE99   Brown, Waln K. "Cultural Learning through Game
        Structure: A Study of Pennsylvania German Children's
        Games." *Pennsylvania Folklife* 23:4 (Summer 1974):
        2-11.

Theoretical article which attempts to analyze the socialization process of Pennsylvania Dutch children through the structure of games noted by scholars as being typical. Concludes that games emphasize individual ability, self-reliance, physical and mental prowess, and adherence to the existing social system. Mentions 67 games (with sources) in appendix. Includes 2 photographs of game playing and 1 chart depicting various categories through which game structure may be analyzed.

GE100   Brown, Waln K. "The Pennsylvania Dutch Carriage
        Trade." *Pennsylvania Folklife* 22:3 (Spring 1973):
        22-36.

Following a history of the horse and carriage as a mode of transportation from the 19th century to World War I, author focuses on the Old Order Amish and Old Order Mennonites, who still rely on this form of movement. Explains reasons for persistence, delineates types of carriages, occasions for their uses, categories of users, differences between Amish and Mennonite styles of construction, as well as older order versus more progressive trends. Focuses on 2 carriage makers in Lancaster County to describe fully the processes involved in carriage making. Includes 7 photographs of carriage advertisements, 12 of carriage making, 2 of coach work company.

GE101   Brumbach, Paul D. "Funerals in My Childhood Days."
         Pennsylvania Folklife 14:1 (October 1964):30-34.

         Reminiscences by the son of a preacher about his
         experiences while accompanying his father to funerals.
         Topics discussed include burial preparation, burial,
         home and church services, funeral meals, and transpor-
         tation of the dead. Includes 3 photographs of funeral
         procession.

GE102   Brumbaugh, G. Edwin. *Colonial Architecture of the
         Pennsylvania Germans*. Norristown, Pa.: Norristown
         Herald, 1933. Pp. 60.

         Discussion of the history, characteristics, and types
         of Pennsylvania German colonial architecture. Examples
         drawn from various settlements. Description of
         building methods. Includes 105 plates, with captions
         illustrating the variety of colonial architecture.

GE103   Bryan, William Jay. "Folk Medicine in Butler County,
         Pennsylvania." *Pennsylvania Folklife* 17:4
         (Summer 1968):40-43.

         Attempt to reconstruct widespread use of folk medicine
         in Butler County during the period 1875-1900, based on
         interviews with over 10 residents. After noting
         historical shift from "supernatural" to "practical"
         usages of medicines, lists types of herbs, teas, and
         poultices and the illnesses they sought to cure.
         Includes 3 photographs of informants and 1 map of
         Butler County.

GE104   Bucher, Robert C. "The Continental Log House."
         Pennsylvania Folklife 12:4 (Summer 1962):14-19.

         Pictorial report (with 19 photographs) of the existence
         and variety of the continental log cabin. Provides
         descriptions of 16 specific cabins from various parts
         of the country and statement by 1 informant about the
         functions of such cabins. Argues that the log cabin
         is distinctively Pennsylvania Dutch.

GE105   Bucher, Robert C. "Grain in the Attic." *Pennsylvania
         Folklife* 13:2 (Winter 1962-1963):7-15.

         Attempt to explain where grain was stored on Pennsyl-
         vania Dutch farms in the 18th century, before barns
         were built. Demonstrates that grain was placed in
         attics of houses. Provides detailed illustrated

descriptions of 4 such houses in Lebanon and Montgomery counties. Explains reasons for attic storage and notes that present-day Pennsylvania Dutch are unaware of such a tradition. Includes 15 photographs of storage places.

GE106   Bucher, Robert C. "The Long Shingle." *Pennsylvania Folklife* 18:4 (Summer 1969):51-56.

Examination of long-shingle roofing from Pricetown in Berks County, Pennsylvania, with emphasis on the question of origin. Author hypothesizes a long chain of European tradition continued by Pennsylvania Dutch immigrants, but notes that more study is needed of contiguous areas settled by the English and Scotch-Irish. Includes 9 photographs and 1 sketch of shingles and the shingle-making process.

GE107   Bucher, Robert C. "Steep Roofs and Red Tiles." *Pennsylvania Folklife* 12:2 (Summer 1961):18-26, 55.

Demonstrates the continuity in red tile roofs between Germany and the United States and considers the steep roof a unique Pennsylvania Dutch contribution to American architecture. Discusses the manufacture of tile, methods of laying it, and advantages and dis-advantages of using tile. Includes a detailed map of locations of buildings with red tile roofs and 14 photographs of various roofs.

GE108   Buffington, Albert F. *Dutchified German Spirituals.* Proceedings and Addresses of the Pennsylvania German Society 62. Lancaster, Pa., 1966. Pp. viii, 249.

Collection of 104 religious folksongs and their variants (in German, with English translations) which were developed and sung at camp meetings (i.e., re-vival and prayer meetings) of the German revivalistic churches in Pennsylvania during the second half of the 19th and the first half of the 20th century. Songs arranged by title, obtained from 31 informants between 1946 and 1959, accompanied by comparative notes and tune transcriptions.

GE109   Buffington, Albert F. "Pennsylvania German Humor: Some Representative Samples." *Keystone Folklore Quarterly* 8:2 (1963):75-80.

Presentation of 10 Pennsylvania German humorous tales, including 3 about preachers, some involving dialect.

*GE110   Burkhart, Charles.   "The Church Music of the Old Order
         Amish and Old Colony Mennonites." *The Mennonite
         Quarterly Review* 27:1 (1953):34-54.

         Discussion of hymn singing and music among North
         American Old Order Amish and Old Colony Mennonites.
         Includes listings of hymns sung at regular religious
         services and at Amish weddings. Provides brief history
         of the hymns and music, tracing their roots to Old
         World models and emphasizing the influence of published
         hymnals on the continuity of the tradition. Includes
         musical transcriptions of 2 "mediant formulae" and of
         2 hymns (1 recorded in Iowa in 1939).
              (Cross-listed as *SW3.)

 GE111   Burrison, John A.   "Pennsylvania German Folktales:
         An Annotated Bibliography." *Pennsylvania Folklife*
         15:1 (Autumn 1965):30-38.

         Comprehensive bibliography of references to published
         articles on and collections of folktales. Divided
         into 2 sections: 1) 55 entries covering general works
         and articles found in various folklore and folklore-
         related sources, and 2) 282 entries to works published
         specifically in the *Pennsylvania Dutchman* and *Pennsyl-
         vania Folklife*.

 GE112   Byington, Robert H.   "Powwowing in Pennsylvania."
         Keystone Folklore Quarterly 9:3 (1964):111-117.

         Description and discussion of two printed sources
         (*The Sixth and Seventh Books of Moses* and *The Long
         Hidden Friend*) frequently consulted by Pennsylvania
         Germans for instructions for powwowing, conjuring,
         or practicing *Brauche*.

*GE113   "A Christmas Eve Custom." *Keystone Folklore
         Quarterly* 1:4 (1956-57):58-59.

         Brief description of the Christmas Eve custom known
         as "Billsnickle," involving an individual's dressing
         in golden rye straw with attached chain and wandering
         about frightening children. Custom reported as being
         popular in Germany. Parallels cited with masquerading
         individuals of Greek and Slovak descent living in
         Luzerne and Schuylkill counties in Pennsylvania, as
         reported in 1939 by an informant from New Ringgold,
         Pennsylvania.
              (Cross-listed as *GR1, *SK2.)

GE114 "Christmas Folk Beliefs of the Pennsylvania Dutch
       Country." *Pennsylvania Dutchman* 3:14 (15 December
       1951):2

       Reprint of previously published piece from 1892 in
       which are enumerated 7 folk beliefs relevant to the
       hour of 11:00 p.m. to midnight on Christmas Eve, as
       found in Berks County, Pennsylvania.

GE115 "Christmas Money." *Pennsylvania Dutchman* 3:14 (15
       December 1951):3.

       Reprint of 1895 piece describing how children earned
       Christmas money by selling dried hog bristles.

GE116 Cline, Ruth H. "Belsnickles and Shanghais." *Journal
       of American Folklore* 71:280 (1958):164-165.

       Report of the author's recollection (from early 20th
       century) of the Christmas and New Year's customs of
       belsnickling and shanghaiing in the Shenandoah Valley
       of Virginia. Also includes quotations from a late 19th-
       century historian's letter describing belsnickling in
       the same area, with comparative references to other
       relevant works. Author hypothesizes customs to be
       of German origin.

GE117 Coffroth, Frederick F. "The Legend of Spooky Hollow
       and Other Somerset Co. Tales." *Pennsylvania
       Dutchman* 3:7 (1 September 1951):2.

       Presentation of 6 legends collected from 2 women in
       Somerset County, Pennsylvania, of events that occurred
       in the past involving ghosts, Halloween, treasure,
       and place names.

GE118 Collier, G. Loyd. "The Cultural Geography of Folk
       Building Forms in Texas." In *Built in Texas*,
       edited by Francis Edward Abernethy, pp. 21-43.
       Publications of the Texas Folklore Society 42
       (1979).

       Discussion of various cultural contributions to Texas
       traditional architecture, with mention of that of
       German immigrants.

GE119 Cooper, Philip D. "The Scheel (Schäl) and Tünnes
       Cycle." *Tennessee Folklore Society Bulletin* 30:3
       (1964):81-87.

       Presentation of 10 numskull tales/jokes (in English),
       recorded from German university students and a German-
       American professor at the University of Kansas,
       Lawrence, Kansas, in 1962-63. Tales said to be part
       of a cycle common in the Cologne area of Germany.

GE120 Cox, Suzanne. "The Use of Speech at Two Auctions."
       Pennsylvania Folklife 24:1 (Fall 1974):39-44.

       Comparison of verbal interaction in two different
       auctions held at a farmer's market near Ephrata,
       Pennsylvania. Includes 1 photograph of each auction.

GE121 Craige, Carter W. "Tanning in Chester County,
       Pennsylvania, 1711-1850." *Pennsylvania Folklife*
       18:1 (Autumn 1968):2-15.

       Description of the history and function of tanning
       in Chester County, Pennsylvania. Detailed descrip-
       tion of leather making process, exemplified by illus-
       trations of its uses as harness, of tools used in
       peeling bark, and of mills in preparing bark for
       tannery. Tanning viewed as significant to under-
       standing rural life of Pennsylvania farmer. Includes
       4 photographs of tools used in tanning and 7 of
       inventories and advertising, 1 sketch of a harness.
       Concludes with a list of 140 tanners and township
       abbreviations.

GE122 Crawley, Donald. "The New Year's Shoot at Cherry-
       ville." *North Carolina Folklore* 10:2 (1962):21-27.

       Discussion of the German-derived custom of visiting
       homes, shooting off muskets, and reciting cries and
       poems on New Year's Eve and Day, in Cherryville,
       North Carolina. Includes excerpts about the custom
       from local newspapers, a text of 1 speech cry and
       of 1 poem, illustrated with 5 photographs of indi-
       viduals involved in the shootings in earlier years.

GE123 Creighton, Helen. *The Folklore of Lunenburg County,
       Nova Scotia.* National Museum of Canada, Bulletin
       No. 11. Ottawa: E. Cloutier, King's Printer, 1950.
       Pp. 163.

       Collection of folk traditions characteristic of
       German people living in Lunenburg County, many of

whom earn their livelihood from the sea trade. Work
divided into such categories as treasure (47 items),
superstitions (109), omens (44), ghosts (72), witchcraft (60), customs and crafts (18), foods (47),
toasts (1), crops (23), dances (13), games (31),
songs (7), cures (96), animals (20), weather (32),
expressions (83), old sayings and proverbs (52),
puzzles and riddles (53), anecdotes (69), tall tales
(23), folktales (2), legends (16). Appendix contains
calls for 10 folk dances.

GE124   Creighton, Helen. "Local Anecdotes from Lunenburg."
        In *Folklore of Canada*, edited by Edith Fowke, pp.
        275-279. Toronto: McClelland and Stewart Limited,
        1976.

        Presentation of 22 anecdotes recorded by the author
        from individuals of German ancestry in Lunenburg
        County, Nova Scotia, Canada. Reprinted from a 1950
        book.

GE125   Cummings, John. "Painted Chests from Bucks County."
        Pennsylvania Folklife 9:3 (Summer 1958):20-23.

        Attempt to argue for a local style of chest making
        in Bucks County by studying design, construction,
        and ornamentation of several pieces. Concludes that
        the several chests discussed were made by one person
        and were unique. Includes 3 photographs of chests
        and 1 map.

*GE126 Curtis, Otis F. (Jr.). "The Curtis Collection of
        Songs, I." *New York Folklore Quarterly* 9:2 (1953):
        94-103.

        Presentation of 9 song texts (in English) from a
        scrapbook compiled in the 19th century, including 1
        song in the German dialect popular during this period,
        and 1 Irish song.
        (Cross-listed as *IR17.)

*GE127 Curtis, Wardon Allan. "'The Light Fantastic' in the
        Central West: Country Dances of Many Nationalities
        in Wisconsin."

        (Cross-listed as *IR18, *NO8, *SW4.)
        (See *SW4 for full citation and annotation.)

GE128 Deischer, Claude K. "My Experience with the Dialect."
    Pennsylvania Folklife 23:4 (Summer 1974):47-48.

    Confessions of a Moravian who grew up in Emmaus, Penn-
    sylvania, in the 20th century, of the value of Pennsyl-
    vania Dutch morals and language. Refers to the embar-
    rassment of many when speaking Pennsylvania Dutch,
    especially with the onset of World War II, and the sub-
    sequent personal rediscovery of the value of the mother
    tongue.

GE129 Dell, Jennie Scott. "Lore from Colton." *New York
    Folklore Quarterly* 12:2 (1956):136-139.

    Characterization of lore collected from the area of
    Colton, New York, including 9 humorous stories about
    local characters (2 of whom are identified as German),
    5 remedies, and 1 saying in German dialect.

GE130 De Long, Nancy. "Bonnets! Bonnets! Bonnets!"
    Pennsylvania Folklife 26 (Supplement 1977):2-5.

    Discussion of history and importance of bonnets for
    Pennsylvania Dutch women. Includes description of
    production process, styles, and differences between
    such Pennsylvania German groups as the Amish, Old
    Mennonites, and New Mennonites. Includes 4 photo-
    graphs showing various types of bonnets.

GE131 "Dialect Similes." *Pennsylvania Dutchman* 1:18
    (1 September 1949):1.

    Listing of 16 similes using the formula "so ... as ..."
    submitted by I.B. Palmyra.

GE132 Dieffenbach, Victor C. "Building a Pennsylvania
    Barn." *Pennsylvania Folklife* 12:3 (Fall 1961):20-24.

    Step-by-step description of processes involved in
    barn raising. Six photographs provide illustration
    of barn raising as a community activity.

GE133 Dieffenbach, Victor C. "Butter Making in Berks
    County." *Pennsylvania Dutchman* 4:1 (May 1952):5.

    Description of making butter remembered from the
    practices of parents and neighbors. Includes aspects
    of churning, butter molds, and coloring.

GE134   Dicffenbach, Victor C. "Cabbage in the Folk-Culture
        of My Pennsylvania Dutch Elders." *Pennsylvania
        Dutchman* 3:22 (15 April 1952):1, 2, 4.

        Description of growing cabbage and its role in the
        cuisine of Pennsylvania Dutch, especially in the
        making and uses of sauerkraut. Importance character-
        ized by folk beliefs (5) and sayings utilizing cabbage
        as a theme (5).

GE135   Dieffenbach, Victor C. "Cow Lore from Berks County."
        Pennsylvania Dutchman 4:2 (June 1952):6-7.

        Investigation of cow lore based on firsthand experience
        from working on father's farm. Divides lore into 16
        categories, including folk beliefs, milking, and uses
        of cow dung.

GE136   Dieffenbach, Victor C. "The Cow That Was Erhexed."
        Pennsylvania Dutchman 4:2 (June 1952):11.

        Account of a stranger who diagnosed a cow as be-
        witched and who offered a cure.

GE137   Dieffenbach, Victor C. "Diaper Lore." *Pennsylvania
        Folklife* 8:1 (Summer 1956):23.

        Presentation of over 50 folk beliefs associated with
        care and use of children's diapers, as well as 1 folk
        narrative in which a man's first diaper was used by
        a healer to save his life from an apparent heart attack.

GE138   Dieffenbach, Victor C. "Eating Wager." *Pennsylvania
        Folklife* 12:2 (Summer 1961):71-72.

        Brief description of custom of wagering who could
        devour the most food in a given amount of time.
        Illustration with 1 such bet.

GE139   Dieffenbach, Victor C. "Guinea Hen Lore." *Pennsyl-
        vania Dutchman* 4:11 (1 February 1953):4-5.

        Remembrances of value of guinea hen for farming when
        author was a boy in Bethel Township, Berks County.
        Includes 2 narratives relating incidents involving hens.

*GE140 Dieffenbach, Victor C. "Gypsy Stories from the
        Swatara Valley." *Pennsylvania Folklife* 16:1
        (Autumn 1966):15-19.

        Author's boyhood reminiscences of prejudicial atti-
        tudes held by Pennsylvania Dutch toward Gypsies as

reflected in 11 folk stories. Includes 4 sketches
depicting contents of stories and 1 photograph of a
Gypsy camp.
(Cross-listed as *GY4.)

GE141 Dieffenbach, Victor C. "Husking Time." *Pennsylvania
Dutchman* 5:6 (October 1953):9, 12.

Process of husking corn as remembered when author was
a youngster, particularly in Bethel Township, Berks
County. Describes various methods used by Amish and
Mennonites. Provides 3 folk beliefs regarding planting
and husking corn.

GE142 Dieffenbach, Victor C. "Of Plows and Plowing."
Pennsylvania Dutchman 5:1 (May 1953):10-11.

Summary of role of plowing among Pennsylvania Dutch,
including types of plows, plowing processes, and
animals used. Presents experiences of individuals
engaged in plowing without wheels and perfecting
their techniques, along with proverbs (10) and old
sayings (11).

GE143 Dieffenbach, Victor C. "Old Funeral Customs."
Pennsylvania Dutchman 1:16 (18 August 1949):3.

Remembrances of funeral customs told to Dieffenbach
by his grandfather. Mention of preburial practices
and of strange tombstone inscriptions.

GE144 Dieffenbach, Victor C. "Peddlers I Remember."
Pennsylvania Folklife 14:1 (October 1964):38-48.

Childhood reminiscences of author concerning peddlers
who lived around 1890. Includes 25 personal experience
narratives describing traits of peddler, his ethnic
background, and relationship to farmers and farm
families, with 9 sketches depicting folk characters.

GE145 Dieffenbach, Victor C. "Powwowing among the Pennsylvania Germans." *Pennsylvania Folklife* 25:2
(Winter 1975-1976):29-46.

General survey of powwowing, including characterizations of the faith healing process, the role of the
faith healer, and personalities of the faith healer.
Events surrounding healing amply exemplified by
author's personal experiences and by the many narratives (over 20) told to him of powwowing power.

Modern application discussed through use of telephone.
Addenda list over 20 cures. Includes 2 photographs of
curing and 13 cover titles of influential books,
advertisements, and testimonials.

GE146   Dieffenbach, Victor C. "Riddles." *Pennsylvania
        Dutchman* 5:12 (15 February 1954):15.

        Presentation of 8 riddles in German (with English
        translation).

GE147   Dieffenbach, Victor C. "Some Lore on Hens." *Pennsyl-
        vania Dutchman* 4:7 (November 1952):6.

        Presentation of 5 tales concerning the hen, heard
        from parents and neighbors.

GE148   Dieffenbach, Victor C. "Tramps of My Youth."
        Pennsylvania Folklife 10:1 (Spring 1959):8-13.

        Remembrances of youth in the 1890s when tramps were
        common in Berks County. Description of physical
        appearance, eccentric behavior, types of tramps, their
        hideouts, pernicious acts, lore told about them, pow-
        wowing held by them, and tales told by them. Includes
        5 drawings, reflecting themes in article.

GE149   Dieffenbach, Victor C. "Weather Signs and Calendar
        Lore from the 'Dumb Quarter.'" *Pennsylvania Folk-
        life* 17:1 (Autumn 1967):26-30.

        Listing of 79 beliefs concerning the weather and
        calendrical events in Pennsylvania Dutch dialect
        (with English translation). Recollection of author's
        experiences in Berks County. Each entry compared
        with standard works on folk beliefs and proverbs by
        the editor of *Pennsylvania Folklife* and evaluated for
        their traditionality.

GE150   Dieffenbach, Victor C. "A Witch and Her Dog."
        Pennsylvania Dutchman 4:14 (April 1953):2-3, 10.

        Presentation of 3 tales told by relatives and friends
        concerning witchcraft.

*GE151 Dinkel, Phyllis A. "Old Marriage Customs in Herzog
        (Victoria), Kansas."

        (Cross-listed as *RU7.)
        (See *RU7 for full citation and annotation.)

GE152   Dluge, Robert L. "My Interview with a Powwower."
        Pennsylvania Folklife 21:4 (Summer 1972):39-42.

        Far from being a past phenomenon, author notes rise
        in interest in powwowing. Presents excerpt of an
        interview with a practicing powwower in East Central
        Pennsylvania concerning the nature of powwowing, its
        transmission, effects, and requirements for powwowing.
        Includes 3 photographs: 2 of patent medicine advertise-
        ments and 1 of a book cover from a treatise on powwowing.

GE153   Doering, J. Frederick. "More Folk Customs from Western
        Ontario." *Journal of American Folklore* 58:228
        (1945):150-155.

        Listing of miscellaneous beliefs and customs associated
        with agriculture and husbandry (14), weather (24),
        omens, tokens, and luck (54), medicine (34), plus
        descriptions of traditional games (9) and toys (4),
        recorded in western Ontario, Canada, principally from
        individuals of German ancestry. Supplements earlier
        essays (see GE157 and GE158).

GE154   Doering, J. Frederick. "Pennsylvania German Folk
        Medicine in Waterloo County, Ontario." *Journal of
        American Folk-Lore* 49:193 (1936):194-198.

        Brief historical sketch of Pennsylvania German
        farmers who settled in Waterloo County, Ontario,
        Canada, in the early 19th century, with emphasis on
        health beliefs and healing practices obtained by the
        author in the mid-1930s. Includes characterizations
        of 32 beliefs and cures common at the time and mention
        of 6 others no longer employed. Also includes a re-
        printing from a newspaper story of 1935 of a "powwow
        ritual" carried out in Williamsport, Pennsylvania.

GE155   Doering, J. Frederick. "The Tramp's Bed." *Southern
        Folklore Quarterly* 10:2 (1946):159.

        Brief note describing the practice among Pennsylvania
        Dutch Mennonites from Ontario, Canada, of providing
        lodging for tramps (usually in outbuildings or wash
        houses). Includes summary of a personal experience
        story about the practice.

GE156   Doering, John Frederick. "Note on the Dyeing of *halb*
        Leinich among the Pennsylvania-Dutch of Ontario."
        Journal of American Folk-Lore 52:203 (1939):124-125.

        Brief note about the dyeing of a kind of cloth known
        as *halb Leinich*, earlier in common use among the
        Pennsylvania Dutch. Brief mention of means of dyeing
        the cloth and its uses as a fabric for clothing.

GE157   Doering, John Frederick, and Doering, Eileen Elita.
        "Some Western Ontario Folk Beliefs and Practices."
        Journal of American Folk-Lore 51 (1938):60-68.

        Listing of folk beliefs from Western Ontario, Canada,
        which show strong influence of Pennsylvania Dutch
        culture on other ethnic groups. Includes beliefs on
        husbandry (36), omens (55), folk medicine (40), house-
        wifery (15), children's rhymes (14), charms (12), and
        provincialisms (51).

GE158   Doering, John Frederick, and Doering, Eileen Elita.
        "Some Western Ontario Folk Beliefs and Practices."
        Journal of American Folklore 54:213-214 (1941):197.

        Brief note presenting 13 "omens, tokens, luck signs,"
        obtained from individuals of Pennsylvania Dutch back-
        ground in Western Ontario, Canada. No sources or
        dates provided.

GE159   Dornbusch, Charles H., and Heyl, John K. "The
        Pennsylvania German Barns." Pennsylvania German
        Folklore Society, *Yearbook* 21 (1956):1-300.

        Pictorial survey of 11 types of barns delineated by
        the author and collaborator John K. Heyl, the latter
        of whom prepared an introductory survey on the struc-
        ture and geographical distribution of barns and
        descriptive notes for the photographs.

*GE160 Dorson, Richard M. "Blood Stoppers."

        (Cross-listed as *FN2, *FR50, *IR20, *SL1, *SS8.)
        (See *FR50 for full citation and annotation.)

*GE161 Dorson, Richard M. "Folklore at a Milwaukee Wedding."
        Hoosier Folklore 6:1 (1947):1-13.

        Presentation of miscellaneous folklore items recorded
        by the author at a Milwaukee wedding in 1946. In-
        cludes 7 dream interpretations and 2 dream accounts

and their consequences, 2 sayings (in German), and 1
tale, recorded from an informant of German ancestry,
and 1 anecdote/joke about a Swede.
(Cross-listed as *SS10.)

GE162 Dorson, Richard M. "Pennsylvania Dutchman." In
       *Buying the Wind: Regional Folklore in the United
       States*, pp. 107-161. Chicago: University of Chicago
       Press, 1964.

       Survey and exemplification of kinds of folklore found
       among the Pennsylvania Dutch. Includes reprinted
       texts of 7 tales of magic and witchcraft, 30 folk
       belief statements, 3 belief tales, 3 noodle tales,
       82 proverbs and Wellerisms, 3 proverbial tales, 23
       riddles, and 3 songs.

GE163 Dorson, Richard M. "Regional Folk Cultures: German
       Pennsylvania." In *American Folklore*, pp. 76-90.
       Chicago: University of Chicago Press, 1959.

       Brief survey of various kinds of folklore found among
       the Pennsylvania Dutch. Includes 24 proverbs, 6 riddles,
       summaries of 14 tales, examples of 9 statements of be-
       lief, 4 cures, 2 summaries of narratives about witch
       detection and driving away evil spirits. Describes
       briefly popular folksongs and folk art motifs.

GE164 Dow, James R. "The Hand Carved Walking Canes of
       William Baurichter." *Keystone Folklore Quarterly*
       15:3 (1970):138-147.

       Description of canes made by a Columbus, Indiana,
       man of German background, illustrated with 10 photo-
       graphs. Emphasis on motifs and carving techniques.

GE165 Dow, James R., and Roemig, Madeline. "Amana Folk
       Art and Craftsmanship." *The Palimpsest* 58:2 (1977):
       54-63.

       Description of various kinds of crafts produced in the
       Amana, Iowa, communities by individuals of German
       ancestry. Includes 15 color photographs of selected
       objects, ranging from items of furniture to toys.

GE166 Druckenborg, Richard. "Some Parson Tales." *Pennsyl-
       vania Dutchman* 5:14 (15 March 1954):5.

       Presentation of 7 tales about preachers, recorded in
       Adamstown, Pennsylvania, in 1949.

GE167   Dubbs, Joseph Henry. "Christmas among Pennsylvania-
        Germans." *The Pennsylvania-German* 12:xii (December
        1911):705-708.

        Reprint of a previously published piece in which the
        author traces Christmas customs brought from Germany
        and notes how they have fared in America. Notes
        revival of neglected Christmas customs among the
        Moravians.

GE168   Dubbs, Joseph Henry. "Reminiscences." *Pennsylvania
        Dutchman* 1:25 (April 1950):2.

        Presentation of the author's childhood recollections
        of Easter egg hiding and hunting.

GE169   "Dutchman Jests." *Pennsylvania Dutchman* 2:20 (15
        March 1951):3.

        Presentation of 4 jests excerpted from previously
        published works, 2 of which deal with humorous aspects
        of the law.

GE170   E., J.W. "Funerals in Pennsylvania and Massachusetts--
        A Contrast." *The Pennsylvania-German* 12:viii
        (August 1911):479-485.

        Comparison of funerals among the Pennsylvania Dutch
        and the Puritans in order to prove the detestable
        behavior of both. Pennsylvania Dutch funerals (in-
        cluding associated foodways) observed first hand,
        while New England funeral practices gleaned from a
        New York paper.

GE171   Ellis, Susan J. "Traditional Food on the Commercial
        Market: The History of Pennsylvania Scrapple."
        Pennsylvania Folklife 22:3 (Spring 1973):10-21.

        Analysis of the effects of commercialization and urban
        production on a variety of pork products. Traces the
        development of scrapple as a distinctly Pennsylvania
        Dutch food, describes variability in the definition of
        scrapple, and indicates consumer reaction to changing
        scrapple production. Study based on questionnaires
        and personal interviews conducted in 1971. Author
        demonstrates the ethnic roots of commercialized pro-
        ducts and notes that they are de-emphasized in com-
        mercial advertisements. Includes 5 photographs of
        advertisements.

*GE172   Erdely, Stephen. "Research on Traditional Music of Nationality Groups in Cleveland and Vicinity."

       (Cross-listed as *GL41, *CR3, *FN11, *HU14, *IR26, *RO3, *SC12, *SK4.)
       (See *GL41 for full citation and annotation.)

GE173   Estep, Glenn, and Pietchke, William. "A Study of Certain Aspects of Spiritualism and Pow-Wow in Regard to the Folklore of Lancaster County." *Pennsylvania Dutchman* 5:13 (1 March 1954):10-11, 15.

       Discussion of the nature of folk cures, based on the study of 2 traditional healers in Lancaster County. Includes healers' responses to questions about the development of their powers, types of diseases cured and methods of healing, necessity of patients' faith in healer, and the role of scientific medicine. Reveals some differences in healers' attitudes. Includes detailed account of authors' research methods and their admission of their sceptical view toward folk curing.

GE174   Estill, Julia. "Children's Games." In *The Sky is My Tipi*, edited by Mody C. Boatright, pp. 231-236. *Publications of the Texas Folklore Society* 22 (1949).

       Characterizations, from the author's and 1 other informant's memories, of 8 children's games, of German origin, commonly played in Fredericksburg, Texas, during the late 19th and early 20th century. Titles and some words of 7 games given (in German, with English translations). Includes text of 1 chant (a version of "London Bridge") in German (with English translation).

GE175   Estill, Julia. "Customs among the German Descendants of Gillespie County." In *Coffee in the Gourd*, edited by J. Frank Dobie, pp. 67-74. *Publications of the Texas Folklore Society* 2 (1923).

       General discussion of the town of Fredericksburg, Gillespie County, Texas, founded by Germans in 1846. Includes description of the Sunday or temporary in-town houses built by farmers; Christmas, Easter, and other holiday and life-cycle customs; foods served during coffee circles. Customs presumed to be of German origin.

GE176   Etter, Russell C.   "Extemporaneous Hymn-Making among
         the Pennsylvania Dutch." *Journal of American Folk-
         lore* 44:173 (1931):302-305.

         Presentation of an example of extemporaneous hymn-
         making among Pennsylvania Dutch members of the United
         Christian Church in Lebanon County, Pennsylvania, with
         description of how an extemporaneous hymn was composed
         and how it was changed and communicated by oral tradi-
         tion and sung in 2 other churches in the area in 1927.
         Includes texts of the original and additional verses
         for the 2 variants.

*GE177   Evanson, Jacob A.   "Folk Songs of an Industrial City."

         (Cross-listed as *GL42, *FN12, *GR8, *IR27, *SK5.)
         (See *GL42 for full citation and annotation.)

GE178   Fabian, Monroe H.   *The Pennsylvania-German Decorated
         Chest.* New York: Universe Books, 1978.   Pp. 230,
         bibliography.

         Description of the history and nature of Pennsylvania
         German decorated chests.   Includes chapters on European
         background, the chest in Pennsylvania, cabinet making,
         construction, hardware, decoration, paint, decorators,
         and chests outside Pennsylvania.   Includes 216 photo-
         graphs with explanatory notes.

GE179   Fabian, Monroe H.   "Sulfur Inlay in Pennsylvania
         German Furniture." *Pennsylvania Folklife* 27:1
         (Fall 1977):2-9.

         Reinforces Frances Lichten's thesis that inlaid chests
         are of Pennsylvania German origin (i.e., there are no
         European antecedents).   By contrast with Lichten's
         contention that decoration is of wax, demonstrates
         that the design was made with sulfur.   Includes 10
         photographs of furniture.

GE180   Fike, Tedford E.   "The Prophetic Harp." *Pennsylvania
         Dutchman* 2:19 (March 1951):2.

         Presentation of 10 legends collected in Somerset
         County, Pennsylvania, and involving ghosts.

GE181   Fike, Tedford E.   "Somerset County Folk Beliefs."
         Pennsylvania Dutchman 13:8 (15 September 1951):8.

         Listing of 6 folk beliefs concerning money, babies,
         and animals.

GE182   Fike, Tedford E. "Two Epitaphs." *Pennsylvania Dutch-*
        man 3:9 (1 October 1951):6.

        Presentation of 2 epitaphs from in and around Ursina,
        Pennsylvania, found on gravestones of individuals who
        died in 1826 and 1836.

GE183   Finckh, Alice. "In the Candle's Glow." *American-*
        German Review 14:ii (December 1947):4-6.

        Attempt to discover the first mention of the Christmas
        tree and the attitude of individuals who introduced it.
        Mention made of early kinds of ornamentation.

GE184   Fogel, Edwin Miller. *Beliefs and Superstitions of the*
        Pennsylvania Germans. Philadelphia: American
        Germanica Press, 1915. Pp. iv, 387, supplement.

        Listing of 2,085 beliefs (in German, with English
        translations) pertaining to everyday life, arranged
        under 40 headings. Purpose of the collection stated
        to be to prove that virtually all superstitions are
        German and British importations and survivals. Supple-
        ment presents beliefs relating to sex, which were
        purposely omitted from the main body of the work.

GE185   Fogel, Edwin M. "Of Months and Days." The Pennsyl-
        vania German Folklore Society, *Yearbook*, Section III
        5 (1940):1-23.

        Catalog of Pennsylvania Dutch names for months of the
        year, with reference to specific holidays falling
        under each month.

GE186   Fogel, Edwin Miller. *Proverbs of the Pennsylvania*
        Germans. Fogelsville, Pa.: The Germanica Press,
        1929. Pp. 222.

        Collection of 1,938 proverbs, arranged alphabetically
        (in German, with English translations) and accompanied
        by variants gleaned from published sources. Intro-
        duction discusses the nature of the Pennsylvania
        German proverb.

GE187   "Folk Beliefs." *Pennsylvania Dutchman* 1:22 (January
        1950):1.

        Presentation of 3 folk beliefs concerning the milking
        of cows, Good Friday, and St. Patrick's Day, submitted
        by a correspondent from Elizabethtown, Pennsylvania.

GE188   Franz, Eleanor. "'Gemutlichkeit.'" *New York Folklore*
        Quarterly 25:2 (1969):137-159.

        Historical sketch of German settlers in Dolgeville,
        New York, in the late 19th century, with emphasis on
        the role of the immigrants in transforming the community
        from a small, nondescript town to one of handsome
        Victorian homes and cultural activities. Includes
        passing mention of foods prepared and served, games
        played, and festivals. Presents 3 recipes.

GE189   Frazier, Paul. "Some Lore of Hexing and Powwowing."
        Midwest Folklore 2:2 (1952):101-107.

        Discussion of beliefs and practices relating to
        witchcraft and healing, recorded from a Pennsylvania
        German female informant from Allentown, Pennsylvania.
        Includes brief descriptions of hexers and hexing,
        spell-breaking and healing by *brauchers*, 8 retold
        tales (1 witch story, 3 tales of death portents, 4
        of returning dead or ghosts).

GE190   Frey, H.C. "'Mr. Munteeth': The Wit from Pumkin
        Center." *Pennsylvania Dutchman* 5:8 (December 1953):7.

        Characterization of a noted eccentric in Margaretta
        Furnace, York County, who was known for his witty
        remarks, especially while under the influence of liquor.

GE191   Frey, Howard C. "Conestoga Wagoners." In *Pennsyl-*
        vania Songs and Legends, edited by George Korson,
        pp. 237-257. Philadelphia: University of Pennsyl-
        vania Press, 1949.

        Historical discussion of Conestoga wagoners (most of
        whom were Pennsylvania Germans) who transported freight
        between Philadelphia and Pittsburgh beginning about
        1750. Includes description of the wagons and their
        equipment, characterizations of 3 tall tales and 2
        jokes, 2 statements of belief, partial reprinting of
        1 poem, presentation of 5 song texts (1 in German,
        with English translation, and 4 in English only, all
        with tune transcriptions), most of them parodies of
        other well-known songs.

GE192   Frey, J. William. "Amish Triple-talk." *American*
        Speech 20:2 (1945):85-98.

        Examination of the characteristics of the Pennsylvania
        Dutch dialect and the High German language used by the
        Old Order Amish. Author discusses the linguistic
        features of each, as well as the differing occasions

for which they were designed. Relevance of the third
part of the "triple-talk," American English, mentioned,
but not discussed.

GE193 Frey, J. William. "Pennsylvania Dutch." *Pennsylvania
       Folklife* 12:3 (Fall 1961):12-13.

Argues that the Pennsylvania Dutch language is a folk
speech and flexible to the needs of the New World.
Examples presented in cartoon form.

GE194 Frey, William. "Amish Hymns as Folk Music." In *Penn-
       sylvania Songs and Legends*, edited by George Korson,
       pp. 129-162. Philadelphia: University of Pennsylvania
       Press, 1949.

Brief historical sketch of the Amish who settled in
Pennsylvania, followed by a discussion of the nature
of their hymns and hymn singing. Includes texts of
16 Amish hymns (9 with musical transcriptions, all in
German with accompanying English translations).

GE195 Funk, H.H. "Marriage Superstitions." *The Pennsylvania-
       German* 9:viii (August 1908):372-373.

Presentation of 4 beliefs concerning marriage among
the Pennsylvania Dutch, with many more examples of
such beliefs found throughout the world.

GE196 Gamon, Albert T. "Story of a Stove." *Pennsylvania
       Folklife* 28:4 (Summer 1979):12-16.

In the process of restoring an 18th-century farm
located in Montgomery County, Pennsylvania, author
concluded that not all Pennsylvania Dutch built their
houses around a central chimney, as had been commonly
supposed. Includes 13 photographs of reconstruction
and 2 diagrams showing placement of fireplace.

*GE197 Gardner, Emelyn E. "Folk-Lore from Schoharie County,
       New York." *Journal of American Folk-Lore* 27:105
       (1914):304-325.

General comment on various ethnic groups who have
settled in Schoharie County and of the imprint that
each has left on the folklore of the area. Includes
13 tales (1 told by a man of Irish ancestry, 1 by a
man of English and Dutch descent), approximately a
dozen beliefs obtained from informants of English and
German backgrounds, and 1 counting-out rhyme (all data
in English only).
       (Cross-listed as *DU9, *IR35.)

GE198   Gehman, Henry Snyder. "Ghost Stories and Old Supersti-
        tions of Lancaster County." *Pennsylvania Folklife*
        9:4 (Summer 1970):48-53.

        Presentation of 19 stories of the supernatural, heard
        by the author during his childhood in Lancaster County.
        Tales deal with ghosts and witches, with 2 having
        buried treasure as their subject. Concludes that the
        occult, once part of the rural environment, is losing
        its hold, due to the loss of the Pennsylvania Dutch
        language, while spirituality is perpetuated by the
        continuity of the religion.

GE199   Gehman, Henry Snyder. "What the Pennsylvania Dutch
        Dialect Has Meant in My Life." *Pennsylvania Folk-
        life* 17:4 (Summer 1968):8-11.

        Author's reminiscences about the role of dialect while
        he was growing up in Ephrata Township, Lancaster
        County, Pennsylvania, in the early 1900s. Discusses
        the attitude of the Dutch to the English language,
        occasions on which Dutch and English were used, and
        attitudes of non-Pennsylvania Dutch to the exclusive-
        ness of the dialect. Includes 3 photographs of the
        author and 1 map showing his place of early residence.

GE200   Gehret, Ellen J., and Keyser, Alan G. "Flax Processing
        in Pennsylvania from Seed to Fiber." *Pennsylvania
        Folklife* 22:1 (Autumn 1972):10-34.

        Description of the process of flaxmaking prevalent in
        rural Pennsylvania in the 18th and 19th centuries.
        Data derived from newspapers, diaries, written works,
        and interviews with 3 informants. Includes discussion
        of placement of patch, season for growing, methods of
        harvesting, threshing, and obtaining flax seed. In-
        cludes glossary of flax terms and 24 photographs
        illustrating the flaxmaking process.

GE201   Gellermann Patterson, Nancy Lou. *Swiss-German and
        Dutch-German Mennonite Traditional Art in the
        Waterloo Region, Ontario.* Canadian Centre for Folk
        Culture Studies, Paper No. 27. Ottawa: National
        Museum of Man, 1979. Pp. iii, 210, biographies,
        bibliography.

        Contrast of home arts and crafts--both past and
        present--produced in Ontario by Swiss-German Mennonites
        (Pennsylvania Dutch) and Dutch-German Mennonites

(Russian), on the basis of style and the different types of art created by each. Examples of specific artists and their works drawn from discussions with 76 informants. Concludes that the Swiss-German Mennonites produce works in the "folk/vernacular" style derived from peasant Europe, while the Dutch-German Mennonites perpetuate elements of adopted German formal and urban styles. Includes 130 photographs.

GE202 Gerhard, Elmer. "Pennsylvania Germans Not Alone Superstitious." *'S Pennsylvaanisch Deitsch Eck,* 25 November 1950.

Defense of Pennsylvania German folk beliefs as being not uncommon, but rather found among many ethnic groups. Traces origins of many superstitions to the Old Country and lists approximately 30 examples under such categories as signs of the moon, hex signs, and charms.

GE203 "German Proverbs Collected in Los Angeles." *California Folklore Quarterly* 4:4 (1945):432-434.

Listing of 18 proverbs in German and English, from the Southern California Writers' Project of the Work Projects Administration (WPA).

GE204 "German Proverbs from around Fort Hays, Kansas." *Western Folklore* 18:2 (1959):98.

Listing of 21 proverbs (in German, with English translations), recorded in the Fort Hays, Kansas, area.

GE205 Geschwindt, Don F. "Holidays in the Dutch Country." *Pennsylvania Dutchman* 2:21 (1 April 1951):3, 8.

Presentation of data relating to 18 holidays and their associated customs in Berks, Monroe, and Northampton counties of Pennsylvania, recorded by students in a folklore class at Franklin and Marshall College.

GE206 Gibbons, J.H. "Tramp Wilhelm--Working Stroller." *Pennsylvania Dutchman* 3:7 (1 September 1951):4.

Presentation of tales of a folk character known in York County in the 1870s and 1880s and noted for his wanderings through corn harvests, ability to get free lodging, either in homes or in jails.

GE207   Gibbons, Phebe Earle. "Pennsylvania Dutch." *'S
         Pennsylvaanisch Deitsch Eck*. 3, 10, 17, 24 February
         and 3 March 1962.

         Reprinting of an *Atlantic Monthly* article of 1869
         credited with having brought the Pennsylvania Dutch
         nationwide attention. Includes sections on religion,
         language, politics, farming, festivals, weddings,
         quiltings, holidays, manners, and customs.

GE208   Gibbons, Phebe Earle. *Pennsylvania Dutch and Other
         Essays*. 3rd ed., rev. and enl. Philadelphia: J.B.
         Lippincott & Co., 1882. Pp. 427.

         Compilation of essays (some previously published) on
         the Pennsylvania Dutch and other German sects.
         Pennsylvania Dutch folklore examples presented in
         appendix, including mention of festivals, weddings,
         quiltings, holiday customs (Easter, Halloween, Christ-
         mas, New Year's), medical beliefs, and general folk
         beliefs.

GE209   Gilbert, Russel W. "Cloth and Clothes." *Pennsylvania
         Dutchman* 12:7 (1 September 1950):7.

         From an examination of 18th-century wills, author is
         able to determine that although the Pennsylvania
         Dutch did not believe in "showy" clothes, they did
         have a concern for proper attire.

GE210   Gilbert, Russel Wieder. "The Pennsylvania German in
         His Will." *American-German Review* 17:iii (February
         1951):24-26.

         Study of Pennsylvania German wills from 15 counties,
         dating back to the late 1700s. Topics reflected in
         wills include family life, property, food, rights and
         obligations.

GE211   Gilbert, Russel Wieder. "Pennsylvania German Wills."
         The Pennsylvania German Folklore Society, *Yearbook*,
         Section I, 15 (1950):5-107.

         Analysis of basic ethnographic detail that can be
         inferred from investigation of the wills of the
         Pennsylvania Dutch in 17 counties during the 18th and
         19th centuries. Contents include material objects,
         foodways, rights of husbands and wives, education,
         religion, and burial.

GE212 Gilbert, Russel Wieder. *A Picture of the Pennsylvania Germans*. Gettysburg: The Pennsylvania Historical Association, 1962. Pp. v, 84, bibliography.

Historical overview of Pennsylvania Dutch, with mention of the full range of folkloric expression and its integration with the Pennsylvania Dutch folk character. Includes 9 photographs.

GE213 Gilbert, Russel Wieder. "Some Characteristics of Pennsylvania German Wills." *'S Pennsylvaanisch Deitsch Eck*, 18, 25 September 1948.

Based on an evaluation of wills from 13 Pennsylvania counties, argues that wills provide insights into Pennsylvania Dutch religious, social, educational, and culinary habits.

GE214 Gillespie, Angus K. "Gravestones and Ostentation: A Study of Five Delaware County Cemeteries." *Pennsylvania Folklife* 19:2 (Winter 1970):34-43.

Attempt to determine criteria for measuring levels of ostentatiousness and reasons for its decline between the 1940s and 1960s. Focuses on different religious denominations and uses statistical charts and photographs to demonstrate that elaborate gravestones declined as there was a lessening in the need to show off one's wealth. Includes 10 photographs of gravestones and 10 tables of measuring mean lines and heights of various gravestones.

GE215 Gingerich, Melvin. "Mennonite Attire Through Four Centuries." *Publications of the Pennsylvania German Society* 4 (1970):4-192, appendices, index.

Study of the history of Mennonite dress, tracing conservative trends and documenting changes that have led to uniformity in custom. Demonstrates the dialectic contrast between new fashion and traditional dress as expressed in numerous debates among Mennonite churches and groups. Uses as examples men's coats and headwear and women's dresses, headdresses, and footwear. Includes 66 photographs.

GE216 Glassie, Henry. "A Central Chimney Continental Log House." *Pennsylvania Folklife* 18:2 (Winter 1968): 33-39.

Identification of continental folk house type in southeastern Pennsylvania, with one specific example

from Cumberland County, complete with illustration of
the floor plan and mode of construction. Argues that
there is value in such studies for delineating folk
cultural regions. Includes 7 photographs and 6
sketches of parts of the house.

GE217   Glassie, Henry. "The Pennsylvania Barn in the South."
        Pennsylvania Folklife 15:2 (Winter 1965-66):8-19.

Study of house types once prevalent in the South but
no longer found in Pennsylvania that owe their character to Pennsylvania Dutch architecture. Indicates
that a study of Pennsylvania-derived barn types still
found in the South can provide insights into Pennsylvania Dutch architecture of the past. Includes 12
photographs and 6 sketches of house types and 2 maps
showing house type distribution.

GE218   Glassie, Henry. "The Pennsylvania Barn in the South,
        Part II." *Pennsylvania Folklife* 15:4 (Summer 1966):
        12-25.

Continuation of an earlier study about the influence
of Pennsylvania Dutch architecture on barns in the
South (see GE217). Focuses on two-level barns extant
in southeastern Pennsylvania that have come to symbol-
ize that area's material folk culture. Barn types
discussed in terms of their formal features and construction techniques, which leads the author to
hypothesize an evolutionary sequence for barn types
in southeastern Pennsylvania. Includes 17 photographs of barns by type and 3 distributional maps.

GE219   Gottshall, Marie. "Band Boxes." *Pennsylvania Folklife*
        28 (Folk Festival Supplement 1979):8-9.

Brief history of the nature and uses of band boxes,
with reasons offered for their disappearance and
instructions on how to make them. Includes 4 photographs.

GE220   Gougler, Richard C. "Amish Weddings." *Pennsylvania
        Folklife* 22 (Folk Festival Supplement 1973):12-13.

Description of Amish weddings, including the wedding
and its aftermath, community participation, and
relationships between civil and religious marriage.
Discusses status change from single to married state.
Includes 2 photographs of Amish weddings.

GE221 Gourley, Norma Mae. "About Powwowing." *Pennsylvania Dutchman* 5:14 (15 March 1954):7-8.

Reprinting of a chapter from the author's M.A. thesis on Pennsylvania German witchcraft. Includes information on learning, who practices the art, curing methods, and special cures for toothaches and burns.

GE222 Graeff, Arthur D. "Humor in Pennsylvania German Almanacs." *American-German Review* 5:v (June 1939): 30-33, 37-38.

Selection from German almanacs of humorous material, the distinctiveness of which comes from dialect, figures of speech, and themes. Summarizes the nature of Pennsylvania Dutch humor, exemplified by jokes.

GE223 Graeff, Arthur D. "Pennsylvania German Humor." *'S Pennsylvaanisch Deitsch Eck*, 12 November-3 December 1949.

Distinguishes dialect humor used by the outsider to poke fun at the Pennsylvania Dutch from humor used by the Pennsylvania Dutch themselves, the latter including jokes about preachers, drunkards, politics, marriage, and dialect translations of English classics; epitaphs; similes, puns, tongue twisters, and whoppers. Examples mostly in German (with a few translated into English) because of the author's contention that translations lead to the loss of original flavor. Speculates on the nature and functions of Pennsylvania Dutch humor.

GE224 Graeff, Arthur D. "Remedies in Pennsylvania German Almanacs." *American-German Review* 6:i (October 1939):10-12, 40.

Presents approximately 50 non-occult folk cures from Pennsylvania German almanacs relating to stopping of bleeding, dysentery, warts, rabies, coughs, and burns. Includes 1 illustration of knives used in wet cupping.

GE225 Graeff, Arthur D. "Weather Prophecies in Pennsylvania German Almanacs." *American-German Review* 6:vi (August 1940):10-14.

Listing of approximately 50 prophecies, most based on the actions of animals (spiders, birds, pets, sheep, and donkeys), and 2 anecdotes extolling the virtues of weather prophecy using the donkey and the cow.

GE226   Graham, Robert L. "The Pow-Wow Doctor." *Pennsylvania
        Dutchman* 2:21 (1 April 1951):2.

        Report of a casual conversation with a chance informant
        about his grandfather's powwowing practices. List of
        about 10 cures effected by the grandfather. Experiment
        by the author to seek cure from a 75-year-old Lancaster
        woman, with the discovery that her cures are well-
        integrated into modern television.

GE227   Grey, Sara. "Children's Games Among Lancaster County
        Mennonites." *Pennsylvania Folklife* 16:4 (Summer
        1967):46-47.

        Discussion of 7 categories of Mennonite children's
        games recorded by the author in Lancaster County in
        1966. Included in recreational activities are holiday
        programs, music sung by children in a Mennonite home.

GE228   Groah, Patrick. "The Bay of Hounds Tale." *Pennsyl-
        vania Dutchman* (1 September 1951):2, 4.

        Presentation of 4 tales told by a 90-year-old man who
        lived in Fettersville, Pennsylvania, and recorded on
        notebook paper. Stories relate to hunting, town
        characters, and cattle kneeling.

GE229   Gruber, Wayne H. "Reminiscences of Life in North
        Heidelberg Township, Berks Co." *Pennsylvania
        Dutchman* (1 April 1952):2, 4, 6.

        Listing of folk beliefs (6) and sayings (2) by author
        from his parents, who lived in North Heidelberg Town-
        ship, and which represent the period 1876-1893.
        Beliefs relate to cures (3) and weather signs, and
        subsumed under sayings are 19 cuss words.

GE230   Gudde, Erwin G. "The Miner's A B C." *California
        Folklore Quarterly* 6:2 (1947):112-114.

        Discussion of a German illustrated alliterating
        alphabet, published in 1856 in San Francisco,
        California, composed and illustrated by two Californi-
        ans, presumably of German background. Includes a
        reproduction of the work, followed by texts in German
        and English translation.

GE231 "Guessing Riddles." *Pennsylvania Dutchman* 1:1 (5 May 1949):2.

Listing of 6 riddles sent to the journal by William P. Shoemaker of Maple Grove, Berks County, in German with English translation.

GE232 "Guessing Riddles." *Pennsylvania Dutchman* 1:2 (12 May 1949):2.

Listing of 6 riddles contributed by Norman A. Smith of Lenhartsville, Berks County, in German with English translations.

GE233 Hale, Leon. "A Lesson on Playing Muhle." In *Some Still Do: Essays on Texas Customs*, edited by Francis Edward Abernethy, pp. 75-76. *Publications of the Texas Folklore Society* 39 (1975).

Characterization of 3 games of German origin (identified as "Muhle," "Mench Arger Dicht Nich," and "Sautreiben") still played in Winedale, Texas. Includes description of play rules and a diagram of the board arrangement on which Muhle is played.

GE234 Hall, Connie. "The Old Koch House." In *Built in Texas*, edited by Francis Edward Abernethy, pp. 107-119. *Publications of the Texas Folklore Society* 42 (1979).

Description (illustrated with 23 photographs) of a house built by German immigrant settlers in Blanco County, Texas, in 1856. House described as typical of those built by German immigrants in Texas and as illustrative of the blending of Old and New World building materials, techniques, and architecture.

*GE235 Hand, Wayland D. "California Miners' Folklore: Above Ground."

(Cross-listed as *CH8, *CO5, *IR39, *IT28, *SS15.)
(See *CO5 for full citation and annotation.)

GE236 Hand, Wayland D. "Folklore Research in North America: German American Folklore." *Journal of American Folklore* 60:238 (1947):366-372.

Survey of research possibilities in German-American folklore to 1947. Includes discussion of methodology, theory, techniques, needs, and standards. Cites

numerous references throughout on classic studies in
German-American folklore, ethnic folklore, German
language, and theory and techniques.

GE237   Hand, Wayland D. "A German House-Raising Ceremony in
          California." *Western Folklore* 13:3 (1954):199-202.

        Description of a 1953 German house-raising in Alamo,
        California, including customs of hoisting a tree to
        the rafters and providing gifts for the workmen
        (illustrated with 2 photographs).

GE238   "The Happy Dumpling: A Plaat Deutsch Nursery Rhyme."
          Colorado Folksong Bulletin 2 (1963):43.

        Presentation of a text of 1 sung nursery rhyme (in
        German, with English translation and tune transcription),
        reproduced from a manuscript submitted by a Boulder,
        Colorado, woman in 1963, who learned the song in her
        childhood from daughters of German-speaking Russian
        Mennonites.

GE239   Hark, Ann. *Blue Hills and Shoofly Pie, in Pennsyl-
          vania Dutchland*. Philadelphia: J.B. Lippincott,
          1952. Pp. 284.

        Nostalgic remembrances of time spent among rural
        Pennsylvania Dutch in Mt. Gretna, Lebanon County.
        Chapters divided monthly from July to June chronicling
        significant events and customs, such as picnics,
        magical practices, production of fine foods, contact
        with Indians, rug making, wood carving, and Christmas
        ritual. Over 25 samples of poetry and song, and
        approximately 20 recipes sprinkled throughout the
        book. Glimpses into many Pennsylvania Dutch person-
        alities.

GE240   Hark, Ann. *Hex Marks the Spot, in the Pennsylvania
          Dutch Country*. Illustrations by Eleanor Hart
          Levis. Philadelphia: J.B. Lippincott, 1938. Pp. 316.

        General descriptions of religious customs and cere-
        monies found among several Pennsylvania Dutch sects,
        including the Amish, Reformed Mennonites, and Moravians,
        derived from extensive field inquiry. Findings of
        fieldwork are recounted through reconstructed dialogue.
        Introduction relates meaning of hex symbols. Customs
        covered are use of hex symbols, incantations as protec-
        tion against witchcraft, baptism rituals, Christmas
        celebrations, folk expressions, folk singing. Special

attention is given to the food customs of several towns (with over 400 recipes at end of the book) and to the contributions of noted Pennsylvania Dutchmen to the development of Pennsylvania Dutch culture.

GE241 Hark, Ann. "Trauer-Lieder." *American-German Review* 27:i (October-November 1960):27-30.

Discussion of composition, content, and composers of tragic ballads among Pennsylvania Dutch. Focus on ballad about hanging of Susanna Cox in 1809 and reasons for its popularity.

GE242 Hark, Ann, and Barba, Preston A. *Pennsylvania German Cookery: A Regional Cookbook*. Allentown, Pa.: Schlecter's, 1950. Pp. xix, 258.

Cookbook with accompanying explanations as to the significance of each of the categories of foods included. Introduction describes the nature of Pennsylvania Dutch cooking. Index to foods provided, along with 14 sketches of foods, containers, and storage places.

GE243 Hartman, Harvey H. "The Dutchman's Branding Iron." *Pennsylvania Dutchman* 3:11 (1 November 1951):2.

Presentation of approximately 100 nicknames out of 300 collected by the author over a 50-year period.

GE244 Hartman, Harvey H. "Jests and Legends from Upper Bucks." *Pennsylvania Dutchman* 2:7 (1 September 1950):2.

Presentation of 16 humorous tales, 5 of which concern religious themes.

GE245 Hartman, Joel. "Hex Pegs." *Pennsylvania Dutchman* 3:2 (15 May 1951):4.

Report of felled trees containing wooden pegs used as a hex to harm someone near Nashville, Pennsylvania. Mention of other techniques applied to trees to inflict pain.

GE246 Hartman, Joel A. "Old Weather Lore." *Pennsylvania Dutchman* 2:8 (15 September 1950):8.

General reminiscences of previous generation's ability to foretell weather. Half (10 of 20) concern observation of animal behavior.

GE247   Hartmann, Gail Eaby. "Quilts, Quilts, Quilts."
         Pennsylvania Folklife 25 (Folk Festival Supplement
         1976):2-9.

         Discusses history of quilting among Pennsylvania
         Dutch, popular patterns and their common designations,
         and changes between colonial and contemporary quilting.
         The present quilter, the author contends, has greater
         choice in color, pattern, and material and is able to
         use machinery for better efficiency. Includes 10
         photographs of quilting patterns.

GE248   Haughon, Synnove. "Religious and Educational Refer-
         ences in Lancaster County Wills." *Pennsylvania
         Folklife* 15:1 (Autumn 1965):20-23.

         Demonstrates religiosity of Pennsylvania Dutch as
         reflected through wills found in Lancaster County,
         and which refer to the late 18th and early 19th
         centuries. Topics include soul and body, willed
         objects, funeral instructions, authority of elders,
         and education.

GE249   Heller, Edna Eby. "Butchering--Then and Now."
         Pennsylvania Dutchman 5:11 (1 February 1954):4.

         Evaluation of changing role of butchering from a
         period of close relationship with the farm. Data
         drawn from interview with a neighbor who describes
         the differences between farm and modern living with
         regard to butchering, storing meat, and canning meat.
         Presentation of 1 recipe for bologna.

GE250   Heller, Edna Eby. "Cookies Just for Nice." *Pennsyl-
         vania Dutchman* 6:3 (Winter 1954-55):8-10.

         Discourse on Christmas cookies and methods of prepara-
         tion, such as dropped and rolled. Includes 2 recipes
         and 5 photographs showing 38 cookie cutters.

GE251   Heller, Edna Eby. "Drinks in Dutchland." *Pennsyl-
         vania Folklife* 8:1 (Summer 1956):8-9.

         Survey of popular drinks among men, women, and
         children that were passed down from grandparents to
         grandchildren. Examples of occasions during which
         drinks were served. Includes 2 recipes for vinegar
         punch and ginger water, 2 for raspberry syrup, and 2
         for wine.

GE252 Heller, Edna Eby. "Dutch Cheeses." *Pennsylvania
       Dutchman* 6:5 (Summer 1955):39.

       Argues for special quality and variety of cheeses made
       in Lancaster and Berks counties. Describes how the
       C.H. Shenk family began their factory and notes prob-
       lems created by modern technology.

GE253 Heller, Edna Eby. "Dutch Treats for Breakfast."
       Pennsylvania Folklife 10:1 (Spring 1959):30-31.

       Ingredients that make up a typical Pennsylvania Dutch
       large breakfast include meat and potatoes, deep-fat
       fried foods, stewed crackers, homemade breads, and
       desserts. Includes 3 recipes and 3 photographs of
       breakfast foods.

GE254 Heller, Edna Eby. "Feeding Them by the Hundred."
       Pennsylvania Dutchman 7:2 (Fall 1955):38-39.

       Recommendation for items to be served for dinner in
       order to create a typically Pennsylvania Dutch meal.
       Provides 9 recipes to be prepared for 100 people.

GE255 Heller, Edna Eby. "'If You Married a Dutchman'...."
       Pennsylvania Dutchman 4:15 (Easter 1953):15, 13.

       In giving advice to a prospective bride who is about
       to enter Pennsylvania Dutch culture, author evaluates
       the relative importance of breakfast, dinner, and
       supper for the Pennsylvania Dutch farmer.

GE256 Heller, Edna Eby. "It's Sticky--But We Love It."
       Pennsylvania Folklife 9:4 (Summer 1970):18-19.

       Enumeration of variety of uses for syrup in Pennsyl-
       vania Dutch cooking, including for the table, baking,
       and as home remedy for laziness. Notes confusion
       between molasses and syrup, and laments the disappear-
       ance of barrel molasses. Includes 2 recipes for egg
       cheese and corn meal mush, and 3 photographs of use
       of syrup.

GE257 Heller, Edna Eby. "Let's Have a Taffy Pull."
       Pennsylvania Dutchman 4:12 (15 February 1953):5.

       Description of children's party during author's child-
       hood in Hammer Creek, Pennsylvania, in which taffy
       making followed an evening of ice skating. Includes
       1 recipe for "pulling taffy."

GE258 Heller, Edna Eby. "Lititz Specialties." *Pennsylvania
          Dutchman* 6:4 (Spring 1955):35-36.

   Discussion of role of foods author feels are distinctly
   Moravian: Lititz pretzel, strussel buns, sugar cakes,
   ginger cookies, and mints. Includes 1 recipe for sugar
   cake, ginger cookies, and mints, and 2 photographs of
   Moravian women preparing foods and 1 of a worship service.

GE259 Heller, Edna Eby. "Morning Glory Cake." *Pennsylvania
          Folklife* 13:1 (Fall 1962):33.

   Description of a fancy floral cake, variety of terms
   used to refer to it, ingredients used in its preparation, and the occasions for its serving, such as for
   birthdays, bridal showers, weddings, Memorial Day, and
   Fourth of July. Includes 1 recipe and 1 photograph.

GE260 Heller, Edna Eby. "Much Ado About Cookies." *Pennsyl-
          vania Folklife* 13:3 (July 1963):24-27.

   Discussion of variety of cookies popular among
   Pennsylvania Dutch. Speculates that large size of
   cookies due to general largeness of other foods served.
   Includes 6 recipes for sugar and honey cakes, heifer
   tongues, sandtarts, chocolate jumbles, and brown
   Moravian cookies. Presents 4 photographs of cookies,
   illustrating multiplicity of shapes.

GE261 Heller, Edna Eby. "Pennsylvania Dutch Cooking Is
          Corny." *Pennsylvania Dutchman* 8:4 (Summer-Fall
          1957):12-13.

   Describes variety of uses of corn: as dried or stewed,
   in pies, puddings, and soups, and as fried. Also
   details methods for preserving corn. Includes 5
   recipes using corn.

GE262 Heller, Edna Eby. "Pennsylvania Dutch Cooking Today
          and Yesterday." *Pennsylvania Folklife* 17:4 (Summer
          1968):38-39.

   Brief description of the general nature of Pennsylvania
   Dutch cooking, including similarities to German and
   Swiss foods and outlining distinctive ingredients
   found in typical Pennsylvania Dutch cookery. Includes
   1 photograph of author at a 1967 folk festival.

GE263   Heller, Edna Eby. "Pies in Dutchland." *Pennsylvania Folklife* 9:2 (Spring 1958):44-45.

Discussion of the importance of pie eating among the Pennsylvania Dutch, with a description of many pies. Evolution of pie making discussed, as well as speculation about the reasons for the popularity of pie. Includes 6 recipes for pies.

GE264   Heller, Edna Eby. "Restaurants, Too, Go Dutch." *Pennsylvania Dutchman* 6:1 (June 1954):9, 23.

Notice of revival of public interest in Pennsylvania Dutch culture as reflected in increase in number of restaurants that serve Pennsylvania Dutch food. Menus of several restaurants included and mention made of most popular Dutch foods served.

GE265   Heller, Edna Eby. "Rye Bread, Lehigh County Style." *Pennsylvania Folklife* 12:1 (Spring 1961):38-39.

Description of the bread baking of a 74-year-old widow, who used traditional starter yeast and baked bread in an outdoor oven. Includes 1 recipe for rye bread and 3 photographs of the breadmaker, together with 1 map of Slatedale, Lehigh County.

GE266   Heller, Edna Eby. "Saffron Cookery." *Pennsylvania Folklife* 13:4 (July 1964):40-41.

Discussion of the history and uses of saffron in Pennsylvania Dutch cooking. Mention made of uses no longer current, such as for medicine and for dyeing cloth. Includes 3 recipes calling for saffron and 3 photographs of foods with saffron as an ingredient.

GE267   Heller, Edna Eby. "A Saffron Fruit Cake, Please." *Pennsylvania Dutchman* 5:8 (December 1953):15.

Discussion of the uses of saffron as a flavor enhancer in bread and potato fillings, pot pie, potatoes, noodles, egg cheese, and chicken corn soup, but not as common an ingredient in cakes. Quote from 1 informant of Boyertown, Pennsylvania, as to how saffron was prepared. Provides brief history of how saffron came to be introduced to the Pennsylvania Dutch.

GE268   Heller, Edna Eby. "Soup's On." *Pennsylvania Folklife*
        18:4 (Summer 1969):20-22.

        Stresses the importance of soup as a main meal, with
        descriptions of often-served soups and their basic
        ingredients. Includes 4 recipes and 2 photographs and
        1 painting of women preparing and serving soup.

GE269   Heller, Edna Eby. "The Staff of Life." *Pennsylvania
        Dutchman* 5:2 (June 1953):10.

        Description of multiple uses of bread for main meals,
        snacks, and as food for the sick, with indication of
        the amount of bread made daily. Includes 1 recipe
        for egg bread.

GE270   Heller, Edna Eby. "That's a Lot of Boloney."
        Pennsylvania Dutchman 6:2 (September 1954):5.

        Description of bologna making, from aging of beef to
        smoking. Example drawn from the successful Palmyra
        Bologna Company, which started as a small enterprise
        and grew to national prominence.

GE271   Heller, Edna Eby. "Traditional Favorites Go Modern."
        Pennsylvania Folklife 16:4 (Summer 1967):44-45.

        Presentation of 3 recipes--for scrapple, apple butter,
        and chow chow--as examples of foods that can be
        easily adapted from rural to urban settings.

GE272   Heller, Edna Eby. "We Waste Not." *Pennsylvania
        Folklife* 21 (Folk Festival Supplement 1972):12-13.

        Illustrates that Pennsylvania Dutch use foods fully
        by referring to the use of leftovers to prepare new
        dishes. Includes 2 recipes using leftover potatoes
        and 2 photographs of bread baking.

GE273   Hemhauser, Robert. "The Pennsylvania Dutch and Some
        of Their Lore." *Pennsylvania Dutchman* 2:22 (15
        April 1951):2.

        Field-based study of powwowing practices in Lancaster
        County, conducted by students in a folklore class.
        Also includes mention of Ascension Day customs.

GE274   Henneberger, George. "Franklin County Lore."
        Pennsylvania Dutchman 2:5 (July 1950):3.

        Presentation of 2 legends told by an 80-year-old
        resident of Franklin County, one concerning the

successful keeping ahead of a rainstorm, the other about sheep stealing.

GE275   Henneberger, George F. "Weather Lore in Franklin County." *Pennsylvania Dutchman* 3:16 (15 January 1952):3.

Presentation of lore describing approximately 10 methods for predicting weather, obtained from 5 informants in Franklin County.

GE276   Henry, James. "Christmas with the Moravians." *American-German Review* 27:ii (December 1960-January 1961):4-7.

Reprinting from an 1859 work of a description of Moravian Christmas celebrations, with information on food, decoration, church activities, and family gatherings. Custom of keeping diaries and reading portions on New Year's Eve also mentioned.

GE277   Henry, Ruth. "Knights of the Road and One-Crust Onion Pie." *Pennsylvania Dutchman* 3:15 (1 January 1952):1, 3.

Description of 2 tramps who lived in Mt. Bethel in the late 1800s, of ways they obtained free food and lodging from local families, and of ways devised by local residents to get rid of the tramps (including serving them onion pie).

GE278   Henry, Ruth. "Old-time Cures and Beliefs." *Pennsylvania Dutchman* 4:5 (September 1952):4.

Presentation of 15 folk cures, most remembered by the author from her mother's practices, others recorded from friends in Mt. Bethel.

GE279   Hering, Irwin M. "Folklore and Superstitions among the Pennsylvania Germans." *'S Pennsylvaanisch Deitsch Eck*, 7 September-19 October 1968.

A series of articles on such subjects as superstitions, powwowing, and weather lore. Data presented based on author's reminiscences and abstracted from a typescript for the period of the 1880s and 1890s.

GE280   Herr, Charlotte C. "Litiz." *Journal of American Folk-Lore* 8:31 (1895):308-312.

Ethnographic description of the Moravian village of Litiz (now spelled Lititz) in eastern Pennsylvania,

settled in 1755 by Germans from Bohemia and Switzer-
land. Comments that the village and life there have
changed little over the years. Focuses on such topics
as the spelling of names, language, holiday customs,
building practices, weddings, and funeral customs.

*GE281 Herrmann, Walter. "Anecdotes About Hitler." *New York
        Folklore Quarterly* 6:4 (1950):258-259.

        Characterization of 3 anecdotes told about Hitler and
        conditions in Germany during the period of his control.
        (Cross-listed as *JE31.)

GE282 Hershey, Mary Jane. "A Study of the Dress of the
       (Old) Mennonites of the Franconia Conference, 1700-
       1953." *Pennsylvania Folklife* 9:3 (Summer 1958):
       24-47.

       Reprint of a 1957 thesis surveying the costume of
       Franconia Mennonites, including bonnets and hats,
       dresses, shawls and capes, cap coverings and veilings,
       aprons and accessories, and men's clothing. Author
       suggests reasons for changes from uniformity, typical
       of the first part of this century, to simplicity and
       modesty of present period. Appendices of conferences
       and recordings of their session by 2 preachers pro-
       vided. Includes 62 photographs.

GE283 Hertzog, Phares H. "Pennsylvania German Snakelore."
       Pennsylvania Folklife 17:4 (Summer 1968):16-19.

       Author relates, in a third and last of a 3-part series,
       reports of tales from informants concerning 3 snakes,
       illustrating importance of environment in producing
       folklore. Includes also 1 tale told of rattlesnake,
       7 concerning the black snake, and 5 of an imaginary
       snake (the "hoop" or "horn" snake). Over 10 beliefs
       identified in tales. Presents 2 photographs of
       author and snakes, and 4 sketches depicting folk
       beliefs.

GE284 Hertzog, Phares H. "Snakelore in Pennsylvania
       German Folk Medicine." *Pennsylvania Folklife* 17:2
       (Winter 1967-1968):24-26.

       Discussion of positive and negative aspects of snake
       medicine, as represented by 6 cures recorded from 4
       informants, and by a listing of 21 different plants
       that have been dubbed "snake root." Includes 1 illus-
       tration of snake bite cure depicted in fraktur.

GE285   Hertzog, Phares H. "Snakes and Snakelore of Pennsyl-
           vania." *Pennsylvania Folklife* 17:1 (Autumn 1967):
           14-17.

        Comparison between folk beliefs concerning snakes and
        scientific thinking on those same beliefs. Discussion
        of 6 beliefs embedded in folk stories, told by an
        informant to illustrate each belief, and then compared
        with scientific "facts." Provides additional 9
        miscellaneous belief tales and 4 tall tales. Includes
        1 photograph of author holding snakes and 2 drawings
        illustrating commonly held folk beliefs.

GE286   Hoffman, George K. "Riddles." *Pennsylvania Dutchman*
           4:15 (Easter 1953):13.

        Listing of 8 riddles in German (with English transla-
        tions).

GE287   Hoffman, W.J. "Folk Snake Cures." *Pennsylvania
           Dutchman* 3:7 (1 September 1951):3.

        Reprint and translation from 1897 newspaper of author's
        observations of powwowing related specifically to
        snake cures, and based, in part, on information re-
        ceived from 2 informants.

GE288   Hoffman, W.J. "Folk-Lore of the Pennsylvania Ger-
           mans." *Journal of American Folk-Lore* 1:2 (1888):
           125-135.

        Brief history of Pennsylvania Germans and the origin
        of their dialect, which the author notes is incorrectly
        known as Pennsylvania Dutch. Examples of name changes
        and a guide to pronunciation of the dialect. Descrip-
        tions and examples of many customs and superstitions
        surviving among Pennsylvania Germans living in rural
        districts: house and barn designs, agricultural beliefs
        and practices, courtship and marriage customs (in-
        cluding bundling), work activities, parties, and
        beliefs about witches.

GE289   Hoffman, W.J. "Folk-Lore of the Pennsylvania Germans.
           II." *Journal of American Folk-Lore* 2:4 (1889):23-35.

        Descriptions of customs and beliefs of the Pennsylvania
        Germans. Examples of foods, holiday dishes, household
        and traditional remedies for childhood and other
        diseases, death and burial customs, and witch and
        ghost stories.

GE290   Hoffman, W.J. "Folk-Lore of the Pennsylvania Germans.
        III." *Journal of American Folk-Lore* 2:6 (1889):
        191-202.

        Comments on problems encountered by the Pennsylvania
        Germans in pronouncing English. Presents 4 tale texts
        (ghost, witch, and haunted locale stories) from
        Fayette County and Crackersport, Lehigh County, in
        Pennsylvania German dialect (with English translations).
        Examples of poetry recited by children and a descrip-
        tion of a children's game, as well as 79 proverbs
        arranged alphabetically by first word, accompanied by
        English translations and/or English proverbs equivalent
        in meaning.

GE291   Hoffman, Walter James. "Folk-Medicine of the Pennsyl-
        vania Germans." *Proceedings of the American Philo-
        sophical Society* 26 (1889):329-352.

        After a general discussion of the nature of Pennsyl-
        vania Dutch folk medicine, author lists and explains
        the significance of over 150 cures under 38 categories,
        such as coughs, dog bites, epilepsy, itch, rheumatism,
        snake bites, tonsilitis, and warts. Author also
        discusses the methods used by conjurers, such as
        hexing and powwowing, and also the processes of
        transferring disease.

GE292   Hohman, John George. *The Long Lost Friend; or Book
        of Pow-Wows: A Collection of Mysterious and In-
        valuable Remedies*. 1820. Reprint. Harrisburg,
        Pa.: The Aurand Press, 1930. Pp. 82.

        Listing of approximately 200 folk remedies, charms,
        and beliefs, with explanations as to their effective-
        ness, based on personal testimony of author and
        acquaintances. These prescriptions employ the method
        of powwowing and are cast in a religious frame.

GE293   Hoke, N.C. "Folk-Custom and Folk-Belief in North
        Carolina." *Journal of American Folk-Lore* 5:17
        (1892):113-120.

        Collection of customs, beliefs, signs, sayings,
        remedies, children's games, and counting-out rhymes
        from an area of North Carolina settled by Germans.
        Subjects covered include agriculture, the dead, babies,
        doggerel, and bread-making. People of this area
        characterized as very conservative.

GE294 Hollenbach, Ida V. "Dialect Jottings." *Pennsylvania
       Dutchman* 4:1 (May 1952):15.

       Listing of 4 sayings and 1 jingle, in German (with
       English translations).

GE295 Hollenbach, Raymond E. "Fasenacht Kuche." *Pennsyl-
       vania Dutch* 5:11 (1 February 1954):3.

       Reply to column written by Alfred L. Shoemaker in a
       1945 *Reading Eagle*, in which he expressed opposition
       to church groups serving round *fasnachts*. Author
       argues that the shape has nothing at all to do with
       determining genuineness; rather, criterion is lack of
       yeast. Gives recipe and describes how food is to be
       eaten. Mentions belief concerning effects of "last
       one out of bed," associated with Shrove Tuesday and
       Ash Wednesday.

GE296 Hommel, Martha Hill. "Quirls or Twirling Sticks:
       Primitive Egg Beaters." *Pennsylvania Dutchman* 5:2
       (June 1953):11.

       Description of the use of branches by pioneer
       Pennsylvania Dutch to beat eggs, as evidence of
       Dutch creativity.

GE297 Horne, Abraham Reeser. "Proverbs and Sayings of the
       Pennsylvania Germans." Pennsylvania German Society,
       Proceedings and Addresses 2 (1892):47-54.

       Argues that proverbs and sayings are indexes of
       Pennsylvania Dutch character. Lists 49 proverbs and
       sayings, in German (with English translations),
       accompanied by brief explanations.

GE298 Hostetler, Beulah S. "An Old Order River Brethren
       Love Feast." *Pennsylvania Folklife* 24:2 (Winter
       1974-1975):8-20.

       Description of a love feast held by Old Order River
       Brethren in 1973, in Lancaster County, including the
       forenoon and communion services. Presents historical
       background of the Brethren, the nature of the sect as
       compared with others, internal divisions, and the
       importance of costume as an expression of religious
       belief. Includes 1 photograph of meeting place, 1
       sketch of internal arrangements, 1 of internal divi-
       sions, and 2 of costume. Appendix contains outline
       of events.

GE299   Hostetler, John. "Amish Costume: Its European Origins."
         American-German Review 22:vi (August-September 1956):
         11-14.

         Discussion of the origin of such costumes as beard and
         hair, buttons, pants, caps, skirts, and bustle.
         Hypothesizes that Amish clung to these older forms in
         order to distinguish themselves from non-German
         neighbors.

GE300   Hostetler, John A. "Amish Family Life: A Sociologist's
         Analysis." *Pennsylvania Folklife* 12:3 (Fall 1961):
         28-39.

         Analysis of selected features of Amish social life,
         including patterns of authority, marital relationships,
         parent-child relationships, and the roles of courtesy
         and conversation. Includes 8 photographs of farm
         life and 1 map.

GE301   Hostetler, John A. *Amish Society*. Rev. ed. Baltimore
         and London: Johns Hopkins University Press, 1968.
         Pp. xviii, 369, bibliography, index.

         Examination of the forces influencing both continuity
         and change in a "self-contained" ethnic group as a
         result of contact with the larger, more modernized
         American society. Resulting problems and tensions
         are related to the group level of interaction as well
         as to personal means of adjustment. Folkloric data
         relating to dress, language, courting, recreation,
         leisure, ceremony, birth, marriage, and death contrib-
         ute to the existence of a "symbolic" community and
         hence to the stability of the group.

GE302   Hostetler, John A. "Folk and Scientific Medicine in
         Amish Society." *Human Organization* 22:4 (Winter
         1963-64):269-275.

         Analysis of the relationship between science and folk-
         lore in the treatment of disease among Amish. Dis-
         cussion of the concept of sickness among Amish, rele-
         vant illnesses treated by medical doctors and folk
         practitioners, and the relationship between medical
         doctors and Amish patients. Concludes with a list of
         general characteristics attributable to the Amish
         view of science and folk medicine. Table I lists 54
         ailments and corresponding cures offered by both
         medical doctors and folk practitioners. Data for

study based on review of 26 issues of the newspaper
Budget and interviews with 46 physicians who serve
the Amish.

GE303 Hostetler, Patricia. "Pennsylvania Dutch Folklore."
Pennsylvania Dutchman 1:12 (21 July 1949):4.

Argues that folklore reflects the ethos of Pennsylvania
Dutch conservative values, as represented through
sayings (1), mottos (1), medical cures (3), planting
by the sign of the moon, and powwowing.

GE304 Hudson, Arthur Palmer. "The New Year's Shoot."
Southern Folklore Quarterly 11:4 (1947):235-243.

Discussion of the custom of "shooting in the New Year,"
as practiced among individuals of German descent in
North Carolina. Includes reprinting of a 1946 newspaper account of the practice, together with texts of
1 speech made traditionally on the occasion and of
1 poem written by a participant. Also presents a
letter written to the author by a participant in
response to questions raised in correspondence between
the two. Comparison made with a similar French custom,
reported from Missouri, and with the English mummers'
plays.

GE305 Hudson, Arthur Palmer. "The Singstunde in Old
Wachovia." *North Carolina Folklore* 14:2 (1966):
4-11.

Historical sketch of the *Singstunde* or "church
service largely of singing" among Moravians, first in
Germany and later in Pennsylvania and North Carolina
(in the latter in the Wachovia, North Carolina, area,
principally between the years 1753 and 1783). Includes information, based on published records, of
the *Singstunde* during the height of its popularity
and speculations concerning its eventual demise in
North Carolina.

GE306 "Humorous Dialect Prayers." *Pennsylvania Dutchman*
1:1 (5 May 1949):2.

Presentation of 2 prayers (1 recorded from Berks
County) recited in dialect and considered to be
humorous and satirical.

GE307   Hurwitz, Elizabeth Adams. "Decorative Elements in the
        Domestic Architecture of Eastern Pennsylvania."
        Pennsylvania Dutchman 7:2 (Fall 1955):6-29.

        Illustrated survey (with 20 photographs) of ornamental
        gateways, porch railings and galleries, and window
        gratings characteristic of early industrial period in
        America. Background of domestic architecture in towns
        and rural settings discussed.

GE308   Huyett, Laura. "Straw Hat Making Among the Older
        Amish." *Pennsylvania Folklife* 12:3 (Fall 1961):40-41.

        Brief description of processes involved in making
        straw hats, from cutting to braiding rye straw. In-
        cludes 1 photograph of a Lancaster County woman
        braiding straw.

GE309   Hyde, Louise. "Herb: Vinegars, Jellies, and Salad
        Dressings." *Pennsylvania Folklife* 28 (Folk Festival
        Supplement 1979):30-31.

        Discussion of the use of herbs in making vinegars,
        jellies, and salad dressings, accompanied by typical
        ingredients contained in these condiments. Includes
        1 recipe for herb jellies and 2 photographs of various
        herb vinegars, salad dressings, and jellies.

GE310   Jack, Phil R. "Amusements in Rural Homes Around the
        Big and Little Mahoning Creeks, 1870-1912." *Pennsyl-
        vania Folklife* 9:2 (Spring 1958):46-49.

        Description of pastimes popular in the early 19th
        century among residents of northern Indiana County
        and southern Jefferson County, Pennsylvania, based
        on fieldwork among 13 informants and information
        derived from newspapers. Includes 7 riddles and
        description of holiday celebrations (both public and
        family). Includes 2 photographs of typical turn-of-
        the-century farm activities.

GE311   Jack, Phil R. "Gravestone Symbols of Western Pennsyl-
        vania." In *Two Penny Ballads and Four Dollar
        Whiskey*, edited by Kennth S. Goldstein and Robert H.
        Byington, pp. 165-173. Hatboro, Pa.: Folklore
        Associates, 1966.

        Classification of gravestone symbols into 23 basic
        "motif categories" and 8 general categories and
        suggestion for future research on gravestones based

on structural, geographical, chronological, and individual considerations. Enumerates 13 basic factors that might account for symbols used.

GE312   Jack, Phil R. "Western Pennsylvania Epitaphs."
        Pennsylvania Folklife 13:4 (July 1964):58-64.

Listing of 51 epitaphs and description of their main themes. Includes 6 photographs of burial plots and stones and 1 map.

GE313   Jack, Phil R. "A Western Pennsylvania Graveyard,
        1787-1967." *Pennsylvania Folklife* 17:3 (Spring
        1968):40-48.

Survey, description, and functional analysis of 525 gravestones (dated 1787-1967) in a cemetery located in North Bethlehem Township, Washington County, Pennsylvania. Discusses composition of stones, symbols and motifs used (16 categories listed), and themes of epitaphs (32 themes enumerated). Includes 36 photographs of tombstones.

GE314   Jackson, George Pullen. "The American Amish Sing
        Medieval Folk Tunes Today." *Southern Folklore
        Quarterly* 10:2 (1946):151-157.

Discussion of tunes referred to in Amish hymnals, with emphasis on their age. Suggests that even though musical transcriptions are absent in such works, references to tunes to which songs are to be sung suggest that many go back hundreds of years, some to the Middle Ages.

GE315   Jackson, George Pullen. "The Strange Music of the
        Old Order Amish." *The Musical Quarterly* 31 (1945):
        275-288.

Presentation of the results of the author's comparisons of tunes recommended for hymns in the 16th-century Amish *Ausbund*, those documented in Pennsylvania and transcribed and published by Joseph Yoder (1942), and those found in German and American folksong and folk music collections. Reveals that tunes have been adapted or shifted over time, with changes in tunes or alternative tunes used in place of those recommended in the *Ausbund*.

GE316   Jentsch, Theodore W. "Old Order Mennonite Family Life
        in the East Penn Valley." *Pennsylvania Folklife*
        24:1 (Fall 1974):18–27.

        Ethnographic descriptions of courtship and marriage,
        home activities, family life, leisure time activities,
        and sickness and death among Old Order Mennonites.
        Emphasizes the permeating influence of religion.
        Includes reprinting of 4 memorial poems written by
        family members.

GE317   Johnson, Hildegard B. "Immigrant Traditions and
        Rural Midwestern Architecture." *American-German
        Review* 9:v (June 1943):17–20.

        Comments on the impact of German influence on rural
        architecture in the Midwest. Concludes that with the
        advent of the machine age, the individual craftsman
        disappeared.

*GE318 Jones, Louis C. "The Devil in York State."

        (Cross-listed as *GL50, *FR69.)
        (See *GL50 for full citation and annotation.)

*GE319 Jordan, Terry G. "A Russian-German Folk House in
        North Texas."

        (Cross-listed as *RU11, *UK4.)
        (See *RU11 for full citation and annotation.)

GE320   Kadelbach, Elizabeth. "Christmas in a German
        Pastor's Home." *The Pennsylvania-German* 9:xii
        (December 1908):534–537.

        Comment on importance of symbols used in Christmas
        celebrations, including the tree, food, and beliefs.

GE321   Kauffman, Henry J. "Church Architecture in Lancaster
        County." *Pennsylvania Dutchman* 6:5 (Summer 1955):
        16–27.

        Survey of the church architecture of several religious
        groups in Lancaster County, Pennsylvania. Includes
        16 photographs with detailed descriptions.

GE322   Kauffman, Henry J. "Decorated Chests in the Pennsyl-
        vania Dutch Country." *Pennsylvania Dutchman* 1:8
        (23 June 1949):1.

        Presentation of the history of chest making,
        especially of dower chests. Argues that these

chests are distinctively Pennsylvanian because
of motifs, materials, and craftsmanship.

GE323   Kauffman, Henry J. "Moravian Architecture in
        Bethlehem." *Pennsylvania Dutchman* 6:4 (Spring
        1955):12-19.

        Discussion of how architecture fits into the religious
        climate of 19th-century Moravian life. Description of
        early architecture by reference to specific homes in
        Bethlehem, and mention of modernization trends. In-
        cludes 21 photographs of various architectural
        examples.

GE324   Kauffman, Henry J. *Pennsylvania Dutch American Folk
        Art*. 1946. Reprint. New York: Dover Publications,
        1964. Pp. 146.

        Survey of various kinds of Pennsylvania Dutch folk
        art, including architecture, furniture, pottery, glass,
        metalwork, textiles and needlework, and certificates
        and manuscripts. Brief historical sketch of the
        Pennsylvania Dutch and their art. Includes 271
        photographs.

GE325   Kauffman, Henry J. "Philadelphia Butter." *Pennsyl-
        vania Folklife* 8:2 (Fall-Winter 1956-1957):8-13.

        Description of the butter-making process, from care
        of cows to the handling of milk and churning of butter.
        Includes 9 accompanying illustrations of motifs found
        on butter molds.

GE326   Kauffman, Henry J. "Punched Tinware." *Pennsylvania
        Dutchman* 5:10 (15 January 1954):3.

        Distinction made between tin and tin-plate, the latter
        being the material used for folk art objects because
        of its decorative and functional adaptability. In-
        cludes 3 photographs of punched tin objects.

GE327   Kauffman, Henry J. "The Riddle of Two Front Doors."
        Pennsylvania Dutchman 6:3 (Winter 1954-55):27.

        Brief commentary about possible origin of two front
        doors in Pennsylvania Dutch architecture, followed by
        a discussion of the development of architectural
        structures since the 18th century, especially in terms
        of room size and placement. Includes 1 photograph of
        a Lancaster County house with two front doors.

GE328   Kauffman, Henry J. "The Summer House." *Pennsylvania*
        Folklife 8:1 (Summer 1956):2-7.

        Discusses structures built as adjuncts to the main
        house in which many domestic chores were carried out.
        Includes 9 photographs showing the move from detached
        to attached ancillary structures.

GE329   Kemp, Alvin F. "More Dialect Stories." *Pennsylvania*
        Folklife 28:2 (Winter 1978/1979):43-45.

        Reprinting of 5 dialect stories emphasizing the
        virtues of minding one's own business, taking good
        advice, and using good judgment. Supplements earlier
        essay (see GE330).

GE330   Kemp, Alvin F. "Pennsylvania Dutch Dialect Stories."
        Pennsylvania Folklife 28:2 (Winter 1978/1979):27-35.

        Reprinting of 15 stories told by Alvin F. Kemp, a
        well-known storyteller. Majority of tales (in German,
        with English translations) are didactic, extolling
        truth, thrift, and modesty. Includes reports from
        4 individuals who remembered Kemp.

GE331   Kessler, Carol. "Ten Tulpehocken Inventories: What
        Do They Reveal About a Pennsylvania German Community?"
        Pennsylvania Folklife 23:2 (Winter 1973-1974):16-30.

        Analysis of 10 inventories of those who died between
        1723 and 1815 in Tulpehocken, Pennsylvania, for in-
        sight into material possessions. Information abstract-
        ed about clothing, yardgoods, foodstuffs, kitchen
        utensils, furnishings, books, and agricultural imple-
        ments. Infers community composition through skills
        noted in inventories. Includes 3 photographs of
        inventory lists.

GE332   Keyser, Alan G. "Eagle Date Boards." *Pennsylvania*
        Folklife 12:4 (Summer 1962):13-14.

        Brief pictorial survey (with 12 photographs) of types
        of eagle date boards commonly found on houses in
        Montgomery County between 1801 and 1840. Argues that
        this art is distinctively Pennsylvania Dutch.

GE333   Keyser, Alan G. "Gardens and Gardening among the
        Pennsylvania Germans." *Pennsylvania Folklife* 20:3
        (Spring 1971):2-15.

        Detailed account of kitchen gardens and gardening
        among the Pennsylvania Dutch, based on interviews

with 15 informants. Topics include fencing, garden
layout, planting by the signs (5 systems described),
planting and care of onions, watering techniques, and
use of scarecrows. Lists approximately 150 plants
and areas of gardens in which they were grown. Includes 16 photographs.

GE334   Keyser, Mildred D. "Pennsylvania Dutch Pottery."
        Pennsylvania Dutchman 2:1 (1 May 1950):7.

        Argues that Pennsylvania Dutch art has a unique style
        and is perhaps the only true folk art in the United
        States. Describes materials used in making pottery,
        as well as molds, forms of decoration, and techniques
        of firing kilns.

GE335   Kirchner, Francis X. "Place Name Lore." *Pennsylvania
        Dutchman* 3:2 (15 May 1951):2.

        Discussion of the legend of "the face on Carter's
        hill," recorded from an informant in Lancaster County,
        and the legend of "Cabbage Hill," obtained from
        several informants. Provides various explanations
        for these place names.

GE336   Klees, Fredric. *The Pennsylvania Dutch*. New York:
        The Macmillan Co., 1950. Pp. ix, 451.

        History of the Pennsylvania Dutch, with sections on
        folkways (including brief descriptions of powwowing,
        hexerei, dialect humor, legends, country life,
        dancing, social gatherings, rites of passage, holidays
        such as Christmas and New Year's) and the arts (in-
        cluding music, folk art, architecture, gardens,
        furniture, and food).

GE337   Klein, H.M.J. *History and Customs of the Amish People*.
        York, Pa.: The Maple Press, 1946. Pp. 73.

        Brief survey of the history, social structure, and
        occupations of the Amish, as well as descriptions of
        their dress, weddings, and holidays. Includes 9
        sketches.

GE338   Knohr, E.L. "Customs and Beliefs in South-Eastern
        Pennsylvania Concerning the Holidays of the Year."
        Pennsylvania Dutchman 2:20 (15 March 1951):5-7.

        Report of fieldwork among 12 informants, conducted in
        Gratz, Dauphin County, Pennsylvania, in 1950. Brief

mention of miscellaneous customs and beliefs associated
with the Easter season. Concludes that these traditions are rapidly dying out and must be recorded
quickly.

GE339 Korson, George. *Black Rock: Mining Folklore of the
       Pennsylvania Dutch*. Baltimore: The Johns Hopkins
       University Press, 1960. Pp. xi, 453.

       Demonstrates that not all Pennsylvania Dutch were in-
       volved in rural farming, but that many contributed
       to the development of the hard-coal industry. Pre-
       sents a history of Pennsylvania Dutch involvement in
       the industry, as well as a description of activities
       necessary to the continuation of the industry,
       exemplified by personal experience narratives,
       legends, tales of heroism, involvement with the devil
       and ghosts (19), local events (7), folk speech items
       (20), courtship and marriage customs (6), folk
       medicine items (4), religious folklore (6), foodways
       (2), and housing (2). Experiences of the miners also
       expressed through songs and ballads (13 texts pre-
       sented, together with 11 tunes). Data for study
       obtained primarily from residents of Schuylkill
       County, who commuted between their farm homes and the
       coal mines.

GE340 Korson, George Gershon. *Minstrels of the Mine Patch:
       Songs and Stories of the Anthracite Industry*.
       1938. Reprint. Hatboro, Pa.: Folklore Associates,
       1964. Pp. xviii, 460.

       Characterization of the singing traditions of miners
       as reflected in themes on all aspects of mining.
       Musical examples (including some tunes) refer to the
       coal camp, the company store, love and courtship,
       play, types of miners, transportation, personnel,
       crafts, superstitions and legends, luck, mine disasters,
       strikes, rebellions, and future hopes. Each song
       accompanied by the name of the singer and the place
       and date of recording.

GE341 Kreider, Mary C. "'Dutchified English'--Some Lebanon
       Valley Examples." *Pennsylvania Folklife* 12:1
       (Spring 1961):40-43.

       Discussion of the unique speech of the "United Chris-
       tians" of Lebanon County, Pennsylvania, a Pennsylvania

Dutch dialect whose continuity is attributed to cultural isolation. Describes phonology, morphology, syntax, and lexicon. Includes 1 map of Lebanon County.

GE342   Kuhns, Levi Oscar. *The German and Swiss Settlements of Colonial Pennsylvania: A Study of the So-Called Pennsylvania Dutch.* Harrisburg, Pa.: The Aurand Press, 1945. Pp. xiii, 268.

Characterization of the 17th- and 18th-century German settlements in Pennsylvania. Includes a chapter on manners and customs, which provides information on architecture, folk beliefs, weather signs, amulets, incantations, and funeral rites.

GE343   Kulp, Clarence. "A Dunker Weekend Love Feast of 100 Years Ago." *Pennsylvania Folklife* 11:1 (Spring 1960):2-9.

Survey of the Brethren's most popular celebration, which reached its peak between 1840 and 1880. Describes spiritual and material preparations for the Saturday service and the accompanying meal. Assesses the significance of the love feast for Brethren and notes changes which have occurred in the celebration. Includes 3 photographs of Indian Creek Brethren meeting houses and 1 of a Lebanon County woman making love feast bread.

GE344   Kulp, Clarence. "A Study of the Dialect Terminology of the Plain Sects of Montgomery County, Pa." *Pennsylvania Folklife* 12:2 (Summer 1961):41-47.

List of folk terms used by Dunkers, "Old" Mennonites, and Schwenkfelders of Montgomery County. Terms divided into those relating to material culture (21 items) and those dealing with the religious or philosophical (not discussed). Includes 7 photographs of meeting houses.

GE345   Lamont, Karen Wells. "Fritz G. Vogt: Itinerant Artist." *New York Folklore* 1:1&2 (1975):45-55.

Biographical sketch of a German immigrant itinerant artist "who drew pencil and crayon farm scenes, town residences, businesses, cemeteries, and in at least one instance, a church" during the closing decade of the 19th century. Includes photographs of 5 of Vogt's house sketches and 9 photographs of the actual sites he sketched (all in New York State).

GE346   Landis, Henry Kinzer. *Early Kitchens of the Pennsyl-
         vania Germans*. Norristown, Pa.: The Pennsylvania
         German Society, 1939. Pp. 130.

         Discussion of the history, characteristics, and types
         of early Pennsylvania Dutch kitchens, including
         descriptions of fireplaces, tools, cooking methods,
         furniture, design and decoration, and activities
         centered in the kitchen. Includes 89 photographs of
         kitchens and their contents.

GE347   Lawton, Arthur J. "The Ground Rules of Folk Architec-
         ture." *Pennsylvania Folklife* 23:1 (Autumn 1973):
         13-19.

         Analysis in geometric terms of the central fireplace-
         three-room-plan house, introduced by German settlers
         in the early 18th century. Building plans communicated
         and learned at first hand rather than through blue-
         prints. Includes 8 photographs showing the various
         geometric designs inherent in house plans.

GE348   Leeds, Wendy. "Fraktur: An Annotated Bibliography."
         Pennsylvania Folklife 25:4 (Summer 1976):35-46.

         Annotated bibliography of over 175 entries. Brief
         description of approaches taken to the study of
         fraktur (single artist, single genre, single collec-
         tion, catalog accompanying museum exhibitions).

GE349   Lefcourt, Charles R. "A Rose by Any Other Name:
         Ethnic Conflict in Berlin, Ontario." *Keystone
         Folklore Quarterly* 12:2 (1967):119-126.

         Discussion of anti-German sentiment in Berlin, Ontario,
         Canada, during World War I and of the change of the
         city's name to Kitchener as a consequence. Includes
         discussion of the reactions of citizens of German
         ancestry to the name change.

GE350   Leh, Leonard L. "Shooting in the New Year." *Pennsyl-
         vania Dutchman* 4:9 (1 January 1953):3.

         Reminiscences of a "shooting" that took place on New
         Year's Eve. Discussion of the shooters' and hosts'
         behavior and wishes.

GE351 Lehr, Robert J. "The Lore of the Moon in the Dutch
       Country." *Pennsylvania Dutchman* 3:7 (1 September
       1951):3.

       Report of fieldwork conducted in Intercourse, Pennsyl-
       vania, and surrounding counties among 5 people who
       plant by the signs of the moon. Includes mention of
       types of vegetation planted according to particular
       moon positions, with 4 proverbs on moon lore.

GE352 Lerch, Lila. "Hex Signs or Fire Marks?" *'S Pennsyl-
       vaanisch Deitsch Eck*, 10 December 1949.

       Traces the history of a Pennsylvania Dutch hex mark
       to sun fire symbols and notes that the sign has been
       chosen by many fire insurance companies because of
       its protective powers.

GE353 Lestz, Gerald S. "How Much Snow Next Winter?" *Key-
       stone Folklore Quarterly* 6:3 (1961):12-14.

       Description of 6 ways to forecast the weather, 1 of
       which is reportedly of Pennsylvania Dutch origin.

GE354 Lich, Glen, and Taylor, Lera. "When the Creeks Run
       Dry: Water Milling in the German Hill Country." In
       Built in Texas, edited by Francis Edward Abernethy,
       pp. 227-245. *Publications of the Texas Folklore
       Society* 42 (1979).

       Discussion of mills in the Hill Country, near
       Fredericksburg, Texas, built in the 1880s by German
       immigrants to the area. Emphasis on the first mill,
       constructed in 1851, with quotations from letters sent
       to Germany by its designer. Includes 5 photographs
       and 2 sketches.

GE355 Lichten, Frances. *Folk Art of Rural Pennsylvania*.
       New York: Charles Scribner's Sons, 1946. Pp. xiv,
       276.

       Survey of Pennsylvania Dutch folk art, with information
       on artists and their works, discussion of themes and
       historical development of various art styles. Demon-
       strates diversity of materials made from clay (pottery),
       flax (linens), wool (coverlets), straw (baskets), wood
       (furniture), stone (gravestones), iron (hardware),
       tin (cooking utensils), textiles (quilts, rugs), and
       paper (manuscripts). Includes over 300 photographs,
       drawings, and sketches.

GE356   Lichten, Frances. *Fraktur: The Illuminated Manuscripts
        of the Pennsylvania Dutch.* Philadelphia: The Free
        Library of Philadelphia, 1958. Pp. 26.

        Description of the nature of fraktur writing, with
        specific references to notable collections and
        prominent categories of fraktur.

GE357   Lichten, Frances. "Pennsylvania Dutch Needlework:
        Where Did the Worker Find Her Patterns?" *Pennsyl-
        vania Dutchman* 7:4 (Spring 1956):18-21.

        Argues that the traditional motifs and themes in
        Pennsylvania Dutch embroidery are common to the whole
        range of Pennsylvania Dutch art. Includes 6 photo-
        graphs of embroidered rugs.

GE358   Lichten, Frances. "'TRAMP WORK'! Pen Knife Plus
        Cigar Boxes." *Pennsylvania Folklife* 10:1 (Spring
        1959):2-7.

        Survey of "tramp work," a broad range of old-time
        crafts made from wooden cigar boxes by the Pennsylvania
        Dutch. Deals specifically with such items as match
        holders, comb and brush holders, caskets, and mirror
        frames. Discusses production techniques and decorative
        uses. Includes 5 photographs of such objects.

GE359   Lick, David E., and Brendle, Thomas R. *Plant Names
        and Plant Lore Among the Pennsylvania Germans.*
        Lancaster, Pa.: The Pennsylvania German Society,
        1923. Pp. xix, 300.

        Alphabetical listing, in Pennsylvania Dutch dialect,
        of plant names reported from Pennsylvania German in-
        formants. Entries provide English, scientific, and
        Pennsylvania German name, the county in which the name
        was noted, folklore relating to the name, and compara-
        tive notes.

GE360   "Local Folk Customs." *Illinois Folklore* 2:1 (1948):
        8-13.

        Miscellaneous collection of Illinois customs, including
        a description of the German custom of "shooting in the
        New Year" as observed in St. Clair and Monroe counties.
        Includes description of the wandering celebrants and
        their visits to homes, with mention of foods provided
        and the text of 1 verse (in German, with English
        translation) recited at the homes visited.

GE361 Long, Amos, Jr. "Bakeovens in the Pennsylvania Folk-
Culture." *Pennsylvania Folklife* 14:2 (December
1964):16-29.

Discussion of the history, construction, design, use,
and significance of early Pennsylvania Dutch bakeovens.
Presents excerpts from local 19th-century newspapers
and information obtained from 6 informants about the
use of bakeovens and their products, together with 2
folk stories, 2 anecdotes, more than 25 folk beliefs,
1 saying, 2 rhymes, and 4 riddles (all from printed
sources). Illustrated with 19 photographs.

GE362 Long, Amos, Jr. "Bank (Multi-Level) Structures in
Rural Pennsylvania." *Pennsylvania Folklife* 20:2
(Winter 1970-71):31-39.

Discussion of the history and variety of bank houses
(illustrated with 15 photographs), including barns,
houses, spring houses, icehouses, and root cellars.

GE363 Long, Amos, Jr. "Chickens and Chicken Houses in
Rural Pennsylvania." *Pennsylvania Folklife* 18:3
(Spring 1969):34-43.

Description of the role of chickens in rural 19th-
century Pennsylvania Dutch farm life, including information on their housing (illustrated with 10 photographs and 2 sketches), care and feeding, and egg
production. Importance of chickens to farming illustrated by rhymes (5), riddles (9), jokes (1), folk
beliefs (5), folk cures (52) having chickens as their
subject.

GE364 Long, Amos, Jr. "Dry Houses in the Pennsylvania Folk-
Culture." *Pennsylvania Folklife* 13:2 (Winter 1962-
1963):16-23.

Discussion of the origin, structure, and uses of the
dry house on Pennsylvania Dutch farms and alternative
methods of drying. Provides firsthand accounts from
9 informants about dry houses that once existed on
their farms and from 2 informants about dry houses
still standing, especially among the Amish and Mennonites of Lancaster County. Includes 7 photographs of
dry houses.

GE365   Long, Amos, Jr. "Dutch Country Scarecrows." *Pennsyl-
         vania Folklife* 12:3 (Fall 1961):55-59.

         Discussion of the role of the scarecrow on Pennsylvania
         Dutch farms, based, in part, on reports from over 10
         informants, 3 anecdotes, 8 stories, and 2 folk beliefs.
         Notes other methods for keeping birds away. Includes
         3 photographs of scarecrows.

GE366   Long, Amos, Jr. "Fences in Rural Pennsylvania."
         Pennsylvania Folklife 12:2 (Summer 1961):30-35.

         Description of types of fences and their common uses
         on Pennsylvania Dutch farms. Provides reasons for
         the decline in the use of fences. Includes 7 photo-
         graphs of various fence types.

GE367   Long, Amos, Jr. "Grout-Kootch, Coldframe and Hotbed."
         Pennsylvania Folklife 13:4 (July 1964):21-27.

         Description of various types of frames used for grow-
         ing vegetables, especially cabbage. Includes reports
         from more than 20 informants concerning their child-
         hood remembrances of such frames. Also includes
         section on planting lore, including 15 folk beliefs
         drawn from the Pennsylvania Folklife Society files
         and from Fogel's book *Beliefs and Superstitions of
         the Pennsylvania Germans*. Includes 12 photographs
         of frames.

GE368   Long, Amos, Jr. "The Ice-House in Pennsylvania."
         Pennsylvania Folklife 14:4 (Summer 1965):47-55.

         Discussion of the history, structure, and uses of
         icehouses and of the ice harvesting process, with
         reports from 11 informants of their experiences with
         dangerous ice-waters. Includes 11 photographs of
         icehouses and ice tools.

GE369   Long, Amos, Jr. "Outdoor Privies in the Dutch Country."
         Pennsylvania Folklife 13:3 (July 1963):33-38.

         Description of the role of outhouses in Pennsylvania
         Dutch culture, including information on their struc-
         ture, design, decorative motifs, methods of going to
         the outhouse, and other uses to which the privies
         were put. Section on privy lore includes 7 anecdotes,
         3 folk beliefs, and 1 prank. Notes continued but
         waning use of privies. Includes 9 photographs.

GE370   Long, Amos, Jr. "Pennsylvania Cave and Ground Cellars."
        Pennsylvania Folklife 11:2 (Fall 1960):36-41.

        Description of various kinds of ground cellars and
        their uses for storing and preserving foods. Presents
        reports from 2 informants who remember having been in
        such cellars during their childhood. Includes 8
        photographs of cellars, particularly those of a farm
        house in Lebanon County.

GE371   Long, Amos, Jr. "Pennsylvania Corncribs." *Pennsyl-
        vania Folklife* 14:1 (October 1964):17-23.

        Discussion of the history, structure, design, and
        function of corncribs and other activities related to
        the uses of corn. Refers to festive gatherings at
        corn husking time and to stories (4) of outwitting
        corncrib thieves (recorded from 4 informants) and 1
        custom related to stacking ears of corn. Includes 12
        photographs of corncribs.

GE372   Long, Amos, Jr. "Pennsylvania Limekilns." *Pennsyl-
        vania Folklife* 15:3 (Spring 1966):24-37.

        Discussion of the history and nature of the early
        Pennsylvania lime industry, based on an analysis of
        existing limekilns and conversations with knowledge-
        able individuals. Topics discussed include limekiln
        design, quarrying and transporting lime, and commercial
        lime-burning. Reports from 3 individuals who worked
        on limekilns, with consideration of the pros and cons
        of using lime. Concludes with a section on folk
        remedies using lime, with mention of 8 such remedies.
        Includes 18 photographs of various limekilns, 1 of
        an informant, and 2 sketches of limekiln dimensions.

GE373   Long, Amos, Jr. "Pennsylvania Summer-Houses and
        Summer-Kitchens." *Pennsylvania Folklife* 15:1
        (Autumn 1965):10-19.

        Discussion of the history and structure of 18th- and
        19th-century summer houses, including information on
        building measurements and construction techniques,
        objects found in such rooms, and functions served by
        such rooms besides that of providing a place in which
        to prepare, serve, and eat meals. Includes 18 photo-
        graphs of summer houses.

GE374   Long, Amos, Jr. "Pigpens and Piglore in Rural Pennsyl-
        vania." *Pennsylvania Folklife* 19:2 (Winter 1970):
        19-33.

        Discussion of the role of pigs on Pennsylvania Dutch
        farms and comments on the care, feeding, and housing
        of these animals. Speculates on reasons for the
        decline in pork production in the late 1800s. Provides
        examples of various types of pig lore, such as sayings
        (7), rhymes (5), tales (6), folk beliefs (over 40),
        folk cures (25), and customs (7). Includes 18 photo-
        graphs of pigpens.

GE375   Long, Amos, Jr. "Pumps, Rams, Windmills and Water
        Wheels in Rural Pennsylvania." *Pennsylvania Folk-
        life* 17:3 (Spring 1968):28-40.

        Review of methods used to obtain and maintain water
        from the ground on Pennsylvania Dutch farms in the
        early 19th century. Includes sections on pumps, wells,
        rams (with statements from 5 informants about their use),
        windmills, watermills, and methods of divining water
        used by dowsers. Includes 18 photographs and sketches.

GE376   Long, Amos, Jr. "The Rural Village." *Pennsylvania
        Folklife* 29:3 (Spring 1980):124-132.

        Description of the settlement, chief sources of
        revenue, forms of entertainment, naming practices,
        architectural styles, types of buildings, churches,
        gardens, and yards in the rural village. Notes that
        rural village life is on the rise despite the trend
        toward urbanization. Includes 6 photographs of
        village architecture.

GE377   Long, Amos, Jr. "Smokehouses in the Lebanon Valley."
        Pennsylvania Folklife 13:1 (Fall 1962):24-32.

        Description of the structure and uses of smokehouses,
        including processes of curing, smoking, and ventilating
        meat and substitutes for smoking. Concludes with over
        20 short stories concerning early smokehouses and the
        raiding of them and thefts of their contents. Pre-
        sents reasons for the decline of smokehouses. Includes
        14 photographs.

GE378   Long, Amos, Jr. "Springs and Springhouses." *Pennsyl-
        vania Folklife* 11:1 (Spring 1960):40-43.

Notes the importance for pioneer families of homes
built along part of a spring. Describes types of
houses built, their multiple uses, and reasons for
their eventual demise. Includes 5 photographs.

GE379   Long, Amos, Jr. "The Woodshed." *Pennsylvania Folk-
        life* 16:2 (Winter 1966-1967):38-45.

Description of the history and uses of woodsheds and
of the processes of cutting, transporting, storing,
and burning wood in the home for heat and cooking.
Includes reports from over 10 informants about the
tasks of obtaining wood and the importance of wood
in the folklife of rural Pennsylvania Dutch culture.

*GE380 Lund, Jens. "The Legend of the King and the Star."

        (Cross-listed as *DA6, *IT43, *JE44.)
        (See *JE44 for full citation and annotation.)

GE381   McDonald, Frank E. "Pennsylvania German Tombstone
        Art in Lebanon County, Pennsylvania." *Pennsylvania
        Folklife* 25:1 (Autumn 1975):2-19.

Discussion of tombstones found in 91 cemeteries in
Lebanon County, with detailed charts and illustrations
of dominant motifs found in each cemetery, the composition of the stones, and tombstone styles. Discusses
changes during the 18th and 19th centuries and considers the debate over the origin of particular motifs.
Includes 11 photographs, 14 sketches of tombstones and
markers, 12 distributional maps, 3 figures representing
variant motifs, and an index to the cemeteries studied.

GE382   "Mahantongo Humor.... Recorded from Willy Brown."
        Pennsylvania Dutchman 4:2 (June 1952):2.

Listing of 6 jokes (in German, with English translations).

GE383   Mankin, Carolyn. "Tales the German Texans Tell." In
        Singers and Storytellers, edited by Mody C. Boat-
        right, Wilson M. Hudson, and Allen Maxwell, pp. 260-
        265. *Publications of the Texas Folklore Society* 30
        (1961).

Characterization (in English) of 10 tales told to the
author by German immigrant informants from Dallas.
Includes stories about Frederick the Great and about
mines in Germany.

*GE384   Martens, Helen. "The Music of Some Religious
         Minorities in Canada." *Ethnomusicology* 16:3 (1972):
         360-371.

         Brief characterization of the music and songs recorded
         from Mennonites, Hutterites, and Doukhobors in Canada.
         National backgrounds of these peoples cited as German,
         Russian, Dutch, Swiss, and Austrian. Presents examples
         of 4 songs/hymns (with musical transcriptions) and a
         text of 1 Mennonite song (in a Mennonite dialect, with
         English translation).
         (Cross-listed as *AU2, *DU13, *RU14, *SW6.)

*GE385   "Maryland Superstitions."

         (Cross-listed as *FR80.)
         (See *FR80 for full citation and annotation.)

 GE386   Master, Marie. "The Cat's at the 'Dippy.'" *Pennsyl-*
         vania Dutchman 5:10 (15 January 1954):2.

         Listing of 7 folktales, 2 of which involve preachers
         and 3 eating.

*GE387   Mead, Jane Thompson. "Proverbs: Sayings from West-
         field, Chautauqua Co."

         (Cross-listed as *IR67, *WE8.)
         (See *IR67 for full citation and annotation.)

 GE388   Meade, Alma B. "Fianna the Dunkard." *Pennsylvania*
         Folklife 12:4 (Summer 1962):38-48.

         Author's memories of her "plain" Dunkard grandmother
         (1847-1930), with the role of religious folk beliefs
         as the central focus. Sections include information
         about magic, buried treasure, haunted houses, Christmas
         customs, foodways, and church services in Lancaster,
         Lebanon, and Berks counties.

 GE389   Meyer, T.P. "County Funerals and Mortuary Customs
         of Long Ago." *The Pennsylvania-German* 9:ix (Septem-
         ber 1908):403-407.

         Presentation of the author's childhood remembrances
         from the 1850s of funeral customs in eastern Pennsyl-
         vania, including information on coffin making,
         mortuary practices, burial processions, and the role
         of illness in the community.

GE390 Meyer, T.P. "Grandmother Home Remedies." *The Pennsylvania-German* 10:vi (June 1909):272-278.

Account of home remedies used in eastern Centre County after 1774. Description of physical healing methods employing roots. Division of roots into 28 categories, with description of how they were used.

GE391 "Mifflin County Folk Beliefs." *Pennsylvania Dutchman* 2:22 (15 April 1951):8.

Presentation of 2 folk beliefs, one concerning a pregnant woman, the other a newborn baby.

GE392 Miller, Daniel K. "Tin Peddlers and Scouring Day." *Pennsylvania Dutchman* 5:12 (15 February 1954):9.

Reminiscences about tin peddlers who brought household utensils from house to house in Birdsboro and southern Berks County before the turn of the century. Notes methods of cleaning and repairing tin.

GE393 Milnes, Humphrey. "German Folklore in Ontario." *Journal of American Folklore* 67:263 (1954):35-43.

Brief historical sketch of the settlement in Waterloo County, Ontario, Canada, of German immigrants and their descendants, followed by a sampling of the kinds of folklore still available for collecting. Includes texts of 9 proverbial expressions (in German, with English translations), 2 field-recorded and 1 reprinted anecdotes (in English), 2 poems (in German, with English translations), 1 prayer (in German), and 5 songs (with tune transcriptions, 3 in German with English translations).

GE394 Milspaw, Yvonne J. "Witchcraft Belief in a Pennsylvania German Family." *Pennsylvania Folklife* 27:4 (Summer 1978):14-24.

Study of 3 generations of faith healers in Dauphin County, Pennsylvania, based on interviews with 7 informants that focused on the degree of belief in witchcraft (*hexerei*). Hypothesizes and confirms that succeeding generations deny power of witchcraft, in part because of embarrassment due to one who was accused of murdering through witchcraft. Notes that contemporary generation seeks to introduce powers of witchcraft as a result of the popularity of the occult, but states that emphasis is now on healing rather than

on harming. Includes 1 photograph of a powwow manuscript, 1 family tree diagram of powwow practitioners,
and 1 reproduction of the title page of Hohman's
The Long Lost Friend.

GE395   Montgomery, Morton L. "Games of Reading in Last
         Century." *Pennsylvania Dutchman* 1:17 (25 August
         1949):2.

         Description of games popular in Reading in the 19th
         century, including "Leap-Frog," "Shinney," "Pitching
         Buttons," "Throwing Knives," and "Cracking the Whip."

GE396   Mook, Maurice. "Nicknames among the Amish." *Keystone
         Folklore Quarterly* 5:4 (1960):3–12.

         Discussion of kinds of nicknames and nicknaming
         practices common among the Amish of Lancaster and
         Mifflin counties, Pennsylvania.

GE397   Mook, Maurice A. "The Big Valley Amish of Central
         Pennsylvania: A Community of Cultural Contrasts."
         Pennsylvania Folklife 26:2 (Winter 1976–1977):30–33.

         Notes that Amish of the Big Valley in central Pennsyl-
         vania (Mifflin County) are not homogeneous. Cultural
         differences exist not only between Old Order and New
         Order Amish, but also among Old Order groups. Varia-
         tions in custom followed due to the traditions of
         each bishop. Includes 1 map.

GE398   Mook, Maurice A. "Bread Baking in Mifflin County,
         Pennsylvania: Commentary for the Documentary Film
         in the 'Encyclopedia Cinematographica.'" *Pennsyl-
         vania Folklife* 21:2 (1971):42–45.

         Interspersed with comments on bread-making film made
         in 1965 is a description of traditional vs. present-
         day bread-making practices and various occasions for
         their use. Includes 2 recipes for white bread and 3
         sayings regarding the importance of bread in Pennsyl-
         vania Dutch culture. Includes 2 photographs of bread-
         making.

GE399   Mook, Maurice A., ed. "The Changing Pattern of
         Pennsylvania German Culture, 1855–1955: A Panel
         Discussion." *Pennsylvania History* 23 (1956):311–339.

         Presentation of individual essays on changes in
         Pennsylvania German culture, with emphasis on family

life and recreation, language, church life and work,
the Mennonites and the Amish, and arts and crafts.

GE400   Mook, Maurice A. "Nicknames among the Amish."
        Pennsylvania Folklife 17:4 (Summer 1968):20-23.

        Discussion of the nature and variety of nicknames
        among the Amish of Lancaster and Mifflin counties.
        Enumerates 8 criteria for choosing nicknames, in-
        cluding geography, occupation, physical and behavioral
        characteristics, and notable events in which the indi-
        vidual participated. Includes 1 photograph and 1
        painting depicting Amish life.

GE401   Mook, Maurice A. "Old Fashioned Bread Baking in Rural
        Pennsylvania." *'S Pennsylvaanish Deitsch Eck*, 19
        February 1966.

        Text of a script for a film on bread baking, made in
        Mifflin County in 1965. Includes discussion of the
        importance of bread baking, methods used, and a well-
        known baker (subject of the film).

GE402   Moore, George L. "Dunkard Life in Lebanon Valley
        Sixty Years Ago." *Pennsylvania Folklife* 12:1
        (Spring 1961):10-23.

        Description of various aspects of cultural life of
        the Dunkards, including information on meeting-house
        architecture, plain dress, and funeral customs. In-
        cludes drawings of 6 meeting houses, 1 of a loaf of
        communion bread, and 1 map of Lebanon Valley.

GE403   Moore, George L. "My Childhood Games." *Pennsylvania
        Folklife* 13:4 (July 1964):42-57.

        Reprint from author's memoirs of his childhood memories
        of life in Lebanon Valley, especially of the games
        played. Includes enumeration of games organized into
        46 categories, with 11 sketches indicating how selected
        games were played.

GE404   Moore, George L. "My Mother's Kitchen." *Pennsyl-
        vania Folklife* 13:1 (Fall 1962):9-12.

        Author's reminiscences of his childhood, especially
        of the family kitchen and its objects, such as the
        stove, table, and sewing machine (illustrated with
        4 sketches).

GE405   Moore, George L. "Weather Rhymes." *Pennsylvania
        Dutchman* 2:11 (1 November 1950):2.

        Listing of 6 traditional rhymes concerning the weather
        (in German, with English translations), recorded in
        Lebanon County.

GE406   Moser, Esther. "Dutch Folksay." *Pennsylvania Dutchman*
        5:9 (1 January 1954):15.

        Presentation of 7 folk sayings (in German, with indica-
        tions in English as to appropriate contexts for use).

GE407   Moser, Helen J. "Couple of Riddles and a Dutch Rhyme."
        Pennsylvania Dutchman 3:22 (15 April 1952):2, 5.

        Listing of 2 riddles (in German, 1 with English trans-
        lation).

GE408   Moser, Helen J. "Riddles." *Pennsylvania Dutchman*
        4:7 (November 1952):11.

        Listing of 3 riddles (in German, with English transla-
        tions).

GE409   Moser, Helen J. "Riddles." *Pennsylvania Dutchman*
        5:14 (15 March 1954):15.

        Listing of 7 riddles (in German, with English transla-
        tions).

GE410   Mueller, Esther L. "Log Cabins to Sunday Houses." In
        Diamond Bessie & The Shepherds, edited by Wilson M.
        Hudson, pp. 51-59. *Publications of the Texas Folk-
        lore Society* 36 (1972).

        Discussion of the arrival of German immigrants in the
        Fredericksburg, Texas, area in 1846 and of their settle-
        ment in central Texas. Emphasis on the building and
        use of in-town "Sunday houses," which the immigrants
        and their families utilized as temporary day-long or
        overnight residences when they came to town to attend
        Sunday church services, to shop or trade, or to receive
        medical treatment. Notes that most Sunday houses have
        now been transformed into permanent residences since
        the introduction of good roads and automobiles no
        longer makes the trip into town and back home difficult
        for rural families.

GE411   Mumaw, John R. "Mennonite Folklore." *Pennsylvania*
        Folklife 11:1 (Spring 1960):38-39.

        Excerpts from the author's 1931 M.A. thesis on Pennsyl-
        vania German folklore in Wayne County, Ohio. Includes
        5 proverbs (in German, with English translations), 11
        folk beliefs, 2 riddles (in German, with English
        translations), 6 customs, 2 folktales (in German, with
        English translations), and 6 rhymes (in German, with
        English translations).

GE412   Murtagh, William J. "Half-Timbering in American
        Architecture." *Pennsylvania Folklife* 9:1 (Winter
        1957-58):3-11.

        Discussion of the use of half-timber construction
        (illustrated with 5 photographs) among early Pennsyl-
        vania Dutch immigrants and the disappearance of such
        housing among later generations. Also compares the
        half-timber method used in Pennsylvania with that
        common elsewhere.

GE413   Myers, Anna Balmer. "The Dutch Touch." *Pennsylvania*
        Dutchman 5:11 (1 February 1954):14-15.

        Reprint of a 1929 essay concerning the combination of
        old and new elements in Pennsylvania Dutch folklife.
        Includes a listing of 8 sayings.

GE414   Myers, George H. "Folk Cures." *Pennsylvania Dutch-*
        man 5:9 (1 January 1954):10.

        Presentation from 4 Lehigh County informants of 18
        folk cures, together with an example of a cure for
        styes known to the author.

GE415   Neifert, William W. "Witchcraft." *The Pennsylvania-*
        German 9:iii (March 1908):114-121.

        General discussion of the efficacy of witchcraft,
        with emphasis on practitioners and reasons for their
        popularity. Includes 3 hexing charms and 17 powwowing
        cures.

*GE416 Nettl, Bruno. "The Hymns of the Amish: An Example of
        Marginal Survival." *Journal of American Folklore*
        70 (1957):323-328.

        Notes that the music of Amish hymns illustrates that
        folklore may be better preserved in immigrant communi-

ties than in places from which individuals emigrate.
Distinctiveness and antiquity of Amish hymns noted
as being due to style of singing, tempo, and rhythmic
complexity. Includes 3 sample musical transcriptions.
(Cross-listed as *SW7.)

GE417 "New Year's Eve in the Olden Time." *Pennsylvania
       Dutchman* 11:1 (1 January 1951):1.

       Reprinting from an 1882 publication of 2 descriptions
       of a New Year's Eve shooting practice, one involving
       an exchange of wishes between hosts and guests.

GE418 "A New Year's Wish for a Young Girl." *Pennsylvania
       Dutchman* 3:15 (1 January 1952):7.

       Example of a New Year's Eve wish (in German, with
       English translation), taken from an old manuscript
       in the Unger collection.

GE419 Newell, W.W. "Tales of the Blue Mountains in
       Pennsylvania." *Journal of American Folk-Lore* 11:40
       (1898):76-78.

       Summaries of 3 tales about fairies as mountain dwellers
       and a belief in witchcraft and magic, with 2 of the
       tales noted as being German in origin. Refers to Rip-
       van-Winkle-types of stories of the Pennsylvania Germans
       and urges recording these examples of Blue Mountain
       folklore while they still survive.

GE420 Newell, William H. "Schuylkill Folktales." *Pennsyl-
       vania Folklife* 9:3 (Summer 1958):18-19.

       Presentation of 12 folktales, recorded from informants
       in Schuylkill County and pertaining to bewitchment
       and farming. Includes 2 sketches of themes depicted
       in the stories.

GE421 Nielson, George R. "Folklore of the German-Wends in
       Texas." In *Singers and Storytellers*, edited by
       Mody C. Boatright, Wilson M. Hudson, and Allen
       Maxwell, pp. 244-259. *Publications of the Texas
       Folklore Society* 30 (1961).

       Brief historical sketch of the Wends and their emigra-
       tion from Germany to Texas in 1854, followed by a
       miscellany of their lore. Includes descriptions of
       15 cures, 1 healing verse (in German, with English
       translation), 8 sayings, 2 ways to prevent theft of

farm animals, 5 personal experience narratives, and
miscellaneous beliefs and customs relating to marriage,
death, Easter, and planting. Distinguishes between
lore perpetuated from the Old World and that developed
in Texas. Based on the author's experiences and interviews conducted in 1958-59.

GE422   Nitzsche, George E. "The Christmas Putz of the Pennsyl-
        vania Germans." The Pennsylvania German Society,
        Yearbook, Section I, 6 (1941):3-28.

Description of Pennsylvania German Christmas nativity
scenes, based on the author's childhood experiences in
Nazareth, Pennsylvania, and on interviews with over 10
informants from Bethlehem, Pennsylvania. Relates *putz*
to the Moravian religion and other aspects of the
Christmas celebration. Argues that although *putz* is
found among other peoples, it can be considered a
traditional Pennsylvania Dutch phenomenon. Includes
16 plates depicting *putzes* from individual homes and
churches in 1941.

GE423   Noll, Ronald W. "Cemetery Tale." *Pennsylvania
        Dutchman* 3:7 (1 September 1951):1, 4.

Recounting of a story told to the author by his
father and grandfather about fear being instilled in
one when he passed a cemetery and overheard a conversation that was presumed to be between God and the
devil.

*GE424 Norlin, Ethel Todd. "Present-Day Superstitions at
        La Harpe, Ill., Survivals in a Community of English
        Origin."

        (Cross-listed as *DU14, *FR88, *IR78, *SC30.)
        (See *IR78 for full citation and annotation.)

GE425   Novak, Anton. "A Few Words About Fraktur." *Canadian-
        German Folklore* 1 (1961):101-102.

Brief history of the introduction of fraktur into
Pennsylvania Dutch folk art, with 2 photographs of
fraktur examples.

GE426   Olsen, Louise P. "Signs and Omens." *Western Folklore*
        9:3 (1950):267-268.

Summaries of 7 personal experience stories involving
signs and omens of impending or near-death, including

unusual sounds, glimpses of the dead, lightning, and
feelings portending death, elicited from a Minnesota
woman of German background in 1949.

GE427   Owens, J.G.   "Folk-Lore from Buffalo Valley, Central
        Pennsylvania." *Journal of American Folk-Lore* 4
        (1891):115-128.

        General description of frontier life among immigrant
        settlers in the 1700s (including comments on foodways
        and harvesting), followed by a listing of superstitions
        of the Pennsylvania Dutch. Includes moon lore (22),
        omens (20), weather signs (18), wart causes and cures
        (5), cures (15), witch lore (18), and stories associated
        with powwowing (2).

*GE428 Peacock, Kenneth. "Establishing Perimeters for Ethno-
        musicological Field Research in Canada: On-Going
        Projects and Future Possibilities at the Canadian
        Centre for Folk Culture Studies."

        (Cross-listed as *GL66, *CH21, *FR91, *HU25, *IC4,
        *ID2, *IT57, *JA9, *LI5, *NO19, *RU19, *UK32.)
        (See *GL66 for full citation and annotation.)

*GE429 Peacock, Kenneth. *Twenty Ethnic Songs from Western
        Canada.*

        (Cross-listed as *CZ10, *HU26, *RU21, *UK33.)
        (See *RU21 for full citation and annotation.)

GE430   "Pennsylvania Dutch Humor." *Pennsylvania Dutchman*
        5:4 (August 1953):8-9.

        Reprinting from 1824-1886 newspapers of 18 anecdotes.

GE431   "Pennsylvania Jests." *Pennsylvania Dutchman* 3:3
        (1 June 1951):2.

        Reprinting from 1876-1880 magazines of 6 jokes
        depicting the Pennsylvania Dutchman in a humorous
        light.

GE432   Pitchon, Miriam. "Widows' Wills for Philadelphia
        County, 1750-1784: A Study of Pennsylvania German
        Folklife." *Pennsylvania Folklife* 26:1 (Fall 1976):
        19-26.

        From an examination of wills of 19 widows who lived
        in Philadelphia County from 1750 to 1784, author obtained

and presents information on property rights, religion, education, slavery, dress, kitchens, furnishings, foodstuffs, and the production of cloth.

GE433 Pocius, Gerald L. "Veterinary Folk Medicine in Susquehanna County, Pennsylvania." *Pennsylvania Folklife* 25:4 (Summer 1976):2-15.

Argues that the study of animal folk healing practices is an important supplement to the study of human healing in that it helps one understand the nature of community cooperation, the role of animals, the value of traditional faith healing, and changing farming practices. Focuses on "cow" men and their evaluations of their roles as reported in interviews. Includes 4 photographs of informants, 2 sketches of curing and 2 of title pages from well-known healing books.

GE434 "Proverbs." *Pennsylvania Dutchman* 1:7 (16 June 1949): 2.

Listing of 6 proverbs (in German, with English translations), recorded from an informant in Lititz, Pennsylvania.

GE435 "Proverbs." *Pennsylvania Dutchman* 1:23 (February 1950):2.

Listing of 4 proverbs (in German, with English translations), submitted by a correspondent from Schenectady, New York.

GE436 "Proverbs." *Pennsylvania Dutchman* 1:24 (March 1950):2.

Listing of 5 proverbs (in German, with English translations).

GE437 "Proverbs." *Pennsylvania Dutchman* 1:25 (April 1950):3.

Listing of 5 proverbs (in German, with English translations), contributed by a woman from Coopersburg, Lehigh County.

GE438 "Proverbs." *Pennsylvania Dutchman* 1:26 (1 May 1950):2.

Listing of 4 proverbs (in German, with English translations), 1 of which is accompanied by an illustration.

GE439 "Proverbs." *Pennsylvania Dutchman* 2:5 (July 1950):2.

Listing of 5 proverbs (in German, with English translations), contributed by a Berks County informant.

GE440   Rahn, Rev. Clarence R. "Pennsylvania German Humor."
        In *Intimate Glimpses of the Pennsylvania Germans*,
        edited by Homer Tope Rosenberger, pp. 43-54.
        Gettysburg: The Pennsylvania German Society, 1966.

        Presentation of 12 jokes (in English, with original
        German) containing a cross section of typical types
        of Pennsylvania German humor. Discussion of categories
        of humor and functions of the jokes, especially for
        Pennsylvania Dutch who adhere to either the Lutheran
        or the Reformed faith.

GE441   Raichelson, Richard. "The Social Context of Musical
        Instruments within the Pennsylvania German Culture."
        Pennsylvania Folklife 25:1 (Autumn 1975):35-44.

        Reconstruction of the contexts in which dancings were
        held and musical instruments were used among the
        Pennsylvania Germans during the 18th and 19th centuries.
        Includes 2 photographs of dancing, 5 of musical instru-
        ments, and a bibliography of more than 50 entries.

GE442   Rauchle, Bob. "Reminiscences from the Germantown
        Settlement in Gibson County, Tennessee." *Tennessee
        Folklore Society Bulletin* 45:2 (1979):62-67.

        Reminiscences of an 81-year-old woman of German descent
        from Gibson County, Tennessee, an area inhabited by
        German immigrants since the 1880s. Includes 6 personal
        experience narratives, 4 superstitions, and 4 examples
        of practical jokes.

GE443   Reagan, William A. "The Blacksmith and His Tools."
        Pennsylvania Folklife 17:2 (Winter 1967-1968):27-29.

        Discussion of blacksmithing in the 17th and 18th
        centuries among the Pennsylvania Dutch. Presents a
        listing of 18 tools used by blacksmiths and statements
        concerning their use. Illustrated by over 50 drawings
        of tools, with Pennsylvania Dutch names.

GE444   Reimensnyder, Barbara. "Annotated Bibliography of
        Pennsylvania Folk Medicine." *Pennsylvania Folklife*
        27:1 (Fall 1977):40-48.

        Annotated bibliography of over 180 entries on folk
        medicine in Pennsylvania, with summary of existing
        data and suggestions for future research.

GE445   "Reminiscences of Belsnickling." *Pennsylvania Dutch-
        man* 3:14 (15 December 1951):1, 3.

        Reminiscences from 1895 of a 65-year-old man concerning
        the practice of belsnickling. Compares the jovial
        atmosphere of the practice in Berks County, where
        teenagers dressed in costumes, carried switches, and
        threw chestnuts while visiting house to house, with the
        seriousness of the Quakers and Amish. Compares night
        activities involving the contemporary Santa Claus with
        the daytime activities involving Belsnickel.

*GE446 Rennick, Robert M. "Successive Name-Changing: A
        Popular Theme in Onomastic Folklore and Literature."

        (Cross-listed as *JE52, *SC35, *YU10.)
        (See *JE52 for full citation and annotation.)

GE447   Rhoads, Collier. "Pennsylvania German Groundhog
        Lodges." *Keystone Folklore Quarterly* 5:1-2 (1960):
        7-9.

        Brief general discussion (reprinted from a newspaper)
        of groundhog lodge suppers held annually by Pennsyl-
        vania Germans in late January or early February.
        Includes brief mention of foods eaten and songs sung
        (by titles only) and an enumeration of existing lodges.

GE448   "Riddles." *Pennsylvania Dutchman* 1:3 (19 May 1949):2.

        Listing of 6 riddles (in German, with English transla-
        tions), from a contributor from Berks County.

GE449   "Riddles." *Pennsylvania Dutchman* 1:4 (26 May 1949):2.

        Listing of 6 riddles (in German, with English transla-
        tions), from a contributor from Reinholds, Pennsylvania.

GE450   "Riddles." *Pennsylvania Dutchman* 1:5 (2 June 1949):2.

        Listing of 5 riddles (in German, with English transla-
        tions), from a contributor from Berks County.

GE451   "Riddles." *Pennsylvania Dutchman* 1:6 (9 June 1949):2.

        Listing of 6 riddles (in German, with English transla-
        tions), from a contributor from Reading, Pennsylvania.

GE452   "Riddles." *Pennsylvania Dutchman* 1:7 (16 June 1949):2.

        Listing of 5 riddles (in German, with English transla-
        tions), from contributors from Bethel and Lititz,
        Pennsylvania.

GE453   "Riddles." *Pennsylvania Dutchman* 1:9 (30 June 1949):2.

Listing of 7 riddles (in English, with German translations), from contributors in Lititz and New Ringgold, Pennsylvania.

GE454   "Riddles." *Pennsylvania Dutchman* 1:10 (7 July 1949):2.

Listing of 5 riddles, from a manuscript of William P. Shoemaker of Maple Grove, Pennsylvania.

GE455   "Riddles." *Pennsylvania Dutchman* 1:11 (14 July 1949): 2.

Listing of 6 riddles (in English, with German translations), from a manuscript of William P. Shoemaker of Maple Grove, Pennsylvania.

GE456   "Riddles." *Pennsylvania Dutchman* 1:12 (21 July 1949): 2.

Listing of 6 riddles (in English, with German translations), from a contributor from Reinholds, Pennsylvania.

GE457   "Riddles." *Pennsylvania Dutchman* 1:13 (28 July 1949): 2.

Listing of 5 riddles (in German, with English translations), from a contributor from Bally, Pennsylvania.

GE458   "Riddles." *Pennsylvania Dutchman* 1:14 (4 August 1949): 2.

Listing of 3 riddles (in English, with German translations), from a contributor from Reading, Pennsylvania.

GE459   "Riddles." *Pennsylvania Dutchman* 1:15 (11 August 1949):2.

Listing of 4 riddles (in German, with English translations), from a contributor from Allentown, Pennsylvania.

GE460   "Riddles." *Pennsylvania Dutchman* 1:16 (18 August 1949):2.

Listing of 4 riddles (in German, with English translations), from a contributor from Tamaqua, Pennsylvania.

GE461   "Riddles." *Pennsylvania Dutchman* 1:17 (25 August 1949):2.

Listing of 6 riddles (in German, with English translations), from a contributor from Maple Grove, Pennsylvania.

GE462   "Riddles." *Pennsylvania Dutchman* 1:19 (15 September
        1949):2.

        Listing of 5 riddles (in English, with German transla-
        tions), from a contributor from Schenectady, New York.

GE463   "Riddles." *Pennsylvania Dutchman* 1:20 (November 1949):
        2.

        Listing of 6 riddles (in German, with English transla-
        tions), from an anonymous contributor from Middleburg,
        Pennsylvania.

GE464   "Riddles." *Pennsylvania Dutchman* 1:22 (January 1950):
        2.

        Listing of 4 riddles (in English, with German transla-
        tions), from a contributor from Berne, Pennsylvania.

GE465   "Riddles." *Pennsylvania Dutchman* 1:23 (February 1950):
        2.

        Listing of 5 riddles (in German, with English transla-
        tions), from contributors from Barto and Berne,
        Pennsylvania.

GE466   "Riddles." *Pennsylvania Dutchman* 1:24 (March 1950):2.

        Listing of 4 riddles (in German, with English transla-
        tions), from contributors from Palmyra and Reading,
        Pennsylvania.

GE467   "Riddles." *Pennsylvania Dutchman* 1:25 (April 1950):4.

        Listing of 2 riddles (in German, with English transla-
        tions), from a contributor from West Hamburg, Pennsyl-
        vania.

GE468   "Riddles." *Pennsylvania Dutchman* 5:13 (1 March 1954):
        15.

        Listing of 5 riddles (in German, with English transla-
        tions).

GE469   Riegel, Lewis Edgar. "Reminiscences of Centerport,
        1876-1885." *Pennsylvania Folklife* 14:2 (December
        1964):34-47.

        Recollections from girlhood of activities, customs,
        events, and personalities of Centerport, Berks County,
        Pennsylvania. Includes descriptions of Christmas,

New Year's customs, men's and women's clothing,
foodways, games, and characterization of changing
customs. Illustrated with 4 sketches.

GE470   Roan, Donald. "Deivels-Dreck (Asafoetida) Yesterday
        and Today." *Pennsylvania Folklife* 14:2 (December
        1964):30-33.

        Description of the asafoetida bag, its content and
        uses for humans and animals, and its role in the
        development of Pennsylvania Dutch folk medicine.
        Illustrated with 3 photographs.

GE471   Robacker, Earl F. "Antiques for Fancy and for Fun."
        Pennsylvania Dutchman 6:5 (Summer 1955):2-6.

        Description of folk art objects made "just for fancy,"
        that is, for ornamental rather than utilitarian
        purposes. Includes mention of various toys, Noah's
        Ark, miniature utensils, dolls and doll accessories.
        Illustrated with 12 photographs.

GE472   Robacker, Earl F. "Art in Christmas Cookies."
        Pennsylvania Dutchman 6:3 (Winter 1954-55):3-7.

        Discussion of the origin and design of Christmas
        cookie cutters and indication of their ages, based on
        types of designs, condition of the tin, and the solder-
        ing process used. Notes role of symbolism in folk art
        and motifs found in several kinds of objects. Illus-
        trated with 12 photographs of cookie molds.

GE473   Robacker, Earl F. "Basketry, A Pennsylvania Dutch
        Art." *Pennsylvania Dutchman* 7:2 (Fall 1955):2-5.

        Brief survey of Pennsylvania Dutch basketry as an
        example of a lost art. Includes information about
        the construction, form, materials, size, decoration,
        and motifs, with 11 accompanying photographs.

GE474   Robacker, Earl F. "Butter Molds." *Pennsylvania
        Dutchman* 6:1 (June 1954):6-8.

        Description of homemade molds used to imprint pats of
        butter with distinctive designs. Discusses variety
        of molds, ways of evaluating their quality, and 17th-
        and 18th-century origins of many molds described.
        Illustrated with 5 photographs.

GE475   Robacker, Earl F. "Christmas--Back Along." *Pennsyl-*
        vania Folklife 16:2 (Winter 1966-1967):2-13.

        Argues that there is no single Christmas tradition,
        but rather several among the Pennsylvania Dutch,
        depending on religious sect and locale. Provides
        specific examples of customs, foodways, folk characters,
        material objects, and Christmas decorations. Illus-
        trated with 22 photographs.

GE476   Robacker, Earl F. "Cutting for Fancy." *Pennsylvania*
        Folklife 10:2 (Fall 1959):2-10.

        Discussion of paper cutting art in terms of Pennsyl-
        vania Dutch themes, methods, functions, varieties,
        and artists. Includes 13 photographs of paper cuts.

GE477   Robacker, Earl F. "Dream in Dutchland." *New York*
        Folklore Quarterly 12:4 (1956):287-290.

        Discussion of the 3 major ethnic forces that impinged
        on Pennsylvania in the colonial period (English-Quaker,
        Swiss-German, and Scotch-Irish), of the effects of
        pressure toward greater acculturation on the Amish
        way of life, and of educational goals and potential
        of the Dutch village near Bethel, Pennsylvania.

GE478   Robacker, Earl F. "The Dutch Touch in Iron."
        Pennsylvania Dutchman 8:3 (Spring 1957):2-6.

        Description of tulip and heart motifs found on various
        kinds of ironwear. Argues that ironwear containing
        these motifs is distinctively Pennsylvania Dutch.
        Illustrated with 12 photographs.

GE479   Robacker, Earl F. "Knife, Fork, and Spoon: A Collec-
        tor's Problem." *Pennsylvania Folklife* 9:2
        (Spring 1958):28-33.

        Argues that cooking and eating utensils which are
        antiques must be considered in terms of the contexts
        for which they were designed, and these have changed
        in the Pennsylvania Dutch country over the years.
        Describes utensils and eating habits of the 17th-
        century Pennsylvania Dutch. Illustrated with 12
        photographs depicting 30 objects.

GE480   Robacker, Earl F. "Let's Talk About Slate." *Pennsylvania Folklife* 22:4 (Summer 1973):2-10.

        Discussion of slate used to create a myriad of objects
        and description of textures, motifs, and uses.
        Describes the slate industry, production, ornamentation, and function, especially in Carbon, Lehigh, and
        Northampton, Pennsylvania. Illustrated with 15
        photographs.

GE481   Robacker, Earl F. "Long Lost Friends." *New York
        Folklore Quarterly* 12:1 (1956):25-31.

        Discussion of the parallel traditions of *braucherei*
        (white magic) and *hexerei* (black magic) among the
        Pennsylvania Dutch, as evidenced particularly in
        weather lore. Includes 1 charm, 1 remedy, and 1
        weather sign.

GE482   Robacker, Earl F. "Major and Minor in Fractur."
        Pennsylvania Dutchman 7:3 (Winter 1956):2-7.

        Discussion of types of fraktur, occasions for production, motifs, and ways to determine age, with 18
        photographs of fraktur works.

GE483   Robacker, Earl F. "Of Cookies and Cooky Cutters."
        Pennsylvania Dutchman 4:8 (December 1952):5.

        Description of themes, shapes, materials, and use of
        cookie cutters from the author's own collection.
        Illustrated with photographs of 25 cookie cutters.

GE484   Robacker, Earl F. "The Paint-Decorated Furniture of
        the Pennsylvania Dutch." *Pennsylvania Folklife*
        13:1 (Fall 1962):2-8.

        Description of paint decoration techniques used on
        such furniture as chairs, dower chests, footstools,
        benches, and cabinets, which became popular in the
        late 18th and early 19th century. Discusses "unique"
        vs. "non-unique" aspects of Pennsylvania Dutch folk
        art. Illustrated with 19 photographs.

GE485   Robacker, Earl F. "Painted Tin or 'Tole.'" *Pennsylvania Dutchman* 6:4 (Spring 1955):2-7.

        Discussion of the controversy over the origin of
        toleware. Argues that some tinware is of Pennsylvania Dutch origin, and defends argument with examples

of Pennsylvania Dutch design and techniques. Includes 14 photographs showing 50 painted tin objects.

GE486　Robacker, Earl F. "The Peacock in Pennsylvania." *Pennsylvania Folklife* 11:1 (Spring 1960):10-16.

Discussion of the role of birds, especially the peacock, as a motif in Pennsylvania Dutch folk art. Includes 13 photographs of various objects with peacock motif.

GE487　Robacker, Earl F. "Pennsylvania Chalkware." *Pennsylvania Folklife* 9:3 (Summer 1958):2-7.

Discussion of the history, composition, and motifs of chalkware art among the Pennsylvania Dutch. Includes 12 photographs depicting a variety of objects and designs.

GE488　Robacker, Earl F. *Pennsylvania Dutch Stuff: A Guide to Country Antiques.* Philadelphia: University of Pennsylvania Press, 1944. Pp. 163.

Survey of Pennsylvania Dutch folk art categorized by type of object, such as specific pieces of furniture (chairs, beds, desks, etc.), utensils, kitchen objects, miniature toys, and ornamental objects. Includes 15 photographs.

GE489　Robacker, Earl F. "Pennsylvania Pewter and Pewterers." *Pennsylvania Folklife* 13:2 (Winter 1962-1963):2-6.

Discussion of the origins and continuities of pewtermaking in order to show American and Pennsylvania Dutch contributions to its development. Includes 6 photographs of pewter objects.

GE490　Robacker, Earl F. "Pennsylvania Redware." *Pennsylvania Folklife* 8:2 (Fall-Winter 1956-57):2-7.

Description (illustrated with 14 photographs showing 24 objects) of redware pottery, with discussion of production techniques, decoration, themes, and assessment of value.

GE491　Robacker, Earl F. "Piece-Patch Artistry." *Pennsylvania Folklife* 13:3 (July 1963):2-10.

Description of quilts made from scraps of dress material, with information on patterns, motifs, construction, function, variety, and quality vs. non-quality art. Identifies unique Pennsylvania Dutch quilt designs and quilts. Includes 19 photographs.

GE492   Robacker, Earl F. "The Rise of Interest in Folk Art." *Pennsylvania Folklife* 10:1 (Spring 1959):20-29.

Discussion of the rise of serious recognition of American folk art—including that of the Pennsylvania Dutch—from the founding of the first American museum of art in Charleston in 1773 to early 19th-century collectors and to authors whose works stimulated an interest in the subject. Includes 17 photographs of various objects.

GE493   Robacker, Earl F. "The Rise of Interest in Pennsylvania Dutch Antiques." *Pennsylvania Folklife* 8:1 (Summer 1956):18-22.

Bibliographical survey of important works that have brought greater attention to Pennsylvania Dutch antiques. Includes 8 photographs.

GE494   Robacker, Earl F. "The Shape of Food That Was." *Pennsylvania Folklife* 14:2 (December 1964):10-15.

Description of types of molds used to make foods and give them a distinctive flavor. Argues that the use of such molds among the Pennsylvania Dutch illustrates their penchant for decorating utilitarian objects. Includes 15 photographs showing 56 objects.

GE495   Robacker, Earl F. "The Sheen of Copper." *Pennsylvania Folklife* 14:1 (October 1964):10-15.

History of coppersmithing in America, with references to items suited to the Pennsylvania Dutch country and 13 photographs of copper objects.

GE496   Robacker, Earl F. "Spatterware." *Pennsylvania Dutchman* 6:2 (September 1954):2-4.

Demonstrates that table pottery commonly assumed to be of Pennsylvania Dutch origin has English roots and became known as Dutch because of its enormous popularity. Includes 9 photographs of objects and their designs.

GE497   Robacker, Earl F. "Stitching for Pretty." *Pennsylvania Folklife* 15:3 (Spring 1966):2-9.

Description of needlework popular in "past" generations, as found in such items as samplers, towels, pillow cases, pin cushions, and friendship quilts. Hints at the possibility of designating a style of needlework as Pennsylvania Dutch. Includes 19 photographs.

GE498   Robacker, Earl F. "Stoneware--Stepchild of Early Pottery." *Pennsylvania Folklife* 13:4 (July 1964): 3-7.

Discussion of the evolution of pottery from redware to stoneware in the 18th century. Describes basic characteristics of stoneware and methods of production and design. Gives reasons for the discontinuation of stoneware use. Includes 12 photographs showing 22 stoneware objects.

GE499   Robacker, Earl F. "Tin--With Holes In." *Pennsylvania Folklife* 12:1 (Spring 1961):2-7.

Survey of objects made with tin and pierced or punched, such as pie cupboards, cheese molds, and coffee pots. Description of techniques and motifs used, as well as a disclaimer of certain tinware objects as being particularly Pennsylvania Dutch. Includes 14 photographs of objects made with tin.

GE500   Robacker, Earl F. "The Township Weavers of Pennsylvania." *Pennsylvania Folklife* 12:2 (Summer 1961):3-7.

Discussion of the history, function, construction techniques, and design of woven bed covers, with 11 photographs.

GE501   Robacker, Earl F. "Victorian Wall Mottoes." *Pennsylvania Folklife* 23:3 (Spring 1974):2-10.

Discussion of difficulty of determining pure ethnic origin of any aspect of material culture. Illustrates the origin of wall mottoes by surveying their style, themes, and construction techniques. Includes 21 photographs of wall mottoes.

GE502   Robacker, Earl F. "The Winding Road to Stick Spatter." *Pennsylvania Folklife* 20:1 (Autumn 1970):16-22.

Description of processes of making spatterware and of the variety of designs that have become popular since

1960. Spatterware considered in the class of objects which have a foreign origin, but which have been adopted by the Pennsylvania Dutch and have come to be considered by others to be Pennsylvania Dutch. Includes 18 photographs showing 44 spatterware objects.

GE503   Robacker, Earl F. and Ada F. "Ancient of Days--Plus Tax!" *Pennsylvania Folklife* 16:4 (Summer 1967):2-9.

Survey of objects collected by antique dealers, in part because of nostalgia for an earlier era during which objects were handmade. Includes 14 photographs of antiques, such as food utensils, candle sticks, cookie cutters, furniture, fraktur, and chalkware.

GE504   Robacker, Earl F. and Ada F. "Antique or Folk Art: Which?" *Pennsylvania Folklife* 12:3 (Fall 1961):8-11.

Distinction made between antiques and products of folk art, noting that the former refers to age relative to type of object, while the latter refers to the process of creating among a certain group of people. Includes 4 photographs of folk art objects.

GE505   Robacker, Earl F. and Ada F. "Antiques in Dutch Land." *Pennsylvania Folklife* 12:3 (Fall 1961):2-7.

Guide to the would-be collector of Pennsylvania Dutch antiques. Demarcates 3 periods of art, lists well-known and reliable dealers, and enumerates 20 terms commonly used in reference to Pennsylvania Dutch antiques. Includes 9 photographs.

GE506   Robacker, Earl F. and Ada F. "Decorative Painting." *Pennsylvania Folklife* 28 (Folk Festival Supplement 1979):34-39.

Describes painting techniques of a variety of folk artists used on glass, velvet, stencil, tin, and furniture. Includes 12 photographs.

GE507   Robacker, Earl F. and Ada F. "The Far-From-Lonely Heart." *Pennsylvania Folklife* 17:2 (Winter 1967-1968):2-11.

Discussion of the role of the heart motif among the Pennsylvania Dutch, with 18 photographs illustrating the heart motif found on 30 objects. Discusses regional styles, including that of Berks County, which is common to Dutch country as a whole.

GE508   Robacker, Earl F. and Ada F. "Flight of the Distelfink."
         Pennsylvania Folklife 20:4 (Summer 1971):2-8.

         Pictorial overview showing the role of birds in Pennsyl-
         vania Dutch folk art, with 23 photographs showing 46
         objects. Describes physical appearances of birds on
         Pennsylvania Dutch art objects and refers to mytho-
         logical and legendary notions about birds.

GE509   Robacker, Earl F. and Ada F. "Floral Motifs in
         Dutchland's Art." *Pennsylvania Folklife* 17:4
         (Summer 1968):2-7.

         Discussion of the flower motif found on a variety of
         Pennsylvania Dutch objects, from plates to furniture
         and samplers. Describes types of flowers and kinds of
         objects they adorn, as illustrated in 16 photographs
         showing 24 objects with floral motifs.

GE510   Robacker, Earl F. and Ada F. "Folk Whittling in
         Pennsylvania." *Pennsylvania Folklife* 22 (Folk
         Festival Supplement 1973):38-48.

         Description of wood carving as a utilitarian and an
         ornamental art. Focuses on a 19th-century German-
         speaking itinerant carver from Carlisle, Pennsylvania,
         whose specialty was birds and animals. Contemporary
         practice of the art exemplified with reference to the
         work of 4 modern carvers. Includes 26 photographs of
         carved objects and their makers.

GE511   Robacker, Earl F. and Ada F. "Fraktur: An Enduring
         Art Form." *Pennsylvania Folklife* 26 (Supplement
         1977):48-55.

         History of fraktur, with illustrations of types of
         manuscripts and focus on contemporary artists who
         attempt to replicate older pieces. Includes 22
         photographs of fraktur examples.

GE512   Robacker, Earl F. and Ada F. "How Far that Little
         Candle Throws...." *Pennsylvania Folklife* 29:4
         (Summer 1980):34-40.

         Discussion of the history and variety of candles and
         candle making in Pennsylvania, illustrated with 12
         photographs showing 39 candles and their enclosures.

GE513   Robacker, Earl F. and Ada F. "Look Back, Once!"
        Pennsylvania Folklife 15:4 (Summer 1966):6-11.

        Survey of various types of antiques prevalent in early
        Pennsylvania, including butter pots, redware, pierced
        tin cheese molds, flower pots, butter bowls, ironwork,
        and toys. Implicit assumption that there is inherent
        value in objects no longer used, and comments made con-
        cerning the uniqueness to Pennsylvania Dutch culture of
        some of the mentioned antiques. Includes 16 photographs
        of different kinds of antiques.

GE514   Robacker, Earl F. and Ada F. "Quilting Traditions of
        the Dutch Country." *Pennsylvania Folklife* 21
        (Folk Festival Supplement 1972):31-38.

        Discussion of the historical roots of quilting in
        America, and description of techniques and patterns
        used by Pennsylvania Dutch women. Includes 15 photo-
        graphs of various quilt patterns.

GE515   Robacker, Earl F. and Ada F. "Tin, Tole--and Inde-
        pendence." *Pennsylvania Folklife* 25 (Supplement
        1976):48-56.

        Discussion of the history of toleware, various types
        and decorations, notable artists, and contemporary
        vs. antique examples. Includes 13 photographs showing
        37 toleware objects.

GE516   Robacker, Earl F. and Ada F. "Whittling: Dumb Dutch
        Pastime." *Pennsylvania Folklife* 9:4 (Summer 1970):
        2-9.

        Discussion of the term "dumb Dutch," which was trans-
        formed from a pejorative word used by non-Dutch to a
        positive term used by the Pennsylvania Dutch to mean
        distinctive, desirable, or peculiar. Illustrates the
        creativity of the Dutch by a variety of homemade wood
        objects (illustrated with 25 photographs showing 42
        objects).

GE517   Robbins, Walter L. "Christmas Shooting Rounds in
        America and Their Background." *Journal of American
        Folklore* 86:339 (1973):48-52.

        Cites five 19th- and early 20th-century descriptions
        of the practice of shooting guns at Christmas in the
        American Midwest and South. Compares this with the

custom of "shooting in the New Year," as reported in
the United States and Germany. Hypothesizes that the
two are related and that both are derived from the
German New Year ritual.

GE518   Robbins, Walter L. "Wishing in and Shooting in the New
        Year among the Germans in the Carolinas." In *American
        Folklife*, edited by Don Yoder, pp. 257-279. Austin:
        University of Texas Press, 1976.

        Historical account and description of the German-
        derived custom of groups of men visiting homes,
        shooting off guns, and being served refreshments on
        New Year's Eve and Day. Includes 1 reprinted 1914
        text (in English) of a "household wish" or speech
        delivered on the occasion, with comparisons made to
        reprinted portions of German and other American texts
        and with hymns, psalms, poems (also reprinted) and to
        segments of texts (some in German, some in English)
        from North Carolina, Pennsylvania, South Carolina, and
        Virginia.

GE519   Rosenberger, Homer. "The Witch of Werner's Mill."
        Keystone Folklore Quarterly 2:4 (1957-58):104-108.

        Brief discussion of witchcraft beliefs in the area of
        Tylersville, Pennsylvania, an area settled largely by
        German immigrants in the late 18th century, followed
        by the text of 1 long tale about a miller's wife who
        haunts his mill in the form of a black cat and whose
        identity is eventually discovered. Includes descrip-
        tion of 3 beliefs as well as the 1 tale text.

GE520   Rosenberger, Jesse Leonard. *The Pennsylvania Germans:
        A Sketch of Their History and Life, of the Mennonites,
        and of the Side Lights from the Rosenberger Family.*
        Chicago: University of Chicago Press, 1923. Pp. x,
        173.

        Historical sketch of the Mennonites includes a chapter
        listing 30 proverbs and 21 folk beliefs, as well as
        references to folk cures and planting by the signs
        (pp. 127-138). Includes 28 photographs.

*GE521 Ross, Terri. "Alsatian Architecture in Medina County."

        (Cross-listed as *FR98.)
        (See *FR98 for full citation and annotation.)

GE522   Roth, Juliana. "Travel Journal as a Folklife Research
        Tool: Impressions of the Pennsylvania Germans."
        Pennsylvania Folklife 21:4 (Summer 1972):28-38.

        Discussion of the value of analyzing 18th- and 19th-
        century travel journals to gain insights into the folk-
        life of the early Pennsylvania Dutch colony. Provides
        information about foodways, disease, recreation, and
        language, and demonstrates stereotypes growing out of
        travelers' knowledge of Pennsylvania Dutch culture.
        Includes 4 drawings of early Pennsylvania Dutch life.

GE523   Rupp, I.D. "Old Wedding Customs." *Pennsylvania
        Dutchman* 4:3 (July 1952):6-8.

        Reprinting of 1 of 21 articles written by Rupp for the
        Cumberland Valley Journal that appeared between 1866
        and 1868 under the general title "The Olden Time of
        Pennsboro Township." Includes brief mention of several
        weddings in different counties, with attendant customs
        and information about the participants' dress and
        dancing.

GE524   Rupp, William J. *Bird Names and Bird Lore among the
        Pennsylvania Germans*. Norristown, Pa.: The
        Pennsylvania German Society, 1946. Pp. xi, 337.

        Discussion of the role of birds in Pennsylvania Dutch
        life and lore, as expressed through dialect names,
        beliefs (114 listed, all in English), sayings (202
        given, all in German), and songs (28, in German) and
        stories (6, in German).

GE525   Rupp, William J. "'Der Huns John,' A Unique Character."
        Pennsylvania Dutchman 3:6 (1 August 1951):3, 7.

        Description of a popular folk character of Berks and
        Lehigh counties in the early 1900s, including 5
        stories of his occupation of selling dogs.

GE526   Sachse, Julius. "Popular Beliefs and Superstitions
        [in Pa.]." *Lancaster County Society Papers and
        Addresses* 7 (6 February 1903):75-101.

        Discussion of prognostication based on popular German
        almanacs, including lucky and unlucky days, blood
        letting, incantations, talismans, and powwowing a burn
        (exorcism by fire).

*GE527 Sackett, S.J. "The Hammered Dulcimer in Ellis County,
        Kansas." *Journal of the International Folk Music
        Council* 14 (1962):61-64.

        Brief sketch of German-Russian immigration to Kansas
        between 1875 and 1878, with emphasis on immigrant
        dulcimer makers from Walker and Hays, Kansas. Includes
        descriptions of dulcimer making, tuning, and performing.
        Based on interviews conducted in 1958 and 1961.
        (Cross-listed as *RU22.)

GE528   Sauers, Ray W. "Fruit Harvesting and Preservation in
        Early Pennsylvania." *Pennsylvania Folklife* 22:3
        (Spring 1974):38-43.

        Survey of types of fruit prevalent on 19th-century
        Pennsylvania Dutch farms, along with information on
        fruit preservation and drying. Comments on the lore
        of fruit harvesting in terms of several folk beliefs
        from almanacs. Includes 2 folk sayings, 2 poems
        gleaned from a questionnaire.

GE529   Schaffer, Sharon A. "Scherenschnitte of the Pennsyl-
        vania Dutch." *Pennsylvania Folklife* 29:4 (Summer
        1980):14-15.

        Description of the little-known art form of scissor
        cutting. Traces history, provides a variety of names,
        and presents various uses in fraktur, love letters,
        and valentines. Includes 4 photographs and directions
        for a small project.

GE530   Scheuttle, Frank A. "Fritz G. Vogt: The Brookman's
        Corners Drawings." *New York Folklore* 1:1&2 (1975):
        57-74.

        Description of selected sketches of a German-born
        immigrant itinerant artist of New York State, with
        emphasis on works produced in the mid-1890s. Includes
        photographs of 10 of Fritz Vogt's sketches (of houses
        and farm scenes), 9 photographs of the sites sketched,
        1 diagram of the area in which the set of sketches
        under discussion was made.

GE531   Schillinger, Alvin W. "Hell's Bells and Panther
        Tracks: Lore of Western Sullivan County." *New York
        Folklore Quarterly* 9:1 (1953):28-39.

        Miscellany of folklore items recorded from informants
        of German ("Dutch") descent in Sullivan County, New

York. Includes characterizations of 6 tall tales
about a local character, 4 other tall tales, 2 anecdotes about local characters, 1 local legend, 10
sayings and retorts, 7 weather sayings, a discussion
of hexes and 4 tales involving hex, and 7 epitaphs.

GE532   Schmidt, Kenneth R. "Outdoor Games of Wyomissing,
        Pennsylvania." *Pennsylvania Dutchman* 5:9 (1 January
        1954):6–7.

Presentation of 13 games recorded from 15 children,
aged 10–14, in Wyomissing, Pennsylvania. Includes
frequency count of games played, listing of 10 counting-out rhymes used by girls in jumping rope, and
description of how the "it" person was chosen (including 4 rhymes). Includes a brief history of Wyomissing and the rationale for choosing the subjects
for study.

GE533   Schneider, Robert I. "Country Butcher: An Interview
        with Newton Bachman." *Pennsylvania Folklife* 20:4
        (Summer 1971):17–21.

Transcription of a 45-minute interview with a Berks
County butcher, conducted at the Pennsylvania Dutch
Folk Festival at Kutztown in 1970. Interview provides
information on butchering techniques, preparation of
parts of the animal, and final processing and storage.

GE534   Schreiber, William I. "Amish Wedding Days." *Journal
        of American Folklore* 73:287 (1960):12–17.

Discussion of the preference for Tuesdays and Thursdays
as wedding days among the Amish in Europe and America,
tracing the custom back to pre-Christian Germanic
traditions. Also includes 2 proverbial expressions
relating to weddings (1 in German with English translation, 1 in English only).

GE535   Schreiber, William I. "The Obituaries of the *Sugarbush
        Budget*." *Midwest Folklore* 5:4 (1955):221–228.

Discussion of the kinds of information about deceased
persons included in obituaries published in the widely-
circulated Amish-Mennonite newspaper the *Sugarbush
Budget*. Notes that obituaries conclude with 4-20-line
poems or verses. Includes examples of 25 such poems-
verses, excerpted and reprinted from the newspaper for
the year 1949.

GE536   Schreiber, William I.   "The Pennsylvania Dutch Barn in
        Ohio." *Journal of the Ohio Folklore Society* 2:1
        (1967):15-28.

        General discussion of the "Bank barn" built by Pennsyl-
        vania Germans in Wayne County, Ohio, during the 19th
        and early 20th centuries. Includes description of
        building materials used, general description of the
        appearance of the barns, with some differentiation of
        barn architectural types based on visible exterior
        openings.

GE537   Schuler, H.A.   "Shooting in the New Year: A Peculiar
        Pennsylvania German Custom." *The Pennsylvania-
        German* 8:i (January 1907):15-18.

        Discussion of the importance of New Year's Eve
        celebrations involving giving gifts to children,
        wishing relatives and friends well, and shooting
        firearms. Includes examples of 3 verse wishes (in
        German), 1 of them rhymed. Notes varying attitudes
        toward customs, depending on the degree of rowdiness
        involved.

GE538   Schuman, John F.   "Dutch Sayings." *Pennsylvania
        Dutchman* 3:3 (1 June 1951):3.

        Presentation of 1 saying relating to chickens and
        eggs and 1 folk belief concerning powwowing, with
        accompanying formula and cure.

GE539   Seely, Daniel Clayton.   "New Orleans Survivals of
        Alsatian Superstitions." *Louisiana Folklore
        Miscellany* 2:2 (1965):105-107.

        Listing of 18 statements of belief/superstitions
        recorded from members of a German-speaking family
        from Alsace living in New Orleans. Includes beliefs
        relating to bad luck and various taboos.

GE540   "Shafely Gay Hame!" *Pennsylvania Dutchman* 3:5
        (1 July 1951):1, 3.

        Response of a former York County resident to a request
        for information about the game "Sheep, Sheep, Come
        Home." Describes rules of game and accompanying
        rhymes.

GE541   Shaner, Richard H. "The Amish Barn Dance." *Pennsyl-vania Folklife* 13:2 (Winter 1962-63):24-26.

Discussion of the role of the barn dance among Amish
youths and assessment of the technical problems involved in staging the dance, accommodating the many
attendants, and providing for acoustical quality.
Makes comparisons between the Amish and "Gay Dutch"
with regard to type, structure, and role of the barn
dance. Includes 2 photographs.

GE542   Shaner, Richard H. "Distillation and Distilleries
among the Dutch." *Pennsylvania Folklife* 13:3
(July 1963):39-42.

Description of distilling practices in the Pennsylvania
Dutch country and the uses to which whiskey was put.
Special emphasis on the Stein Distillery in Durtztown.
Mention also made of distilleries producing non-alco-
holic beverages from birch, sassafras, and wintergreen,
the oils of which were used for medicinal purposes.
Includes 6 photographs depicting distilling practices.

GE543   Shaner, Richard H. "Festival Foods: The Original
Touch of the Dutch." *Pennsylvania Folklife* 25
(Supplement 1976):35-39.

Discussion of regional foods introduced to the annual
Kutztown Folk Festival, with accompanying comments on
the history and meaning of selected foods. Includes
9 photographs of foods and their preparation.

GE544   Shaner, Richard H. "Hex Signs: A Living Tradition."
Pennsylvania Folklife 27 (Supplement 1978):2-5.

Notes that hex signs are not found universally among
the Pennsylvania Dutch, but are concentrated in the
Lehigh-Berks-Montgomery counties area. Discusses
the placement on barns and as traditional decorations
and assesses the present state of hex artistry, with
comments on its declining popularity.

GE545   Shaner, Richard H. "Living Occult Practices in Dutch
Pennsylvania." *Pennsylvania Folklife* 12:3 (Fall
1961):62-63.

Based on responses to a special exhibit on the occult
held at Kutztown in 1961, author concludes that
magical practices are still prevalent among the

Pennsylvania Dutch. Conclusion contrasts with
Brendle's and Unger's claim that witchcraft is a past
phenomenon. Includes 2 photographs of paper charms
and reprintings of 3 letters.

GE546   Shaner, Richard H. "The Oley Valley Basketmaker."
        Pennsylvania Folklife 14:1 (October 1964):2-9.

Description of Freddie Bieber of Berks County as
typical of the traditional Pennsylvania Dutchman:
self-reliant, self-sufficient, speaks only Pennsylvania
Dutch, and attends Pennsylvania Dutch celebrations.
Describes the Ascension Day Vendues, which the Biebers
used to attend regularly. Includes 10 photographs
of Freddie demonstrating basket weaving techniques.

GE547   Shaner, Richard H. "Powwow Doctors." *Pennsylvania
        Folklife* 12:2 (Summer 1961):72.

Analysis of the change in role of powwowing from overt
to covert, and a listing of differences between
powwowing in eastern and western Pennsylvania and
between powwowing and hexing. Illustration of 1
powwowing activity and 1 hex doctor's practices.

GE548   Shaner, Richard H. "Recollections of Witchcraft in
        the Oley Hills." *Pennsylvania Folklife* 21 (Folk
        Festival Supplement 1972):39-43.

Recounting of a quest to understand in greater detail
the role of witchcraft among the Pennsylvania Dutch.
From personal experiences with witchcraft practices
of his aunt and uncle and their neighbors, the author
describes specific incidents of hexing and methods used
to alleviate hexing. Refers to traditional hexing
tombs used by hexers and amulets worn to avert the
evil eye. Includes 8 photographs of paraphernalia
used in hexing.

GE549   Shaner, Richard H. "Taverns and Tavern Lore of
        Dutchland." *Pennsylvania Folklife* 22 (Folk Festival
        Supplement 1973):30-35.

Discussion of the role of the tavern for the traveler
and, even more importantly, for the community, as a
trading, social, and entertainment center. Describes
forms of recreation in the tavern and refers to their
typically German character. Focuses on 1 tavern,
which dates from 1740. Includes 2 anecdotes, 1

concerning a traveler, the other about pride in the
tavern profession. Includes 5 photographs of taverns.

GE550 Shaner, Richard H. "Uni Day's Herb Garden." *Pennsylvania Folklife* 14:3 (Spring 1965):46–48.

Report of a meeting with Uni Day of Rockland Township,
Berks County, concerning his interest in herbs. Includes a catalog of various herbs and their medicinal
uses, with 5 photographs of Uni.

GE551 Shaner, Richard H. "Waffles and Wafers." *Pennsylvania
Folklife* 12:4 (Summer 1962):20–23.

Description of waffles and utensils used to prepare
them. Also notes the importance of waffles and wafer-
making for the Pennsylvania Dutch housewife. Notes
changes in the waffle iron from the 18th through the
20th century. Includes 10 photographs.

GE552 Shea, John. *The Pennsylvania Dutch and Their Furniture.*
New York: Van Nostrand Reinhold Co., 1980. Pp. 226.

Survey of various forms of Pennsylvania Dutch arts and
crafts, including chapters on farm houses, metalwork,
textiles, fraktur, ceramics, glass, woodenware, furniture design (chairs, tables, desks), as well as "how
to do it" chapters on furniture construction, painting,
decorating, and measurements. Latter chapters
accompanied by 96 photographs, 64 sketches, and 55
measurement diagrams.

GE553 Shelley, Donald A. *The Fraktur-Writings or Illuminated
Manuscripts of the Pennsylvania Germans.* Allentown,
Pa.: Schlechters, 1961. Pp. viii, 375.

History and development of fraktur-writing showing
unique Pennsylvania German style created between 1750
and 1850. Includes information on European relationships, techniques, designs, art of different schools,
modes of printing, and relationships between fraktur
and other forms of Pennsylvania German folk art.
Appendices list fraktur, illuminators, printing
centers, and printers.

GE554 Shenton, Donald R. "The Blessing of the Sowing of the
Seed." *Keystone Folklore Quarterly* 1:4 (1956–57):
55–57.

Brief description of a ritual involving blessing the
sown seed and its sowers, held annually on a Sunday

in May by individuals of German descent in Pennsylvania. Includes brief description of the setting, participants, and religious service.

GE555   Shively, Jacob G. "Occult Tales from Union County."
        Pennsylvania Folklife 16:1 (Autumn 1966):32-33.

Presentation of 6 tales told by a Union County narrator concerning supernatural beliefs and beings (witches). Includes 1 map of Union County.

GE556   Shoemaker, Alfred L. "About Apees." *Pennsylvania Dutchman* 5:13 (1 March 1954):5.

Discussion of the etymology of the name of a cookie called *Apees*, arguing that this popular Pennsylvania Dutch food was borrowed from the general American cuisine. Presents as proof references to this dessert in early American cookbooks.

GE557   Shoemaker, Alfred L. "Barricading the Road." *Pennsylvania Dutchman* 5:13 (1 March 1954):2.

Presentation of printed material on the custom of barricading the road in the path of a married couple so that they cannot pass without paying a "toll." Traces earliest reference to the Lancaster *Volksfreund* of 20 January 1824. Notes that the custom disappeared with the passing of the horse-drawn carriage.

GE558   Shoemaker, Alfred L. "Barring Out the Schoolmaster." *Pennsylvania Dutchman* 7:3 (Winter 1956):14-17.

Compilation of clippings from 1873 onward dealing with a custom of refusing entrance to a teacher on either Christmas or Shrove Tuesday, depending on the region. Illustrated with 3 drawings.

GE559   Shoemaker, Alfred L. "Bellschniggle." *Pennsylvania Dutchman* 3:14 (15 December 1951):3.

Reprinting of earliest account of Belsnickel customs (from the 1827 *Pennsylvania Gazette*). Includes information on costumes, Belsnickel's attire, and comparisons between rural and city rituals.

GE560   Shoemaker, Alfred L. "Belsnickel Lore." *Pennsylvania Dutchman* 6:3 (Winter 1954-55):34-38.

Compilation of published literature on Belsnickel from newspapers, diaries, periodicals, and from student term papers. Contains 18 accounts, the earliest from 1827, with 1 photograph of a Belsnickel Christmas card and 1 of a Belsnickel cookie cutter.

GE561 Shoemaker, Alfred L. "Belsnickel Parties in Grand-father's Day." *Pennsylvania Dutchman* 3:14 (15 December 1951):3.

Reprinting of an 1892 article describing Berks County Belsnickel customs, such as decorating trees, gathering moss and Christmas greens, and baking Christmas cakes.

GE562 Shoemaker, Alfred L. "Blacksmith Lore." *Pennsylvania Dutchman* 3:6 (1 August 1951):2.

Presentation of blacksmithing lore reported from 6 informants. Includes examples of folksongs, rhymes, folk beliefs, folk healing, and views of the changing role of the blacksmith.

GE563 Shoemaker, Alfred L. "Christmas Customs around the Year 1822." *Pennsylvania Dutchman* 2:14 (15 December 1950):3.

Reprinting of an 1881 newspaper account considered to contain the earliest reference in the Pennsylvania Dutch country to the Christmas tree. Describes physical features of the tree, decorations, and other Christmas customs, such as gift-giving and the Bels-nickel.

GE564 Shoemaker, Alfred L. "Christmas Folk Beliefs of the Pennsylvania Dutch Country." *Pennsylvania Dutchman* 3:14 (15 December 1951):2.

Reprinting of an 1892 article listing over 15 beliefs from Berks County related to the period from 11:00 to midnight on Christmas Eve.

GE565 Shoemaker, Alfred L. *Christmas in Pennsylvania: A Folk-Cultural Study*. Kutztown: The Pennsylvania Folklore Society, 1959. Pp. 116.

Review of the histories of the Christmas celebration among Pennsylvania ethnic groups and of the debate concerning its value, followed by a sampling of the histories of such Pennsylvania Dutch traditions as foodways, Christmas characters (Kris Kringle), customs, tree, Belsnickling, carnivals, and decorations (*putzes*). Includes 33 photographs and 27 drawings and sketches.

GE566   Shoemaker, Alfred L. "Christmas Topics." *Pennsylvania Dutchman* 2:14 (15 December 1950):1, 3.

Attempt to determine the origin of several Christmas customs, including divining the future, the Belsnickel tradition, and the Christmas cookie and cookie cutter.

GE567   Shoemaker, Alfred L. "Church and Meetinghouse Stables and Sheds." *Pennsylvania Folklife* 11:1 (Spring 1960):22-33.

Historical study of shelters used for horses and buggies (illustrated with 13 photographs) which facilitated church and meetinghouse gatherings.

GE568   Shoemaker, Alfred L. "A Dog on His Breast." *Pennsylvania Dutchman* 3:8 (15 September 1951):4.

Characterization of a story told by an elderly woman about her brother, who had nightmares nightly because of bewitchment and who was cured by a local hex doctor.

GE569   Shoemaker, Alfred L. "Dutch Folk-Beliefs." *Pennsylvania Dutchman* 5:2 (June 1953):12.

Reprinting of an 1890 newspaper article on popular beliefs in Lancaster County. Lists beliefs concerning Good Friday (7), good luck (4), omens (2), and witchcraft (4).

GE570   Shoemaker, Alfred L. "Dutchman Jests." *Pennsylvania Dutchman* 4:4 (August 1952):11.

Reprinting of 3 jokes, taken from 1 English and 2 German newspapers published between 1832 and 1853.

GE571   Shoemaker, Alfred L. "Dutchman Jests from the Germantown Telegraph." *Pennsylvania Dutchman* 3:16 (15 January 1952):4.

Reprinting of 12 jokes culled from newspapers and published originally between 1830 and 1860.

GE572   Shoemaker, Alfred L. "Easter Lore." *Pennsylvania Dutchman* 4:15 (Easter 1953):3, 5, 11.

Discussion of the importance of the contribution of the Easter rabbit and egg to American religion. Describes techniques for preparing and picking eggs, occasions for eating eggs, and egg collectors and decorators. Includes 2 photographs of Easter eggs.

GE573   Shoemaker, Alfred L. "Easter Monday." *Pennsylvania*
         Dutchman 4:15 (Easter 1953):2.

         Discussion of the importance of Easter Monday as a
         rest day from farm work.

GE574   Shoemaker, Alfred L. "The Easter Tree." *Pennsylvania*
         Dutchman 4:15 (Easter 1953):5.

         Reprinting of an 1895 article describing Easter tree
         decorations, with 1 photograph of such a tree.

GE575   Shoemaker, Alfred L. *Eastertide in Pennsylvania: A*
         Folk Cultural Study. Kutztown: The Pennsylvania
         Folklife Society, 1960. Pp. 96.

         Descriptions of customs and ceremonies surrounding
         Easter, arranged by days preceding and following Easter,
         such as Shrove Tuesday, Ash Wednesday, Maundy Thursday,
         Easter, and Easter Monday, as well as Ascension Day
         and Whitsuntide. Included are chapters on the Easter
         rabbit, scratch-carved Easter eggs, and the Easter egg
         tree. Concludes with a short story by James N. Beck,
         taken from the 1858 *Evening Bulletin* describing the
         celebration of Whitsuntide in Lancaster County. In-
         cludes 42 photographs and 19 sketches and drawings.

GE576   Shoemaker, Alfred L. "Famous 'Doctor' Hageman."
         Pennsylvania Dutchman 5:4 (August 1953):12-14.

         Reprinting of a 1900 newspaper article describing
         several cases of bewitchment brought to a "doctor"
         Hageman of Reading, Pennsylvania. Author concludes,
         after visiting Hageman, that the doctor is "a fool."

GE577   Shoemaker, Alfred L. "Fantasticals." *Pennsylvania*
         Dutchman 4:15 (Easter 1953):16.

         Attempt to pinpoint locales in which the custom of
         males disguising themselves and scaring children on
         New Year's Day is practiced and to determine whether
         or not this custom is also practiced on other holidays.
         Includes 1 reproduction of a plate depicting men
         dressed as women.

GE578   Shoemaker, Alfred L. "Fantasticals." *Pennsylvania*
         Folklife 9:1 (Winter 1957-58):28-31.

         Traces the early history of the custom of grotesquely-
         clad men parading in the streets on horseback while

making noise, on New Year's morning, in order to scare
young children. Author notes that custom has been
accepted by the Pennsylvania Dutch, but is probably
of British origin.

GE579   Shoemaker, Alfred L. "February Lore." *Pennsylvania
        Dutchman* 5:11 (1 February 1954):11.

        Discussion of beliefs surrounding unlucky and lucky
        days in the month of February. Speculates on etymology
        of Pennsylvania Dutch word *Der Harning* for February.

GE580   Shoemaker, Alfred L. "Fingernail Lore." *Pennsylvania
        Dutchman* 1:2 (12 May 1949):3.

        Mention made of folklore associated with white spots
        on fingernails, called "gifts." Includes 3 folk
        beliefs and 1 rhyme.

GE581   Shoemaker, Alfred L. "The First Week of Lent in
        Pennsylvania Dutch Lore." *Pennsylvania Dutchman*
        1:23 (February 1950):3.

        Discussion of customs associated with Shrove Tuesday
        and Ash Wednesday, including foods eaten and nicknames
        given to late risers on each of the days of Lent.

GE582   Shoemaker, Alfred L. "The Folklore of Bread."
        Pennsylvania Dutchman 1:2 (12 May 1949):3.

        Discussion of folk beliefs concerning bread, such as
        the use of bread to induce cows to chew their cud.
        Also includes names for various stages of bread-making,
        based on information provided by 4 informants.

GE583   Shoemaker, Alfred L. "Folklore on Snow." *Pennsylvania
        Dutchman* 5:12 (15 February 1954):5.

        Listing of approximately 24 folk beliefs (in German,
        with English translations) having snow as their subject
        and 10 relating to predicting the "blooming" of snow.
        Includes 2 expressions and 2 rhymes.

GE584   Shoemaker, Alfred L. "Games a Century Ago." *Pennsyl-
        vania Dutchman* 5:12 (15 February 1954):12-13.

        Reprint of an 1890 newspaper article describing 19
        outdoor games played by boys in Reading, Pennsylvania.

GE585   Shoemaker, Alfred L. "The 'Glingelsock.'" *Pennsyl-*
        vania Folklife 12:2 (Summer 1961):53-55.

        Historical survey from colonial times to the 1850s of
        the use of the "collection bag" in Lutheran and
        Reformed churches, with 2 artists' renderings of the
        use of the glingelsock in church services.

GE586   Shoemaker, Alfred L. "Good Friday Lore." *Pennsylvania*
        Dutchman 4:15 (Easter 1953):2.

        Mention of 1862 Pennsylvania legislation making Good
        Friday a legal holiday, with Good Friday lore about
        farm and household work taboos, curative powers of
        eggs, and 4 weather prognostications.

GE587   Shoemaker, Alfred L. "Hex Doctor Rides Tomcat."
        Pennsylvania Dutchman 5:12 (15 February 1954):2.

        Presentation of 2 folktales recorded in 1953 from an
        87-year-old retired farmer of Rockland Township,
        Berks County, concerning incidents involving hex
        doctors.

GE588   Shoemaker, Alfred L. "Hex Lore." *Pennsylvania Dutch-*
        man 5:4 (August 1953):4.

        Reprint of an 1885 note describing an incident during
        which a "Dr. Hageman" diagnosed a sick child as having
        been bewitched and almost killed. Child cured by a
        reputable physician.

GE589   Shoemaker, Alfred L. "Hex Marks! But Who Says So?"
        Pennsylvania Dutchman 1:6 (9 June 1949):2.

        Refutes the notion that hex signs are found in all
        Pennsylvania Dutch counties and that they are
        necessarily used to ward off evil spirits.

GE590   Shoemaker, Alfred L. "Hexes in Berks." *Pennsylvania*
        Dutchman 2:19 (1 March 1951):3.

        Reprint of an 1862 newspaper article relating the
        story of a woman whose illnesses were said to have
        been caused by an evil-minded person and who was cured
        when the harmful person was found.

GE591   Shoemaker, Alfred L. "In Search of Folklore Around
        the Grubba Karrich." *Pennsylvania Dutchman* 3:8
        (15 September 1951):3.

        Presentation of miscellaneous folklore items
        (approximately 10, including examples of hexing,

play, party games, folksongs, parodies, and folk
beliefs) obtained from a visit to the neighborhood
of Grubba Karrich, located in Snyder County, Pennsylvania.

GE592   Shoemaker, Alfred L. "Is the Easter Egg Tree
        Traditionally Pa. Dutch?" *Pennsylvania Dutchman*
        1:25 (April 1950):2.

        Demonstrates that the Pennsylvania Dutch custom of
        making Easter egg trees did not originate in Germany
        and is very recent in origin. No information provided
        about possible ethnic source of the custom.

GE593   Shoemaker, Alfred L. "Longswamp Gallery." *Pennsyl-
        vania Dutchman* 3:9 (1 October 1951):2.

        Notes that folksongs found in well-known Pennsylvania
        Dutch collections are of European origin. Calls for
        studies of indigenous Pennsylvania German songs. From
        recorded songs about people in Longswamp, Pennsylvania,
        author concludes that many local songs are humorous.
        Includes 4 song verses (in German).

GE594   Shoemaker, Alfred L. "March Lore." *Pennsylvania
        Dutchman* 5:13 (1 March 1954):9.

        Listing of approximately 25 folk beliefs associated
        with the month of March, some recorded from informants
        and others derived from well-known literature. Notes
        that the body of belief relating to March is relatively
        small, since March is an uneventful month.

GE595   Shoemaker, Alfred L. "Mock Dutch-English." *Pennsyl-
        vania Dutchman* 3:5 (1 July 1951):1, 3.

        Notes that the 1920s are important for an understanding
        of mock Pennsylvania Dutch-English. Includes re-
        printing of a 1922 newspaper column to illustrate types
        of humor. Reprint presents 13 categories of jokes,
        with summaries of approximately 25 jokes using Dutch-
        English puns.

GE596   Shoemaker, Alfred L. "Moshey and Bellyguts." *Pennsyl-
        vania Folklife* 8:1 (Summer 1956):16-17, 59.

        Discussion of the etymologies of moshey and bellyguts
        (two types of taffy), with comments on the popularity
        of these words throughout the Pennsylvania Dutch
        country.

GE597 Shoemaker, Alfred L. "New Year's Day." *Pennsylvania
       Dutchman* 4:9 (1 January 1953):3.

       Reprinting from an 1881 newspaper of a brief descrip-
       tion of the New Year custom of "shooting," with 2
       examples of the accompanying wishes (in German).

GE598 Shoemaker, Alfred L. "Of Folkloristic Interest."
       Pennsylvania Dutchman 4:13 (1 March 1953):4–5, 14.

       Abstracts from a diary covering the years 1837–44, kept
       by an Episcopalian storekeeper from Morgantown, Berks
       County, Pennsylvania. Includes about 45 entries
       containing information about holidays, witchcraft, and
       water divination.

GE599 Shoemaker, Alfred L. "Old Funeral Customs." *Pennsyl-
       vania Dutchman* 1:5 (2 June 1949):3.

       Description of miscellaneous funeral customs (such as
       community responses to death, preparation of the body,
       transportation of the dead to the funeral, and burial),
       reprinted from a mid–19th–century work.

GE600 Shoemaker, Alfred L. "On the Trail of Epitaphs."
       Pennsylvania Dutchman 1:23 (February 1950):2.

       Listing of 6 "unique" epitaphs, including name of
       deceased and name of cemetery where deceased is buried.

GE601 Shoemaker, Alfred L. "Der Ovvich Uns." *Pennsylvania
       Dutchman* 5:10 (15 January 1954):4.

       Sampling of 200 narratives concerning Sunday desecra-
       tion, referred to as "The Lord Above" tales. Includes
       texts of 3 stories (in German, with English transla-
       tions) and 1 folk belief.

GE602 Shoemaker, Alfred L., ed. *The Pennsylvania Barn.*
       Lancaster, Pa.: Pennsylvania Dutch Folklore Center,
       1955. Pp. 96.

       Compilation of 16 brief essays (12 by the editor) on
       various aspects of Pennsylvania Dutch barns (barn
       types, terminology, decorations, barn types and sizes
       as reported in 1798 direct tax records, travelers'
       reports of barns, barn raising, brick-end barn decora-
       tion, and log barns). Includes 51 photographs of
       barns, barn facades, and barn decorations.

GE603   Shoemaker, Alfred L. "Pennsylvania Dutch Cookery."
        Pennsylvania Dutchman 4:14 (April 1953):5, 8.

        Reprinting of a 1907 newspaper article describing
        shopping and favorite dishes in Dauphin County,
        Pennsylvania.

GE604   Shoemaker, Alfred L. *The Pennsylvania Dutch Country.*
        Lancaster, Pa.: Pennsylvania Dutch Folklore Center,
        1954. Pp. 38.

        Brief pictorial presentation of essential cultural
        features of the Pennsylvania Dutch, including dress,
        architecture, barns, foodways, fraktur, pottery, art,
        crafts, customs, sports, and recreations.

GE605   Shoemaker, Alfred L. "Pa. Dutch Fairy Lore." *Pennsyl-
        vania Dutchman* 4:12 (15 February 1953):3.

        Information about fairies among the Pennsylvania
        Dutch, contained in a popular periodical published
        between 1867 and 1900. Includes mention of 2 incidents
        involving the citing of fairies.

GE606   Shoemaker, Alfred L. "The Pennsylvania Dutch in Early
        Newspaper Humor." *Pennsylvania Dutchman* 2:14
        (15 December 1950):2.

        Presentation of texts of 9 jests taken from English
        newspapers published between 1820 and 1850 depicting
        the Pennsylvania Dutchman. Author contends that such
        humor is rare in English papers.

GE607   Shoemaker, Alfred L. "Penna. Dutch Jests from Early
        Issues of *Harper's.*" *Pennsylvania Dutchman* 2:17
        (1 February 1951):2.

        Presentation of texts of 8 jokes involving Pennsyl-
        vania Dutch, taken from the "Editor's Drawer" section
        of *Harper's Magazine.*

GE608   Shoemaker, Alfred L. "Pennsylvania Dutch Jests from
        the *Lebanon Courier.*" *Pennsylvania Dutchman* 2:18
        (15 February 1951):2.

        Presentation of texts of 5 jokes reprinted from
        various issues of the *Lebanon Courier* dated 1846-1851.

GE609   Shoemaker, Alfred L.   "The Pennsylvania Dutchman in
        Philadelphia Almanacs." *Pennsylvania Dutchman* 3:10
        (15 October 1951):2.

        Presentation of texts of 11 jests depicting the Pennsyl-
        vania Dutch humorously, excerpted from 400 English
        almanacs.

GE610   Shoemaker, Alfred L.   "Scratch-Carved Easter Eggs."
        Pennsylvania Dutchman 6:4 (Spring 1955):20-23.

        Notes the earliest (1789) reference to the custom of
        scratch-carving Easter eggs, and provides examples
        drawn from newspapers dated from 1874 onward. Includes
        15 photographs showing various egg designs, taken
        from the collection of Fred Wichmann.

GE611   Shoemaker, Alfred L.   "Scratching Tulips on Easter
        Eggs." *Pennsylvania Dutchman* 1:25 (April 1950):2.

        Reprinting of the earliest published reference (from
        the Allentown *Republikaner* of 23 April 1829) to Easter
        eggs. Describes activities of adults and children on
        Good Friday and Easter Sunday to illustrate the lack
        of true religious reverence.

GE612   Shoemaker, Alfred L.   "A Sheaf of Dutchman Jests."
        Pennsylvania Dutchman 4:14 (April 1953):11.

        Reprinting of 8 jokes involving the Pennsylvania
        Dutch, taken from various newspapers and originally
        published between 1824 and 1856.

GE613   Shoemaker, Alfred L.   "A Sheaf of Pennsylvania Dutch
        Folktales." *Pennsylvania Dutchman* 5:11 (1 February
        1954):5.

        Presentation of 6 folktales (all in German, 5 with
        English translations) recorded from a 77-year-old man
        in Berks County in 1953.

GE614   Shoemaker, Alfred L.   "Shrove Tuesday Lore." *Pennsyl-
        vania Dutchman* 5:11 (1 February 1954):3.

        Description of the *fasnach* baked for Shrove Tuesday,
        with mention of special customs associated with that
        holiday.

GE615   Shoemaker, Alfred L. "Some Dutchman Jests." *Pennsyl-*
        vania Dutchman 4:3 (July 1952):4.

        Reprinting of 4 jokes about the Pennsylvania Dutch,
        culled from various English newspapers, indicating
        place of telling and names of narrators and listeners.

GE616   Shoemaker, Alfred L. "Some Old Yule Customs."
        Pennsylvania Dutchman 1:21 (December 1949):1.

        Mention of 2 customs related to Christmas: 1) placing
        a pile of hay in the open in the barnyard an hour
        before midnight on Christmas Eve, and 2) putting out
        a loaf of bread on Christmas Eve, either on the window-
        sill or in the yard. Laments the fact that these
        customs are now practiced by only a few people and
        expresses hope for their revival.

GE617   Shoemaker, Alfred L. "Some Powwow Formulas from
        Juniata County." *Pennsylvania Dutchman* 3:10 (15
        October 1951):1, 4.

        Report of a conversation with a 71-year-old woman
        about her powwowing experiences. Includes information
        about how she learned the art, aids to memory, and
        formula used for curing. Provides examples of 5 cures
        for snakebite, poison, and scurvy.

GE618   Shoemaker, Alfred L. "Some Word Lore in Pennsylvania
        Dutch." *Pennsylvania Dutchman* 3:6 (1 August 1951):3.

        Presentation of folk etymologies for 3 Pennsylvania
        place names and for the word describing the act of
        driving over a ditch.

GE619   Shoemaker, Alfred L. "Somerset County Decorated Barns."
        Pennsylvania Dutchman 6:1 (June 1954):4-5.

        Short note listing 3 types of barn decorations in the
        Pennsylvania Dutch country: the geometric hex around
        Kutztown, the brick-end style in Cumberland and York
        counties, and the less well-known stars found in
        Somerset County. Includes illustrations of each type.

GE620   Shoemaker, Alfred L. "Spring Lore." *Pennsylvania
        Dutchman* 5:13 (1 March 1954):9.

        Listing of some 20 folk beliefs associated with
        spring and comment that the paucity of such beliefs
        serves as evidence that the concept "spring" is not
        old.

GE621   Shoemaker, Alfred L. "The Status of Witchcraft in the
         Pennsylvania Dutch Country Today." *Pennsylvania
         Dutchman* 3:18 (15 February 1952):1–3.

         Report of more than 10 hex tales, recorded from 10
         informants in Berks County and included in a paper
         written by a student for a folklore class. Includes
         the chain of transmission for each informant, and
         emphasizes the belief elements in the tales.

GE622   Shoemaker, Alfred L. "Tales They Tell Down Allegheny-
         ville Way." *Pennsylvania Dutchman* 2:8 (15 September
         1950):3.

         Presentation of 8 stories (3 involving pastors)
         attributed to locales in and around Alleghenyville,
         Pennsylvania. Includes description of the Allegheny-
         ville environment.

GE623   Shoemaker, Alfred L. "There Was Witches in Lebanon
         Wunst." *Pennsylvania Dutchman* 2:18 (15 February
         1951):3, 4.

         Reprinting of an undated newspaper clipping in which
         the author learns of "superstitious" behavior from a
         woman in Lebanon County. Recounts over 50 folk beliefs,
         together with exploits of witches and possible pre-
         ventive techniques.

GE624   Shoemaker, Alfred L. "Tongue Twisters." *Pennsylvania
         Dutchman* 5:9 (1 January 1954):4.

         Presentation of 7 tongue twisters (all in German, 4
         with English translations), submitted to the Pennsyl-
         vania Dutch Folklore Center and gleaned from Pennsyl-
         vania Dutch magazines.

GE625   Shoemaker, Alfred L. *Traditional Rhymes and Jingles
         of the Pennsylvania Dutch*. Lancaster, Pa.: The
         Pennsylvania Dutch Folklore Center, 1951. Pp. 16.

         Anthology of traditional Pennsylvania Dutch rhyme
         types (in German, with English translations), including
         nursery rhymes (5) recorded from informants, rhymes
         found in almanacs (6), those expressing rivalries
         between towns (3), powwow rhymes (3), earthy rhymes
         (9), nonsense rhymes (4), counting-out rhymes (4),
         and rhymes making use of local personal names (4).

GE626   Shoemaker, Alfred L. "Water Witching." *Pennsylvania Folklife* 12:3 (Fall 1961):25-27.

Attempt to demonstrate that waterwitching is a phenomenon typically found among the Pennsylvania Dutch. Evidence taken from correspondence, diaries, and newspapers. Describes practitioners, methods of finding water, sources of power, and reaction from community members. Includes 3 photographs of a Lancaster County dowser searching for water.

GE627   Shoemaker, Alfred L. "Whit-Monday ... Dutch Fourth of July." *Pennsylvania Dutchman* 5:1 (May 1953):5, 12.

Description of a 1780 reference noting ways in which the May 15th holiday was celebrated with races, bands, dancing, and much food and drink.

GE628   Shoemaker, Alfred L. "Whit-Monday in Lancaster." *Pennsylvania Dutchman* 5:2 (June 1953):8-9.

Compilation of best newspaper descriptions (8) of Whit-Monday in Lancaster County from 1843 to 1884.

GE629   Shoemaker, Alfred L. "Williams Township Lore." *Pennsylvania Dutchman* 5:2 (June 1953):11.

Reprinting of information on spirits, powwowing, weather prognostication, and home remedies, from an unpublished manuscript on the history of Williams Township, Northampton County.

GE630   Shoemaker, Alfred L. "Wishbone Lore." *Pennsylvania Dutchman* 1:6 (9 June 1949):3.

Discussion of the lore associated with breaking wishbones, including significance of winning the breaking contest and accompanying signs of the future. Meaning of the Pennsylvania Dutch equivalent taken from contributors to a Reading newspaper and from acquaintances.

GE631   Shoemaker, William. "Two Folktales, the Ghost and a Drunk." *Pennsylvania Dutchman* 1:19 (15 September 1949):2.

Presentation of 2 narratives (in German, with English translations), one involving the confrontation of a drunk with the devil, the other of an alleged plot by the Lord and the devil to divide the dead in a cemetery.

GE632   Shoemaker, William P. "Sitting Up with a Corpse."
         Pennsylvania Dutchman 1:20 (November 1949):2.

         Presentation of 1 narrative about a wager in which
         the winner was the person who could sit up all night
         with a corpse, with the loser of the bet discovering
         that the "corpse" was actually a living man.

GE633   "Shooting in the New Year." *Pennsylvania Dutchman*
         1:21 (December 1949):2.

         Description of New Year's Eve customs, including firing
         guns and wishing people well. Notes that the customs
         have disappeared.

GE634   Showalter, Henry A. "Snitz Pie." *Pennsylvania Dutch-
         man* 5:9 (1 January 1954):16.

         Author's remembrance from his childhood of eating
         schnitz pies, and presentation of his wife's and others'
         comments on the baking process and ingredients used.

GE635   Showalter, M.E. "Christmas Cookery and Customs from
         Greatgrandmother's Day." *American-German Review*
         17:ii (December 1950):7-9.

         Mention of popular foods and desserts made for Christ-
         mas years ago, together with 1 custom and 1 saying
         relevant to the holiday.

GE636   Simmons, Isaac Shirk. "Dutch Folk-Beliefs." *Pennsyl-
         vania Dutchman* 5:14 (15 March 1954):2-3, 15.

         Reprinting of a chapter from the author's 1915 M.A.
         thesis, with listing of 11 beliefs relating to birth
         and child care, 15 relating to marriage, 21 concerning
         death, 36 cures for various diseases, 38 beliefs
         relating to ill luck, 12 beliefs associated with work,
         and 9 miscellaneous beliefs.

GE637   Simons, Isaac Shirk. "Haunted Places and Tales of
         Black Magic." *Pennsylvania Dutchman* 2:11 (1 November
         1950):2.

         Discussion of places frequented by spirits and explana-
         tions as to their character, association with buried
         treasure, and the people who seek them. Also presents
         beliefs concerning witchcraft as it affects children
         and cows. Some information obtained from Lancaster
         County informants. Article derived from the author's
         unpublished 1915 M.A. thesis.

GE638   "Skulls of Horses Used as Charms." *Journal of American Folk-Lore* 9:32 (1896):72.

Notice that 3 or 4 horses' skulls were nailed to an old farmhouse on the road between Wilkes Barre and Bear Creek in Pennsylvania. Explanation that the skulls were to prevent the ghost of the dead owner from crossing the road. People identified as Germans.

GE639   Smith, Clarissa. "Jumping into Spring." *Pennsylvania Folklife* 17:3 (Spring 1968):20-21.

Classification of 21 jump-rope rhymes and verses found among Pennsylvania Dutch children, illustrated with 3 photographs.

GE640   Smith, Edward C., and Thompson, Virginia Van Horn. *Traditionally Pennsylvania Dutch.* New York: Hastings, 1947. Pp. 81.

Brief descriptions of barn signs, furniture, chests, Conestoga wagons, barn raising, foodways, folk art, medicine, quilting, Christmas *putz*, New Year shooting, Halloween, music, and antiques.

GE641   Smith, Elmer L. "The Amish Marriage." *'S Pennsylvaanisch Deitsch Eck*, 1 August 1959.

Discussion of Amish marriage age and how it differs from the norms. Notes that Amish marry later, have more children despite late marriages, and have not significantly changed average age of marriage over the years. Includes statistical data.

GE642   Smith, Elmer L. "Amish Names." *Names* 16 (1968):105-110.

Characterization of limited number of surnames, given names, and middle names common among the Pennsylvania Dutch, a situation which leads to problems of Amish identification. Problem partially alleviated by the use of nicknames. Describes the criteria used in creating and applying nicknames.

GE643   Smith, Elmer L. "The Amish System of Nomenclature (The Surnames, Given Names, and Nicknames among the Amish of Southeastern Pennsylvania)." *'S Pennsylvaanisch Deitsch Eck*, 8 August 1959.

Demonstrates that although the Amish have a small number of different family names and cling to a

relatively few Biblical given names, they distinguish
among individuals through middle names and nicknames.
Includes statistical data based on a study of 2,611
surnames.

GE644   Smith, Elmer L. "The Amish Wedding Season." *'S
         Pennsylvaanisch Deitsch Eck*, 17 January 1959.

Presentation of the results of a study among southeastern Pennsylvania Dutch of Lancaster County analyzing
580 Amish marriages over a period of 15 years (1 July
1939 through 31 July 1954) and noting that the typical
wedding season runs from October through December.
Gives reasons for "out-of-season" weddings.

GE645   Smith, Elmer L. *Bundling Among the Amish*. Lebanon,
         Pa.: Pennsylvania Applied Arts, 1961. Pp. 34.

Attempt to determine the degree to which bundling is
still practiced among the Amish. Presents a history
of bundling in the United States, with reference to
its prevalence in several states, to parallels in
other countries, and to 3 ballads that reflect negative
attitudes toward the practice. Concludes with a
discussion of bundling in courtship, as a moral issue,
in the church, and presents comments by informants as
to reasons for initiating bundling among the Amish.
Includes 17 illustrations.

GE646   Smith, Elmer L., and Stewart, John. "Belling." *'S
         Pennsylvaanisch Deitsch Eck*, 23 January 1965.

Description of the custom of belling, which involves
the visitation by friends on a married couple's wedding
night for purposes of disrupting their honeymoon
activities.

GE647   Smith, Elmer L., and Stewart, John. "The Black Walnut."
         'S Pennsylvaanisch Deitsch Eck, 19 December 1964.

Description of the autumn activity, involving the
entire Pennsylvania Dutch family, of walnut gathering,
drying, picking, hulling, and cracking. Notes that
these social activities contributed to positive social
relationships within families while also serving
practical ends.

GE648   Smith, Elmer L., and Stewart, John. "Grundsau Dag."
        'S Pennsylvaanisch Deitsch Eck, 30 January 1965.

        Description of Groundhog Day and its associated
        weather prognostications in the Shenandoah Valley.
        Notes that the groundhog came to be considered a
        delicacy and became the subject of folksongs. Includes
        2 previously unpublished versions of such songs from
        Virginia (in a dialect of German) and non-German
        variants from Southern Appalachia.

GE649   Smith, Elmer L., and Stewart, John. "Hydrophobia and
        the Madstone." 'S Pennsylvaanisch Deitsch Eck,
        17 July 1965.

        Discussion of the history and nature of curing
        practices employing madstones, especially for dogbites,
        in the Shenandoah Valley.

GE650   Smith, Elmer L., and Stewart, John. "Pennsylvania
        German Folklore in the Shenandoah Valley." 'S
        Pennsylvaanisch Deitsch Eck, 6, 13 April, 8, 15, 22,
        29 June, 6, 13 July, 7, 14, 21, 28 September, 23,
        30 November, 14, 21, 28 December 1963.

        Series of articles on various aspects of Pennsylvania
        Dutch folklore and folklife, including calendar
        customs (mention of 5 holidays), folk cures (20 cate-
        gories), moon signs (8 categories), weather signs
        (over 10), signs of the zodiac, apple-butter boiling,
        sugaring, snake stories, pottery making, rifles,
        stone cutting, recipes, hex signs, belsnickeling, and
        shooting (with examples of rhymed greeting in 7 stanzas).

GE651   Smith, Elmer L., and Stewart, John. "Shenandoah
        Valley Sayings." 'S Pennsylvaanisch Deitsch Eck,
        5 June 1965.

        Listing of over 50 sayings, phrases, and word usages
        from the Shenandoah Valley.

GE652   Smith, Elmer Lewis. "The Amish Today: An Analysis of
        Their Beliefs, Behavior, and Contemporary Problems."
        The Pennsylvania German Folklore Society, Yearbook
        24 (1960):1-346.

        General sociological treatise on Amish life, including
        discussion of folklore related to courtship and
        weddings (chapters 5 and 6).

GE653   Smith, Elmer Lewis; Stewart, John G.; and Kyger, M.
        Ellsworth. "The Pennsylvania Germans of the
        Shenandoah Valley." The Pennsylvania German Folklore
        Society, Yearbook 26 (1962):1-278.

        Survey of beliefs, arts, and crafts among the Pennsyl-
        vania Dutch of the Shenandoah Valley, based on inter-
        views with elderly informants. Topics include calendar
        beliefs, folk medicine, witchcraft, fraktur, folk
        crafts, and tombstones. Includes 5 plates illustrating
        fraktur and 23 photographs.

GE654   Smith, Richard. "Collecting Folk Cures in Lebanon
        County." Pennsylvania Dutchman 2:8 (15 September
        1950):4.

        Listing of approximately 20 folk cures, derived from
        an interview with 1 informant. Several cures concern
        prevention of tooth pain.

GE655   Smith, Rita. "Characteristics of Pennsylvania German
        Food." Canadian-German Folklore 1 (1961):86-88.

        Brief description of basic characteristics of Pennsyl-
        vania Dutch cooking, especially as found in Ontario,
        Canada.

GE656   "The Snake-Bitten Dutchman." Pennsylvania Folklife
        16:1 (Autumn 1966):42-43.

        Reprinting of a sketch from a Pennsylvania scrapbook
        dating from the 1850s typifying the stereotypical
        "Dutchman" joke of the 19th century, found in news-
        papers, almanacs, and joke books. Traits mentioned
        include use of broken English, conservative ways,
        rural stubbornness, and stupidity. Includes 1
        pictorial joke found in a 19th-century newspaper.

GE657   Snellenburg, Betty. "Four Interviews with Powwowers."
        Pennsylvania Folklife 18:4 (Summer 1969):40-45.

        Discussion of interviews with 4 powwowers from York
        and Lancaster counties concerning such aspects of
        powwowing as education, background, and types of prac-
        titioners; relationship between religion and curing;
        source of curing powers. Efficacy of powwowing rein-
        forced and illustrated by stories of miraculous cures.
        Includes 2 photographs of the cover of Hohman's The
        Long Lost Friend, the principal collection of charms
        used by Pennsylvania Dutch powwowers.

GE658   Snyder, Mabel. "How I Make Soap." *Pennsylvania Folklife* 17:4 (Summer 1968):12-15.

Transcription of a recording (in dialect, with English translation) made by the editor of *Pennsylvania Folklife* of Mabel Snyder of Berks County describing how she makes soap. Includes 3 photographs of women making and cutting soap.

GE659   Soldner, Dora. "Serenading on the New Year's Eve." *American-German Review* 18:ii (December 1951):26-28.

Discussion of the origin of serenading and of popular song composition of persons residing in Sonnenberg, Bluffton, and Pandora counties, Ohio. Mentions customs common among serenaders and their hosts. Includes musical transcriptions of 2 songs.

GE660   "Songs by Mrs. Fred Ehrlich, of Windsor, Colorado." *Colorado Folksong Bulletin* 3 (1964):42-45.

Presentation of texts of 3 songs (in German, with English translations and tune transcriptions), recorded in 1963 in Windsor, Colorado, from a Russian-Mennonite immigrant woman who learned the songs from family, friends, and neighbors.

GE661   Spieler, Gerhard G. "Pennsylvania Dutch Place Names." *Pennsylvania Dutchman* 5:7 (November 1953):5-6.

Discussion of naming, origin of place names, and those responsible for early names in Pennsylvania Dutch country. Lists 37 names, with explanations for their origins.

GE662   Spieler, Gerhard G. "The Story of Pennsylvania Dutch Family Names." *Pennsylvania Dutchman* 5:4 (August 1953):2.

Presentation of categories of names based on occupations, place names, nicknames, and baptismal names, with sources of Pennsylvania Dutch names noted. Discusses nature of and reasons for name changing. Comments on the identification of certain names with specific religious sects.

GE663   "Spook Stories." *Pennsylvania Dutchman* 5:9 (1 January 1954):8-9.

Presentation of ghost stories told to the author (who wished to remain anonymous) by approximately

15 informants, mostly family members and friends.
Provides some rational explanations for ghosts.

GE664   Stack, Phil. "Folk Amusements in Western Pennsylvania."
        Pennsylvania Folklife 10:2 (Fall 1959):29-37.

        Sketch of folk amusements prevalent in western Pennsyl-
        vania from 1775 to 1914. Mentions family amusements of
        the rural farm home (frolic), amusements in the home
        in which the public participates (weddings), amusements
        in the community at large (holiday celebrations), and
        amusements unspecified as to place and participants.

GE665   Stair, J. William. "Brick-End Barns." *Pennsylvania
        Dutchman* 6:2 (September 1954):14-33.

        Survey and analysis of brick-end barns popular in the
        1800s, particularly in Pennsylvania Dutch country.
        Includes information on construction techniques,
        designs, and history. Concludes with a note on data-
        gathering techniques and sources. Includes 35 photo-
        graphs and 3 sketches of barns and 1 map.

GE666   Stanbery, Mrs. George A. "Folk-Medicine in Ohio."
        Folk-Lore 8:2 (1897):185-187.

        Presentation of 10 medical cures, obtained by the
        author from relatives of "an old German woman" from
        Somerset, Perry County, Ohio.

GE667   Starr, Frederick. "Some Pennsylvania German Lore."
        Journal of American Folk-Lore 4 (1891):321-326.

        Listing of beliefs gathered over a 10-year period from
        informants living in Northampton and Clinton counties.
        Includes omens (9), dreams (9), moon lore (9), lucky
        days (7), curing warts (5), sympathetic magic (5),
        stories about witchcraft (3) and powwowing (1).

GE668   Stewart, Susan. "Rational Powwowing: An Examination
        of Choice among Medical Alternatives in Rural York
        County, Pennsylvania." *Pennsylvania Folklife* 26:1
        (Fall 1976):12-17.

        Report of a lengthy interview with an elderly York
        County informant. Hypothesizes that belief in powwow-
        ing (including that in the existence of malevolent
        witches) is not inconsistent with belief in other more
        "rational" techniques of faith healing. Contends that
        both these kinds of belief are well integrated in the
        informant's thinking.

GE669   Stewart, Susan. "Sociological Aspects of Quilting in
        Three Brethren Churches in Southeastern Pennsylvania."
        Pennsylvania Folklife 23:3 (Spring 1974):15-29.

        Analysis of the role of quilting among women members
        of Brethren churches in Indian Creek and Spring Creek,
        Pennsylvania. Describes quilting techniques and
        designs, and infers the religious, social, and artistic
        functions for both the church communities and indi-
        vidual women. Study based on interviews, questionnaires,
        correspondence, and participant observation. Includes
        17 illustrations depicting the process of quilting.

GE670   Stitzer, Clarence R. "Some Notes on Easter." *Pennsyl-
        vania Dutchman* 1:25 (April 1950):2.

        Author's recollections of Easter customs practiced by
        his mother and grandmother, including serving of
        greens, coloring of eggs, Easter baskets, egg games,
        and cuisine.

GE671   Stoudt, Fno. Baer. "Pennsylvania German Riddles and
        Nursery Rhymes." *Journal of American Folk-Lore*
        19:73 (1906):113-121.

        Listing of 37 riddles, 5 counting-out rhymes, 10 cradle
        songs, 1 evening prayer, and 2 mock sermons, all in
        Pennsylvania German dialect (with English translations
        for the riddles).

GE672   Stoudt, John Joseph. *Early Pennsylvania Arts and
        Crafts*. New York: A.S. Barnes, 1964. Pp. 364.

        Discussion of Pennsylvania Dutch arts and crafts as
        expressions of immigrant culture and history. Relates
        arts and crafts to different periods in American
        history and to different socioeconomic class levels,
        which reflect conflicting outlooks of aristocratic,
        plain, and primitive views. Exemplifies different
        styles with architecture, furniture, fine arts, crafts,
        and illuminating art. Includes 344 photographs and
        sketches.

GE673   Stoudt, John Joseph. *Pennsylvania German Folk Art: An
        Interpretation*. Rev. ed. Allentown, Pa.:
        Schlechter's, 1966. Pp. xx, 385.

        Treatise on the nature of folk arts, with discussion
        of sources of Pennsylvania German iconography, the
        symbolic mood of Pennsylvania pietism, the relationship

among symbol, image, and literary expression, and the
role of symbolism in folk art. Second half of book
provides a pictorial survey of the art of Ephrata (48
photographs), fraktur writing (65), decorated household
objects (99), ceramics (31), architecture (24), and
tombstones (11).

GE674   Stoudt, John Joseph. "Pennsylvania German Folklore."
         The Pennsylvania German Folklore Society, *Yearbook*
         16 (1951):159-170.

         Discussion of the characteristics of Pennsylvania
         Dutch folklore, with emphasis on folklore as an ongoing
         response to new situations (as opposed to survivals of
         a European past). Categorizes Pennsylvania Dutch
         folklore into 5 groups: folk literature, folk piety,
         arts and crafts, social amusement, and man's place in
         nature.

GE675   Stoudt, John Joseph. *Sunbonnets and Shoofly Pies:*
         A Pennsylvania Dutch Cultural History. South
         Brunswick and New York: A.S. Barnes and Co., 1973.
         Pp. 272.

         Cultural historical survey of Pennsylvania Dutch,
         examining their folk art, folk humor, and foodways
         against the background of Americanization.

GE676   Strong, Leah A. "Humor in the Lehigh Valley." *New*
         York Folklore Quarterly 15:2 (1959):126-130.

         Presentation of 10 tale texts (2 in dialect) and 13
         beliefs about the curing of certain illnesses, recorded
         from a Pennsylvania Dutch informant in Allentown,
         Pennsylvania.

GE677   Swetnam, George. "Sex--the Missing Fascicle." *Key-*
         stone Folklore Quarterly 10:4 (1965):155-171.

         Reprinting of items 1836 through 1912 in a section
         titled "Sex," omitted from published volumes of Edwin
         Miller Fogel's book *Beliefs and Superstitions of the*
         Pennsylvania Germans (Philadelphia, 1915) (see GE184)
         and available to purchasers of the book by special
         request only. Reprinted from the only copy of the
         missing fascicle the author could find--in the Free
         Library of Philadelphia.

GE678   Swope, Martha Ross. "Lebanon Valley Date Stones."
        Pennsylvania Dutchman 6:1 (June 1954):21-22.

        Discussion of stones bearing dates of the erection
        of buildings, including types of stones, designs, and
        buildings on which the stones were placed. Includes
        9 sketches of stones and their markings.

GE679   Taft, Donald E. "Forest County Lore." *Pennsylvania
        Folklife* 26:2 (Winter 1976-77):27-29.

        Results of a 1976 survey (by questionnaire) of beliefs
        and superstitions in Forest County, Pennsylvania.
        Responses categorized as occupational narratives (5),
        home remedies (39), weather lore (14), superstitions
        (7), and omens (12). Includes 1 map.

GE680   "Tales Told About Jessie Pannebecker." *Pennsylvania
        Dutchman* 3:6 (1 August 1951):2.

        Presentation of 6 stories told about a popular local
        character Jessie Pannebecker (also spelled Pennypacker)
        from the Hopeland section of Lancaster County.

GE681   Taube, Kristie. "Family Folklore with a German Flair."
        Journal of the Ohio Folklore Society n.s. 3:1 (1974):
        17-19.

        Transcriptions of 2 legend texts (both involving over-
        coming bewitchment) and 1 example of folk medicine
        (a cure for bed-wetting), recorded in Ohio in 1973
        from 2 American-born informants of German ancestry.

*GE682 Taylor, Archer. "An Old-World Tale from Minnesota."

        (Cross-listed as *FR107, *IR101.)
        (See *IR101 for full citation and annotation.)

GE683   Taylor, Lonn. "Rails, Rocks, and Pickets: Traditional
        Farmstead Fencing in Texas." In *Built in Texas*,
        edited by Francis Edward Abernethy, pp. 177-189.
        Publications of the Texas Folklore Society 42 (1979).

        Description of various kinds of pre-wire farm fencing
        found in Texas, mostly from the 19th century. In-
        cludes brief discussion of split-rail fences built
        by German immigrant settlers. Illustrated with 19
        photographs.

*GE684   Terbovich, Fr. John B.   "Religious Folklore among the
         German-Russians in Ellis County, Kansas."

         (Cross-listed as *RU24.)
         (See *RU24 for full citation and annotation.)

GE685   Thompson, David W.   "Gee, Haw, and Geehaw."   *Pennsyl-
         vania Folklife* 20:4 (Summer 1971):47-57.

         Discussion of specialized terms used to refer and talk
         (cry) to animals. Presents both English and Pennsyl-
         vania Dutch equivalents, tracing their linguistic
         derivation and noting regional and personal variation.

GE686   Todd, Charles Burr.   "The Corpus Christi Festival at
         St. Mary's, Pennsylvania."   *Journal of American
         Folk-Lore* 11:41 (1898):126-128.

         Description of the manner in which the Corpus Christi
         festival is celebrated in the German Catholic town of
         St. Mary's, Pennsylvania. Comments on town decorations,
         procession, mass, and costumes of townspeople. Notes
         that this holiday is observed with more festivity than
         either Christmas or Easter. Includes 6 photographs,
         published in *Journal of American Folk-Lore* 11:42
         (1898):245.

GE687   Tortora, Vincent R.   "The Amish at Play."   *Pennsylvania
         Folklife* 8:4 (Summer-Fall 1957):14-34.

         Description of games played by Amish children and
         youths and of practical jokes carried out by both
         children and adults. Argues that the Amish have
         developed well the art of relaxation and entertainment,
         contrary to the popular view. Includes 25 photographs
         of people playing a variety of games.

GE688   Tortora, Vincent R.   "Amish Barn Raising."   *Pennsyl-
         vania Folklife* 12:3 (Fall 1961):14-19.

         Discussion of barn raising as a cooperative community
         activity reflecting social and religious values.
         Photographs (10) illustrate processes involved in
         barn raising and accompanying activities.

GE689   Tortora, Vincent R.   "Amish Funerals."   *Pennsylvania
         Folklife* 12:2 (Summer 1961):8-13.

         Description of funeral practices in Lancaster County
         (burial preparation, social involvement, family rites,

burial, and religious service). Includes 11 photographs of funeral-related events and 1 map of Lancaster
County.

GE690   Tortora, Vincent R. "The Courtship and Wedding
        Practices of the Old Order Amish." *Pennsylvania
        Folklife* 9:2 (Spring 1958):12-21.

        Detailed description of courtship and wedding practices
        of the Amish, based on the author's firsthand observa-
        tion of 1 wedding. States that the wedding serves as
        an example of the self-sufficiency of Amish society.
        Includes 13 photographs.

GE691   Tortora, Vincent R. "The Get-Togethers of the Young
        Amish Folk." *Pennsylvania Folklife* 11:1 (Spring
        1960):17-21.

        Description of Sunday "singing" get-togethers, with
        explanations of their functions as entertainment,
        opportunity to meet members of the opposite sex, and
        expression of pride in riding a buggy. Includes 18
        photographs of meetings and modes of transportation.

GE692   "Traditional New Year Wish." *Pennsylvania Dutchman*
        4:9 (1 January 1953):4.

        Report of 1 Berks County resident's New Year's wish
        (from 1875) (in German, with English translation).

GE693   Troup, W. Edwin. "A Few Remarks on Our Folk Art."
        Canadian-German Folklore 1 (1961):103-104.

        Notes the differences between Pennsylvania Dutch folk
        art and Canadian Dutch folk art.

GE694   Trout, John D. "In Search of Pow-Wows." *Pennsylvania
        Dutchman* 3:5 (1 July 1951):2, 7.

        Presentation of cures for headaches, rheumatism,
        toothache, and bloated cows, obtained from 5 informants
        in Manheim, Shillington, Pottstown, and Berks County
        by students enrolled in a folklore course at Franklin
        and Marshall College.

GE695   Troyer, Lester O. "Amish Nicknames from Holmes County,
        Ohio." *Pennsylvania Folklife* 17:4 (Summer 1968):24.

        Explains the proliferation of nicknames among Amish
        males. Presents examples of 9 nicknames based on

peculiar physical characteristics, unacceptable
social habits, or strange behavior.

GE696   Troyer, Lester O. "Regionalism among the Holmes
         County Amish." *Pennsylvania Folklife* 17:2 (Winter
         1967-68):42-43.

         Demonstrates internal divisions among the Amish of
         Holmes County, Ohio, based on religious controversy,
         differences in family lineages, topography of the
         land, and stereotypes. Includes 2 maps of the study
         area.

*GE697   Umble, John. "The Old Order Amish, Their Hymns and
         Hymn Tunes." *Journal of American Folk-Lore* 52:203
         (1939):82-95.

         Brief historical sketch of the Old Order Amish (of
         Swiss-German backgrounds) and their hymns. Includes
         12 excerpts (in German) from hymn texts published in
         the 5th edition of the *Ausbund* (Lancaster, Pa., 1815).
         Also includes transcriptions of the words and tunes of
         3 hymns recorded in Iowa and Indiana in 1938.
         (Cross-listed as *SW8.)

GE698   "Valuable Recipes." *Pennsylvania Dutchman* 5:6
         (October 1953):13.

         Reprinting of an 1886 pamphlet (Henry G. Buch, *A
         Compilation of Valuable Recipes*) containing 22 occult
         remedies from the "Dutch country."

*GE699   Wacker, Peter O., and Trindell, Roger T. "The Log
         House in New Jersey: Origins and Diffusion."

         (Cross-listed as *FN26, *SS28, *SW9.)
         (See *FN26 for full citation and annotation.)

*GE700   Walker, Barbara K. "Folklore in the Schools: Collecting
         by Seventh Graders."

         (Cross-listed as *GL82.)
         (See *GL82 for full citation and annotation.)

GE701   Watkins, Margilynn Fox. "Otillia's Moss Rose." *New
         York Folklore Quarterly* 19:4 (1963):279-280.

         Discussion of the origin of a tradition (involving a
         certain type of rose bush) among families of German
         descent in New York and of its persistence in the New
         World.

GE702   Weaver, William Woys. "A Blacksmith's 'Summerkich.'"
        Pennsylvania Folklife 22:4 (Summer 1973):22-26.

        Focuses on the 18th-century Lancaster County summer
        kitchen of one Christian Hauser. Provides detailed
        description of the building and its parts in order to
        determine the amount of German and American influence
        on architecture during and following the Revolutionary
        War period. Notes multiple purposes of summer kitchens.
        Includes 4 photographs and 3 diagrams of the building
        and its parts.

*GE703 Webb, Wheaton Phillips. "The Wart."

        (Cross-listed as *AU6, *SS29.)
        (See *SS29 for full citation and annotation.)

GE704   Weitzel, Louise A. "How Christmas Is Observed by the
        Moravians." *The Pennsylvania-German* 9:xii (December
        1908):531-534.

        Author's recollections of Christmas customs observed
        by the Moravians in Lititz, Pennsylvania, including
        trees, decorations, church services, and Christkindle.

GE705   Weitzel, Louise A. "How Easter Is Observed by the
        Moravians." *The Pennsylvania-German* 10:iv (April
        1909):150-152.

        Description of Moravian Easter week church services in
        Lititz, Pennsylvania, based on the author's experiences
        and observations.

GE706   Weitzel, Louise A. "How New Year Is Observed by the
        Moravians." *The Pennsylvania-German* 10:i (January
        1909):11-12.

        Description of Moravian New Year's Eve and Day church
        services in Lititz, Pennsylvania, based on the author's
        recollections.

GE707   Westkott, Marcia. "Powwowing in Berks County."
        Pennsylvania Folklife 19:2 (1970):2-9.

        Summary of interviews conducted in Berks County with
        3 powwowers, each of whom discusses the meaning faith
        healing has for him and his patients, the procedures
        for successful faith healing, and kinds of cures.
        Hypothesizes that although powwowing is losing its
        hold over increasingly educated and urban peoples,

powwowers are able to adapt their practices to meet
modern needs. Includes 2 photographs of "letters
from heaven" used for protection.

GE708 Wetzel, J. Stuart. "The Wholesale Peddler." *Pennsyl-
        vania Dutchman* 4:2 (June 1952):4.

        Presentation of stories of eccentric Freddy Hilficker,
        who made a living as a peddler and who was the butt
        of jokes.

GE709 Wetzel, John. "Riddles." *Pennsylvania Dutchman* 4:11
        (1 February 1953):5.

        Presentation of 6 riddles (in German, with English
        translations).

GE710 Weygandt, Cornelius. "Beasts in Dutchland." *Pennsyl-
        vania Dutchman* 6:5 (Summer 1955):10-15.

        Survey of most popular animals found among early
        Pennsylvania Dutch and various representations of them.
        Includes mention of Conestoga horses, mules, cattle,
        sheep, deer, dogs, and cats, with 2 photographs
        depicting various beasts.

GE711 Weygandt, Cornelius. "Birds in Dutchland." *Pennsyl-
        vania Dutchman* 6:2 (September 1954):8-11.

        Discussion of the importance of birds as motifs in
        Pennsylvania Dutch culture, including types of birds
        and many objects on which they are depicted. Includes
        14 photographs of objects using birds as their main
        motifs.

GE712 Weygandt, Cornelius. *The Dutch Country: Folks and
        Treasures in the Red Hills of Pennsylvania.* New
        York: D. Appleton-Century Co., 1939. Pp. 352.

        Survey of Pennsylvania Dutch life includes scattered
        references to folk art, powwowing, folk beliefs
        concerning cats, and costumes. Includes 25 photo-
        graphs.

GE713 Whitaker, Alice P. "German Lore of the Holidays in
        Western New York." *New York Folklore Quarterly*
        11:4 (1955):256-261.

        Discussion of German Christmas customs, including
        beliefs about St. Nicholas, *Weihnachtsmann* (Santa

Claus), the *Christkind*, and of some of the related customs among the Pennsylvania Dutch and the Germans in New York State. Includes 3 texts of songs sung to children, 1 song about the Erie Canal, and 6 proverbs (all in German, with English translations). Data recorded from individuals of German descent living in Buffalo and Ithaca, New York, in 1941-42.

GE714 White, Emma Gertrude. "Folk-Medicine among Pennsylvania Germans." *Journal of American Folk-Lore* 10:36 (1897):78-80.

Brief descriptions of methods of powwowing and cures for 8 diseases used by Pennsylvania Germans. Author comments that people using these are not necessarily ignorant, but are superstitious.

GE715 Wieand, Paul R. "Carpet Rag Parties." *Pennsylvania Folklife* 12:2 (Summer 1961):27-29.

Description of a social gathering in which rags are sewn together in preparation for weaving into carpets. Party serves to bring together young and old in a common task. Includes 5 photographs of family members sewing rags.

GE716 Wierman, Nancy K. "The Pennsylvania Dutchman." *Pennsylvania Folklife* 28:2 (Winter 1978/79):2-11.

From a series of interviews with 15 informants who reminisce about early Pennsylvania Dutch life, author attempts to determine the unique qualities of the Pennsylvania Dutch, such as hospitality, hard work, family courage, religion, search for truth, and traditional folklore. Includes 11 photographs depicting families and occupations of informants.

GE717 Wilson, Charles Bundy. "Notes on Folk Medicine." *Journal of American Folk-Lore* 21:80 (1908):68-73.

Defends the study of folk medicine and presents a listing of remedies, cures, and preventives for 10 ailments used by Germans in Iowa. Information obtained from oral tradition and from an 1837 booklet written by a German minister from Pennsylvania.

GE718   Wilson, Marian Ludwig. "Present Day Food Habits of
        the Pennsylvania Dutch." *Pennsylvania Folklife*
        9:4 (Fall 1958):38–39.

        Argues that many Pennsylvania Dutch have perpetuated
        traditional food practices, as evidenced by the con-
        tinuing use of certain food items. Study based on
        fieldwork in York County in which the eating habits
        of Dutch and non-Dutch were compared and contrasted.
        Includes 4 photographs of women preparing food.

GE719   Wilson, Marion B. "Why an Egg Tree?" *Pennsylvania
        Dutchman* 5:15 (1 April 1954):5.

        Notes the importance of the Easter egg tree and
        comments on types and designs.

GE720   Wilson, Marion Ball. "Christmas Eve in Bethlehem."
        Pennsylvania Dutchman 5:8 (December 1953):5.

        Describes a Christmas visit with Moravian friends in
        Bethlehem, Pennsylvania. Focuses on church services,
        children's love feast, candle-lighting ceremony,
        decorations, and special foods.

GE721   Winey, Fay McAfee. "Belsnickling in Paxtonville."
        Pennsylvania Folklife 19:2 (Winter 1970):10–13.

        Argues that the New Year's celebration when people
        acted outlandishly became combined with Halloween
        trick-or-treating, with the Belsnickel, a Santa Claus
        type figure, being transferred from the Christmas-
        New Year period to Halloween, tempering the malicious
        behavior of Halloween participants. Includes 1
        artist's sketch of Belsnickel and 1 of a Belsnickel
        cookie cutter.

*GE722 Winner, Julia Hull. "The Money Diggers of Niagara
        County." *New York Folklore Quarterly* 16:3 (1960):
        221–225.

        Discussion of a local legend concerning some German
        immigrants in Niagara County, New York, who had used
        the *Sixth and Seventh Book of Moses* to assist them
        (unsuccessfully) in finding buried treasure in the
        area in 1870. This book, published in German and
        English in 1849, contains information on Jewish
        incantations, magical practices, alchemy, witchcraft,
        and magical seals. Also includes a brief discussion
        of remedies and beliefs found in the book.
        (Cross-listed as *JE83.)

*GE723 Wintemberg, W.J. "Alsatian Witch Stories." *Journal*
        of American Folk-Lore 20:78 (1907):213-215.

        Presentation of 7 stories, some obtained from author's
        Alsatian immigrant grandparents from Waterloo County,
        Ontario, and from his parents, and 1 story recorded
        from a Bavarian woman. Notes a parallel tale from
        Scotland.
        (Cross-listed as *FR115.)

GE724   Wintemberg, W.J. "German Folk-Tales Collected in
        Canada." *Journal of American Folk-Lore* 19:74 (1906):
        241-244.

        Presentation of 5 tales about supernatural or strange
        occurrences involving the devil, witches, snakes, and
        a fairy wife, 1 from German-Poland and 3 from Alsace,
        with brief comparative notes for 1 tale.

GE725   Wintemberg, W.J. "Items of German-Canadian Folk-Lore."
        Journal of American Folk-Lore 12:44 (1899):45-50.

        Presentation of folklore items collected from German
        speakers in Canada, though author notes that some may
        be of English or Scottish origin. Includes 5 death
        signs, 4 rain signs, 2 storm signs, 1 good luck sign,
        10 bad luck superstitions, beliefs about thunder and
        lightning, folklore related to flora and fauna, cures
        for 14 ailments, moon signs, miscellaneous supersti-
        tions, Halloween and Christmas Eve customs, beliefs
        about witches and witchcraft.

GE726   Wintemberg, W.J. "Superstitions and Popular Beliefs
        in Waterloo County." In *Folklore of Canada*, edited
        by Edith Fowke, pp. 271-275. Toronto: McClelland
        and Stewart Limited, 1976.

        Presentation of 56 cures, 21 bad luck signs, 17 death
        signs, recorded by the author from individuals of
        German ancestry in Waterloo County, Ontario, Canada.
        Listing excerpted and reprinted from a 1950 work.

GE727   Wismer, Helen. "Pennsylvania Deutsch Home Life."
        Canadian-German Folklore 7 (1979):149-174.

        Author's reminiscences about growing up in a Pennsyl-
        vania Dutch home. Includes descriptions of the kitchen,
        washday, cooking, games, hospitality, beliefs, medi-
        cine, housecleaning, Christmas, and the privy.

GE728   "The Witch of Black Creek." *Pennsylvania Dutchman*
3:13 (1 December 1951):2.

Presentation of 1 legend concerning a creek in Luzerne
County, Pennsylvania, said to have been inhabited by
witches and to have brought bad luck to all who lived
near it.

*GE729 Withers, Carl. "Current Events in New York City
Children's Folklore." *New York Folklore Quarterly*
3:3 (1947):213–222.

Discussion of folklore as both a socializing force
and a reflection of social values, with emphasis on
the influence of national events (specifically, World
War II and the presidential election of 1944) on the
content of children's lore. Presentation of 32 rhyme,
chant, and song parody texts, 15 of which represent
anti-German, anti-Italian, or anti-Japanese attitudes.
(Cross-listed as *IT85, *JA13.)

GE730   Witthoff, John. "A Snake Tale from Northern New York."
New York Folklore Quarterly 3:2 (1947):134–137.

Presentation of 2 personal experience narratives and 1
tale text, recorded from an informant of German descent
in St. Lawrence County, New York, from a Hudson River
area source, and from an Ojibwa Indian. Suggests that
these tales are genetically related and of European
origin.

GE731   Wolfe, C.N. "Proverbs." *Pennsylvania Dutchman* 5:12
(15 February 1954):15.

Presentation of 5 proverbs (in German, with English
translations) current in Logan Township, Clinton County,
during the author's childhood.

GE732   Wolpert, Robert. "Ghosts and Dogs." *Pennsylvania
Dutchman* 3:11 (1 November 1951):7.

Presentation of 1 story about a dog which acted
strangely when it approached a haunted house.

GE733   "Yankee Outwits a Dutchman." *Pennsylvania Dutchman*
2:7 (1 September 1950):2.

Presentation of 1 tale concerning a Yankee peddler who
dupes a Dutchman into giving his money for a wine-
making scheme.

GE734   Yerger, Amos. "Pennsylvania Dutch Tall Tales."
        Pennsylvania Dutchman 1:24 (March 1950):2.

        Presentation of stories told to the author about cats,
        snakes, corn, and pigs.

GE735   Yoder, Don. "Christmas Fraktur, Christmas Broadsides."
        Pennsylvania Folklife 14:2 (December 1964):2-9.

        Pictorial presentation (with 7 photographs) of illumi-
        nated manuscripts and broadsides that contain greetings
        appropriate to New Year's and Christmas.

GE736   Yoder, Don. "Folklife Studies Bibliography 1964:
        Periodicals, Part I." *Pennsylvania Folklife* 14:3
        (Spring 1965):60-64.

        Listing of articles on Pennsylvania Dutch found in 25
        journals and magazines. Includes photographs of 3
        journal title pages.

GE737   Yoder, Don. "The Folklife Studies Movement." *Pennsyl-
        vania Folklife* 13:3 (July 1963):43-56.

        Considers individual studies on Pennsylvania Dutch
        culture under the rubric of folklife studies and
        suggests such areas as regional folk culture and
        acculturation as promising for folkloristic analysis.
        Includes 44 notes to sources on the folklife movement,
        with 8 photographs of various folklife scenes and 2
        of fraktur.

GE738   Yoder, Don. "Genealogy and Folk Culture." *Pennsyl-
        vania Folklife* 15:1 (Autumn 1965):24-29.

        Plea for scholars to study genealogies of Pennsylvania
        families for their potential folkloristic content.
        Example drawn from D.B. Shuey, *History of Shuey
        Family in America, From 1732 to 1876*, in which are
        found references to folk beliefs, folk architecture,
        house furnishings, family traditions, and dialect.
        Includes photographs of title pages from folklife-
        centered genealogies, 1 photograph of Shuey, and 1
        sketch of an old schoolhouse, taken from a genealogical
        treatise.

GE739   Yoder, Don. "Harvest Home." *Pennsylvania Folklife*
        9:4 (Fall 1958):2-11.

        Description of a thanksgiving held in summer or early
        autumn to celebrate a good harvest. Comparison made

to an unpopular New England thanksgiving celebration.
Provides historical references from lay and religious
leaders about methods for celebrating, types of
services, church decorations, and customs. Includes
14 photographs.

GE740 Yoder, Don. "Historical Sources for American Tradi-
       tional Cookery: Examples from the Pennsylvania
       German Culture." *Pennsylvania Folklife* 20:3
       (Spring 1971):16-29.

Author discusses problems in foodways research and
suggests the values of and problems with using historical materials from the 18th and 19th centuries. Topics
discussed include acculturation, changes in food
technology, and the relationship between rural and
urban foods. Includes 10 photographs of menus, diet
lists, and scenes taken from early American history
books.

GE741 Yoder, Don. "How Dear to Our Hearts Is ... Sauerkraut?"
       Pennsylvania Dutchman 2:15 (1 January 1951):1.

Traces the history of sauerkraut eating among the
Pennsylvania Dutch and discusses the relationship
between sauerkraut and New Year's celebrations.

GE742 Yoder, Don. "Let's Play 'Gluck un Awdler.'" *Pennsyl-
       vania Dutchman* 1:14 (4 August 1949):2.

Description of a children's game consisting of 2 main
players, the mother hen (Gluck) and the chicken hawk
(Awdler), with accompanying dialogue in question-and-
answer format (in German). Speculates on the origin
of the game.

GE743 Yoder, Don. "Love Feasts." *Pennsylvania Dutchman*
       7:4 (Spring 1956):34-37.

Brief characterization of "love feasts" practiced by
the Dunkers, Moravians, and Methodists, with the former
2 groups integrating food into the religious service
to express communion, while the latter refer not to
food, but to "spiritual" love expressed through
testimony. Includes 7 photographs of women preparing
food for love feasts.

GE744   Yoder, Don. "Men's Costumes among the Plain People."
        Pennsylvania Dutchman 4:15 (Easter 1953):6-7, 9.

        Theoretical statement about differences among members
        of different religious sects, with concrete example
        from the coats, hats, and beards of Brethren and
        Mennonite men. Includes sketches of "plain" coat
        styles available at a Lancaster department store and
        of 2 men (one a Mennonite, the other a Dunkard) in the
        1800s.

GE745   Yoder, Don. "Official Religion Versus Folk Religion."
        Pennsylvania Folklife 15:2 (Winter 1965-66):36-52.

        Analysis of the changing view of Pennsylvania Dutch
        folk practices as judged by official religion in pre-
        and post-1850 America, excerpted from William B.
        Raber's "The Devil and Delusion," which exemplifies
        post-1850 evangelical Protestantism's negative reaction
        to such folk beliefs as witchcraft and powwowing, as
        contrasted with pre-1850 positive attitudes toward
        these phenomena. Includes reprintings of 4 title
        pages from religious works and 5 engravings depicting
        the belief in the supernatural.

GE746   Yoder, Don. "Pennsylvania Dutch Folk Dancing."
        Pennsylvania Dutchman 2:5 (July 1950):1.

        Common reason given for dearth of dancing in contempo-
        rary Pennsylvania Dutch culture is that dancing is
        antithetical to religion, but the author argues that
        this answer is unsatisfactory because the literature
        of the 18th and 19th centuries amply demonstrates
        the importance of dance and dance music.

GE747   Yoder, Don. "Pennsylvania German Folklore Research:
        A Historical Analysis." In *The German Language in
        America: A Symposium*, edited by Glenn G. Gilbert,
        pp. 70-105. Austin: University of Texas Press, 1971.

        Traces the rise and perpetuation of Pennsylvania
        German folklore studies in the United States conducted
        by academic institutions, ethnic societies, and new
        folklore institutions. Case study of the history of
        folksong research. Makes a plea for analysis of
        assimilation and bilingual repertoires. Concludes
        with 4 pages of transcript of a question-and-answer
        session on topics of folk healing, American-Indian
        relationships, and interethnic contacts. Includes
        many bibliographical references.

GE748   Yoder, Don. "The Pennsylvania Germans: A Preliminary
        Reading List." *Pennsylvania Folklife* 21:2 (Winter
        1971-72):2-17.

        Listing of important works on Pennsylvania Dutch
        language, literature, and culture, including sections
        on religion, medicine, the arts, architecture, costume,
        and cookery.

GE749   Yoder, Don. *Pennsylvania Spirituals*. Lancaster, Pa.:
        Pennsylvania Folklife Society, 1961. Pp. xi, 528,
        preface, appendix, maps, indices.

        Historical discussion of the American spiritual tradi-
        tion, with emphasis on revivalist sects among the
        Pennsylvania Dutch (the "bush-meeting religion").
        Includes texts, tunes, translations of 150 spirituals,
        recorded between 1950 and 1961, with comparative notes
        and discussions of the sources, diffusion, print
        history, and themes of songs. Emphasizes the fact
        that spirituals are "American hybrids," brought about
        by "the early American acculturation process."

GE750   Yoder, Don. "Pennsylvanians Called It Mush."
        Pennsylvania Folklife 13:2 (Winter 1962-1963):27-49.

        Detailed analysis of the history of mush making,
        including descriptive terms, introduction to Pennsyl-
        vania Dutch culture, use of mush throughout various
        historical periods, processes involved in preparing
        ingredients for mush, and selected recipes (14). Also
        shows the use of mush as reflected in poetry (4),
        rhymes (10), folk speech (8), folk belief (2), and
        humor (10). Includes 8 sketches taken from various
        newspapers illustrating the importance of mush.

GE751   Yoder, Don. "Pennsylvania's Plain Garb." *Pennsylvania
        Folklife* 12:4 (Summer 1962):2-5.

        Argues that the clothes of the "plain" Dutch represent
        a badge of identity and separation from non-plain
        Dutch (the Amish, for example). Also, while of
        European origin, clothing is American in its develop-
        ment. Specific examples drawn from Quakers, Ephrata,
        Moravian, Dunkard, and Mennonite groups. Includes 7
        photographs of women in plain garb.

GE752 Yoder, Don. "Plain Dutch and Gay Dutch: Two Worlds in
       the Dutch Country." *Pennsylvania Folklife* 8:1
       (Summer 1956):34-55.

       Comprehensive discussion of the contrast between "Gay
       Dutch" (Lutherans, Reformed, and others), who consider
       themselves part of the world, and "Plain Dutch"
       (Mennonites, Amish, Brethren, and related sectarian
       groups), who consider themselves apart from this world.
       Comments on mixture of Pennsylvania Dutch culture,
       history and world view of the "Plain Dutch," evolution
       of the "plain" costume, the Amish as an example of
       "plain" people, methods of maintaining group solidarity,
       and the general role of religion among the Pennsylvania
       Dutch. Includes 28 photographs of various social
       gatherings and 2 sketches of popular dress in the early
       1800s.

GE753 Yoder, Don. "The Saint's Legend in the Pennsylvania
       German Folk-Culture." In *American Folk Legend: A
       Symposium*, edited by Wayland D. Hand, pp. 157-183.
       Publications of the UCLA Center for the Study of
       Comparative Folklore and Mythology 2. Berkeley and
       Los Angeles: University of California Press, 1971.

       Brief historical sketch of the development of saints'
       legends from medieval to post-Reformation times.
       Discussion of saints' lore and legends as used in
       Pennsylvania German folk medicine ("powwowing") and
       magic (especially in healing charms and incantations).
       Characterization of the transplantation of European
       saints' legends, particularly those concerning Saint
       Genoveva of Brabant, and of native saints' legends,
       with emphasis on stories about hermitess Maria Jung,
       known popularly as "Mountain Mary." Includes texts
       of 10 charms, 3 narratives, 1 poetic epitaph, all
       reprinted from other published or manuscript sources.

GE754 Yoder, Don. "Sauerkraut in the Pennsylvania Folk-
       Culture." *Pennsylvania Folklife* 12:2 (Summer 1961):
       56-69.

       Study of the role of sauerkraut among the Pennsylvania
       Dutch. Topics include history, preparation, and
       occasions for eating, as well as mention of sauerkraut
       in folk rhymes (7), poetry (14), folksongs (3),
       medicine, and jests (3). Includes 3 artist's concep-
       tions of sauerkraut making and 1 photograph of a New
       Year's store advertisement for sauerkraut and pork.

GE755   Yoder, Don. "Schnitz in the Pennsylvania Folk-Culture."
        Pennsylvania Folklife 12:3 (Fall 1961):44-53.

        Analysis of the use and significance of dried apples
        in Pennsylvania Dutch culture. Topics include history
        and types of schnitz, its uses in geographical names,
        and rhymes (4), jokes (4), narratives (2), and proverbs
        (6) about or involving schnitz. Includes 6 photographs
        depicting schnitz making.

GE756   Yoder, Don. "Spirituals from the Pennsylvania Dutch
        Country." *Pennsylvania Folklife* 8:2 (Winter 1956-
        57):22-23.

        Discussion of the history and types of Pennsylvania
        Dutch spirituals, with explanations for differences
        between spirituals of the Pennsylvania Dutch and other
        religio-ethnic groups, contributions of the Pennsyl-
        vania Dutch spirituals to American hymnody, and the
        development of themes. Includes 1 photograph and 6
        sketches of camp-meetings and 4 of hymnal title pages.

GE757   Yoder, Don. "The Strouse Dance." *Pennsylvania Folk-
        life* 9:1 (Winter 1957-58):12-17.

        Source study of a popular 19th-century occasion on
        which a dance contest was held and a "Strouse"
        (clothing) prize was awarded to the winner. Includes
        6 photographs of social dance scenes.

GE758   Yoder, Don. "The Themes of the Pennsylvania Dutch
        Spiritual." *Pennsylvania Dutchman* 3:7 (1 September
        1951):1, 5.

        Arrangement by content and purpose of selected verses
        from 5 Pennsylvania Dutch hymns, with discussion of
        the role of social conscience, "otherworldliness,"
        and emotionalism in spirituals.

GE759   Yoder, Don. "Tongue-Twisters." *Pennsylvania Dutchman*
        2:21 (1 April 1951):5.

        Presentation of 3 tongue twisters (in German, with
        English translations) recorded during a riddling
        session.

GE760   Yoder, Don. "Twenty Questions on Powwowing."
        Pennsylvania Folklife 15:4 (Summer 1966):38-40.

        Presentation of questions and answers concerning the
        nature and role of powwowing in Pennsylvania Dutch

culture, including those about origin, power, relationship to official religion and black magic, proof of
cures, and the law. Presents 3 sample charms.

GE761 Yoder, Don. "What To Read on the Amish." *Pennsylvania
       Folklife* 18:4 (Summer 1969):14-19.

       Survey of basic sources on the Amish which, according
       to the author, have come to symbolize Pennsylvania
       Dutch and which include references to folk music,
       art, community, and family.

GE762 Yoder, Don. "Willy Brown of Mahantongo, Our Foremost
       Folksinger." *Pennsylvania Dutchman* 4:2 (June 1952):
       3.

       Discussion of the role of Willy Brown (also known as
       "Papa Gernet") as one of the greatest folksingers of
       the entire Pennsylvania Dutch country. Reports on an
       interview with Brown, including information about how
       he learned his repertoire. Includes 1 photograph of
       Brown.

GE763 Yoder, Don. "Witch Tales from Adams County."
       Pennsylvania Folklife 12:4 (Summer 1962):29-37.

       Transcription of 19 folktales recorded from a single
       narrator in 1958, with background information on the
       informant and comparative and supplemental footnotes.

GE764 Yoder, Eleanor. "Nicknaming in an Amish-Mennonite
       Community." *Pennsylvania Folklife* 23:3 (Spring
       1974):30-37.

       Discussion of the function of nicknaming among the
       Amish and Mennonites in Somerset County, Pennsylvania,
       and Garrett County, Maryland. Cataloging of nick-
       names based largely on responses to a questionnaire,
       returned by 49 out of a total of 210 people. Explains
       the logic behind various types of nicknames and
       supplies a list of over 200 nicknames, with explana-
       tions of their origins. Also characterizes subjects'
       attitudes toward the questionnaire. Includes 1 map.

GE765 Yoder, Jacob H. "Proverbial Lore from Hegins Valley."
       Pennsylvania Dutchman 3:16 (15 January 1952):3.

       Presentation of 9 proverbs recorded from informants
       in Hegins Valley (in German, with English translations
       and historical explanations).

GE766   Yoder, Joseph W. *Amische Lieder*. Huntingdon, Pa.:
        Yoder Publishing Company, 1942. Pp. xii, 114,
        foreword.

        Presentation of texts (in German, with tune transcrip-
        tions) of 94 Amish hymns, recorded by the author from
        singers in Mifflin County, Pennsylvania, and intended
        as a means of insuring consistency in the singing of
        the hymns among members of various Amish communities.

GE767   Zehner, Olive G. "Christmas in Dutch Country."
        American-German Review 20:ii (December 1953):7-9.

        Notes the earliest mention in written literature of
        the Christmas tree and Christmas cookies, and describes
        tree decorations and nativity scenes.

GE768   Zehner, Olive G. "Dutch Quilts." *Pennsylvania Dutch-
        man* 5:10 (15 January 1954):16.

        Comparison of New England and Midwestern quilts to
        determine uniqueness of Pennsylvania Dutch quilts.
        Discussion of design patterns and use of motifs. In-
        cludes 1 photograph and 1 sketch of types of quilt
        designs.

GE769   Zehner, Olive G. "The Egg Tree Recognized as Pa. Dutch
        Custom as Far as Seattle, Washington." *Pennsylvania
        Dutchman* 3:21 (1 April 1952):3.

        Notes that the popular Pennsylvania Dutch Easter
        custom of hanging Easter eggs from a tree, popularized
        by Katherine Milhous in her book *The Egg Tree*, has
        begun to spread among different ethnic and religious
        groups. Includes 1 photograph of mother and children
        peering at their egg tree.

GE770   Zehner, Olive G. "A Master Blacksmith." *Pennsylvania
        Dutchman* 4:3 (July 1952):10-11.

        Focuses on the renewed blacksmithing career of Albert
        Hersh of Lancaster County, who reminisces about
        blacksmithing as practiced by his father and grand-
        father. Includes 3 folk beliefs associated with
        blacksmiths.

GE771   Zehner, Olive G. "Twentieth Century Pennsylvania
        Dutch Pottery." *Pennsylvania Dutchman* 2:3 (1 June
        1950):3.

        A potter compares older Pennsylvania Dutch folk pottery
        with similar contemporary art. Argues that modern

artists have greater need to be creative than to
reproduce older forms faithfully. Greatest change is
in the area of greater availability of colors. Potter
feels that modern pottery is no less authentic than
older examples.

GE772 Ziegler, Rebecca. "'Strangers and Exiles': Narratives
from the Brethren." *Folklore and Mythology Studies*
1 (1977):23-32.

Presentation and discussion of 7 personal experience
narratives recorded from members of the Church of the
Brethren (a small Protestant denomination of German
origin) between 1973 and 1975 in LaVerne, California,
and Elgin, Illinois. Notes that stories are structured
to contrast the pacifist activities and humanitarian
concerns of the Brethren with the behavior of others,

GE773 Ziemer, Alice. "Folk Medicine." *Pennsylvania Dutchman* 5:14 (15 March 1954):3.

Listing of home remedies current in 19th-century
southeastern Pennsylvania, 4 relating to babies, 10
to medics, and 2 involving the use of tea.

GE774 Zook, Jacob and Jane. *Hexology: The History and the
Meaning of the Hex Symbols.* Lancaster, Pa.:
Jacob and Jane Zook, 1962. Pp. 14.

Brief pictorial representation of the art of hexing,
with explications of 22 hex signs.

GE775 Zupan, Joyce Goodhart. "A Look at Pa. Dutch Folk Art
Through the Eye of a Needle." *Pennsylvania Folklife*
28 (Folk Festival Supplement 1979):28-29.

After tracing the history of embroidery in Europe and
the United States, author discusses the creative
processes involved in her own production of embroideries, from choice of design to the making of embroidery
kits for sale. Includes 1 photograph of the author
wearing one of her embroidered creations.

XX.   GREEK (GR) (1-39)

*GR1   "A Christmas Eve Custom."

    (Cross-listed as *GE113, *SK2.)
    (See *GE113 for full citation and annotation.)

GR2   Burgess, Thomas. *Greeks in America: An Account of Their
    Coming, Progress, Customs, Living, and Aspirations.*
    1913. Reprint. New York: Arno Press, 1970. Pp. xiv,
    256.

    In a work that has as its principal objective to explain
    Greek immigration to the United States from the 1880s
    to 1913, author includes a chapter on celebrations (pp.
    87-112) which provides information on customs, religious
    and secular holidays, church music, household icons,
    weddings, and funerals. Includes 16 photographs.

GR3   Doering, Eileen Elita. "A Charm of the Gulf of Mexico
    Sponge Fishers." *Journal of American Folklore* 52:
    203 (1939):123.

    Brief note enumerating 2 sailing taboos and 1 charm for
    calming stormy seas among Greek immigrant sponge fisher-
    men in Tarpon Springs, Florida.

GR4   Doering, J. Frederick. "Folk Customs and Beliefs of
    Greek Sponge-Fishers of Florida." *Southern Folklore
    Quarterly* 7:2 (1943):105-107.

    Brief characterization of assorted customs and beliefs
    of Greek sponge fishermen of Tarpon Springs, Florida.
    Includes mention of Epiphany Day ceremonies, sailing
    taboos, rituals for finding sponges, charms for calming
    stormy seas and for insuring good luck, traditional
    medical beliefs and practices (including "cupping").

*GR5   Dorson, Richard M. "Is There a Folk in the City?"

    (Cross-listed as *GL34, *CR1, *SE1.)
    (See *GL34 for full citation and annotation.)

*GR6   Dorson, Richard M. "Tales of a Greek-American Family
    on Tape." *Fabula* 1:1-2 (1957):114-143. Errata
    published in *Fabula* 2:1-2 (1958):202-203.

    Presentation of a transcription of a tape-recorded
    interview held by the author with members of a Greek-

American family in Iron Mountain, Michigan, in 1955.
Includes 2 accounts of cursing, 2 descriptions of
customs, 1 account of an encounter with the devil, 8
beliefs, cures, and accounts of individuals' experiences
with the evil eye, 1 account of a healing, 3 humorous
tales, 3 personal experience narratives (historical),
13 accounts of encounters with and miracles performed
by saints, 15 beliefs and stories relating to supernatural beings, 1 joke about a Jewish convert to
Catholicism.
(Cross-listed as *JE17.)

*GR7   Erdely, Stephen. "Ethnic Music in the United States:
        An Overview."

        (Cross-listed as *GL40, *AR5, *CR2, *GY5, *JE22,
        *SC11, *SE2.)
        (See *GL40 for full citation and annotation.)

*GR8   Evanson, Jacob A. "Folk Songs of an Industrial City."

        (Cross-listed as *GL42, *FN12, *GE177, *IR27, *SK5.)
        (See *GL42 for full citation and annotation.)

*GR9   Foster, James R. "Brooklyn Folklore."

        (Cross-listed as *GL43, *IR31, *IT21, *JE24, *PL28,
        *PO6, *SP7.)
        (See *GL43 for full citation and annotation.)

GR10   Georges, Robert A. "Feedback and Response in Story-
        telling." *Western Folklore* 38:2 (1979):104-110.

        Discussion of audience- and self-generated feedback
        and responses to it during storytelling. Includes
        description of a Greek-American narrator's emotional
        response to self-feedback while he was telling a
        version of *The Forty Thieves*.

GR11   Georges, Robert A. *Greek-American Folk Beliefs and
        Narratives*. New York: Arno Press, 1980. Pp. iv,
        230, 2 appendices, bibliography.

        A 1964 Indiana University dissertation focusing on
        selected folk beliefs and narratives of Greek immigrants
        and their American-born descendants, based on 1961-62
        fieldwork in Tarpon Springs, Florida; Savannah, Georgia;
        Wichita Falls, Texas; Cincinnati, Ohio; and New York
        City. Provides a brief survey and assessment of
        American immigrant folklore studies, an historical

sketch of Greek immigration to and settlement in the
United States and in Tarpon Springs, Florida. Surveys
beliefs and narratives associated with religion;
occupational beliefs, customs, and tales of Greek-
American sponge fishermen in Tarpon Springs, Florida;
beliefs, customs, and narratives relating to supernatural beings and magical practices; and the taletelling tradition. Includes texts of 54 narratives,
variously identified as saints' legends, stories
relating to the evil eye, fairy tales, humorous jokes
and anecdotes, stories about encounters with supernatural beings.

GR12   Georges, Robert A. "Greek Folk Remedy in America."
        Southern Folklore Quarterly 26:2 (1962):122-126.

        Discussion and transcription of segments of tape-
        recorded interviews with 5 Greek-Americans (conducted
        in Florida and Georgia in 1961) concerning the practice
        of "cupping" to treat colds, pneumonia, and backache.

GR13   Georges, Robert A. "The Greeks of Tarpon Springs: An
        American Folk Group." *Southern Folklore Quarterly*
        29:2 (1965):129-141.

        Historical sketch of Tarpon Springs, Florida, and
        discussion of selected beliefs and customs of Greek-
        American sponge fishermen of that community. Includes
        descriptions of icon display and use, saints' beliefs
        and legends, Epiphany Day ceremonies, ship and water-
        blessing rituals, sailing taboos. Includes 4 narrative
        texts. Based on fieldwork conducted in 1961 and 1962.

GR14   Georges, Robert A. "Matiasma: Living Folk Belief."
        Midwest Folklore 12:2 (1962):69-74.

        Discussion of the evil eye in Greek-American tradition,
        including informant descriptions of preventives,
        diagnoses, effects, and cures. Based on fieldwork
        conducted in Florida, Georgia, and New York in 1961.

GR15   Gizelis, Gregory. "Foodways Acculturation in the Greek
        Community of Philadelphia." *Pennsylvania Folklife*
        20:2 (Winter 1970-1971):9-15.

        Argues that processes of urbanization and Americanization
        do not destroy traditional Greek cooking, but rather
        create a unique Greek-American blend. Provides reasons
        for continuity and transformations, derived from inter-

views with 8 Greek-Americans in Philadelphia, 4 of whom
are first generation and 4 of whom are second generation.
Presents 3 pages of selected transcripts of interview
sessions, and provides a list of informants. Includes
10 photographs of informants preparing foods.

GR16   Gizelis, Gregory. "The Function of the Vision in
        Greek-American Culture." *Western Folklore* 33:1
        (1974):65-76.

        Discussion of religious symbols and words as stimuli
        for visions and of ways visions function for Greek-
        Americans: to ease spiritual ills, to reinforce faith,
        and to gain entry and achieve status in sub-groups
        within the ethnic community. Includes transcriptions
        of 6 interviews and narratives from Philadelphia
        fieldwork.

GR17   Gizelis, Gregory. *Narrative Rhetorical Devices of
        Persuasion: Folklore Communication in a Greek-American
        Community.* Athens: National Centre of Social Research,
        1974. Pp. 155, preface, introduction, 2 appendices,
        bibliography.

        Discussion of storytelling in the Greek-American
        community of Philadelphia, with emphasis on ways stories
        serve as sources of self-identification and differentia-
        tion, as means of self-evaluation, and as ways of
        communicating and reinforcing group norms. Based on
        1970-71 fieldwork. Includes texts of approximately 44
        narratives (variously identified as fables, ethnic
        jokes/slurs, puns, stories), presented within the
        contexts of transcribed segments of tape-recorded
        interviews.

GR18   Gizelis, Gregory. *Narrative Rhetorical Devices of
        Persuasion in the Greek Community of Philadelphia.*
        New York: Arno Press, 1980. Pp. xxxix, 264, preface,
        appendix, bibliography, index.

        A 1972 University of Pennsylvania dissertation, based
        on 1970-71 fieldwork among Greek-Americans in Philadel-
        phia, with emphasis on the ways stories and storytelling
        serve as sources of self-identification and differentia-
        tion, as means of self-evaluation, and as ways of
        communicating and reinforcing group norms. Provides
        an overview and assessment of Greek-American folklore
        scholarship, a discussion of the fieldwork site and
        circumstances, and "the rhetorical aspects of narrative

communication." Includes texts of approximately 40
tales, variously identified as fables, ethnic jokes/
slurs, puns, and stories, presented within the contexts
of transcribed segments of tape-recorded interviews.

GR19   Gizelis, Gregory. "A Neglected Aspect of Creativity
       of Folklore Performers." *Journal of American Folk-
       lore* 86:340 (1973):167-172.

Distinctions made among re-creation, limited creation,
and real creation in folklore performances. Argues
that folklorists have focused on the first of these and
neglected the other two. Presents examples of tales
told by Greek-American narrators in Philadelphia in
1970 to illustrate creativity in storytelling. Includes
texts of 3 narratives.

GR20   Gizelis, Gregory. "The Use of Amulets among Greek-
       Philadelphians." *Pennsylvania Folklife* 20:3 (Spring
       1971):30-38.

Attempts to measure the strength of belief in and use
of amulets by observation and interviews with over 5
informants in Philadelphia in 1969. Describes nature
of amulets and places where they can be obtained.
Discusses the relationship between religion and folk
beliefs. Includes excerpts from tape recordings and
10 photographs of amulets.

*GR21 Jones, Louis C. "The Evil-Eye among European-Americans."

       (Cross-listed as *GL51, *HU17, *IN1, *IR50, *IT35,
       *JE35, *PL39, *RU10, *SZ2.)
       (See *GL51 for full citation and annotation.)

GR22   Kaloyanides, Michael G. "New York and Bouzoukia: The
       Rise of Greek-American Music." *Essays in Arts and
       Sciences* 6:1 (1977):95-103.

Through a discussion of the music of Greek immigrants to
the United States, author demonstrates that Greek-American
culture evolved through 3 states: from a village- or
regionally-based Old World culture (1900-1920) to a
national hellenic one (1920-1930s) to a Greek-American
one (since 1940s). Discusses briefly this evolution
as indicated by the selections played and instruments
used by Greek-American musical groups, revealing the
increasing influences of American popular music on
Greek-American ensembles and the ultimate influence,
in the 1950s and 1960s, of Greek popular music on

Greek-American and American repertoires and musical
styles. Focuses principally on Greek-American music
and musicians in New York City. Includes prefatory
historical sketch of Greek immigration to the United
States.

GR23 Lee, D. Demetracopoulou. "Folklore of the Greeks in
      America." *Folk-Lore* 47:3 (1936):294-310.

      Miscellaneous sampling of folklore recorded from
      Boston-area Greek immigrants in 1934-35. Distinctions
      made among the traditions of three regions: the Pontus,
      the island of Lesbos and adjacent coast of Asia Minor,
      and the district of Arcadia in the Peloponnesus of
      mainland Greece. Includes 6 narrative texts, summaries
      or characterizations of 14 others, descriptions of such
      supernatural beings as *magissa, callicandjari,
      vrykolakas,* and *neraides.* Conclusion is that Old World
      Greek folklore has no place in the New World and cannot
      survive or persist here.

GR24 Lee, D. Demetracopoulou. "Greek Accounts of the
      Vrykolakas." *Journal of American Folklore* 55:217
      (1942):126-132.

      Presentation (in English translation) of 13 accounts of
      encounters with the *vrykolakas,* a non-human being
      believed to be able to leave its grave "every day
      except Saturday," recorded from male Greek immigrant
      informants from Belmont, Cambridge, and Watertown,
      Massachusetts, in 1934.

GR25 Lee, Dorothy D. "Greek Personal Anecdotes of the
      Supernatural." *Journal of American Folklore* 64:253
      (1951):307-312.

      Presentation (in English translation) of 14 accounts of
      the nature of, and encounters with, a wide range of
      supernatural beings and of 5 statements of belief/
      superstitions about "unlucky days," recorded from
      Greek immigrants in the greater Boston area. Comments
      on the degree of transmission to members of the first
      American-born generation.

GR26 Lee, Dorothy D. "Greek Tales of Nastradi Hodjas." *Folk-
      Lore* 57:4 (1946):188-195.

      Presentation (in English translation) of texts of 28
      tales about the trickster-numskull figure Nastradi

Hodjas, recorded by the author in 1934 and 1937 from
Greek immigrants living in the Boston area. Identifies
homelands of informants as being in what is currently
the country of Turkey.

GR27   Lee, Dorothy D. "Greek Tales of Priest and Priestwife."
       Journal of American Folklore 60:236 (1947):163-167.

       Presentation (in English translation) of 9 tales,
       recorded by the author among Greeks in the greater
       Boston area in 1934 and 1937, concerned with priests as
       lechers and/or priestwives as coveted or unfaithful.
       Also includes mention of 1 belief/superstition about
       priests as ill omens and the text (in English transla-
       tion) of 1 song sung to accompany a round dance (about
       a priestwife who desires a shepherd boy rather than her
       priest husband).

*GR28 Lee, Dorothy D. "Three Romances from Pontos." *Folk-
       lore* 62 (1951):388-397, 449-453.

       Presentation of texts of 3 minstrel tales (in English
       translation), recorded by the author from a Greek in-
       formant from Pontos in Watertown, Massachusetts. Tales
       told in the Pontic dialect of Greek and lyrics sung in
       Turkish.
       (Cross-listed as *TU2.)

GR29   Mathews, Ernest S. "Merry Greek Tales from Buffalo."
       New York Folklore Quarterly 5:4 (1949):268-275.

       Characterizations of 8 tales of the street-priest
       Stratouhotdas (Nasreddin Hodja), elicited from a
       Greek-American woman in Buffalo, New York, in 1948.

*GR30 Nichols, Mrs. Priscilla Miller. "Greek Lore from
       Syracuse, N.Y." *New York Folklore Quarterly* 9:2
       (1953):109-117.

       Characterization of 2 personal experience stories
       concerning the evil eye, 1 folksong, brief descriptions
       of customs and beliefs relating to holidays, engage-
       ments and weddings, childbirth and christenings, sick-
       ness and death. Recorded from a Greek-American couple
       in Syracuse, New York.
       (Cross-listed as *TU4.)

GR31 Papanikolas, Helen Z. "Greek Folklore of Carbon County."
      In *Lore of Faith & Folly*, edited by Thomas E. Cheney,
      assisted by Austin E. Fife and Juanita Brooks, pp. 61-
      77. Salt Lake City: University of Utah Press, 1971.

      General discussion of Greek immigrant miners in Carbon
      County, Utah, including brief mention of customs and
      beliefs relating to marriage, childbirth, death, healing,
      the evil eye, and Easter. Includes 1 personal experi-
      ence story and 2 lamentation verses (all in English).
      Author asserts that Old World beliefs and customs are
      dying out among these immigrants and their descendants.

GR32 Papanikolas, Helen Z. "Magerou: The Greek Midwife."
      Utah Historical Quarterly 38:1 (1970):50-60.

      Biographical sketch of a Greek woman who came to the
      Magna, Utah, area in 1909 to live with her Austrian
      immigrant husband. Emphasis on the woman's work as a
      midwife and healer, both in Greece and in Utah.

GR33 Patterson, G. James. *The Greeks of Vancouver: A Study
      in the Preservation of Ethnicity*. Canadian Centre
      for Folk Culture Studies, Paper No. 18. Ottawa:
      National Museum of Man, 1976. Pp. iv, 155, bibli-
      ography.

      Ethnographic description of the Greek community in
      Vancouver, British Columbia, with specific reference
      to history, sense of community, and life histories of
      13 individuals. Data based on interviews and partici-
      pant observation in 1975. Ethnicity viewed through
      discussion of foodways, medicine, folk beliefs, folk-
      tales, dancing, music, language, proxemics, and material
      culture. Conclusion provides reasons for the strength
      of Greek ethnicity in Canada. Includes 28 photographs.

GR34 Teske, Robert Thomas. "The Eikonastasi Among Greek-
      Philadelphians." *Pennsylvania Folklife* 23:1 (1973):
      20-29.

      Study of the placement of icons within the household
      of one extended family of 14 members, based on 10 hours
      of interviewing. Discusses physical locations of the
      icons and relationships between folk and official
      religions. Notes and explains the conflicts among
      differing folk conceptions. Includes 17 photographs
      of icons and their placement in the home.

GR35   Teske, Robert Thomas. "Living Room Furnishings, Ethnic
       Identity, and Acculturation among Greek Philadelphians."
       New York Folklore 5:1-2 (1979):21-31.

       Describes artifacts and color schemes found in living
       rooms of Philadelphia Greeks, noting that the former
       (ranging from Greek postcards to icons to reproductions
       of classical Greek vases) and the latter (the light
       blue and white of the Greek flag) have as their objec-
       tive to make visitors aware of the ethnic identity of
       the householders and also serve as an index of the
       degree of acculturation of the family (based on what
       is displayed and how it is presented).

GR36   Teske, Robert Thomas. "On the Making of *Bobonieres* and
       Marturia in Greek Philadelphia: Commercialism in
       Folk Religion." *Journal of the Folklore Institute*
       16:3 (1977):151-158.

       Discussion of a Greek-American couple's making and
       selling *bobonieres* (almonds tied in netting, distributed
       at Greek weddings) and *marturia* (baptismal ribbons),
       with emphasis on the problems involved and innovations
       made as the couple established and expanded production.
       Based on observations and interviews in Upper Darby,
       Pennsylvania, in 1973. Includes 2 photographs, of a
       boboniere and of a *marturia*.

GR37   Teske, Robert Thomas. "Rules Governing the Presentation
       of Votive Offerings among Greek-Philadelphians."
       Keystone Folklore 18:4 (1974):181-195.

       Discussion of the practice among Greeks of promising
       votive offerings, usually material in nature, to saints
       in exchange for cures for illnesses or answers to
       petitions or requests. Focuses on the behavior of one
       Greek immigrant woman from Philadelphia and on various
       factors involved in making a request, determining what
       to promise for its fulfillment, and deciding where and
       when the offering should be carried out or presented.
       Includes characterizations of 2 personal experience
       stories, photographs of 3 gold- or silver-plated icons
       in Philadelphia Greek Orthodox churches, and 1 photo-
       graph of a votive candle.

GR38   Teske, Robert Thomas. *Votive Offerings among Greek-Philadelphians*. New York: Arno Press, 1980. Pp. xxix, 326, preface, list of illustrations, bibliography, index.

A 1974 University of Pennsylvania dissertation, based on 1972-74 fieldwork among Greek-Americans in Philadelphia and focusing on the practice of making and presenting votive offerings in response to requests or as manifestations of vows made to the Virgin Mary, saints, and other figures in the Greek Orthodox religious pantheon. Provides discussion of the bases for the study, the fieldwork site and circumstances, the history of votive offerings from classical Greek times to the present, a survey of scholarship on votive offerings in Greece and elsewhere in Europe, the "rules governing votive offerings among Greek-Philadelphians," and the "message stored in and transmitted through the votive offering." Presents texts or characterizations of 67 experiences with vows and votive offerings, identified variously as personal experience narratives, legends, and memorates, many involving miraculous healings. Includes 15 photographs of churches, icons, and votive offerings and 1 map of the Philadelphia area in which fieldwork was conducted. Author identifies his approach as one in which ritual is viewed as communication.

GR39   Theophano, Janet. "Feast, Fast, and Time." *Pennsylvania Folklife* 27:3 (1978):25-32.

Discussion of continuity in food customs between members of different generations of Greeks in Philadelphia in the 1970s, based on fieldwork among 25 Greek Orthodox informants. Describes similarities between Greek and American food customs associated with festivals, life-cycle events, calendrical rites, and seasonal changes. Includes a glossary of Greek foods.

XXI.   GYPSY (GY) (1-14)

*GY1   Agogino, George A., and Pickett, David W. "Two Tales
       of Three Nails." *New York Folklore Quarterly* 16:1
       (1960):32-36.

       Brief discussion of the origin of the Gypsies and of
       their origin myth. Presentation of 2 tale texts,
       recorded in the spring and summer of 1958 from Gypsy
       informants (1 of whom is identified as Russian) living
       in New York State. Tales seem to explain the presence
       of the penance motif in the Gypsy origin myth.
       (Cross-listed as *RU1.)

 GY2   Bonos, Arlene Helen. "Roumany Rye of Philadelphia."
       American Anthropologist n.s. 44:2 (1942):257-274.

       Description of a group of Philadelphia Gypsies, with
       emphases upon male-female roles and responsibilities,
       taboos concerning contact and cleanliness, beliefs and
       customs associated with such rites of passage as marriage,
       pregnancy, childbirth, and death.

 GY3   Cotten, Rena M. "Sex Dichotomy among the American
       Kalderaš Gypsies." *Journal of the Gypsy Lore Society*
       3rd series 30:1-2 (1951):16-25.

       General discussion of sex roles among American Kalderaš
       Gypsies, emphasizing the increasing loss of sex role
       distinctions as a result of culture contact and Ameri-
       canization. Includes passing references to menstruation
       and marriage taboos and customs.

*GY4   Dieffenbach, Victor C. "Gypsy Stories from the Swatara
       Valley."

       (Cross-listed as *GE140.)
       (See *GE140 for full citation and annotation.)

*GY5   Erdely, Stephen. "Ethnic Music in the United States:
       An Overview."

       (Cross-listed as *GL40, *AR5, *CR2, *GR7, *JE22,
       *SC11, *SE2.)
       (See *GL40 for full citation and annotation.)

*GY6   Gruszczyńska, Mrs. Valeria. "'Cast Your Bread Upon the
       Waters ...': A 'Good Gypsy' Story."

       (Cross-listed as *PL35.)
       (See *PL35 for full citation and annotation.)

GY7   Gutowski, John. "The Gypsies and Gypsy Hill." *Indiana
       Folklore* 3:1 (1970):95-112.

       Presentation of 13 recollections and tales about Gypsies
       who gathered in the Gypsy Hill, Indiana, area in the
       late 19th and early 20th centuries, based on data
       recorded in 1970 from members of 3 generations of area
       residents.

GY8   "Gypsy Queen in America." *Journal of American Folk-
       Lore* 2:5 (1889):156.

       Reprinted description of the coronation of a Gypsy
       queen near Dayton, Ohio, in 1888.

GY9   Pelly, Francine. "Gypsy Folktales from Philadelphia."
       Keystone Folklore Quarterly 13:2 (1968):83-102.

       Presentation of 11 folktale texts, recorded from members
       of a Philadelphia Gypsy family in 1968. Tales identi-
       fied as ghost stories, a migratory legend, and memorates.
       Includes description of informants' living quarters and
       lifestyles, quotations from taped interviews about the
       Gypsies, their background, and their experiences.

GY10   Salo, Matt T. "The Expression of Ethnicity in R̲om Oral
       Tradition." *Western Folklore* 36:1 (1977):33-56.

       An historical and ethnographic characterization of the
       R̲om Gypsies of North America, with 16 field-recorded
       and 2 reprinted narrative texts (identified as anecdotes,
       legends, and memorates), illustrating the R̲om sense of
       uniqueness and ways they distinguish themselves from
       others. Based on fieldwork conducted from 1972 to 1977
       in Ontario, Quebec, Illinois, Ohio, New York, Louisiana,
       Florida, and Mississippi.

GY11   Salo, Matt T., and Salo, Sheila M.G. *The Kalderas in
       Eastern Canada.* Canadian Centre for Folk Culture
       Studies, Paper No. 21. Ottawa: National Museum of
       Man, 1977. Pp. 268, bibliography.

       An analysis of ethnic identity of the Kalderas Gypsies
       in eastern Canada, based on fieldwork in the Montreal
       and Toronto areas in 1973 and 1976. Expression of
       ethnic identity illustrated through religion, life-
       cycle events, clothing, food, music, dance, and narra-
       tives. Concept of ethnic boundaries used to explain
       continuity of ethnicity despite changes. Appendices
       contain 15 memorates and belief tales, 7 legends and
       fabulates, 2 origin and family legends, 2 anecdotes,
       and 7 proverbs.

GY12   Sinclair, A.T. "Gypsies." *Journal of American Folk-
        Lore* 19:74 (1906):261.

        Listing of 10 questions directed to readers of the
        Journal of American Folk-Lore requesting information
        about any Gypsies they know living in their home locales.

GY13   Sinclair, A.T. "Notes on the Gypsies." *Journal of
        American Folk-Lore* 19:74 (1906):212-213.

        Discussion of the author's personal experiences with
        Gypsies, both in the United States and Europe. De-
        scribes commonly held stereotypes: Gypsies' reputation
        for stealing children, their attitude toward honesty,
        and their attitude toward chastity.

GY14   Stiver, Shawn. "Gypsy Hill." *Indiana Folklore* 5:1
        (1972):31-55.

        Presentation of excerpts from 52 interviews with
        residents of the Gypsy Hill, Indiana, area, concerning
        their recollections or knowledge about the Gypsies who
        frequented the area in the late 19th and early 20th
        centuries. Emphasizes the stereotypic nature of
        people's conceptions of Gypsies.

                      XXII. HUNGARIAN (HU) (1-31)

*HU1   Barbour, Frances M. "Some Foreign Proverbs in Southern
        Illinois."

        (Cross-listed as *DA1, *DU2, *FR21, *GE33, *IT3.)
        (See *GE33 for full citation and annotation.)

HU2   Blumstock, Robert, ed. *Bekevar: Working Papers on a
        Canadian Prairie Community.* Canadian Centre for
        Folk Culture Studies, Paper No. 31. Ottawa: National
        Museum of Man, 1979. Pp. ix, 308.

        Presentation of 6 reports of a multidisciplinary in-
        vestigation conducted by a National Museum of Man
        research team in 1974 and 1975 on the Hungarian-Canadian
        community of Kipling, Saskatchewan, formerly known as
        Békévar. Focus is on changes in the community and the
        erosion of its ethnic distinctiveness. Includes folk-
        lore-related essays by Linda Dégh ("Folklore of the

Békévar Community," see HU3), Mária Kresz ("Békévar,
Children, Clothing, Crafts," see HU20), and Hélène
Stålfelt-Szabó and Mátyás Szabó ("The Architecture of
Békévar," see HU28).

HU3   Dégh, Linda. "Folklore of the Békévar Community." In
      Bekevar: Working Papers on a Canadian Prairie Community,
      edited by Robert Blumstock, pp. 13-64. Canadian Centre
      for Folk Culture Studies, Paper No. 31. Ottawa:
      National Museum of Man, 1979.

      Survey of folklore forms among Hungarians of Kipling,
      Saskatchewan, based on fieldwork conducted in 1975 among
      93 informants. Narratives described according to themes,
      such as heroic pioneers, spiritualism, ghosts, magical
      beliefs and legends, historical events, and jokes and
      anecdotes. Use of folk medicine discussed. Describes
      the religious nature of Békévar folklore, as well as the
      effects of modern technology on folklore transmission.

HU4   Dégh, Linda. "Grape Harvest Festival of Strawberry
      Farmers: Folklore or Fake?" Ethnologia Europaea 10:2
      (1977-78):114-131.

      Description of the community of Árpádhon, Louisiana, and
      its inhabitants of Hungarian ancestry, whose sole source
      for perpetuating their sense of ethnic identity is an
      annual harvest festival held each October since the
      first decade of the 20th century. Author notes that
      neither the dances, costumes, nor music for the festival
      are based on authentic Hungarian folk or peasant models,
      but rather are combinations of aspects and elements from
      peasant and popular Hungarian and American life and of
      imaginative notions about what was "traditional" in
      Hungary, suggesting that the festival should be regarded
      as "fake" rather than "folk." Argues that the 70+-year
      history of the festival, with its obvious continuities,
      as well as some slight changes, seems to warrant one's
      viewing the festival as a tradition or as traditional
      for those who celebrate it. Includes brief descriptions
      of dances performed, costumes worn, music played,
      instruments used, food prepared and served.

HU5   Dégh, Linda. People in the Tobacco Belt: Four Lives.
      Canadian Centre for Folk Culture Studies, Paper No.
      13. Ottawa: National Museum of Man, 1975. Pp. xx, 277.

      Presentation of life history as a unique prose genre.
      Data taken from 1972 recordings of life stories of 4

Hungarian immigrants who settled in Delhi, Canada, and whose occupations revolved around tobacco farming. Each life history arranged in 4 sections: 1) introduction of narrators and their environment, 2) summary of chronology of narrative events, 3) narrative accompanied by annotations, 4) analytical comments.

*HU6   Dégh, Linda. "Prepared Comments by Linda Dégh."

(Cross-listed as *GL27.)
(See *GL27 for full citation and annotation.)

*HU7   Dégh, Linda. "Survival and Revival of European Folk Culture in America."

(Cross-listed as *GL29.)
(See *GL29 for full citation and annotation.)

HU8   Dégh, Linda. "Symbiosis of Joke and Legend: A Case of Conversational Folklore." In *Folklore Today: A Festschrift for Richard M. Dorson*, edited by Linda Dégh, Henry Glassie, and Felix J. Oinas, pp. 101-122. Bloomington, Ind.: Research Center for Language and Semiotic Studies, Indiana University, 1976.

Description of a Székely-Hungarian-American immigrant couple, based on fieldwork begun in the Calumet region of Indiana in 1964, which focuses on the husband's role as anecdote and joke teller and wife's role as narrator of legends concerned with extranormal experiences. Presents transcribed segments of tape-recorded interviews (including 14 narratives) to exemplify kinds of tales the two tell and to demonstrate ways they respond to and complement each other during storytelling. Notes four kinds of social groups that constitute audiences for the narrators.

HU9   Dégh, Linda. "Two Hungarian-American Stereotypes." *New York Folklore Quarterly* 28:1 (1972):3-14.

Biographical sketches of 2 Hungarian immigrants, 1 who came to the United States after World War I with the express intention of returning to Hungary, but who settled permanently instead in East Chicago, Indiana, and sent for his wife after four decades of separation, the other a man who migrated with his family to Canada around 1900 and settled in the Békévar community with the intention of remaining permanently in the New World. Examples cited to illustrate "that the initial attitude of the peasant immigrant acts decisively on his fate, social adjustment, acculturation, language use and mental development."

HU10   Dégh, Linda. "Two Letters from Home." *Journal of American Folklore* 91:361 (1978):808-822.

Notes that letters between New World immigrants and their homeland friends and relatives are important research resources, often containing folklore or allusions to homeland traditions. Discussion of two letters from Hungarians to relatives living in Canada, with accompanying analyses of the folklore which they transmit or upon which they draw. Letters written in 1955, 1971.

HU11   Dégh, Linda. "Two Old World Narrators in Urban Setting." In *Kontakte und Grenzen: Probleme der Volks-, Kultur- und Sozialforschung. Festschrift für Gerhard Heilfurth zum 60. Geburtstag*, pp. 74-86. Göttingen: Otto Schwartz, 1969.

Characterization of the storytelling of 2 Hungarian immigrant women (ages 86 and 75) living in Gary, Indiana, based on observation and interviewing begun in 1964. Includes biographical sketches of the two women, characterizations of the ways they tell stories both face-to-face and over the telephone, and ways that local happenings and media presentations (particularly on television) provide source material for storytelling and stimulate recall of stories learned and told in the women's homeland (anecdotes, jokes, legends, and personal experience stories).

*HU12   Dorson, Richard M. "The Ethnic Research Survey of Northwest Indiana."

(Cross-listed as *GL30.)
(See *GL30 for full citation and annotation.)

HU13   Erdely, Stephen. "Folksinging of the American Hungarians in Cleveland." *Ethnomusicology* 8:1 (1964):14-27.

Presentation of 19 examples of songs (with transcriptions of tunes and handwritten words in Hungarian) recorded in 1961-62 from Hungarian immigrants in Cleveland, Ohio. Emphasis on the classification of the songs into old style, new style, and mixed genera.

*HU14   Erdely, Stephen. "Research on Traditional Music of
         Nationality Groups in Cleveland and Vicinity."

         (Cross-listed as *GL41, *CR3, *FN11, *GE172, *IR26,
         *RO3, *SC12, *SK4.)
         (See *GL41 for full citation and annotation.)

HU15   Erdely, Stephen. "Traditional and Individual Traits in
         the Songs of Three Hungarian-Americans." *Selected
         Reports in Ethnomusicology* 3:1 (1978):98-151.

         Biographical sketches of 3 Hungarian-American singers
         from the Cleveland, Ohio, area from each of whom the
         author has recorded between 80 and 100 songs, followed
         by a discussion of "the traditional elements and princi-
         ples" which characterize their music and songs and
         "their individual peculiarities." Includes presentation
         of divisions usually made in Hungarian music and com-
         parisons of the 3 singers' songs and music with examples
         reported in the literature from Hungarian informants.
         Includes 1 map, 5 sets of musical transcriptions
         illustrating structures and features of the music, 39
         transcribed musicological examples from both the
         repertoires of the singers and from previously published
         works on Hungarian music, English translations of
         stanzas, lines, and parts of stanzas and lines of 40
         song texts, 5 photographs of the singers studied, the
         home of 1, and a Cleveland Hungarian hall.

HU16   Halpert, Herbert. "Hungarian Lying-Contest Tales About
         America." *New York Folklore Quarterly* 1:4 (1945):
         236-237.

         Presentation of 2 texts (in English) with explanatory
         notes illustrating the type of exaggeration which
         developed in tales (told in Hungary) dealing with the
         economic possibilities in America. Recorded from a
         Hungarian informant in New York City.

*HU17   Jones, Louis C. "The Evil-Eye among European-Americans."

         (Cross-listed as *GL51, *GR21, *IN1, *IR50, *IT35,
         *JE35, *PL39, *RU10, *SZ2.)
         (See *GL51 for full citation and annotation.)

HU18   Kolozy, Raymond. "Folktales: 1. *King Matt and the Wise
         Old Farmer.*" *West Virginia Folklore* 5:3 (1955):45-46.

         Characterization (in English) of 1 folktale, told to
         the author by his Hungarian immigrant grandmother, about

a king who poses 3 riddles to his ministers, based on his encounter with an old farmer. Farmer agrees to answer the riddle for the ministers after first requesting and receiving 10 gold pieces for the answer to each.

HU19   Kolozy, Raymond. "Stories of Witches and Ghosts: 1. *Witchcraft on the Farm.*" *West Virginia Folklore* 5:3 (1955):42.

Characterization (in English) of 1 personal experience story, related about the author's Hungarian great-grandmother, about a bewitched cow that failed to give milk until the owner carried out prescribed rituals for uncovering the witch and breaking the spell.

HU20   Kresz, Mária. "Békévar, Children, Clothing, Crafts." In *Bekevar: Working Papers on a Canadian Prairie Community*, edited by Robert Blumstock, pp. 127-166. Canadian Centre for Folk Culture Studies, Paper No. 31. Ottawa: National Museum of Man, 1979.

Analysis of Békévar traditional folklife, including child-rearing and growing up in an agricultural community, as well as a description of clothing worn, the interior of houses, crafts produced, and the cemetery structure. Each topic illustrated with folk beliefs. Concludes with reasons for the breakdown in these traditional values and practices.

HU21   Makar, Janos. *The Story of an Immigrant Group in Franklin, New Jersey.* Translated by August J. Molnar. Franklin, N.J.: by the author, 1969. Pp. 170.

Ethnography of Hungarian life in Franklin, New Jersey, as well as a reconstruction of the history of the Franklin Hungarian Church. Description of folklife (presented in chapter 3, pp. 83-111) includes such topics as customs, christenings, weddings, funerals, folk dress, patriotic holidays, and Christmas caroling (4 tunes, words in German with English translations). Chapter 4 (pp. 112-170) surveys the types of Hungarian folksongs (with 42 examples, in German, with English translations and tune transcriptions) prevalent in America which reflect both Old (village life) and New (immigrant) World experiences.

*HU22   Musick, Ruth Ann. "Chapter 16, Immigrant Ghosts."

(Cross-listed as *CZ6, *IT50, *YU7.)
(See *CZ6 for full citation and annotation.)

*HU23   Musick, Ruth Ann. "European Folktales in West Virginia."
        (Cross-listed as *AU3, *CZ7, *IT51.)
        (See *AU3 for full citation and annotation.)

*HU24   Musick, Ruth Ann. *Green Hills of Magic: West Virginia
        Folktales from Europe.*
        (Cross-listed as *AR9, *AU4, *CZ8, *IR74, *IT52,
        *PL52, *RO4, *RU16, *TU3, *YU8.)
        (See *IT52 for full citation and annotation.)

*HU25   Peacock, Kenneth. "Establishing Perimeters for Ethno-
        musicological Field Research in Canada: On-Going
        Projects and Future Possibilities at the Canadian
        Centre for Folk Culture Studies."
        (Cross-listed as *GL66, *CH21, *FR91, *GE428, *IC4,
        *ID2, *IT57, *JA9, *LI5, *NO19, *RU19, *UK32.)
        (See *GL66 for full citation and annotation.)

*HU26   Peacock, Kenneth. *Twenty Ethnic Songs from Western
        Canada.*
        (Cross-listed as *CZ10, *GE429, *RU21, *UK33.)
        (See *RU21 for full citation and annotation.)

*HU27   Richman, Hyman. "The Saga of Joe Magarac." *New York
        Folklore Quarterly* 9:4 (1953):282-292.

        Investigation of the legend of Joe Magarac, folk hero
        of Hungarian and Slavic steelworkers. Examines informa-
        tion from printed sources and personal interviews, and
        draws the conclusion that this figure is a fabrication
        of special interest groups within the steel industry
        and is not attested in oral tradition.
        (Cross-listed as *GL73, *SI2.)

HU28   Ståfelt-Szabó, Hélène, and Szabó, Mátyás. "The Archi-
        tecture of Békévar." In *Bekevar: Working Papers on
        a Canadian Prairie Community,* edited by Robert Blum-
        stock, pp. 210-256. Canadian Centre for Folk Culture
        Studies, Paper No. 31. Ottawa: National Museum of
        Man, 1979.

        Analysis of the processes involved in establishing new
        buildings on a farm settlement. Provides reasons for
        the types of buildings constructed in terms of economy,
        style, technology, and construction, as well as a survey
        of the kinds of buildings commonly found on the farm
        for both humans and animals.

HU29   Stofan, Sandra. "Sources of Change in Hungarian-American
       Cooking." *Journal of the Ohio Folklore Society* n.s.
       3:1 (1974):38-45.

       Brief listing of some traditional Hungarian foods and
       general description of ingredients and ways they are
       prepared, followed by notes on reasons for both conti-
       nuity and change in foods among Americans of Hungarian
       ancestry. Based on experiential data in the author's
       family environment in Toledo, Ohio.

HU30   Vázsonyi, Andrew. "The *Cicisbeo* and the Magnificent
       Cuckold: *Boardinghouse Life and Lore in Immigrant
       Communities.*" *Journal of American Folklore* 91:360
       (1978):641-656.

       Discussion of Hungarian immigrant boarding houses and
       reported liaisons between male boarders and their land-
       ladies. Indicates that while relationships between
       wives of boarding house owners and male boarders often
       created tensions and resulted in divorces or broken
       marriages, they also contributed to household stability
       and economic success. Based on fieldwork begun in 1967
       in the Calumet region of Indiana. Includes reprinted
       segments of 2 songs and 6 poems illustrative of the
       nature and effects of "star-boarders'" relationships
       with wives of their landlords.

HU31   Ware, Helen. "The American-Hungarian Folk-Song." *The
       Musical Quarterly* 2:3 (1916):434-441.

       Discussion of folksongs recorded from a Hungarian
       immigrant roaming fiddler and ballad singer in South
       Bend, Indiana. Songs describe immigration experiences,
       the immigrant's impressions of the new land and longing
       for the old. Includes texts of or excerpts from 11
       songs (in English translations, 3 with tune transcrip-
       tions).

XXIII. ICELANDIC (IC) (1-4)

IC1 Einarsson, Magnus. "Icelandic Pular." In *Folklore of Canada*, edited by Edith Fowke, pp. 287-290. Toronto: McClelland and Stewart Limited, 1976.

Presentation (in English) of 2 *pular* ("rhapsodic enumerative nonstrophic" poems), recorded by the author in 1966 in Gimli, Manitoba, from a Canadian immigrant woman born in Iceland. Texts identified as variants of "The Mouse Regains Its Tail" and "The Twelve Kinds of Food."

*IC2 Hopkins, Pandora. "Individual Choice and the Control of Musical Change." *Journal of American Folklore* 89:354 (1976):449-462.

Asserts that there are reasons for change, as well as for stability, in traditional music and that individual choice, rather than degeneration, is often responsible for change. Discusses 2 Icelandic-Americans (encountered in 1965) who had learned and retained in the United States their skill at transforming well-known Icelandic legends into a versified musical form called *rimur*, a process common in early 20th-century Iceland but since discontinued there. Includes 1 transcribed musicological example to illustrate the *rimur* style. Also discusses the song-learning experiences of Irish-American folk-singer Sara Cleveland (of Hudson Falls, New York) to illustrate the point that singers often distinguish "old" and "new" songs and that the former may be precisely learned and performed, while the latter may be free from such restrictions. Includes a musical transcription of 1 song by Sara Cleveland.
(Cross-listed as *IR45.)

*IC3 Klymasz, Robert B. "The Ethnic Joke in Canada Today."

(Cross-listed as *GL53, *FR71, *IT38, *JE40, *UK10.)
(See *GL53 for full citation and annotation.)

*IC4 Peacock, Kenneth. "Establishing Perimeters for Ethno-musicological Field Research in Canada: On-Going Projects and Future Possibilities at the Canadian Centre for Folk Culture Studies."

(Cross-listed as *GL66, *CH21, *FR91, *GE428, *HU25, *ID2, *IT57, *JA9, *LI5, *NO19, *RU19, *UK32.)
(See *GL66 for full citation and annotation.)

XXIV. INDIAN (ID) (1-4)

*ID1   Hoe, Ban Seng. "Asian-Canadian Folklore Studies: An
       Interdisciplinary and Cross-Cultural Approach."

       (Cross-listed as *CH9, *JA3.)
       (See *CH9 for full citation and annotation.)

*ID2   Peacock, Kenneth. "Establishing Perimeters for Ethno-
       musicological Field Research in Canada: On-Going
       Projects and Future Possibilities at the Canadian
       Centre for Folk Culture Studies."

       (Cross-listed as *GL66, *CH21, *FR91, *GE428, *HU25,
       *IC4, *IT57, *JA9, *LI5, *NO19, *RU19, *UK32.)
       (See *GL66 for full citation and annotation.)

*ID3   Qureshi, Regula. "Ethnomusicological Research among
       Canadian Communities of Arab and East Indian Origin."

       (Cross-listed as *EG1, *LE4, *PA1, *SZ4.)
       (See *SZ4 for full citation and annotation.)

 ID4   Vatuk, Ved Prakash. "Panjabi Riddles from the West
       Coast." *Western Folklore* 29:1 (1970):35-46.

       Discussion of riddles and riddling in India, followed
       by a listing of 39 riddles (in Panjabi, with English
       translations), recorded from Indian immigrants in the
       El Centro and Yuba City, California, areas in 1965.
       Includes comments on riddle form and style and on
       differences between riddling in India and among Indian
       immigrants in the United States.

                 XXV. IRANIAN (IN) (1)

*IN1   Jones, Louis C. "The Evil-Eye among European-Americans."

       (Cross-listed as *GL51, *GR21, *HU17, *IR50, *IT35,
       *JE35, *PL39, *RU10, *SZ2.)
       (See *GL51 for full citation and annotation.)

XXVI.   IRISH (IR) (1-119)

*IR1   Augar, Pearl Hamelin. "French Beliefs in Clinton County."

        (Cross-listed as *FR5.)
        (See *FR5 for full citation and annotation.)

IR2   Bacon, A.M., and Parsons, E.C. "Folk-Lore from Elizabeth
        City County, Virginia." *Journal of American Folk-Lore*
        35:137 (1922):250-327.

        Preface by Parsons notes that the 114 tales and 136
        riddles presented are from various sources, with most of
        the tales recorded around the turn of the century by
        Bacon from Afro-Americans at the Mapton Institute and
        others recorded by Parsons in 1920 at Hampton. "Irish-
        men stories" (texts 72, 73, 75-108) relevant to this
        bibliography.

*IR3   Barbeau, C.M. "Folk-Songs." *Journal of American Folk-
        Lore* 31:120 (1918):170-179.

        Presentation of 6 songs (in English, with tune transcrip-
        tions). Primary informant of French-Canadian and
        Scottish-Canadian descent. Songs learned from Irishmen.
        (Cross-listed as *FR6, *SC1.)

*IR4   Barrick, Mac E. "Racial Riddles & the Polack Joke."

        (Cross-listed as *GE43, *IT6, *JE4, *PL5.)
        (See *PL5 for full citation and annotation.)

IR5   Barry, Phillips. "Irish Come-All-Ye's." *Journal of
        American Folk-Lore* 22:86 (1909):374-388.

        Notes Irish contributions to the preservation of tradi-
        tional songs and ballads in the United States. Presents
        9 song texts ("Come-All-Ye's," with tune transcriptions),
        recorded in Boston. States that Irish ballad singers
        make no distinction between earlier and later balladry,
        but sing those songs with good melodies that are appeal-
        ing. Comments on the re-creative process by which a
        "ballad mosaic" may be composed of several ballads and
        on ballad refrains.

IR6   Barry, Phillips. "Irish Folk-Song." *Journal of Ameri-*
       can Folk-Lore 24:93 (1911):332-343.

       Differentiates between "art-song" and "folk-song" on the
       basis of communal re-creation, with 2 examples of
       ancient and 2 of later ballads. Presents words and
       music of Irish songs recorded in Boston and others from
       an unpublished manuscript of one Dr. Henry Hudson, who
       recorded his songs (primarily melodies) in Ireland.
       Notes that Irish immigrants brought many songs to the
       northern United States, but few have become "Americanized."

IR7   Barry, Phillips. "New Ballad Texts." *Journal of Ameri-*
       can Folk-Lore 24:93 (1911):344-349.

       Presentation of 6 ballad texts from the author's collec-
       tion made from 1903 to 1911, 2 of which were recorded
       from Irish immigrants or their descendants.

IR8   Barry, Phillips. "Some Aspects of Folk-Song." *Journal*
       of American Folk-Lore 25:95 (1912):274-283.

       Presentation of 8 ballad texts (with tune transcriptions,
       plus an additional 4 tunes), 1 of which is identified as
       Irish. Notes the beauty of the melodies and stresses
       the changes different ballads have undergone, apparently
       due to the process of re-creation.

*IR9   Bethke, Robert. "Chester County Widow Wills (1714-1800):
       A Folklife Source." *Pennsylvania Folklife* 18:1 (1968):
       16-20.

       Examination of wills left by widows in Chester County,
       Pennsylvania, during the 18th century. Argues importance
       of wills as folk-cultural documents in revealing atti-
       tudes toward immigration, settlement patterns, religious
       affiliation, educational practices, property rights, and
       monetary values among individuals of Welsh, English,
       Scotch-Irish, and Quaker backgrounds.
       (Cross-listed as *SC2, *WE1.)

*IR10 Blegen, Theodore C. "Singing Immigrants and Pioneers."

       (Cross-listed as *DA2, *FN1, *NO2, *SS3.)
       (See *NO2 for full citation and annotation.)

IR11 Booker, Louise Robertson. "A Folk Story from Ireland."
      North Carolina Folklore 20:4 (1972):157-158.

      Characterization of 1 story, reportedly of Irish origin
      but heard in the United States, about the transformation
      of a woman into a rat and the way this was discovered.

*IR12 Botkin, Ben A. (Moderator). "The Folksong Revival: A
      Symposium."

      (Cross-listed as *JE9, *SC3.)
      (See *JE9 for full citation and annotation.)

IR13 Brewster, Paul G. "Folk-Tales from Indiana and Missouri."
      Folk-Lore 50:3 (1939):294-310.

      Presentation of 17 folktale texts, 14 recorded by the
      author in 1938 from 2 informants of Irish ancestry in
      Princeton, Indiana, and St. Louis, Missouri, and 3
      remembered by the author from his childhood from un-
      known sources.

IR14 Cazden, Norman. "Song: 'The Foggy Dew' (Irish)."
      New York Folklore Quarterly 10:3 (1954):213-217.

      Discussion of the theme of the mist-maiden, or mermaid,
      and its roots in ancient Irish lore and even earlier
      forms of siren imagery; of the appearance of this theme
      in "The Foggy Dew" and other traditional songs; and of
      other printed versions of this song and their possible
      relationships. Presentation of 1 text of this song
      (with tune) as recorded from George Edwards of the
      Catskills.

IR15 Cohen, Norman. "'The *Persian's* Crew'--The Ballad, Its
      Author, and the Incident." *New York Folklore
      Quarterly* 25:4 (1969):289-296.

      Author traces the ballad "The *Persian's* Crew" to a poem
      written by an Irish immigrant to Oswego, New York, and
      published in a book of poems of his in 1886. Includes
      excerpts from newspaper accounts of the sinking of the
      ship and reprints the presumed poem-model for the
      ballad written by Patrick Fennell.

*IR16 Curtin, Jeremiah. "European Folk-Lore in the United
      States."

      (Cross-listed as *GL21.)
      (See *GL21 for full citation and annotation.)

*IR17   Curtis, Otis F. (Jr.). "The Curtis Collection of Songs, I."

(Cross-listed as *GE126.)
(See *GE126 for full citation and annotation.)

*IR18   Curtis, Wardon Allan. "'The Light Fantastic' in the Central West: Country Dances of Many Nationalities in Wisconsin."

(Cross-listed as *GE127, *NO8, *SW4.)
(See *SW4 for full citation and annotation.)

*IR19   Cutting, Edith. "Peter Parrott and His Songs."

(Cross-listed as *FR47.)
(See *FR47 for full citation and annotation.)

*IR20   Dorson, Richard M. "Blood Stoppers."

(Cross-listed as *FN2, *FR50, *GE160, *SL1, *SS8.)
(See *FR50 for full citation and annotation.)

*IR21   Dorson, Richard M. "Dialect Stories of the Upper Peninsula: A New Form of American Folklore."

(Cross-listed as *CO3, *FN3, *FR53, *IT17, *SS9.)
(See *FR53 for full citation and annotation.)

*IR22   Dorson, Richard M. "Personal Histories."

(Cross-listed as *DU6, *FR56, *SS11.)
(See *SS11 for full citation and annotation.)

IR23   Duncan, Gwyneth. "Irish Customs and Beliefs in North Carolina." *North Carolina Folklore* 18:3 (1970): 148-153.

Characterization of customs and beliefs associated with New Year's, Lent and Easter, May Day, Halloween, and women, recorded from an Irish immigrant woman in Winston-Salem, North Carolina. Includes 2 personal experience stories, comparative notes and discussions.

*IR24   Dunn, Adda Ann. "Songs, Riddles, and Tales from Saratoga County." *New York Folklore Quarterly* 5:3 (1949):211-219.

Presentation of lore collected from Saratoga County, New York. Includes 2 ballad texts (no tunes; discussion of the events to which one of the ballads alludes),

1 ballad fragment, 1 hymn parody, 5 riddle texts, 1
trickster tale (set in Ireland), and 1 tale involving
fairies (from an informant of Irish descent); also
includes a brief discussion of 1 Scottish superstition,
1 custom, and 1 legend explaining how the thistle became the emblem of Scotland.
(Cross-listed as *SC8.)

*IR25 Eames, Frank. "Landon's Ould Dog and Hogmanay Fair."

       (Cross-listed as *FR58, *SC10.)
       (See *FR58 for full citation and annotation.)

*IR26 Erdely, Stephen. "Research on Traditional Music of
       Nationality Groups in Cleveland and Vicinity."

       (Cross-listed as *GL41, *CR3, *FN11, *GE172, *HU14,
       *RO3, *SC12, *SK4.)
       (See *GL41 for full citation and annotation.)

*IR27 Evanson, Jacob A. "Folk Songs of an Industrial City."

       (Cross-listed as *GL42, *FN12, *GE177, *GR8, *SK5.)
       (See *GL42 for full citation and annotation.)

IR28   Evers, Alf. "Bluestone Lore and Bluestone Men." *New
       York Folklore Quarterly* 18:1 (1962):86-107.

       Discussion of the relationship of the physical environ-
       ment to the type of lore which the people of an area
       produce (in this instance, Ulster County, New York);
       of the gradual dominance in the area (which produces
       dark bluestone) of the "quarry Irish" and the wakes
       associated with this period; of the decline of quar-
       rying in Woodstock; of the many uses of bluestone,
       some of the mysterious bluestone structures in the area,
       and the use of bluestone as a form of currency; and of
       the transition of Woodstock into an artists' colony
       (the Irish-American plays of Dan Sully were written
       here) and the uses made of bluestone by this new group.
       Includes presentation (or characterization) of 2 epi-
       taphs, 1 anecdote, 2 tall tales, and 4 stories from the
       area.

IR29   "Folk-Lore Scrap-Book." *Journal of American Folk-Lore*
       12:46 (1899):226-228.

       Presentation of 7 "Irishman stories" or tales about
       Irishmen told by Afro-Americans as quoted from *Southern
       Workman* (May 1899). Notes that in these stories the
       Irishman is responsible for simplistic or rustic deeds.

IR30   Forster, J. Margaret. "Folklore of County Monaghan,
       Ireland, Twenty Years Later." *California Folklore
       Quarterly* 2:4 (1943):309-314.

       Characterizations of 3 place legends, 6 stories involving
       fairies and witches, 2 personal experience stories of a
       curse and a fire of stones, 1 tale of a tabooed fort, 1
       story of a tabooed bush, 1 Halloween story, 6 ghost
       tales, 1 buried treasure tale, 9 superstitions, 1 healing
       charm. Information obtained from 2 California Irish-
       American families.

*IR31 Foster, James R. "Brooklyn Folklore."

       (Cross-listed as *GL43, *GR9, *IT21, *JE24, *PL28,
       *P06, *SP7.)
       (See *GL43 for full citation and annotation.)

IR32   Foster, John Wilson. "Some Irish Songs in the Gordon
       Collection." *Northwest Folklore* 3:2 (1968):16-29.

       Brief discussion of an Irish song manuscript included
       in the Gordon Collection at the University of Oregon,
       followed by the presentation of 6 songs.

IR33   Fox, C. Milligan. "Irish Songs from America." *Journal
       of the Irish Folk Song Society* 9 (1911):13-16.

       Presentation of texts of 3 songs (in English, with tune
       transcriptions), recorded from "the singing of two
       Sligo girls" in New York.

IR34   Gard, R. Max. "Tales of Dungannon, A Spot of Ireland
       in Ohio." *Keystone Folklore Quarterly* 8:2 (1963):
       84-90.

       Brief historical sketch of Irish immigrants to the
       Dungannon, Ohio, area during the early 1800s, with
       emphasis on one canal boat owner and 6 anecdotes about
       his outrageous antics.

*IR35 Gardner, Emelyn E. "Folk-Lore from Schoharie County,
       New York."

       (Cross-listed as *DU9, *GE197.)
       (See *GE197 for full citation and annotation.)

IR36   Halpert, Herbert. "Aggressive Humor on the East Branch."
       New York Folklore Quarterly 2:2 (1946):85-97.

       Discussion of aggression as a prominent element in
       American folk tradition, as exemplified in tales recorded

from former raftsmen and lumbermen in the east branch
of the Delaware River area. Presentation of 21 texts
(in English), which include 11 numskull stories, 4
trickster tales, 4 *retorts*, 2 unclassified tales, and
notes on parallels and analogues, with 8 of these texts
specifically identified as "Irishman stories."

*IR37   Halpert, Herbert. "Legends of the Cursed Child."

(Cross-listed as *GL48, *SC19.)
(See *GL48 for full citation and annotation.)

IR38   Halpert, Lt. Herbert. "Pennsylvania Fairylore and
Folktales." *Journal of American Folklore* 58:228
(1945):130-134.

Presentation of texts of 11 tales, 3 about fairies or
concerned with beliefs in the existence of fairies,
recorded from a man of Irish background in Wayne County,
Pennsylvania, in 1941.

*IR39   Hand, Wayland D. "California Miners' Folklore: Above
Ground."

(Cross-listed as *CH8, *CO5, *GE235, *IT28, *SS15.)
(See *CO5 for full citation and annotation.)

*IR40   Hand, Wayland D. "The Folklore, Customs, and Tradi-
tions of the Butte Miner."

(Cross-listed as *CO7, *FI2, *FN14, *IT29, *SE4.)
(See *CO7 for full citation and annotation.)

IR41   Harper, Jared, and Hudson, Charles. "Irish Traveler
Cant in Its Social Setting." *Southern Folklore
Quarterly* 37:2 (1973):101-114.

Discussion of "secret language" or cant used by itinerant Irish-Americans in the South. Brief historical
sketch of the Travelers (tinkers), examples of the cant
words they use for secret communication, and descriptions of kinds of social settings in which the cant is
used. States that the learning and use of this cant
are on the decline.

IR42   Haufrecht, Herbert, and Cazden, Norman. "Music of the
Catskills." *New York Folklore Quarterly* 4:1 (1948):
32-46.

Discussion of the singers, songs, musicians, and dancers
encountered while doing fieldwork in the Catskill

Mountains of New York. Includes a brief discussion
(with exemplification) of the variation which occurs
with the importation of songs, and a presentation of
the following: 2 texts of an Irish comic song (1 stanza
each, both with tune), 1 ballad text (1 stanza, with
tune, of an American version of Child #20, "The Cruel
Mother"), 1 text of an "immigrant" ballad (1 stanza of
an Irish ballad, no tune), and 1 text of a Civil War
ballad (2 stanzas only, no tune). Also presented is a
list of the tunes documented in the area, with an
indication of informants: vocal music (142) and
instrumental music (45).

IR43 Healy, William M. "Instrumentation and Repertoire in
      Commercially Recorded Irish Instrumental Music in
      the United States, 1900-1930." *Folklore and Mythology
      Studies* 2 (1978):16-19.

An introductory survey, based on commercial phonograph
records and recording company catalogues, of the kinds
of music selected and the instruments used for early
20th-century sound recordings of Irish music in the
United States. Emphasizes the fact that phonograph
recordings are an important source of information about
Irish instrumental music in an era during which fieldwork was minimal.

IR44 Hogan, Virginia. "A Matchless Old Man." *Western Folk-
      lore* 13:1 (1954):1-6.

Characterization of stories and jokes about an Irishman
who emigrated to San Diego in the 1850s, drawing on and
reprinting selections from the San Diego *World* concerning the man's exploits.

*IR45 Hopkins, Pandora. "Individual Choice and the Control
      of Musical Change."

      (Cross-listed as *IC2.)
      (See *IC2 for full citation and annotation.)

IR46 Hudson, Arthur Palmer. "Ballads and Songs from Missis-
      sippi." *Journal of American Folk-Lore* 39:152 (1926):
      93-194.

Presentation of 88 ballad and song texts, with comparative references and notes on informants and sources, 2
of which were obtained from a woman of English and Irish
ancestry living in Lee County, Mississippi.

*IR47 Humphrey, Linda T. "'It Ain't Funny, Buster': The Ethnic
       Riddle-Joke at Citrus Community College."

       (Cross-listed as *GL49, *CH13, *IT32, *JA5, *SS17.)
       (See *GL49 for full citation and annotation.)

IR48   "Irish Lore from New York State's Capital District."
       New York Folklore Quarterly 10:1 (1954):35-39.

       Presentation of 1 tale text and 5 song texts recorded
       from 1932 to 1940 from informants of Irish descent by
       teachers enrolled in a folk literature course at Albany
       State College for Teachers.

IR49   Jeffers-Johnson, Stratford. "Lore from Leitrim." *New
       York Folklore Quarterly* 5:4 (1949):276-296.

       Presentation of tales and songs (in English) recorded
       from informants of Irish descent. Includes characteri-
       zations of 1 local legend (set in Ireland), 2 folktales,
       and 1 tale about a witch, and the presentation of 4
       song texts: 1 anti-Protestant song (a fragment), 1 love
       song, 1 song for playing with children (infants), and
       1 ballad.

*IR50 Jones, Louis C. "The Evil-Eye among European-Americans."

       (Cross-listed as *GL51, *GR21, *HU17, *IN1, *IT35,
       *JE35, *PL39, *RU10, *SZ2.)
       (See *GL51 for full citation and annotation.)

IR51   Jones, Louis C. "The Little People." *New York Folk-
       lore Quarterly* 18:4 (1962):243-264.

       Presentation of miscellaneous folklore items concerning
       fairies, recorded from informants of Irish descent by
       the author's students at New York State College for
       Teachers, Albany, from 1940 to 1946. Includes 1) a dis-
       cussion of folk hero Bill Greenfield of Saratoga County,
       New York, and tales told about him, including characteri-
       zation of 1 tale involving "little people"; 2) 2 stories
       about fairies (1 involving a changeling and set in the
       United States); 3) a discussion of types of fairies and
       certain individual fairies; 4) a discussion of beliefs
       about leprechauns and their physical appearance, in-
       cluding several descriptions of them; 5) a description
       of fairy forts and fairy rings and beliefs about them;
       6) a discussion of bushes associated with fairies and
       1 story about a fairy bonfire; 7) 2 stories about fairy
       music; 8) a discussion of holidays celebrated by the

fairies, and 1 tale about Halloween; 9) a discussion of
the proper behavior toward fairies, with 2 stories
illustrating this; 10) a discussion of the mischievous
nature of fairies, illustrated by 3 stories; 11) a
discussion of beliefs about changelings, illustrated
by 1 story; and 12) a discussion of beliefs about the
goodness of fairies, illustrated by 1 story.

IR52 Kelly, Catherine. "Irish Sayings and Irish Fairies."
      New York Folklore Quarterly 1:3 (1945):174-178.

      Brief presentation of 19 Irish proverbs and a miscellany
      of traditional greetings (all in English), followed by
      a discussion of beliefs about fairies and the souls of
      the dead, recorded in New York from informants of Irish
      descent.

IR53 Kidder, H.R. "Why the Poplar Stirs--Superstitions of
      Miners in Michigan." *Journal of American Folk-Lore*
      13:50 (1900):226.

      Report of an Irish work foreman in Michigan who refused
      to cut down poplar trees to build a road because the
      Saviour's cross was made of such a tree.

IR54 Kittredge, G.L. "The Robber Maid." *Journal of American
      Folk-Lore* 39:152 (1926):214-217.

      Brief comment on the relationship between 2 ballad texts
      ("The Undaunted Female" and "The Tinker and Stafford-
      shire Maid"), the former recorded in 1925 from an Irish
      servant.

IR55 Kittredge, G.L. "Various Ballads." *Journal of American
      Folk-Lore* 26:100 (1913):174-182.

      Presentation of 6 ballad texts, including 1 recorded
      from an Irish servant-maid in 1909.

*IR56 Korson, George. "Coal Miners."

      (Cross-listed as *GL55, *SK7, *WE7.)
      (See *GL55 for full citation and annotation.)

IR57 Larson, Mildred R. "Lore from Snow Country." *New York
      Folklore Quarterly* 11:4 (1955):262-274.

      Presentation of miscellaneous folklore items recorded
      in Camden, New York. Includes stories and anecdotes
      about snow (6), stories about pioneer life in the area

(8), local legends (4), tall tales (2), stories involving trickster figures (2), stories about unusual
people (2), 1 tale about an Indian cure, and 2 Pat-and-
Mike tales (about Irish immigrants). Also includes
discussion of 1 superstition and presentation of 5 folk
sayings and 1 song text.

*IR58   Larson, Mildred R. "The Taller the Better." *New York
        Folklore Quarterly* 18:3 (1962):217-234.

Presentation of miscellaneous humorous tales from New
York State. Includes 9 tall tales; 3 legends about the
folk hero Herb Stevens; 2 Frank-and-Sylvester tales from
Rome, New York (with accompanying brief discussion); 4
stories about superstitions (2 recorded from an informant of Irish descent); 3 stories about New York City
life (1 involving 2 Italian brothers); 1 immigrant story
about Russian Jews; and 1 stupid fellow story.
        (Cross-listed as *IT40, *JE43, *RU12.)

IR59   Laws, G. Malcolm, Jr. "Anglo-Irish Balladry in North
        America." In *Folklore in Action: Essays for Discus-
        sion in Honor of MacEdward Leach*, edited by Horace P.
        Beck, pp. 172-183. Publications of the American Folk-
        lore Society. Bibliographical and Special Series 14.
        Philadelphia: American Folklore Society, 1962.

General discussion of Irish love, criminal, and satiric
ballads in English reported from Ireland and North
America, with texts of or excerpts from 15 previously
published ballads. Asserts that Anglo-Irish ballad is
"almost entirely fictional," that it "largely ignores
journalistic subject matter and suppresses sensational-
ism and violence," that it "has almost no interest in
anti-English propaganda or in Irish nationalism," that
it "leans heavily towards the romantic in content and
treatment."

*IR60   Leeson, Alice M. "Certain Canadian Superstitions."
        Journal of American Folk-Lore 10:36 (1897):76-78.

Comments that the Irish, Scots, and French Canadians in
the Canadian far west are all similar in many of their
customs. Notes some belief about lucky and unlucky
days, dreams, signs, charms, and omens recorded from
Irish and Scottish Canadians.
        (Cross-listed as *SC24.)

*IR61 Lewis, Mary Ellen Brown. "Folk Elements in Scotch-
       Irish Presbyterian Communities."

       (Cross-listed as *SC25.)
       (See *SC25 for full citation and annotation.)

IR62   Logan, Nancy A. "Look for a Post!" *New York Folklore
       Quarterly* 12:4 (1956):283-286.

       Characterization of 5 tall tales and anecdotes about
       the Erie Canal (2 of which are about Irish immigrants),
       recorded from a boatman who lived during that era.

IR63   McCombs, Hazel A. "Erie Canal Lore." *New York Folk-
       lore Quarterly* 3:3 (1947):205-212.

       Brief discussion of the songs of the canalers ("canawl-
       ers") and laborers (mostly Irish) on the Erie Canal and
       of a number of communities that developed along the
       canal (Harbor, Howard's Bush, and Rock City). Includes
       presentation of 4 song texts.

IR64   McCullough, Larry. "Fife and Fiddle: Chicago's Irish
       Musical Tradition." *Sing Out!* 26:4 (1978):14-16.

       Brief historical sketch of Irish music and musicians in
       Chicago from the 1850s to the present. Includes
       comments on the collecting and publications of Francis
       O'Neill and James O'Neill, mention of music and dancing
       clubs. Includes 3 photographs, 2 of Irish musicians
       and 1 of a music club group.

IR65   McCullough, Lawrence E. "An American Maker of Uilleann
       Pipes: Patrick Hennelly." *Éire-Ireland* 10:4 (1975):
       109-115.

       Biographical sketch of a Chicago Irish immigrant man,
       maker of uilleann pipes, with description of the incep-
       tion of the man's skills as a craftsman in Ireland and
       of the individuals in the United States from whom he
       learned pipe-making. Includes brief description of
       construction procedures and materials, as well as some
       of the innovations introduced by Patrick Hennelly over
       time.

IR66   Maloney, Thomas Vincent. "Mary Neil." *New York Folk-
       lore Quarterly* 1:2 (1945):99-100.

       Presentation of 1 ballad text, recorded from an Irish
       informant in Buffalo, New York, with references to
       other published versions of the ballad.

*IR67   Mead, Jane Thompson (Mrs.). "Proverbs: Sayings from
        Westfield, Chautauqua Co." *New York Folklore
        Quarterly* 10:3 (1954):226-227.

        Presentation of 11 sayings, recorded in Chautauqua
        County, New York, 4 of which are identified as being
        Irish, Welsh, and German in origin.
        (Cross-listed as *GE387, *WE8.)

IR68   Meltz, Adrienne. "Why the Sea Waters Taste Like Salt."
        New York Folklore Quarterly 14:1 (1958):59-64.

        Presentation of 1 tale text, recorded from an Irish-
        English informant.

IR69   Michaelis, Kate Woodbridge. "An Irish Folk-Tale."
        Journal of American Folk-Lore 23:90 (1910):425-428.

        Presentation of 1 tale text, recorded from an Irish
        immigrant woman in Cambridge, Massachusetts.

*IR70   Millard, Eugenia L. "A Sampling of Guessing Games."
        New York Folklore Quarterly 13:2 (1957):135-143.

        Discussion of principles involved in traditional
        guessing games as used by promoters of current radio
        and television quiz shows and of traditional games
        played by children in New York State. Includes pre-
        sentation of 17 game descriptions, 5 game rhymes, and
        2 game formulas, with 1 game description recorded from
        an informant of Irish descent and mention of Scottish
        parallels to some games discussed.
        (Cross-listed as *SC29.)

IR71   Moloney, Michael. "Medicine for Life: A Study of a
        Folk Composer and His Music." *Keystone Folklore*
        20:1-2 (1975):3-37.

        Brief discussion of Irish music and its study to date,
        followed by a biographical sketch of a single Irish
        immigrant musician living in Philadelphia. Emphasis
        on the man's composing experiences and techniques and
        quotes from interviews about the backgrounds or sources
        for the songs/tunes he composed. Based on fieldwork
        conducted in the Philadelphia area between 1973 and
        1975.

IR72 Moloney, Mick. "Irish Traditional Music in America."
      Sing Out! 25:4 (1976):3-5, 15.

      Brief survey of Irish dances and dance music, with
      emphasis on changes that have occurred in America with
      immigration and cultural revivals. Includes brief
      mention of musical instruments played, dances performed,
      and recording industry influences.

IR73 Moses, Louise von Blittersdorf. "Irish Fairies in
      Texas." In *Straight Texas*, edited by J. Frank Dobie
      and Mody C. Boatright, pp. 185-189. *Publications of
      the Texas Folklore Society* 13 (1937).

      Reconstruction of 2 tales told to the author by an Irish
      immigrant from Thorndale, Texas, one concerning the
      informant's encounter with a woman in black in Ireland
      who predicted his future with playing cards, the other
      about the destruction of an Irish lord's castle on the
      night of his daughter's betrothal and the restoration
      of the castle and its inhabitants by God, at the request
      of the fairies, and its transference to Texas, where it
      remained away from Irish eyes until settlement in that
      state required it to sink into the ground at the site
      on which the informant built his Texas home.

*IR74 Musick, Ruth Ann. *Green Hills of Magic: West Virginia
      Folktales from Europe.*

      (Cross-listed as *AR9, *AU4, *CZ8, *HU24, *IT52,
      *PL52, *RO4, *RU16, *TU3, *YU8.)
      (See *IT52 for full citation and annotation.)

IR75 Neely, Charles. "Why the Irish Came to America."
      Journal of American Folk-Lore 46:179 (1933):90-91.

      Presentation of the text of 1 version of the Swan
      Maiden story, which concludes with an explanation as to
      why the Irish emigrated from Ireland and settled in
      America, recorded "in an Irish settlement in the Ozark
      Mountain foothills of southern Illinois."

IR76 Nestler, Harold. "Songs of the Hudson Valley." *New
      York Folklore Quarterly* 5:2 (1949):78-112.

      Brief discussion of ways songs from the British Isles
      became a part of American tradition, and presentation
      of 31 miscellaneous song texts from New York's Hudson
      Valley. Includes 4 Irish songs (1 love song, 1 sea

chantey, 1 ballad, 1 anti-British song) and 1 anti-
Irish song, with 5 songs reportedly from an Irish
informant.

IR77   Newell, Jane H. "Superstitions of Irish Origin in
       Boston, Mass." *Journal of American Folk-Lore* 5:18
       (1892):242-243.

       Listing of 17 superstitions recorded in Boston from
       individuals of Irish ancestry.

*IR78 Norlin, Ethel Todd. "Present-Day Superstitions at La
       Harpe, Ill., Survivals in a Community of English
       Origin." *Journal of American Folk-Lore* 31:120
       (1918):202-215.

       Listing of 123 superstitions, arranged according to
       topic and recorded in 1915 at La Harpe, Hancock County,
       Illinois. Informants primarily of English, Irish, and
       Scottish descent, with others of French, Dutch, and
       German backgrounds.
       (Cross-listed as *DU14, *FR88, *GE424, *SC30.)

IR79   O'Beirne, James. "The Ghostly Priest Who Says Mass."
       New York Folklore Quarterly 2:3 (1946):213-214.

       Presentation of 1 folktale text, recorded from an
       Irish informant in New York City.

IR80   O'Beirne, James. "Una Ban: An Irish Song and Story."
       New York Folklore Quarterly 2:4 (1946):269-272.

       Presentation of 1 song text, recorded from an informant
       of unspecified nationality in New York City, with
       discussion of the tale upon which the song is based
       and references to other printed versions of the song.

*IR81 O'Neill, Capt. Francis. *Irish Folk Music, A Fascinating
       Hobby, with Some Account of Allied Subjects Including
       O'Farrell's Treatise on the Irish or Union Pipes and
       Touhey's Hints to Amateur Pipers.* 1910. Reprint edi-
       tion. Darby, Pa.: Norwood Editions, 1973. Pp. xi, 359,
       3 appendices, index.

       Reprinting of a 1910 work about the author's collecting
       and studying Irish songs, music, dances, musical instru-
       ments, with sketches of individuals of Irish and
       Scottish ancestry in Chicago. Includes 13 tune tran-
       scriptions (appendix C), some reprinted from other
       sources, some known to or recorded by the author in
       Chicago.
       (Cross-listed as *SC31.)

IR82   O'Neill, Capt. Francis. *Irish Minstrels and Musicians,*
        with Numerous Dissertations on Related Subjects.
        1913. Reprint edition. Darby, Pa.: Norwood Editions,
        1973. Pp. viii, 497, introduction, preface, index.

        Reprinting of a 1913 work containing sketches of "191
        Uilleann pipers, 54 fiddlers, 38 harpers, 19 pipe-makers,
        12 fluters, 10 warpipers, 8 music collectors, one
        accordion player, and one ceili band," many of whom are
        American immigrants from Ireland, the majority resettled
        in the Chicago area.

IR83   O'Neill, Capt. Francis. *O'Neill's Music of Ireland:*
        Eighteen Hundred and Fifty Melodies, Airs, Jigs,
        Reels, Hornpipes, Long Dances, Marches, Etc., Many
        of which are now Published for the First Time. Chica-
        go: Lyon & Healy, 1903. Pp. 366, introduction, index.

        Presentation of tune transcriptions of 1,850 songs,
        jigs, reels, hornpipes, long dances, marches, more than
        half of which were documented by the author from musi-
        cians of Irish ancestry in Chicago.

*IR84   Osborn, Lettie. "Fiddle Tunes from Orange County, New
        York." *New York Folklore Quarterly* 8:3 (1952):211-215.

        Brief discussion of traditional fiddling, the musicians,
        styles, and tunes played. Presents a list of the names
        of 57 tunes recorded in Orange County, New York, and
        observes that most of the tunes are of Irish, Scottish,
        or native origin.
        (Cross-listed as *SC32.)

*IR85   Owen, Mary A. "Coyote and Little Pig." *Journal of*
        American Folk-Lore 15:56 (1902):63-65.

        Presentation of 1 text of "The Three Little Pigs,"
        obtained from an 82-year-old woman who learned it from
        her grandmother, a Scotch-Irish woman who arrived in
        Londonderry, New Hampshire, in 1718. Author notes that
        this is a version of the story "Coyote and Little Pig"
        reported from the Flathead Indians of Idaho.
        (Cross-listed as *SC33.)

IR86   Pocius, Gerald L. "'The First Day that I Thought of It
        Since I Got Wed': Role Expectations and Singer Status
        in a Newfoundland Outport." *Western Folklore* 35:2
        (1976):109-122.

        Discussion of the community status and repertoires of
        2 traditional singers (husband and wife) in a Newfound-

land Irish Catholic community, based on 1974 fieldwork.
Emphasizes the fact that while the male singer had
community-wide recognition as a performer and was
frequently called upon to sing publicly, the female was
the better singer (though not acknowledged or recognized
as such by others). Includes transcribed segments of
interviews during which the 2 singers discuss songs and
their learning of them. Presents text of 1 song as sung
by the male singer and accompanied (and corrected) by
his wife.

*IR87   Preston, Michael J. "A Typescript Ethnic Joke Anthology."

        (Cross-listed as *IT61, *PL65.)
        (See *IT61 for full citation and annotation.)

IR88   Rapp, Marvin A. "Canawl Water and Whiskey." *New York
        Folklore Quarterly* 11:4 (1955):296-300.

        Discussion of the part played by Irish workers in the
        building of the Erie Canal, and of the Niagara Frontier
        as a center for smuggling activities between the United
        States and Canada. Includes characterization of 1
        legend about the building of the canal and presentation
        of a dialogue between a customs officer and an Irish
        woman arrested for smuggling whiskey from Canada into
        the United States. (Dialogue taken from the personal
        recollections of Charles R. Edward, c. 1860.)

IR89   Relihan, Catherine. "Farm Lore: Folk Remedies." *New
        York Folklore Quarterly* 3:2 (1947):166-169.

        Presentation of a miscellany of 48 remedies (in English),
        2 of which are specifically identified as Irish.

IR90   Rogers, W. Stuart. "Irish Lore Collected in Schenectady."
        New York Folklore Quarterly 8:1 (1952):20-30.

        Presentation (in English) of a miscellany of folklore
        items recorded from an Irish informant in Schenectady,
        New York. Categories include: "Banshee and Other
        Fairies" (11 tale texts), "The Church and the Clergy"
        (6 texts; this category also includes a discussion of
        the preparation for the return of the dead on the eve
        of All Souls' Day), and "Miscellaneous Beliefs in the
        Supernatural" (a brief discussion of funerals, omens,
        omens of itching, and a miscellaneous category), and
        1 prophecy concerning the end of the world.

IR91   Scanlon, Rosemary. "The Handprint: Biography of a
       Pennsylvania Legend." *Keystone Folklore Quarterly*
       16:2 (1971):97-107.

   Discussion of a legend, well known and frequently told
   by individuals of Irish descent, about an accused
   murderer who, just before being hanged in 1877 and in
   protest about his conviction, pressed his hand against
   his cell wall in the Carbon County, Pennsylvania, jail
   and vowed that it would remain forever as a sign of his
   innocence. Handprint remains even today, despite
   efforts to eradicate it. Includes 2 texts of the
   legend, recorded from informants in Philadelphia and
   Middletown, Pennsylvania, and the reprinting of the
   text of 1 ballad reflecting Irish sentiment after the
   trial. Emphasis on re-creating the background of the
   legend and discussing it in terms of the treatment of
   Irish immigrants in the coal mining regions of Pennsylvania around Jim Thorpe (formerly Mauch Chunk). Includes 2 photographs (of the Carbon County Prison and
   the ineradicable handprint).

IR92   Sharp, Dean. "Folktales: 2. *The Man Who Sold His
       Shadow.*" *West Virginia Folklore* 5:3 (1955):47.

   Characterization (in English) of 1 folktale, told to
   the author by a relative of Irish ancestry, about a
   man who sells his shadow to a stranger for an ever-full
   purse of gold and who is suspected and then accused and
   convicted of being a thief and is cast into prison for
   the rest of his life.

IR93   Skeel, Mary H. "To Kill Cats is Unlucky." *Journal of
       American Folk-Lore* 3:10 (1890):241.

   Recording of an incident in which an Irishman refused
   to kill a cat maimed in a hay-cutting machine. When
   neighbors also refused for fear of bad luck, a man of
   American birth was found to put the animal out of its
   misery.

IR94   Smith, Grace Partridge. "Folklore from 'Egypt.'"
       Journal of American Folklore 54:211-212 (1941):48-59.

   Presentation of 15 tale texts, 22 remedies, 10 superstitions, recorded by the author in Southern Illinois
   ("Egypt" or "Little Egypt"). Includes 2 tales of
   bewitched cows, recorded from informants of Irish
   background.

IR95   Smith, Grace Partridge. "Four Irish Ballads from
       'Egypt.'" *Hoosier Folklore* 5:3 (1946):115-119.

       Presentation of 4 ballad texts traced to Irish sources
       and recorded from Irish-American singers living in
       that part of southern Illinois known as "Egypt."

IR96   Stoner, Michael. "Narratives Associated with Irish
       Fiddle Tunes: Some Contextual Considerations." *New
       York Folklore* 2:3&4 (1977):17-27.

       Based upon fieldwork conducted among Irish-American
       musicians in Rochester, New York. Author argues that
       these performers seldom identify selections by titles
       and rarely know titles with which stories are associated.
       Includes characterization of kinds of settings in which
       Irish-American musicians play.

IR97   Struder, Norman. "Boney Quillen of the Catskills."
       New York Folklore Quarterly 7:4 (1951):276-282.

       Discussion of the life of Boney Quillen, an Irish song-
       maker of the Catskills. Includes stories and anecdotes
       about his life, and presentation of 1 of his songs
       (text and tune, in English).

*IR98 Tallmadge, William H. "Anglo-Saxon vs. Scotch-Irish."
       Mountain Life & Work 45:2 (1969):10-12.

       On the basis of immigration statistics and the kinds
       of ballads collected in Kentucky, author argues that
       the ancestry of most of that state's residents is
       Scotch-Irish and not Anglo-Saxon, as many researchers
       have assumed.
       (Cross-listed as *SC37.)

*IR99 Tallmadge, William H. "The Scotch-Irish and the British
       Traditional Ballad in America." *New York Folklore
       Quarterly* 24:4 (1968):261-274.

       Author contends that many so-called "British traditional
       ballads" recorded in North America were brought to the
       New World by Scottish and Irish immigrants, not by
       emigrants from England. Cities immigration information,
       historical sources to defend the thesis.
       (Cross-listed as *SC38.)

*IR100   Taylor, Archer. "The 'Dream-Bread' Story Once More."
         Journal of American Folk-Lore 34:133 (1921):327-328.

         Presentation of verses (sung to the tune of "Pop Goes
         the Weasel") composed by a Mr. Frank Wolff conveying
         the story about 2 Irishmen and a Hebrew who must
         determine which one will get the remaining provisions.
         They decide that the one with the best dream will get
         the food. In the morning when the dreams are recounted,
         the Hebrew, who goes last, notes that he dreamed the
         other two had gone to heaven, so he ate the last of the
         food.
         (Cross-listed as *JE76.)

*IR101   Taylor, Archer. "An Old-World Tale from Minnesota."
         Journal of American Folk-Lore 31:122 (1918):555-556.

         Presentation of 1 tale about an Irish tramp who outwits
         his hosts, as well as a German and a Frenchman, when
         he divides the chicken for dinner. Tale obtained from
         an individual who heard it in Minnesota around 1885
         from a Dane who had learned it from an Irishman in
         North Dakota. History of the tale briefly explored.
         (Cross-listed as *FR107, *GE682.)

IR102   Thompson, Ellen Powell. "Folklore from Ireland. I."
         Journal of American Folk-Lore 6:23 (1893):259-268.

         Brief descriptions of many popular festivals, legends,
         miracles, and fairy activities as celebrated or told
         in Ireland. Information provided by 2 women informants,
         1 from Roscommon County, Connaught, living in Washing-
         ton, D.C., and the other from Covan, Ireland. Some
         footnotes with brief comparative comments and supple-
         mentary data from printed sources. Author comments
         that first informant, although willing to cooperate,
         stopped providing information when she was scolded by
         fellow Irishmen.

IR103   Thompson, Ellen Powell. "Folk-Lore from Ireland. II."
         Journal of American Folk-Lore 7:26 (1894):224-227.

         Brief descriptions of various beliefs and customs
         related to animal life, popular medical practices, and
         other superstitions and customs, noted by a single
         Irish informant living in the United States.

*IR104   Thompson, Harold W. "Proverbs and Sayings." *New York Folklore Quarterly* 5:4 (1949):296-300.

Presentation of 48 texts of proverbs and sayings (2 specifically identified as Irish, 1 as Armenian). (Cross-listed as *AR10.)

*IR105   Thompson, Marion. "Folklore in the Schools: Collecting in Cortland."

(Cross-listed as *GL80, *IT77, *JE77.)
(See *GL80 for full citation and annotation.)

IR106   Travis, James. "Three Irish Folk Tales." *Journal of American Folklore* 54:213-214 (1941):199-203.

Presentation of texts (in English) of 3 folktales learned by the author from his parents, both of Irish ancestry. Tales of a midwife asked to aid in a fairy birth, a priest who curses a blasphemous landlord, and a priest who drives away the devil in the form of a cat.

IR107   Travis, James. "Two Irish Folk Tunes." *Journal of American Folklore* 55:217 (1942):169-170.

Brief note presenting partial transcriptions of the melodies of 2 Irish folk tunes, learned by the author from his American-born father, who learned them from his mother, a native of County Donegal, Northern Ireland, and a pre-Civil War immigrant to the United States. Tunes are previously unreported from America. Brief discussion of tune structure.

IR108   Waffner, Laura M. "Seumas O'Connor's Bagpipes." *New York Folklore Quarterly* 3:1 (1947):60-61.

Presentation of 1 tale text (in English), recorded from an informant (nationality unspecified), presumably in New York.

IR109   Walton, Ivan. "Folk Singing on Beaver Island." *Midwest Folklore* 2:4 (1952):243-250.

Brief history of the 19th-century Irish settlement of Beaver Island on Lake Michigan, followed by an inventory of 100 songs (by title only) of both American and European (Irish, English, Scottish) backgrounds, recorded there principally between 1932 and 1940. Includes brief descriptions of 4 highly-regarded local singers.

IR110   Ward, Peter A. "Tales from Colton." *New York Folklore Quarterly* 22:2 (1966):143-146.

Presentation of 4 stories, 1 description of a picnic, 1 description of snow-clearing methods, reported from Colton, New York, from informants of Irish background.

*IR111   Warner, Frank. "A Salute and a Sampling of Songs." *New York Folklore Quarterly* 14:3 (1958):202-223.

Article includes presentation of 1 stanza of a hobo song, 1 Revolutionary War song, 1 prisoner's song, and 1 song of separation, recorded in New York and Long Island; also lists the titles of 56 and 78 songs which were recorded from 2 singers in New York, and presents 3 texts of Irish songs (1 stanza from each song) from the first informant, and 2 song texts (1 stanza of a milkmaid's song, 1 stanza of an anti-conscription song) from the second informant. (Repertoires of both informants include Scottish, Irish, and English songs, though not designated as such.) Also includes presentation of 4 ballad texts and tunes from each of the 2 informants (1 of which is an Irish song of the French-Indian War). All titles and texts in English. (Cross-listed as *SC40.)

IR112   Warner, Frank L. "Songs My Uncle Taught Me." *North Carolina Folklore* 9:1 (1963):23-33.

Presentation of 11 folksong and ballad texts, 2 of which are identified as of Irish origin ("Blue Mountain Lake" and "Gilgorry Mountain," recorded from informants from New York's Hudson Valley and East Jaffrey, New Hampshire, respectively).

*IR113   Webb, Wheaton P. "Witches in the Cooper Country."

(Cross-listed as *DU25.)
(See *DU25 for full citation and annotation.)

IR114   Wilgus, D.K. "The Early American Influence on Narrative Songs in Ireland." In *Folklore Studies in Honour of Herbert Halpert: A Festschrift*, edited by Kenneth S. Goldstein and Neil V. Rosenberg, pp. 377-395. St. John's, Newfoundland: Memorial University of Newfoundland, 1980.

Discussion of English-language Irish narrative songs imported into Ireland from America or re-introduced into the native country from abroad, with assertion

that the process began in the 17th century, but became
more prevalent during the 19th and 20th centuries.
Includes texts of or excerpts from 7 songs (some reprinted from previously published sources).

*IR115 Willis, Alice. "Tales from a Mountain Homestead."

(Cross-listed as *DU27, *SC41.)
(See *DU27 for full citation and annotation.)

*IR116 Wintemberg, W.J. "Folk-Lore Collected at Roebuck,
        Grenville County, Ontario." *Journal of American
        Folk-Lore* 31:120 (1918):154-157.

Listing of 19 items obtained in 1912 from Irish
Protestants, Scots, and persons of English descent
in Roebuck, Grenville County, Ontario. No indication
given of which items are from which ethnic group.
Included are items of folk medicine, folk belief,
book rhymes, and counting-out rhymes.
(Cross-listed as *SC42.)

*IR117 Wintemberg, W.J. and Katherine H. "Folk-Lore from
        Grey County, Ontario." *Journal of American Folk-
        Lore* 31:119 (1918):83-124.

Listing of 426 items obtained from Canadians in a
Scotch-Irish community in Normanby Township, Grey
County, Ontario. Most data provided by one of the
authors and her mother, of Irish descent. Includes
beliefs and lore about natural phenomena, customs,
proverbs, rhymes, games, tongue twisters, and riddles.
(Cross-listed as *SC43.)

IR118   Woodward, Robert H. "Addenda." *New York Folklore
        Quarterly* 19:4 (1963):296-298.

Article discusses John Fitzgerald Kennedy's remarks
concerning the nature of fairies (the "little people")
written in response to a letter received from a young
boy in 1963 (quotation from the letter and Kennedy's
reply are reprinted from a newspaper article), and
adds some comments on folklore related to the Prince
Albert Tobacco can (addenda to 1962 and 1963 articles
appearing in the *New York Folklore Quarterly*).

IR119   Wright, Robert L., ed. *Irish Emigrant Ballads and
        Songs*. Bowling Green, Ohio: Bowling Green Univer-
        sity Popular Press, 1975. Pp. 712, preface, intro-
        duction, 3 appendices, discography, bibliography.

        Presentation of 402 texts and 136 tunes (reprinted
        from other sources) of Irish ballads and songs relating
        to emigration to and settlement in America (with 2
        texts in Gaelic, with English translations, all others
        in English). History of Irish emigration to America
        sketched in introduction.

                    XXVII. ITALIAN (IT) (1-86)

IT1   Agonito, Rosemary. "*Il Paisano*: Immigrant Italian
        Folktales of Central New York." *New York Folklore
        Quarterly* 23:1 (1967):52-64.

        Presentation (in English) of texts of 8 folktales,
        recorded by the author from Italian immigrants in the
        Syracuse, New York, area in 1962. Includes a brief
        sketch of the south-central Italian village of
        Guardiaregia, from which the informants emigrated.

IT2   Ainsworth, Catherine Harris. "Some Italian Folktales
        of the Niagara Frontier." *New York Folklore
        Quarterly* 27:4 (1971):385-392.

        Presentation (in English) of texts of 4 tales, obtained
        by the author from college students in Niagara, New
        York, in 1963-64.

*IT3   Barbour, Frances M. "Some Foreign Proverbs in
        Southern Illinois."

        (Cross-listed as *DA1, *DU2, *FR21, *GE33, *HU1.)
        (See *GE33 for full citation and annotation.)

IT4   Barrese, Pauline N. "A Child of the Thirties." *New
        York Folklore Quarterly* 25:2 (1969):129-136.

        Autobiographical account of the author's childhood in
        an Italian immigrant family and her growing up in
        Greenwich Village, New York City, in the 1930s.
        Describes household activities, pastimes of children,
        kinds of foods eaten daily. Includes 3 traditional
        remedies/cures.

IT5   Barrese, Pauline N. "Southern Italian Folklore in
        New York City." *New York Folklore Quarterly* 21:3
        (1965):184-193.

        Presentation of miscellaneous folklore items, recorded
        from Italians in New York City. Includes 3 riddles, 3
        proverbs, 4 superstitions, descriptions of 2 games and
        2 religious customs, and 6 recipes, with 2 photographs
        (one of men playing *bocce*, one of an 1876 view of New
        York City).

*IT6   Barrick, Mac E. "Racial Riddles & the Polack Joke."

        (Cross-listed as *GE43, *IR4, *JE4, *PL5.)
        (See *PL5 for full citation and annotation.)

IT7   Basile, James. "Mining Experiences and Other Events
        in the Life of Luigi Basile." *West Virginia Folklore*
        12:3 (1962):34-43.

        Biographical sketch of the author's Italian grandfather,
        his immigration to West Virginia, and his experiences
        in the coal mines. Includes 2 personal experience
        stories concerning the man's negative reaction toward
        Italians with Mafia connections and his narrow escape
        from death in a coal mine explosion.

IT8   Bianco, Carla. "Folklore and Immigration among Italian-
        Americans." *Journal of the Folklore Institute* 11:1-
        2 (1974):141-144.

        Brief characterization of the author's fieldwork
        experiences among Italian-Americans in the 1960s.

IT9   Bianco, Carla. *Italian and Italian-American Folklore:
        A Working Bibliography.* Folklore Forum Bibliographic
        and Special Series No. 5 (1970). Pp. ii, 37,
        introduction.

        A bibliography of 398 entries, 87 devoted to Italian-
        American history, culture, and folklore, with brief
        descriptions following entries.

IT10   Bianco, Carla. "Migration and Urbanization of a Tradi-
        tional Culture: An Italian Experience." In *Folklore
        in the Modern World*, edited by Richard M. Dorson,
        pp. 55-63. The Hague: Mouton Publishers, 1978.

        Brief "cultural profile" of the Italian-American com-
        munity of Roseto, Pennsylvania, comparing and contrast-
        ing its people and their behaviors with those of Roseto,

Italy, the south Italian mountain village from which
the original immigrants to the Pennsylvania community
came. States that some traditional homeland practices
and forms continue unaltered in Roseto, Pennsylvania,
some have been modified in response to the new environment and modern-day influences, and some have been discontinued or forgotten. Notes the need to develop a
new interdisciplinary methodology to comprehend and
study change as it affects and is resisted by traditional ways.

IT11 Bianco, Carla. *The Two Rosetos*. Bloomington, Ind.:
      Indiana University Press, 1974. Pp. xv, 234, preface,
      notes, bibliography, index.

      Comparative study of folklore in two related communities:
      Roseto, Pennsylvania, and Roseto Valfortore, Italy,
      noting both continuities and changes in traditions in
      the two communities. Includes an historical sketch of
      Italian immigration to America; descriptions of the two
      communities; settlement of Italian immigrants in
      Roseto, Pennsylvania; contemporary life in Roseto,
      Pennsylvania. Includes texts of 49 proverbs, 14 songs,
      11 folktales, 2 jokes, 6 stories involving supernatural
      beings, 8 personal experience narratives (about the
      immigration experience, early days in Roseto, Pennsyl-
      vania, return visits to the homeland), 1 dialect story,
      1 historical legend, description of 1 game, and descrip-
      tions of various beliefs and customs associated with
      such rites of passage as pregnancy, childbirth, marriage,
      and death. Includes 20 photographs (of persons and
      scenes in the two communities) and 2 maps.

*IT12 Boswell, George W. "Ole Miss Jokes and Anecdotes."

      (Cross-listed as *GL9, *JE8, *PL7.)
      (See *PL7 for full citation and annotation.)

IT13 Brunetti, Michael. "Italian Folklore." *New York Folk-
      lore Quarterly* 28:4 (1972):257-262.

      Presentation of miscellaneous folklore items collected
      by the author from his Italian-born grandmother. In-
      cludes 8 statements of belief; 4 preventives, diagnoses,
      and cures for the evil eye; 5 tales (1 about an exorcism
      carried out by the author's great-grandfather).

IT14   "Calling on the Devil To Cure Disease." *Journal of
        American Folk-Lore* 5:18 (1892):238.

        Account of an Italian ill with pneumonia who hired two
        other Italians to cure him by exorcising the devil.
        Description of the treatment and subsequent legal case,
        reprinted from an unnamed New York newspaper of April
        1892.

IT15   "The Cat on the Mountain." *Colorado Folksong Bulletin*
        1:3 (1962):30.

        Presentation of 1 song text (in Italian, with English
        translation and tune transcription), recorded from an
        Italian immigrant woman in Santa Fe, New Mexico, in
        1961.

IT16   Culin, Stewart. "Italian Marionette Theatre in Brook-
        lyn, N.Y." *Journal of American Folk-Lore* 3:9 (1890):
        155-157.

        Account of a tour of an Italian puppet theater and
        observations made of a performance, taken from the
        Public Ledger, Philadelphia, 19 April 1890.

*IT17   Dorson, Richard M. "Dialect Stories of the Upper
        Peninsula: A New Form of American Folklore."

        (Cross-listed as *CO3, *FN3, *FR53, *IR21, *SS9.)
        (See *FR53 for full citation and annotation.)

IT18   Feintuch, Burt. "Frank Boccardo: Toward an Ethnography
        of a Chairmaker." *Pennsylvania Folklife* 22:3 (1973):
        2-9.

        Study of an Italian-American who immigrated to Newton,
        Pennsylvania, in 1908 and who became a noted chairmaker.
        Discusses the effects of his Italian background on his
        lifestyle and on his standards for chairmaking. Enumer-
        ates processes involved in making chairs and analyzes
        the buyers' influences. Includes 16 photographs of
        chairmaking.

IT19   "The Fishing for the Ring (La Pesca dell' Anello)."
        Colorado Folksong Bulletin 2 (1963):44-45.

        Presentation of 1 song text (in Italian, with English
        translation), recorded in Canon City, Colorado, in
        1962 from 2 Italian immigrant women.

IT20   Forchi, Violet. "Folktales: 4. Fortune." *West Vir-*
       ginia Folklore 5:3 (1955):49-59.

       Characterization (in English) of 1 folktale, told to
       the author by her Italian immigrant uncle, a resident
       of West Virginia.

*IT21 Foster, James R. "Brooklyn Folklore."

       (Cross-listed as *GL43, *GR9, *IR31, *JE24, *PL28,
       *PO6, *SP7.)
       (See *GL43 for full citation and annotation.)

IT22   Francello, Elvira. "An Italian Version of 'Maid Freed
       from the Gallows.'" *New York Folklore Quarterly*
       2:2 (1946):139-140.

       Presentation of 1 ballad text (in Italian, with English
       translation), recorded from an Italian informant and
       identified as a version of "The Maid Freed from the
       Gallows" (Child 95).

IT23   Fratto, Toni F. "Cooking in Red and White." *Pennsyl-*
       vania Folklife 19:3 (1970):2-15.

       Report on interviews with 6 informants from South
       Philadelphia (2 first and 4 second generation) concern-
       ing the degree of traditionality of Italian-American
       cooking. Includes biographical sketches of informants
       and gives reasons for similarities in their cooking.
       Lists approximately 100 traditional foods, especially
       those served on holidays. Concludes with generaliza-
       tions concerning the acculturative process for members
       of the first, second, and third generations. In post-
       script, lists 6 possible sources for the study of
       traditional foodways. Includes 26 photographs.

IT24   Garofalo, Alexander J. "The Oven of the Seven *Montelli*."
       New York Folklore Quarterly 2:4 (1946):273-275.

       Presentation of 1 tale text (in English), recorded from
       Italian informants in Ridgefield Park, New Jersey.

IT25   Giuliano, Bruce B. *Sacro o Profano? A Consideration*
       of Four Italian-Canadian Religious Festivals.
       Canadian Centre for Folk Culture Studies, Paper No.
       17. Ottawa: National Museum of Man, 1976. Pp. iv,
       64.

       Description of 4 religious festivals held in Toronto
       in the summer of 1972, with comments on their origins

and changes in festival behavior through the years.
Includes information about festival preparation,
organization, participation, community involvement,
and attitudes of participants toward the meaningfulness
of the events. Festivals related to the debate over
the value of continuing Old World traditions in modern
society and to the dynamics of ethnic identification
in a pluralistic framework. Includes 18 photographs
of festivals.

IT26   Greco, Joseph V. "Three Men on the Bridge." *Keystone
       Folklore Quarterly* 15:1 (1970):1-2.

       Presentation of 1 personal experience story (identified
       as a memorate) about 3 Italian immigrants' experiences
       in outwitting a bridge tolltaker when they did not have
       enough money to pay the toll across the bridge. Story
       set in Pittsburgh, Pennsylvania.

*IT27 Greenberg, Andrea. "Form and Function of the Ethnic
       Joke."

       (Cross-listed as *GL47, *FR63, *JE28, *PL33.)
       (See *GL47 for full citation and annotation.)

*IT28 Hand, Wayland D. "California Miners' Folklore: Above
       Ground."

       (Cross-listed as *CH8, *CO5, *GE235, *IR39, *SS15.)
       (See *CO5 for full citation and annotation.)

*IT29 Hand, Wayland D. "The Folklore, Customs, and Tradi-
       tions of the Butte Miner."

       (Cross-listed as *CO7, *FI2, *FN14, *IR40, *SE4.)
       (See *CO7 for full citation and annotation.)

IT30   Hartman, Peter, and McIntosh, Karyl. "Evil Eye Beliefs
       Collected in Utica, New York." *New York Folklore*
       4:1-4 (1978):61-69.

       Discussion of evil eye beliefs among Italian-Americans
       of Utica, New York, focusing on the transcription of
       an interview with a third-generation Italian-American
       woman. Includes 1 photograph of traditional amulets
       utilized to ward off the evil eye.

IT31 Hoffman, Dan G. "Stregas, Ghosts, and Werewolves."
      New York Folklore Quarterly 3:4 (1947):325-328.

      Characterization of a number of discussions with an
      Italian informant in New York City in 1946-47 on the
      topics of *stregas* (spirits), werewolves, funerals, and
      dreams about the dead.

*IT32 Humphrey, Linda T. "'It Ain't Funny, Buster': The
      Ethnic Riddle-Joke at Citrus Community College."

      (Cross-listed as *GL49, *CH13, *IR47, *JA5, *SS17.)
      (See *GL49 for full citation and annotation.)

IT33 "Il Magg (Welcome May)." *Colorado Folksong Bulletin*
      1:3 (1962):32-33.

      Presentation of 1 song text (in Italian, with English
      translation and tune transcription), recorded from an
      Italian immigrant woman in Boulder, Colorado, in 1962.

IT34 Jagendorf, M. "Italian Tales in New York City." *New
      York Folklore Quarterly* 11:3 (1955):177-182.

      Characterization of 4 tales recorded from an informant
      of Italian descent in New York City.

*IT35 Jones, Louis C. "The Evil-Eye among European-Americans."

      (Cross-listed as *GL51, *GR21, *HU17, *IN1, *IR50,
      *JE35, *PL39, *RU10, *SZ2.)
      (See *GL51 for full citation and annotation.)

*IT36 Jones, Louis C. "Italian Werewolves." *New York Folk-
      lore Quarterly* 6:3 (1950):133-138.

      Discussion of werewolf traditions among individuals of
      Italian descent in the United States, including beliefs
      about, the appearance of, and methods to ward off were-
      wolves. Includes characterizations of 2 stories (in
      English) about werewolves (set in Italy), indicating
      several parallel beliefs in French-Canadian tradition.
      Makes the observation that French-Canadians give the
      material an American locale, while Italians give these
      stories an Italian setting.
      (Cross-listed as *FR70.)

*IT37   King, C. Richard. "Old Thurber." In *Singers and Story-
        tellers*, edited by Mody C. Boatright, Wilson M.
        Hudson, and Allen Maxwell, pp. 107-114. *Publications
        of the Texas Folklore Society* 30 (1961).

        Description of Thurber, Texas, when coal was mined
        there for locomotives. Includes brief characterization
        of wedding and funeral customs of Polish immigrant
        residents and of wedding and other celebrations and the
        game of *bocce* among Italian immigrant residents of the
        town.
        (Cross-listed as *PL42.)

*IT38   Klymasz, Robert B. "The Ethnic Joke in Canada Today."

        (Cross-listed as *GL53, *FR71, *IC3, *JE40, *UK10.)
        (See *GL53 for full citation and annotation.)

IT39   "La Monaca Sposa." *Colorado Folksong Bulletin* 1:2
        (1962):24-25.

        Presentation of 1 song text (in Italian, with English
        translation and tune transcription), recorded from an
        Italian immigrant woman in Santa Fe, New Mexico, in
        1952.

*IT40   Larson, Mildred. "The Taller the Better."

        (Cross-listed as *IR58, *JE43, *RU12.)
        (See *IR58 for full citation and annotation.)

IT41   LeNoir, Phil. "The Hermit of Las Vegas." In *Tone the
        Bell Easy*, edited by J. Frank Dobie, pp. 124-126.
        Publications of the Texas Folklore Society 10 (1932).

        Brief biographical sketch of an Italian immigrant man
        who settled in the Las Vegas, New Mexico, area and
        lived most of his life as a hermit atop a mountain
        which was subsequently to bear the commemorative name
        Hermit Peak.

IT42   "Little Margaret: An Italian Song." *Colorado Folksong
        Bulletin* 1:1 (1962):11.

        Presentation of 1 song text (in Italian, with English
        translation and tune transcription), recorded from an
        Italian immigrant woman in Santa Fe, New Mexico, in
        1952. Song identified by the informant as "Easter Day
        Song," by the transcriber/translator as "Ghitin."

*IT43   Lund, Jens. "The Legend of the King and the Star."
        (Cross-listed as *DA6, *GE380, *JE44.)
        (See *JE44 for full citation and annotation.)

IT44   McNaughton, Barbara J. Taft. "Calabrian Folklore from
        Giovanna." *Journal of the Ohio Folklore Society*
        n.s. 3:1 (1974):20-28.

        Brief biographical sketch of an Italian immigrant
        woman's emigration to America (the author's grandmother),
        followed by presentation of 4 personal experience
        stories (in English and identified as legends/memorates)
        and 2 statements of belief (identified as superstitions).
        Tales concern the sighting of dead individuals and the
        marking of children whose mothers were deprived of
        craved foods during pregnancy. Based on 1973 fieldwork
        in Newark, Ohio.

IT45   Maiolo, Melia Rose. "Italian Tales Told in Shinnston."
        West Virginia Folklore 8:1 (1957):8-16.

        Characterization (in English) of 3 folktales, told to
        the author by her Italian-raised mother, 1 about a
        prince's marriage to a poor peasant girl with magical
        powers, 1 about an adulterous woman who tries unsuccess-
        fully to blind and then kill her husband, and 1 about a
        woman and her husband who trick 12 priests who proposi-
        tion the woman and who end up being embarrassed and
        revealed to the bishop.

IT46   Mankins, Jerilyn. "More Italian Beliefs." *West Vir-
        ginia Folklore* 12:2 (1962):24-29.

        Miscellany of beliefs recorded from Italian immigrants
        in West Virginia. Includes descriptions of death omen
        and portents, the evil eye, childbirth beliefs, ways
        of determining one's future spouse. Includes 10 person-
        al experience stories, 1 having to do with an encounter
        with a monster.

*IT47   Mason, Wilton. "The Music of the Waldensians in
        Valdese, North Carolina." *North Carolina Folklore*
        8:1 (1960):1-6.

        Brief historical sketch of immigrants from the Cottian
        Alps of Italy, members of the Waldensian religious
        movement, who arrived in Valdese, North Carolina, in
        1893. Includes texts (with musical transcriptions) of

1 Italian song (in Italian) welcoming spring and the
return of the cuckoo and 2 French songs (in French),
one about a shepherdess and the other a hymn.
(Cross-listed as *FR81.)

IT48   Mathias, Elizabeth. "The Game as Creator of the Group
        in an Italian-American Community." *Pennsylvania
        Folklife* 23:4 (1974):22-30.

        Ethnographic description of the bowling game *bocce*
        played by Italian-Americans in South Philadelphia,
        based on interviews with and observations of approxi-
        mately 5 informants. Concludes that playing *bocce*
        continues a long-standing Italian tradition and has
        special significance for older Italian-Americans in
        giving value to their lives and for recent Italian
        immigrants in helping them make the transition between
        Italian, Italian-American, and American cultures.
        Includes 8 photographs of *bocce* playing, players, and
        social clubs supporting the game.

IT49   Mathias, Elizabeth. "The Italian-American Funeral:
        Persistence through Change." *Western Folklore* 33:1
        (1974):35-50.

        Brief historical and ethnographic sketch of South
        Italian peasant immigrants to South Philadelphia,
        followed by a discussion of the post-immigration trans-
        formation of their funerals from ones based upon
        Italian peasant models to ones patterned after those of
        Italian landowners. Indicates changes from funeral
        customs concerned with the pacification of souls of
        the deceased to those stressing display of the body and
        symbols of status. Argues that folk religious beliefs
        which previously manifested themselves in overt be-
        haviors have become covert, but remain strong, while
        concern with social status and sanctions has supplanted
        the preoccupation with the fate of the soul as the
        principal basis for uniformity. Based on fieldwork
        conducted in Philadelphia. Includes 11 photographs
        of tombstones and tombstone plaques.

*IT50   Musick, Ruth Ann. "Chapter 16, Immigrant Ghosts."

        (Cross-listed as *CZ6, *HU22, *YU7.)
        (See *CZ6 for full citation and annotation.)

*IT51   Musick, Ruth Ann. "European Folktales in West Virgina."
        (Cross-listed as *AU3, *CZ7, *HU23.)
        (See *AU3 for full citation and annotation.)

*IT52   Musick, Ruth Ann. *Green Hills of Magic: West Virginia
        Folktales from Europe.* Lexington, Ky.: University
        of Kentucky Press, 1970. Pp. xvi, 312, introduction,
        notes, motif index, bibliography.

        Presentation of 79 folktale texts (all in English),
        recorded by the author and her students in West Vir-
        ginia from European immigrants and their American-born
        descendants between 1948 and 1967. Tales identified
        as Armenian (1), Austrian (5), Czech (3), Hungarian (9),
        Irish (8), Italian (24), Polish (12), Romanian (2),
        Russian (2), Turkish (3), and Yugoslav (2). Some texts
        reprinted from previously published sources. Tales
        identified according to tale type and motif numbers,
        with some additional comparative notes included.
        (Cross-listed as *AR9, *AU4, *CZ8, *HU24, *IR74,
        *PL52, *RO4, *RU16, *TU3, *YU8.)

IT53   [Musick, Ruth Ann.] "Tales Told by Mr. Rocco Pantalone
        of Fairmont." *West Virginia Folklore* 11:1 (1960):
        2-16.

        Characterization (in English) of 7 folktales, recorded
        from an Italian immigrant informant in Fairmont, West
        Virginia. Includes brief biographical sketch of the
        informant.

*IT54   Musick, Ruth Ann. "The Trickster Story in West Vir-
        ginia." *Midwest Folklore* 10:2 (1960):125-132.

        Presentation of 3 trickster tale texts, recorded from
        informants of Russian, Yugoslav, and Italian backgrounds
        in West Virginia.
        (Cross-listed as *RU17, *YU9.)

IT55   Navarra, Anthony. "Old Tales and New Tongues." *New
        York Folklore Quarterly* 18:1 (1962):12-15.

        Discussion of the Sicilian backgrounds of the author's
        mother and grandfather and of their repertoires as
        storytellers and his own storytelling in New York (no
        texts or examples presented).

IT56   N[ewell], W[illiam] W[ells]. "Italian Marionettes in
       Boston." *Journal of American Folk-Lore* 7:25 (1894):
       153.

       Notice that puppets in a Boston marionette show (identi-
       fied as South Italian in character) were damaged by
       fire. Continuance of the theater despite the disaster
       noted and hope expressed that modernization of the
       scenery and other aspects of the theater do not result
       from repairs made.

*IT57 Peacock, Kenneth. "Establishing Perimeters for Ethno-
       musicological Field Research in Canada: On-Going
       Projects and Future Possibilities at the Canadian
       Centre for Folk Culture Studies."

       (Cross-listed as *GL66, *CH21, *FR91, *GE428, *HU25,
       *IC4, *ID2, *JA9, *LI5, *NO19, *RU19, *UK32.)
       (See *GL66 for full citation and annotation.)

IT58   Pietropaoli, Lydia Q. "Folklore from the Heart of
       Italy, Part 1." *New York Folklore Quarterly* 19:3
       (1963):163-182.

       Characterization of miscellaneous folklore items:
       1) 5 folktales; 2) 1 invocation to a grandmother; 3)
       a discussion of customs associated with the Feast of
       Saint John; 4) a brief discussion of the life and works
       of Saint Angelo, beliefs about him, activities associated
       with his feast day, the fountain of Saint Angelo and its
       waters, and 1 legend about the statue of the saint (set
       in Italy); and 5) 3 Italian proverbs (in English),
       which conclude 3 of the folktales noted above. Material
       either sent to the author by relatives in Italy or
       recorded from informants of Italian descent in New York.

IT59   Pietropaoli, Lydia Q. "Folklore from the Heart of
       Italy, Part II." *New York Folklore Quarterly* 19:4
       (1963):283-295.

       Characterization of miscellaneous folklore items: 5
       folktales, 1 story about the feast day of Saint Anthony
       of Padua, and 1 counting-out game from Italy. Also
       includes a discussion of the fairies (*le fate*) which
       are believed to haunt a particular Italian castle, and
       2 sayings (1 in English and 1 in Italian, with English
       translation). Material either sent to the author by
       relatives in Italy or recorded from informants of
       Italian descent in New York.

IT60   Pietropaoli, Lydia Q. "The Italians Came Up Watertown
       Way." *New York Folklore Quarterly* 29:1 (1973):58-79.

       Discussion of some of the contributions made by Italians
       to the settlement of the New World in general and of
       Watertown, New York, in particular, with passing refer-
       ences made to foods eaten, games played, dialect spoken,
       marriage customs, and funeral traditions. Includes a
       listing of 10 superstitions.

*IT61 Preston, Michael J. "A Typescript Ethnic Joke Anthology."
       New York Folklore 1:3&4 (1975):229-234.

       Presentation of a list of ethnic jokes from a typescript,
       obtained by the author from an acquaintance, illustrating
       that much folklore is communicated in writing or print.
       Includes 30 riddle jokes involving Italians, 6 involving
       Irish, and 10 involving Poles.
       (Cross-listed as *IR87, *PL65.)

IT62   Ramírez, Manuel D. "Italian Folklore from Tampa,
       Florida: Introduction." *Southern Folklore Quarterly*
       5:2 (1941):101-106.

       Brief sketch of the Italian settlement in Tampa, Florida,
       followed by texts of 3 folksongs in Sicilian dialect
       (no English translations).

IT63   Ramírez, Manuel D. "Italian Folklore from Tampa,
       Florida, Series No. II: Proverbs." *Southern Folklore
       Quarterly* 13:2 (1949):121-132.

       Bilingual listing of 115 proverbs, recorded from Italian-
       Americans in Tampa, Florida, in the 1940s, with brief
       introductory comments.

IT64   Regnoni-Macera, Clara. "The Song of May." *Western
       Folklore* 23:1 (1964):23-26.

       Presentation (in Italian, with English translation) of
       1 folksong text, recorded from an Italian immigrant in
       Colorado. Includes musical transcription and historical
       and comparative discussion of the May Day ritual during
       which young girls sing the song presented.

IT65   Roberts, Leonard. "Folktales from the Italian Alps."
       Tennessee Folklore Society Bulletin 12:4 (1956):99-108.

       Presentation (in English) of 6 tale and legend texts,
       written down for the author by a woman of Italian descent
       from Wooldridge, Tennessee, who heard the tales when a
       child from her Italian immigrant father.

IT66   Roberts, Leonard. "More Folktales from the Italian
       Alps." *Tennessee Folklore Society Bulletin* 13:4
       (1957):95-104.

       Presentation (in English) of 4 tale texts, written
       down for the author by a woman of Italian descent from
       Wooldridge, Tennessee, who heard the tales when a child
       from her Italian immigrant father.

IT67   Simmons, Donald C. "Anti-Italian-American Riddles in
       New England." *Journal of American Folklore* 79:313
       (1966):475-478.

       Brief discussion of anti-Italian lore in New England
       between the mid-1940s and the mid-1960s, suggesting
       that increased competition brought about by the rising
       status of Italian-Americans is probably responsible for
       the generation and popularity of anti-Italian jokes and
       riddles. Includes characterizations of 3 anecdotal
       tales, 26 anti-Italian riddles, and 4 other ethnic
       slurs/riddles from various parts of Massachusetts and
       Connecticut.

IT68   Smith, M. Estellie. "Folk Medicine among the Sicilian-
       Americans of Buffalo, New York." *Urban Anthropology*
       1:1 (1972):87-106.

       Discussion of folk medical data recorded by the author
       from Sicilian-Americans in Buffalo, New York. Includes
       1 account of a cure by a healer, 1 of an encounter with
       a witch, 2 tales about curses and their consequences,
       2 about evil eye curings. Also includes a list of 6
       beliefs about ways to prevent or cure the evil eye.
       Argues that even fourth-generation Sicilian-Americans
       in Buffalo may resort to traditional cures and healers
       when other methods or remedies fail.

IT69   "Spazzacamino: The Chimney Sweep." *Colorado Folksong
       Bulletin* 1:3 (1962):31.

       Presentation of 1 song text (in Italian, with English
       translation and tune transcription), recorded from an
       Italian immigrant man in Lafayette, Colorado, in 1962.

*IT70 Speroni, Charles. "California Fishermen's Festivals."
       Western Folklore 14:2 (1955):77-91.

       Characterization of fishermen's festivals in San Fran-
       cisco (Italian), Monterey (Sicilian), San Pedro (Italian

and Slavonian), and Point Loma (Portuguese), California, including descriptions of religious processions and sea and ship blessings (illustrated with 4 photographs). (Cross-listed as *PO22, *SJ1.)

IT71 Speroni, Charles. "The Development of the Columbus Day Pageant of San Francisco." *Western Folklore* 7:4 (1948):325-335.

Brief historical sketch of Columbus Day celebrations in the United States, followed by a chronology of such festivals among Italians in San Francisco since 1869. Includes brief description of the 1947 San Francisco celebration witnessed by the author.

IT72 Speroni, Charles. "Five Italian Wellerisms." *Western Folklore* 7:1 (1948):54-55.

Presentation of 5 Wellerism texts (in Italian, with English translations), recorded from California informants of Italian background, with 1 explanatory tale concerning the origin of 1 of the sayings.

IT73 Speroni, Charles. "The Observance of Saint Joseph's Day Among the Sicilians of Southern California." *Southern Folklore Quarterly* 4:3 (1940):135-139.

Description of festive altars prepared, drama enacted (Mary, Joseph, and Jesus seeking and eventually obtaining shelter), and food prepared and consumed by California Italian (Sicilian) immigrants to commemorate Saint Joseph's Day. Includes texts of segments of 2 dramas enacted (presented in Sicilian dialect, with English translations).

IT74 Spicer, Dorothy Gladys. "Health Superstitions of the Italian Immigrant." *Hygeia* 4:5 (1926):266-269.

Discussion of ways to break down traditional Italian health beliefs and healing practices among immigrants to America and to motivate the immigrants to seek care from doctors and hospitals. Includes mention of 1 story about a girl who sought a saint's help for a cure and was actually healed with diet modification, 1 story about a man with tuberculosis who at first preferred to consult a healer before going to a sanitorium, and mention of 1 custom relating to toasting the health of the newborn. Includes 4 photographs of Italian immigrants.

IT75   Stingo, Sandra Voldeck. "III. Witch Stories of
        European Origin: 4. The Night Visitor." *West Vir-
        ginia Folklore* 6:1 (1955):15.

        Characterization (in English) of 1 story, told to the
        author by her Italian grandfather, about the mysterious
        appearance and disappearance of a woman in black shortly
        before a family member was reported to have died.

IT76   Stingo, Sandra Voldeck. "III. Witch Stories of
        European Origin: 5. The Strange Power." *West Vir-
        ginia Folklore* 6:1 (1955):16.

        Characterization (in English) of 1 personal experience
        story, told to the author by her Italian immigrant
        grandmother, about a woman who mysteriously appeared to
        another woman and told her of impending deaths.

*IT77   Thompson, Marion. "Folklore in the Schools: Collecting
        in Cortland."

        (Cross-listed as *GL80, *IR105, *JE77.)
        (See *GL80 for full citation and annotation.)

IT78   Trop, Sylvia. "An Italian Rip Van Winkle." *New York
        Folklore Quarterly* 1:2 (1945):101-105.

        Presentation of 1 folktale text (in English) which the
        author feels is of interest because of its similarity
        to Washington Irving's *Rip Van Winkle*. Tale recorded
        from an Italian informant in Granville, New York.

IT79   Turner, Kay F. "The Virgin of Sorrows Procession: A
        Brooklyn Inversion." *Folklore Papers of the Univer-
        sity* [of Texas at Austin] *Folklore Association*,
        October 1980, pp. 1-26.

        Description, analysis, interpretation, and discussion
        of the meaning of a Good Friday "Procession of Maria
        SS Addolorato (the Virgin of Sorrows)" held annually
        by South Italian immigrants and their American-born
        descendants in an Italian neighborhood in Brooklyn,
        New York. Author uses the example to present a defini-
        tion of the procession, to illustrate the process of
        "symbolic inversion" of which the procession under study
        is a manifestation, and to demonstrate continuities from
        the Old World to the New World of traditional practices
        and underlying concepts and assumptions. Comparisons
        made between the Virgin of Sorrows procession as cele-

brated in Brooklyn and in Bari, Italy, the area from
which the majority of the Brooklyn procession participants emigrated.

IT80 Urick, Mildred. "The San Rocco Festival at Aliquippa,
      Pennsylvania: A Transplanted Tradition." *Pennsyl-
      vania Folklife* 19:1 (1969):14-22.

Argues that despite forces leading to acculturation
among members of many ethnic groups, the Italians of
Aliquippa, Pennsylvania, maintain many Old World traditions, including the custom of celebrating a saint's
day with the San Rocco festival, held annually during
the weekend nearest to August 16, the feast day of San
Rocco. Includes a discussion of the origin of the
festival, comparison of Italian and Italian-American
festivals commemorating the saint, and primary aspects
of the festival. Illustrated with 4 photographs of
the celebration, 1 prayer card, and 1 calendar.

IT81 Valetta, Clement L. "Friendship and Games in Italian-
      American Life." *Keystone Folklore Quarterly* 15:4
      (1970):174-187.

General discussion of Italian immigrants who settled in
Roseto, Pennsylvania, during the 1890s, followed by a
description of social relationships and tensions in the
community. Describes card and hand games played by the
men, noting their correlations with social relations
and stratification. Includes mention of the role of
gossip, name-fixing, and 2 personal experience stories
and 1 dream interpretation.

IT82 Voiles, Jane. "Genoese Folkways in a California Mining
      Camp." *California Folklore Quarterly* 3:3 (1944):
      212-216.

Presentation of miscellaneous items of lore from
Italian (Genoese) immigrants living in a California
mining camp, as recalled by the author. Includes
descriptions of ways of preventing, diagnosing, and
curing the evil eye; of healing stomach and other
ailments; of marking such calendrical events as May
Day, Saint John's Day, Christmas, and New Year's Day.

*IT83 Weiner, Harvey. "Folklore in the Los Angeles Garment
       Industry." *Western Folklore* 23:1 (1964):17-21.

Brief characterization of miscellaneous customs, beliefs,
and taboos recorded by the author in 1962 from workers

in the Los Angeles garment industry, with 5 items
being identified as Italian and 5 as Jewish.
(Cross-listed as *JE80.)

IT84   Williams, Phyllis H. *South Italian Folkways in Europe
        and America: A Handbook for Social Workers, Visiting
        Nurses, School Teachers, and Physicians.* New Haven,
        Conn.: Yale University Press, 1938. Pp. xviii, 216,
        index.

Comparison and contrast of the folkways of South Italians
from 6 southern Italian states (including Sicily) and
in the United States, based on research conducted in
the Italian community of New Haven, Connecticut. Topics
discussed focus on employment, housing, diet and household economy, dress, marriage and the family, recreation
and hospitality, education, religion and superstition,
health and hospitals, care of the aged and of other
dependents, and death and mortuary practices. Emphasizes
the fact that traditional folkways and mores of Italian
immigrants in America cannot be changed easily and often
persist even among members of the second generation born
in the United States. States that an understanding of
the cultural background of South Italians is a useful
prerequisite for the work of American social workers,
visiting nurses, schoolteachers, and physicians. Includes 8 illustrations and photographs and 1 map of the
area of Italy from which those studied emigrated.

*IT85   Withers, Carl. "Current Events in New York City
        Children's Folklore."

        (Cross-listed as *GE729, *JA13.)
        (See *GE729 for full citation and annotation.)

IT86   Zappacosta, Bob. "Italian Beliefs." *West Virginia
        Folklore* 12:2 (1962):18-24.

Characterization of a variety of traditional beliefs/
superstitions recorded from 2 Italian immigrants in
West Virginia. Includes those concerning witches and
witchcraft, 1 cure for headaches, 2 rituals for pro-
tecting one's home from lightning and storms, 1 ritual
for breaking droughts, 2 customs relating to the dead,
1 ritual practiced on Saint Agnes's Day to enable young
girls to dream of their future husbands, 1 All Souls'
Day custom, 1 preventive for the evil eye, 1 belief
relating to longevity and happiness, 2 beliefs relating
to pregnancy and childbirth, 1 cooking taboo, and 1
taboo about behavior following one's viewing of the dead.
Includes 3 personal experience narratives.

XXVIII. JAPANESE (JA) (1-13)

*JA1 Bryant, Margaret M. "Folklore in the Schools: Folklore
      in College English Classes."

      (Cross-listed as *GL11, *JE11.)
      (See *GL11 for full citation and annotation.)

JA2   Hewes, Gordon W. "American Japanese Place Names."
      American Speech 21:2 (1946):100-105.

      Discussion of the methods used by immigrant Japanese to
      translate American place names into Japanese writing.
      Lists 38 names of American cities and their Japanese
      equivalents. Speculates that new written forms may in-
      fluence the spoken word. Notes that the process of
      translation of names into Japanese may be a sign of
      anti-assimilation tendencies.

*JA3 Hoe, Ban Seng. "Asian-Canadian Folklore Studies: An
      Interdisciplinary and Cross-Cultural Approach."

      (Cross-listed as *CH9, *ID1.)
      (See *CH9 for full citation and annotation.)

JA4   Hofmann, Charles. "Japanese Folksongs in New York City."
      Journal of American Folklore 59:233 (1946):325-326.

      Brief description of folksong recordings made by Japanese
      singers in New York City in June 1945, with emphasis on
      the combining of traditional Japanese music and songs
      and Western classical music and hence on the "synthesis"
      of two traditions. Some songs recorded identified by
      titles, but no actual examples provided.

*JA5 Humphrey, Linda T. "'It Ain't Funny, Buster': The
      Ethnic Riddle-Joke at Citrus Community College."

      (Cross-listed as *GL49, *CH13, *IR47, *IT32, *SS17.)
      (See *GL49 for full citation and annotation.)

JA6   Kawamoto, Fumi. "Folk Beliefs among Japanese in the Los
      Angeles Area." *Western Folklore* 21:1 (1962):13-26.

      Listing of 216 statements of belief recorded from indi-
      viduals of Japanese ancestry in the Los Angeles area.
      Includes body superstitions, dream interpretations, cures
      and home remedies, luck and charms, birth beliefs, court-
      ship and marriage beliefs and customs, death supersti-
      tions, domestic superstitions, food superstitions, animal
      and fish beliefs, and weather and astronomy beliefs.

JA7   May, Elizabeth. "Encounters with Japanese Music in Los
      Angeles." *Western Folklore* 17:3 (1958):192-195.

      Account of the author's search for Japanese traditional
      music and songs among her Japanese students and in Los
      Angeles music stores. Includes partial transcription
      of the music of 1 children's folksong, mention of musical
      instruments brought to her classes by students. Notes
      that Japanese music and song are still played and sung
      in the Los Angeles area.

JA8   Opler, Marvin K. "Japanese Folk Beliefs and Practices,
      Tule Lake, California." *Journal of American Folklore*
      63:250 (1950):385-397.

      Discussion of the revival and dissemination of tradition-
      al Japanese peasant folk beliefs and practices among
      Japanese-Americans interned at Tule Lake, California,
      during World War II. Includes examples of stories
      relating to the appearance of a fireball (*hidama*) or
      fluorescent-like light (*hitodama*) as a ghostlike omen
      of death (6 illustrative texts); tales of animal-spirit
      possession and bewitchment (5 textual examples); narra-
      tives about swordsmen and sorcerer's apprentices capable
      of shape-shifting, disappearing, levitating the body,
      hypnotizing others (illustrative endings for 3 such
      stories). Also included are brief descriptions of
      selected death and bad luck omens (9 examples), pregnancy
      beliefs and taboos (10 examples), ways to predict the
      sex of unborn children (8 examples), birth and infancy
      beliefs, and brief descriptions of healers and cures.
      Notes that revival and dissemination of these phenomena
      are attributable to stresses and anxieties caused by in-
      ternment and uncertainty about the environment and the
      future, but that follow-up fieldwork after the end of
      internment revealed an indifference toward or rejection
      of such beliefs and practices.

*JA9 Peacock, Kenneth. "Establishing Perimeters for Ethno-
      musicological Field Research in Canada: On-Going
      Projects and Future Possibilities at the Canadian
      Centre for Folk Culture Studies."

      (Cross-listed as *GL66, *CH21, *FR91, *GE428, *HU25,
      *IC4, *ID2, *IT57, *LI5, *NO19, *RU19, *UK32.)
      (See *GL66 for full citation and annotation.)

JA10   Preston, W.D. "Japanese Riddle Materials." *Journal of
       American Folklore* 61:240 (1948):175-181.

       Two-part essay consisting of 1) translation into English
       of a Russian article on types of Japanese riddles and
       2) presentation (in Japanese, then literal and "free"
       English translations) of 5 riddles recorded from 2
       Japanese informants in Philadelphia in 1945-46. The 5
       riddles recorded in the United States discussed in terms
       of the classification scheme outlined in the translated
       Russian essay.

JA11   Radin, Paul. "Folktales of Japan as Told in California."
       Journal of American Folklore 59:233 (1946):289-308.

       Presentation (in English translation) of 16 folktale
       texts, recorded in 1934 from individuals of Japanese
       ancestry in Berkeley and Oakland, California, by a
       "Miss N.I." and edited for publication by author Radin.
       Includes brief comments about general familiarity or
       unfamiliarity of informants with specific tales and
       about knowledge of Japanese folktales among second- and
       third-generation Japanese-Americans.

JA12   Radin, Paul. "Japanese Ceremonies and Festivals in
       California." *Southwestern Journal of Anthropology*
       2:2 (1946):152-179.

       Comparative study of Japanese life-cycle and calendrical
       festivals, celebrations, and customs in Japan and among
       Japanese-Americans living in Berkeley and Oakland,
       California, based on data gathered in 1934. Includes
       descriptions of birth, marriage, and funeral ceremonies
       in the two communities and New Year, Empire Day, Doll,
       Flag, Dead, Moon Gazing, Chrysanthemum, Emperor's
       Birthday, and miscellaneous religious festivals and
       ceremonies. Emphasis on contrasts, changes, adaptations,
       and discontinuation of traditional Japanese ceremonies
       and festivals among California Japanese-Americans.

*JA13 Withers, Carl. "Current Events in New York City
       Children's Folklore."

       (Cross-listed as *GE729, *IT85.)
       (See *GE729 for full citation and annotation.)

XXIX.   JEWISH (JE) (1-86)

*JE1   Abrahams, Roger D.   "Folklore in the Definition of
       Ethnicity: An American and Jewish Perspective."

       (Cross-listed as *GL2.)
       (See *GL2 for full citation and annotation.)

JE2   Armistead, S.G., and Silverman, J.H.   "A Judeo-Spanish
       Kompla and Its Greek Counterpart."   *Western Folklore*
       23:4 (1964):262-264.

       Brief note presenting a Judeo-Spanish *kompla* (couplet)
       recorded by the authors in Los Angeles in 1958 from a
       Sephardic Jewish immigrant woman from the Greek island
       of Rhodes, with comparison of the text to Greek analogues.
       Asserts that the *kompla* under discussion, as well as
       others known among Judeo-Spanish peoples, was probably
       modeled after, or influenced by, Greek distiches.

JE3   Armistead, Samuel G., and Silverman, Joseph H.   "Hispanic
       Balladry among the Sephardic Jews of the West Coast."
       Western Folklore 19:4 (1960):229-244.

       Brief historical sketch of the Sephardic Jews, followed
       by the presentation (in Judeo-Spanish, with English
       translation) of 7 ballad or *romancero* texts, recorded
       from Sephardic Jewish informants in 1957 and 1958 in
       Los Angeles and Seattle.   Includes discussion of events
       that the ballads depict and provides historical and
       comparative notes.

*JE4   Barrick, Mac E.   "Racial Riddles & the Polack Joke."

       (Cross-listed as *GE43, *IR4, *IT6, *PL5.)
       (See *PL5 for full citation and annotation.)

JE5   Bauman, Richard.   "Y.L. Cahan's Instructions on the
       Collecting of Folklore."   *New York Folklore Quarterly*
       18:4 (1962):284-289.

       Discussion of the inaccessibility of much American folk-
       lore because of its linguistic diversity; of the life
       and work of the Jewish folklorist Y.L. Cahan in New York;
       and of Cahan's ideas regarding scientific folklore
       collecting.

JE6   Ben-Amos, Dan. "The Americanization of 'The King and
      the Abbot.'" *Indiana Folklore* 2:1 (1969):115-123.

      Presentation of 2 reprinted Jewish variants of the tale
      "The King and the Abbot," followed by 1 text of the tale
      recorded in Indianapolis in 1963 from a Jewish immigrant
      informant from Poland. Brief description of the story-
      teller and discussion of how the American text cited
      differs from usual Jewish versions of the tale, revealing
      the transformation in roles and genre in an American
      environment.

JE7   Ben-Amos, Dan. "The 'Myth' of Jewish Humor." *Western
      Folklore* 32:2 (1973):112-131.

      Challenges the views, first suggested by Sigmund Freud,
      that Jewish humor is self-critical, self-mocking, and
      masochistic. Argues that joking among Jews is indicative
      of the complexity, segmentation, and socioeconomic
      stratification of their communities and that when jokes
      are analyzed within their communicative contexts, they
      can be shown to be vehicles for distinguishing tellers
      and listeners from Jews of other socioeconomic classes
      or strata rather than as means of criticizing or mocking
      Jews collectively. Includes 3 reprinted and 2 field-
      recorded joke texts.

*JE8 Boswell, George W. "Ole Miss Jokes and Anecdotes."

      (Cross-listed as *GL9, *IT12, *PL7.)
      (See *PL7 for full citation and annotation.)

*JE9 Botkin, Ben A. (Moderator). "The Folksong Revival: A
      Symposium." *New York Folklore Quarterly* 19:2 (1963):
      83-142.

      Transcription of discussions during the meeting of the
      New York Folklore Society on 2 March 1963 concerning
      problems raised in the definition and conceptualization
      of "folk music" as a result of the folksong revival in
      America. Includes brief discussion of the character-
      istics of Anglo-Scots-Irish tradition, of the fact that
      the most complete body of Yiddish folksong is preserved
      in the United States, and of the use of *hassidic* songs
      by the *mitnaggedim* movement. Also includes presentation
      of 1 stanza of an Irish rebel song heard in New York City,
      1 stanza of a ballad, and 1 stanza of an anti-Hitler song
      written by Woody Guthrie (all in English).
      (Cross-listed as *IR12, *SC3.)

*JE10 Brunvand, Jan Harold. "Some Thoughts on the Ethnic-
       Regional Riddle Joke."

       (Cross-listed as *GL10, *PL8.)
       (See *GL10 for full citation and annotation.)

*JE11 Bryant, Margaret M. "Folklore in the Schools: Folklore
       in College English Classes."

       (Cross-listed as *GL11, *JA1.)
       (See *GL11 for full citation and annotation.)

JE12   Clarfield, Geoffrey. "Music in the Moroccan Jewish
       Community of Toronto." *Canadian Folk Music Journal*
       4 (1976):31-38.

       General discussion of kinds of music and song found in
       the Moroccan-Jewish (Sephardic) community of Toronto.
       Mention made of 2 ballads (*romanceros*) about which in-
       formants spoke, with plot of 1 summarized. Suggests
       that use rather than content may be the basis for cate-
       gorizing music and song.

JE13   Cray, Ed. "The Rabbi Trickster." *Journal of American
       Folklore* 77:306 (1964):331-345.

       Presentation of 18 field-recorded and 4 reprinted
       Jewish jokes, most concerning the exploits and inter-
       actions of rabbis and others, recorded between 1960 and
       1963, principally in Los Angeles. Contrasts made be-
       tween Old World Jewish jokes and those spawned by
       experiences in and told in the United States.

JE14   Dantzker, Sondra. "Some Jewish Folk Habits and Super-
       stitions." *New York Folklore Quarterly* 14:2 (1958):
       148-149.

       Brief discussion of 3 superstitions and 3 customs, 1
       toast, and the practice of drinking liquor at the time
       of someone's death. Information recorded from the
       author's mother (in New York City) and Jewish friends
       and relatives.

JE15   Dorson, Richard M. "Jewish-American Dialect Stories on
       Tape." In *Studies in Biblical and Jewish Folklore*,
       edited by Raphael Patai, Francis Lee Utley, and Dov
       Noy, pp. 111-174. Indiana University Folklore Series
       No. 13 (1960). Also published as *Memoirs of the
       American Folklore Society* 51 (1960).

       Presentation of texts of 81 Jewish-American dialect
       stories, 68 recorded from Jewish-Americans, 13 from

Americans not of Jewish background, based on fieldwork conducted principally in Indiana and Michigan and mostly from 4 informants. Includes brief discussion of the style and form of the jokes, and provides comparative notes.

JE16   Dorson, Richard M. "More Jewish Dialect Stories." *Midwest Folklore* 10:3 (1960):133-146.

Presentation of 16 Jewish dialect story texts, recorded at Indiana University in 1959 from a man from Brooklyn, New York.

*JE17   Dorson, Richard M. "Tales of a Greek-American Family on Tape."

(Cross-listed as *GR6.)
(See *GR6 for full citation and annotation.)

JE18   Dresser, Norine. "'Is It Fresh?' An Examination of Jewish-American Shopping Habits." *New York Folklore Quarterly* 27:1 (1971):153-160.

Description of food-buying habits of Jewish-American women, based on observations made in Los Angeles in 1969. Includes 13 anecdotes, numerous examples of questions and answers exchanged between buyers and sellers of foods in a section of small shops in a Jewish business area of Los Angeles. Brief comparative data provided to contrast attitudes and shopping habits of the daughters of Jewish immigrants with those of their immigrant mothers.

JE19   Dresser, Norine, and Schuchat, Theodor. "In Search of the Perforated Page." *Western Folklore* 39:4 (1980): 300-306.

Discussion of 2 stories about Jewish men whose pictures were printed on perforated pages in their schools' yearbooks so the pages could be removed by anyone who objected to the individuals' photographs being included because of their ethnic background (Jewish), followed by a characterization of the search to determine whether or not the stories had any basis in fact (which they did). Includes 2 photographs of a page (front and back) that may have served as the basis for the stories.

*JE20   Dundes, Alan. "A Study of Ethnic Slurs: The Jew and the Polack in the United States."

(Cross-listed as *PL26.)
(See *PL26 for full citation and annotation.)

*JE21   Elish, Karl M. "Death and the Old Man." *New York Folk-
        lore Quarterly* 2:1 (1946):59.

        Characterization of 1 folktale (in English) heard by
        the author in Yiddish from his Russian immigrant parents.
        (Cross-listed as *RU8.)

*JE22   Erdely, Stephen. "Ethnic Music in the United States:
        An Overview."

        (Cross-listed as *GL40, *AR5, *CR2, *GR7, *GY5,
        *SC11, *SE2.)
        (See *GL40 for full citation and annotation.)

JE23   Firestone, Melvin M. "Sephardic Folk-Curing in Seattle."
        Journal of American Folklore 75:298 (1962):301-310.

        Brief sketch of the settlement of Sephardic Jews in
        Seattle, followed by a description of healing incanta-
        tions and rites for the evil eye and demon-fright. In-
        cludes texts of 7 incantations/spells and descriptions
        of miscellaneous healing rituals.

*JE24   Foster, James R. "Brooklyn Folklore."

        (Cross-listed as *GL43, *GR9, *IR31, *IT21, *PL28,
        *PO6, *SP7.)
        (See *GL43 for full citation and annotation.)

*JE25   Frantz, Mrs. Gilda. "The Cheerapakas." *Polish Folk-
        lore* 5:4 (1960):55-56.

        Characterization (in English) of 1 moral tale, told to
        children to counter their protests about having their
        hair combed, about some animals in Poland named *cheera-
        pakas*, who were hairy, but who refused to let their
        mother comb their hair until it was so tangled that
        birds began to nest in it--and still do. Author-
        contributor--from Sherman Oaks, California--learned the
        tale from her Polish-Jewish mother.
        (Cross-listed as *PL29.)

JE26   Glanz, Dr. Rudolf. *The Jew in the Old American Folk-
        lore.* New York: Waldon Press, Inc., 1961. Pp. vi,
        234, acknowledgments, appendix, notes.

        Survey of the image of the Jew as revealed in ethnic
        slurs, sayings, statements of belief, jokes, legends,
        tales, and games, with a variety of examples reprinted
        from previously published sources. Asserts that cer-
        tain stereotypes of the Jew were common among various

European peoples, who brought them to America and perpetuated them in the New World, with some traits viewed stereotypically as Jewish also at times transferred to such other figures as the Yankee. Notes a gradual evolution in the image of the Jew in folk and popular literature from the "Christ-killer" to a figure in "business folklore."

*JE27 Gorelick, J. "Two Anecdotes of Immigrant Life." *New York Folklore Quarterly* 18:1 (1962):65-67.

Brief discussion of the types of stories that were told by Russian Jews about the Jews who had migrated to America, and characterization of 2 anecdotes about such immigrants in America (1 involving the author). (Cross-listed as *RU9.)

*JE28 Greenberg, Andrea. "Form and Function of the Ethnic Joke."

(Cross-listed as *GL47, *FR63, *IT27, *PL33.) (See *GL47 for full citation and annotation.)

JE29 Hand, Wayland D. "Jewish Popular Beliefs and Customs in Los Angeles." In *Studies in Biblical and Jewish Folklore*, edited by Raphael Patai, Francis Lee Utley, and Dov Noy, pp. 309-326. Indiana University Folklore Series No. 13 (1960). Also published as *Memoirs of the American Folklore Society* 51 (1960).

Presentation of 113 statements of belief and descriptions of related customs, recorded mostly from students of Jewish background beginning in 1948 in Los Angeles. Includes examples of customs and beliefs relating to birth, infancy, and childhood; naming; evil eye; medical beliefs; culinary and domestic practices; beliefs relating to sewing and the garment industry; moving into new houses; marriage and weddings; death; animal and plant lore; and religious lore.

JE30 Hand, Wayland D. "Reply to Parzen." *Journal of American Folklore* 74:293 (1961):250-251.

Reply to criticisms by Herbert Parzen (see JE51) concerning the author's essay "Jewish Popular Beliefs and Customs in Los Angeles" (see JE29). Largely a defense of method and a plea for more collecting of Jewish-American folklore.

*JE31   Herrmann, Walter. "Anecdotes about Hitler."

        (Cross-listed as *GE281.)
        (See *GE281 for full citation and annotation.)

JE32   Hurvitz, Nathan. "Blacks and Jews in American Folklore."
        Western Folklore 33:4 (1974):301-325.

        Discussion and exemplification of negative attitudes
        toward Afro-Americans and Jews communicated through the
        folklore of the dominant white Christian society, with
        emphasis on similarities in the portrayal of the two.
        Includes texts of 1 game rhyme (reprinted), 4 verses/
        rhymes (2 reprinted, 2 recorded by the author), 19 jokes
        (16 reprinted, 3 field-recorded), 2 examples of graffiti,
        and 1 riddle joke.

JE33   Hurvitz, Nathan. "Jews and Jewishness in the Street
        Rhymes of American Children." *Jewish Social Studies*
        16:2 (1954):135-150.

        Characterization of American children's rhymes and song
        parodies containing references or allusions to Jews or
        Jewishness, reported from both Jewish and non-Jewish
        sources. Suggests that some rhymes may have been
        intentionally derogatory or prejudicial, while others--
        especially bilingual rhymes known and recited by Jews--
        may be indicative of differences in attitudes between
        first- and second-generation American Jews. Includes
        texts of 42 rhymes and song parodies known or reported
        to the author by informants from the 1920s to 1940s
        from cities throughout the United States and 9 rhymes
        reprinted from previously published sources.

JE34   Jason, Heda. "The Jewish Joke: The Problem of Defini-
        tion." *Southern Folklore Quarterly* 31:1 (1967):48-54.

        Response to an essay by Ed Cray (see JE13) objecting
        to attempts to define "*the* Jewish joke" as if there
        were only one kind, to view all European Jews collec-
        tively (rather than distinguishing Eastern European
        from Central and Western European Jews), and to regard
        American Jews and their jokes as distinctive (instead
        of as derivatives from and transformations of Old World
        counterparts). Stresses the need for extensive and
        systematic fieldwork before generalizations are made.

*JE35 Jones, Louis C. "The Evil-Eye among European-Americans."
(Cross-listed as *GL51, *GR21, *HU17, *IN1, *IR50,
*IT35, *PL39, *RU10, *SZ2.)
(See *GL51 for full citation and annotation.)

JE36 Katz, Naomi, and Katz, Eli. "Tradition and Adaptation
in American Jewish Humor." *Journal of American Folklore* 84:332 (1971):215-220.

Comparison and contrast of East European Jewish and
Jewish-American dialect jokes, positing that the former
reflect and comment humorously on the East European
Jew's experiences in a segregated environment and a
technological age, while the latter reveal the American-
born Jew's ambivalence toward Yiddish-speaking immigrants
and toward his own acceptance by the majority culture
in the United States. Includes 3 reprinted joke texts.

JE37 Kirshenblatt-Gimblett, Barbara. "The Concept and
Varieties of Narrative Performance in East European
Jewish Culture." In *Explorations in the Ethnography
of Speaking*, edited by Richard Bauman and Joel
Sherzer, pp. 283-308. New York: Cambridge Univer-
sity Press, 1974.

Characterization of various social settings in which
and speech events during which storytelling occurs
among East European Jews, based in part on fieldwork conducted in Toronto from 1968 to 1971. Distinguishes among
stories told as glosses on conversations and inter-
actions, stories as topics in discourse, storytelling
rounds, and solo storytelling. Notes that storytelling
is always subordinate to non-narrative discourse and
that the nature of the speech events during which
stories are told affects performance and genre choice.
Includes transcribed excerpts from tape-recorded interviews with 2 East European Jewish immigrants in
Toronto and the text of 1 parable.

JE38 Kirshenblatt-Gimblett, Barbara. "Culture Shock and
Narrative Creativity." In *Folklore in the Modern
World*, edited by Richard M. Dorson, pp. 109-122.
The Hague: Mouton Publishers, 1978.

Discussion of "situations of radical change and culture
shock" experienced by immigrants as sources and stimuli
for the generation of stories and the continued popularity of storytelling, based on fieldwork among East

European (mostly Polish) Jews in Toronto in 1968-70.
Includes texts of 1 joke, 1 personal experience narrative. Discusses style of telling stories about early
immigrant experiences. Distinguishes between "classics"
(tales based on early immigrant days whose humor is due
as much to style of telling as to punchlines and which
are repeatedly told and enjoyed) and "oncers" (stories
viewed as funny only once). Notes that traditional
tales may be "immigrantized," immigrant experiences
"folklorized," with resulting tales and tellings
sharing characteristics and styles.

JE39 Kirshenblatt-Gimblett, Barbara. "A Parable in Context:
      A Social Interactional Analysis of Storytelling
      Performance." In *Folklore: Performance and Communi-
      cation*, edited by Dan Ben-Amos and Kenneth S. Gold-
      stein, pp. 105-130. The Hague: Mouton, 1975.

Detailed analysis of the ways in which a parable told
by a Jewish woman in Toronto in 1968 correlated with
the dynamics of the social interactional situation that
generated it and during which it was communicated.
Includes transcribed text of the narrator's report of
her performance of the tale and of a second informant's
characterization of a parable told to him by another
individual on a specific occasion. Emphasis placed on
the fact that such stories are not autonomous entities,
but are meaningful only in terms of the individuals and
specific social contexts by and in which they are
communicated.

*JE40 Klymasz, Robert B. "The Ethnic Joke in Canada Today."
      (Cross-listed as *GL53, *FR71, *IC3, *IT38, *UK10.)
      (See *GL53 for full citation and annotation.)

JE41 Koskoff, Ellen. "Contemporary Nigun Composition in an
      American Hasidic Community." *Selected Reports in
      Ethnomusicology* 3:1 (1978):153-173.

Characterization of *nigunim* (melodies) composed by
practitioners of Lubavitcher Hasidim who are members
of Hasidic Jewish communities in Brooklyn, New York,
and Pittsburgh, Pennsylvania. Includes brief sketches
of the 4 composers, their communities, their composi-
tions. Based on fieldwork and interviews conducted
between the late 1960s and mid-1970s. Includes musicological transcriptions of 6 *nigunim* (4 by the composers, 2 by others provided for comparison and contrast).

JE42 Krauss, Friedrich S. "Jewish Folk-Life in America."
      Journal of American Folk-Lore 7:24 (1894):72-75.

      A plea for members of the American Folklore Society to
      promote the study of Jewish folklore, particularly in
      the United States, based on the assumption that Jews
      (and particularly German Jews) moving to America are
      discarding their traditional ways and are becoming
      assimilated. Mention made of the work of European
      folklore collectors (especially Ignaz Bernstein in
      Warsaw and his interest in Jewish proverbs) who lament
      the lack of data from Jews in America.

*JE43 Larson, Mildred. "The Taller the Better."

      (Cross-listed as *IR58, *IT40, *RU12.)
      (See *IR58 for full citation and annotation.)

*JE44 Lund, Jens. "The Legend of the King and the Star."
      Indiana Folklore 8:1-2 (1975):1-37.

      Description of 3 variants of a rumor-based story about
      the king of Denmark and/or non-Jewish Danes wearing,
      or threatening to wear, yellow armbands with stars of
      David on them when the Nazis ordered Danish Jews to do
      so during World War II. Includes discussion of pro-
      Jewish sentiment among Danes and other Europeans, plus
      5 reprinted versions and 31 elicited responses to
      questions about the incident which the story depicts
      (1 from an Italian-American, 2 from Americans of German
      background, 1 from a Dane, and 2 from Anglo-Americans).
      (Cross-listed as *DA6, *GE380, *IT43.)

*JE45 Meltzer, Herbert S. "Jewish Tales." *New York Folklore
      Quarterly* 6:1 (1950):21-30.

      Characterization of 6 Jewish folktales, 2 of which
      involve the Ukrainian trickster figures Mottke Chabud
      and Herschel Stopoler, recorded from 3 Jewish informants
      in New York City.
      (Cross-listed as *UK29.)

JE46 Mintz, Jerome R. *Legends of the Hasidim: An Introduc-
      tion to Hasidic Culture and Oral Tradition in the
      New World.* Chicago: University of Chicago Press,
      1968. Pp. 462, bibliography.

      Analysis of Hasidic life, society, and culture, based
      on a corpus of over 370 tales recorded from 59 in-
      formants in New York City between 1959 and 1961 and in

1963. Part one provides background on the Hasidic
movement in Europe and New York, characterizes the
social system based on the central role of the rabbis
and their followers, outlines the basic value system
of Hasidism, and explains the functions that storytelling fulfills within the community. Part two
presents the narrative texts--arranged around the exploits of leading rabbis in Europe and America--con-
cerning the basic values of Hasidism, reaction to ad-
versity, and adjustment to secular values in the United
States. Appendices correlate tellers' ages and occupations with particular stories, list prominent "Rebbes"
mentioned in the study, and provide a glossary of
Hebrew and Yiddish terms. Includes 32 photographs.

JE47   Mlotek, Eleanor Gordon. "America in East European
       Yiddish Folksong." In *The Field of Yiddish: Studies
       in Yiddish Language, Folklore, and Literature*, edited
       by Uriel Weinreich, pp. 179-195. New York: Publica-
       tions of the Linguistic Circle of New York No. 3,
       1954.

       Discussion of images of and attitudes toward immigration
       to and life in America as revealed in folksongs sung by
       Jews in Eastern Europe. Includes texts of 29 sample
       songs (in English translation) revealing attitudes of
       women toward emigrating husbands, positive and negative
       impressions and experiences of Jewish immigrants to
       America, and attitudes toward American wealth.

JE48   Myerhoff, Barbara. *Number Our Days*. New York: E.P.
       Dutton, 1979. Pp. xiii, 306, bibliography.

       Analysis of the ways in which elderly Jews living in
       Venice, California, cope with old age by interacting
       intensely in a senior citizens' center. The nature of
       participation in the center and the dynamics of social
       interaction viewed against the background of the author's
       identity as a Jewess as well as an eventual elder.
       Problems highlighted through a series of portraits of
       specific members of the community derived from life-
       history interviews and partially resolved through the
       creation of secular rituals.

JE49 Myerhoff, Barbara G. "We Don't Wrap Herring in a
      Printed Page: Fusion, Fictions and Continuity in
      Secular Ritual." In *Secular Ritual*, edited by Sally
      F. Moore and Barbara G. Myerhoff, pp. 199-224.
      Amsterdam: Van Gorcum, Assen, 1977.

      Analysis of the role of secular ritual among elderly
      California Jews who created a unique ceremony at a
      senior citizens' home in which a religious and a secular
      graduation celebration were fused. Through an examina-
      tion of the components of the ritual, the author
      demonstrates how the fundamental Jewish values of
      "being a Jew" and learning are dramatized against the
      backdrop of Old and New World experiences.

JE50 Nusbaum, Philip. "Some Notes on the Construction of
      the Jewish-American Dialect Story." *Keystone Folk-
      lore* 23:1-2 (1979):28-52.

      Discussion of recurrent themes, character types,
      settings, language use, and names in a corpus of Jewish-
      American dialect jokes recorded by Richard M. Dorson.
      Notes that the jokes communicate stereotypes of Jews
      and "make what is perceived as Jewish appear strange."
      Includes an appendix identifying jokes by title, kinds
      of narrative themes, settings, and kinds of language
      used.

JE51 Parzen, Herbert. "Observations on a Study of Jewish
      Folklore in Los Angeles." *Journal of American Folk-
      lore* 74:293 (1961):246-250.

      Response to an essay by Wayland D. Hand on Jewish be-
      liefs and customs (see JE29) in which Parzen questions
      the reliability of Hand's data and criticizes him for
      failing to distinguish clearly between Jewish law and
      folklore. Emphases on naming practices, food and eating
      customs, and "rules" concerning menstruation and co-
      habitation. (For Hand's reply, see JE30.)

*JE52 Rennick, Robert M. "Successive Name-Changing: A Popular
      Theme in Onomastic Folklore and Literature." *New York
      Folklore Quarterly* 25:2 (1969):119-128.

      Discussion of the process of multiple name changes, with
      emphasis on anecdotes/stories exemplifying the process.
      Includes texts of 6 such stories involving Jews (1 a
      reprinting), 2 involving Scotsmen (reprinted), 1 in-

volving a Yugoslav (reprinted), 2 involving Germans
(1 reprinted), and 5 involving individuals of unspecified ethnic backgrounds (4 reprinted).
(Cross-listed as *GE446, *SC35, *YU10.)

JE53   Richman, Irwin. "The Bungalow Colony Industry." *Key-
        stone Folklore Quarterly* 17:1 (1972):3-10.

        Discussion of the nature and development of "bungalow
        colonies"--clusters of summer rental cottages--in
        Sullivan County, New York, with emphasis on their Jewish
        clientele from New York City. Traces changes in furnish-
        ings and amenities, as well as in renters, from the late
        1850s to the present time. Includes general descrip-
        tions of the bungalows and casinos, swimming pools, and
        other recreational facilities developed over time in the
        bungalow colonies.

JE54   Rosenberg, Bernard, and Shapiro, Gilbert. "Marginality
        and Jewish Humor." *Midstream* 4:2 (1958):70-80.

        Discussion of jokes and anecdotes about Jews told by
        Jews to other Jews in the United States. Emphasis on
        the fact that the telling of Jewish anecdotes and jokes
        is not only "a response to anti-Semitism," but also
        "a reaction to the special problem of questionable
        status which the Jew has faced in many lands, but most
        clearly and most notably in the United States." In-
        cludes texts or characterizations of 32 jokes and anec-
        dotes exemplifying such themes and stereotypes as inter-
        group marriage, religious conversion, conspicuous con-
        sumption, and economic and social competition for status.

JE55   Rubin, Ruth. "Chanukkah, a Jewish Holiday." *New York
        Folklore Quarterly* 9:4 (1953):255-260.

        Brief historical discussion of the "Hellenizing" of the
        Jews of the commercial classes which preceded the
        struggle of the Maccabees, and examination of the
        possible origin and development of Hanukkah. Also
        discusses the evolution of a literature on the Macca-
        bean theme in America and the rituals, customs, and
        songs associated with Hanukkah in the United States.

JE56   Rubin, Ruth. "From a Collector's Notebook: Yiddish
        Anecdotes, Jokes, and Sayings." *New York Folklore
        Quarterly* 20:4 (1964):289-295.

        Presentation (in English) of texts of 12 anecdotes, 3
        jokes, and 2 personal experience narratives relating to

the immigration experience, recorded by the author at unspecified places from unidentified informants, all of Jewish background and all Yiddish speakers.

JE57   Rubin, Ruth. "Nineteenth-Century History in Yiddish Folksong." *New York Folklore Quarterly* 15:3 (1959): 220-228.

Discussion of the interest Jewish folklore holds for scholars in the humanities and social sciences, especially in illuminating the life of the East European Jewish communities no longer in existence, and of 6 historical patterns of the 19th century and their relationship to several songs of that era. Includes presentation of 9 song texts (in Yiddish, with English translations): 1) a song about the poverty of the Jews of this period (utilizing the letters of the Hebrew alphabet), 2) an anti-Hassidic song, 3) an anti-conscription song from Russia, 4) the song of a young recruit, 5) a song about the Odessa pogrom of 1871, 6) a political workingman's song from Lithuania, 7) a song of Zionist women in Bessarabia, 8) a parody of a well-known Zionist folksong, and 9) 4 stanzas of a lullaby by Sholem Aleichem. Also includes a description of the conscription of Jewish children into the army of the czar during the 19th century, by a Russian singer of this period.

JE58   Rubin, Ruth. "Slavic Influences in Yiddish Folk Songs." In *Folklore & Society: Essays in Honor of Benj. A. Botkin*, edited by Bruce Jackson, pp. 131-152. Hatboro, Pa.: Folklore Associates, 1966.

Discussion of possible Slavic models for, and influences on, Yiddish folksongs. Includes texts (in Yiddish, Russian, Ukrainian, and Polish, with English translations and brief tune transcriptions) of 18 songs, 5 recorded by the author from Jewish informants in New York City in 1946, 1948, and 1962.

JE59   Rubin, Ruth. "Some Aspects of Comparative Jewish Folksong." *New York Folklore Quarterly* 12:2 (1956): 87-95.

Brief discussion of the development of parallel traditions within the body of Jewish folklore, and presentation of excerpts from a miscellany of Jewish folksongs: 1) 1 stanza of a Passover song (in Hebrew, with English translation); 2) 1 stanza of a Passover song sung by Franco-Americans in Woonsocket, Rhode Island (in French);

3) 1 stanza of another Passover song (in Aramaic, with
English translation, accompanied by 3 stanzas of a
version of this song in English recorded by W.W. Newell
in New England in 1908); 4) 2 stanzas of a Yiddish
riddle song (in Yiddish, with English translation),
accompanied by the remaining riddles posed in the song
(in Yiddish, with English translations), and 2 stanzas
(in English) of a riddle song from Anglo-American tradition; 5) 2 stanzas of a version of "Our Goodman"
(Child 274) recorded from a Lithuanian informant in
New York City (in Lithuanian, with English translation),
accompanied by 1 stanza from an American parallel of
this ballad (in English and titled "The Sailor's
Return").

*JE60   Rubin, Ruth. "Some Aspects of Comparative Jewish Folk-
        song." In *Studies in Biblical and Jewish Folklore*,
        edited by Raphael Patai, Francis Lee Utley, and Dov
        Noy, pp. 235-252. Indiana University Folklore Series
        No. 13 (1960). Also published as *Memoirs of the
        American Folklore Society* 51 (1960).

        Presentation of selected stanzas of 6 Jewish folksongs
        (in Hebrew or Yiddish, with English translations),
        with analogous stanzas from American folksongs presented
        for purposes of comparison and contrast. Of examples
        presented, 2 were recorded from Jewish informants from
        Lithuania living in New York City.
        (Cross-listed as *LI10.)

*JE61   Rubin, Ruth. "Songs: 'Chanuke, O Chanuke!' (Jewish)."
        New York Folklore Quarterly 10:4 (1954):308-309.

        Presentation of 1 song text and tune (in Yiddish, with
        English translation) which the author sang as a child.
        Text attributed to a Lithuanian and tune identified as
        Hassidic.
        (Cross-listed as *LI11.)

JE62   Rubin, Ruth. *Voices of a People: The Story of Yiddish
        Folksong*. 1963. 2d ed. New York: McGraw-Hill
        Book Company, 1973. Pp. 558, preface, prologue, 2
        appendices, map, bibliography, general index, song
        index.

        General discussion (with examples) of the development
        of Yiddish folksong, with a chapter titled "To America"
        (pp. 342-367) that includes texts of 20 songs (in
        Yiddish, with English translations) relating to the

immigration, settlement, and experiences of Yiddish-speaking Jews in the New World. Includes 54 tune transcriptions, 17 of which were tunes known to the author or recorded by her from Jewish immigrants and their descendants in New York City and Montreal (see p. 522).

JE63   Rubin, Ruth. "Y.L. Cahan and Jewish Folklore." *New York Folklore Quarterly* 11:1 (1955):34-45.

Discussion of the life and work of Jewish and Yiddish folklorist Y.L. Cahan and some of the information available in *Yidisher Folklore*, a small journal which first appeared in 1954.

JE64   Rubin, Ruth. "Yiddish Folksong in New York City." *New York Folklore Quarterly* 2:1 (1946):15-23.

Brief discussion of Jewish immigration from Eastern Europe to New York in the 1880s and 1890s, followed by a discussion of the development of Yiddish secular folksong. Discusses particular songs and presents texts or excerpts (in Yiddish, with English translations) of lullabies, wedding songs, work songs, love songs, humorous songs, Hassidic songs, and anti-Hassidic songs. Includes some historical discussion of the tunes of particular songs, but presents no tune transcriptions.

JE65   Rubin, Ruth. "Yiddish Folk Songs Current in French Canada." *Journal of the International Folk Music Council* 12 (1960):76-78.

Brief sketch of Jewish immigration to Canada, followed by a list of 8 types of songs current among Yiddish-speaking immigrants and their descendants living in Montreal and Toronto (no song examples given).

JE66   Rubin, Ruth. "Yiddish Folksongs of Immigration and the Melting Pot." *New York Folklore Quarterly* 17:3 (1961):173-182.

Brief discussion of the ideals of freedom, equality, and economic security that America came to represent for East European Jews, especially those of czarist Russia in the late 19th century. Includes presentation of 8 song texts (in Yiddish, with English translations and discussion of the historical and social background of each song): 1) 3 songs about immigration to America, 2) 1 song about homesickness, 3) 1 "letter song," 4)

1 lullaby adapted from a poem about social conditions,
5) 1 song about the sinking of the *Titanic*, and 6) 1
song denouncing the Russian autocracy (adapted from a
poem).

JE67   Rubin, Ruth. "Yiddish Riddles and Problems." *New York
        Folklore Quarterly* 12:4 (1956):257-260.

        Presentation of 16 Yiddish riddles and 3 arithmetical
        problems (all in English) which were posed by the
        author's mother for amusement during the Hanukkah
        holiday.

JE68   Rubin, Ruth. "Yiddish Sayings and English Equivalents."
        New York Folklore Quarterly 15:2 (1959):91-92.

        Presentation of 26 Yiddish sayings (in Yiddish, with
        English translations), followed by equivalent proverbs
        or sayings in English.

JE69   Rubin, Ruth. "Yiddish Sayings and Some Parallels from
        the Sayings of Other Peoples." *New York Folklore
        Quarterly* 22:4 (1966):268-273.

        Listing (without sources or dates of recording) of 48
        Yiddish proverbial expressions (in Yiddish, with
        English translations).

JE70   Rubin, Ruth. "Yiddish Tales for Children." In *Folk-
        lore of Canada*, edited by Edith Fowke, pp. 291-294.
        Toronto: McClelland and Stewart Limited, 1976.

        Presentation (in English) of texts of 2 tales, recol-
        lected by the author from her childhood days in Montreal
        and identified as Yiddish tales.

JE71   Schaechter, Mordche. "On Children's Nonsense Oaths in
        Yiddish." In *The Field of Yiddish: Studies in
        Yiddish Language, Folklore, and Literature*, edited
        by Uriel Weinreich, pp. 196-198. New York: Publica-
        tions of the Linguistic Circle of New York No. 3, 1954.

        Presentation of 7 nonsense oaths (in Yiddish), recorded
        from Yiddish-speaking East European Jewish informants
        in New York City. Suggests that these nonsense oaths
        probably originated among adults, though they have come
        to be uttered principally by children.

JE72   Schlesinger, Emma Adatto. "Two Judeo-Spanish Folktales
       Having the Same Theme: One from Skolpje, South Mace-
       donia, One from Seattle, Washington." *Folklore* 83
       (1972):41-60.

       Presentation (in English translation) of 2 Judeo-
       Spanish variants of a tale identified as "The Twins or
       Blood Brothers," 1 of which was obtained by the author
       from her mother, a Judeo-Spanish (Sephardic Jewish)
       immigrant living in Seattle. Includes brief survey of
       published works on Judeo-Spanish folktales.

*JE73 Simmons, Donald C. "Protest Humor: Folkloristic Reac-
       tion to Prejudice." *American Journal of Psychiatry*
       120:6 (1963):567-570.

       Characterization of 12 narratives identified by the
       author as "protest tales" of American minority groups,
       9 involving Jews (7 of which involve interactions be-
       tween Jews and Catholics and/or Protestants, 1 exchange
       between a Jew and a Chinese). Asserts that the tales
       "primarily function to preserve the ego identity of
       minority group members compelled to suffer attacks on
       their group image through repeated contacts with the
       majority group's unflattering stereotypes."
       (Cross-listed as *CH25.)

JE74   Slobin, Mark. "The Uses of Printed Versions in Studying
       the Song Repertoire of East European Jews: First
       Findings." In *The Field of Yiddish: Studies in
       Language, Folklore, and Literature*, Fourth Collection,
       edited by Marvin I. Herzog, Barbara Kirshenblatt-
       Gimblett, Dan Miron, and Ruth Wisse, pp. 329-370.
       Philadelphia: Institute for the Study of Human Issues,
       1980.

       Discussion (with examples) of the interplay among oral
       tradition, printed song sheets for piano, phonograph
       recordings, theatrical performances and the resultant
       songs sung by East European Jewish immigrants in America.
       Demonstrates that traditional songs may be altered (in
       words, but not necessarily in tunes) by printed and
       recorded versions and that popular art songs and tunes
       may be modified by individuals who re-create them in
       accordance with traditional folksinging styles.

JE75   Stern, Stephen. *The Sephardic Jewish Community of Los Angeles.* New York: Arno Press, 1980. Pp. 417, introduction, conclusion, 5 appendices, bibliography.

A 1977 Indiana University dissertation focusing on ethnic identity as it is conceived and expressed among Sephardic Jews in Los Angeles. Includes surveys and assessments of studies of ethnicity in the United States, historical sketch of the development of Sephardic Jewish communities in Los Angeles, descriptions and analyses of conflicting images of the communities, survey of supernatural beliefs and related narratives, humorous anecdotes and jokes, folk religion, traditional speech and proverbial expressions, foodways, and community events. Argues that there is no one agreed-upon source or combination of criteria that serves as the basis for Sephardic identity in the Los Angeles communities. Includes texts or characterizations of approximately 45 narratives (identified variously as anecdotes, jokes, tales about supernatural beings, Čoha tales, personal experience narratives, tales, and trickster stories), texts of 6 songs (in Ladino, with English translations), texts of approximately 45 proverbs. Includes descriptions and discussions of beliefs, customs, and/or tales associated with ghosts, the evil eye, healing, luck, speech, naming, and life-cycle and calendrical customs and celebrations. Based on 1974 fieldwork in Los Angeles.

*JE76   Taylor, Archer. "The 'Dream-Bread' Story Once More."

(Cross-listed as *IR100.)
(See *IR100 for full citation and annotation.)

*JE77   Thompson, Marion. "Folklore in the Schools: Collecting in Cortland."

(Cross-listed as *GL80, *IR105, *IT77.)
(See *GL80 for full citation and annotation.)

JE78   Tull, Marc. "Kosher Brownies for Passover." *New York Folklore* 4:1-4 (1978):81-88.

Presentation of 1 recipe for brownies made and served at Passover by a Jewish woman in Utica, New York. Includes 5 photographs with captions presenting the informant's instructions on how to make the brownies, step by step.

*JE79   Walerstein, Marcia. "Ethnic Folklore in the Primary School Classroom."

       (Cross-listed as *GL81, *SP16.)
       (See *GL81 for full citation and annotation.)

*JE80   Weiner, Harvey. "Folklore in the Los Angeles Garment Industry."

       (Cross-listed as *IT83.)
       (See *IT83 for full citation and annotation.)

JE81   Weinreich, Beatrice S. "The Americanization of Passover." In *Studies in Biblical and Jewish Folklore*, edited by Raphael Patai, Francis Lee Utley, and Dov Noy, pp. 329-366. Indiana University Folklore Series No. 13 (1960). Also published as *Memoirs of the American Folklore Society* 51 (1960).

       Sketch of the "traditional way" of celebrating Passover in Eastern Europe, based on an interview with a Jewish immigrant informant living in the United States, followed by a description and discussion of changes which have occurred in the celebration of the holiday in American urban environments. Based on questionnaire responses, observations, and interviews begun in 1949.

JE82   Wheatley, Richard. "The Jews in New York." *The Century Magazine* 43:3 (1892):323-342.

       Historical sketch of Jewish immigration to New York City, with discussion of settlement and adjustment patterns, modes of daily living and work. Includes brief descriptions of major religious holiday celebrations, with 12 photographs of religious structures and events.

*JE83   Winner, Julia Hull. "The Money Diggers of Niagara County."

       (Cross-listed as *GE722.)
       (See *GE722 for full citation and annotation.)

JE84   Yoffie, Leah R.C. "Present-Day Survivals of Ancient Jewish Customs." *Journal of American Folk-Lore* 29:113 (1916):412-417.

       An apparent response to a request of the Folk-Lore Society of Missouri that the customs and beliefs of all migrants to that state be studied. Presents

descriptions of burial ceremonies and mourning customs,
as well as of some religious practices, recorded from
Jews from Russia, Poland, and Galicia living in St.
Louis. Provides brief comments about possible origins
of selected practices. Includes 1 text (in English)
of a religious chant frequently recited at Passover.

JE85   Yoffie, Leah Rachel. "Popular Beliefs and Customs
       among the Yiddish-Speaking Jews of St. Louis, Mo."
       Journal of American Folk-Lore 38:149 (1925):375-399.

       Presentation of popular beliefs, customs, and supersti-
       tions recorded from Russian Jews who had lived in the
       United States for 20-30 years. Includes descriptions
       of the evil eye; amulets; spirits and magic; exorcism;
       spitting; numbers, days, times, and seasons; foretelling
       the future; dreams; love and marriage; human and bodily
       functions; household objects; lost articles; clothing;
       food; death and mourning. Cites Frazer's explanations
       for certain customs and suggests that these customs and
       beliefs are dying out in St. Louis.

JE86   Yoffie, Leah Rachel. "Yiddish Proverbs, Sayings, etc.
       in St. Louis, Mo." *Journal of American Folk-Lore*
       33:128 (1920):134-165.

       Listing of non-scriptural proverbs and sayings (420 of
       them, in Lithuanian and Yiddish, with English transla-
       tions), arranged topically (e.g., God and fate, wisdom
       and folly, death) and based on data recorded from
       Russian and Lithuanian Jews in St. Louis. Includes
       comparative and explanatory notes.

XXX. KOREAN (KO) (1)

KO1 Song, Bang-Song. *The Korean-Canadian Folk Song: An
      Ethnomusicological Study.* Canadian Centre for Folk
      Culture Studies, Paper No. 10. Ottawa: National
      Museum of Man, 1974. Pp. xiii, 222, bibliography.

      Musicological analysis of 229 folksongs recorded from
      Korean immigrant informants in Toronto in 1973. In-
      cludes general information about the Korean people,
      specific information about their settlement in Toronto,
      description of their music, and an assessment of the
      unique style of Korean music. Includes 21 songs (in
      Korean), with musical scores and transcriptions, followed
      by explanatory comments. Also presents scores for 9
      instrumental pieces produced by 2 instruments. Appendix
      includes information about audio and visual documentation,
      field notebook, and questionnaire forms. Concludes that
      data are insufficient to predict the vitality of Korean
      folksong beyond the immigrant generation. Includes 39
      photographs of informants and musical instruments.

                    XXXI. LATVIAN (LA) (1-3)

LA1 Carpenter, Inta Gale. *A Latvian Storyteller.* New York:
      Arno Press, 1980. Pp. ii, 259, bibliography, indices
      of tale types and motifs.

      An Indiana University M.A. thesis focusing on the narra-
      tive repertoire of a Latvian immigrant storyteller (the
      author's maternal grandfather), based on interviews con-
      ducted in Bloomington and Indianapolis, Indiana, from 1972
      to 1974. Presents a brief cultural history of Latvia to
      1945, a brief survey of Latvian folksong and folktale
      research, and a biographical sketch of the informant and
      his storytelling skills and repertoire. Includes auto-
      biographical narratives (divided into 5 periods from 1886
      to 1973); 20 personal history stories; 38 tales, anec-
      dotes, and jokes; 17 puzzles, riddles, and verses; and
      6 songs (all translated into English from the Latvian).

*LA2 Mitchell, John Fletcher, and Driedger, Leo. "Canadian
      Ethnic Folk Art: An Exploratory Study in Winnipeg."
      Ethnicity 5:3 (1978):252-265.

      Results of a survey conducted by questionnaire in Winni-
      peg, Canada, among individuals of Latvian and Ukraianian
      backgrounds who create folk art objects. Concludes that
      artists make folk art objects to maintain the continuity
      of their cultural heritage, that art forms are viewed as
      symbolic of ethnicity, that art reinforces ethnic identi-
      ty by "providing it with a material image," that the
      usual and best critics of folk art are members of ethnic
      communities rather than museum personnel or art critics.
      (Cross-listed as *UK30.)

 LA3 Niles, Christina. "The Revival of the Latvian *Kokle* in
      America." *Selected Reports in Ethnomusicology* 3:1
      (1978):211-239.

      Description of the *kokle*, "a small, wing-shaped zither,"
      of increasingly declining popularity in Latvia, and of
      its revival in the United States as a craft and as a
      symbol of national identity among post-World-War-II
      Latvian immigrants to America and their children. Pro-
      vides an historical sketch of the instrument and its
      uses in Latvia; a discussion of construction techniques
      brought to, and employed in, America; and a brief discus-
      sion of *kokle* playing and its use in musical performing
      groups. Concludes that while the instrument has been
      revived in America, it is not used to perpetuate tradi-
      tional songs (folksongs) or music (folk music), but
      instead to play "standardized, written material" which
      appeals to "the musical taste and aesthetic preferences
      of an urban, middle-class community." Includes 5 sample
      song texts (in Latvian, with English translations), 1
      diagram of the *kokle*, 2 photographs of a *kokle* at various
      stages of construction, 3 photographs of finished hand-
      crafted *kokle* instruments, 2 photographs of microphones
      strapped to the *kokle* to amplify performances, 1 set of
      diagrams of finger positions used in playing the *kokle*,
      1 photograph of a *kokle* performance in Los Angeles, 4
      musical transcriptions of tunes and songs played on the
      kokle, with accompanying texts of 2 of the selections
      (in English translation).

XXXII. LEBANESE (LE) (1-4)

LE1 Bratcher, James T. "An Arabic Romance in Austin, Texas."
     In *Tire Shrinker to Dragster*, edited by Wilson M.
     Hudson, pp. 187-202. *Publications of the Texas
     Folklore Society* 34 (1968).

     Presentation (in English) of the text of 1 heroic tale,
     recorded from an Austin, Texas, man of Lebanese back-
     ground who learned the story from his Lebanese immigrant
     father. Also includes excerpts from a written version
     of the tale for comparison and contrast. Author indi-
     cates that other individuals of Lebanese background in
     Austin also know the story.

LE2 Joseph, Suad. "Where the Twain Shall Meet--Lebanese in
     Cortland County." *New York Folklore Quarterly* 20:3
     (1964):175-191.

     Brief discussion of the arrival and settlement of
     Lebanese immigrants in Cortland County, New York, in the
     early 20th century and their subsequent assimilation in-
     to American society. Includes 2 immigration experience
     stories, 3 song texts (2 in English, 1 in Lebanese with
     English translation), brief description of a traditional
     drum (*derbakke*), traditional foods, and 1 festival. In-
     cludes 2 photographs (of a man playing the *derbakke* drum
     and of 2 women dancing).

*LE3 Naff, Alixa. "Belief in the Evil Eye Among the Chris-
     tian Syrian-Lebanese in America." *Journal of American
     Folklore* 78:307 (1965):46-51.

     Discussion of causes, diagnoses, and cures for the evil
     eye as reported by Christian Syrian-Lebanese-American
     informants in 1962. Includes the text of 1 exorcising
     prayer. Suggests that the belief in the evil eye is
     questioned or rejected by most immigrants after they
     settle in the United States.
     (Cross-listed as *SZ3.)

*LE4 Qureshi, Regula. "Ethnomusicological Research among
     Canadian Communities of Arab and East Indian Origin."

     (Cross-listed as *EG1, *ID3, *PA1, *SZ4.)
     (See *SZ4 for full citation and annotation.)

XXXIII. LITHUANIAN (LI) (1-11)

LI1   Balys, Jonas. "Fifty Lithuanian Riddles." *Journal of
       American Folklore* 63:249 (1950):325-327.

       Presentation (in English translation) of 50 riddles,
       recorded by the author from a Lithuanian immigrant
       woman in Chicago. Includes a brief biographical sketch
       of the informant and a characterization of other kinds
       of folklore recorded from her.

LI2   Balys, Jonas. "Lithuanian Folk Songs in the United
       States." *Journal of the International Folk Music
       Council* 3 (1951):67-70.

       Brief characterization of 3 kinds of songs recorded
       among Lithuanian immigrants and their descendants in
       the United States (identified as *sutartines* or round
       form, old meter, and modern songs). Includes English
       summaries of 2 songs, sample stanza and refrain of 1
       song (also in English only). Includes brief description
       of selected musical characteristics of the songs.

LI3   Balys, Jonas. "Lithuanian Ghost Stories from Pittsburgh,
       Pennsylvania." *Midwest Folklore* 2:1 (1952):47-52.

       Presentation of 3 ghost stories (edited), recorded from
       a Lithuanian immigrant woman in Pittsburgh in 1949.

*LI4   Clar, Mimi. "Russian Folk Beliefs Collected in Los
       Angeles." *Western Folklore* 17:2 (1958):123-126.

       Listing of 70 statements of belief, recorded in 1956
       from the author's grandmother, an immigrant from
       Lithuania.
       (Cross-listed as *RU5.)

*LI5   Peacock, Kenneth. "Establishing Perimeters for Ethno-
       musicological Field Research in Canada: On-Going
       Projects and Future Possibilities at the Canadian
       Centre for Folk Culture Studies."

       (Cross-listed as *GL66, *CH21, *FR91, *GE428, *HU25,
       *IC4, *ID2, *IT57, *JA9, *NO19, *RU19, *UK32.)
       (See *GL66 for full citation and annotation.)

LI6   Peacock, Kenneth. *A Garland of Rue: Lithuanian Folk-
      songs of Love and Betrothal*. Ottawa: National Museum
      of Man Publications in Folk Culture No. 2, 1971.
      Pp. viii, 60, summary, introduction, acknowledgments,
      biographical note.

      Presentation of 28 folksong texts (in Lithuanian, with
      English translations and tune transcriptions), recorded
      by the author in 1967-68 from individuals of Lithuanian
      ancestry in Toronto and Ontario, Canada. Songs focus
      on "the mating cycle," and include those dealing with
      courtship, matchmaking, seduction, and marriage.

LI7   Poleway, Bette. "Lithuanian Wedding Customs of Fifty
      Years Ago." *West Virginia Folklore* 3:3 (1953):51.

      Characterization of 9 customs associated with marriage
      and weddings, recorded from an informant of Lithuanian
      descent. Includes brief description of dowries,
      arranged marriages, and wedding receptions.

LI8   Reaver, J. Russell. "Four Lithuanian-American Folk
      Tales." *Southern Folklore Quarterly* 12:4 (1948):
      259-265.

      Presentation of 4 translated folktale texts, recorded
      from a Lithuanian immigrant woman in Illinois in 1948.

LI9   Reaver, J. Russell. "Lithuanian Tales from Illinois."
      Southern Folklore Quarterly 14:3 (1950):160-168.

      Presentation of 6 translated folktale texts, recorded
      from a Lithuanian immigrant woman in Illinois in 1949.

*LI10 Rubin, Ruth. "Some Aspects of Comparative Jewish Folk-
      song."

      (Cross-listed as *JE60.)
      (See *JE60 for full citation and annotation.)

*LI11 Rubin, Ruth. "Songs: 'Chanuke, O Chanuke!' (Jewish)."

      (Cross-listed as *JE61.)
      (See *JE61 for full citation and annotation.)

XXXIV.   MACEDONIAN (MA) (1-2)

*MA1   Montgomery, Margaret. "A Macedonian Wedding in Indian-
         apolis."

         (Cross-listed as *BU2.)
         (See *BU2 for full citation and annotation.)

MA2   Tilney, Philip V.R. "The Immigrant Macedonian Wedding
         in Ft. Wayne." *Indiana Folklore* 3:1 (1970):3-34.

         Description of 2 Macedonian weddings witnessed by the
         author in 1963 and 1969 in Fort Wayne, Indiana, with
         additional information obtained from interviews with 5
         informants. Comparison and contrast of Macedonian and
         Macedonian-American customs, including those relating
         to engagement, pre-marriage festivities, the wedding
         ceremony, and the reception. Demonstrates that Old and
         New World customs are combined in the United States and
         that some homeland practices are discontinued because
         of their incompatibility with the new environment. In-
         cludes 7 photographs depicting dancing before and after
         the wedding ceremony, the bride's departure from her
         parents' home, the receiving line outside the church,
         and the wedding cakes.

                        XXXV.   MONGOL (MO) (1)

MO1   Snellenburg, Betty. "An Introduction to Some Kalmyks'
         Ideas on Proverbs." *Keystone Folklore Quarterly*
         13:4 (1968):275-279.

         Brief historical and ethnographic sketch of the Kalmyk
         Mongols and of immigrant Kalmyks living in Philadelphia
         and neighboring parts of New Jersey, followed by a
         listing of 10 proverbs (in English) and a summary of
         informants' comments about what proverbs are, why and
         when they are used. Based on fieldwork carried out in
         the Philadelphia area.

XXXVI. NORWEGIAN (NO) (1-22)

NO1 Blegen, Theodore C. "The Ballad of Oleana: A Verse
     Translation." *Norwegian-American Studies and Records*
     14 (1944):117-121.

     Presentation of a verse translation into English of 1
     popular satiric ballad, composed in Norway in 1853,
     about the disastrous Norwegian colony in Oleana, Potter
     County, Pennsylvania. Ballad exaggerates the plenty
     and productivity of the fated New World colony.

*NO2 Blegen, Theodore C. "Singing Immigrants and Pioneers."
     In *Studies in American Culture: Dominant Ideas and
     Images*, edited by Joseph J. Kwiat and Mary C. Turpie,
     pp. 171-188. Minneapolis: University of Minnesota
     Press, 1960.

     Discussion of the themes of hope and disillusionment
     found in ballads and songs reported from immigrants to
     America. Includes texts of and excerpts from 35 ballads
     and songs, all in English (1 identified as Danish, 1 as
     Finnish, 2 as Irish, 6 as Norwegian, 3 as Swedish).
     Argues that ballads and songs are an important and
     little-explored source of information about emigration,
     settlement, and adjustment of immigrants to a new land.
     (Cross-listed as *DA2, *FN1, *IR10, *SS3.)

NO3 Blegen, Theodore C., and Ruud, Martin B. *Norwegian
     Emigrant Songs and Ballads*. Minneapolis: University
     of Minnesota Press, 1936. Pp. 350, introduction.

     Reprintings of 60 poetic texts (54 from the 19th century,
     2 from the 20th century, 4 undated) from letters, news-
     papers, pamphlets, manuscripts, immigrant magazines, all
     concerned with aspects of Norwegian immigration to the
     New World (e.g., about enthusiasm for and opposition to
     emigration, first impressions of the new environment,
     problems of settlement and adjustment, feelings of
     alienation and homesickness, similarities and differ-
     ences between the homeland and the new land). Includes
     11 tunes (harmonized for the piano).

NO4 Blegen, Theodore C., and Ruud, Martin B. "The Seven-
     teenth of May in Mid-Atlantic: Ole Rynning's Emigrant
     Song." *Norwegian-American Studies and Records* 8
     (1934):18-22.

     Presentation of 1 song text (in Norwegian, with English
     translation) composed by one Ole Rynning while on board

a ship headed from Norway to America in 1837. Song
subsequently became popular both in oral tradition and
in print. Song written to commemorate Norway's inde-
pendence day and the celebration of it by immigrants
at sea.

NO5 Bøhn, Tora. "A Quest for Norwegian Folk Art in America."
     Norwegian-American Studies and Records 19 (1956):
     116-141.

     Characterization of the author's 1949-50 tour to visit
     museums and families in order to discover the nature and
     extent of Norwegian traditional arts and crafts in the
     United States (particularly in Iowa, Minnesota, and
     Wisconsin). Includes a brief survey of large and small
     museums and their holdings, some description of objects
     in selected Norwegian-American homes, and brief mention
     of craftspeople of Norwegian descent producing objects
     in traditional ways in America.

NO6 Brunvand, Jan Harold. "Norwegian-American Folklore in
     the Indiana University Archives." *Midwest Folklore*
     7:4 (1957):221-228.

     Presentation of a statistical count, by genre, of
     Norwegian-American folklore items on deposit in the
     Indiana University Archives, followed by the reprinting
     of 7 archival versions of an historical legend.

NO7 Brunvand, Jan Harold. *Norwegian Settlers in Alberta*.
     Canadian Centre for Folk Culture Studies, Paper No. 8.
     Ottawa: National Museum of Man, 1974. Pp. iv, 71,
     biographies of key informants, bibliography.

     Survey of folklore among first- and second-generation
     Norwegians in Alberta, Canada. Analysis of folk music,
     folk narratives, customs, festivals, anecdotes, and
     material culture based on interviews with 50 informants.
     Argues that the disappearance of Old World folklore forms
     is counterbalanced by the creation of anecdotes and folk
     architecture growing out of New World experiences, with
     anecdotes reflecting the settlement experience, particu-
     larly the problem of coping with the English language.
     Includes 31 photographs.

*NO8 Curtis, Wardon Allan. "'The Light Fantastic' in the
      Central West: Country Dances of Many Nationalities in
      Wisconsin."

      (Cross-listed as *GE127, *IR18, *SW4.)
      (See *SW4 for full citation and annotation.)

NO9   Field, Jerome P. "Folk Tales from North Dakota, 1910."
        Western Folklore 17:1 (1958):29-33.

        Presentation of 6 personal experience stories (most
        involving the devil), told in Los Angeles by the author's
        mother, who learned them from her Norwegian immigrant
        mother in North Dakota about 1910.

NO10   Haugen, Einar. "A Norwegian-American Pioneer Ballad."
        Norwegian-American Studies and Records 15 (1949):1-19.

        Historical study of an 1878 ballad "How Things Have
        Gone," a song "which tells in simple but appealing words
        the story of Norwegian pioneers in early Wisconsin" and
        which "appears to have been the most popular of all
        songs written in this country in a Norwegian rural
        dialect." Includes text of the presumed original (in
        Norwegian, with English translation), which depicts
        "the immigrant's struggles with the language, his
        economic subservience to the native 'Yankee,' his un-
        wise choice of land, and his overtones of viking pride."
        Traces the published history of the ballad and dis-
        cusses attempts made by others to claim authorship of
        the work.

NO11   Haugen, Einar. "Norwegian Emigrant Songs and Ballads."
        Journal of American Folk-Lore 51:199 (1938):69-75.

        Brief discussion of the contrasting attitudes toward
        immigration by Norwegians to America as found in
        ballads and songs, followed by the reprinting of a song
        published in Chicago in 1894 presenting a debate between
        an established and settled Norwegian immigrant and a
        recent Norwegian arrivee to the New World about the
        values of immigration to and resettlement in America.
        Norwegian emigrant songs and ballads viewed as important
        indices of conflicting attitudes toward emigration from
        Norway.

NO12   Haugen, Einar. "Thor Helgeson: Schoolmaster and
        Raconteur." *Norwegian-American Studies* 24 (1970):1-28.

        Discussion of the writings and folklore collecting of
        a Norwegian immigrant schoolmaster who settled in
        Waupaca County, Wisconsin. Includes texts or charac-
        terizations of 17 tales and anecdotes, excerpts from 3
        ballads and the text of 1 poem written by Helgeson.
        Many examples drawn from unpublished writings, including
        a collection of folklore made by and also about the
        immigrant schoolmaster, himself a noted raconteur.

NO13   Hustvedt, Lloyd. "The Folktale and Norwegian Migration."
       Journal of Popular Culture 2:4 (1969):552-562.

       Advances the thesis that motives for Norwegian immigra-
       tion to the United States--"escape from poverty, release
       from a traditional social order, and ... relief from
       family or community conditions found oppressive"--were
       themes found both in Norwegian folktales popular prior
       to the immigration period and in popular novels pub-
       lished in America during settlement periods.

*NO14 Munch, Peter A. "Ten Thousand Swedes: Reflections on a
       Folklore Motif."

       (Cross-listed as *SS20.)
       (See *SS20 for full citation and annotation.)

NO15   Olsen, Louise P. "Four Scandinavian Ghost Stories."
       Hoosier Folklore 9:1 (1950):25-27.

       Transcriptions (from the author's shorthand notes) of
       4 ghost stories, 3 involving sightings of dead people,
       1 concerning a ghostlike figure warning a sailor not to
       set sail on a doomed ship, told by a Norwegian-American.

NO16   Olsen, Louise P. "A Norwegian Circle Charm." *Midwest
       Folklore* 4:4 (1954):216.

       Second-hand report of a personal experience story
       portraying a man capable of restricting movements of a
       snake and a swarm of bees by "drawing three circles in
       the air" with his cane. Restricted animals freed when
       circle-drawing was reversed.

NO17   Olsen, Louise P. "Norwegian Tales from Minnesota."
       Midwest Folklore 4:1 (1954):37-39.

       Presentation of 6 personal experience stories involving
       supernatural phenomena, including witches, trolls, and
       strange sounds, recorded from informants of Norwegian
       background in Minnesota.

NO18   Olson, Sandi. "Ethno Cuisine: Lefse, Lutefish and
       Rommegrøt." *AFFword, Publication of Arizona Friends
       of Folklore* 3:1 (1973):44-45.

       Presentation of 3 recipes for traditional Norwegian
       foods prepared and eaten on Christmas Eve, recorded
       from a woman of Norwegian descent from Tucson, Arizona.

*NO19   Peacock, Kenneth. "Establishing Perimeters for Ethno-
        musicological Field Research in Canada: On-Going
        Projects and Future Possibilities at the Canadian
        Centre for Folk Culture Studies."

        (Cross-listed as *GL66, *CH21, *FR91, *GE428, *HU25,
        *IC4, *ID2, *IT57, *JA9, *LI5, *RU19, *UK32.)
        (See *GL66 for full citation and annotation.)

NO20   Rølvaag, Ella Valborg. "Norwegian Folk Narratives in
        America." *Norwegian-American Studies and Records*
        12 (1941):33-59.

        Brief discussion of the nature of folk narratives
        brought to America by Norwegian immigrants, with
        emphasis on legends involving supernatural beings, such
        as the *hulder* people. Includes characterizations of 34
        legend plots, passing mention of traditional beliefs
        and customs, 1 rhyme (in Norwegian), most from previous-
        ly published sources, several apparently from Norwegian-
        American informants living in Wisconsin.

NO21   Ruud, Martin B. "Norwegian Emigrant Songs." *Publica-
        tions of the Norwegian-American Historical Associa-
        tion, Studies and Records* 2 (1927):1-19.

        Presentation of rough English translations of 13
        Norwegian emigrant songs written between 1837 and 1925
        and previously published in Norwegian. Songs focus on
        such subjects as the farewell and departure from the
        homeland, the reasons for emigrating, expectations
        about the new homeland, and the ocean crossing by ship.

*NO22   Wilden, Albin. "Scandinavian Folklore and Immigrant
        Ballads."

        (Cross-listed as *DA7, *SS30.)
        (See *SS30 for full citation and annotation.)

                    XXXVII. PAKISTANI (PA) (1)

*PA1   Qureshi, Regula. "Ethnomusicological Research among
        Canadian Communities of Arab and East Indian Origin."

        (Cross-listed as *EG1, *ID3, *LE4, *SZ4.)
        (See *SZ4 for full citation and annotation.)

XXXVIII. POLISH (PL) (1-87)

PL1   Ainsworth, Catherine Harris. "Polish-American Church
      Legends." *New York Folklore Quarterly* 30:4 (1974):
      286-294.

      Characterization (in English) of 5 legends, obtained in
      writing by the author from students of Polish background
      living in New York State and submitted in 1964, 1965,
      1967, and 1971. Tales concern a painting of Christ that
      bleeds.

PL2   Ainsworth, Catherine Harris. *Polish-American Folktales*.
      Buffalo: The Clyde Press, 1977. Pp. 102, headnotes.

      A miscellany of tales and descriptions of beliefs and
      customs submitted to the author by her students (of
      Polish descent) in writing in the Niagara Falls-Buffalo,
      New York, area between 1961 and 1977. Includes examples of
      2 Christmas customs; 10 superstitions; descriptions of
      3 customs relating to the determination of one's future
      spouse, the sex of an unborn child, and to marriage; 1
      remedy for the evil eye; 13 tales; 31 legends; 15 per-
      sonal experience stories; and 3 memorates.

PL3   Baker, T. Lindsay. "Silesian Polish Folk Architecture
      in Texas." In *Built in Texas*, edited by Francis Edward
      Abernethy, pp. 131-135. *Publications of the Texas
      Folklore Society* 42 (1979).

      Brief discussion (illustrated with 3 photographs) of log
      and stone houses built by Polish immigrants to the Panna
      Maria and Bandera, Texas, areas beginning in the mid-
      1850s.

PL4   Baretski, Charles Allan. "A Fatal Choice, A Polish Tale."
      New York Folklore Quarterly 8:2 (1952):104-110.

      Presentation of 1 folktale text, recorded from a Polish
      informant. Tale contains 2 proverbs (in Polish, with
      English translations provided in footnotes).

*PL5 Barrick, Mac E. "Racial Riddles & the Polack Joke."
      Keystone Folklore Quarterly 15:1 (1970):3-15.

      General discussion of racial and ethnic jokes and
      riddle-jokes, followed by a listing of 52 Polack jokes
      and riddle-jokes recorded from college students and
      faculty members in Pennsylvania. Also includes reprint-
      ings of 3 Irish jokes, 5 jokes about Afro-Americans, 7

Jewish jokes, 5 Italian jokes, 1 Swabian (Pennsylvania
Dutch) joke, 7 Polish jokes heard on television, and 5
Slobbovian jokes (reprinted).
(Cross-listed as *GE43, *IR4, *IT6, *JE4.)

PL6   Barry, Phillips. "Polish Ballad: Trzy Siostry (The
        Three Sisters)." *Bulletin of the Folk-Song Society
        of the Northeast* 10 (1935):2-5; 11 (1936):2-4.

        Presentation of an English summary and also 2 texts
        (in Polish, with English translations and with tune of
        1 transcribed) of a ballad recorded in 1934 and again
        in 1935 from a woman of Polish ancestry in Springfield,
        Vermont. Ballad identified as a version of "The Two
        Sisters." Extensive comparisons made between informant's
        texts and other variants.

*PL7   Boswell, George W. "Ole Miss Jokes and Anecdotes."
        Tennessee Folklore Society Bulletin 42:2 (1976):72-82.

        Listing of 104 jokes and riddle-jokes recorded by
        students at the University of Mississippi. Includes
        18 Polish jokes, 3 Italian jokes, and 1 Jewish joke.
        (Cross-listed as *GL9, *IT12, *JE8.)

*PL8   Brunvand, Jan Harold. "Some Thoughts on the Ethnic-
        Regional Riddle Joke."

        (Cross-listed as *GL10, *JE10.)
        (See *GL10 for full citation and annotation.)

PL9   Burczak, Helen. "A Fairy Tale from Poland." *New York
        Folklore Quarterly* 1:2 (1945):110-112.

        Presentation of 1 folktale text (in English translation),
        recorded from a Polish informant in New York City in
        1944.

PL10   Chuck, Charles. "'And He Shall Reign ...': A Legend of
        Christianity in Early Poland." *Polish Folklore* 4:1
        (1959):1-3.

        Characterization (in English) of 1 legend, told to the
        author by a Polish aunt, about the appearance, among
        pagan Poles, of a Christian who converts the son of the
        chief and who is about to be burned at the urging of 13
        priests with the young man, when a thunderbolt and
        lightning destroy the statue of their chief pagan god
        and send the 13 priests running into the forest, after
        which the community as a whole was converted to Chris-
        tianity. Author-source from Chicago.

PL11   Clements, William M. *The Types of the Polack Joke.*
       Folklore Forum Bibliographic and Special Series No. 3
       (1969). Pp. 56, introduction.

       Presentation of a classification scheme for Polack
       jokes, based on data in the Michigan State and Indiana
       University student folklore archives and, to a lesser
       extent, on printed sources. Includes brief characteri-
       zations of the jokes identified as distinctive types.

PL12   Coleman, Marion Moore (Mrs.). "The Diabolical Hat, A
       Polish Tale from Amsterdam, N.Y." *New York Folklore
       Quarterly* 8:1 (1952):60-64.

       Presentation of 1 tale text, recorded from an informant
       of Polish descent in Amsterdam, New York.

PL13   Coleman, Marion Moore. "Podhalan Plant Lore from
       Connecticut." *Polish Folklore* 2:3 (1957):44-45.

       Description of herbs grown by a Polish immigrant woman
       in Cheshire, Connecticut. Includes mention of mugwort,
       wormwood, abrotanum, thyme, comfrey, iris root, leached
       oak leaves and description of their traditional uses to
       drive off evil spirits, to make a plaster for infection,
       to heal women's diseases and ease childbirth and men-
       strual pain, to make cough medicine, and to rid one of
       lice.

PL14   Coleman, Marion Moore. "Polish Lore from Eastern New
       York." *New York Folklore Quarterly* 6:4 (1950):246-251.

       Discussion of beliefs about water sprites (*topielcy*)
       and characterization of 2 tales about them, recorded
       from an informant of Polish descent in Waterford, New
       York. Includes comparison of the beliefs among Poles
       in the Waterford area regarding *topielcy* with those
       held in western Poland. Presents 1 tale about the
       appearance of the hand of a dead woman, recorded from
       the same informant (all data in English).

PL15   Conley, Anne. "Folktales: 3. The Golden Duck." *West
       Virginia Folklore* 5:3 (1955):47-49.

       Characterization of 1 folktale (in English), told to
       the author by a Polish immigrant uncle, about the search
       for a golden duck that stole golden apples from a king's
       tree. Only part of the story included, with the rest
       promised, but never published, in a future issue of the
       journal.

PL16   Conley, Anne. "Twardowsky and the Devil." *West Vir-
       ginia Folklore* 2:2 (1952):14-16.

       Characterization (in English) of 1 legend about a man
       who works for, and then outwits, the devil and wins
       freedom from his labors in hell. Source purportedly
       an informant of Polish descent.

PL17   Conley, Anne Kukuchka. "How Mushrooms Came To Be."
       Polish Folklore 3:1 (1958):16-17.

       Characterization (in English) of 1 story about Christ
       and Saint Peter walking in a forest with only a crust
       of bread to eat. Walking behind, Peter sneaks bites of
       the bread, has to spit them out when Christ asks him
       questions. Peter throws bread on the ground, Christ
       transforms it into mushrooms, which have been plentiful
       and holy in Poland ever since. Tale told by the author's
       Polish mother.

PL18   Corso, Mrs. Rose. "The Evil Eye." *Polish Folklore*
       4:1 (1959):6.

       Brief note by a woman of Polish descent from Chicopee
       Falls, Massachusetts, about bewitchment of a cow by
       the evil eye and of the way to break the evil spell by
       finding and destroying a half-moon-shaped fungus growing
       in a tree.

PL19   Costanzo, William. "Memories of a Grandmother."
       Polish Folklore 3:4 (1958):62-64.

       Characterization (in English) of 2 tales--recorded from
       a Polish immigrant woman from Lansford, Pennsylvania--
       one about a returning dead boy, killed by his stepmother,
       who asked the narrator 3 times for masses for his soul,
       the other about a milkmaid who befriends a snake, gives
       it milk daily, and is rewarded on her wedding day when
       the snake appears and spits out a tiny gold crown for
       the new bride.

PL20   Davis, Susan G. "Old-Fashioned Polish Weddings in
       Utica, New York." *New York Folklore* 4:1-4 (1978):
       89-102.

       Description of traditional Polish weddings (from
       courting to post-wedding festivities) as commonly
       held among Polish-Americans in Utica, New York, from
       about 1900 to the beginning of World War II. Based on
       interviews conducted by the author in 1978 with in-
       formants who recollected such events. Includes
       excerpts from interviews.

PL21 Davis, Susan G. "Utica's Polka Music Tradition." *New York Folklore* 4:1-4 (1978):103-124.

Discussion of polka music among Polish-Americans in Utica, New York, based on observations and interviews conducted by the author in 1978. Includes descriptions of where and when polka music was and is played in the community, kinds of instruments used, reasons for changes in musical styles and performance settings. Includes excerpts from interviews with informants.

PL22 Davis, Susan G. "Women's Roles in a Company Town: New York Mills, 1900-1951." *New York Folklore* 4:1-4 (1978):35-47.

Discussion of the role of Polish immigrant women in the textile mills of New York Mills, New York, from 1900 to 1951, based on interviews with women of the community held in 1978. Includes excerpts from interviews describing working conditions and aspects of social life.

PL23 Dorson, Richard M. "Polish Tales from Joe Woods." *Western Folklore* 8:2 (1949):131-145.

Presentation of texts of 12 tales (identified as humorous tales, hero legend, moral tales, *novelle*, and true story), recorded from a Polish immigrant narrator in the Upper Peninsula of Michigan in 1946 and 1947.

PL24 Dorson, Richard M. "Polish Wonder Tales of Joe Woods." *Western Folklore* 8:1 (1949):25-52.

Presentation of 6 tale texts (identified as *Märchen* or fairy tales) recorded in 1946 and 1947 from a Polish immigrant informant living in the Upper Peninsula of Michigan.

PL25 Dundes, Alan. "Polish Pope Jokes." *Journal of American Folklore* 92:364 (1979):219-222.

Presentation of texts of 27 Polish jokes, most involving Pope John Paul II. Argues that attempts to end the telling of ethnic jokes are futile, since ethnic humor is "more of a symptom than a cause of ethnic stereotyping and ethnic prejudice."

*PL26 Dundes, Alan. "A Study of Ethnic Slurs: The Jew and the Polack in the United States." *Journal of American Folklore* 84:332 (1971):186-203.

Characterization of behaviors of Jews and Poles as portrayed in jokes, joke-riddles, and sayings identi-

fied by the author as "ethnic slurs." Includes 26 jokes
(18 involving Jews, 2 concerning Poles), 55 joke-riddles
(18 involving Jews, 46 concerning Poles), 2 sayings
(both involving Jews). Indicates that ethnic slurs are
important means of teaching and reinforcing stereotypes.
(Cross-listed as *JE20.)

PL27   Fish, Lydia. "Is the Pope Polish? Some Notes on the
       Polack Joke in Transition." *Journal of American
       Folklore* 93:370 (1980):450-454.

       Discussion of the transition, following the election of
       Pope John Paul II, from Polish to Polish Pope jokes in
       the United States. Includes examples of 33 jokes
       recorded by the author from her students and colleagues
       in Buffalo, New York, and a brief discussion of possible
       functions of the jokes, particularly for individuals of
       Polish background.

*PL28 Foster, James R. "Brooklyn Folklore."

       (Cross-listed as *GL43, *GR9, *IR31, *IT21, *JE24,
       *PO6, *SP7.)
       (See *GL43 for full citation and annotation.)

*PL29 Frantz, Mrs. Gilda. "The Cheerapakas."

       (Cross-listed as *JE25.)
       (See *JE25 for full citation and annotation.)

PL30   Gicewicz, The Reverend Edmund. "Lore of the Saints: 1.
       St. John Kanty." *Polish Folklore* 4:3 (1959):42-43.

       Characterization (in English) of 2 saints' legends,
       told by the author, a priest in Erie, Pennsylvania, in
       1958, both concerning Jan of Kety (St. John Kanty),
       Polish patron saint of students. Tales concern the
       miraculous appearance of a plate filled with food in
       place of one the saint had just given a hungry person
       and the miraculous reconstitution and refilling of a
       little girl's accidentally smashed pitcher full of milk.

PL31   Glofcheskie, John Michael. *Folk Music of Canada's
       Oldest Polish Community.* Canadian Centre for Folk
       Culture Studies, Paper No. 33. Ottawa: National
       Museum of Man, 1980. Pp. viii, 82, bibliography.

       Study of the musical life of the Kashubs of Renfrew Coun-
       ty, Ontario, based on fieldwork conducted in 1973. Music
       discussed in context of occasions for its performance
       (during weddings, wakes, and daily life), and comments
       made as to change, function, form, and style of Kashubian

music. Instrumental music and dance also treated. Final
chapter notes changes in texts over time. Some texts accompanied by musical transcriptions. Illustrated with
16 photographs.

PL32 Goldstein, Elizabeth, and Green, Gail. "Pierogi- and
      Babka-Making at St. Mary's." *New York Folklore* 4:1-4
      (1978):71-79.

Description of the activities of a Polish-American
women's group in New York Mills, New York, that makes
pierogi and *babka* (traditional Polish foods) at Christmas and Easter for sale to the community, with proceeds
going to their local Catholic church. Includes description of how the women prepare the foods, the money
earned, and the ways profits are spent. Includes 3
photographs of women cooking, as well as excerpts from
interviews conducted in 1978.

*PL33 Greenberg, Andrea. "Form and Function of the Ethnic
      Joke."

      (Cross-listed as *GL47, *FR63, *IT27, *JE28.)
      (See *GL47 for full citation and annotation.)

PL34 Gruszcyński, Joseph. "'For the Gods See Everywhere....'"
      Polish Folklore 5:3 (1960):44-45.

Characterization of 1 personal experience (in English)
from Poland, by a man of Polish background from Ambridge, Pennsylvania, of a girl who takes candles from
all graves in a cemetery on All Soul's Day, though in-
structed to take those candles only from her grandfather's grave. Girl takes all candles but those from
her grandfather's grave when ghostly voices instruct
her to do so.

*PL35 Gruszczyńska, Mrs. Valeria. "'Cast Your Bread Upon the
      Waters ...': A 'Good Gypsy' Story." *Polish Folklore*
      4:3 (1959):40-41.

Characterization (in English) of 1 story, known to the
author (a woman of Polish background from Ambridge,
Pennsylvania), about a man who saves a convicted Gypsy
from death by using all the money he has to pay the
man's fine and who, in turn, is made wealthy through
the Gypsy's clever strategies to get the man's favored
brother to share with him the family fortune which he
alone had inherited.
      (Cross-listed as *GY6.)

PL36 Gruszczyńska, Mrs. Valeria. "Three Nails, and a Fourth."
      Polish Folklore 5:1 (1960):4.

Brief note in which the author (of Polish descent, from
Ambridge, Pennsylvania) characterizes 1 story--about the
blacksmith who made the nails for Christ's crucifixion,
threw the fourth one away after he watched in horror as
the first three were driven into Christ's body. Tale
includes explanation about why Polish blacksmiths make
only 3 nails on Good Friday and then go home.

PL37 Hartman, Peter, and Tull, Marc. "Photographic Documenta-
tion of a Polish-American Community." *New York Folklore* 4:1-4 (1978):21-34.

Authors cite responses of Polish-Americans in New York
Mills, New York, to photographs of buildings within
their community. Responses reveal attitudes toward
Polish ethnicity, Polish immigrants' experiences in the
town, and the Americanization of Polish immigrants and
their American-born children. Includes 5 photographs
shown to informants for their comments.

PL38 Jarka, Matthew. "The Phantom Surveyor." *Polish Folklore* 3:2 (1958):30.

Characterization (in English) of 1 story, told by the
author's Polish mother, about a surveyor who makes an
unfair land division and haunts the area after his death
until a proper boundary line is established.

*PL39 Jones, Louis C. "The Evil-Eye among European-Americans."

(Cross-listed as *GL51, *GR21, *HU17, *IN1, *IR50,
*IT35, *JE35, *RU10, *SZ2.)
(See *GL51 for full citation and annotation.)

PL40 Kennon, Peg Korsmo; Mahoney, Libby; and Wolter, Marcia
Britton. "Teaching and Collecting Folklore at St.
Mary's School." *New York Folklore* 4:1-4 (1978):
125-147.

Description of a folklore project involving 7th graders
of Polish background, conducted in New York Mills, New
York, in 1978. Characterizes kinds of activities in
which students engaged and kinds of information they
were asked to obtain through observation and interviewing. Includes 3 photographs of students at work, sample
pages from a "family archive book" that each student
was asked to compile.

PL41 Kerman, Judith B. "The Light-Bulb Jokes: Americans
Look at Social Action Processes." *Journal of American
Folklore* 93:370 (1980):454-458.

Discussion of "spin-offs" from the "Polish light-bulb
joke," with identity *Pole* being replaced by such names
as Californians, psychiatrists, feminists, educators,
WASPs, etc. Includes 11 examples of such jokes, recorded by the author during 1980 in Buffalo, New York;
Ann Arbor, Michigan; and Cambridge, Massachusetts.

*PL42   King, C. Richard. "Old Thurber."

     (Cross-listed as *IT37.)
     (See *IT37 for full citation and annotation.)

PL43   Kulikowska, Mrs. Frances, and Orze, Mrs. Helen. "The
       Two Eyes." *Polish Folklore* 2:3 (1957):47-48.

Characterization (in English) of 1 story about a church
in a Polish village in which 2 huge eyes (1 representing
the good angel and 1 the devil) were painted, with names
listed on a parchment under each. Devil's list constantly
growing with names of evil villagers, while "the good
eye" could find no one whose name could be put on its
parchment. Told by an informant of Polish ancestry from
New Brighton, Pennsylvania.

PL44   Kuzmirek, Mrs. Sophia, and Orze, Helen. "The Miraculous
       Apple Tree." *Polish Folklore* 2:3 (1957):36-38.

Characterization (in English) of 1 story about gold
coins transformed to stones, found under an uprooted
tree following a man's encounter with a spectral child
and his father's earlier meeting with 2 white spectral
calves in the same Polish village, told by a Youngstown,
Ohio, Polish informant.

PL45   Laskowski, Rev. Cornelius J. "Polish Tales of the
       Supernatural Collected in Albany, N.Y." *New York
       Folklore Quarterly* 10:3 (1954):165-175.

Characterization of 11 tales involving the supernatural,
recorded from informants of Polish descent in Albany,
New York.

PL46   Liedtke, Harriet. "Recollections of Witching in Poland."
       Journal of the Ohio Folklore Society n.s. 3:1
       (1974):5-16.

Presentation of 9 transcriptions (in English and identified as personal narratives, superstitions, and a
legend) of segments of tape-recorded interviews about
witches and "witch doctors." Includes brief sketches
of the 4 Polish immigrant informants and a discussion of
their attitudes toward witches and witchcraft.

PL47   Lonczkowska, Helen, and Orze, Helen. "The Ghost Below."
       Polish Folklore 3:1 (1958):11-13.

       Characterization (in English) of 1 story set in Karnkowo,
       Poland, about the annual spring appearance of a ghostly
       figure in a cherry tree grove at the base of a famous
       hill and of a nearby house haunted by the same ghost,
       recorded from a woman of Polish ancestry in Youngstown,
       Ohio.

*PL48 Luciw, Wasyl O., and Wynnsky, George. "Pysanka and
       Other Decorated Easter Eggs in Pennsylvania."
       Pennsylvania Folklife 21:3 (1972):3-7.

       Description of Easter egg decorating processes among
       Poles, Ukrainians, and Russians, with information from
       5 informants about color extraction and designs, illus-
       trated with 8 photographs.
       (Cross-listed as *RU13, *UK27.)

PL49   Maron, Frank and Louise. "Better to Have Played for
       Love." *Polish Folklore* 2:3 (1957):50-51.

       Characterization (in English) of 1 story about a Polish
       fiddler who willingly plays at weddings for no pay,
       decides he should be compensated for his efforts, and
       agrees to play for gold at a wedding of mysterious
       strangers. Fiddler returns to playing at weddings for
       the love of it after gold coins given to him by strangers
       turn to manure.

PL50   Maron, Louise. "Polish Sayings." *Polish Folklore*
       2:3 (1957):51.

       Listing of 7 statements of belief, recorded from indi-
       viduals of Polish ancestry.

PL51   Maziarz, Robert. "Polish Customs in New York Mills,
       N.Y." *New York Folklore Quarterly* 24:4 (1968):
       302-307.

       Presentation of miscellaneous folklore items recorded
       by the author from his Polish-born grandmother, an
       immigrant to New York Mills, New York. Includes 6
       examples of beliefs/superstitions, descriptions of 12
       holiday customs, descriptions of 2 children's games,
       texts of 4 proverbial expressions, 1 recipe, 2 remedies,
       1 song, 3 tales, and miscellaneous descriptions of
       holiday and other foods.

*PL52 Musick, Ruth Ann. *Green Hills of Magic: West Virginia Folktales from Europe.*

(Cross-listed as *AR9, *AU4, *CZ8, *HU24, *IR74, *IT52, *RO4, *RU16, *TU3, *YU8.)
(See *IT52 for full citation and annotation.)

*PL53 Musick, Ruth Ann. "West Virginia Stories: European Folktales in West Virginia."

(Cross-listed as *AU5.)
(See *AU5 for full citation and annotation.)

PL54 Nagorka, Suzanne. "The Life of Felicia Nagorka." *New York Folklore Quarterly* 28:4 (1972):286-292.

Biographical sketch of a Polish immigrant woman who came to the United States as a child and settled in New York State. Includes passing references to traditional Polish Christmas and Easter customs, tales about the woman's experiences as an immigrant.

PL55 Nagorka, Suzanne. "Traditional Polish Cooking." *New York Folklore Quarterly* 28:4 (1972):271-285.

Presentation of 21 recipes for traditional Polish foods, with brief biographical sketches of the 2 cooks who were the sources of the information.

PL56 Nawrocka, Victoria. "More Plant Magic." *Polish Folklore* 2:3 (1957):46.

Brief note about grains and flowers blessed on Assumption Day (August 15), dried, and used to cure earaches and illnesses of animals. Reported from individuals of Polish descent in Browerville, Minnesota.

PL57 Olszowka, Frank. "How Superstitions Grow Up and Spread." *Polish Folklore* 2:4 (1957):69.

Brief explanatory note about the origin of a superstition among Polish people in Oil City, Pennsylvania, that black dogs are dangerous, and mention of a taboo against taking rosaries or prayer books which have been inadvertently left by others in churches.

PL58 Orze, Helen. "How St. Roch Came to Lubotyń." *Polish Folklore* 2:4 (1957):66-69.

Characterization (in English) of 1 story about the strange appearance of parrots on All Souls' Day

(November 2) in the cemetery of the village of
Lubotyń, Poland. Story told by a Polish immigrant
woman from Beaver Falls, Pennsylvania.

PL59   Orze, Helen. "Lilies in the Snow." *Polish Folklore*
       4:4 (1959):65-69.

       Characterization (in English) of 2 stories related to
       the author by a Polish immigrant man in Youngstown,
       Ohio—one tale about an unwed pregnant girl cursed by
       her mother, the other about 7 sisters lost in a snow-
       storm and found in the spring, huddled together and dead.

PL60   Orze, Helen. "The Siren Boots." *Polish Folklore* 3:2
       (1958):22-24.

       Characterization (in English) of 1 story, set in Poland,
       about a young fiddler and herder who encounters a woman
       who spends 23 hours of each day in hell and 1 hour on
       earth, as punishment for her transgressions. Fiddler
       plays for the woman, who promises help when the man
       needs it. Man is punished when he violates the woman's
       interdiction.

PL61   Pajewski, Bernard. "The Headless Ghost of Panna Maria."
       Polish Folklore 4:1 (1959):11-12.

       Brief description of lore about a purportedly Polish
       ghost, a headless man in shiny black boots and black
       cloak, sighted intermittently in Kearns County, Texas,
       since 1867, when an old Polish graveyard was dug up and
       the buried bodies exhumed. Includes brief characteriza-
       tion of 2 personal experience stories involving the
       appearance of the non-malevolent, headless ghost.

PL62   Piasecki, Mrs. Sally. "The Vengeful Stork." *Polish
       Folklore* 5:3 (1960):45.

       Characterization (in English) of 1 experience involving
       a stork whose annual nests in the eaves of 1 house were
       destroyed by the homeowner, with the stork taking re-
       venge. Tale illustrates the Polish belief "Never harm
       a stork's nest. You will pay for it if you do."
       Author-contributor of Polish descent from Harrison,
       New Jersey.

PL63   Pike, Alfred J. "Transitional Aspects of Polish-American
       Music." *Polish Review* 3:4 (1958):104-111.

       Assessment of stylistic changes in the general Polish
       popular and folk musical repertoire as a result of the

American immigrant and ethnic experience, with comments
on which Polish features remain and which American
elements have been introduced. Concludes that American
influence has led to a predominance of instrumental
styles with secondary vocal characteristics and to the
popularity of dance types over purely vocal styles.

PL64   Preston, Kathleen A. and Michael J. "A Note on Visual
       Polack Jokes." *Journal of American Folklore* 86:340
       (1973):175-177.

       Description of 2 visual Polack jokes, with accompanying
       illustration for 1, from Colorado. Emphasizes the need
       for more study of "visual jokes."

*PL65 Preston, Michael J. "A Typescript Ethnic Joke Antholo-
       gy."

       (Cross-listed as *IR87, *IT61.)
       (See *IT61 for full citation and annotation.)

PL66   Preston, Michael J. "Xerox-Lore." *Keystone Folklore*
       19:1 (1974):11-26.

       Characterization and exemplification of lore that is
       disseminated by means of photocopying machines. Includes
       mention of 1 and illustrations of 2 additional "visual"
       Polack jokes.

PL67   Rudzińska, Mrs. Katherine, and Orze, Helen. "Doomed
       Be the Cold of Heart." *Polish Folklore* 3:4 (1958):
       59-61.

       Characterization (in English) of 1 legend about 3 girls
       who deceive a priest, are cursed by him, and are de-
       stroyed with their father's castle when a bolt of
       lightning in the form of a cross strikes the structure.
       Tale learned by one of the authors, of Youngstown, Ohio,
       from her Polish grandmother.

PL68   Sękowska, Agnes. "A Mountain Circe." *Polish Folklore*
       5:3 (1960):47-48.

       Characterization (in English) of 1 story about a woman
       who transforms men into beautiful horses. Blacksmith
       apprentice discovers the bewitchment and brings about
       the breaking of the spell. Author-contributor of Polish
       descent from Gallitzin, Pennsylvania.

PL69   Sękowska, Mrs. Agnes. "Spring Madness." *Polish Folk-*
       lore 5:1 (1960):11.

       Characterization (in English) of 1 Polish story about a
       fight between Saint Michael and the devil and involving
       the stone that closed the entrance to hell, followed by
       a brief description of a festival held each spring on
       the site and of pilgrimages made to the area. Author-
       contributor of Polish descent from Gallitzin, Pennsyl-
       vania.

PL70   Sękowski, Mrs. Agnes. "The Miraculous Gun." *Polish*
       Folklore 4:2 (1959):29-30.

       Characterization (in English) of 1 story known to the
       author (of Polish descent from Gallitzin, Pennsylvania),
       about a miraculous gun that could identify and kill
       thieves.

PL71   Sidwa, Anne. "The Devil and the Long, Long Thread."
       Polish Folklore 3:2 (1958):28-29.

       Characterization (in English) of 1 story, told to the
       author by a Polish immigrant from Saginaw, Michigan,
       about a poor tailor who sells his soul to the devil and
       then saves himself by outwitting the devil in a sewing
       contest.

PL72   Sidwa, Anne. "A Graveyard Taboo." *Polish Folklore*
       2:4 (1957):58-59.

       Characterization (in English) of 1 story told by a
       Polish woman about a girl who walked through a
       cemetery with her dog at night, violating 2 taboos.

PL73   Sidwa, Anne H. "The Whipping Bag." *Polish Folklore*
       5:1 (1960):2-4.

       Characterization (in English) of 1 tale, traditionally
       told in the author's family, about a husband who
       manages, by trickery, to get his lazy wife to do house-
       hold chores.

PL74   Spottswood, Richard. "Karol Stoch and Recorded Polish
       Folk Music from the Podhale Region." *JEMF Quarterly*
       13:48 (1977):196-204.

       Brief characterization of the Podhale region in the
       Tatra Mountains in southeastern Poland, followed by a
       sketch of 1 immigrant from that area who made early

"foreign" music phonograph records beginning in 1927.
Includes 4 photographs of Stoch and other musicians
and of the cover and pages from the Victor catalog.
Also includes a discography of Podhale music and of
Stoch and other musicians from the area.

PL75   Stróżik, Joseph. "Alliance Has a Ghost." *Polish
       Folklore* 4:4 (1959):57.

Brief description of a whistling sound, first heard by
the author in the environs of Alliance College, Cambridge Springs, Pennsylvania, in 1917, which reportedly
is made when the dead daughter of the manager of the
college whistles for her collie dog. Includes 1 personal experience narrative depicting the event.

PL76   Stróżik, Joseph. "The Golden Flowers of St. John's
       Eve." *Polish Folklore* 3:2 (1958):19-21.

Characterization (in English) of 1 story, told to the
author by his Polish mother, about a boy born blind who
follows the advice of an old woman whom he and his
mother befriend and goes with his mother on St. John's
Eve to a place deep in a forest to find golden flowers
of the St. John's fern, which, when applied to his eyes,
enable him to see. Narrator is a Polish immigrant from
Syracuse, New York.

PL77   Stróżik, Joseph. "The Wages of Greed." *Polish Folk-
       lore* 3:1 (1958):3-5.

Characterization (in English) of 1 story, told to the
author by his Polish mother, about a castle in which
3 brothers were killed and which was subsequently inhabited by bandits and/or evil spirits. Man who
attempts to steal a bag of gold from the castle is made
hunchbacked, aged, and speechless for life.

PL78   Suchecki, Mrs. Evelyn. "The Earth Is the Lord's."
       Polish Folklore 4:2 (1959):23-24.

Characterization (in English) of 1 story, told to the
author (from Dorchester, Massachusetts) by her Polish
mother, about an impatient and inhumane Polish lord
who kills a priest who is late to begin mass and who
is struck dead afterwards by a lightning bolt. Dead
lord cannot rest in his grave until his body is ex-
humed, blessed, and eventually burned.

PL79 Taylor, Archer. "Polish Riddles from Michigan."
      Journal of American Folklore 62:244 (1949):189.

      Presentation (in English) of 8 riddle texts, recorded
      by Richard M. Dorson in Crystal Falls, Michigan, in
      1946, and annotated by Archer Taylor with comparative
      notes to a riddle collection from Poland.

PL80 "Three Devil Stories." *Polish Folklore* 5:1 (1960):
      12-17.

      Characterization of 3 stories involving the devil (in
      English), contributed by individuals of Polish descent
      from Ambridge, Pennsylvania; Syracuse, New York; and
      North Lima, Ohio.

PL81 Welsch, Roger L. "American Numskull Tales: The Polack
      Joke." *Western Folklore* 26:3 (1967):183-186.

      Brief discussion of Polack jokes and possible reasons
      for and places of origin. Includes 12 sample jokes,
      recorded in 1965-66 in Lincoln, Nebraska.

PL82 Wolanin, Adam. "The Spectral Rider of Ulanów." *Polish
      Folklore* 2:1 (1957):6-8.

      Characterization (in English) of 1 personal experience
      story, recorded from a Polish immigrant man near Youngs-
      town, Ohio, about his sighting of a spectral figure on
      horseback and a gallows with a hanged person near two
      odd-shaped mounds in his home village of Ulanów, Poland.

PL83 Wong, Celia. "Magic in the Mullein Stalk." *Polish
      Folklore* 2:3 (1957):46.

      Brief mention of mullein and the procedure and incanta-
      tion used with it to cure animals of worms. Known to
      the author from individuals of Polish descent in
      Milwaukee.

PL84 Wong, Celia. "The Soul That Would Not Stay Put."
      Polish Folklore 2:1 (1957):12-13.

      Characterization (in English) of 1 personal experience
      story, learned by the author in Milwaukee from indi-
      viduals of Polish descent, about the soul of a sleeping
      man emerging from his mouth in snake form and disappear-
      ing into, then re-emerging from, a pine tree while a
      second man looked on in amazement. Sleeping man awakens,
      reports dreaming of seeing a treasure in the tree. The
      men dig, find a pot of gold, and become rich. Tale set
      in Litwa, Poland.

PL85   Wood, Arthur. "Polish Heritage and Survivals." In
        American Minorities: A Textbook of Readings in Inter-
        group Relations, edited by Milton L. Barron, pp. 296–
        308. New York: Alfred A. Knopf, 1957.

        Chapter excerpted from the author's book *Hamtramck--*
        Then and Now (1955, pp. 29–45) in which language and
        customs are viewed as providing continuity for Polish
        immigrants in the United States. Includes 30 proverbs
        to demonstrate Polish language persistence and a listing
        of customs associated with the seasons, as well as Polish
        wedding and funeral customs practiced in the United
        States.

PL86   Wright, Betty Jane. "The Orange County Onion Harvest
        Festivals." *New York Folklore Quarterly* 2:3 (1946):
        197–204.

        Description of the onion harvest festivals held in
        Orange County, New York, in 1939 and 1940 (revivals of
        the Polish harvest festival *Dozynki Pod Debami*), in-
        cluding information on preparations, costumes, activi-
        ties, music, and dances.

PL87   Zimniewicz, Helene. "The Accusing Hand." *Polish Folk-*
        lore 2:1 (1957):14.

        Characterization (in English) of 1 story about an in-
        delible handprint, burned into a wooden door at the
        time of the death of a Polish priest in Wisconsin who,
        during his lifetime, neglected to say mass as ordered
        on 3 occasions.

                   XXXIX. PORTUGUESE (PO) (1-22)

PO1   Aman, Reinhold, and Monteiro, George. "Portuguese
        Nicknames." *Maledicta, The International Journal of*
        Verbal Aggression 3:1 (1979):69-70.

        Enumeration of 45 off-color and scatological nicknames
        found among individuals of Portuguese background in
        southern New England and New Bedford, Massachusetts.

PO2 Fagundes, Francisco Cota. "Carnival Dances in Terceira
     and California." In *Portuguese and Brazilian Oral
     Traditions in Verse Form: Symposium Papers Presented
     on May 2-3, 1975 at the University of Southern Cali-
     fornia*, edited by Joanne B. Purcell, with the collabora-
     tion of Samuel G. Armistead, Eduardo Mayone Dias, and
     Joanne E. March, pp. 117-118. Los Angeles, 1976.

     English summary of an essay published in its entirety in
     Portuguese in the volume ("As Danças Carnavalescas na
     Terceira e na Califórnia," pp. 119-127) in which the
     author characterizes 3 types of medieval carnival dances
     brought to California by Portuguese immigrants from the
     island of Terceira in the Azores. Includes examples of
     the dance types and descriptions of performances of them,
     the costumes worn by performers, and the similarities
     and differences among the dances and their performances.

PO3 Fontes, Manuel da Costa. "*Dona Maria* and *Batalha de
     Lepanto*: Two Rare Luso-American Ballads." In *Portu-
     guese and Brazilian Oral Traditions in Verse Form:
     Symposium Papers Presented on May 2-3, 1975 at the
     University of Southern California*, edited by Joanne B.
     Purcell, with the collaboration of Samuel G. Armistead,
     Eduardo Mayone Dias, and Joanne B. March, pp. 148-157.
     Los Angeles, 1976.

     Presentation (in Portuguese) of the texts of 2 versions
     of the ballad "Dona Maria," recorded from Portuguese
     immigrants in Manteca and Crows Landing, California, in
     1970 and 1972 and of 1 version of the ballad "Batalha de
     Lepanto," recorded from a Portuguese immigrant woman in
     Manteca, California, in 1970. Includes comparisons and
     contrasts between the 2 "Dona Maria" texts and with a
     variant recorded in Portugal and between the "Lepanto"
     text recorded in California and those reported from
     mainland Portugal and the Azores.

PO4 Fontes, Manuel da Costa. "*Lizarda*: A Rare Vicentine
     Ballad in California." *Romance Philology* 32 (1979):
     308-314.

     Presentation of texts of 2 versions of a ballad identi-
     fied as "Lizarda," recorded by the author in 1971 and
     1972 from Portuguese-American informants in Manteca and
     Modesto, California. Compares the California texts with
     Gil Vicente's play *Tragicomedia de Don Duardos* (c. 1525)
     and with other earlier Portuguese versions of the ballad.

PO5   Fontes, Manuel da Costa. "A New Portuguese Ballad
      Collection from California." *Western Folklore* 34:4
      (1975):299-310.

      Description of ballads recorded, since 1970, from Portu-
      guese immigrant informants throughout California. Empha-
      sis on the need to collect ballads while they are still
      remembered, since American-born children of immigrants
      and young people in Portugal do not seem to be learning
      the songs. Includes excerpts from 5 ballads, lists of
      titles of other songs recorded. Notes that most ballads
      were recited rather than sung and that most came from
      female informants.

*PO6 Foster, James R. "Brooklyn Folklore."

      (Cross-listed as *GL43, *GR9, *IR31, *IT21, *JE24,
      *PL28, *SP7.)
      (See *GL43 for full citation and annotation.)

PO7   Gayton, A.H. "The '*Festa da Serreta*' at Gustine."
      Western Folklore 7:3 (1948):251-265.

      Description of the festival of Our Lady of Miracles,
      held annually from September 8 to 15 in Gustine, California.
      Includes descriptions of the novena, mass, religious
      processions, extemporaneous song contests, commercial
      carnival, the "banquet of milk," and bullfights (illus-
      trated with 6 photographs and sketches), based on the
      author's 1947 observations and documentation. Provides
      historical background on the origins of the festival,
      begun in Gustine in 1932 by Portuguese immigrants from
      the Azores, most of them from Terceira Island.

PO8   Hare, Maud Cuney. "Portuguese Folk-Songs from Province-
      town, Cape Cod, Mass." *The Musical Quarterly* 14:1
      (1928):35-53.

      Characterization of seafaring and dance songs and music
      recorded by the author in Provincetown, Cape Cod, Massa-
      chusetts, from Portuguese immigrants from the Azores.
      Includes 3 sample tunes; 9 song texts in Portuguese
      (with English translations and tune transcriptions); 1
      song tune (with text in English translation only); 2
      texts (in English translations without tune transcrip-
      tion); summary (in English) of plot of 1 folktale. Also
      includes brief descriptions of dances performed and
      kinds of musical instruments played by Portuguese-
      Americans.

PO9   Lang, Henry R. "The Portuguese Element in New England."
       Journal of American Folk-Lore 5:6 (1892):9–18.

       General historical and ethnographic discussion of the
       Azorean Portuguese in New England, particularly in New
       Bedford, Massachusetts. Examples of folk speech, songs,
       superstitions, proverbs, games, and name changes cited
       as the kinds of folklore that can be recorded from these
       people. Appendix presents additional comments and notes.

PO10   Monteiro, George. "*Alcunhas* among the Portuguese in
       Southern New England." *Western Folklore* 20:2 (1961):
       103–107.

       Discussion of the custom among Portuguese immigrants
       and the first American-born generation of utilizing
       nicknames (*alcunhas*) and substitute surnames (*apelidos*)
       in place of given or family names. Examples illustrate
       the means by which such names are chosen and given to
       individuals. Based on data recorded in the Blackstone
       Valley area of Rhode Island.

PO11   Monteiro, George. "*As Palavras Sao Como as Cerejas:
       Umas Puxam as Outras*: Proverbs of Mainland Portuguese
       in the United States." *Revista de Etnografia* 11:1
       (1968):33–68.

       Listing (in Portuguese only) of 709 proverbs, recorded
       by the author in Rhode Island from Portuguese immi-
       grants and their American-born descendants. Prefatory
       comment about the dearth of folklore fieldwork among
       Portuguese-Americans. Includes list of informants,
       with brief biographical information. Informants born
       between 1896 and 1937.

PO12   Monteiro, George. "Conjecture on a Portuguese Proverb."
       Proverbium 12 (1969):336.

       Brief note on 2 Portuguese proverbs (presented in Portu-
       guese, with English translations), recorded frequently
       by the author from "Portuguese natives now living in
       the United States." Postulates a genetic relationship
       between the two, with one having its source in Scrip-
       ture and the other being a more modern variant of it.

PO13   Monteiro, George. "*The Portuguese Element in New
       England* by Henry Lang: Notes from Another Country."
       Revista de Etnografia 13:2 (1969):339–352.

       Brief historical sketch of Portuguese immigration to
       the United States, followed by a "sampling" of Portu-

guese-American folklore recorded by the author. Includes excerpts from 5 ballads, 1 proverb, 1 tale,
description of 1 game, and 2 riddles.

PO14 Monteiro, George. "Proverbs and Proverbial Phrases of
      the Continental Portuguese." *Western Folklore* 22:1
      (1963):19-45.

      Collection of 457 proverbs and proverbial phrases re-
      corded from continental Portuguese immigrants living
      in the Blackstone Valley area of Rhode Island. Portu-
      guese-language texts with English translations arranged
      alphabetically by first words. Appendix provides brief
      biographical data on 9 informants.

PO15 Monteiro, George. "The Unhistorical Uses of Peter
      Francisco." *Southern Folklore Quarterly* 27:2 (1963):
      139-159.

      Reconstruction of the process by which Peter Francisco,
      a Revolutionary War soldier apparently of Portuguese
      birth, has become a hero and a source of ethnic identity
      among Portuguese-Americans.

PO16 Parsons, Elsie Clews. "Accumulative Tales Told by
      Cape Verde Islanders in New England." *Journal of
      American Folk-Lore* 33:127 (1920):34-42.

      Presentation of 3 tales (in Portuguese dialect, with
      English translations) recorded in New England.

PO17 Parsons, Elsie Clews. "Folklore of the Cape Verde
      Islanders." *Journal of American Folk-Lore* 34:131
      (1921):89-109.

      Sampling of miscellaneous folklore items recorded from
      Portuguese-speaking Blacks from the Cape Verde Islands
      living in Rhode Island and Massachusetts. Includes
      beliefs and practices relating to conception, pregnancy,
      and childbirth; childrearing, courtship and marriage;
      death and funerals; black magic; good and bad luck;
      summaries of some legends; descriptions of religious
      feast days and holidays (including some songs, in
      Portuguese, with English translations and tune tran-
      scriptions). Notes briefly the advantages and dis-
      advantages of studying the folklore of a country
      through information obtained from emigrants from that
      country.

PO18   Parsons, Elsie Clews. "Ten Folk-Tales from the Cape
       Verde Islands." *Journal of American Folk-Lore* 30:
       116 (1917):230-238.

       Presentation of 10 tales, recorded from Black Portuguese
       immigrants in Rhode Island and Massachusetts. Texts
       identified as part of the "Lob and Subrinha cycle" of
       tales and presented in the Portuguese dialect of Fogo
       Island (with English translations). Includes limited
       vocabulary and information on informants, with some
       comparative data.

PO19   Parsons, Elsie Clews. "Three Games of the Cape Verde
       Islands." *Journal of American Folk-Lore* 33:127
       (1920):80-81.

       Description of 3 Cape Verde Island games (guessing,
       ring, and counting-out games) (in English, with terms
       in Portuguese).

PO20   Purcell, Joanne B. "Traditional Ballads Among the
       Portuguese in California: Part I." *Western Folklore*
       28:1 (1969):1-19.

       General characterization of the traditional ballads as
       sung or recited by Portuguese-speaking immigrants in
       California, followed by a more detailed examination of
       several versions of 3 selected ballads: "Nau Catrineta,"
       "A Condessa," and "Frei Joao." Analysis based on
       notion of "narrative stages." Includes musical tran-
       scriptions and comparative references to other Luso-
       Brazilian and Hispanic texts. Based on 1967 fieldwork.

PO21   Purcell, Joanne B. "Traditional Ballads Among the
       Portuguese in California: Part II." *Western Folklore*
       28:2 (1969):77-90.

       Presentation of 4 ballad texts (in Portuguese, with
       2 sample musical transcriptions and identified as
       "Casamento da Filha do Galo," "Dom Varão," "Noiva
       Arriana," and "Jesus Peregrino"), recorded in 1967
       from informants of Portuguese ancestry in California.
       Continuation of an earlier essay (see PO20).

*PO22 Speroni, Charles. "California Fishermen's Festivals."

       (Cross-listed as *IT70, *SJ1.)
       (See *IT70 for full citation and annotation.)

XL.   ROMANIAN (RO) (1-7)

RO1   Coss, Carol. "Ethno Cuisine: Romanian Immigrant Recipes."
      AFFword: Publication of Arizona Friends of Folklore
      4:4 (1975):44-48.

      Presentation of 3 recipes (for bread, noodles, and pan-
      cakes), 4 remedies, and 1 personal experience story,
      recorded from the author's Romanian immigrant aunt in
      Phoenix, Arizona.

RO2   Coss, Carol Ann. "The Immigrant: Craft and Celebration."
      Southwest Folklore 2:1 (1978):40-48.

      Characterization, based on recollections of the author's
      Romanian immigrant aunt and uncle, of various practices
      and celebrations in their native village. Includes
      descriptions of making wool yarn, flax linen, leather
      and of celebrating a church dedication, Christmas, May
      Day, and weddings. Includes 1 text (in English) of a
      "Song of Krist Kringel." Brief discussion of the func-
      tions of these traditions included.

*RO3 Erdely, Stephen. "Research on Traditional Music of
      Nationality Groups in Cleveland and Vicinity."

      (Cross-listed as *GL41, *CR3, *FN11, *GE172, *HU14,
      *IR26, *SC12, *SK4.)
      (See *GL41 for full citation and annotation.)

*RO4 Musick, Ruth Ann. *Green Hills of Magic: West Virginia
      Folktales from Europe.*

      (Cross-listed as *AR9, *AU4, *CZ8, *HU24, *IR74,
      *IT52, *PL52, *RU16, *TU3, *YU8.)
      (See *IT52 for full citation and annotation.)

RO5   Patterson, G. James. *The Romanians of Saskatchewan:
      Four Generations of Adaptation.* Canadian Centre for
      Folk Culture Studies, Paper No. 23. Ottawa: National
      Museum of Man, 1977. Pp. v, 85, bibliography.

      Ethnographic description of Romanians in Saskatchewan,
      with specific reference to their history and sense of
      ethnic identity. Data based on interviews with and
      observations of individuals in Regina and focusing on
      the degree of adaptation of religious holidays, rites
      of passage, social events, foodways, folk beliefs,
      medicine, dance, music, language, and proxemics.

Verbatim transcripts of 10 individuals' life histories
presented to illustrate ethnicity. Author concludes
that despite the disappearance of traditional folklore
forms, four generations of Romanians have a high degree
of awareness of their ethnic identification. Includes
48 photographs and 6 sketches.

RO6 Thigpen, Kenneth A. *Folklore and the Ethnicity Factor
     in the Lives of Romanian-Americans.* 2 volumes in 1.
     New York: Arno Press, 1980. Pp. 586, list of inform-
     ants, motif and tale type indices, bibliography.

A 1973 Indiana University dissertation which attempts
"to explain the nature of Romanian ethnicity of some
Americans via the folklore mode of expression," noting
that "a typical Romanian-American type does not exist"
since "personal fragmentation of experience ... is inte-
gral to American ethnicity." Relationships between
folklore and "the ethnicity factor" exemplified through
discussion and presentation, in the main body of the
work, of 9 personal experience stories about Old World
life and experiences, 5 anecdotes about local traditions
and characters in Romania, 7 legends, 1 *Märchen* text,
7 jokes and anecdotes on such subjects as priests' behavior and adultery, 6 songs, 1 charm text, 21 stories
and anecdotes about the experiences of immigrating and
settling in the New World, 1 rhyme, and 1 poem. Second
half of work presents texts of 14 historical traditions,
53 fictional narratives, 66 beliefs and legends, and 31
texts from the Wayne State University folklore archive
(recorded in 1939, 1940, 1948, and 1964). Work based on
interviews with over 100 Romanian-American informants,
conducted in Detroit, Cleveland, Indianapolis, and Miami
in 1972-73, with additional data obtained from informants
in Fort Wayne, Indiana, and in Chicago (the latter via
correspondence). All textual examples in English only.

RO7 Thigpen, Kenneth A. "Romanian-American Folklore in
     Detroit." In *Ethnic Studies Reader (Immigrants and
     Migrants: The Detroit Experience)*, edited by David W.
     Hartman, pp. 189-201. Detroit: New University Thought
     Publishing Co., 1974.

Brief discussion of Romanian immigration to the United
States, emphasizing distinctions among early 20th-century
peasant immigrants, their American-born progeny, and
post-World-War-II educated urban immigrants. Includes
texts (in English) and brief discussions of 2 traditional

folktales, 4 legends about General George Pomutz (an
American Civil War hero of Romanian background), 1
"refugee story," and 1 joke about life under Communist
rule in contemporary Romania, all recorded by the author
in Detroit in 1973.

XLI. RUSSIAN (RU) (1-24)

*RU1   Agogino, George A., and Pickett, David W. "Two Tales
       of Three Nails."

       (Cross-listed as *GY1.)
       (See *GY1 for full citation and annotation.)

RU2   Alexander, Alex Edward. "The Russian Chastushka Abroad."
       Journal of American Folklore 89:353 (1976):335-341.

       Discussion of the nature, characteristics, and themes of
       the Russian *chastushka*, sung folk rhymes ranging in
       length from 2 to 8 lines, but usually composed in quatrains.
       Asserts that the form is a 19th-century development,
       heavily influenced by foreign models and literary works.
       Includes texts of 13 *chastushka*, recorded from Russian
       immigrants in New York City, and 7 texts reprinted from
       published sources. Notes that the form is not known among
       younger Russian immigrants or American-born children of
       immigrants, suggesting that it is too rooted in the Russian
       cultural environment to persist in America.

RU3   Braddy, Haldeen. "Vashka." *Journal of American Folk-
       lore* 59:231 (1946):70.

       Brief note presenting 1 tale text, contributed by a
       student of Russian descent and recorded in New York
       City, about a peasant whose eagerness to catch a rabbit
       and to prosper from his catch results in his frightening
       and losing his prey.

RU4   Clar, Mimi. "Childhood Beliefs from Stockton, Califor-
       nia." *Western Folklore* 18:1 (1959):41-42.

       Listing of 34 statements of belief (including remedies,
       cures, and signs), recorded in Stockton, California, by
       the author from her Russian immigrant grandmother. Notes
       that the beliefs "were not confined to any particular
       ethnic group," but were generally known among immigrants
       of diverse national backgrounds in Stockton.

*RU5   Clar, Mimi. "Russian Folk Beliefs Collected in Los
       Angeles."

      (Cross-listed as *LI4.)
      (See *LI4 for full citation and annotation.)

*RU6   Crosby, Rev. John R. "Modern Witches of Pennsylvania."

      (Cross-listed as *AR3.)
      (See *AR3 for full citation and annotation.)

*RU7   Dinkel, Phyllis A. "Old Marriage Customs in Herzog
       (Victoria), Kansas." *Western Folklore* 19:2 (1960):
       99-105.

      Description of courting, engagement, and wedding
       customs prevalent among Russian-German immigrants to
       Kansas in the late 1800s and early 1900s, based on
       recollections of informants interviewed in Victoria,
       Kansas, in 1957-58.
      (Cross-listed as *GE151.)

*RU8   Elish, Karl M. "Death and the Old Man."

      (Cross-listed as *JE21.)
      (See *JE21 for full citation and annotation.)

*RU9   Gorelick, J. "Two Anecdotes of Immigrant Life."

      (Cross-listed as *JE27.)
      (See *JE27 for full citation and annotation.)

*RU10 Jones, Louis C. "The Evil-Eye among Euopean-Americans."

      (Cross-listed as *GL51, *GR21, *HU17, *IN1, *IR50,
       *IT35, *JE35, *PL39, *SZ2.)
      (See *GL51 for full citation and annotation.)

*RU11 Jordan, Terry G. "A Russian-German Folk House in
       North Texas." In *Built in Texas*, edited by Francis
       Edward Abernethy, pp. 136-139. *Publications of the
       Texas Folklore Society* 42 (1979).

      Brief description of 1 house in Hurnville, Clay County,
       Texas, built by a Russian-German immigrant family
       shortly after the resettlement of Russian-Germans in
       that area beginning in 1893. Includes 2 photographs
       and 1 map.
      (Cross-listed as *GE319, *UK4.)

*RU12   Larson, Mildred. "The Taller the Better."

       (Cross-listed as *IR58, *IT40, *JE43.)
       (See *IR58 for full citation and annotation.)

*RU13   Luciw, Wasyl O., and Wynnsky, George. "Pysanka and
       Other Decorated Easter Eggs in Pennsylvania."

       (Cross-listed as *PL48, *UK27.)
       (See *PL48 for full citation and annotation.)

*RU14   Martens, Helen. "The Music of Some Religious Minorities
       in Canada."

       (Cross-listed as *AU2, *DU13, *GE384, *SW6.)
       (See *GE384 for full citation and annotation.)

RU15   Moore, Willard Burgess. *Molokan Oral Tradition:
       Legends and Memorates of an Ethnic Sect.* University
       of California Folklore Series No. 28. Berkeley and
       Los Angeles: University of California Press, 1973.
       Pp. vii, 82, acknowledgments, introduction, appendix,
       bibliography.

       Study of the Spiritual Christian Molokan community of
       Los Angeles, based on the author's 1970 fieldwork, with
       emphasis on oral narratives through which members
       express and perpetuate their religious traditions.
       Includes an historical sketch of the Molokans in Russia
       and their settlement in the New World, a characteriza-
       tion of the Molokan world view, a description of the
       Los Angeles community and of a typical religious
       service, and a presentation and analysis of selected
       legends and memorates (all in English). Includes
       transcribed texts of 37 legends, memorates, and per-
       sonal experience narratives relating to prophecies,
       healings, consequences of violating religious taboos,
       and text of 1 saying. Mention made in passing of food,
       songs, and their role in community life.

*RU16   Musick, Ruth Ann. *Green Hills of Magic: West Virginia
       Folktales from Europe.*

       (Cross-listed as *AR9, *AU4, *CZ8, *HU24, *IR74,
       *IT52, *PL52, *RO4, *TU3, *YU8.)
       (See *IT52 for full citation and annotation.)

*RU17   Musick, Ruth Ann. "The Trickster Story in West Virginia."

       (Cross-listed as *IT54, *YU9.)
       (See *IT54 for full citation and annotation.)

RU18   Neidle, Cecyle S. "Immigrant's Idyll: Maurice Hindus
       in Upstate New York." *New York Folklore Quarterly*
       21:1 (1965):49-57.

       Characterization of selected experiences of a Russian
       immigrant in New York State, derived from the book
       Green Worlds (1938) written by the immigrant, Maurice
       Hindus. Through excerpts and paraphrases from the book,
       illustrates Hindus' longings for Old World rural life
       and the contrasts he drew between life in Russia and
       in the United States.

*RU19 Peacock, Kenneth. "Establishing Perimeters for Ethno-
       musicological Field Research in Canada: On-Going
       Projects and Future Possibilities at the Canadian
       Centre for Folk Culture Studies."

       (Cross-listed as *GL66, *CH21, *FR91, *GE428, *HU25,
       *IC4, *ID2, *IT57, *JA9, *LI5, *NO19, *UK32.)
       (See *GL66 for full citation and annotation.)

RU20   Peacock, Kenneth. *Songs of the Doukhobors: An Intro-
       ductory Outline.* National Museums of Canada Bulletin
       No. 231, Folklore Series No. 7. Ottawa, 1970. Pp.
       ix, 167, foreword, introduction, 4 flexidiscs.

       Presentation of 27 song and hymn texts (in Russian,
       with English translations and tune transcriptions),
       recorded by the author in 1963-64 among Doukhobors of
       Russian ancestry in Alberta, British Columbia, and
       Saskatchewan. Introductory essay includes historical
       sketch of the Doukhobors. Includes 27 photographs of
       singers and singing groups.

*RU21 Peacock, Kenneth. *Twenty Ethnic Songs from Western
       Canada.* National Museum of Canada Bulletin No. 211,
       Anthropological Series No. 76. Ottawa, 1966. Pp. 89.

       Presentation of 20 folksong and hymn texts, 5 from
       Russian Doukhobors of British Columbia (in Russian,
       with English translations and tune transcriptions), 5
       from German-Russian Mennonites of Manitoba (in German,
       with English translations and tune transcriptions), 5
       from Hungarians of Saskatchewan (in Hungarian, with
       English translations and tune transcriptions), 4 from
       Ukrainians of Ontario and Manitoba (in Ukrainian, with
       English translations and tune transcriptions), and 1
       from a Czech informant of Manitoba (in Czech, with
       English translation and tune transcription). Based on
       fieldwork conducted in 1950, 1962, and 1963. Includes

brief sketches of the ethnic groups and selected
informants and of musical features of the songs and
hymns, with 20 photographs of informants and communities.
(Cross-listed as *CZ10, *GE429, *HU26, *UK33.)

*RU22   Sackett, S.J.   "The Hammered Dulcimer in Ellis County,
        Kansas."

        (Cross-listed as *GE527.)
        (See *GE527 for full citation and annotation.)

RU23   Tarasoff, Koozma J.   *Traditional Doukhobor Folkways:
       An Ethnographic and Biographic Record of Prescribed
       Behaviour.*   Canadian Centre for Folk Culture Studies,
       Paper No. 20.   Ottawa: National Museum of Man, 1977.
       Pp. xxviii, 391, list of informants, bibliography.

       Evaluation of the persistence and change of Doukhobor
       folklife among those emigrating from Russia to Canada,
       based on interviews with 63 informants conducted in
       1975 in British Columbia and Saskatchewan.   Includes
       transcriptions of tape-recorded interviews, with
       accompanying analytical remarks about the cultural life
       and values of the Doukhobors.   Following an analysis
       of 13 "cultural values" (including marriage, death,
       singing, narration, art, healing, clothing, foodways,
       retirement, child rearing, language, and ideology) among
       members of 3 Doukhobor sub-groups, author concludes that
       in the areas of family life, cultural activities, and
       decision making, there is a trend toward secularization,
       modernization, and professionalism.   Elements of
       ideology, however, remain traditional and reflect Old
       World values.   Includes 66 photographs and 1 map.

*RU24   Terbovich, Fr. John B.   "Religious Folklore among the
        German-Russians in Ellis County, Kansas."   *Western
        Folklore* 22:2 (1963):79-88.

        Survey of folklore relating to Catholicism, religious
        holidays, and rites of passage, recorded in the towns
        of Hays, Catherine, and Victoria in Ellis County,
        Kansas.   Includes beliefs and customs relating to
        childbirth, marriage, death, Christmas, New Year's,
        and Easter.
        (Cross-listed as *GE684.)

XLII. SCANDINAVIAN (SA) (1-2)

*SA1 Cheney, Thomas E. "Scandinavian Immigrant Stories."

          (Cross-listed as *DA3, *SS4.)
          (See *DA3 for full citation and annotation.)

 SA2 Wahlgren, Erik. "Scandinavian Folklore and Folk Culture
          in the Trans-Mississippi West." *Northwest Folklore*
          3:1 (1968):1-16.

          General discussion of the lack of folklore collecting
          among Scandinavian immigrants in the United States, with
          emphasis on the need to do more fieldwork and a general
          discussion of some of the kinds of folklore available
          and sources for future research. Includes excerpts (in
          English) from 4 songs and ballads.

                    XLIII. SCOTTISH (SC) (1-45)

*SC1 Barbeau, C.M. "Folk-Songs."

          (Cross-listed as *FR6, *IR3.)
          (See *IR3 for full citation and annotation.)

*SC2 Bethke, Robert. "Chester County Wills (1714-1800): A
          Folklife Source."

          (Cross-listed as *IR9, *WE1.)
          (See *IR9 for full citation and annotation.)

*SC3 Botkin, Ben A. (Moderator). "The Folksong Revival: A
          Symposium."

          (Cross-listed as *IR12, *JE9.)
          (See *JE9 for full citation and annotation.)

 SC4 Bundy, Colleen. "A Method for Removing Warts."
          Journal of American Folklore 59:231 (1946):70.

          Description of the way the author's Scottish-born grand-
          mother removed approximately 39 warts from the hands
          and feet of the author's 10-year-old cousin, in Paoli,
          Indiana, in 1935.

SC5   Creighton, Helen, and MacLeod, Calum. *Gaelic Songs in Nova Scotia*. National Museum of Canada Bulletin No. 198, Anthropological Series No. 66. Ottawa, 1964. Pp. xii, 302, introduction, bibliography, index.

Presentation of 94 songs (in Gaelic, with English translations and tune transcriptions), recorded since 1933 in Cape Breton, Nova Scotia, and Prince Edward Island, Canada. Introduction provides information about the fieldwork sites and circumstances. Includes 22 photographs (of dance groups, singers, musicians, local scenes, and game-playing) and brief informant notes and comparative references.

SC6   Doering, J. Frederick. "'Donald Monroe,' A Canadian Version of a Scottish Folksong." *Journal of American Folklore* 55:217 (1942):170-174.

Presentation of 1 song text (identified as a version of "Donald Monroe"), recorded by the author from a singer of Scotch-Irish background in Ontario, Canada.

SC7   Dundes, Alan. "Advertising and Folklore." *New York Folklore Quarterly* 19:2 (1963):143-151.

Discussion of the effects of the mass media upon American folklore, of the media as an impetus for the formation of new folklore, and of advertising as a "cultural idiom." Includes 9 jokes involving puns on the name of a product (1 of which is a riddle which alludes to Scottish stinginess); 7 jokes involving puns on advertising slogans or songs; 1 joke involving a conglomeration of product names; 2 jokes involving advertising claims; and 2 jokes about the advertising industry.

*SC8 Dunn, Adda Ann. "Songs, Riddles, and Tales from Saratoga County."

(Cross-listed as *IR24.)
(See *IR24 for full citation and annotation.)

SC9   Dunn, Charles W. "Gaelic Proverbs in Nova Scotia." *Journal of American Folklore* 72:283 (1959):30-35.

Presentation (in Scottish Gaelic, with English translations) of 59 proverbs, recorded by the author from Gaelic-speaking Scots in Nova Scotia between 1941 and 1943. Also includes characterization of 1 anecdote (in English) and brief introduction to the proverbs, with comments on form and style.

*SC10   Eames, Frank. "Landon's Ould Dog and Hogmanay Fair."

        (Cross-listed as *FR58, *IR25.)
        (See *FR58 for full citation and annotation.)

*SC11   Erdely, Stephen. "Ethnic Music in the United States:
        An Overview."

        (Cross-listed as *GL40, *AR5, *CR2, *GR7, *GY5,
        *JE22, *SE2.)
        (See *GL40 for full citation and annotation.)

*SC12   Erdely, Stephen. "Research on Traditional Music of
        Nationality Groups in Cleveland and Vicinity."

        (Cross-listed as *GL41, *CR3, *FN11, *GE172, *HU14,
        *IR26, *RO3, *SK4.)
        (See *GL41 for full citation and annotation.)

SC13   Fraser, Alexander. "The Gaelic Folk-Songs of Canada."
        *Proceedings and Transactions of the Royal Society of
        Canada.* 2d series. 9, section II (May 1903):49-60.

        Discussion of the importance of traditional songs in
        the lives of Scottish immigrants to Canada, with texts
        of or excerpts from 16 songs and poems included (6 in
        Gaelic with English translations, 3 in Gaelic only,
        and 7 in English translations only). Includes songs
        relating to the experiences of immigrating and settling
        in the new land.

SC14   Fraser, C.A. "Scottish Myths from Ontario." *Journal
        of American Folk-Lore* 6:22 (1893):185-198.

        Presentation of 4 ghost stories, noted in the author's
        own words, heard from third-generation Canadian farmers
        in Ontario, descendants of Scottish Highlanders from
        Glenelg. Includes summaries of several other stories
        of strange happenings and weird incidents in the
        community. Comments on the "authenticity" of ghost
        stories and the tendency for narrators to "invent"
        evidence to support them.

SC15   Frazier, Paul. "The Legend of Nellie MacQuillie."
        Midwest Folklore 1:3 (1951):165-166.

        Summary of 1 legend told in North Carolina about a
        Scottish immigrant girl and her dog who were scalped
        by Indians in the late 18th century. When mist shrouds
        the murder site even today, the girl and dog can be seen.

SC16   Gaillard, Mary Lou. "Folklore from Nova Scotia and
       Prince Edward Island." *Southwest Folklore* 3:2 (1979):
       59-66.

       Presentation of texts of 8 tales, told by the author's
       mother and father, both of Scottish background and born
       and raised in Nova Scotia and Prince Edward Island,
       respectively. Includes stories involving ghosts and
       other supernatural phenomena, seafaring, personal
       experiences, and religion.

SC17   Glover, Waldo F. "Old Scotland in Vermont." *Vermont
       History* n.s. 23:2 (1955):92-103.

       Brief discussion of Scottish immigration to and settle-
       ment in Ryegate, Vermont, and environs in the late 18th
       century, with emphasis on the few Scottish-style stone
       houses built in the area between 1797 and 1812. In-
       cludes descriptions of construction materials and
       additions made over the years. Illustrated with 5
       photographs of selected houses.

*SC18 Grame, Theodore C. *America's Ethnic Music.*

       (Cross-listed as *GL45.)
       (See *GL45 for full citation and annotation.)

*SC19 Halpert, Herbert. "Legends of the Cursed Child."

       (Cross-listed as *GL48, *IR37.)
       (See *GL48 for full citation and annotation.)

SC20   Haviland, Thomas P. "An Early American Folk-Song."
       Journal of American Folklore 63:247 (1950):94-96.

       Reprinting of 1 folksong text (titled "Scots Song upon
       America"), recorded in the late 18th century by a Swiss-
       born immigrant to Philadelphia. Song characterizes a
       Scottish immigrant's observations and evaluations of
       experiences in America.

SC21   Jackson, Kenneth. "More Tales from Port Hood, Nova
       Scotia." *Scottish Gaelic Studies* 6:2 (1949):176-188.

       Presentations of texts of 4 tales (in Scottish Gaelic,
       with appended English plot summaries), recorded by the
       author in Port Hood, Nova Scotia, in 1946. One tale
       identified as a version of "The Dragon Slayer." In-
       cludes brief comparative notes. Supplements an earlier
       essay (see SC22).

SC22   Jackson, Kenneth. "Notes on the Gaelic of Port Hood,
       Nova Scotia." *Scottish Gaelic Studies* 6:1 (1947):
       89-109.

       Description of the phonology and morphology of the
       Scottish Gaelic spoken in Port Hood, Nova Scotia,
       followed by a transcription (in Scottish Gaelic) of
       1 folktale recorded by the author in 1946. Includes
       an English summary of the plot of the tale, identified
       as a version of "The Monster's Bride."

*SC23 Jamison, Mrs. C.V. "Signs and Omens from Nova Scotia."

       (Cross-listed as *FR68.)
       (See *FR68 for full citation and annotation.)

*SC24 Leeson, Alice M. "Certain Canadian Superstitions."

       (Cross-listed as *IR60.)
       (See *IR60 for full citation and annotation.)

*SC25 Lewis, Mary Ellen Brown. "Folk Elements in Scotch-
       Irish Presbyterian Communities." *Pennsylvania Folk-
       life* 18:1 (1968):21-25.

       Presentation of folk elements abstracted from 18th-
       century diaries of Presbyterian ministers John McMillan
       and John Cuthbertson. Reminiscences reflect importance
       of witchcraft and folk remedies (16 examples given) for
       immigrant Scotch-Irish.
       (Cross-listed as *IR61.)

SC26   MacKenzie, W. Roy. "Ballad-Singing in Nova Scotia."
       Journal of American Folk-Lore 22:85 (1909):327-331.

       Observations about and explanations for the decline of
       ballad singing among descendants of Scottish immigrants
       to the north shore counties of Nova Scotia. Notes that
       many French-Swiss in Nova Scotia have learned the
       Scottish ballads and continue the tradition. Comparison
       made between a singer of Scottish descent who has for-
       gotten most of the ballads he learned as a young man and
       a French-Swiss singer who learned the Scottish ballads
       and continues to sing them.

SC27   Marshall, Alexander. "The Days of Auld Lang Syne."
       Pennsylvania Folklife 13:4 (1964):8-19.

       Author's reminiscences of pioneer life among the Scotch-
       Irish Presbyterians in northwestern Chester County of

Pennsylvania, reprinted from 1877-78 newspapers. Includes information on farming, cooking, clothing, education, and recreation. Illustrated with 9 sketches of
farming life.

SC28   Mazzei, Maureen. "Scottish Folklore in Brooklyn."
       New York Folklore Quarterly 11:3 (1955):205-208.

       Characterization of 1 personal experience story, discus-
       sion of 1 practical joke, and presentation in English
       of proverbs and sayings concerning "industry and thrift"
       (7), "love, marriage, and family life" (9), "cynical
       observation" (14), "warning" (2), "drinking" (2), and
       "comfort" (3). Data obtained from informants of
       Scottish descent living in Brooklyn, New York.

*SC29 Millard, Eugenia L. "A Sampling of Guessing Games."

       (Cross-listed as *IR70.)
       (See *IR70 for full citation and annotation.)

*SC30 Norlin, Ethel Todd. "Present-Day Superstitions at La
       Harpe, Ill., Survivals in a Community of English
       Origin."

       (Cross-listed as *DU14, *FR88, *GE424, *IR78.)
       (See *IR78 for full citation and annotation.)

*SC31 O'Neill, Capt. Francis. *Irish Folk Music, A Fascinating
       Hobby with Some Account of Allied Subjects Including
       O'Farrell's Treatise on the Irish or Union Pipes and
       Touhey's Hints to Amateur Pipers.*

       (Cross-listed as *IR81.)
       (See *IR81 for full citation and annotation.)

*SC32 Osborn, Lettie. "Fiddle Tunes from Orange County, New
       York."

       (Cross-listed as *IR84.)
       (See *IR84 for full citation and annotation.)

*SC33 Owen, Mary A. "Coyote and Little Pig."

       (Cross-listed as *IR85.)
       (See *IR85 for full citation and annotation.)

SC34   Pound, Louise. "A Nebraska Folk-Song." *Folk-Lore*
       37:1 (1922):113-115.

       Presentation of a text of 1 New Year's song obtained by
       the author from a man of Scottish ancestry living in

Lincoln, Nebraska, in 1919. Song reported to accompany house-to-house visits by boys and girls on New Year's, with visitors being rewarded with food and drink after singing the song.

*SC35   Rennick, Robert M. "Successive Name-Changing: A Popular Theme in Onomastic Folklore and Literature."

(Cross-listed as *GE446, *JE52, *YU10.)
(See *JE52 for full citation and annotation.)

SC36   Rose, H.J. "Canadian Folklore." *Folk-Lore* 32:2 (1921):124-131.

Presentation of miscellaneous folklore items gathered by McGill University students. Includes 2 beliefs/ superstitions and 1 tale about second sight from Prince Edward Island, recorded "from the Scots population of this Province."

*SC37   Tallmadge, William H. "Anglo-Saxon vs. Scotch-Irish."

(Cross-listed as *IR98.)
(See *IR98 for full citation and annotation.)

*SC38   Tallmadge, William H. "The Scotch-Irish and the British Traditional Ballad in America."

(Cross-listed as *IR99.)
(See *IR99 for full citation and annotation.)

SC39   Teit, J.A. "Water-Beings in Shetlandic Folk-Lore, As Remembered by Shetlanders in British Columbia." *Journal of American Folk-Lore* 3 (1918):180-201.

Discussion of the Norwegian and general Scandinavian character of Shetlandic folklore due to the history and settlement of the Shetland Islands and of the Scottish influence since the beginning of the 17th century. Presents descriptions of various water-beings, based on the author's own knowledge obtained as a boy in Shetland and from elderly Shetlanders living in North America, particularly in British Columbia. Physical characteristics of water-beings noted, as well as commentary about their activities and narratives about encounters and experiences with such creatures. Author comments that because Scandinavian settlement in Canada has been slight, there is no Shetland-Canadian folklore as there is French-Canadian folklore.

*SC40   Warner, Frank. "A Salute and a Sampling of Songs."

        (Cross-listed as *IR111.)
        (See *IR111 for full citation and annotation.)

*SC41   Willis, Alice. "Tales from a Mountain Homestead."

        (Cross-listed as *DU27, *IR115.)
        (See *DU27 for full citation and annotation.)

*SC42   Wintemberg, W.J. "Folk-Lore Collected at Roebuck,
        Grenville County, Ontario."

        (Cross-listed as *IR116.)
        (See *IR116 for full citation and annotation.)

*SC43   Wintemberg, W.J. and Katherine H. "Folk-Lore from Grey
        County, Ontario."

        (Cross-listed as *IR117.)
        (See *IR117 for full citation and annotation.)

 SC44   Wright, Estelle. "Sammy Lingo and Bobby Cuso."
        Journal of American Folklore 54:213-214 (1941):197-199.

        Presentation (in English) of the text of a version of
        a "Magic Flight" tale, told to the author by her mother,
        who learned it from her mother, a member of "the Scotch
        colony in North Carolina." Includes brief transcrip-
        tions of portions of tunes to songs sung as an integral
        part of the tale.

 SC45   Wright, Ruth C. "Songs: 'Gypsy Davy' (Child 200)."
        New York Folklore Quarterly 10:1 (1954):52-53.

        Presentation of 1 ballad text and tune (in English),
        identified as a version of the Scottish ballad "The
        Gypsy Laddie" (Child #200).

                    XLIV.   SERBIAN (SE) (1-8)

*SE1   Dorson, Richard M. "Is There a Folk in the City?"

        (Cross-listed as *GL34, *CR1, *GR5.)
        (See *GL34 for full citation and annotation.)

*SE2 Erdely, Stephen. "Ethnic Music in the United States:
       An Overview."

       (Cross-listed as *GL40, *AR5, *CR2, *GR7, *GY5, *JE22,
       *SC11.)
       (See *GL40 for full citation and annotation.)

*SE3 Forry, Mark. "*Bécar* Music in the Serbian Community of
       Los Angeles: Evolution and Transformation." *Selected
       Reports in Ethnomusicology* 3:1 (1978):174-209.

       Description of the "social situation, performing style,
       and native concepts" of *bécar* music and performance among
       Yugoslav immigrants (perticularly Serbians) in Los Ange-
       les, with emphasis on both similarities and differences
       between music and performances in Yugoslavia and the
       United States, on the one hand, and between turn-of-the-
       century and post-World-War-II Yugoslav immigrants, on
       the other. Discusses Yugoslav immigration to the United
       States, tamburitza performing groups, the tambura and
       accordion, dances, repertoires of musicians, musical
       elements and stylistic characteristics, informants' con-
       ceptions of *bécar* music. Includes 2 photographs of
       tamburitza orchestras, 1 map of Yugoslavia, 10 brief
       musical transcriptions of *bécar* selections, 2 full tune
       transcriptions with words of songs (in Serbo-Croatian,
       with English translations). Based on observations and
       interviews conducted during the 1970s.
       (Cross-listed as *YU4.)

*SE4 Hand, Wayland D. "The Folklore, Customs, and Traditions
       of the Butte Miner."

       (Cross-listed as *CO7, *FI2, *FN14, *IR40, *IT29.)
       (See *CO7 for full citation and annotation.)

*SE5 March, Richard. "The Tamburitza Tradition in the Calumet
       Region."

       (Cross-listed as *CR6, *YU5.)
       (See *CR6 for full citation and annotation.)

SE6   Milanovich, Anthony. "Serbian Tales from Blanford."
       Indiana Folklore 4:1 (1971):1-60.

       Reprinting of 12 folktale texts (in English translations
       only), recorded by Milanovich from Serbian immigrants
       in Blanford, Indiana, and originally presented as part
       of an M.A. thesis in 1942. Includes a foreword by Stith
       Thompson; a description of contemporary Blanford by

Yvonne J. Milspaw (with 2 photographs of town buildings, 3 of a Serbian immigrant musician playing traditional instruments); and a description of the author-collector and his 2 principal narrator informants by Linda Dégh.

*SE7   Soland, Craig. "Ethno-Cuisine: Serbo-Flemish Christmas Cookery." *AFFword: Publication of Arizona Friends of Folklore* 3:3 (1973):39-42.

Presentation of 3 recipes, contributed by the author's mother, 2 for Serbian pastries served at Christmastime and 1 for Flemish honey bread.
(Cross-listed as *BE3.)

SE8   Soland, Craig. "How To Make a Sve-Te Saba." *AFFword: Publication of Arizona Friends of Folklore* 4:1 (1974): 1-7.

Description, from an informant's recollections, of the way Serbian immigrants and their children in Omaha, Nebraska, celebrated saints' days. Includes 3 recipes (for cabbage rolls, paprika chicken, and dumplings) and general descriptions of home blessings by the priest, musicians, and foods and drinks served.

XLV. SLAVIC (SI) (1-2)

SI1   Perkowski, Jan L. *Vampires, Dwarves, and Witches among the Ontario Kashubs.* Canadian Centre for Folk Culture Studies, Paper No. 1. Ottawa: National Museum of Man, 1972. Pp. 85, bibliography.

Demonstration of the continuity of Old World Kashubian daemonology in the New World. Description of the role of vampires, *succuba*, dwarfs, and witches. Study based on interviews with 15 informants in Ontario in 1968-69. Reports of each informant presented in Kashubian, accompanied by brief biographical data. Includes 17 photographs, 3 maps.

*SI2   Richman, Hyman. "The Saga of Joe Magarac."

(Cross-listed as *GL73, *HU27.)
(See *HU27 for full citation and annotation.)

XLVI. SLAVONIAN (SJ) (1)

*SJ1 Speroni, Charles. "California Fishermen's Festivals."
(Cross-listed as *IT70, *PO22.)
(See *IT70 for full citation and annotation.)

XLVII. SLOVAK (SK) (1-10)

*SK1 Babcock, C. Merton. "Czech Songs in Nebraska."
(Cross-listed as *CZ2.)
(See *CZ2 for full citation and annotation.)

*SK2 "A Christmas Eve Custom."
(Cross-listed as *GE113, *GR1.)
(See *GE113 for full citation and annotation.)

*SK3 Cincura, Andrew. "Slovak and Ruthenian Easter Eggs in
America: The Impact of Culture Contact on Immigrant
Art and Custom." *Journal of Popular Culture* 4:1
(1970):155-193.

Description and discussion of traditional Easter egg
decorating as practiced by Slovak and Ukrainian (Ruthenian) immigrants and their descendants in Cleveland, with
emphasis on implements and materials used, designs,
techniques, and customs involving decorated eggs. Based
on 1969 fieldwork. Includes 12 photographs of decorated
eggs and of artists decorating eggs.
(Cross-listed as *UK1.)

*SK4 Erdely, Stephen. "Research on Traditional Music of
Nationality Groups in Cleveland and Vicinity."
(Cross-listed as *GL41, *CR3, *FN11, *GE172, *HU14,
*IR26, *RO3, *SC12.)
(See *GL41 for full citation and annotation.)

*SK5 Evanson, Jacob A. "Folk Songs of an Industrial City."
(Cross-listed as *GL42, *FN12, *GE177, *GR8, *IR27.)
(See *GL42 for full citation and annotation.)

SK6   Hatas, Kristina. "Czechoslovakian Folklore." *Journal*
       of the Ohio Folklore Society n.s. 3:1 (1974):33-37.

       Collectanea from the author's Slovak immigrant grandmother
       and American-born mother, recorded in Rossford, Ohio, in
       1973. Includes 1 folktale text, 1 proverb (in Slovak,
       with English translation), 1 children's game (in Slovak,
       with English translation), and 1 recipe (for sausage).

*SK7   Korson, George. "Coal Miners."

       (Cross-listed as *GL55, *IR56, *WE7.)
       (See *GL55 for full citation and annotation.)

*SK8   Nettl, Bruno, and Moravcik, Ivo. "Czech and Slovak
       Songs Collected in Detroit."

       (Cross-listed as *CZ9.)
       (See *CZ9 for full citation and annotation.)

*SK9   Pirkova-Jakobson, Svatava. "Harvest Festivals among
       Czechs and Slovaks in America."

       (Cross-listed as *CZ11.)
       (See *CZ11 for full citation and annotation.)

SK10   Seckar, Alvena V. "Slovak Wedding Customs." *New York*
       Folklore Quarterly 3:2 (1947):189-205.

       Description of a typical wedding and the activities
       associated with it in the town of Novotoy, Slovakia,
       including variations in a neighboring province, followed
       by a description of a Slovak wedding the author attended
       in McMechen, West Virginia. Includes descriptions of
       wedding preparation, the bridal procession, food,
       activities on the wedding night. Includes 6 song texts
       (in Slovakian, with English translations and tune
       transcriptions for 5).

XLVIII. SLOVENIAN (SL) (1-3)

*SL1   Dorson, Richard M. "Blood Stoppers."

       (Cross-listed as *FN2, *FR50, *GE160, *IR20, *SS8.)
       (See *FR50 for full citation and annotation.)

SL2 Kess, Joseph F. "Ribence Tales among the American
     Slovenians." *Journal of the Ohio Folklore Society*
     n.s. 3:4 (1968):201-209.

     Presentation of 11 numskull tale texts (in English
     translations), recorded from post-World-War-I Slovenian
     immigrants to Cleveland. Tales concern an imaginary
     Slovenian town called Ribence and describe the behavior
     of its naive or stupid inhabitants.

SL3 Montgomery, Margaret. "Slovenian Folklore in Indianapo-
     lis." *Hoosier Folklore* 6:4 (1947):121-132.

     Presentation of miscellaneous folklore items, recorded
     by the author from a Slovenian woman in Indianapolis in
     1947. Includes descriptions of Christmas and Easter
     customs, name-day celebrations, 2 recipes, and 2 folk-
     tales.

                XLIX. SPANISH (SP) (1-16)

SP1 Boggs, Ralph Steele. "Spanish Folklore from Tampa,
     Florida." *Southern Folklore Quarterly* 1:3 (1937):
     1-12.

     Brief historical and ethnographic description of the
     Spanish-speaking population of Tampa, Florida, followed
     by the presentation of 5 riddles.

SP2 Boggs, Ralph Steele. "Spanish Folklore from Tampa,
     Florida: (No. V) Folktales." *Southern Folklore
     Quarterly* 2:2 (1938):87-106.

     Presentation of 19 folktale texts (in Spanish), recorded
     in Tampa, Florida.

SP3 Boggs, Ralph Steele. "Spanish Folklore from Tampa,
     Florida: (No. III) *Una Ledi de Naso.*" *Southern Folk-
     lore Quarterly* 1:4 (1937):9-13.

     Presentation (in a combination of Cuban Spanish and
     English, with English translation) of the text of 1
     poem recited by "street urchins" in Tampa, Florida.

SP4   Campa, Arthur L.   "Spanish Folksongs in Metropolitan
      Denver."   *Southern Folklore Quarterly* 24:3 (1960):
      179-192.

      Discussion of various periods of Spanish immigration to
      and settlement in the Denver area, from the period of
      original Spanish exploration and colonization to recent
      influxes of Mexican immigrants, with emphasis on songs
      remembered and still sung from earliest settlement days
      to the present and of songs composed about local
      happenings in recent years. Includes texts of or
      excerpts from 38 songs (in Spanish).

SP5   Claudel, Calvin.   "Spanish Folktales from Delacroix,
      Louisiana."   *Journal of American Folklore* 58:229
      (1945):209-224.

      Presentation (in English) of texts of 16 folktales, 2
      recorded in 1935, 14 written down by schoolchildren in
      1941, in Delacroix, Saint Bernard Parish, Louisiana.
      Informants descendants of Spanish settlers from the
      Canary and other islands.

SP6   Claudel, Calvin.   "Three Spanish Folktales."   *California
      Folklore Quarterly* 3:1 (1944):21-28.

      Presentation of 3 tale texts (in English), recorded in
      San Diego, California, and Tolleson, Arizona, from an
      informant of "Spanish, Portuguese, and Mexican" back-
      ground.

*SP7 Foster, James R.   "Brooklyn Folklore."

      (Cross-listed as *GL43, *GR9, *IR31, *IT21, *JE24,
      *PL28, *PO6.)
      (See *GL43 for full citation and annotation.)

SP8   Hauptmann, O.H.   "Spanish Folklore from Tampa, Florida:
      (No. IV) Superstitions."   *Southern Folklore Quarterly*
      2:1 (1938):11-30.

      Listing of 99 superstitions, arranged alphabetically by
      subject nouns, with comparative notes to American,
      German, Cuban, and Chilean collections.

SP9   McCarthy, Paul T.   "The Minorcan 'Fromajardis' and 'La
      Guignolée.'"   *The French Folklore Bulletin* 7:40
      (1949):5-6.

      Brief note describing a custom reported from Spanish
      Minorcans of Saint Augustine, Florida, of a singing

group that paraded through the streets on Easter eve, stopping at homes for refreshments. Includes text of 1 folksong sung on the occasion (in Spanish, with English translation). Notes that custom is no longer observed.

SP10 MacCurdy, Raymond R., Jr. "Spanish Folklore from St. Bernard Parish, Louisiana." *Southern Folklore Quarterly* 13:4 (1949):180-191.

Ethnographic and historical description of the Spanish-speaking population of St. Bernard Parish, Louisiana, followed by texts of 7 tales about the protagonist Quevedo (in Spanish). Based on 1941 and 1947 fieldwork.

SP11 MacCurdy, Raymond R., Jr. "Spanish Folklore from St. Bernard Parish, Louisiana: Part III, Folktales." *Southern Folklore Quarterly* 16:4 (1952):227-250.

Presentation of 12 folktale texts (in Spanish), recorded in St. Bernard Parish, Louisiana, in 1947.

SP12 MacCurdy, Raymond R., Jr. "Spanish Riddles from St. Bernard Parish, Louisiana." *Southern Folklore Quarterly* 12:2 (1948):129-135.

Presentation of 22 riddles (in Spanish), recorded in Delacroix, St. Bernard Parish, Louisiana.

SP13 Minor, Eugene R. "III. Witch Stories of European Origin: 2. Maria's Sorrow." *West Virginia Folklore* 6:1 (1955): 12-13.

Characterization (in English) of 1 tale, recorded in West Virginia from an informant from Spain.

SP14 Rybak, Shulameth. "Puerto Rican Children's Songs in New York." *Midwest Folklore* 8:1 (1958):5-20.

Report on a study of traditional songs known to 2 groups of Puerto-Rican-American children in New York—1 group that had lived there for more than, and 1 that had been there for less than, 2 years. Includes texts and tune transcriptions for 11 songs, with comparisons and contrasts of the songs known to the members of the 2 groups.

SP15   Schinhan, Jan Philip. "Spanish Folklore from Tampa,
       Florida: (No. VI) Folksongs." *Southern Folklore
       Quarterly* 3:3 (1939):129-163.

       Description of Spanish songs in Tampa, Florida, based
       on 25 field recordings made by Ralph Steele Boggs.
       Analysis of selected music according to characteristics
       of scale, structure, melody, rhythm, harmony, and rendi-
       tion.

*SP16 Walerstein, Marcia. "Ethnic Folklore in the Primary
       School Classroom."

          (Cross-listed as *GL81, *JE79.)
          (See *GL81 for full citation and annotation.)

                    L. SWEDISH (SS) (1-31)

SS1   Archibald, Edith. "Swedish Folklore from the Idaho
       White Pines." *Western Folklore* 24:4 (1965):275-280.

       Characterization of folklore recorded in 1963-64 from
       individuals of Swedish ancestry in the Troy, Idaho,
       area. Includes texts of 2 personal experience stories,
       1 joke, 8 sayings (in Swedish, with English transla-
       tions), 3 game descriptions (with accompanying rhymes),
       1 Wellerism (in Swedish, with English translation), and
       1 ball-bouncing rhyme (with 3 variant endings).

SS2   Barry, Phillips. "Swedish Ballad: 'De Tva Systrarna'
       (Swedish: The Two Sisters)." *Bulletin of the Folk-
       Song Society of the Northeast* 7 (1934):14.

       Presentation of the tune transcription of 1 ballad,
       identified as a version of "The Two Sisters," recorded
       from a singer of Swedish ancestry in Cambridge Massa-
       chusetts. Author notes, "As far as is known, this is
       the first Swedish *folkvisa* or popular ballad ever
       recorded in America."

*SS3   Blegen, Theodore C. "Singing Immigrants and Pioneers."

          (Cross-listed as *DA2, *FN1, *IR10, *NO2.)
          (See *NO2 for full citation and annotation.)

*SS4   Cheney, Thomas E. "Scandinavian Immigrant Stories."
        (Cross-listed as *DA3, *SA1.)
        (See *DA3 for full citation and annotation.)

SS5   Danielson, Larry. "The Dialect Trickster among the
        Kansas Swedes." *Indiana Folklore* 8:1-2 (1975):39-59.

        Discussion of jokes, anecdotes, and personal reminiscences
        about Alfred Bergin, a Lindsborg, Kansas, pastor, in-
        cluding 15 illustrative texts and excerpts from inter-
        views conducted in 1966. Comparisons made between these
        tales and Old World pastor tales, American dialect
        stories, American Indian trickster tales, and Mormon
        stories about J. Golden Kimball. Includes inferences
        about social and psychological functions of the narratives.

SS6   Danielson, Larry. "Public Swedish-American Ethnicity in
        Central Kansas: A Festival and Its Functions." *The
        Swedish Pioneer Historical Quarterly* 25:1 (1974):13-36.

        Description of the *Svensk Hyllings Fest* held in Lindsborg,
        Kansas, in 1969, including characterization of costumes
        worn, dances performed, parades held, foods served, and
        crafts made and sold, followed by an assessment of the
        social and psychological functions of the festival,
        regarded as "fairly representative of other ethnic and
        quasi-ethnic festivals in the contemporary American
        small town." Festival viewed as an example of "cultural
        revivalism," with display of ethnic identity being one
        (but not necessarily the most important) of its purposes.
        Includes 3 photographs taken during the festival described.

SS7   Danielson, Larry. "Swedish-American Mothers: Conservators
        of the Tradition." In *Folklore on Two Continents:
        Essays in Honor of Linda Dégh*, edited by Nikolai
        Burlakoff and Carl Lindahl, pp. 338-347. Bloomington,
        Ind.: Trickster Press, 1980.

        Discussion of the role of women in general and mothers
        in particular as vehicles for the transmission of ethnic
        culture. Discusses the differential adjustment of men
        and women to immigrant life. Concludes that, while
        women have greater difficulty adjusting to the New World,
        they are the primary transmitters of ethnic folklore.
        Data based on historical research and interviews with
        women in Lindsborg, Kansas.

*SS8   Dorson, Richard M. "Blood Stoppers."

        (Cross-listed as *FN2, *FR50, *GE160, *IR20, *SL1.)
        (See *FR50 for full citation and annotation.)

*SS9   Dorson, Richard M. "Dialect Stories of the Upper
        Peninsula: A New Form of American Folklore."

        (Cross-listed as *CO3, *FN3, *FR53, *IR21, *IT17.)
        (See *FR53 for full citation and annotation.)

*SS10   Dorson, Richard M. "Folklore at a Milwaukee Wedding."

        (Cross-listed as *GE161.)
        (See *GE161 for full citation and annotation.)

*SS11   Dorson, Richard M. "Personal Histories." *Western
        Folklore* 7:1 (1948):27-42.

        Characterization of 17 personal experience stories told
        by 4 narrators (2 of Swedish, 1 of Irish-French, and 1
        of Dutch-Irish backgrounds), recorded in 1946 in
        Michigan's Upper Peninsula.
        (Cross-listed as *DU6, *FR56, *IR22.)

 SS12   "The Drowned Tailor." *Colorado Folksong Bulletin* 1:1
        (1962):11-12.

        Presentation of 1 song text (in Swedish, with English
        translation and tune transcription), recorded from a
        Swedish immigrant man in Boulder, Colorado, in 1951.

 SS13   Eisen, Gustav A. "A Swedish Rhyme for Counting Out."
        Journal of American Folk-Lore 2:6 (1889):235.

        Presentation of 1 counting-out rhyme (in Swedish),
        remembered by the author (apparently a Swedish immigrant
        to Delano, California) from his childhood days. Comments
        on the meaning and possible origins of individual words
        in the rhyme.

*SS14   Gronow, Pekka. "Recording for the 'Foreign' Series."
        JEMF Quarterly 12:41 (1976):15-20.

        Presentation of excerpts from interviews with a Swedish
        and a Ukrainian musician concerning their experiences
        as artists on early "foreign" music phonograph recordings
        in the United States, with historical background and
        commentary by the author. Includes photographs of 4
        catalog covers and 1 book cover and 1 of one of the
        artists.
        (Cross-listed as *UK3.)

*SS15   Hand, Wayland D. "California Miners' Folklore: Above
        Ground."

        (Cross-listed as *CH8, *CO5, *GE235, *IR39, *IT28.)
        (See *CO5 for full citation and annotation.)

SS16   Houser, George J. *The Swedish Community at Eriksdale,
        Manitoba.* Canadian Centre for Folk Culture Studies,
        Paper No. 14. Ottawa: National Museum of Man, 1976.
        Pp. v, 109, biographies of key informants, bibliog-
        raphy.

        Study of changes in folklife among Swedes following
        their immigration to Canada, based on interviews con-
        ducted in 1975 with 38 informants who at one time or
        another resided in Eriksdale, Manitoba. Describes and
        analyzes foodways, maternity care and home remedies,
        rites of passage, holiday observances, material culture,
        folk music, weather lore, and folktales, legends, and
        anecdotes. Author finds the anecdote to be the most
        popular form of New World expression.

*SS17   Humphrey, Linda T. "'It Ain't Funny, Buster': The
        Ethnic Riddle-Joke at Citrus Community College."

        (Cross-listed as *GL49, *CH13, *IR47, *IT32, *JA5.)
        (See *GL49 for full citation and annotation.)

SS18   Klein, Barbro Sklute. *Legends and Folk Beliefs in a
        Swedish American Community.* 2 vols. New York: Arno
        Press, 1980. Pp. 826, bibliography.

        A 1970 Indiana University dissertation focusing on folk
        beliefs and legends recorded between 1964 and 1967 by
        the author from Swedish immigrants and their American-
        born descendants in New Sweden, Maine. Includes dis-
        cussion of fieldwork methodology; an historical sketch
        and description of the community of New Sweden; descrip-
        tions of the 29 principal informants and the nature of
        their folklore repertoires and attitudes toward beliefs
        and legends; description of supernatural concepts and
        beings and their manifestations in narratives; and both
        continuities and changes in the kinds of folklore
        described and discussed. Passing mention made in volume
        I of food, material culture, ethnic organizations, and
        local characters in New Sweden, illustrated with excerpts
        from 43 interview sessions, 1 joke, 1 numskull tale, 1
        memorate, 10 legends, 2 tales, and miscellaneous folk
        beliefs. Presentation of 139 texts and interview

segments in volume II, some in English, some in combina-
tions of Swedish and English, some in Swedish only
(with English translations). Includes 2 maps (1 of
Sweden and 1 of New Sweden).

SS19   Lahikainen, Dean. "The Folk Sculpture and Violins of
        Gustaf Nyman." *The Swedish Pioneer Historical
        Quarterly* 17:4 (1976):270-285.

Biographical sketch of a Swedish immigrant man who
settled in Gardner, Massachusetts, and who further
developed and perfected woodcarving skills learned
firsthand in his native Sweden. Traces the evolution
of the artist from a maker of violins to a creator of
wood sculpture representing a variety of human beings
and types common in his adopted homeland. Includes 16
photographs of the artist and his works.

*SS20   Munch, Peter A. "Ten Thousand Swedes: Reflections on a
        Folklore Motif." *Midwest Folklore* 10:2 (1960):61-69.

Discussion of the expression "Ten thousand Swedes/ran
through the weeds,/--chased by one Norwegian," including
commentary on its possible relationship to actual
historical events and to a late 18th-century ballad
(the "Sinclair Ballad"). Hypothesizes that the saying
and associated anecdotes and jests may have originated
in an interethnic milieu in America in which individuals
wished to differentiate socially between Swedes and
Norwegians.
        (Cross-listed as *NO14.)

SS21   Nordquist, Del. "Olaf Krans, Folk Painter from Bishop
        Hill, Illinois." *American-Swedish Historical Founda-
        tion Yearbook*, 1961, pp. 45-58.

Biographical sketch of a Swedish immigrant man who was
a member of the Janssonist colony of Bishop Hill,
Illinois, and who became a painter following the
colony's dissolution, painting scenes of colony life
as well as a variety of other things, ranging from
billboards to portraits to ceilings in public buildings
to animals and hunting scenes. Includes brief characterization of the painter's techniques and outputs.

SS22   Olsen, Louise P. "Tomte." *Journal of American Folk-
        lore* 63:247 (1950):97-98.

Characterization of 2 tales involving the informant's
grandmother's experiences with the *tomte*, a supernatural

being, in Sweden prior to the woman's immigration to Roberts County, South Dakota, in the late 19th century.

SS23 Peterson, Walter F. "Swedish Christmas in Iowa in 1879." *The Swedish Pioneer Historical Quarterly* 12:4 (1961): 160-161.

Re-publication of an 1879 newspaper description, written by an American editor, of the Swedish Christmas celebration in a small Iowa community.

SS24 "The Returning Cavalryman." *Colorado Folksong Bulletin* 1:2 (1962):22-24.

Presentation of 1 song text (in Swedish, with English translation and tune transcription), recorded from a Swedish immigrant man in Boulder, Colorado, in 1951.

SS25 Sklute, Barbro. "Folkstories about Supernatural Beings and Occurrences in Swedish-American Life: A Fading Tradition." *The Swedish Pioneer Historical Quarterly* 17:1 (1966):22-35.

Presentation of transcriptions of portions of tape-recorded interviews with a Swedish immigrant woman in Indianapolis and an American-born man of Swedish ancestry in New Sweden, Maine, based on the author's 1963-64 fieldwork. Emphasis on beliefs in and stories about supernatural beings, illustrated with 6 tale texts. Predicts the decline and eventual demise of such beliefs and tales in the New World.

SS26 "Swedish Song: Lilla Klara." *Colorado Folksong Bulletin* 2 (1963):42-43.

Presentation of 1 song text (in Swedish, with English translation and tune transcription), recorded from a woman in Longmont, Colorado, who learned it from a Swedish immigrant man.

SS27 Torre, Luis. "Of Swedish Roots: A Fiddler Returns to His Home Roof." *The Swedish Pioneer Historical Quarterly* 19:4 (1978):277-287.

Biographical sketch of an immigrant man who learned how to fiddle in his native Sweden and who began fiddling and making and repairing fiddles once again after settling in Minnesota. Describes the man's teaching fiddling to his sons and grandsons, who achieved local and then national fame for their traditional style and

who were honored during a trip to the man's native
Sweden in 1977, where the three generations of Swedish-
American fiddlers played and were singled out as "pre-
servers of the Swedish fiddlers' tradition in America."
Includes 9 photographs of the fiddler, his family, and
performances.

*SS28 Wacker, Peter O., and Trindell, Roger T. "The Log House
       in New Jersey: Origins and Diffusion."

       (Cross-listed as *FN26, *GE699, *SW9.)
       (See *FN26 for full citation and annotation.)

*SS29 Webb, Wheaton Phillips. "The Wart." *New York Folklore
       Quarterly* 2:2 (1946):98-106.

       Humorous survey of cures for warts (with mention also
       made of 1 remedy for goiter and 1 for burns), based on
       data recorded in the Schenevus Valley, New York, from
       individuals of Swedish, German, and Austrian ancestry.
       (Cross-listed as *AU6, *GE703.)

*SS30 Wilden, Albin. "Scandinavian Folklore and Immigrant
       Ballads." *Bulletin of the American Institute of
       Swedish Arts, Literature and Science* n.s. 2:1 (1947):
       2-44.

       Description of ballads, songs, poems, and rhymes by
       American immigrants of Danish, Norwegian, and Swedish
       backgrounds, based on previously published or written
       sources. Includes texts of or excerpts from 25 Swedish
       examples (in Swedish, with English translations), 6
       Danish and 6 Norwegian examples (in English translations
       only). Includes brief prefatory historical sketch of
       Scandinavian immigration to and settlement in the United
       States, particularly in the upper Midwest.
       (Cross-listed as *DA7, *NO22.)

 SS31 Wright, Robert L. *Swedish Emigrant Ballads*. Lincoln,
       Neb.: University of Nebraska Press, 1965. Pp. 209,
       introduction, bibliography, explanatory note,
       appendix, acknowledgments.

       Presentation of texts of 40 Swedish emigrant ballads
       (in Swedish, with English translations), with transcrip-
       tions of 19 tunes included in the appendix. Prefatory
       essay about Swedish immigration to and settlement in
       America. Ballad texts reprinted from previously pub-
       lished 19th- and early 20th-century sources.

LI. SWISS (SW) (1-9)

*SW1 Bronner, Simon J. "'We Live What I Paint and I Paint
      What I See': A Mennonite Artist in Northern Indiana."

      (Cross-listed as *GE97.)
      (See *GE97 for full citation and annotation.)

SW2   Bucher, Robert C. "The Swiss Bank House in Pennsylvania."
      Pennsylvania Folklife 18:2 (1968-1969):3-11.

      Detailed discussion of bankhouses of 18th-century Swiss
      immigrants who settled in the Lebanon-Lancaster area,
      eastern Berks county, and the Oley Valley, Pennsylvania.
      Provides identification of house types, focusing on
      Weinbauren houses, which are well known for their asso-
      ciation with the liquor industry.

*SW3 Burkhart, Charles. "The Church Music of the Old Order
      Amish and Old Colony Mennonites."

      (Cross-listed as *GE110.)
      (See *GE110 for full citation and annotation.)

*SW4 Curtis, Wardon Allan. "'The Light Fantastic' in the
      Central West: Country Dances of Many Nationalities in
      Wisconsin." *The Century Magazine* 73:4 (1907):570-579.

      General description of social dances held among individuals
      of Irish, German, Swiss, and Norwegian backgrounds living
      in Wisconsin in the late 19th century. Includes passing
      references to traditional customs, music, dances, with 15
      photographs of representative "ethnic types," 1 church
      (Swiss), 1 dance scene (Swiss). Argues that the distinc-
      tive ethnicity of these groups is rapidly fading and
      doomed to extinction as the Americanization process
      continues.
      (Cross-listed as *GE127, *IR18, *NO8.)

SW5   Hand, Wayland D. "*Schweizer Schwingen*: Swiss Wrestling
      in California." *California Folklore Quarterly* 2:2
      (1943):77-84.

      Description of a Swiss wrestling match and accompanying
      festivities witnessed in Holtville, California, in 1942.
      Includes comments on wrestlers' training and attire, the
      wrestling pit, the wrestling itself, and festival activi-
      ties held in conjunction with the wrestling (dancing,
      music-making, and an awards ceremony).

*SW6   Martens, Helen. "The Music of Some Religious Minorities
       in Canada."

       (Cross-listed as *AU2, *DU13, *GE384, *RU14.)
       (See *GE384 for full citation and annotation.)

*SW7   Nettl, Bruno. "The Hymns of the Amish: An Example of
       Marginal Survival."

       (Cross-listed as *GE416.)
       (See *GE416 for full citation and annotation.)

*SW8   Umble, John. "The Old Order Amish, Their Hymns and
       Hymn Tunes."

       (Cross-listed as *GE697.)
       (See *GE697 for full citation and annotation.)

*SW9   Wacker, Peter O., and Trindell, Roger T. "The Log House
       in New Jersey: Origins and Diffusion."

       (Cross-listed as *FN26, *GE699, *SS28.)
       (See *FN26 for full citation and annotation.)

LII. SYRIAC (SY) (1)

SY1   Lethin, Joyce Bynum. "Syriac Proverbs from California."
       Western Folklore 31:2 (1972):87-101.

       Brief historical sketch of Syriac-speaking Christians or
       "Assyrians," followed by a listing of 35 proverbs (in
       Syriac, with English translations), recorded in 1970 from
       individuals of Syriac ancestry in San Francisco. Relates
       proverbs to well-known stories and customs and includes
       explanations of meanings informants provide for proverbs.

LIII. SYRIAN (SZ) (1-5)

SZ1 Hanna, Marion. "Around the Narghile: Lore of Old Syria."
     New York Folklore Quarterly 3:3 (1947):223-230.

Miscellaneous folklore items derived from personal
recollections of informants of Syrian descent. Includes
characterization of 1 saint's legend, 2 *atobas*, 1 competi-
tive song involving animals, 1 numskull tale, 1 tall tale,
1 story involving a priest, 1 story about the devil, 1
animal tale, text of 1 funeral and 1 wedding song (all
in English), followed by the presentation of 2 proverbs,
a discussion of superstitions, death customs, and courtship and marriage customs.

*SZ2 Jones, Louis C. "The Evil-Eye among European-Americans."

(Cross-listed as *GL51, *GR21, *HU17, *IN1, *IR50,
*IT35, *JE35, *PL39, *RU10.)
(See *GL51 for full citation and annotation.)

*SZ3 Naff, Alixa. "Belief in the Evil Eye Among the Christian
      Syrian-Lebanese in America."

(Cross-listed as *LE3.)
(See *LE3 for full citation and annotation.)

*SZ4 Qureshi, Regula. "Ethnomusicological Research among
      Canadian Communities of Arab and East Indian Origin."
      Ethnomusicology 16:3 (1972):381-396.

Brief historical sketches of the immigration to and
settlement in Canada of Arabs from Syria, Lebanon, and
Egypt and of East Indians, mostly from India and Pakistan,
followed by a discussion of kinds of performance contexts
in which music is played. Categorizes music as classical,
folk, popular, and religious and enumerates research
accomplishments and prospects. Based principally on a
survey conducted in Alberta, Canada, in 1971-72.
(Cross-listed as *EG1, *ID3, *LE4, *PA1.)

SZ5 Wilson, Howard Barrett. "Notes of Syrian Folk-Lore
     Collected in Boston." *Journal of American Folk-Lore*
     16:62 (1903):133-147.

Listing of miscellaneous folklore items obtained from
Syrians living in the Boston area. Includes 19 dreams,
12 riddles, 24 superstitions, brief descriptions of
curing and tattooing customs, games, marriage customs, 1
folktale, and 1 allegorical narrative (all in English),
preceded by a brief comment on the Syrians of Boston.

LIV.   TURKISH (TU) (1-5)

TU1   Jansen, William Hugh. "Some Turkish Folktales."
      Hoosier Folklore 5:4 (1946):136-149.

      Presentation of 24 folktale texts, written out by
      Turkish students studying at Indiana University in 1946
      (10 Nasreddin Hodja tales, 4 Bektashi tales, and 10
      miscellaneous tales).

*TU2   Lee, Dorothy D. "Three Romances from Pontos."

      (Cross-listed as *GR28.)
      (See *GR28 for full citation and annotation.)

*TU3   Musick, Ruth Ann. *Green Hills of Magic: West Virginia
      Folktales from Europe.*

      (Cross-listed as *AR9, *AU4, *CZ8, *HU24, *IR74,
      *IT52, *PL52, *RO4, *RU16, *YU8.)
      (See *IT52 for full citation and annotation.)

*TU4   Nichols, Mrs. Priscilla Miller. "Greek Lore from
      Syracuse, N.Y."

      (Cross-listed as *GR30.)
      (See *GR30 for full citation and annotation.)

TU5   Wilson, Barbara. "Merry Tales from Turkey." *New York
      Folklore Quarterly* 7:2 (1951):125-130.

      Characterization of 10 Turkish folktales (6 about
      Nasreddin Hodja), recorded from a Turkish informant in
      New York.

LV.   UKRAINIAN (UK) (1-35)

*UK1   Cincura, Andrew. "Slovak and Ruthenian Easter Eggs in
      America: The Impact of Culture Contact on Immigrant
      Art and Custom."

      (Cross-listed as *SK3.)
      (See *SK3 for full citation and annotation.)

*UK2   Cutting, Edith E. "Easter Eggs in the Triple Cities."
        (Cross-listed as *CZ4.)
        (See *CZ4 for full citation and annotation.)

*UK3   Gronow, Pekka. "Recording for the 'Foreign' Series."
        (Cross-listed as *SS14.)
        (See *SS14 for full citation and annotation.)

*UK4   Jordan, Terry G. "A Russian-German Folk House in North
        Texas."
        (Cross-listed as *GE319, *RU11.)
        (See *RU11 for full citation and annotation.)

UK5   Joyce, Rosemary. "Pysanky: The Ukrainian Easter Egg in
        Ohio." *Journal of the Ohio Folklore Society* n.s.
        5 (1978):3-9.

        Discussion of the wax-resist process of decorating Easter
        eggs (*pysanky*) as found among individuals of Ukrainian
        descent in Ohio. Includes brief descriptions of deco-
        rating techniques, implements used, and technological
        changes made in the process in the United States,
        accompanied by 4 legends.

UK6   Klymasz, Robert B. *A Bibliography of Ukrainian Folklore
        in Canada, 1902-64.* National Museum of Canada,
        Anthropology Papers No. 21. Ottawa, 1969. Pp. vi, 53.

        Bibliography of 463 items with brief descriptive annota-
        tions, arranged in 14 categories (history of Ukrainian
        folklore in Canada, 1902-64; folklore; customs, beliefs,
        traditions, rituals; verbal folklore; folktales and
        anecdotes; fictitious immigrant heroes in popular publi-
        cations; folksong and folk music; the immigrant theater
        and folk drama; folk dance; minor folklore genres; folk
        speech; namelore; folk arts; recordings; unpublished
        collections; films). Includes an introductory survey
        essay (pp. 1-5).

UK7   Klymasz, Robert B. "The Case for Slavic Folklore in
        Canada." In *Slavs in Canada*, vol. 1, pp. 110-120.
        Proceedings of the First National Conference on
        Canadian Slavs. Edmonton: Inter-University Committee
        on Canadian Slavs, 1966.

        Notes that Slavic folklore has been ignored in Canada
        and that work done tends to view folklore negatively by

contrasting it with literary works. Focuses on Ukrainian-
Canadian folksongs recorded by the author in western
Canada in 1963–64, with emphasis on traditional songs
which reflect "the process of acculturation and Canadianization." Songs discussed categorized as casual or non-
ritual and non-casual or ritual, the latter of which are
regarded as survivals in Canada because they are "divorced
from the old, calendaric rituals and various ceremonies
with which they were genetically associated." Includes
excerpts from 16 folksongs (15 in English translations,
1 in Ukrainian) that depict such experiences as the departure for and arrival and settlement in Canada. Asserts
that "the Ukrainian-Canadian immigrant folksong cycle is
non-ritual (casual) in essence."

UK8   Klymasz, Robert B. *Continuity and Change: The Ukrainian
      Folk Heritage in Canada.* Canadian Centre for Folk
      Culture Studies of the National Museum of Man. Ottawa,
      1972. Pp. 56.

      Catalog describing Ukrainian arts and crafts presented as
      an exhibit at the Canadian Centre for Folk Culture Studies
      of the National Museum of Man, Ottawa. Introductory essay
      distinguishes among arts and crafts brought to Canada by
      turn-of-the-century Ukrainian immigrants, arts and crafts
      that emerged as multiple waves of Ukrainian immigrants
      intermingled in Canada and forged a "national Ukrainian
      art" stressing common symbols of ethnic identity, and arts
      and crafts of contemporary times characterized by experi-
      mentation with new materials and transformations of familiar
      objects, motifs, and symbols for mass consumption. Includes
      3 color and 8 black-and-white photographs and descriptions
      of 121 exhibit objects, including household utensils,
      clothing and accessories, jewelry, textiles, musical in-
      struments, foods, dolls, cookbooks, and campaign buttons.

UK9   Klymasz, Robert B. "The Ethnic Folk Festival in North
      America Today." In *Ukrainians in American and Canadian
      Society: Contributions to the Sociology of Ethnic Groups*,
      edited by Wsevolod W. Isajiw, pp. 199–211. Jersey City:
      M.P. Kots Publishing, 1976.

      Distinguishes among "closed, in-group" ethnic festivals,
      single-ethnic-group-oriented public festivals, and multi-
      ethnic public festivals, with emphasis on the second, illus-
      trated by a description and analysis of the National
      Ukrainian Festival in Dauphin, Manitoba, Canada, initiated

in 1966. Asserts that the "Festival affords the ethnic
group with an outlet for cultural self-expression that
no other festive occasion is able to match." Characterizes the festival as "a unique blend of the old and
the new" which builds "on the ruins of a shattered
immigrant folk heritage" and assigns "added social and
cultural status to a minority group which has succeeded
in relating its particular sense of ethnicity to the
needs of the community at large."

*UK10 Klymasz, Robert B. "The Ethnic Joke in Canada Today."

      (Cross-listed as *GL53, *FR71, *IC3, *IT38, *JE40.)
      (See *GL53 for full citation and annotation.)

UK11 Klymasz, Robert B. *Folk Narrative among Ukrainian-*
      Canadians in Western Canada. Canadian Centre for
      Folk Culture Studies, Paper No. 4. Ottawa: National
      Museum of Man, 1973. Pp. 133, bibliography.

Survey of folk narratives among Ukrainian-Canadians in
western Canada, based on fieldwork conducted from 1963 to
1966 and in 1968. Assesses the effects of immigration on
Old World forms and the creation of new ethnic phenomena.
Narratives reflect the pioneering experience, the transplantation of Old World ideas to the New World, and the
embarrassing incidents emerging from the immigrant period.
Includes texts of 46 tales and 28 anecdotes and jokes
(in English) in appendices, an index of motifs and tale
types, and 17 photographs of Ukrainian-Canadians, their
homes and churches, and their work sites.

*UK12 Klymasz, Robert B. "From Immigrant to Ethnic Folklore:
      A Canadian View of Process and Transition."

      (Cross-listed as *GL54.)
      (See *GL54 for full citation and annotation.)

UK13 Klymasz, Robert B. *An Introduction to the Ukrainian-*
      Canadian Folksong Cycle. National Museums of Canada,
      Bulletin No. 234, Folklore Series No. 8. Ottawa,
      1970. Pp. ix, 106, foreword, introduction, list of
      singers, appendix, 4 flexidiscs.

Presentation of 28 folksong texts (in Ukrainian, with
English translations and tune transcriptions), recorded
by the author from individuals of Ukrainian ancestry in
1963-65 in western Canada. Emphasis on casual or non-
ritual songs that focus on the experiences of emigrating,

reactions (both positive and negative) of the immigrants
to Canada, everyday life experiences of the immigrants,
and life-cycle events (illustrated with 4 wedding songs,
1 funeral lament, and 1 commemorative lament). Includes
34 photographs of singers, musicians, dancers, and
scenes from the communities in which the data were
recorded. Emphasis on songs composed in Canada or those
from the Old World that have undergone considerable
"Canadianization."

UK14   Klymasz, Robert B.   "The Letter in Canadian Ukrainian
        Folklore." *Journal of the Folklore Institute* 6:1
        (1969):39-49.

Discussion of the dilemma faced by Ukrainian immigrants
to Canada who are no longer able to interact face-to-
face with relatives and friends at home. Asserts that
the concept of communication via letter manifests itself
in revisions of old, and in the creation of new, folksongs in which letters and letter-writing motifs appear;
of folksongs that are intended to function as letters;
and of published letter-parodies which stereotype the
letter-writing process.

UK15   Klymasz, Robert B.   "Social and Cultural Motifs in
        Canadian Ukrainian Lullabies." *The Slavic and East
        European Journal* 12:2 (1968):176-183.

Discussion of lullabies recorded by the author in 1963-
64 from Ukrainian immigrants and their descendants in
western Canada. Argues that lullabies function as a
form of female protest and as an outlet for repressed
emotions brought about by various conflicts. Includes
texts of 5 and partial texts of another 10 lullabies
(in Ukrainian).

UK16   Klymasz, Robert B.   "'Sounds You Never Heard Before':
        Ukrainian Country Music in Western Canada."
        Ethnomusicology 16:3 (1972):372-380.

Notes that Anglo-American country music and the commercial phonograph recording industry have contributed
significantly to the devolution of the folksong and
folk music heritage of Ukrainian-Canadians. Characterizes recorded Ukrainian-Canadian music and song as transformations of traditional old country music, on the one
hand, and as due to new needs, on the other, and illustrates the adaptation and translation of Anglo-American
country music into Ukrainian. States that Ukrainian

country music in western Canada "is largely a product
of the on-going acculturative process." Includes texts
(in Ukrainian, with English translations) of 1 old
carol and 1 Anglo-American song translated into Ukrainian
("This Land Is Your Land"--text in Ukrainian and English).

UK17 Klymasz, Robert B. "Syllabo-Stanzaic Stability and the
   Ukrainian *Kolomyjka*: A Case Study." In *Studies*
   Presented to Professor Roman Jakobson by His Students,
   pp. 149-164. Cambridge, Mass.: Slavica Publishers,
   Inc., 1968.

Linguistic, content, structural, and musical analyses
of a parody of a Ukrainian church mass, recorded by the
author in Winnipeg, Manitoba, Canada, in 1961, with
emphasis on "the divergencies from the normal 14-syllable
line of the *kolomyjka*." Notes that verses of the
kolomyjka are chanted and the chorus sung. Transcribed
text of the mass parody and excerpts from it presented
in Ukrainian.

UK18 Klymasz, Robert B. "Ukrainian-Canadian Folktales." In
   Folklore of Canada, edited by Edith Fowke, pp. 279-287.
   Toronto: McClelland and Stewart Limited, 1976.

Presentation of 3 folktale texts (reprinted from an un-
dated previously published work), recorded by the author
from individuals of Ukrainian ancestry in Alberta and
Saskatchewan, Canada, in 1964 and 1965.

UK19 Klymasz, Robert B. *The Ukrainian Easter Egg in Canada*.
   Ottawa: National Museums of Canada, 1969. Pp. 8.

Brief discussion of the origins and history of egg
decoration among Ukrainians from pre-Christian to contemporary times, with emphasis on the craft as it is
carried out among Ukrainian immigrants and their New
World descendants in Canada. Includes brief descriptions
of ornamentation techniques, major motifs painted on
eggs, beliefs and customs relating to eggs in general
and eggs prepared for Easter in particular, changes in
ornamentation techniques introduced since World War II,
largely as a result of an influx of new Ukrainian immigrants. Notes that "the Ukrainian Easter egg in Canada
has become the vivid symbol of Ukrainian ethnicity."
Written to accompany an exhibit of Ukrainian-Canadian
arts and crafts at the National Museum of Man in Ottawa,
spring 1969. (Also available in a French-language
edition.)

UK20   Klymasz, Robert B. *Ukrainian Folklore in Canada.* New
          York: Arno Press, 1980. Pp. iv, 324, bibliography.

          A 1970 Indiana University dissertation focusing on
          changes in ethnic folklore from an immigrant to an ethnic
          stage among Ukrainians of 3 areas: Dauphin in Manitoba,
          Yorkton in Saskatchewan, and Vegreville in Alberta.
          Data recorded from 1963 to 1966 and in 1968 from over 100
          informants. Author argues that Old World traditions
          have given way to new, more dynamic contemporary ethnic
          expression. Evidence for change based on the study and
          analysis of Old and New World narratives, folk beliefs,
          humor, rituals, music, and festivals. Includes 46 Old
          World narratives, 28 New World anecdotes (in appendices),
          an index of tale types and motifs, a list of informants,
          and a discography of 42 long-playing phonograph records.

UK21   Klymasz, Robert B. "Ukrainian Folklore in Canada: The
          Big Put-Down." *Journal of Ukrainian Graduate Studies*
          3:1 (1978):66-77.

          Historical sketch of Ukrainian-Canadian folklore study,
          followed by a description of various stages through
          which the tradition can be said to have evolved. Empha-
          sis on the shift from community participation in tradi-
          tions to a division between performers and audience,
          from oral transmission to mechanical means of learning,
          transmitting, and perpetuating folklore, from an emphasis
          on verbal to that on audible and visual phenomena.
          States the need for more fieldwork, explores the role
          folklore plays in perpetuating a sense of Ukrainian
          cultural heritage in Canada. Includes 14 riddle jokes
          about Ukrainians (without answers), 1 story recorded by
          the author in 1965 about Ukrainians' tendency to talk
          excessively.

UK22   Klymasz, Robert B. "The Ukrainian Folksong in Canada."
          *Blue Yodel: Indiana University Folksong Club News-
          letter* 3:3 (1965):3-4.

          Brief note indicating the richness of folklore in general
          and folksongs in particular among Ukrainian immigrants
          and their Canadian-born descendants in western Canada,
          speculating about possible reasons for folklorists'
          failure to document this rich heritage and describing
          the author's preliminary field surveys in the summers
          of 1963-64 of Ukrainian-Canadian folksong cycle tradi-
          tions.

UK23   Klymasz, Robert B.   "Ukrainian Incest Ballads from
       Western Canada." *Canadian Folk Music Journal* 1
       (1973):35-37.

       Presentation of 3 ballad texts (in English translations),
       recorded by the author from individuals of Ukrainian
       ancestry in western Canada in 1964 to 1965. Ballads
       describe and characterize reactions to incest.

UK24   Klymasz, Robert B. *The Ukrainian Winter Folksong Cycle
       in Canada.* Musical transcriptions by Kenneth Peacock.
       National Museum of Canada, Bulletin No. 236, Folklore
       Series No. 9. Ottawa, 1970. Pp. ix, 156, bibliog-
       raphy, discography, 4 flexidiscs.

       Presentation of 50 folksong texts from the Ukrainian
       winter folksong cycle (in Ukrainian, with English
       translations and tune transcriptions), categorized as
       secular carols, religious carols, and mummers' songs.
       Songs recorded from 1963 to 1966 from 30 Ukrainian-
       Canadian informants. The origin and evolution of the
       songs, their traditional form and style, and the effects
       of immigration and modernization on song form, style,
       and function discussed in introduction. Includes 26
       photographs.

UK25   Klymasz, Robert B.   "We Shall Live in Our Art." *Craft
       Dimensions artisanales* 2 (1971):2-4.

       Brief characterization of Ukrainian immigration to
       Canada, stressing the kinds of folk arts, crafts, and
       music from the homeland of the immigrants which crystal-
       lized into recognizable ethnic symbols in Canada, blur-
       ring regional distinctions common in the western
       Ukraine. Written to accompany an exhibit of Ukrainian
       folk arts and crafts "acquired by the Museum of Man in
       recent years" and exhibited at the National Library,
       Ottawa, in October 1971. Includes 1 photograph of an
       embroidered Ukrainian woman's jacket blouse and sash.
       Text in English and French.

UK26   Klymasz, Robert B., and Porter, James. "Traditional
       Ukrainian Balladry in Canada." *Western Folklore*
       33:2 (1974):89-132.

       Brief discussion of the history of Ukrainian ballad
       scholarship, followed by a characterization of a corpus
       of 56 ballads recorded from Ukrainian-Canadians from
       1961 to 1966. Includes commentary on ballad functions,

content, changes, poetics, structure, and style. Emphasizes the fact that ballads are retained and perpetuated
as the most popular narrative folksong genre and that
these songs both transmit, and comment positively and
negatively upon, a traditional "code of behavior."
Presents 11 ballad texts (in Ukrainian, with English
translations and tune transcriptions), 5 additional
musical examples, and a list of singer-informants.

*UK27 Luciw, Wasyl O., and Wynnsky, George. "Pysanka and
        Other Decorated Easter Eggs in Pennsylvania."

        (Cross-listed as *PL48, *RU13.)
        (See *PL48 for full citation and annotation.)

UK28   Medwidsky, Bohdan. "A Ukrainian Assassination Ballad
        in Canada." *Canadian Folk Music Journal* 6 (1978):
        30-37.

        Discussion of a Ukrainian ballad that evolved following
        "the assassination of Empress Elizabeth of Austria-
        Hungary in Geneva on September 10, 1898." Includes
        reprinted descriptions of the assassination, reprinted
        and translated text of 1 version of the ballad, excerpts
        from 2 interviews in which the ballad and its possible
        origin are discussed, and 2 texts (in English transla-
        tions) of the ballad recorded from individuals of
        Ukrainian ancestry in Canada.

*UK29 Meltzer, Herbert S. "Jewish Tales."

        (Cross-listed as *JE45.)
        (See *JE45 for full citation and annotation.)

*UK30 Mitchell, John Fletcher, and Driedger, Leo. "Canadian
        Ethnic Folk Art: An Exploratory Study in Winnipeg."

        (Cross-listed as *LA2.)
        (See *LA2 for full citation and annotation.)

UK31   Moran, Joyce Demcher. "Miz Ukraini: 'We are from the
        Ukraine.'" *Pennsylvania Folklife* 28:2 (1978/79):12-17.

        Reconstruction of Ukrainian immigration based on
        reminiscences of the author's grandparents. Includes
        information about the hardships of the immigrant, work,
        family relationships, contacts with relatives in the
        Ukraine, and celebration of holidays.

*UK32   Peacock, Kenneth. "Establishing Perimeters for Ethno-
musicological Field Research in Canada: On-Going
Projects and Future Possibilities at the Canadian
Centre for Folk Culture Studies."

       (Cross-listed as *GL66, *CH21, *FR91, *GE428, *HU25,
*IC4, *ID2, *IT57, *JA9, *LI5, *NO19, *RU19.)
(See *GL66 for full citation and annotation.)

*UK33   Peacock, Kenneth. *Twenty Ethnic Songs from Western
Canada.*

       (Cross-listed as *CZ10, *GE429, *HU26, *RU21.)
(See *RU21 for full citation and annotation.)

UK34   Proracki, Anthony, and Henderson, Alan. "Ukrainian-
Canadian Folk Music of the Waterford Area." *Canadian
Folk Music Journal* 2 (1974):19-28.

       Presentation of 6 secular folksong texts (in Ukrainian,
with English translations and tune transcriptions),
recorded by the author from Ukrainian immigrants and
their Canadian-born descendants in Norfolk County,
Ontario, Canada, in 1974.

UK35   Waibel, John. "Ukrainian Student Folklore." *Journal
of the Ohio Folklore Society* n.s. 3:1 (1974):29-32.

       Presentation of 2 anecdotes, 1 tale involving bewitch-
ment and human-to-bird transformation, 1 description of
water battles engaged in by children following the church
celebration of the baptism of Christ. Recorded from 2
informants of Ukrainian background in Lorain, Ohio, in
1973.

LVI.   WELSH (WE) (1-8)

*WE1   Bethke, Robert. "Chester County Widow Wills (1714-
1800): A Folklife Source."

       (Cross-listed as *IR9, *SC2.)
(See *IR9 for full citation and annotation.)

WE2   Biondi, Mary H. "Take the Gray Basin...." *New York*
          Folklore Quarterly 19:3 (1963):183-195.

          Discussion of favorite family recipes (over several
          generations) and traditions associated with cooking.
          Includes 27 recipes for food and beverages, 2 cough
          remedies, 1 cure for asthma, 1 cure for colds, 1 recipe
          for soap liniment, 1 set of ingredients for fertilizer,
          and the presentation of 1 Welsh grace (in Welsh, with
          English translation).

WE3   Cowan, John L. "Welsh Superstitions." *Journal of*
          American Folk-Lore 15:57 (1902):131-132.

          Notes presenting 2 beliefs commonly held by Americans of
          Welsh descent, with description of the occasions on
          which the author learned these beliefs (in Pennsylvania).

WE4   Edwards, Jane Spencer. "Wills and Inventories of the
          First Purchasers of the Welsh Tract." *Pennsylvania*
          Folklife 23:2 (1973-1974):2-15.

          Analysis of the wills of 14 individuals who came from
          Penllyn, Wales, to the newly purchased land in Merion,
          Philadelphia, in the late 17th and early 18th century.
          Argues that wills and inventories provide clues to the
          standards of living within a community and to items in
          general use at particular times. Lists 14 persons and
          the contents of their wills, as well as 9 categories of
          information found in wills, including slaves and servants,
          livestock, tools, crops and foodstuffs, household
          utensils, wearing apparel, and furniture. Appendix
          presents inventories from the wills of 7 people.

WE5   Halpert, Lt. Herbert. "Three Tales from Gwent." *Journal*
          of American Folklore 58:227 (1945):51-52.

          Presentation of 3 folktale texts, recorded by the author
          in 1944 in Calgary, Alberta, Canada, from a native of
          Wales.

WE6   Kirkland, Edwin C. "Welsh Folksongs." *Tennessee Folk-*
          lore Society Bulletin 9:4 (1943):1-7.

          Presentation (in English) of texts of 2 rhymes (recited
          at Christmastime) and 4 songs (with musical transcrip-
          tions), recorded in 1942 from an informant of Welsh
          background, from Knoxville, Tennessee.

*WE7 Korson, George. "Coal Miners."

    (Cross-listed as *GL55, *IR56, *SK7.)
    (See *GL55 for full citation and annotation.)

*WE8 Mead, Mrs. Jane Thompson. "Proverbs: Sayings from
    Westfield, Chautauqua Co."

    (Cross-listed as *GE387, *IR67.)
    (See *IR67 for full citation and annotation.)

LVII. YUGOSLAV (YU) (1-10)

YU1 Delovich, Homer W. "III. Witch Stories of European
    Origin: 3. The Deceased Needed a Shave." *West
    Virginia Folklore* 6:1 (1955):14-15.

    Characterization (in English) of 1 story, told to the
    author by his Yugoslav grandfather, about a man's en-
    counter with the devil.

*YU2 Dunin, Elsie Ivancich. *South Slavic Dance in California:
    A Compendium for the Years 1924-1977.* Palo Alto,
    Calif.: Ragusan Press, 1979. Pp. v, 204, acknowledg-
    ments, introduction, sample dance description, inter-
    pretation.

    Listing of South Slavic (Bulgarian and Yugoslav) folk
    dances documented in books, periodicals, and record
    syllabi and taught by folk dance instructors in Califor-
    nia between 1924 and 1977. Includes 5 tables which
    identify dances by name, sources of information about
    South Slavic dances in California, instructors, dates
    on which and places in which instruction occurred.
    Survey indicates that of 1,810 dances to which reference
    is made, 50% were "taught in the 1970's (seven years),"
    33% "were taught in the 1960's (ten years)," and 17%
    "were taught in the 1950's (ten years)." Notes that folk
    dance instruction is "an important indicator of dance
    repertoire."
    (Cross-listed as *BU1.)

YU3   Dunin, Elsie Ivancich. "Winter Dance Events among South
         Slavic Immigrants in California." *Makedonski Folklor
         (Le Folklore Macedonien)* 8:15-16 (1975):165-175.

         Description of 4 winter "events" held by Yugoslav-Ameri-
         cans in California in 1974-75 at which social dancing
         occurred, with a listing of the specific dances in which
         participants engaged. Social dances seen as source of
         cultural continuity. Emphasis on structural similarities
         among social dance events and on dance repertoires in
         events of differing kinds (e.g., pre-Christmas and pre-
         Easter events and fund-raising events).

*YU4   Forry, Mark. "*Bécar* Music in the Serbian Community of
         Los Angeles: Evolution and Transformation."

         (Cross-listed as *SE3.)
         (See *SE3 for full citation and annotation.)

*YU5   March, Richard. "The Tamburitza Tradition in the Calumet
         Region."

         (Cross-listed as *CR6, *SE5.)
         (See *CR6 for full citation and annotation.)

*YU6   Monahan, Kathleen. "The Role of Ethnic Record Companies
         in Cultural Maintenance: A Look at Greyko."

         (Cross-listed as *GL60, *CR7.)
         (See *GL60 for full citation and annotation.)

*YU7   Musick, Ruth Ann. "Chapter 16, Immigrant Ghosts."

         (Cross-listed as *CZ6, *HU22, *IT50.)
         (See *CZ6 for full citation and annotation.)

*YU8   Musick, Ruth Ann. *Green Hills of Magic: West Virginia
         Folktales from Europe.*

         (Cross-listed as *AR9, *AU4, *CZ8, *HU24, *IR74,
         *IT52, *PL52, *RO4, *RU16, *TU3.)
         (See *IT52 for full citation and annotation.)

*YU9   Musick, Ruth Ann. "The Trickster Story in West Virginia."

         (Cross-listed as *IT54, *RU17.)
         (See *IT54 for full citation and annotation.)

*YU10   Rennick, Robert M. "Successive Name-Changing: A Popular
         Theme in Onomastic Folklore and Literature."

         (Cross-listed as *GE446, *JE52, *SC35.)
         (See *JE52 for full citation and annotation.)

INDEXES

I. FOLKLORE FORMS AND TOPICS INDEX

amulets
    GE342; GR20; IT30; JE85
architecture
    GE317; GE323; GE324; GE327; GE336; GE342; GE347; GE376;
    GE402; GE412; GE567; GE604; GE672; GE673; GE678; GE738;
    GE748; HU28; NO7; PL37; SS16; SW2
  barns and barn raising
    DU15; DU24; GE2; GE132; GE159; GE212; GE217; GE218; GE288;
    GE355; GE362; GE536; GE544; GE589; GE602; GE604; GE619;
    GE640; GE665; GE672; GE688
  barracks
    DU24
  churches
    GE321; GE376
  houses and outbuildings
    DU5; FN9; *FR98 (*GE521); GE17; GE23; GE102; GE118; GE175;
    GE188; GE196; GE216; GE234; GE237; GE288; GE307; GE327;
    GE328; GE332; GE346; GE347; GE362; GE364, GE368; GE369;
    GE370; GE371; GE373; GE376; GE377; GE378; GE379; GE404;
    GE410; GE412; GE552; GE702; HU20; JE53; PL3; *RU11 (*GE319,
    *UK4); SC17; SW2
  log houses
    *FN26 (*GE699, *SS28, *SW9); GE104
  saunas
    FN9; FN18; FN23; FN24
  water mills
    GE354
art
    GE3; GE95; *GE97 (*SW1); GE163; GE201; GE212; GE324;
    GE336; GE345; GE471; GE472; GE486; GE488; GE492; GE493;
    GE503; GE504; GE505; GE506; GE507; GE508; GE509; GE530;
    GE552; GE604; GE640; GE672; GE673; GE675; GE693; GE711;
    GE712; GE748; GE761; *LA2 (*UK30); NO5; RU23; UK8; UK25
    See also painting and painters.
  baptismal certificates
    GE79

fraktur
    GE3; GE75; GE212; GE324; GE348; GE355; GE356; GE425; GE482;
    GE503; GE511; GE552; GE553; GE604; GE653; GE672; GE673;
    GE735
artists
    GE345; GE348; GE355; GE511; GE530
    See also painting and painters.
  performing
    See fiddling and fiddlers; groups, performing; musicians;
    singing and singers; storytelling and storytellers.
Ascension Day
    DA5; GE89; GE273; GE338; GE546; GE575
Assumption Day
    PL56
auctions and auctioneers
    GE84; GE120
ballads
    See songs, ballads.
baptism
    GE240; GR36; HU21
    See also art, baptismal certificates.
Bar Mitzvah and Bat Mitzvah
    JE75
beliefs
    GL13; GL33; *GL43 (*GR9, *IR31, *IT21, *JE24, *PL28, *PO6,
    *SP7); *GL48 (*IR37, *SC19); GL58; *GL75 (*FR103); GL76;
    *AR3 (*RU16); BU3; CH5; CH15; CH16; CH19; CO2; *CO5 (*CH8,
    *GE235, *IR39, *IT28, *SS15); CO6; *CO7 (*FI2, *FN14,
    *IR40, *IT29, *SE4); CO9; CZ12; *DU3 (*FR22, *GE36);
    DU10; DU21; DU23; FI6; *FN5 (*CO4, *FR54); FN22; FR1;
    *FR5 (*IR1); FR27; *FR50 (*FN2, *GE160, *IR20, *SL1,
    *SS8); *FR80 (*GE385); FR96; FR97; FR104; FR117; GE4; GE11;
    GE12; GE14; GE17; GE24; GE38; GE40; GE41; GE47; GE53; GE54;
    GE64; GE71; GE79; GE83; GE89; *GE113 (*GR1, *SK2); GE114;
    GE123; GE134; GE135; GE137; GE141; GE149; GE153; GE154; GE157;
    GE158; GE162; GE163; GE181; GE184; GE187; GE189; GE191;
    GE195; GE202; GE208; GE212; GE229; GE279; GE283; GE285;
    GE288; GE289; GE292; GE293; GE320; GE340; GE342; GE361;
    GE363; GE365; GE367; GE369; GE374; GE391; GE394; GE411;
    GE419; GE421; GE427; GE442; GE519; GE520; GE524; GE526;
    GE528; GE538; GE539; GE555; GE562; GE564; GE569; GE580;
    GE582; GE583; GE591; GE594; GE601; GE620; GE623; GE630;
    GE636; GE638; GE653; GE668; GE676; GE677; GE679;
    GE712; GE713; GE714; GE717; *GE722 (*JE83); GE725; GE726;
    GE727; GE738; GE750; GE753; GE770; GE773; *GR6 (*JE17);
    GR11; GR13; GR14; GR20; GR25; GR27; *GR30 (*TU4); GR31;
    GR33; GY2; GY3; HU3; IR23; IR30; IR51; IR53; IR57; *IR58
    (*IT40, *JE43, *RU12); *IR60 (*SC24); IR77; *IR78 (*DU14,

*FR88, *GE424, *SC30); IR90; IR93; IR103; *IR116 (*SC42);
*IR117 (*SC43); IR118; IT5; IT11; IT13; IT30; IT31; IT44;
IT46; IT49; IT58; IT60; IT64; IT68; IT74; *IT83 (*JE80);
IT84; IT86; JA6; JE14; JE26; JE29; JE30; JE75; JE85; *LE3
(*SZ3); *LI4 (*RU5); NO20; PL2; PL14; PL46; PL50; PL51;
PL56; PL62; PO9; PO17; RO5; RO6; RU4; *RU24 (*GE684); SC36;
SC39; SP8; SS18; SS25; SZ1; SZ5; UK19; WE3

Belsnickel and Belsnickling
    GE60; *GE113 (*GR1, *SK2); GE116; GE445; GE475; GE559;
    GE560; GE561; GE563; GE565; GE566; GE650; GE713
birth
    See pregnancy and childbirth.
bundling
    GE15; GE74; GE287; GE645
cant
    IR41
carnivals
    GE565; PO2
carols
    See songs, carols.
chants
    JE84; SZ1; UK17
charms
    *AR3 (*RU6); CO8; FN7; FN8; *FR80 (*GE385); GE98; GE154;
    GE157; GE202; GE208; GE292; GE293; GE481; GE545; GE760;
    GR3; GR4; IR30; *IR60 (*SC24); IT13; JA6; NO16; PL83; RO6;
    *SS29 (*AU6, *GE703); UK35
childbirth
    See pregnancy and childbirth.
children's folklore
    See folklore, children's.
Christmas
    CZ3; CZ12; DA5; DU4; DU5; DU23; GE24; GE27; GE60; GE67;
    GE89; *GE113 (*GR1, *SK2); GE114; GE115; GE116; GE167;
    GE175; GE183; GE208; GE227; GE239; GE240; GE250; GE276;
    GE310; GE320; GE336; GE422; GE442; GE469; GE472; GE475;
    GE517; GE558; GE559; GE560; GE561; GE563; GE564; GE565;
    GE566; GE616; GE635; GE640; GE704; GE720; GE721; GE725;
    GE727; GE735; GE767; HU21; IT82; NO18; PL2; PL32; PL51;
    PL54; RO2; *RU24 (*GE684); *SE7 (*BE3); SL3; SS23; WE6;
    YU3
    See also Belsnickel and Belsnickling.
circumcision
    GE10; JE75
clothing
    See costume and dress.

Columbus Day
    IT71
conjuring
    FR27; FR55; GE112; GE291
Corpus Christi Day
    GE86
costume and dress
    CH3; CH5; GE22; GE63; GE130; GE209; GE215; GE282; GE298;
    GE299; GE301; GE337; GE402; GE468; GE604; GE686; GE712;
    GE744; GE748; GE751; GE752; GE753; GY11; HU4; HU20; HU21;
    IT84; JE85; PL86; PO2; RU23; SC27; SS6; SW5; UK8; UK25
couplets
    JE2
courtship and marriage
    GL58; FR96; GE10; GE11; GE26; GE71; GE195; GE220; GE301;
    GE421; GE636; GE641; GR31; GY2; GY3; IT11; IT60; IT84;
    JA6; JA12; JE29; JE85; LI6; LI7; MA2; PO17; RU23; *RU24
    (*GE684); SZ1; SZ5
    See also weddings.
curses and cursing
    CH19; *GR6 (*JE17); IT68; PL59; PL67
customs
    *GL29 (*HU7); *GL43 (*GR9, *IR31, *IT21, *JE24, *PL28,
    *PO6, *SP7); *GL45 (*SC18); *AR3 (*RU6); AR4; BA1; BU3;
    CH3; CH5; CH12; CO2; *CO5 (*CH8, *GE235, *IR39, *IT28,
    *SS15); CO6; *CZ11 (*SK9); DA5; DU5; FI6; FR4; *FR5 (*IR1);
    FR83; FR87; FR95; FR110; GE68; GE83; *GE113 (*GR1, *SK2);
    GE122; GE123; GE153; GE175; GE205; GE207; GE212; GE237;
    GE276; GE280; GE288; GE289; GE293; GE304; GE336; GE338;
    GE342; GE350; GE360; GE371; GE374; GE389; GE402; GE411;
    GE421; GE442; GE447; GE468; GE518; GE523; GE534; GE557;
    GE558; GE560; GE561; GE563; GE565; GE566; GE572; GE579;
    GE598; GE599; GE604; GE614; GE616; GE633; GE635; GE650;
    GE653; GE701; GE704; GE713; GE739; GR2; *GR6 (*JE17);
    GR11; *GR30 (*TU4); GR31; GR39; GY2; GY3; HU21; IR23;
    *IR24 (*SC8); IR103; *IR117 (*SC43); IT5; *IT37 (*PL42);
    IT49; IT58; IT59; IT60; IT64; IT73; IT74; IT80; IT82;
    *IT83 (*JE80); IT84; IT86; JA12; JE14; JE29; JE30; JE51;
    JE55; JE75; JE81; JE82; JE84; JE85; *LE3 (*SZ3); LI7;
    MA2; NO7; NO20; PL2; PL51; PL54; PL85; PO2; PO7; PO17;
    RO2; *RU7 (*GE151); *RU24 (*GE684); SC34; *SK3 (*UK1);
    SK10; SL3; SP9; SS23; *SW4 (*GE127, *IR18, *NO8); SW5;
    SY1; SZ1; SZ5; UK19; WE6
dances and dancing
    GL22; *GL60 (*CR7, *YU6); AR2; BA1; CR4; FR19; FR57; FR110;
    GE9; GE123; GE441; GE541; GE746; GE757; GR33; GY11; HU4;
    IR42; IR64; IR72; *IR81 (*SC31); IR83; PL31; PL63; PL86;
    PO2; PO8; RO5; *SE3 (*YU4); SS6; *SW4 (*GE127, *IR18,
    *NO8); SW5; SZ1; *YU2 (*BU1); YU3

death and the dead
  *GL21 (*IR16); *GL43 (*GR9, *IR31, *IT21, *JE24, *PL28,
  *PO6, *SP7); *GL45 (*SC18); GL58; *GL80 (*IR105, *IT77,
  *JE77); AR1; *AU5 (*PL53); CH15; CZ5; DU10; DU16; *DU27
  (*IR115, *SC41); GE10; GE11; GE26; GE38; GE61; GE71; GE189;
  GE293; GE301; GE316; GE421; GE426; GE636; GE725; GE726;
  GR24; *GR30 (*TU4); GR31; GY2; IR52; *IR60 (*SC24); IR79;
  IR90; IT11; IT31; IT44; IT46; IT49; IT75; IT76; IT84; IT86;
  JA6; JA8; JE29; JE84; JE85; NO15; PL14; PL19; PL38; PL45;
  PL47; PL75; PL78; PO17; RU23; *RU24 (*GE684); SC15; SZ1;
  YU1
demons
  See supernatural beings, demons.
devil, the
  See supernatural beings, the devil.
dialect
  GE13; GE128; GE192; GE341; GE344; GE738
  jokes
  See jokes, dialect.
  songs
  See songs, dialect.
  stories
  See tales, dialect.
divination
  CZ12; GE60
dowsers and dowsing
  GE375; GE598; GE626
dreams
  *AR3 (*RU6); AR4; FR96; GE10; GE11; GE38; *GE161 (*SS10);
  GE667; *IR60 (*SC24); IT31; IT81; JA6; JE85; SZ5
dress
  See costume and dress.
Easter
  AR4; *CZ4 (*UK2); CZ12; DA5; FN8; GE25; GE68; GE89; GE168;
  GE175; GE187; GE208; GE295; GE303; GE310; GE421; GE558;
  GE572; GE573; GE574; GE575; GE581; GE586; GE592; GE610;
  GE611; GE614; GE627; GE628; GE670; GE705; GE719; GE769;
  *GR30 (*TU4); GR31; IR23; IT42; PL32; PL36; PL48; PL51;
  PL54; *RU24 (*GE684); *SK3 (*UK1); SL3; SP9; UK19; YU3
  eggs
  See handicrafts, egg decorations and decorating.
epitaphs
  GE182; GE312; GE313; GE531; GE600; IR28
erotica
  FI3
ethnic slurs
  See slurs, ethnic.

evil eye
    *GL43 (*GR9, *IR31, *IT21, *JE24, *PL28, *P06, *SP7);
    *GL51 (*GR21, *HU17, *IN1, *IR50, *IT35, *JE35, *PL39,
    *RU10, *SZ2); GL58; GL76; *AR3 (*RU6); AU1; *FR5 (*IR1);
    FR116; GE10; GE548; *GR6 (*JE17); GR11; GR14; *GR30 (*TU4);
    GR31; IT11; IT13; IT30; IT46; IT68; IT84; IT86; JE23;
    JE29; JE75; JE85; *LE3 (*SZ3); PL2; PL18; R06
exorcism
    JE85; *LE3 (*SZ3)
fables
    See tales, fables.
fairies
    See supernatural beings, fairies.
family folklore
    See folklore, family.
festivals
    GL22; *GL45 (*SC18); CH10; CH12; CH14; CH15; CH19; *CZ11
    (*SK9); *FR58 (*IR25, *SC10); GE188; GE207; GE208; GE543;
    GE686; GE739; GR39; HU4; IR102; IT11; IT25; *IT70 (*P022,
    *SJ1); IT71; IT79; IT80; JA12; LE2; N07; PL69; PL86; P07;
    SS6; SW5; UK9
fiddling and fiddlers
    *GL40 (*AR5, *CR2, *GR7, *GY5, *JE22, *SC11, *SE2); HU31;
    IR71; *IR84 (*SC32); PL49; PL60; SS27
folklore
  children's
    *GL11 (*JA1, *JE11); *GL80 (*IR105, *IT77, *JE77); CH5;
    *CZ9 (*SK8); DA5; DU4; DU5; FN18; *FR47 (*IR19); FR60;
    GE7; GE99; GE114; GE157; GE174; GE290; GE293; GE532; GE639;
    GE671; GE713; *GE729 (*IT85, *JA13); GE742; IR49; *IR70
    (*SC29); IT59; JA7; JE33; JE71; SK6; SP14; SP15; UK15
  commercialization of
    GE271
  educational uses of
    GL12; *GL81 (*JE79, *SP16); FR79; PL40
  family
    GE738; PL40; PL73
  functions of
    GL1; *GL47 (*FR63, *IT27, *JE28, *PL33); *GL53 (*FR71,
    *IC3, *IT38, *JE40, *UK10); GL65; CR4; GE764; GR16; GR17;
    GR18; *PL26 (*JE20); PL27; PL31; SS5
  occupational
    *GL42 (*FN12, *GE177, *GR7, *IR27, *SK5); *GL55 (*IR56,
    *SK7, *WE7); GL58; *GL73 (*HU27, *SI2); *C05 (*CH8, *GE235,
    *IR39, *IT28, *SS15); C06; *C07 (*FI2, *FN14, *IR40, *IT29,
    *SE4); DU7; FN17; GE230; GE339; GE340; GE383; GE531;
    GE562; GE586; GE679; GE770; GR3; GR4; GR11; GR13; IR28;
    IR36; IR57; *IR58 (*IT40, *JE43, *RU12); IR62; IR63; IR76;

IR88; IR91; IT7; *IT37 (*PL42); *IT70 (*PO22, *SJ1); IT82; *IT83 (*JE80); JE29; JE57; JE64; PL22; PL36; PO8; SC16; SW5
organizations
GL5; FR79
urban
GL64; GE171; IT10; JE33; JE41; JE54; JE75; JE81; LA3
See also folklore studies, urban.
folklore studies
approaches to
GL3; GL25; GL26; *GL27 (*HU6); *GL30 (*HU12); GL32; *GL34 (*CR1, *GR5, *SE1); GL35; GL36; GL37; GL68; GL79; *CH9 (*ID1, *JA3); FI6; FN22; GE737; IT8; IT79; JE5; JE63; RO6
interethnic relationships
GL25; GL26; *GL34 (*CR1, *GR5, *SE1); GE477; GE747; RO6
surveys of
GL1; GL5; GL6; *GL20 (*FR46); GL23; GL24; GL28; GL31; GL36; GL37; GL57; *GL66 (*CH21, *FR91, *GE428, *HU25, *IC4, *ID2, *IT57, *JA9, *LI5, *NO19, *RU19, *UK32); GL68; GL79; *CH9 (*ID1, *JA3); FR30; GE236; GE747; JE42; UK6; UK21; UK22
urban
*GL27 (*HU6); *GL34 (*CR1, *GR5, *SE1); RO6
See also folklore, urban.
foodways
GL22; *GL29 (*HU7); GL56; CH3; CH12; CH14; *CO7 (*FI2, *FN14, *IR40, *IT29, *SE4); CZ3; DU19; FI6; FR3; GE7; GE8; GE9; GE10; GE25; GE27; GE30; GE35; GE60; GE62; GE68; GE76; GE82; GE95; GE123; GE133; GE138; GE170; GE171; GE175; GE188; GE212; GE239; GE240; GE242; GE249; GE250; GE251; GE252; GE253; GE254; GE255; GE256; GE257; GE258; GE259; GE260; GE261; GE262; GE263; GE264; GE265; GE266; GE267; GE268; GE269; GE270; GE272; GE276; GE289; GE293; GE295; GE309; GE320; GE336; GE339; GE343; GE361; GE370; GE398; GE401; GE447; GE468; GE472; GE475; GE479; GE483; GE494; GE522; GE543; GE551; GE556; GE565; GE566; GE582; GE603; GE604; GE614; GE634; GE635; GE640; GE647; GE650; GE655; GE670; GE675; GE718; GE727; GE740; GE741; GE743; GE748; GE750; GE754; GE755; GR15; GR33; GR39; GY11; HU4; HU29; IT4; IT23; IT25; *IT37 (*PL42); IT60; IT73; IT84; JA6; JE18; JE51; JE75; JE85; LE2; PL32; PL51; RU23; SC27; SE8; SK10; SS6; SS16; SS18; UK8; WE2
recipes
GL74; BE2; CH28; CO2; CO9; CZ13; DU4; GE8; GE15; GE27; GE35; GE67; GE83; GE188; GE240; GE242; GE249; GE250; GE251; GE253; GE254; GE256; GE257; GE258; GE259; GE260; GE261; GE263; GE265; GE266; GE268; GE269; GE271; GE272; GE295; GE309; GE386; GE650; GE750; JE78, NO18; PL51; PL55; RO1; *SE7 (*BE3); SE8; SK6; SL3; WE2

fortunetelling and fortunetellers
    CH16; *FR25 (*GE72); IR73
frolic
    GE664
funerals
    CH4; CH5; CH10; CH19; DU17; DU28; GE15; GE17; GE38; GE101;
    GE142; GE170; GE280; GE289; GE342; GE389; GE402; GE599;
    GE689; GR2; GR31; HU21; IR28; IT31; *IT37 (*PL42); IT49;
    IT60; IT84; JA12; JE75; JE84; JE85; PL31; PL85; PO17; SZ1;
    UK13
    See also death and the dead.
games and sports
    AR4; CH5; DU5; FR19; *FR58 (*IR25, *SC10); GE7; GE15; GE99;
    GE123; GE153; GE174; GE188; GE227; GE233; GE290; GE293; GE310;
    GE340; GE395; GE403; GE468; GE532; GE540; GE584; GE591;
    GE604; GE670; GE687; GE727; GE742; *IR70 (*SC29); *IR117
    (*SC43); IT5; IT11; *IT37 (*PL42); IT48; IT59; IT60; IT81;
    JE26; PL51; PO9; PO13; PO19; SC5; SS1; SW5; SZ1; SZ5
  board
    GE233
  card
    BA1; IT81
  finger and hand
    GE39; IT81; PO19; SK6
  parlor
    FR111; FR112
ghosts
    See supernatural beings, ghosts.
giants
    See supernatural beings, giants.
gossip
    IT81
graffiti
    JE32
Groundhog Day
    GE338; GE648
groups, performing
    *GL40 (*AR5, *CR2, *GR7, *GY5, *JE22, *SC11, *SE2); *GL41
    (*CR3, *FN11, *GE172, *HU14, *IR26, *RO3, *SC12, *SK4);
    *GL60 (*CR7, *YU6); CH22; CR4; *CR6 (*SE5, *YU5); GR22;
    LA3; SC5; *SE3 (*YU4)
Halloween
    GE7; GE208; GE640; GE721; GE725; IR23; IR30; IR51
handicrafts
    GL22; CZ1; FR72; GE44; GE123; GE165; GE219; GE358; GE399;
    GE473; GE480; GE503; *GE527 (*RU22); GE604; GE653; GE672;
    HU20; NO5; RO2; SS6; SS19; UK8; UK25

baskets and basketmaking
  GE355; GE473; GE546
cane and caning
  GE164
chalkware
  GE487
copper and coppersmithing
  GE495
dyeing
  GE156
egg decorations and decorating
  *CZ4 (*UK2); GE68; GE73; GE572; GE575; GE610; GE611; GE670;
  GE719; *PL48 (*RU13, *UK27); *SK3 (*UK1); UK5; UK19
embroideries and embroidering
  GE357; GE775
flax and flaxwork
  GE200; RO2
glass and glassmaking
  CZ1; GE324; GE552; GE672
hats and hatmaking
  GE308
ironware
  GE478; GE513
lace and lacemaking
  BE2
leather and leatherwork
  GE121; RO2
metalwork
  GE552
needlework
  GE324; GE497; GE501
paper cutting
  GE476; GE529
pottery
  GE212; GE239; GE334; GE355; GE488; GE490; GE496; GE498;
  GE502; GE513; GE552; GE604; GE650; GE672; GE673; GE771
quilts and quiltmaking
  GE9; GE207; GE208; GE247; GE288; GE355; GE491; GE497;
  GE514; GE640; GE669; GE768
rugs and rugmaking
  GE239; GE355; GE715
tinware and tinsmithing
  GE85; GE326; GE355; GE392; GE485; GE499; GE506; GE515;
weaving
  GE355; GE500
woodcarving and woodcarvers
  GE239; GE510; GE516; SS19
  See also material culture; technology.

Hanukkah
    JE55; *JE61 (*LI11); JE67
haunted houses and places
    CH20; IR73; PL47
heroes
    *GL73 (*HU27, *SI2); FR34; FR35; GE339; LE1; PO5
hex signs and hexing
    GE2; GE90; GE94; GE95; GE98; GE112; GE136; GE189; GE202;
    GE240; GE245; GE279; GE291; GE336; GE352; GE394; GE415;
    GE481; GE531; GE544; GE547; GE548; GE568; GE587; GE588;
    GE589; GE590; GE602; GE621; GE629; GE650; GE760; GE774
history, folklore and
    GL31; GL35; GL36; GL37
humor
    CH23; FI3; FR2; *FR47 (*IR19); GE42; GE96; GE169; GE222;
    GE223; GE306; GE336; GE430; GE440; GE606; GE609; GE675;
    GE750; JE7; JE75
    See also jokes; songs, humorous; tales, humorous.
hymns
    See songs, hymns.
icons
    GR2; GR13; GR34; GR35; GR37; GR38
instruments, musical
    *GL40 (*AR5, *CR2, *GR7, *GY5, *JE22, *SC11, *SE2); *GL66
    (*CH21, *FR91, *GE428, *HU25, *IC4, *ID2, *IT57, *JA9,
    *LI5, *NO19, *RU19, *UK32); GL69; AR2; CH22; *CR6 (*SE5,
    *YU5); FR29; FR57; *GE527 (*RU22); GE672; GR22; HU4; IR43;
    IR65; IR72; *IR81 (*SC31); IR82; IR83; JA7; KO1; LA3; LE2;
    PL21; PL86; PO8; *SE3 (*YU4); SS19; SS27; SZ1; UK8
jokes
    FI6; FN4; *FN5 (*CO4, *FR54); FN22; FR2; FR49; GE16; GE82;
    GE96; GE119; *GE161 (*SS10); GE169; GE191; GE222; GE363;
    GE382; GE431; GE440; GE442; GE570; GE571; GE606; GE607;
    GE608; GE609; GE612; GE615; GE656; GE754; GE755; *GR6
    (*JE17); GR11; GR17; GR18; HU3; HU8; HU11; IR44; IT11;
    *IT61 (*IR87, *PL65); JE6; JE7; JE13; JE15; JE26; JE32;
    JE38; JE54; JE56; JE75; LA1; PL11; *PL26 (*JE20); RO6;
    RO7; SC7; SC28; SS1; SS5; SS18; UK11; UK21
  dialect
    GL33; *GL47 (*FR63, *IT27, *JE28, *PL33); GE96; GE223;
    GE595; JE16; JE36; JE50
    See also tales, dialect.
  ethnic
    *GL2 (*JE1); *GL10 (*JE10, *PL8); GL14; GL33; GL35; GL38;
    *GL47 (*FR63, *IT27, *JE28, *PL33); *GL49 (*CH13, *IR47,
    *IT32, *JA5, *SS17); *GL53 (*FR71, *IC3, *IT38, *JE40,
    *UK10); FI5; GR17; GR18; *IT61 (*IR87, *PL65); JE34;
    *JE73 (*CH25); JE75; *PL5 (*GE43, *IR4, *IT6, *JE4); *PL7
    (*GL9, *IT12, *JE8); PL11; PL25; PL27; PL41; PL64; PL66;
    PL81

practical
    SC28
riddle
    *GL10 (*JE10, *PL8); GL38; *GL47 (*FR63, *IT27, *JE28,
    *PL33); *GL49 (*CH13, *IR47, *IT32, *JA5, *SS17); *GL53
    (*FR71, *IC3, *IT38, *JE40, *UK10); *IT61 (*IR87, *PL65);
    JE32; *PL5 (*GE43, *IR4, *IT6, *JE4); *PL7 (*GL9, *IT12,
    *JE8); PL11; PL25; *PL26 (*JE20); UK21
visual
    PL64; PL66
legends
    See tales, legends.
local characters
    DU1; GE34; GE87; GE90; GE129; GE144; GE148; GE190; GE206;
    GE228; GE277; GE475; GE525; GE531; GE680; GE708; GE733;
    IR44; IR51; *IR58 (*IT40, *JE43, *RU12); IR97; IT41; RO6;
    SS5; SS18
love songs
    See songs, love.
luck
    *GL43 (*GR9, *IR31, *IT21, *JE24, *PL28, *PO6, *SP7);
    GL58; *DU3 (*FR22, *GE36); GE11; GE71; GE153; GE157; GE158;
    GE340; GE526; GE539; GE569; GE579; GE636; GE667; GE725;
    GE726; GR4; GR25; IR23; *IR60 (*SC4); IR93; JA8; JE75;
    PO17
lullabies
    See songs, lullabies.
Märchen
    See tales, Märchen.
mardi gras
    FR55
marriage
    See courtship and marriage; weddings.
material culture
    GR33; RO5; SS16; SS18
  bake ovens
    BE1; FI6; GE362
  boats
    FR72
  buttermolds and buttermaking
    GE133; GE325; GE474
  chairs and chairmaking
    IT18
  cooking utensils
    GE296; GE355; GE474; GE479; GE494; GE499; GE503; GE513;
    GE551; GE566; GE721
  fireplaces and stoves
    GE196; GE346; GE347

furniture
  GE9; GE17; GE125; GE165; GE178; GE179; GE322; GE336; GE346;
  GE404; GE484; GE488; GE503; GE505; GE508; GE552; GE640;
  GE672; GE738
  See also material culture, chairs and chairmaking.
gravestones
  GE28; GE29; GE31; GE38; GE143; GE214; GE311; GE313; GE355;
  GE381; GE653; GE673; IT49
industrial equipment
  GE372
pewter and pewtermaking
  GE489
roofs
  GE106; GE107
tools
  CH26; GE82; GE346; GE355; GE443
toys
  GE153; GE165; GE471; GE488; GE513; UK8
walls and fences
  GE366; GE683
  See also architecture; handicrafts; technology.
May Day
  IR23; IT64; IT82; RO2
medicine
  BU3; CH5; GE11; GE25; GE153; GE157; GE208; GE266; GE302;
  GE339; GE433; GE444; GE542; GE640; GE727; GE748; GE753;
  GE754; GR4; GR33; HU3; IR103; *IR116 (*SC42); IT84; PL13;
  RO5; SS16
cures
  *GL43 (*GR9, *IR31, *IT21, *JE24, *PL28, *PO6, *SP7);
  *GL51 (*GR21, *HU17, *IN1, *IR50, *IT35, *JE35, *PL39,
  *RU10, *SZ2); GL59; *AR3 (*RU6); AR4; CO8; DU19; DU21;
  *FN5 (*CO4, *FR54); FN7; FN8; FN18; *FR5 (*IR1); *FR50
  (*FN2, *GE160, *IR20, *SL1, *SS8); FR117; GE12; GE18; GE19;
  GE71; GE92; GE93; GE98; GE103; GE123; GE129; GE145; GE153;
  GE154; GE163; GE173; GE224; GE278; GE284; GE291; GE292;
  GE293; GE302; GE303; GE363; GE372; GE374; GE390; GE394;
  GE414; GE415; GE421; GE427; GE469; GE481; GE520; GE522;
  GE562; IT14; IT68; IT74; IT81; IT84; IT86; JA6; JA8; JE23;
  JE29; JE75; PL13; PL51; PL56; PL83; RO1; RO6; RU4; RU23;
  SC4; *SS29 (*AU6, *GE703); SZ5; WE2
healing and healers
  GL76; CO8; *FR50 (*FN2, *GE160, *IR20, *SL1, *SS8); FR55;
  GE137; GE173; GE707; GE747; *GR6 (*JE17); GR11; GR31;
  GR32; IT68; IT74; JA8; *SC25 (*IR61)
midwifery and midwives
  GL76; GR32; IR106
  See also powwowing and powwowers.

menstruation
    GY3; JE51; PL13
music
    *GL20 (*FR46); GL22; *GL40 (*AR5, *CR2, *GR7, *GY5, *JE22,
    *SC11, *SE1); *GL41 (*CR3, *FN11, *GE172, *HU14, *IR26,
    *RO3, *SC12, *SK4); GL44; *GL45 (*SC18); GL46; GL57, *GL60
    (*CR7, *YU6); GL62; GL63; GL64; *GL66 (*CH21, *FR91, *GE428,
    *HU25, *IC4, *ID2, *IT57, *JA9, *LI5, *NO19, *RU19, *UK32);
    GL67; GL68; GL69; GL78; AR2; CH22; *CR6 (*SE5, *YU5);
    *CZ9 (*SK8); FN13; FN25; FR13; FR14; FR15; FR17; FR18;
    FR19; FR28; FR29; FR33; FR55; FR62; FR64; FR73; FR74; FR89;
    GE7; GE9; GE17; GE52; *GE110 (*SW3); GE191; GE212; GE314;
    GE315; GE336; *GE384 (*AU2, *DU13, *RU14, *SW6); GE393;
    *GE416 (*SW7); GE441; GE640; *GE697 (*SW8); GE761; GR2;
    GR22; GR33; GY11; HU4; HU15; *IC2 (*IR45); IR42; IR43;
    IR51; IR64; IR71; IR72; *IR81 (*SC31); IR82; IR83; *IR84
    (*SC32); IR96; IR107; *IT47 (*FR81); IT64; IT69; JA7; *JE9
    (*IR12, *SC3); JE12; JE41; *JE61 (*LI11); JE62; JE74; KO1;
    LA3; LI2; LI6; NO3; NO7; PL21; PL31; PL63; PL74; PL86; PO8;
    RO5; RU20; *RU21 (*CZ10, *GE429, *HU26, *UK33); SC5; SC44;
    *SE3 (*YU4); SP15; *SS14 (*UK3); SS16; SS27; *SW4 (*GE127,
    *IR18, *NO8); SW5; *SZ4 (*EG1, *ID3, *LE4, *PA1); UK16
    instrumental
        *GL40 (*AR5, *CR2, *GR7, *GY5, *JE22, *SC11, *SE2); GE441;
        IR42; IR43; PL31
musicians
    *GL40 (*AR5, *CR2, *GR7, *GY5, *JE22, *SC11, *SE2); *GL45
    (*SC18); FN13; GR22; HU4; HU31; IR42; IR64; IR71; *IR81
    (*SC31); IR82; *IR84 (*SC32); IR96; JE41; LA3; PL74; SC5;
    *SE3 (*YU4); SE8; *SS14 (*UK3); SS27
myths
    See tales, myths.
name changing
    GL72; *JE52 (*GE446, *SC35, *YU10); GE662
name days
    SL3
names and naming
    GL57; *FR5 (*IR1); GE79; GE212; GE280; GE288; GE516;
    GE524; GE643; GE662; GE685; IT81; JE29; JE51; JE85; PO9;
    PO10
    building
        FN21
    calendrical
        GE185
    food
        GE596
    personal
        GL72; GE625; GE662

place
    GL18; GL19; GL61; GL70; GL71; *DU18 (*FR101); GE335; GE349;
    GE617; GE661; GE662; JA2
plant
    GE359
street
    CH11
    See also nicknames and nicknaming.
New Year (Chinese)
    CH5; CH16
New Year's Eve and Day
    CZ3; DU5; *FR58 (*IR25, *SC10); FR83; FR110; GE64; GE66;
    GE80; GE116; GE122; GE208; GE276; GE304; GE310; GE336;
    GE350; GE360; GE417; GE418; GE469; GE517; GE518; GE537;
    GE577; GE578; GE597; GE633; GE640; GE650; GE659; GE692;
    GE706; GE721; GE735; GE741; GE754; *GR30 (*TU4): IR23;
    IT82; PL51; *RU24 (*GE684); SC34
nicknames and nicknaming
    FR55; GE59; GE243; GE396; GE400; GE642; GE643; GE662;
    GE695; GE764; PO1; PO10
nonsense speech
    JE71
    See also rhymes, nonsense.
nursery songs
    See songs, nursery.
oaths
    FR76; FR87; JE71
occupational folklore
    See folklore, occupational.
omens
    *FR5 (*IR1); *FR68 (*SC23); FR96; GE38; GE71; GE123; GE153;
    GE157; GE158; GE289; GE426; GE427; GE481; GE569; GE667;
    GE679; GE726; GR13; *IR60 (*SC24); IR90; IT46; IT75; IT76;
    JA8; NO15
painting and painters
    *GE97 (*SW1); GE506; GE672; SS21
parades
    SS6
parodies
    *FR53 (*CO3, *FN3, *IR21, *IT17, *SS9); GE191; GE591;
    GE671; *GE729 (*IT85, *JA13); *IR24 (*SC8); JE33; JE57;
    UK14; UK17
parties
    GE257; GE287
Passover
    JE59; JE78; JE81; JE84
performing groups
    See groups, performing.

personal experience narratives
  See tales, personal experience.
photographers and photography
  GE65
picnics
  FR92; GE239; IR110
poems and verses
  *CO7 (*FI2, *FN14, *IR40, *IT29, *SE4); FR24; FR41; FR48;
  FR109; GE58; GE83; GE122; GE191; GE290; GE293; GE304;
  GE316; GE360; GE393; GE421; GE518; GE528; GE535; GE750;
  GE754; GR31; HU30; IC1; IR15; JE2; JE32; LA1; NO12; RO6;
  RU2; SC13; SP3; *SS30 (*DA7, *NO22)
powwowing and powwowers
  GE12; GE18; GE19; GE20; GE21; GE69; GE98; GE112; GE145;
  GE148; GE152; GE154; GE189; GE221; GE226; GE240; GE273;
  GE279; GE287; GE291; GE292; GE303; GE336; GE394; GE415;
  GE427; GE481; GE526; GE538; GE547; GE576; GE617; GE625;
  GE629; GE657; GE667; GE668; GE694; GE707; GE712; GE714;
  GE645; GE753; GE760
pranks
  GE369; GE687; JE19; SC28
prayers
  *FN5 (*CO4, *FR54); GE45; GE98; GE306; GE393; GE671; *LE3
  (*SZ3); WE2
pregnancy and childbirth
  *GL43 (*GR9, *IR31, *IT21, *JE24, *PL28, *PO6, *SP7):
  *GL48 (*IR37, *SC19); GE10; GE301; GE391; GE636; *GR30
  (*TU4); GR31; GR32; GY2; IT11; IT44; IT46; IT74; IT84;
  IT86; JA6; JA8; JA12; JE29; JE75; PL13; PO17; *RU24
  (*GE684)
profanity
  FR67; GE229
proverbs and proverbial speech
  *GL11 (*JA1, *JE11); GL38; *GL80 (*IR105, *IT77, *JE77);
  BU4; CO2; CZ3; DU23; DU28; FI6; FN10; FN18; *FR5 (*IR1);
  *GE33 (*DA1, *DU2, *FR21, *HU1, *IT3); GE45; GE96; GE123;
  GE131; GE142; GE149; GE162; GE163; GE186; GE203; GE204;
  GE290; GE297; GE351; GE393; GE410; GE434; GE435; GE436;
  GE437; GE438; GE439; GE520; GE534; GE713; GE731; GE755;
  GE765; GY11; IR52; *IR67 (*GE387, *WE8); *IR104 (*AR10);
  *IR117 (*SC43); IT5; IT11; IT58; IT59; IT63; IT72; JE68;
  JE69; JE75; JE86; MO1; PL4; PL51; PL85; PO9; PO11; PO12;
  PO13; PO14; SC9; SC28; SK6; SY1; SZ1
  See also sayings; tongue twisters; Wellerisms.
recipes
  See foodways, recipes.

religion
    GL22; *GL29 (*HU7): *GL40 (*AR5, *CR2, *GR7, *GY5, *JE22,
    *SC11, *SE2); *GL45 (*SC18); *GL80 (*IR105, *IT77, *JE77);
    AR4; CH3; CH19; *DA3 (*SA1, *SS4); DA5; DU4; DU5; FN22;
    FN25; *FR5 (*IR1); FR49; FR90; GE42; GE81; GE82; GE89;
    *GE110 (*SW3); GE176; GE194; GE198; GE214; GE220; GE244;
    GE248; GE292; GE298; GE305; GE314; GE315; GE316; GE323;
    GE339; GE343; *GE384 (*AU2, *DU13, *RU14, *SW6); *GE416
    (*SW7); GE422; GE554; GE585; GE601; GE614; GE662; GE669;
    GE673; GE686; *GE697 (*SW8); GE704; GE705; GE706; GE720;
    GE739; GE743; GE745; GE748; GE749; GE752; GE756; GE760;
    GE766; GE772; GR2; *GR6 (*JE17); GR11; GR13; GR16; GR20;
    GR34; GR36; GR37; GR38; GY11; HU3; IT5; IT25; *IT47
    (*FR81); IT49; *IT70 (*PO22, *SJ1); IT73; IT79; IT82;
    IT84; IT86; JE29; JE41; *JE45 (*UK29); JE46; JE48; JE49;
    JE55; JE57; JE59; *JE61 (*LI11); JE81; JE82; JE84; PL10;
    PL43; PL56; PL57; PO7; PO17; RO2; RO5; RU15; *RU21 (*CZ10,
    *GE429, *HU26, *UK33); *RU24 (*GE684); SC16; SE8; SZ1
remedies
    See medicine, cures.
rhymes
    *CZ9 (*SK8); DA5; *DU3 (*FR22, *GE36); *FN5 (*CO4, *FR54);
    *FR47 (*IR19); GE45; GE157; GE361; GE363; GE374; GE405;
    GE411; GE562; GE650; *GE729 (*IT85, *JA13); GE750; GE754;
    GE755; *IR117 (*SC43); JE32; JE33; NO20; RO6; RU2; *SS30
    (*DA7, *NO22)
  ball-bouncing
    *GL11 (*JA1, *JE11); SS1
  counting-out
    *GL11 (*JA1, *JE11); AR4; CH5; *GE197 (*DU9, *IR35);
    GE293; GE531; GE625; GE671; *IR116 (*SC42); IT59; PO19;
    SS13
  finger
    DU19; GE39
  game
    *GL80 (*IR105, *IT77, *JE77)
  jump-rope
    *GL11 (*JA1, *JE11); GE531; GE580; GE583; GE639
  nonsense
    DU19; GE625
  nursery
    DU19; GE238; GE671
riddle jokes
    See jokes, riddle.
riddles
    AR4; CH2; *FR47 (*IR19); FR55; GE83; GE123; GE146; GE162;
    GE163; GE231; GE232; GE286; GE310; GE361; GE363; GE407;

GE408; GE409; GE411; GE448; GE450; GE451; GE452; GE453; GE455; GE456; GE457; GE458; GE459; GE460; GE461; GE462; GE463; GE464; GE465; GE466; GE467; GE468; GE671; GE709; HU18; ID4; *IR117 (*SC43); IT5; IT67; JA10; JE59; JE67; LA1; LI1; PL79; PO13; SP1; SP12; SZ5
  See also jokes, riddle; songs, riddle.
rituals
  *AR3 (*RU6); *CZ11 (*SK9); FN23; GE154; GR4; GR13; GR38; IT49; IT64; IT82; IT86; JE48; JE49; JE55; *LE3 (*SZ3)
rumors
  *JE44 (*DA6, *GE380, *IT43)
saints and saints' days
  GE26; GE187; IT11; IT34; IT58; IT59; IT65; *IT70 (*PO22, *SJ1); IT73; IT74; IT78; IT80; IT82; PL17; PL76; PO7; SE8
sayings
  *CO5 (*CH8, *GE235, *IR39, *IT28, *SS15); *DU3 (*FR22, *GE36); DU28; GE13; GE123; GE129; GE134; GE142; *GE161 (*SS10); GE293; GE294; GE297; GE303; GE361; GE374; GE406; GE413; GE421; GE481; GE528; GE531; GE538; GE583; GE635; GE651; IR57; *IR60 (*SC24); *IR67 (*GE387, *WE8); *IR104 (*AR10); JE26; JE68; JE69; JE75; JE86; RU15; SC28; SS1; *SS20 (*NO14); WE3
  See also proverbs and proverbial speech; Wellerisms.
science, folklore and
  GE14; GE302
shivaree
  FR4; *FR5 (*IR1)
singing and singers
  *GL40 (*AR5, *CR2, *GR7, *GY5, *JE22, *SC11, *SE2); *GL45 (*SC18); FN13; FR7; FR16; GE762; HU15; HU31; *IC2 (*IR45); IR5; IR42; IR86; IR97; IR109; SC5; SC26
  See also songs.
slurs, ethnic
  GL4; GL8; *GL11 (*JA1, *JE11); GL15; GL16; GL17; GL18; GL19; GL38; GL39; GL59; GL61; GL70; GL71; *GL81 (*JE79, *SP16); CH6; DU11; DU22; FI1; FI6; FN15; GE516; *IT61 (*IR87, *PL65); IT67; JE26; *JE73 (*CH25); *PL5 (*GE43, *IR4, *IT6, *JE4); *PL26 (*JE20); UK11; UK21
songs
  *GL7 (*FR23); *GL20 (*FR46); GL33; GL35; *GL40 (*AR5, *CR2, *GR7, *GY5, *JE22, *SC11, *SE2); *GL41 (*CR3, *FN11, *GE172, *HU14, *IR26, *RO3, *SC12, *SK4); *GL42 (*FN12, *GE177, *GR7, *IR27, *SK5); *GL45 (*SC18); *GL55 (*IR56, *SK7, *WE7); GL62; *GL66 (*CH21, *FR91, *GE428, *HU25, *IC4, *ID2, *IT57, *JA9, *LI5, *NO19, *RU19, *UK32); *GL80 (*IR105, *IT77, *JE77); AR2; BA1; CO2; *CZ2 (*SK1); *CZ9 (*SK8); DA5; DU4; DU5; FI3; FI6; FN8; FN9; FN13; FN17;

FN18; FN25; FR7; FR8; FR11; FR12; FR13; FR14; FR15; FR16;
FR17; FR18; FR19; FR20; FR26; FR28; FR29; FR32; FR33;
FR41; *FR47 (*IR19); FR48; *FR53 (*CO3, *FN3, *IR21, *IT17,
*SS9); FR57; *FR58 (*IR25, *SC10); FR62; FR64; FR73; FR74;
FR78; FR83; FR89; FR90; FR93; FR106; FR110; FR111; FR114;
FR118; GE6; GE52; GE81; GE82; GE91; GE123; *GE126 (*IR17);
GE162; GE191; GE238; GE240; GE339; GE340; GE393; GE447;
GE524; GE562; GE591; GE593; GE660; GE713; GE747; GE754;
GR27; *GR30 (*TU4); HU13; HU15; HU21; HU30; HU31; *IC2
(*IR45); *IR3 (*FR6, *SC1); IR5; IR6; IR14; IR32; IR33;
IR42; IR46; IR48; IR49; IR57; IR63; IR71; IR76; IR80;
*IR81 (*SC31); IR82; IR86; IR97; *IR100 (*JE76); IR109;
*IR111 (*SC40); IR112; IR114; IR119; IT11; IT33; *IT47
(*FR81); IT62; IT64; IT69; JA4; JA7; *JE9 (*IR12, *SC3);
JE12; JE33; JE47; JE55; JE57; JE58; JE59; *JE60 (*LI10);
*JE61 (*LI11); JE62; JE64; JE65; JE66; JE74; JE75; KO1;
LA1; LE2; LI2; LI6; *NO2 (*DA2, *FN1, *IR10, *SS3); NO3;
NO4; NO11; NO12; NO21; PL51; PL63; PL74; PO7; PO8; PO17;
RO2; RO6; RU2; RU15; RU20; *RU21 (*CZ10, *GE429, *HU26,
*UK33); RU23; SA2; SC5; SC13; SC20; SC34; SC44; *SE3
(*YU4); SK10; SP4; SP9; SP14; SP15; SS26; *SS30 (*DA7,
*NO22); SZ1; *SZ4 (*EG1, *ID3, *LE4, *PA1); UK7; UK13;
UK14; UK16; UK17; UK22; UK24; UK34; WE6
ballads
*GL45 (*SC18); *CO7 (*FI2, *FN14, *IR40, *IT29, *SE4);
*CZ2 (*SK1); FN6; FN7; *FR5 (*IR1); FR32; FR66; FR119;
GE32; GE77; GE78; GE241; GE340; GE645; GE735; HU31; IR5;
IR6; IR7; IR8; IR15; *IR24 (*SC8); IR42; IR46; IR49; IR54;
IR55; IR59; IR66; IR76; IR91; IR95; *IR98 (*SC37); *IR99
(*SC39); *IR111 (*SC40); IR112; IR119; IT15; IT19; IT22;
IT39; IT42; *IT46 (*FR81); JE3; *JE9 (*IR12, *SC3); JE12;
JE47; JE59; NO1; *NO2 (*DA2, *FN1, *IR10, *SS3); NO3;
NO10; NO11; NO12; PL6; PO3; PO4; PO5; PO9; PO13; PO20;
PO21; SA2; SC6; SC26; SC45; SP4; SS2; SS12; *SS20 (*NO14);
SS24; *SS30 (*DA7, *NO22); SS31; UK23; UK26; UK28
carols
HU21; UK21
dialect
GE88; GE648
humorous
JE64
hymns
GL22; FN25; FR90; GE82; *GE110 (*SW3); GE176; GE194; GE227;
GE305; GE314; GE315; *GE384 (*AU2, *DU13, *RU14, *SW6);
*GE416 (*SW7); GE518; *GE697 (*SW8); GE749; GE758; GE766;
*IT47 (*FR81); RU20; *RU21 (*CZ10, *GE429, *HU26, *UK33)
love
FR11; JE64

lullabies
   FN17; JE57; JE64; JE66; UK15
nursery
   FN18; GE671
religious
   GE108; JE59
riddle
   JE59
satirical
   NO1
spirituals
   GE78; GE749; GE756; GE758
   See also singing and singers.
speeches
   GE304
spirituals
   See songs, spirituals.
sports
   See games and sports.
stereotypes and stereotyping
   *GL12 (*JE1); GL14; GL38; GE656; GE696; GY13; GY14; JE26;
   JE32; JE50; JE54; *JE73 (*CH25); PL25; *PL26 (*JE20); RO6
storytelling and storytellers
   BA2; FN19; FN20; FR2; FR7; FR49; FR64; FR65; FR109; GE82;
   GE330; GR10; GR17; GR18; GR19; HU8; HU11; IT55; JE37;
   JE38; JE39; JE46; LA1; NO12; PL23; PL24; SE6; *SS11 (*DU6,
   *FR56, *IR22)
   See also tales.
street cries
   GE1
supernatural beings
   FR49; FR51; FR52; FR77; FR113; GE163; *GR6 (*JE17); GR23;
   GR24; GR25; IT11; IT31; *IT36 (*FR70); JE46; JE75; PL14;
   PL34; PL44; PL45; PL49; PL82; RO6; SC16; SC39; SI1; SS18;
   SS22; SS25; SZ1; UK35
demons
   JE23; SI1
devil, the
   *GL43 (*GR9, *IR31, *IT21, *JE24, *PL28, *PO6, *SP7);
   *GL50 (*FR69, *GE318); DU12; DU21; *FR5 (*IR1); FR100;
   FR102; FR104; FR105; GE7; GE90; GE339; GE423; GE631;
   GE724; *GR6 (*JE17); IR49; IR51; IR90; IR106; IT14; IT66;
   NO9; PL12; PL16; PL43; PL45; PL69; PL71; PL80; RO6; SS18
fairies
   CE1; *FR5 (*IR1); GE605; GE724; IR30; IR38; IR49; IR51;
   IR52; IR73; IR90; IR102; IR106; IR118; IT59

ghosts
   AU1; CH15; CH18; CH19; CH20; CH27; *CZ6 (*HU22, *IT50,
   *YU7); DU16; DU28; *FR5 (*IR1); FR27; FR49; FR82; FR104;
   GE35; GE40; GE123; GE180; GE189; GE198; GE289; GE290;
   GE339; GE637; GE638; GE663; GE732; GY9; HU3; IR30; IR90;
   IT31; JE75; LI3; NO15; PL45; PL47; PL61; PL75; RO7; SC14;
   SC15; SC16
giants
   CE1
trolls
   NO17; SS18
werewolves
   GL58; *GL75 (*FR103); FR102; IT11; IT31; *IT36 (*FR70);
   PL45
witches
   *GL75 (*FR103); *AR3 (*RU16); AU1; BU3; *DU25 (*IR113);
   *DU27 (*IR115, *SC41); DU28; *FR5 (*IR1); FR27; FR84;
   FR85; GE5; GE10; GE11; GE14; GE20; GE21; GE40; GE90; GE94;
   GE123; GE150; GE162; GE189; GE198; GE212; GE240; GE288;
   GE289; GE290; GE415; GE419; GE519; GE545; GE548; GE555;
   GE569; GE598; GE623; GE637; GE653; GE667; GE681; *GE723
   (*FR115); GE724; GE725; GE728; GE745; HU19; IR30; IR49;
   IR94; IT11; IT68; IT84; IT86; NO17; PL46; PL68; RO6;
   *SC25 (*IR61); SI1; UK35
superstitions
   See beliefs.
taboos
   *AR3 (*RU6); CZ5; GE539; GR3; GR4; GR13; *GR30 (*TU4);
   GY2; GY3; IR30; *IT83 (*JE80); IT84; IT86; PL57; PL60;
   PL72
tales
   GL13; GL33; *GL43 (*GR9, *IR31, *IT21, *JE24, *PL28,
   *PO6, *SP7); *GL50 (*FR69, *GE318); *GL80 (*IR105, *IT77,
   *JE77); *GL82 (*GE700); AR1; *AR3 (*RU6); AR6; AR7; *AU3
   (*CZ7, *HU23, *IT51); *AU5 (*PL53); BA2; BO1; CE1; CH14;
   CH15; CH20; CH24; CH27; CO2; *CO5 (*CH8, *GE235, *IR39,
   *IT28, *SS15); CO6; CO9; CR5; *CZ6 (*HU22, *IT50, *YU7);
   DU9; DU20; FN18; FN19; FR2; *FR5 (*IR1); FR7; FR9; FR10;
   FR27; FR31; FR34; FR35; FR36; FR37; FR38; FR39; FR40;
   FR42; FR43; FR44; FR45; *FR47 (*IR19); FR49; FR51; FR55;
   FR59; FR60; FR64; FR65; FR82; FR100; FR104; FR109; FR113;
   FR116; GE5; GE34; GE37; GE40; GE61; GE86; GE87; GE109;
   GE111; GE123; GE137; GE139; *GE140 (*GY4); GE145; GE147;
   GE150; GE154; *GE161 (*SS10); GE162; GE163; GE166; GE189;
   *GE197 (*DU9, *IR35); GE198; GE206; GE228; GE283; GE285;
   GE288; GE289; GE290; GE361; GE365; GE371; GE374; GE377;
   GE383; GE386; GE393; GE410; GE419; GE420; GE423; GE426;
   GE519; GE524; GE555; GE562; GE587; GE601; GE605; GE613;

GE621; GE622; GE631; GE632; GE650; GE664; GE667; GE678;
GE679; GE680; *GE723 (*FR115); GE724; GE732; GE733; GE755;
GE763; GR10; GR19; GR23; GR25; *GR28 (*TU2); GR33; GY7;
GY11; HU18; IR2; IR11; IR13; IR29; IR36; IR38; IR48; IR49;
*IR58 (*IT40, *JE43, *RU12); IR68; IR69; IR73; IR75; IR79;
IR80, *IR85 (*SC33); IR92; IR94; *IR101 (*FR107, *GE682);
IR106; IR108; IR110; IT1; IT2; IT11; IT13; IT20; IT24;
IT31; IT34; *IT36 (*FR70); IT41; IT45; *IT52 (*AR9, *AU4,
*CZ8, *HU24, *IR74, *PL52, *RO4, *RU16, *TU3, *YU8);
IT53; IT58; IT59; IT65; IT66; IT68; IT72; IT74; IT78; JA8;
JA11; JE6; JE19; *JE21 (*RU8); JE26; *JE27 (*RU9); JE37;
*JE45 (*UK29); JE70; JE72; JE75; LA1; LE1; LE2; LI3; LI8;
LI9; NO7; NO12; NO13; NO15; NO20; PL2; PL4; PL9; PL12;
PL14; PL15; PL17; PL19; PL24; *PL35 (*GY6); PL36; PL38;
PL43; PL44; PL45; PL47; PL51; PL59; PL60; PL68; PL70;
PL71; PL72; PL73; PL76; PL77; PL78; PL80; PO8; PO18; RO6;
RO7; RU3; RU15; RU18; SC14; SC16; SC21; SC22; SC36; SC39;
SC44; SE6; SK6; SL3; SP2; SP5; SP6; SP10; SP11; SP13;
SS16; SS18; SY1; SZ5; TU1; TU5; UK11; UK18; UK21; UK35;
WE5; YU1

anecdotes
AR7; CO1; *CO5 (*CH8, *GE235, *IR39, *IT28, *SS15); *CO7
(*FI2, *FN14, *IR40, *IT29, *SE4); DU1; DU7; *DU27 (*IR115,
*SC41); *FN5 (*CO4, *FR54); FN17; FN18; FR52; FR86; GE16;
GE90; GE96; GE123; GE124; *GE161 (*SS10); GE225; *GE281
(*JE31); GE361; GE365; GE369; GE393; GE430; GE530; GE549;
GE676; *GR6 (*JE17); GR11; GR17; GR18; GY10; GY11; HU3;
HU8; HU11; IR34; IR62; IR97; IT67; JE18; JE26; *JE27
(*RU9); *JE52 (*GE446, *SC35, *YU10); JE54; JE56; JE75;
LA1; NO7; NO12; RO6; *SS20 (*NO14); SC9; SS5; SS16; UK11;
UK35

animal
*GL43 (*GR9, *IR31, *IT21, *JE24, *PL28, *PO6, *SP7); BA2;
*DU27 (*IR115, *SC41); *FR5 (*IR1); FR35; FR43; FR99;
FR116; GE730; *IR58 (*IT40, *JE43, *RU12); SZ1

cante-fables
SC44

cumulative
AR7; PO16

dialect
GL33; GL35; CO1; *FN5 (*CO4, *FR54); FR51; *FR53 (*CO3,
*FN3, *IR21, *IT17, *SS9); GE109; GE329; GE330; GE676;
GR17; GR18; IT11; JE15; JE16; JE50; SS5

fables
*GL80 (*IR105, *IT77, *JE77); GR17; GR18

humorous
   AR7; *AU5 (*PL53); DU1; DU7; *DU27 (*IR115, *SC41); *FR47
   (*IR19); FR94; FR99; GE90; GE109; GE129; GE244; GE531;
   *GR6 (*JE17); GR27; HU16; IR48; IR57; IT45; IT58; IT59;
   PL23; RO7; TU5
legends
   GL13; *GL43 (*GR9, *IR31, *IT21, *JE24, *PL28, *PO6, *SP7);
   *GL48 (*IR37, *SC19); *AR3 (*RU6); AR7; CH1; DU12; DU16;
   *DU18 (*FR101); DU19; *DU27 (*IR115, *SC41); FN20; FR10;
   FR51; FR75; FR99; FR105; GE37; GE90; GE117; GE123; GE180;
   GE274; GE335; GE336; GE339; GE340; GE531; GE681; GE701;
   *GE722 (*JE83); GE728; GR11; GR38; GY9; GY10; GY11; HU3;
   HU8; HU11; *IC2 (*IR45); *IR24 (*SC8); IR30; IR49; IR57;
   *IR58 (*IT40, *JE43, *RU12); IR88; IR91; IR102; IT11;
   IT34; IT44; IT58; IT65; JE26; *JE44 (*DA6, *GE380, *IT43);
   JE46; NO6; NO20; PL1; PL2; PL10; PL16; PL23; PL46; PL67;
   PO17; RO6; RO7; RU15; SC15; SS16; SS18; SS25; UK5
legends, saints'
   DU4; GE753; *GR6 (*JE17); GR11; GR13; GR38; IT11; IT34;
   IT65; PL30; PL58; PL69; SZ1
Märchen
   AR7; CE1; FN4; FR60; FR99; GR11; RO6; SP5
memorates
   CZ5; GE40; GR24; GR38; GY9; GY10; GY11; PL2; SS25
moralistic
   *JE25 (*PL29); PL23; PL49; PL77
myths
   AR7; *GY1 (*RU1)
numskull
   CO1; DA4; DU7; FI4; FR34; FR35; FR37; FR40; FR43; FR108;
   GE119; GE162; GR26; GR29; IR2; *IR58 (*IT40, *JE43, *RU12);
   IT58; PL81; SL2; SS18; SZ1
nursery
   FR60; FR61
parables
   JE37; JE39
personal experience
   *GL21 (*IR16); *GL51 (*GR21, *HU17, *IN1, *IR50, *IT35,
   *JE35, *PL39, *RU10, *SZ2); AU1; CH18; *CO7 (*FI2, *FN14,
   *IR40, *IT29, *SE4); CZ5; *DA3 (*SA1, *SS4); *DU27 (*IR115,
   *SC41); FI5; FR27; FR49; *FR50 (*FN2, *GE160, *IR20, *SL1,
   *SS8); FR52; FR102; GE101; GE144; GE155; GE339; GE368;
   GE388; GE421; GE426; GE442; GE730; GE772; *GR6 (*JE17);
   GR12; GR13; GR14; GR16; GR24; *GR30 (*TU4); GR31; GR37;
   GR38; HU8; HU11; HU19; IR23; IR30; IR73; IT4; IT7; IT11;
   IT26; IT44; IT46; IT75; IT76; IT81; IT86; JE38; JE56;
   JE75; NO9; NO16; NO17; PL2; PL22; PL34; PL46; PL54; PL61;
   PL62; PL75; PL82; PL84; RO1; RO6; RU15; SC16; SC28; SS1;
   SS5; *SS11 (*DU6, *FR56, *IR22); SS18; SS22; UK31

sagas
  AR7
tall
  DU7; FN4; *FR47 (*IR19); FR65; FR86; GE90; GE123; GE191;
  GE285; GE531; GE734; IR28; IR57; *IR58 (*IT40, *JE43,
  *RU12); IR62; PO15; SZ1
trickster
  AR8; BA2; CH17; FN16; FR2; FR36; FR37; FR40; FR43; GR26;
  GR29; IR36; IR57; *IT54 (*RU17, *YU9); JE13; *JE45 (*UK29);
  JE75; SP10; SS5; TU1; TU5
  See also storytelling and storytellers.
technology
  GE740
  beekeeping
    GE83
  blacksmithing and blacksmiths
    GE443; GE562; GE770
  butchering and butchers
    GE249; GE533
  distilling and distilleries
    GE542
  soapmaking
    GE658
  See also architecture; handicrafts; material culture.
theater
  drama
    IT73
  puppet
    IT16; IT56
toasts
  JE14
tongue twisters
  GE624; GE759; *IR117 (*SC43)
urban folklore
  See folklore, urban; folklore studies, urban.
visions
  GR16
votive offerings
  GR37; GR38
weather, the
  *GL80 (*IR105, *IT77, *JE77); BU3; DA5; *DU3 (*FR22, *GE36);
  DU26; DU28; FR96; GE11; GE26; GE71; GE123; GE149; GE153;
  GE225; GE229; GE246; GE275; GE279; GE342; GE353; GE405;
  GE427; GE481; GE531; GE586; GE629; GE648; GE650; GE679;
  GE725; JA6
weddings
  *GL45 (*SC18); *BU2 (*MA1); CH10; CH19; CZ5; FR3; *FR5
  (*IR1); GE17; GE57; GE58; *GE110 (*SW3); GE207; GE208;

GE220; GE280; GE288; GE316; GE337; GE339; GE523; GE534;
GE557; GE644; GE646; GE652; GE664; GE690; GR2; *GR30
(*TU4); GR36; HU21; *IT37 (*PL42); IT60; IT84; JE29; JE64;
JE75; LI6; LI7; MA2; PL20; PL31; PL49; PL51; PL85; RO2;
*RU7 (*GE151); *RU24 (*GE684); SK10; SZ1; UK13
    See also courtship and marriage.
Wellerisms
    IT72; SS1
werewolves
    See supernatural beings, werewolves.
witches
    See supernatural beings, witches.
Xerox lore
    PL66

II.   GENERAL SUBJECT INDEX

acculturation
    See culture change.
agriculture
    GE41; GE46; GE55; GE70; GE105; GE153; GE287; GE293; GE333;
    GE365; GE367; GE371; GE554; HU5; NO7; SC27
    harvesting
    *CZ11 (*SK9); CZ12; GE26; GE46; GE56; GE141; GE528
    herbs and herbalists
    GE550; PL13
    planting
    GE4; GE41; GE45; GE141; GE153; GE288; GE303; GE351; GE359;
    GE367; GE421; GE520; GE650
    plowing
    GE142
All Souls' Day
    IR90; PL34; PL58
almanacs
    GE222; GE224; GE225; GE526; GE609; GE625; GE656
alphabet books
    GE230
Amish
    GE4; GE5; GE17; GE22; GE74; GE100; GE130; GE141; GE192;
    GE194; GE220; GE240; GE299; GE300; GE301; GE302; GE308;
    GE314; GE315; GE337; GE364; GE396; GE397; GE399; GE400;
    *GE416 (*SW7); GE445; GE477; GE534; GE541; GE642; GE643;
    GE644; GE645; GE687; GE688; GE689; GE690; GE691; GE695;
    GE696; *GE697 (*SW8); GE752; GE761; GE764; GE766
animals and animal husbandry
    GE47; GE135; GE139; GE147; GE153; GE157; GE325; GE363;
    GE374; GE685; GE710; ĜE711; GE712; GE734
archives and archiving
    GL57; FR12; FR79
assimilation
    See culture change.
astronomy
    JA6
bibliographies
    GE111; GE348; GE444; GE493; GE736; GE748; GE761; IT9; UK6

bilingualism
    GE192; SS18
Brethren
    GE298; GE343; GE669; GE752; GE772
cartoons
    FN15; GE16; GE193
Catholics
    FR90; GE686; IT79; *JE73 (*CH25); PL25; PL27; PL32; PL57;
    PO7; *RU24 (*GE684)
cemeteries
    GE17; GE214; GE600; HU20; PL61; PL72
Christ
    PL17; PL36
clergy
    See ministers; priests; rabbis.
code-switching
    FR109; SS18
coronations
    GY8
culture change
    GL3; GL13; *GL54 (*UK12); FN24; FR109; GE22; GE282; GE301;
    GE323; GE399; GE674; GE675; GE737; GE740; HU2; IR72; IT10;
    IT23; IT25; JE38; JE74; JE81; PL21; PL37; PL63; RO6; RU23;
    SS6; SS18; UK7; UK11; UK16; UK21
diaries, journals, and letters
    GE304; GE522; GE545; GE598; HU10; UK14
Doukhobors
    *GE384 (*AU2, *DU13, *RU14, *SW6)
Dunkards
    GE388; GE402; GE744; GE751
Dunkers
    GE743
Epiphany
    DA5; DU5; FR95; GR4; GR13; PL51
ethnic identity
    See identity, ethnic.
ethnic organizations
    See organizations, ethnic.
ethnicity
    *GL2 (*JE1); GL3; GL23; GL24; GL28; GL52; GL56; GL65;
    GL79; GR33; GY10; SS7
  maintenance of
    GL1; GE752; IT48; IT80; SS7
  public display of
    GL1; GL3; GL25
gambling
    CH3; GE138

gardens and gardening
    GE333; GE336; GE376
genealogies
    GE738
herbs and herbalists
    See agriculture, herbs and herbalists.
Hitler
    *GE281 (*JE31)
housekeeping
    GE48; GE49; GE50; GE51; GE53; GE54; GE289; GE727
Hutterites
    *GE384 (*AU2, *DU13, *RU14, *SW6)
identity, ethnic
    GL1; *GL2 (*JE1); GL52; GL65; FN23; GE716; GE751; GR35;
    GY10; GY11; IT25; IT48; JE75; *LA2 (*UK30); LA3; PL37;
    PO5; RO5; RO6; RO7; SS6
immigration
    GL36; GL37; *GL54 (*UK12); GL56; BA1; CO8; CO9; CR4; FN17;
    HU5; HU9; HU10; HU21; IR119; IT10; IT11; JE47; JE56; JE66;
    JE75; JE82; LE2; NO1; NO3; NO10; NO11; NO13; NO21; PL54;
    RO6; RU18; SC13; *SE3 (*YU4); SS31; UK7; UK13; UK26; UK31
inventories
    GE331
journals
    See diaries, journals, and letters.
kites and kite-flying
    CH19
letters
    See diaries, journals, and letters.
life histories
    HU5; HU9; HU15; JE48; LA1; PL22
mass media
    GL46; *FR25 (*GE72); HU3; HU11; IT10; JE74; SC7
    See also newspapers; phonograph records; radio; television.
Mennonites
    GE22; GE35; GE76; *GE97 (*SW1); GE100; GE130; GE141;
    GE155; GE215; GE240; GE282; GE316; GE344; GE364; *GE384
    (*AU2, *DU13, *RU14, *SW6); GE393; GE399; GE520; GE660;
    GE744; GE751; GE752
ministers
    GE42; GE90; GE109; GE166; GE386; GE622; *JE73 (*CH25); SS5
Moravians
    GE57; GE128; GE167; GE240; GE258; GE276; GE280; GE305;
    GE323; GE422; GE704; GE705; GE706; GE720; GE743
museums
    NO5; UK25
Nazis
    *JE44 (*DA6, *GE380, *IT43)

newspapers
    GE304; GE535; GE606; GE656
obituaries
    GE535
organizations, ethnic
    CH4; CR4; DU4; IR64; SS18
phonograph recording companies
    *GL60 (*CR7, *YU6); GL77; GL78; IR43
phonograph records
    *GL60 (*CR7, *YU6); GL77; GL78; FN13; FR89; IR43; JE74;
    PL74; *SS14 (*UK3)
popular culture
    GL3
priests
    *GL43 (*GR9, *IR31, *IT21, *JE24, *PL28, *PO6, *SP7);
    *GL50 (*FR69, *GE318); BA2; GR13; GR27; IR79; IR90; IR106;
    IT45; *JE73 (*CH25); PL12; PL67; PL78; RO6; SZ1
Protestants
    FR90; GE745; IR49; *JE73 (*CH25)
rabbis
    *GL43 (*GR9, *IR31, *IT21, *JE24, *PL28, *PO6, *SP7);
    JE13; *JE45 (*UK29); JE46; *JE73 (*CH25)
radio
    GL46
  stations
    GL46
restaurants
    GE264
Schwenkfelders
    GE62; GE63; GE344
sex
    GE677; JE51
sheet music
    JE74
snakes
    GE71; GE283; GE284; GE285; GE287; GE650; GE724; GE730;
    GE734; NO16; PL19; PL84
socialization
    DU5; FN23; GE7; GE9; GE99; GE300; GE316; *GE729 (*IT84,
    *JA13); HU20
taverns
    GE549
television
    GL46; FR109
  stations
    GL46
transportation, modes of
    GE17; GE100; GE191; GE640; GE691

United Christians
    GE341
vacation facilities
    JE53
Waldensians
    *IT47 (*FR81)
Wends
    GE421
wills
    GE209; GE210; GE211; GE213; GE248; GE432; *IR9 (*SC2,
    *WE1); WE4
World War I
    IR76
World War II
    *JE44 (*DA6, *GE380, *IT43)

III.   GEOGRAPHICAL INDEX

Alberta (Canada)
    NO7; RU20; *SZ4 (*EG1, *ID3, *LE4, *PA1); UK18; UK20; WE5
    Vegreville
    UK20
Arizona
    GL46
    Flagstaff
    CH28
    Phoenix
    RO1
    Tolleson
    SP6
    Tucson
    NO18
Békévar
    See Saskatchewan, Kipling.
British Columbia (Canada)
    RU20; *RU21 (*CZ10, *GE429, *HU26, *UK33); RU23; SC39
    Vancouver
    GR33
California
    GL18; GL46; AR8; CH15; CH26; *CO5 (*CH8, *GE235, *IR39,
    *IT28, *SS15); *CO7 (*FI2, *FN14, *IR40, *IT29, *SE4);
    CO9; FI3; FI5; IR30; IT72; IT73; IT82; JE49; PO2; PO5;
    PO20; PO21; *YU2 (*BU1); YU3
    Alamo
    GE237
    Azusa
    *GL49 (*CH13, *IR47, *IT32, *JA5, *SS17)
    Berkeley
    JA11; JA12
    Crow's Landing
    PO3
    Delano
    FI6; SS13
    El Centro
    ID4

Fresno
  AR2
Gustine
  PO7
Holtville
  SW5
La Verne
  GE772
Los Angeles
  GL19; AR2; BO1; GE203; *IT83 (*JE80); JA6; JA7; JE2; JE3;
  JE13; JE18; JE29; JE30; JE75; LA3; *LI4 (*RU5); NO9;
  RU15; *SE3 (*YU4)
Manteca
  PO3; PO4
Modesto
  PO4
Monterey
  *IT70 (*PO22, *SJ1)
Monterey County
  FI6
Oakland
  JA11; JA12
Point Loma
  *IT70 (*PO22, *SJ1)
San Diego
  IR44; SP6
San Francisco
  *GL81 (*JE79, *SP16); CH2; CH11; CH12; CH16; CH22; GE230;
  *IT70 (*PO22, *SJ1); IT71; SY1
San Pedro
  *IT70 (*PO22, *SJ1)
Sherman Oaks
  *JE25 (*PL29)
Stockton
  RU4
Tule Lake
  GL33; JA8
Venice
  JE48
Yuba City
  ID4
Canada (locales unspecified)
  *GL40 (*AR5, *CR2, *GR7, *GY5, *JE22, *SC11, *SE2); *GL53
  (*FR71, *IC3, *IT38, *JE40, *UK10); *GL54 (*UK12); *GL66
  (*CH21, *FR91, *GE428, *HU25, *IC4, *ID2, *IT57, *JA9,
  *LI5, *NO19, *RU19, *UK32); GL67; *CH9 (*ID1, *JA3); FR8;
  FR9; FR10; FR11; FR12; FR13; FR15; FR16; FR17; FR19; FR20;

FR28; FR45; FR75; FR94; FR104; FR106; *GE384 (*DU13, *RU14, *SW6); GE425; GE693; GE727; SC13; UK6; UK7; UK8; UK11; UK13; UK14; UK15; UK16; UK19; UK21; UK22; UK23; UK24; UK25; UK26; UK28
See also specific locales in Canada, by name.
Cape Breton, Nova Scotia (Canada)
  CE1; SC5
Charlevoix County, Quebec (Canada)
  FR7
Colorado
  GL46; IT64; PL64
 Boulder
  GE6; GE238; IT33; SS12; SS24
 Canon City
  IT19
 Central City
  CO1
 Denver
  SP4
 Lafayette
  IT69
 Longmont
  SS26
 Windsor
  GE660
Connecticut
  GL46; IT67
 Cheshire
  PL13
 New Haven
  IT84
Delhi, Ontario (Canada)
  HU5
Florida
  GL46; GR12; GR14; GY10
 Miami
  RO6
 Saint Augustine
  SP9
 Tampa
  IT62; IT63; SP1; SP2; SP3; SP8; SP15
 Tarpon Springs
  GR3; GR4; GR11; GR13
Georgia
  GR12; GR14
 Savannah
  GR11

Idaho
  Boise
    BA1
  Troy
    SS1
Illinois
    GL46; FN19; FR110; *GE33 (*DA1, *DU2, *FR21, *HU1, *IT3);
    GY10; IR75; IR94; IR95; LI8; LI9
  Bishop Hill
    SS21
  Chicago
    BO1; IR64; IR65; *IR81 (*SC31); IR82; IR83; LI1; PL10;
    RO6
  Elgin
    GE772
  Hancock County
    *IR78 (*DU14, *FR88, *GE424, *SC30)
  Monroe County
    GE360
  St. Clair County
    GE360
Indiana
    *GL10 (*JE10, *PL8); FR110; *GE697 (*SW8); JE15; PL11
  Blanford
    SE6
  Bloomington
    LA1; NO6
  Caernarvon
    GE445
  Calumet Region
    *GL27 (*HU6); *GL29 (*HU7); GL32; *CR6 (*SE5, *YU5); HU8;
    HU30
  Columbus
    GE164
  East Chicago
    GL26; *GL30 (*HU12); *GL34 (*CR1, *GR5, *SE1); CR5; HU9
  Elkhart County
    *GE97 (*SW1)
  Fort Wayne
    MA2; RO6
  Gary
    GL26; *GL30 (*HU12); *GL34 (*CR1, *GR5, *SE1); HU11
  Gypsy Hill
    GY7; GY14
  Indianapolis
    *BU2 (*MA1); JE6; LA1; SL3; SS25

Paoli
    SC4
Princeton
    IR13
South Bend
    HU31
Iowa
    CZ12; DU24; *GE110 (*SW3); *GE697 (*SW8); GE717; NO5; SS23
Amana
    GE165
Kansas
    CZ13
Ellis County
    *RU24 (*GE684)
Fort Hays
    GE204
Hays
    *GE527 (*RU22)
Lawrence
    GE119
Lindsborg
    SS5; SS6; SS7
St. Mary's
    BE1
Victoria
    *RU7 (*GE151)
Walker
    *GE527 (*RU22)
Kentucky
    *IR98 (*SC37)
Louisiana
    GL46; FR14; FR26; FR29; FR34; FR35; FR36; FR38; FR39;
    FR40; FR41; FR42; FR43; FR44; FR48; FR55; FR60; FR61;
    FR72; FR89; FR90; FR93; FR108; FR114; GY10
Árpádhon
    HU4
Avoyelles Parish
    FR37; FR74; FR99; FR100
Delacroix (Saint Bernard Parish)
    SP5; SP12
Goudeau
    FR43
Iberia Parish
    FR37
Lafayette Parish
    FR37
Lafourche Parish
    FR4

Mamou
  FR2
Natchitoches
  FR66
New Orleans
  CH7; FR37; FR95; GE539
Orleans Parish
  FR37
Pointe Coupee Parish
  FR37
Saint Bernard Parish
  FR37; SP5; SP10; SP11; SP12
  See also Louisiana, Delacroix (Saint Bernard Parish).
St. Mary's Parish
  FR59
Vermilion Parish
  FR27
Maine
 New Sweden
  SS18; SS25
Manitoba (Canada)
  *RU21 (*CZ10, *GE429, *HU26, *UK33); FN24; UK9; UK20
 Dauphin
  UK20
 Eriksdale
  SS16
 Gimli
  IC1
 Winnipeg
  *LA2 (*UK30); UK17
Maritime provinces (Canada)
  *GL20 (*FR46); FR32
Maryland
  GL46
 Garrett County
  GE764
 Washington County
  *FR80 (*GE385)
Massachusetts
  GL46; IT67; PO17; PO18
 Belmont
  GR24
 Boston
  *GL40 (*AR5, *CR2, *GR7, *GY5, *JE22, *SC11, *SE2); AR4;
  CH3; FI1; GR23; GR25; GR26; GR27; IR5; IR6; IR77; IT56;
  SZ5
 Cambridge
  GR24; IR69; PL41; SS2

Chicopee Falls
  PL18
Dorchester
  PL78
Gardner
  SS19
New Bedford
  PO1; PO9
Watertown
  GR24; *GR28 (*TU2)
Michigan
  GL46; CO9; DU21; IR53; IR109; JE15; PL11
Ann Arbor
  PL41
Detroit
  AR6; AR7; *CZ9 (*SK8); *CZ11 (*SK9); RO6; RO7
Iron Mountain
  *GR6 (*JE17)
Midland
  FR24
Ridge
  FN17
Saginaw
  PL71
Upper Peninsula
  GL33; CO2; FN4; *FN5 (*CO4, *FR54); FN16; FN18; FN23;
  FR49; FR51; FR52; *FR53 (*CO3, *FN3, *IR21, *IT17, *SS9);
  PL23; PL24
Midwest, the (locales unspecified)
  GE517; GE768
Minnesota
  CZ12; FN6; FN7; FN8; FN9; FN10; FN19; FN22; GE426; *IR101
  (*FR107, *GE682); NO5; NO17; SS27
Browerville
  PL56
Cokato
  FN25
Crystal
  FN25
Mississippi
  GY10; *PL7 (*GL9, *IT12, *JE8)
Lee County
  IR46
Missouri
  FR34; FR83; FR110; GE304
Johnson County
  GE58

Lafayette County
    GE58
Old Mines
    FR31
Pettis County
    GE58
St. Louis
    IR13; JE84; JE85; JE86
Saline County
    GE58
Montana
    CO9
Butte
    *CO7 (*FI2, *FN14, *IR40, *IT29, *SE4)
Montreal, Quebec (Canada)
    GY11; JE62; JE65; JE70
Nebraska
    *CZ2 (*SK1)
  Lincoln
    SC34; PL81
  Omaha
    SE8
Nevada
    GL46; CH19
New Brunswick (Canada)
    FR73
New England (locales unspecified)
    GL33; FR19; GE768; IT67; PO1; PO9; PO16
Newfoundland (Canada)
    IR86
  Port-au-Port Peninsula
    FR109
New Hampshire
  East Jeffrey
    IR112
  Londonderry
    *IR85 (*SC33)
New Jersey
    GL46; *FN26 (*GE699, *SS28, *SW9); MO1
  Franklin
    HU21
  Harrison
    PL62
  Hightstown
    *CZ11 (*SK9)
  Raritan Valley
    DU24
  Ridgefield Park
    IT24

New Mexico
  GL46
 Las Vegas
  IT41
 Santa Fe
  IT15; IT39; IT42
New York
    *GL11 (*JA1, *JE11); GL46; *GL50 (*FR69, *GE318); *GL80
    (*IR105, *IT77, *JE77); AR1; CZ5; DU1; DU5; DU7; DU17;
    *DU27 (*IR115, *SC41); *FR25 (*GE72); GE345; GE530; GE701;
    GR14; *GY1 (*RU1); GY10; IR14; IR52; *IR58 (*IT40, *JE43,
    *RU12); IR63; *IR70 (*SC29); IR108; *IR111 (*SC40); IT14;
    *IT36 (*FR70); JE5; PL1; PL54; RU18; SC45; TU5; WE2
 Albany
  DU4; DU23; IR48; *IR104 (*AR10); PL45
 Amsterdam
  PL12
 Binghamton
  GL22; *CZ4 (*UK2)
 Brooklyn
  *GL43 (*GR9, *IR31, *IT21, *JE24, *PL28, *PO6, *SP7);
  DU12; FN21; IT79; JE16; JE41; SC28
 Broome County
  GL22
 Buffalo
  GE713; GR29; IR66; IR88; IT68; PL2; PL27; PL41
 Camden
  IR57
 Catskill area
  IR36; IR42; IR97
 Chautauqua
  *IT67 (*GE387, *WE8)
 Colton
  GE129; IR110
 Cooper County
  *DU25 (*IR113)
 Cornwall
  *GL82 (*GE700)
 Cortland County
  LE2
 Dolgeville
  GE188
 Dutchess County
  *DU3 (*FR22, *GE36)
 Endicott
  GL22; *CZ4 (*UK2)
 Franklin County
  *FR58 (*IR25, *SC10)

Granville
  IT78
Hudson Falls
  *IC2 (*IR45)
Hudson Valley
  IR76; IR112
Ithaca
  GE713
Johnson City
  GL22
Long Island
  *GL50 (*FR69, *GE318); CZ1; *IR111 (*SC40)
Mohawk Valley
  DU16
Montgomery County
  DU28
Motteville
  CZ3
New York City
  GL58; CH7; CH14; CH27; *CZ11 (*SK9); GR11; GR22; HU16;
  IR33; IR49; *IR58 (*IT40, *JE43, *RU12); IR79; IR80; IT4;
  IT5; IT31; IT34; IT55; JA4; *JE9 (*IR12, *SC3); JE14;
  *JE45 (*UK29); JE46; JE53; JE58; JE59; *JE60 (*LI10);
  JE62; JE64; JE71; JE82; PL9; RU2; RU3
New York Mills
  PL22; PL32; PL37; PL40; PL51
Niagara County
  *GE722 (*JE83); IR88
Niagara Falls
  IT2; PL2
Onondaga County
  CZ3
Orange County
  *IR84 (*SC32); PL86
Oswego
  IR15
Otsego County
  *DU25 (*IR113)
Otter Lake
  *GL75 (*FR103)
Redford
  *FR47 (*IR19); FR92
Rochester
  IR96
Rome
  *IR58 (*IT40, *JE43, *RU12)
St. Lawrence County
  GE730

Saratoga County
  *IR24 (*SC8); IR51
Schenectady
  GE435; GE462; IR90
Schenevus Valley
  *SS29 (*AU6, *GE703)
Schoharie County
  *GE197 (*DU9, *IR35)
Sullivan County
  GE530; JE53
Syracuse
  CH1; *GR30 (*TU4); IT1; PL76; PL77; PL80
Troy
  DA5; GE1
Ulster County
  DU19; IR28
Utica
  IT30; JE78; PL20; PL21; SZ1
Waterford
  PL14
Watertown
  IT58; IT59; IT60
Westchester County
  *DU18 (*FR101)
Whitesboro
  IT58; IT59
Woodstock
  DU20; IR28
North Carolina
  GE293; GE304; GE518; SC15; SC44
  Cherryville
    GE122
  Valdese
    *IT47 (*FR81)
  Wachovia
    GE305
  Winston-Salem
    IR23
North Dakota
  NO9
Nova Scotia (Canada)
  *FR68 (*SC23); FR73; SC5; SC9; SC16; SC26
  Lunenburg County
    GE123; GE124
  Port Hood
    SC21; SC22
Ohio
  GL46; AR1; FR85; GE681; GY10; UK5

Bluffton
  GE659
Cincinnati
  GR11
Cleveland
  *GL40 (*AR5, *CR2, *GR7, *GY5, *JE22, *SC11, *SE2);
  *GL41 (*CR3, *FN11, *GE172, *HU14, *IR26, *RO3, *SC12,
  *SK4); HU13; HU15; PL46; RO6; *SK3 (*UK1); SL2
Darke County
  FR82; FR84
Dayton
  GY8
Dungannon
  IR34
Holmes County
  GE695; GE696
Newark
  IT44
North Lima
  PL80
Pandora
  GE659
Perry County
  GE666
Rossford
  SK6
Sonnenberg
  GE659
Toledo
  HU29
Wayne County
  GE411; GE536
Youngstown
  PL44; PL47; PL59; PL67; PL82
Ontario (Canada)
  GL46; FR32; FR33; GE4; GE153; GE155; GE156; GE157; GE158;
  GE201; GE349; GE655; GY10; LI6; *RU21 (*CZ10, *GE429, *HU26,
  *UK33); SC6; SC14; SI1; UK34
Berlin
  GE349
Brant County
  GE157
Bruce County
  GE157
Essex County
  FR117
Grenville County
  *IR116 (*SC42)

Grey County
  *IR117 (*SC43)
Huron County
  GE157
Norfolk County
  UK34
Perth County
  GE157
Renfrew County
  PL31
Waterloo County
  GE154; GE157; GE393; *GE723 (*FR115); GE726
Wellington County
  GE157
Oregon
  BA2; FN19; IR32
Astoria
  FN22
Pennsylvania
  GL46; *GL55 (*IR56, *SK7, *WE7); CO8; FR102; GE2; GE42;
  GE83; GE91; GE98; GE152; GE194; GE200; GE217; GE218; GE288;
  GE289; GE311; GE315; GE316; GE342; GE363; GE389; GE412;
  GE419; GE447; GE490; GE513; GE518; GE547; GE554; GE586;
  GE589; GE602; GE664; GE712; GE749; GE773; *PL5 (*GE43,
  *IR4, *IT6, *JE4); *PL48 (*RU13, *UK27); WE3
Adams County
  GE69; GE763
Adamstown
  GE166
Aliquippa
  IT80
Alleghenyville
  GE622
Allentown
  GE189; GE459; GE676
Ambridge
  PL34; *PL35 (*GY6); PL36; PL80
Bally
  GE457
Barto
  GE465
Bear Creek
  GE638
Beaver Falls
  PL58
Bechtelsville
  GE61
Bedford County
  *GL75 (*FR103)

Berks County
  GE66; GE74; GE106; GE107; GE114; GE133; GE135; GE139;
  GE141; GE148; GE149; GE205; GE229; GE231; GE232; GE252;
  GE306; GE388; GE392; GE439; GE445; GE450; GE468; GE507;
  GE525; GE533; GE544; GE546; GE550; GE561; GE564; GE587;
  GE590; GE598; GE613; GE621; GE658; GE692; GE694; GE707;
  SW2
Berne
  GE464; GE465
Bethel
  GE452; GE477
Bethlehem
  GE57; GE323; GE422
Blair County
  *GL75 (*FR103)
Boyertown
  GE267
Bradford County
  DU8
Bucks County
  GE125
Buffalo Valley
  GE427
Butler County
  GE103
Cambria County
  *GL75 (*FR103)
Cambridge Springs
  PL75
Carbon
  GE480
Carbon County
  IR91
Carlisle
  GE510
Chester County
  GE121; *IR9 (*SC2, *WE1)
Clinton County
  *GL75 (*FR103); GE667; GE731
Cumberland County
  GE38; GE41; GE216; GE619
Dauphin County
  GE328; GE394; GE603
Delaware County
  GE214
Durtztown
  GE542

Eastern Centre County
  GE390
Elizabethtown
  GE187
Emmaus
  GE128
Enon Valley
  GE5
Ephrata
  GE120
Erie
  PL30
Fayette County
  GE290
Fettersville
  GE228
Forest County
  GE679
Franklin County
  GE274; GE275
Gallitzin
  PL68; PL69; PL70
Hammer Creek
  GE257
Hebe
  GE70
Hegins Valley
  GE765
Indiana County
  *AR3 (*RU6); GE310
Intercourse
  GE351
Jefferson County
  GE310
Jim Thorpe
  IR91
Juniata County
  GE617
Kutztown
  GE543; GE619
Lancaster
  GE744
Lancaster County
  GE17; GE22; GE23; GE74; GE76; GE86; GE100; GE107; GE173;
  GE198; GE199; GE226; GE227; GE248; GE252; GE273; GE298;
  GE308; GE321; GE327; GE335; GE364; GE388; GE396; GE400;
  GE569; GE575; GE626; GE628; GE637; GE644; GE657; GE680;
  GE689; GE702; GE770; SW2

Lansford
  PL19
Lebanon County
  GE74; GE105; GE176; GE239; GE270; GE341; GE343; GE370;
  GE381; GE388; GE405; GE623; GE654; SW2
Lebanon Valley
  GE377; GE402; GE403; GE678
Lehigh County
  GE265; GE290; GE437; GE480; GE525; GE544
Lehigh Valley
  GE67; GE68; GE414; GE676
Lititz
  GE280; GE434; GE452; GE453; GE704; GE705; GE706
Longswamp
  GE593
Luzerne County
  *GE113 (*GR1, *SK2); GE728
Mahantongo Valley
  GE81; GE382; GE762
Manheim
  GE694
Maple Grove
  GE448; GE454; GE455; GE461
Middletown
  IR91
Middleburg
  GE463
Mifflin County
  GE74; GE391; GE396; GE397; GE398; GE400; GE401; GE766
Monroe County
  GE205
Montgomery County
  GE105; GE107; GE196; GE332; GE343; GE344; GE544
Mt. Bethel
  GE277; GE278
Nashville
  GE245
Nazareth
  GE422
New Berlinville
  GE61
New Brighton
  PL43
New Ringgold
  GE453
Newton
  IT18

Northampton County
  GE205; GE480; GE667
Oil City
  PL57
Oley Valley
  SW2
Palmyra
  GE466
Paxtonville
  GE721
Pennsboro Township
  GE523
Perkiomen Valley
  GE60; GE64
Philadelphia
  CH4; FI4; GE171; GE191; GR15; GR16; GR17; GR18; GR19; GR20;
  GR35; GR36; GR37; GR38; GR39; GY2; GY9; IR71; IR91; IT23;
  IT48; IT49; JA10; MO1; SC20; WE4
Philadelphia County
  GE432
Pittsburgh
  *GL42 (*FN12, *GE177, *GR7, *IR27, *SK5); GL44; *GL45
  (*SC18); *GL60 (*CR7, *YU6); GE191; IT26; JE41; LI3
Potter County
  NO1
Pottstown
  GE694
Queenstown
  GE34
Reading
  GE395; GE451; GE458; GE466; GE584
Reinholds
  GE449; GE456
Roseto
  IT10; IT11; IT81
St. Mary's
  GE686
Salisbury Township
  GE32
Schuylkill County
  GE21; GE40; *GE113 (*GR1, *SK2); GE339; GE420
Shillington
  GE694
Snyder County
  GE74; GE591
Somerset County
  GE117; GE180; GE181; GE619; GE764

Spring Creek
  GE669
Steelton
  CR4
Susquehanna County
  GE433
Swatara Valley
  *GE140 (*GY4)
Tamaqua
  GE460
Tulpehocken
  GE331
Tylersville
  GE519
Union County
  GE555
Upper Darby
  GR36
Ursina
  GE182
Washington County
  GE313
Wayne County
  IR38
West Chester County
  SC27
West Hamburg
  GE467
Wilkes-Barre
  GE638
Williamsport
  GE154
Womelsdorf
  GE23
Wyomissing
  GE532
York County
  GE69; GE190; GE206; GE540; GE619; GE657; GE668; GE718
Prince Edward Island (Canada)
  SC5; SC16; SC36
Quebec (Canada)
  FR3; FR15; FR16; FR18; FR62; FR64; FR65; FR67; FR73; FR77;
  FR78; FR96; FR97; FR111; FR112; FR118; GY10
  Beauce County
    FR57
Rhode Island
  PO11; PO17; PO18

Blackstone Valley
   PO10; PO14
Woonsocket
   JE59
Rorketon, Manitoba (Canada)
   FN24
Saskatchewan (Canada)
   GE82; RU20; *RU21 (*CZ10, *GE429, *HU26, *UK33); RU23;
   UK18; UK20
   Kipling (Békévar)
   HU2; HU3; HU9; HU20; HU28
   Regina
   RO5
   Yorktown
   UK20
South, the (locales unspecified)
   GE217; GE218; GE517; IR41
South Dakota
   Roberts County
   SS22
Tennessee
   Knoxville
   WE6
   Wooldridge
   IT65; IT66
Texas
   GL46; FR66; GE118; GE421; GE683
   Austin
   LE1
   Bandera
   PL3
   Bexar County
   GE71
   Blanco County
   GE234
   Clay County
   *RU11 (*GE319, *UK4)
   Dallas
   GE383
   Fredericksburg
   GE174; GE175; GE354; GE410
   Galveston
   FR113
   Kearns County
   PL61
   Medina County
   *FR98 (*GE521)

Panna Maria
  PL3
San Antonio
  GL12
Thorndale
  IR73
Thurber
  *IT37 (*PL42)
Wichita Falls
  GR11
Winedale
  GE233
Toronto, Ontario (Canada)
  FR117; GY11; IT25; JE12; JE37; JE38; JE39; JE65; KO1; LI6
Utah
  CO6; *CO7 (*FI2, *FN14, *IR40, *IT29, *SE4); *DA3 (*SA1,
  *SS4); DA4
  Carbon County
  GR31
  Magna
  GR32
  Salt Lake City
  DU10
Vermont
  FN20
  Ryegate
  SC17
  Springfield
  PL6
Virginia
  FN22; GE518; IR2
  Shenandoah Valley
  GE116; GE646; GE647; GE648; GE649; GE650; GE651; GE653
Washington
  Seattle
  JE3; JE23; JE72
West, the (locales unspecified)
  SA2
West Virginia
  AU1; *AU3 (*CZ7, *HU23, *IT51); *AU5 (*PL53); *CZ6 (*HU22,
  *IT50, *YU7); HU18; IT7; IT20; IT46; *IT52 (*AR9, *AU4,
  *CZ8, *HU24, *IR74, *PL52, *RO4, *RU16, *TU3, *YU8);
  *IT54 (*RU17, *YU9); IT86; SP13
  Fairmont
  IT53
  Gilmer County
  DU26

McMechen
  SK10
Shinnston
  IT45
Wisconsin
  BE1; CO9; NO5; NO10; NO20; *SW4 (*GE217, *IR18, *NO8)
  Milwaukee
    *GE161 (*SS10); PL83; PL84
  Waupaca County
    NO12
Wyoming
  CH6

IV. AUTHOR INDEX

Abrahams, Roger D.
    GL1; *GL2 (*JE1); GL3
Agogino, George A.
    *GY1 (*RU1)
Agonito, Rosemary
    CH1; IT1
Ainsworth, Catherine Harris
    IT2; PL1; PL2
Albrecht, Henry F.
    GE1
Alderfer, Harold F.
    GE2
Alego, John
    GL4
Alexander, Alex Edward
    RU2
Allen, George
    GE3
Aman, Reinhold
    PO1
Ancelet, Barry Jean
    FR2
Anderson, Jack
    AU1
Anderson, Jay A.
    FR3
Anderson, Robert
    DU1
Andrews, Jan
    GE5
Archibald, Edith
    SS1
Armistead, Samuel J.
    JE2; JE3
Atkinson, Robert
    CZ1
Atwood, E. Bagby
    FR4

Augar, Pearl Hamelin
    *FR5 (*IR1)
Aurand, Monroe A.
    GE7; GE8; GE9; GE10; GE11; GE12; GE13; GE14; GE15; GE16
Babcock, C. Merton
    *CZ2 (*SK1)
Bachman, George
    GE17
Bacon, A.M.
    IR2
Bailer, Sophia
    GE18; GE19; GE20; GE21
Baker, T. Lindsay
    PL3
Baldwin, Sioux
    GE22
Balys, Jonas
    LI1; LI2; LI3
Bancroft, Caroline
    CO1
Barakat, Robert A.
    GE23
Barba, Preston A.
    GE24; GE25; GE26; GE27; GE28; GE29; GE30; GE31; GE32; GE242
Barbeau, C. Marius
    GL5; GL6; FR7; FR8; FR9; FR10; FR11; FR12; FR13; FR14;
    FR15; FR16; FR17; FR18; FR19; FR20; *IR3 (*FR6, *SC1)
Barbour, Frances M.
    *GE33 (*DA1, *DU2, *FR21, *HU1, *IT3)
Barbour, John
    GE34
Baretski, Charles Allan
    PL4
Barker, Maxine
    GE35
Barnes, Gertrude
    *DU3 (*FR22, *GE36)
Barrese, Pauline N.
    IT4; IT5
Barrick, Mac E.
    GE37; GE38; GE39; GE40; GE41; GE42; *PL5 (*GE43, *IR4,
    *IT6, *JE4)
Barry, Phillips
    *GL7 (*FR23); IR5; IR6; IR7; IR8; PL6; SS2
Basile, James
    IT7
Bauman, Richard
    JE5

Baver, Florence S.
    GE44
Baver, Russel S.
    GE45; GE46; GE47
Baver, Mrs. Russel S.
    GE48; GE49; GE50; GE51; GE52; GE53; GE54; GE55
Beck, Berton E.
    GE56
Beck, E.C.
    FR24
Beckel, Clarence E.
    GE57
Bek, William G.
    GE58
Ben-Amos, Dan
    JE6; JE7
Bender, Rhoda
    GE59
Bennit, Dorothy V.
    DU4
Bergen, Fanny D.
    AR1
Berkey, Andrew S.
    See Berky, Andrew S.
Berky, Andrew S.
    GE60; GE61; GE62; GE63; GE64; GE65
Berwin, Solomon
    GE66
Best, Martha S.
    GE67; GE68
Bethke, Robert
    *IR9 (*SC2, *WE1)
Bianco, Carla
    IT8; IT9; IT10; IT11
Bieter, Pat
    BA1
Biondi, Mary H.
    WE2
Birnbaum, Mariana D.
    GL8
Bittinger, Lucy Forney
    GE69
Bixler, Leo H.
    GE70
Blegen, Theodore C.
    NO1; *NO2 (*DA2, *FN1, *IR10, *SS3); NO3; NO4
Blumstock, Robert
    HU2

Boggs, Ralph Steele
    SP1; SP2; SP3
Bogusch, E.R.
    GE71
Bøhn, Tora
    NO5
Bolton, Henry Carrington
    *FR25 (*GE72)
Bomberger, Barbara B.
    GE73
Bomberger, C.M.
    GE74
Bonos, Arlene Helen
    GY2
Booker, Louise Robertson
    IR11
Borcherdt, Donn
    AR2
Borneman, Henry S.
    GE75
Boswell, George W.
    *PL7 (*GL9, *IT12, *JE8)
Botkin, Ben A.
    *JE9 (*IR12, *SC3)
Bowman, H.H.M.
    GE76
Boyer, Walter E.
    GE77; GE78; GE79; GE80; GE81
Braddy, Haldeen
    RU3
Brandon, Elizabeth
    FR26; FR27
Brassard, François
    FR28
Bratcher, James T.
    LE1
Brednich, Rolf Wilh.
    GE82
Breininger, Lester
    GE83; GE84; GE85
Brendel, John B.
    GE86; GE87
Brendle, Thomas R.
    GE88; GE89; GE90; GE91; GE92; GE93; GE94; GE359
Brenner, Scott Francis
    GE95
Bressler, Leo Albert
    GE96

Brewster, Paul G.
    IR13
Bronner, Simon J.
    *GE97 (*SW1)
Brown, Carleton
    GE98
Brown, Vonnie R.
    FR29
Brown, Waln K.
    GE99; GE100
Brumbach, Paul D.
    GE101
Brumbaugh, G. Edwin
    GE102
Brunetti, Michael
    IT13
Brunvand, Jan Harold
    *GL10 (*JE10, *PL8); NO6; NO7
Bryan, William J.
    GE103
Bryant, Margaret M.
    *GL11 (*JA1, *JE11)
Bucher, Robert C.
    GE104; GE105; GE106; GE107; SW2
Buffington, Albert F.
    GE108; GE109
Bundy, Colleen
    SC4
Burczak, Helen
    PL9
Burgess, Thomas
    GR2
Burkhart, Charles
    *GE110 (*SW3)
Burrison, John A.
    GE111
Buso, Mildred
    CZ3
Byington, Robert H.
    GE112
Calkins, Charles F.
    BE1
Campa, Arthur L.
    SP4
Carpenter, Inta Gale
    LA1
Carrière, Joseph Médard
    FR30; FR31; FR43; FR44

Cazden, Norman
    IR14; IR42
Chapman, Mary
    CH3
Cheney, Thomas E.
    *DA3 (*SA1, *SS4)
Christenson, Jackie
    GL12
Christiansen, Reidar Th.
    GL13
Chuck, Charles
    PL10
Chute, William S.
    FR74
Cincura, Andrew
    *SK3 (*UK1)
Clar, Mimi
    *LI4 (*RU5); RU4
Clarfield, Geoffrey
    JE12
Claudel, Calvin
    FR34; FR35; FR36; FR37; FR38; FR39; FR40; FR41; FR42;
    FR43; FR44; SP5; SP6
Clements, William M.
    GL14; PL11
Clifton, Merritt
    GL15
Cline, Ruth H.
    GE116
Coffroth, Frederick F.
    GE117
Cohen, Norman
    IR15
Coleman, Marian Moore (Mrs.)
    PL12; PL13; PL14
Collier, G. Loyd
    GE118
Colombo, John Robert
    GL16
Conley, Anne Kukuchka
    PL15; PL16; PL17
Cooper, Philip D.
    GE119
Corso, Rose (Mrs.)
    PL18
Coss, Carol Ann
    RO1; RO2

Costanzo, William
    PL19
Cotten, Rena M.
    GY3
Cowan, John L.
    WE3
Cox, Suzanne
    GE120
Craige, Carter W.
    GE121
Crawley, Donald W.
    GE122
Cray, Ed
    GL17; GL18; GL19; JE13
Creighton, Helen
    *GL20 (*FR46); GE123; GE124; SC5
Crosby, John R. (Rev.)
    *AR3 (*RU6)
Culin, Stewart
    CH4; CH5; IT16
Cummings, John
    GE125
Curtin, Jeremiah
    *GL21 (*IR16)
Curtis, Otis F., Jr.
    *GE126 (*IR17)
Curtis, Wardon Allan
    *SW4 (*GE127, *IR18, *NO8)
Cutting, Edith E.
    GL22; *CZ4 (*UK2); *FR47 (*IR19)
Danielson, Larry
    GL23; GL24; SS5; SS6; SS7
Dantzker, Sondra
    JE14
Davis, Susan G.
    PL20; PL21; PL22
Dégh, Linda
    GL25; GL26; *GL27 (*HU6); GL28; *GL29 (*HU7); HU3; HU4;
    HU5; HU8; HU9; HU10; HU11
Deischer, Claude K.
    GE128
deKay, Eckford J.
    DU5
Dell, Jennie Scott
    GE129
De Long, Nancy
    GE130

Delovich, Homer W.
    YU1
Dieffenbach, Victor C.
    GE132; GE133; GE134; GE135; GE136; GE137; GE138; GE139;
    *GE140 (*GY4); GE141; GE142; GE143; GE144; GE145; GE146;
    GE147; GE148; GE149; GE150
Dinkel, Phyllis A.
    *RU7 (*GE151)
Dluge, Robert
    GE152
Doering, Eileen Elita
    GE157; GE158; GR3
Doering, John Frederick
    FR48; GE153; GE154; GE155; GE156; GE157; GE158; GR4; SC6
Dornbusch, Charles H.
    GE159
Dorson, Richard M.
    *GL30 (*HU12); GL31; GL32; GL33; *GL34 (*CR1, *GR5, *SE1);
    GL35; GL36; GL37; CO2; DU7; FN4; *FN5 (*CO4, *FR54);
    FR49; *FR50 (*FN2, *GE160, *IR20, *SL1, *SS8); FR51;
    FR52; *FR53 (*CO3, *FN3, *IR21, *IT17, *SS9); FR55; *GE161
    (*SS10); GE162; GE163; *GR6 (*JE17); JE15; JE16; PL23;
    PL24; *SS11 (*DU6, *FR56, *IR22)
Dow, James R.
    CH6; GE164; GE165
Doyon, Madeleine
    FR57
Dresser, Norine
    JE18; JE19
Driedger, Leo
    *LA2 (*UK30)
Druckenborg, Richard
    GE166
Dubbs, Joseph Henry
    GE167; GE168
Duncan, Gwyneth
    IR23
Dundes, Alan
    GL38; PL25; *PL26 (*JE20); SC7
Dunin, Elsie Ivancich
    *YU2 (*BU1); YU3
Dunn, Adda Ann
    *IR24 (*SC8)
Dunn, Charles W.
    SC9
E., J.W.
    GE170

Eames, Frank
    *FR58 (*IR25, *SC10)
Edgar, Marjorie
    FN6; FN7; FN8; FN9; FN10
Edwards, G.D.
    AR4
Edwards, Jane Spencer
    WE4
Einarsson, Magnus
    IC1
Eisen, Gustav A.
    SS13
Eisiminger, Sterling
    GL39
Elish, Karl M.
    *JE20 (*RU8)
Ellis, Susan J.
    GE171
Erdely, Stephen
    *GL40 (*AR5, *CR2, *GR7, *GY5, *JE22, *SC11, *SE2); *GL41
    (*CR3, *FN11, *GE172, *HU14, *IR26, *RO3, *SC12, *SK4);
    HU13; HU15
Estep, Glenn
    GE173
Estill, Julia
    GE174; GE175
Etter, Russel C.
    GE176
Evanson, Jacob A.
    *GL42 (*FN12, *GE177, *GR7, *IR27, *SK5)
Evers, Alf
    IR28
Fabian, Monroe H.
    GE178; GE179
Fagundes, Francisco Cota
    PO2
Feintuch, Burt
    IT18
Field, Jerome P.
    NO9
Fike, Tedford E.
    GE180; GE181; GE182
Finckh, Alice
    GE183
Firestone, Melvin M.
    JE23

Fish, Lydia
    PL27
Fogel, Edwin Miller
    GE184; GE185; GE186
Fontes, Manuel da Costa
    PO4; PO5
Forchi, Violet
    IT20
Forry, Mark
    *SE3 (*YU4)
Forster, J. Margaret
    IR30
Fortier, Alcée
    FR59; FR60; FR61
Foster, James R.
    *GL43 (*GR9, *IR31, *IT21, *JE24, *PL28, *PO6, *SP7)
Foster, John Wilson
    IR32
Fowke, Edith Fulton
    FR62
Fox, C. Milligan
    IR33
Francello, Elvira
    IT22
Frantz, Gilda (Mrs.)
    *JE25 (*PL29)
Franz, Eleanor
    GE188
Fraser, Alexander
    SC13
Fraser, C.A.
    SC14
Fratto, Toni F.
    IT23
Frazier, Paul
    GE189; SC15
Freeman-Witthoft, Bonita
    DU8
Frey, Howard C.
    GE190; GE191
Frey, J. William
    GE192; GE193; GE194
Funk, H.H.
    GE195
Gaillard, Mary Lou
    SC16
Gamon, Albert T.
    GE196

Gard, R. Max
    IR34
Gardner, Emelyn E.
    AR6; *GE197 (*DU9, *IR35)
Garofalo, Alexander J.
    IT24
Gayton, A.H.
    PO7
Gehman, Henry Snyder
    GE198; GE199
Gehret, Ellen J.
    GE200
Gellermann Patterson, Nancy-Lou
    GE201
Georges, Robert A.
    GR10; GR11; GR12; GR13; GR14
Gerhard, Elmer
    GE202
Geschwindt, Don F.
    GE205
Gibbons, J.H.
    GE206
Gibbons, Phebe Earle
    GE207; GE208
Gicewicz, Edmund (Rev.)
    PL30
Gilbert, Russel Wieder
    GE209; GE210; GE211; GE212; GE213
Gillespie, Angus K.
    GE214
Gingerich, Melvin
    GE215
Giuliano, Bruce B.
    IT25
Gizelis, Gregory
    GR15; GR16; GR17; GR18; GR19; GR20
Glanz, Rudolf (Dr.)
    JE26
Glassie, Henry
    GE216; GE217; GE218
Glofcheskie, John Michael
    PL31
Glover, Waldo F.
    SC17
Goldstein, Elizabeth
    PL32
Gorelick, J.
    *JE27 (*RU9)

Gottshall, Marie
    GE219
Gougler, Richard C.
    GE220
Gourley, Norma Mae
    GE221
Graeff, Arthur D.
    GE222; GE223; GE224; GE225
Graham, Robert L.
    GE226
Grame, Theodore C.
    GL44; *GL45 (*SC18); GL46
Greco, Joseph V.
    IT26
Green, Gail
    PL32
Greenberg, Andrea
    *GL47 (*FR63, *IT27, *JE28, *PL33)
Greenough, William Parker
    FR64; FR65
Grey, Sara
    GE227
Groah, Patrick
    GE228
Gronow, Pekka
    FN13; *SS14 (*UK3)
Gruber, Wayne H.
    GE229
Gruszcyński, Joseph
    PL34
Gruszczyńska, Valeria (Mrs.)
    *PL35 (*GY6); PL36
Gudde, Erwin G.
    GE230
Gutowski, John
    GY7
Hale, Leon
    GE233
Hall, Connie
    GE234
Halpert, Herbert
    *GL48 (*IR37, *SC19); HU16; IR36; IR38; WE5
Hand, Wayland D.
    *CO5 (*CH8, *GE235, *IR39, *IT28, *SS15); CO6; *CO7 (*FI2,
    *FN14, *IR40, *IT29, *SE4); DU10; GE236; GE237; JE29;
    JE30; SW5
Hanna, Marion
    SZ1

Hare, Maud Cuney
     PO8
Hark, Ann
     GE239; GE240; GE241; GE242
Harper, Jared
     IR41
Hartman, Harvey H.
     GE243; GE244
Hartman, Joel
     GE245; GE246
Hartman, Peter
     IT30; PL37
Hartmann, Gail Eaby
     GE247
Hatas, Kristina
     SK6
Hatcher, Mattie Austin
     FR66
Haufrecht, Herbert
     IR42
Haugen, Einar
     NO10; NO11; NO12
Haughon, Synnove
     GE248
Hauptmann, O.H.
     SP8
Haviland, Thomas P.
     SC20
Healy, William M.
     IR43
Heller, Edna Eby
     GE249; GE250; GE251; GE252; GE253; GE254; GE255; GE256;
     GE257; GE258; GE259; GE260; GE261; GE262; GE263; GE264;
     GE265; GE266; GE267; GE268; GE269; GE270; GE271; GE272
Hemhauser, Robert
     GE273
Henderson, Anthony
     UK34
Henneberger, George F.
     GE274; GE275
Henry, James
     GE276
Henry, Ruth
     GE277; GE278
Hering, Irwin
     GE279
Herr, Charlotte C.
     GE280

Herrmann, Walter
    *GE281 (*JE31)
Hershey, Mary Jane
    GE282
Hertzog, Phares H.
    GE283; GE284; GE285
Hewes, Gordon W.
    JA2
Heyl, John K.
    GE159
Hoe, Ban Seng
    *CH9 (*ID1, *JA3); CH10
Hoffman, Dan G.
    IT31
Hoffman, David F., Jr.
    CR4
Hoffman, George K.
    GE286
Hoffman, Walter James
    GE287; GE288; GE289; GE290; GE291
Hofmann, Charles
    JA4
Hogan, Virginia
    IR44
Hohman, John George
    GE292
Hoke, N.C.
    GE293
Hollenbach, Ida V.
    GE294
Hollenbach, Raymond E.
    GE295
Hommel, Martha Hill
    GE296
Hondius, Katherine N.
    DU11
Hoogasian, Susie
    See Hoogasian-Villa, Susie
Hoogasian-Villa, Susie
    AR6; AR7
Hopkins, Pandora
    *IC2 (*IR45)
Horne, Abraham Reeser
    GE297
Hostetler, Beulah S.
    GE298
Hostetler, John A.
    GE299; GE300; GE301; GE302

Hostetter, Patricia
    GE303
Houser, George J.
    SS16
Hoy, William J.
    CH11; CH12
Hubbard, Lester A.
    DA4
Hudson, Arthur Palmer
    GE304; GE305; IR46
Hudson, Charles
    IR41
Huguenin, Charles A.
    DU12
Humphrey, Linda T.
    *GL49 (*CH13, *IR47, *IT32, *JA5, *SS17)
Hurvitz, Nathan
    JE32; JE33
Hurwitz, Elizabeth Adams
    GE307
Huston, Nancy
    FR67
Hustvedt, Lloyd
    NO13
Huyett, Laura
    GE308
Hwa, Hsü Tsan
    CH23; CH24
Hyde, Louise
    GE309
Jack, Phil R.
    GE310; GE311; GE312; GE313
Jackson, George Pullen
    GE314; GE315
Jackson, Kenneth
    SC21; SC22
Jagendorf, M.
    IT34
Jamison, C.V. (Mrs.)
    *FR68 (*SC23)
Jansen, William Hugh
    CR5; TU1
Jarka, Matthew
    PL38
Jarvenpa, Robert
    FN15
Jason, Heda
    JE34

Jeffers-Johnson, Stratford
    IR49
Jentsch, Theodore W.
    GE316
Johnson, Aili Kolehmainen
    FN16; FN17; FN18
Johnson, Hildegard B.
    GE317
Johnston, Richard
    FR62
Jones, Louis C.
    *GL50 (*FR69, *GE318); *GL51 (*GR21, *HU17, *IN1, *IR50,
    *IT35, *JE35, *PL39, *RU10, *SZ2); IR51; *IT36 (*FR70)
Jordan, Rosan A.
    GL52
Jordan, Terry G.
    *RU11 (*GE319, *UK4)
Joseph, Suad
    LE2
Joyce, Rosemary
    UK5
Kadelbach, Elizabeth
    GE320
Kalčik, Susan
    GL3
Kaloyanides, Michael G.
    GR22
Katz, Eli
    JE36
Katz, Naomi
    JE36
Kauffman, Henry J.
    GE321; GE322; GE323; GE324; GE325; GE326; GE327; GE328
Kawamoto, Fumi
    JA6
Kelly, Catherine
    IR52
Kemp, Alvin F.
    GE329; GE330
Kennon, Peg Korsmo
    PL40
Kerman, Judith B.
    PL41
Kess, Joseph F.
    SL2
Kessler, Carol
    GE331

Keyser, Alan G.
    GE200; GE332; GE333
Keyser, Mildred D.
    GE334
Kidder, H.R.
    IR53
King, C. Richard
    *IT37 (*PL42)
Kirchner, Francis X.
    GE335
Kirkland, Edwin C.
    WE6
Kirshenblatt-Gimblett, Barbara
    JE37; JE38; JE39
Kirwan, Lucile Vartanian
    AR8
Kittredge, G.L.
    IR54; IR55
Klees, Fredric
    GE336
Klein, Barbro Sklute
    See Sklute, Barbro
Klein, H.M.J.
    GE337
Klymasz, Robert B.
    *GL53 (*FR71, *IC3, *IT33, *JE40, *UK10); *GL54 (*UK12);
    UK7; UK8; UK9; UK11; UK13; UK14; UK15; UK16; UK17; UK18;
    UK19; UK20; UK21; UK22; UK23; UK24; UK25; UK26
Knipmeyer, William B.
    FR72
Knohr, E.L.
    GE338
Kolinski, Mieczyslaw
    FR73
Köngäs, Elli Kaija
    See Köngäs-Maranda, Elli Kaija
Köngäs-Maranda, Elli Kaija
    FN19; FN20; FN21; FN22; FR79
Korson, George Gershon
    *GL55 (*IR56, *SK7, *WE7); GE339; GE340
Koskoff, Ellen
    JE41
Krauss, Friedrich S.
    JE42
Kraut, Alan M.
    GL56
Kreider, Mary C.
    GE341

Kresz, Mária
   HU20
Kuhns, Levi Oscar
   GE342
Kulikowska, Frances (Mrs.)
   PL43
Kulp, Clarence
   GE343; GE344
Kuzmirek, Sophia (Mrs.)
   PL44
Laatsch, William G.
   BE1
Lagarde, Marie-Louise
   FR74
Lahaye, Marie
   FR108
Lahikainen, Dean
   SS19
Lamont, Karen Wells
   GE345
Landis, Henry Kinzer
   GE346
Landry, Renée
   GL57
Lang, Henry R.
   PO9
Langlois, Janet
   CH14
Larson, Mildred R.
   DA5; IR57; *IR58 (*IT40, *JE43, *RU12)
Laskowski, Cornelius J. (Rev.)
   PL45
Laws, G. Malcolm, Jr.
   IR59
Lawton, Arthur J.
   GE347
Leach, MacEdward
   CE1
Lee, D. Demetracopoulou
   See Lee, Dorothy Demetracopoulou
Lee, Dorothy
   See Lee, Dorothy Demetracopoulou
Lee, Dorothy D.
   See Lee, Dorothy Demetracopoulou
Lee, Dorothy Demetracopoulou
   GR23; GR24; GR25; GR26; GR27; *GR28 (*TU2)
Lee, Jon
   CH15; CH16

Leeds, Wendy
  GE348
Leeson, Alice M.
  *IR60 (*SC24)
Lefcourt, Charles R.
  GE349
Leh, Leonard L.
  GE350
Lehr, Robert J.
  GE351
LeMoine, J.M.
  FR76
Lerch, Lila
  GE352
Lestz, Gerald S.
  GE353
Lethin, Joyce Bynum
  SY1
Lewis, Mary Ellen Brown
  *SC25 (*IR61)
Li, Lienfung
  CH17
Li, Lillian
  CH18
Lich, Glen
  GE354
Lichten, Frances
  GE355; GE356; GE357; GE358
Lick, David E.
  GE359
Liedtke, Harriet
  PL46
Lockwood, Yvonne R.
  FN23
Logan, Nancy A.
  IR62
Lonczkowska, Helen
  PL47
Long, Amos, Jr.
  GE361; GE362; GE363; GE364; GE365; GE366; GE367; GE368;
  GE369; GE370; GE371; GE372; GE373; GE374; GE375; GE376;
  GE377; GE378; GE379
Loomis, C. Grant
  CH19
Luciw, Wasyl O.
  *PL48 (*RU13, *UK27)
Lumpkin, Ben Gray
  BO1

Lund, Jens
    *JE44 (*DA6, *GE380, *IT43)
McCadden, Helen M.
    GL58
McCarthy, Paul T.
    SP9
McCombs, Hazel A.
    IR63
McCullough, Larry
    IR64
McCullough, Lawrence E.
    IR65
MacCurdy, Raymond R., Jr.
    SP10; SP11; SP12
MacDonald, Frank E.
    GE381
Mackenzie, W. Roy
    SC26
McLaughlin, Valerie
    CZ5
MacLeod, Calum
    SC5
Macmillan, Ernest
    FR78
MacMullen, Jerry
    GL59
McNaughton, Barbara J.
    IT44
Mahoney, Libby
    PL40
Maiolo, Melia Rose
    IT45
Makar, Janos
    HU21
Maloney, Thomas Vincent
    IR66
Mankin, Carolyn
    GE383
Mankins, Jerilyn
    IT46
Maranda, Elli Köngäs
    See Köngäs-Maranda, Elli Kaija
March, Richard
    *CR6 (*SE5, *YU5)
Maron, Frank
    PL49
Maron, Louise
    PL49; PL50

Marshall, Alexander
  SC27
Martens, Helen
  *GE384 (*AU2, *DU13, *RU14, *SW6)
Mason, Wilton
  *IT47 (*FR81)
Master, Marie
  GE386
Mathews, Ernest S.
  GR29
Mathias, Elizabeth
  IT48; IT49
May, Elizabeth
  JA7
Maziarz, Robert
  PL51
Mazzei, Maureen
  SC28
Mead, Jane Thompson
  *IR67 (*GE387, *WE8)
Meade, Alma B.
  GE388
Medwidsky, Bohdan
  UK28
Meltz, Adrienne
  IR68
Meltzer, Herbert S.
  *JE45 (*UK29)
Meñez, Herminia Quimpo
  FI3; FI4; FI5; FI6
Meyer, T.P.
  GE389; GE390
Michaelis, Kate Woodbridge
  IR69
Milanovich, Anthony
  SE6
Millard, Eugenia L.
  *IR70 (*SC29)
Miller, Daniel K.
  GE392
Miller, William Marion
  FR82; FR83; FR84; FR85
Milnes, Humphrey
  GE393
Milspaw, Yvonne J.
  GE394
Minor, Eugene R.
  SP13

Mintz, Jerome R.
    JE46
Mitchell, John Fletcher
    *LA2 (*UK30)
Mlotek, Eleanor Gordon
    JE47
Moloney, Michael
    IR71
Moloney, Mick
    IR72
Monahan, Kathleen
    *GL60 (*CR7, *YU6)
Monteiro, George
    GL61; FR86; PO1; PO10; PO11; PO12; PO13; PO14; PO15
Montgomery, Margaret
    *BU2 (*MA1); SL3
Montgomery, Morton L.
    GE395
Mook, Maurice A.
    GE396; GE397; GE398; GE399; GE400; GE401
Moore, George L.
    GE402; GE403; GE404; GE405
Moore, Willard Burgess
    RU15
Moran, Joyce Demcher
    UK31
Moravcik, Ivo
    *CZ9 (*SK8)
Moser, Esther
    GE406
Moser, Helen J.
    GE407; GE408; GE409
Moses, Louise von Blittersdorf
    IR73
Mueller, Esther L.
    GE410
Mumaw, John R.
    GE411
Munch, Peter A.
    *SS20 (*NO14)
Murtagh, William J.
    GE412
Musick, Ruth Ann
    *AU3 (*CZ7, *HU23, *IT51); *AU5 (*PL53); *CZ6 (*HU22,
    *IT50, *YU7); *IT52 (*AR9, *AU4, *CZ8, *HU24, *IR74,
    *PL52, *RO4, *RU16, *TU3, *YU8); IT53; *IT54 (*RU17, *YU9)
Myerhoff, Barbara G.
    JE48; JE49

Myers, Anna Balmer
    GE413
Myers, George H.
    GE414
Naff, Alixa
    *LE3 (*SZ3)
Nagorka, Suzanne
    PL54; PL55
Navarra, Anthony
    IT55
Nawrocka, Victoria
    PL56
Neely, Charles
    IR75
Neidle, Cecyle S.
    RU18
Neifert, William W.
    GE415
Nestler, Harold
    IR76
Nettl, Bruno
    GL62; GL63; GL64; *CZ9 (*SK8); *GE416 (*SW7)
Newell, Jane H.
    IR77
Newell, W.W.
    See Newell, William Wells
Newell, William H.
    GE420
Newell, William Wells
    FR87; GE419; IT56
Nichols, Priscilla Miller (Mrs.)
    *GR30 (*TU4)
Nielson, George R.
    GE421
Niles, Christina
    LA3
Nitzsche, George E.
    GE422
Noll, Ronald W.
    GE423
Nordquist, Del
    SS21
Norlin, Ethel Todd
    *IR78 (*DU14, *FR88, *GE424, *SC30)
Novak, Anton
    GE425
Nusbaum, Philip
    JE50

O'Beirne, James
    IR79; IR80
Olsen, Louise P.
    CH20; GE426; NO15; NO16; NO17; SS22
Olson, Sandi
    NO18
Olszówka, Frank
    PL57
O'Neill, Francis (Capt.)
    *IR81 (*SC31); IR82; IR83
Opler, Marvin K.
    JA8
Orze, Helen (Mrs.)
    PL43; PL44; PL47; PL58; PL59; PL60; PL67
Osborn, Lettie
    *IR84 (*SC32)
Oster, Harry
    FR89; FR90
Owen, Mary A.
    *IR85 (*SC33)
Owens, J.G.
    GE427
Pajewski, Bernard
    PL61
Papanikolas, Helen Z.
    GR31; GR32
Paredes, Américo
    GL65
Parsons, Elsie Clews
    IR2; PO16; PO17; PO18; PO19
Parzen, Herbert
    JE51
Patterson, G. James
    GR33; RO5
Peacock, Kenneth
    *GL66 (*CH21, *FR91, *GE428, *HU25, *IC4, *ID2, *IT57,
    *JA9, *LI5, *NO19, *RU19, *UK32); LI6; RU20; *RU21 (*CZ10,
    *GE429, *HU26, *UK33)
Pelinski, Ramon
    GL67
Pelly, Francine
    GY9
Perkowski, Jan L.
    SI1
Peterson, Walter F.
    SS23
Petroff, Louis
    BU3; BU4

Piasecki, Sally (Mrs.)
    PL62
Pickett, David W.
    *GY1 (*RU1)
Pietchke, William
    GE173
Pietropaoli, Lydia Q.
    IT58; IT59; IT60
Pike, Alfred J.
    PL63
Pinkowski, Edward
    CO8
Pirkova-Jakobson, Svatava
    *CZ11 (*SK9)
Pitchon, Miriam
    GE432
Pocius, Gerald L.
    GE433; IR86
Poleway, Bette
    LI7
Porter, James
    GL68; GL69
Porter, Kenneth
    GL70; GL71
Porter, Marjorie Lansing
    FR92
Pound, Louise
    SC34
Preston, Kathleen A.
    PL64
Preston, Michael J.
    *IT61 (*IR87, *PL65); PL64; PL66
Preston, W.D.
    JA10
Prévos, André
    FR93
Proracki, Anthony
    WE3
Prudon, Theodore H.M.
    DU15
Purcell, Joanne B.
    PO20; PO21
Qureshi, Regula
    *SZ4 (*EG1, *ID3, *LE4, *PA1)
Radin, Paul
    JA11; JA12
Rahn, Clarence R. (Rev.)
    GE440

Raichelson, Richard
    GE441
Ramírez, Manuel D.
    IT62; IT63
Rapp, Marvin A.
    IR88
Rauchle, Bob
    GE442
Reagan, William A.
    GE443
Reaver, J. Russell
    LI8; LI9
Regnoni-Macera, Clara
    IT64
Reich, Wendy
    FR94
Reimensnyder, Barbara
    GE444
Reinecke, George F.
    FR74; FR95
Relihan, Catherine
    IR89
Rennick, Robert M.
    GL72; *JE52 (*GE446, *SC35, *YU10)
Reynolds, Neil B.
    DU16
Rhoads, Collier
    GE447
Richman, Hyman
    *HU27 (*GL73, *SI2)
Richman, Irwin
    JE53
Riddle, Ronald
    CH22
Riegel, Lewis Edgar
    GE469
Roan, Donald
    GE470
Robacker, Ada F.
    GE503; GE504; GE505; GE506; GE507; GE508; GE509; GE510;
    GE511; GE512; GE513; GE514; GE515; GE516
Robacker, Earl F.
    GE471; GE472; GE473; GE474; GE475; GE476; GE477; GE478;
    GE479; GE480; GE481; GE482; GE483; GE484; GE485; GE486;
    GE487; GE488; GE489; GE490; GE491; GE492; GE493; GE494;
    GE495; GE496; GE497; GE498; GE499; GE500; GE501; GE502;
    GE503; GE504; GE505; GE506; GE507; GE508; GE509; GE510;
    GE511; GE512; GE513; GE514; GE515; GE516

Robbins, Walter L.
    GE517; GE518
Roberts, Leonard
    IT65; IT66
Roemig, Madeline
    GE165
Rogers, W. Stuart
    IR90
Rølvaag, Ella Valborg
    NO20
Rose, E.H.
    FR96; FR97
Rose, H.J.
    FR96; FR97; SC36
Rosenberg, Bernard
    JE54
Rosenberger, Homer
    GE519
Rosenberger, Jesse Leonard
    GE520
Ross, Terri
    *FR98 (*GE521)
Roth, Juliana
    GE522
Rowe, John
    CO9
Rubin, Ruth
    JE55; JE56; JE57; JE58; JE59; *JE60 (*LI10); *JE61 (*LI11);
    JE62; JE63; JE64; JE65; JE66; JE67; JE68; JE69; JE70
Rudzińska, Katherine (Mrs.)
    PL67
Rupp, I.D.
    GE523
Rupp, William J.
    GE524; GE525
Ruud, Martin B.
    NO3; NO4; NO21
Ryan, Lawrence V.
    CZ12
Rybak, Shulameth
    SP14
Sachse, Julius
    GE526
Sackett, Marjorie
    GL74; CZ13
Sackett, S.J.
    BE2; *GE527 (*RU22)

Salo, Matt T.
    GY10; GY11
Salo, Sheila M.G.
    GY11
Sapir, Edward
    CH23; CH24; FR20
Saucier, Corinne Lelia
    FR99; FR100
Sauers, Ray W.
    GE528
Scanlon, Rosemary
    IR91
Schaechter, Mordche
    JE71
Schaffer, Sharon A.
    GE529
Scheuttle, Frank A.
    GE530
Schillinger, Alvin W.
    GE531
Schinhan, Jan Philip
    SP15
Schlesinger, Emma Adatto
    JE72
Schmidt, Kenneth R.
    GE532
Schneider, Robert I.
    GE533
Schreiber, William I.
    GE534; GE535; GE536
Schuchat, Theodor
    JE19
Schuler, H.A.
    GE537
Schuman, John F.
    GE538
Scott, Kenneth
    DU17
Seckar, Alvena V.
    SK10
Seely, Daniel Clayton
    GE539
Sękowska, Agnes (Mrs.)
    PL68; PL69
Sękowski, Agnes (Mrs.)
    PL70
Shaner, Richard H.
    GE541; GE542; GE543; GE544; GE545; GE546; GE547; GE548;
    GE549; GE550; GE551

Shapiro, Gilbert
    JE54
Sharp, Dean
    IR92
Shaw, Ann
    *DU18 (*FR101)
Shea, John
    GE552
Shelley, Donald A.
    GE553
Shenton, Donald R.
    GE554
Shively, Jacob G.
    GE555
Shoemaker, Alfred L.
    GE556; GE557; GE558; GE559; GE560; GE561; GE562; GE563;
    GE564; GE565; GE566; GE567; GE568; GE569; GE570; GE571;
    GE572; GE573; GE574; GE575; GE576; GE577; GE578; GE579;
    GE580; GE581; GE582; GE583; GE584; GE585; GE586; GE587;
    GE588; GE589; GE590; GE591; GE592; GE593; GE594; GE595;
    GE596; GE597; GE598; GE599; GE600; GE601; GE602; GE603;
    GE604; GE605; GE606; GE607; GE608; GE609; GE610; GE611;
    GE612; GE613; GE614; GE615; GE616; GE617; GE618; GE619;
    GE620; GE621; GE622; GE623; GE624; GE625; GE626; GE627;
    GE628; GE629; GE630
Shoemaker, Henry W.
    *GL75 (*FR103); FR102
Shoemaker, William
    GE631
Shoemaker, William P.
    GE632
Showalter, Henry A.
    GE634
Showalter, M.E.
    GE635
Shuttleworth, Barbara
    FR104
Sidwa, Anne H.
    PL71; PL72; PL73
Silverman, Joseph H.
    JE2; JE3
Simmons, Donald C.
    IT67; *JE73 (*CH25)
Simmons, Isaac Shirk
    GE636
Simons, Isaac Shirk
    GE637

Sinclair, A.T.
   GY12; GY13
Skeel, Mary H.
   IR93
Skinner, Charles M.
   FR105
Sklute, Barbro
   SS18; SS25
Slobin, Mark
   JE74
Smith, Agnes Scott
   DU19; DU20
Smith, Clarissa
   GE639
Smith, Edward C.
   GE640
Smith, Elmer Lewis
   GE641; GE642; GE643; GE644; GE645; GE646; GE647; GE648;
   GE649; GE650; GE651; GE652; GE653
Smith, Grace Partridge
   IR94; IR95
Smith, M. Estellie
   IT68
Smith, Richard
   GE654
Smith, Rita
   GE655
Snellenburg, Betty
   GE657; MO1
Snyder, Mabel
   GE658
Soland, Craig
   *SE7 (*BE3); SE8
Soldner, Dora
   GE659
Song, Bang-Song
   KO1
Speroni, Charles
   *IT70 (*PO22, *SJ1); IT71; IT72; IT73
Spicer, Dorothy Gladys
   GL76; IT74
Spieler, Gerhard G.
   GE661; GE662
Spier, Robert F.G.
   CH26
Spottswood, Richard K.
   GL77; GE78; PL74

Stack, Phil
  GE664
Stair, J. William
  GE665
Stålfelt-Szabó, Hélène
  HU28
Stanbery, George A. (Mrs.)
  GE666
Starr, Frederick
  GE667
Stern, Stephen
  GL79; JE75
Stewart, John G.
  GE646; GE647; GE648; GE649; GE650; GE651; GE653
Stewart, Susan
  GE668; GE669
Stingo, Sandra Voldeck
  IT75; IT76
Stitzer, Clarence R.
  GE670
Stiver, Shawn
  GY14
Stofan, Sandra
  HU29
Stoner, Michael
  IR96
Stoudt, Fno. Baer
  GE671
Stoudt, John Joseph
  GE672; GE673; GE674; GE675
Strong, Leah A.
  GE676
Strózik, Joseph
  PL75; PL76; PL77
Struder, Norman
  IR97
Suchecki, Evelyn (Mrs.)
  PL78
Sutyla, Charles M.
  FN24
Swanson, Kenneth Albin
  FN25
Swetnam, George
  GE677
Swope, Martha Ross
  GE678
Szabó, Mátyás
  HU28

Taché, Joseph-Charles
    FR106
Taft, Donald E.
    GE679
Tallmadge, William H.
    *IR98 (*SC37); *IR99 (*SC38)
Tarasoff, Koozma J.
    RU23
Taube, Kristie
    GE681
Taylor, Archer
    DU22; *IR100 (*JE76); *IR101 (*FR107, *GE682); PL79
Taylor, Lera
    GE354
Taylor, Lonn
    GE683
Teit, J.A.
    SC39
Terbovich, Fr. John B.
    *RU24 (*GE684)
Teske, Robert Thomas
    GR34; GR35; GR36; GR37; GR38
Theophano, Janet
    GR39
Thériot, Marie
    FR108
Thigpen, Kenneth A.
    RO6; RO7
Thomas, Gerald
    FR109
Thomas, Rosemary Hyde
    FR110
Thompson, David W.
    GE685
Thompson, Ellen Powell
    IR102; IR103
Thompson, Harold W.
    DU23; *IR104 (*AR10)
Thompson, Marion
    *GL80 (*IR105, *IT77, *JE77)
Tilney, Philip V.R.
    MA2
Todd, Charles Burr
    GE686
Torre, Luis
    SS27
Tortora, Vincent R.
    GE687; GE688; GE689; GE690; GE691

Travis, James
    IR106; IR107
Tremblay, Maurice
    FR111; FR112
Trindell, Roger T.
    *FN26 (*GE699, *SS28, *SW9)
Trop, Sylvia
    IT78
Troup, W. Edwin
    GE693
Trout, John D.
    GE694
Troxell, William S.
    GE90; GE91
Troyer, Lester O.
    GE695; GE696
Tucker, Philip C.
    FR113
Tull, Marc
    JE78; PL37
Turner, Kay F.
    IT79
Umble, John
    *GE697 (*SW8)
Unger, Claude W.
    GE92; GE93; GE94
Urick, Mildred
    IT80
Valetta, Clement L.
    IT81
Vatuk, Ved Prakash
    ID4
Vázsonyi, Andrew
    HU30
Voiles, Jane
    IT82
Wacker, Peter O.
    DU24; *FN26 (*GE699, *SS28, *SW9)
Waffner, Laura M.
    IR108
Wahlgren, Erik
    SA2
Waibel, John
    UK35
Walerstein, Marcia
    *GL81 (*JE79, *SP16)
Walker, Barbara K.
    *GL82 (*GE700)

Walton, Ivan
    IR109
Wang, Joseph
    CH27
Ward, Peter A.
    IR110
Ware, Helen
    HU31
Warner, Frank L.
    *IR111 (*SC40); IR112
Watkins, Margilynn Fox
    GE701
Weaver, William Woys
    GE702
Webb, Wheaton Phillips
    *DU25 (*IR113); *SS29 (*AU6, *GE703)
Weiner, Harvey
    *IT83 (*JE80)
Weinreich, Beatrice S.
    JE81
Weitzel, Louise A.
    GE704; GE705; GE706
Welsch, Roger L.
    PL81
Westkott, Marcia
    GE707
Wetzel, J. Stuart
    GE708
Wetzel, John
    GE709
Weygandt, Cornelius
    GE710; GE711; GE712
Wheatley, Richard
    JE82
Whitaker, Alice P.
    GE713
White, Emma Gertrude
    GE714
Whitfield, Irène-Thérèse
    FR114
Whiting, Clay
    DU26
Wieand, Paul R.
    GE715
Wierman, Nancy K.
    GE716
Wilden, Albin
    *SS30 (*DA7, *NO22)

Wilgus, D.K.
    IR114
Williams, Phyllis H.
    IT84
Willis, Alice
    *DU27 (*IR115, *SC41)
Wilson, Barbara
    TU5
Wilson, Charles Bundy
    GE717
Wilson, Howard Barrett
    SZ5
Wilson, Marian Ludwig
    GE718
Wilson, Marion B.
    GE719
Wilson, Marion Ball
    GE720
Winey, Fay McAfee
    GE721
Winner, Julia Hull
    *GE722 (*JE83)
Wintemberg, Katherine H.
    *IR117 (*SC43)
Wintemberg, W.J.
    FR116; FR117; *GE723 (*FR115); GE724; GE725; GE726; *IR116
    (*SC42); *IR117 (*SC43)
Wismer, Helen
    GE727
Withers, Carl
    *GE729 (*IT85, *JA13)
Witthoff, John
    GE730
Wolanin, Adam
    PL82
Wolfe, C.N.
    GE731
Wolpert, Robert
    GE732
Wolter, Marcia Britton
    PL40
Wong, Celia
    PL83; PL84
Wong, Jason
    CH28
Wood, Arthur
    PL85

Woodward, Robert H.
    IR118
Wright, Barbara
    DU28
Wright, Betty Jane
    PL86
Wright, Estelle
    SC44
Wright, Robert L.
    IR119; SS31
Wright, Ruth C.
    SC45
Wyman, Loraine
    FR118
Wynnsky, George
    *PL48 (*RU13, *UK27)
Yerger, Amos
    GE734
Yoder, Don
    GE736; GE737; GE738; GE739; GE740; GE741; GE742; GE743;
    GE744; GE745; GE746; GE747; GE748; GE749; GE750; GE751;
    GE752; GE753; GE754; GE755; GE756; GE757; GE758; GE759;
    GE760; GE761; GE762; GE763
Yoder, Eleanor
    GE764
Yoder, Jacob H.
    GE765
Yoder, Joseph W.
    GE766
Yoffie, Leah Rachel C.
    JE84; JE85; JE86
Zappacosta, Bob
    IT86
Zehner, Olive G.
    GE767; GE768; GE769; GE770; GE771
Ziegler, Rebecca
    GE772
Ziemer, Alice
    GE773
Zimm, Louise Hasbrouck
    FR119
Zimniewicz, Helene
    PL87
Zook, Jacob
    GE774
Zook, Jane
    GE774
Zupan, Joyce Goodhart
    GE775